T0365639

DISCERNING PERCEPTIvᴇ

Spiritually Revealing Insights with
Sympathetic Understandings
of the Sincere & Inspiring
Word of God.

Sister Glory G. Thompson

Order this book online at www.trafford.com
or email orders@trafford.com

Most Trafford titles are also available at major online book retailers.

All Thanks and Glory be to God!

Printed in the United States of America.

ISBN: 978-1-4269-2351-7 (sc)

Library of Congress Control Number: 2009913885

Trafford rev. 06/10/2011

 www.trafford.com

North America & international
toll-free: 1 888 232 4444 (USA & Canada)
phone: 250 383 6864 ♦ fax: 812 355 4082

Contents:

Preface

Discerning Perceptive is designed by definition against the haters whom indeed oppress, repress, and overwhelmingly seeks to dominate as to have dominion over others. Simultaneously, it's designed for those whom are hated and are oppressed by the enemy. It's design for the Muslims and Christians. This book is for Americans and non-Americans, Republic and Democrat, gays and straights, and all political parties; whether they are apart of a conservative body or liberal. The Author who is a believer of God the Father, the Son, and the Holy Spirit hopes that Discerning Perceptive helps you the readers to possess the key element which compassionately strengthens the weak without accusing or blaming anyone unto God.

The author is not someone who desires to hold the conscious minds of you the readers' hostage nor does she want to confine you in anyway, form, or fashion. She desires to use her converted conscience and righteous spirit to serve the Lord as she encouragingly cries out unto every race of mankind, no matter what their differences are; nor does it matter to her of what a person's sin consist of, because she talks the same way unto all sinners about love, repentance, reconciliation, and redemption; not by her own will, but by the will of the Lord.

The views expressed in this book are solely those of the author and doesn't necessarily reflect the views of the Churches that are named within the contents of this context which she either once attended are presently attends, and none are to be held responsible for her views. She's a free-spirited Christian who used her civil rights as an American citizen to express her own personal spiritual perception which involved many different political factors that affects the lives of all sorts of religious believers; especially the Christians.

INTRODUCTION

> 1Kings3:9 "Give therefore thy servant an understanding heart to judge thy people, that I might discern between good and bad; for who is able to judge this thy great a people?"
>
> 1Kings3:11 "And God said unto him, because thou hast asked this thing, and hast not asked for thyself long life; neither hast asked riches for thyself, nor hast asked the life of thine enemies; but hast asked for thyself understanding to discern judgment;"
>
> 1Kings3:12 "...lo I have given thee a wise and understanding heart;"

"Discerning Perceptive," spiritually describes the revealed sympathetic insights and understandings of the predisposed inherited traditional religious beliefs and customs of Vanity, which kills the Spirit of God within all mankind alike. The content of this context does not judge the conscience of any man, but it does judge the surrounding acts and events which troubles the heart of a great multitude.

Every man's heart goes through a process of forming a hypothesis or theory of something not proven, but assumed to be true for the purpose of implying a greater or superficial likelihood of truth. This technique has always been used by the teachings of The Holy Ghost, for all to perceive and understand the concepts and ideas of the Lord's Divine truth with the righteous sense to know the difference between right and wrong or good and evil. The differences of one man's opinions of the

Lord's anointed teachings, comes from the mannerism in which ones' state of being may perceive the Holy Scriptures and accept the One True Gospel of Jesus Christ as an infallible truth. Discerning Perceptive is a Christian message concerning Christ.

The author; Sister Glory Sanders Thompson, used the inspiring powerful Word of God to reveal to all readers of her spiritual and personal insights with sympathetic understandings of the preexistence of the hardened hearts of the world. All thanks and glory be to God, for blessing her with heavenly wisdom to spiritually process and conclude these particular hypothesis and theories of an inevitable spiritual evolutionary change, which is guided and predestined by God the Father, the Son, and the Holy Spirit.

> Romans11:28 "As concerning the gospel, they are enemies for your sakes: but as touching the election, they are beloved for the father's sakes."
> Romans11:29 "For the gifts and calling of God are without repentance."
> Romans11:30 "For as ye in times past have not believed God, yet have now obtained mercy through their unbelief:"
> Romans11:31 "Even so have these also now not believed, that through your mercy they also may obtain mercy

After the eyes of man has been opened to know good and evil, the prince of the world deludes men's minds and misconstrues the intent of the message of God's Word of Truth. Although many are called by the Lord, most of them are tricked into using vain philosophies and words of deceit to justify their own understandings of right and wrong; in an attempt to answer the calling which the Lord has on their lives. All things which are sown into the heart of an individual or a group of persons are exposed or brought to the light through words phrases or signs that express the thoughts, feelings, or qualities of ones state of being.

Hebrews4:12 "For the Word of God is quick, and powerful, and sharper than any two-edged sword, piercing even to the dividing asunder of soul and spirit, and of the joints and marrow, and is a discerner of the thoughts and intents of the heart."

Although NO MAN STANDS EXEMPT from GOD's Words of Truth, not all men believe on him. They are spiritually and biblically recognized or understood to be busy bodies and scorners. They hate to be reproved and they fail to attain the awareness and understandings of the Holy truth, which lies within the One True Gospel of Jesus Christ. They are so busy being some judges of the Lord's law, till they disable themselves the ability to establish or perceive the wisdom of God, which comes from Heaven.

The authors' perceptions and anointed understandings within "Discerning Perceptive" disclose and acknowledge the worldly created traditions of religious warfare that are denied by the Lord God himself and are described by him to be unfruitful and are enmity against God. Although these worldly traditional beliefs persecuted Christ, many religious peoples are still living by the same old worldly traditions as religious cultists of the 21st century, whom think they are formal representatives of the Spirit of Righteousness and Truth. The contents of this context are provided for all readers who may or may not be capable of acknowledging, recognizing, or accepting the Spirit of Truth.

The Authors' Famous Quote: "If the Holy Spirit is right, then a whole lot of people are living bibliographically wrong!"

<u>MAY GOD BLESS THE HEARS AND DOERS OF HIS WORDS, AMEN!</u>

Messenger's Note:

"THERE'S THREE SIDES TO EVERY STORY. THERE'S YOUR TRUTH, MY TRUTH AND THE HOLY TRUTH." (ST.JOHN18:29-40) IN THE END THE HOLY TRUTH IS THE ONLY TRUTH THAT REALLY MATTERS.

Babes and elders of all ages, please open your hearts and minds concerning the will of God for your own soul's sake (1Peter 1&2). The Lord knows that you desire to make a fair show in the flesh and that

xi

you've been mentally confined by the froward perverse words of those who has made themselves apostles of Christ. (Gal. 6:12-18)

They've mentally seduced you by enslaving your minds into having very little or no faith in Christ's ability to do whatsoever he said he'd do to save you, because they desire for you all to perish. Without heavenly wisdom or understanding, their teachings unto you are hypocrisy. They pretend to be more virtuous or religious than they really are so that they may glory in your flesh. Do not worry, the Lord knows yours sorrows and hears your righteous cry.

> **Ps.34:17 "The righteous cry, and the Lord heareth, and delivereth them out of all their troubles."**
> **1John3:20 "For if our hearts condemn us, God is greater than our heart, and knoweth all things."**

After being delivered out of your troubles, don't be to them as they were to you . . . HYPOCRITES. Instead of throwing stone for stone, evil for evil, or eye for eye let your light shine and love even those who used froward perverseness against you. Bless them that curse you with forgiveness. Do good to them that hate you, and pray for them which despitefully use you, and persecute you. (Matt 5:43-48)

Treat froward men the way you want them to treat you which is equal, fair, and is acceptable unto to God as your reasonable service of sacrifice (Rom.12:1/1Cor.6:20/Rom.9:11-16). Kill their evil with kindness, and be blessed by God. Judge them not, as the Lord forbid you, and remember the Lord isn't partial. That which he says he'll do for one; he'll do for all concerning his promise of life everlasting. (2Peter 3:9)

Romans2:1 "Therefore thou art inexcusable, O man, whosoever thou art that judgest: for where in thou judgest another, thou condemnest thyself; for thou judgest doest the same things." James4:11 "Speak not evil one of another, brethren. He that speaketh evil of his brother, and judgeth his brother, speaketh evil of the law, and judgeth the law: but if you judge the law, thou art not a doer of the law, but a judge."(Rom.2: 1/St. Matt.7:1-2/St. Luke6:36-38)

The fruit of the Spirit identifies one's deeds to be either good or evil, but it's unrighteous to use the fruit of the Spirit to judge one another. Of course perverse disputing of religious and froward men may disagree, but the truth is the light and there's no darkness in that light. (Col.3:1-17)

Of course there is a thing known as righteous judgment, but it solely pertains to the proper usage of identifying which spirit is being presented; so that righteous decisions can be made by the identifier (YOU!).

The author of Discerning Perceptive speaks the Holy truth, which goes beyond worldly definition and beyond tradition; as the anointed truth is given unto her beyond intervention. She speaks of the Holy Truth to interpose between fact vs. fiction, good vs. evil, good vs. bad, and truth vs. lies and old wise fables; in hopes of stopping, settling, and changing the corrupt perception that you as the reader may have of yourself as well as strangers, neighbors, friends, relatives, co-workers etc. by properly using the inspiring Word of God to uplift you.

As you read with an open heart and mind, she prays and believes that the Lord will set you aside from the corrupt perceptions of the Word of God that has been given unto you by the Prince of the World. The worldly and/or traditional religious perceptions you may have of others, subconsciously are the same as the perception you have of yourself. In other words, the same judgments that you assign by measure to judge others by, are mete or assigned back to you again.

The method and patterns of making wrongful judgments are given unto you by the perception of false teachers and false prophets, who stands before you in a pulpit or at an altar. These men command of you to subject your hearts to believe in their false theories and traditional religious practices of the Word of God, which are of evil works and are enmity against God.

It is by faith, the author lives, and it is believed by the author that she is chosen and predestined by God to answer his calling on her life. Sharing her perception of the Word of God, which is made manifest unto her by the Anointed teachings of the Power of God is apart of her calling and is the Will of God.

With sympathetic understandings of the ways of the world, and the way of the Lord; the author presents the manifestations of what the Holy Ghost did during past times and is still doing today, only to mediate between all countrymen who lives in the shadowy shambles of traditional religion and political affairs which cause them to doubt the power of God. Sister Glory's writing emphasizes salvation by faith in the atoning death of Jesus Christ through her personal conversion with the authority of the Holy Scriptures. She also emphasizes the importance of preaching the Gospel of Jesus Christ as contrasted with a formal habitual procedure, custom, or ritual, while trying to awaken religious enthusiasm.

For those of you who can spiritually recognize that we all reap the works of another man's heart, God gives you all the spiritual sense to identify which Fruit is sown unto you. This is done for and by the Spirit of God, which lives in all mankind regardless of ones sin, for us all to obey the Law of God and the true prophets of God. (St. Matt.7:12)

MAY GOD BLESS THE HEARS AND THE DOERS OF HIS WORDS, AMEN!

PERSONAL CONTACT INFORMATION: gloriouswonenterpriselld@yahoo.com

CHAPTER 1 LIFE'S PURPOSE IS TO LIVE IN LOVE & LET LOVE LIVE

> Isaiah60:1 "Arise, shine; for thy light is come, and the glory of the Lord is risen upon thee."
> Isaiah60:2 "For, behold, the darkness shall cover the earth, and gross darkness the people: but the Lord shall arise upon thee, and his glory shall be seen upon thee."

There comes a time in all of our lives when we must one day wake up out of sleep. Sleep symbolically represents the temperament state of having the lack of the Lord's heavenly Wisdom, to spiritual understand the true purpose of our individual lives here on earth. Due to ignorance, the most respected kings and parliaments all around the world; have been coerced for centuries into upholding the rigid traditional religious ways of one of the most ancient and noted sects among the Jews. The religious teachings of the sect of the Pharisees should've been preserved by and for every race of people all around the world after Christ sent the world the Holy Ghost as a comforter, but the harsh strict version of the Old Testament was converted into the Gospel of Jesus Christ without the consent of God by the unawares; who crept in and went against Jesus Christ; the King of kings and Lord of lords. The kings, gods, and lords of the land created parliaments for all to idolize and worship, while making life difficult and uncomfortable for their personally owned menservants and slaves.

The traditional teachings of the sect of the Pharisees; (AKA The 21st Century False Prophets), implies for all the kings, gods, and lords of the land to religiously worship, revere, and devote their complete loyalty; to serve the severe and harsh religious ideas and opinions, which gives the human-race an unjustified reason to adoringly desire to accept the

1

presences of the condemned spirit of the oppressor as a religious veneration. All religious tyrants delude and overtake the pure consciences of the entire human race also seek for world domination, while in quest of the Kingdom of Heaven. They haven't yet understood the meaning of the Holy Scriptures where the Lord says, man can not serve two masters. These people want their cake and want to eat it too. All, whom simultaneously seeks for both royalty and loyalty concerning world domination, and the Kingdom of Heaven, are in error in their ways.

Meanwhile, they are misled into maliciously imposing adversity, obscurity, and desolation upon the hearts of those whom willingly shares their same said religion's vain version and perception of the Word of God. They sit, eat, and drink from the same cup, but yet can't stand each others. Instead of following the path of Christ, which teaches the human race to humbly stand bold on the Word of God in a stern, firm, and uncompromising way with a GENTLE REPROOF, the traditional rigid teachings of the religious sect of the Pharisees seems to motivate the 21st century tutors, scholars, and traditional religious members into standing bold and strong on the words of man which encourages one religion to vs. another in a rough reproof.

Instead of preserving the old wine in old bottles, they believe in retrieving, recovering, and salvaging the old, while adding a reinvented or renewed brand to the old. They do so in false hope of restoring the old dead methods of the Sect of the Pharisees' and Sadducees' ministry. Therefore, they work indeed to bring the rigid ways of both ministries back into existence. When Christ destroyed the old destructive religious ways of these ministries and all others that are similar to them, he made it impossible for such harsh ways of mankind to enter into the Kingdom of God.

In the mist of forcefully coercing the rigid ways of the sect of the Pharisees unto other Christian believers, mockingly a group of professional religious cultists and critiques subconsciously changes the meek and loving appearance of God to resemble the manifestation of a monstrous God within their ministry. They think God desires to devour and send you all to hell, because this desire equals their own desire. Therefore, they themselves feel like they need to direct your steps to follow the false prophets' incomprehensible laws of bondage that are marked and are noticeably identical to the Sect of the Pharisees, Sadducees, and the Scribes. All Christians of today's generation, whom are persecuted by the religious cultists' rigorous religious trainings, are freed by the blood of Jesus Christ to work on working out their own Salvation. The Christians are given the holy gifts of God as the proper tools to use against the traditional religious rituals which hereditarily distort the Lord's truth. The traditional religious rituals are also known for providing the people of the 21st century with false reasons to disbelieve that they are free. Therefore, many are unaware that they and/or their neighbors aren't obligated to do the old burdening law which devours the minds of men to live in a deep state of oppression and bondage. Many religious critiques have changed their own brotherhood, while giving in to the unreasonable assessments of which quality the traditional religious men may think is good for all to follow and which they say is bad to abandon, renounce, and forsake concerning the purest image of their own version of a Christian. In such cases, they all are made hypocrites.

HOW THE UNGODLY PATTERNS OF IRRELIGIOUS MEN EQUALLY COMPARES TO THE METHODS OF TRADITIONAL RELIGION?

Like the sect of the Pharisees and the Sadducees, the traditional religious communities of the 21st century are precise and accurate procedural wise, towards making creative works for themselves; to work their way into Heaven. They as false prophets broadcast the assessment of their works as if they disbelieve that the price Christ paid is enough to save all sinners from sin. They are no more different than any other person or group of people whom Christ came into the world to save, but if they think they are saved by the old law; then they too must do the whole law.

3

They curse themselves and forsake their own mercy into being obligated to do all that of the old law which God's chosen apostles foreseen, and Christ forewarned all to humbly understand that the repercussions and disadvantages of choosing to do the unreasonable traditional religious sacrificial services profits man nothing. The entire human race no longer are made obligated to throw stones at each others like they were commanded to do before the birth of Christ, or during the B.C time period.

After empathizing with the unreasonable services preached by false prophets, the saints and sinners can now spiritually compare the false ministries of today's generation; to know whether or not the today's ministries are equivalent to that of the sect of the Pharisees or of the Lord's ministry. Virtuously after seeing that the today's earthy gods, goddesses, saints, and sinners who are aware of the Gospel of Jesus Christ are gifted by God to spiritually discern and understand the justifiable cause and identifiable reason, which clearly explains the reason why God the Father desired through his love, mercy, and grace to send his only begotten Son into the world in the form of the flesh; was so that he might save all whom believes on his son from the condemning spirit. The greatest sin of all sins; comes from the spirit of condemnation, which provokingly places a yoke of bondage around the necks of all haters and chokes the godly life out of the spirit of them.

As false prophets ridiculously waver or float like a leaf in the wind, according to their faith they preach as doubters and nonbelievers of the Lord's holiest of all Holy Powers, and preach against the Lord's love, mercy, and grace, which is the foundation of God's sternest of all desire and ability to fairly save the least and the most despised race or human-being of the world. They corruptibly preach their unreasonable perceptions of the Gospel of Jesus Christ in a very stern and uncompromising or inflexible way. They train their children up to be despisers and haters of men. Unknowingly, they ignorantly teach their children how to dogmatically influence the legislative governing body of law of the lands to falsely appear to assert positivity, fairness, and godly love, but in reality they only assert iniquity through hatred.

4

In reality, their hypocritical religious theories, opinions, and overviews of agape love upholds the opposite principles and ideas than that which the Anointed teaches. According to the Anointed teachings of the Holy Ghost, God is love. (1Cor13:4) Any religion which discourages us from putting up with one another in despite of our faults and failings isn't humbled to receive the true message of the Lord's messenger whom writes Discerning Perceptive.

Being humbled doesn't make us a fool for man, but the false prophets whom makes themselves ministers of God teaches that an empathic heart makes a person susceptible to be weak and foolish enough to be a fool for man. They view empathy as a man's wickedness which encourages a false image of a person's fleshly weakness, but empathy being empowered by agape love helps us to be considerate and forgiving one towards another. False prophets either doesn't know or don't care to know, that they too are imperfect and have faults and failings. Love enables us to put up with one another, but the false prophets' unfulfilling religion publically proclaims themselves to be praiseworthy and others to be unworthy of receiving God's love, mercy, and grace.

Without wavering in faith, the messenger of Discerning Perceptive declares the value of a man's worth isn't counted as do the advice of false apostles who suggestively count slackness against a person. No man feels worthy, except through Christ Jesus. All who fails to know the Lord also fails to understand that everything and everyone made, is created by and for the love of God. All are created in the image and likeness of God. He loves his creation and all are worthy enough in the beginning of life and shall remain worthy unto the end; too receive his love, mercy, and grace. His Son didn't die in vain. He died to save the worthless, the worthy, and the unworthy alike. He even died to save a wretch like you and I, whom am a distressed people who evokes pity, forgiveness, and mercy.

During the 21st century, the religious pride that hides behind the boastings of the church organizations which false prophets and religious martyrs and scorners subsidizes and gives money too as a charity; subconsciously causes men to feel obligated to help in continuing the traditional functioning of the old law that vengefully promotes anger, hatred, and lies against the Holy Ghost. People are well known for using the traditional defective definition of what once was an acceptable religious behavior long before the birth, life, death, and resurrection of Jesus Christ, but now such traditional religious behaviors are defiantly misleading people to rebel against the good pleasures and the will of the Lord God.

Certain manmade ministers preach the Holy Word of God maliciously. The spiteful role of their ministry gives them a false sense of righteous authority when using the Lord's Word to stone a person to death. If indeed the thoughts of stoning a person to death is taught as an irreversible or permanent process, who then are the students of such teachings? Do they not know the truth or has evil deluded the minds of them into believing people are saved through false ministries, which uses the Word of God to condemn the inner-spiritual consciences of all sinners? If the Word was sent to condemn the inner-spiritual consciences of all sinners, then yes the false teachers would be religiously right about what they preach and practice. If Christ died to send people to Hell, then yes the false ministers are correct for worshiping the Lord under the Old Covenant and not the New.

Using the Word of God to stone a person's faith, equals the violent and disgraceful intent of humiliating sinners under the Old Law. In using the Word of God inappropriately to stone a sinner to death, is like discouraging them so ferociously that they start to have a lack of hope of being redeemed by the Lord and Saviour Jesus Christ. Killing the faith a person has on the Lord, indeed works to destroy and kills all that which is good within the godly spirit of the tutors and the pupils of such ministries. The laboring of false ministers preaches the Word of God without the clarity of the Holy Spirit. Unsurprisingly they misuse the Word of God and twist the holy truth of it with worldly wisdom being their chief successor. The primary intent of a false ministry is to overly exert the process of their own ignorance in an attempt to convince or

6

prove to others that their most important part of reasoning with the reign of terrors makes up the world's most respected cult churches of the 21st century only to save themselves from being persecuted or set outside the traditional religious assembly of men.

Therefore, to appease the focus and foundation of the today's false ministries' stern and viciously inhuman violent methods, patterns, and malicious ways; Satan works towards making all sinners believe in putting away or denying their God given Unalienable Rights as Freethinkers or Free spirits. The sole role and duty of false prophets and false ministers is to convincingly urge all of you sinners to disbelieve on the Power of the Lord who says, except for you sinners who sins the unforgivable sin as a liar against the Holy Ghost, or resides as an unbeliever who shall not receive the Kingdom of God; all others are saved by his blood. Satan knows that without hope no man shall be saved. Therefore, he and his servants work together to strip all hope and faith from the hearts of as many as they can, by convincing you to become a non-believer of the Lord's ability to deliver you out of the temptations of the world, and redeem your soul unto Salvation.

The strength of today's false ministries resides where ever Satan can firmly develop anguish, misery, and desolation within the Body of Christ's church. As Satan bringing about a dissimulation of love to hide his hatred; he works to weaken the faith of the Freethinkers and the Saints by imprisoning the minds of them into thinking that their sin is greater than the Power of God. In so doing, Satan prevents their free spirited hearts from humbly uniting together for the edification of Jesus as one Body in Christ. In other words, as the fusion of agape love works to replenish and restore the primary faith of all sinners so that none shall perish, the descendants of false ministries' increasingly desires to see more sinners made susceptible of having their faith on the Lord depleted. So that they themselves shall not feel persecuted by the Cross of Christ; they made the outer appearance of their ministry appear to be worshipping the Cross of Christ, but inwardly the works of their ministry indeed misleads sinners into having a lack of faith on the Lord. Like the leaders of the Sect of the Pharisees, the leaders of today's

7

false ministries teach its members to believe the strength of the old customs and heritages are the most powerful due to its age. Therefore, they devote their hearts to the oldness of the despots' dogmatic traditional religious standard principles and values, which automatically deludes their minds to believe that their religious loyalty to despotism during today's day of age will allow or make it possible for their main belief of fellowshipping to be exempt or excused from being required by God the Father, the Son, and the Holy Ghost to honor and devote their hearts to live and worship together in peace through the loving, merciful, and powerful Word of God under the New Covenant of Jesus Christ.

Normally they take pride in misusing the Word of God as a motivating religious tool for themselves to support certain particular traditional vain religious beliefs and rituals. Maliciously, they gain up on and against people who desire to renew their minds and repent of their past wrongs. They religiously practice devoting their hearts to feel enthusiastic about keeping hold of the traditional religious procedural standards and principles of the Sect of the Pharisees, which loves to condemn the weak and simple. In America their fairest of way of stoning a person to death is done without physically using rocks of stones, but by misusing the Word of God like a cloak of maliciousness. God sent the Word sent into the world to convict and save sinners from condemnation, but traditional religious martyrs uses the Word of God to restrain and condemn the conscious spirit, hearts, and minds of men in a ferocious way which substitutes the violent act of throwing physical stones and shedding blood.

In order to paint a vivid picture as an illustration to describe the impotence and powerlessness within the feeling of being helplessly stoned to death as a sinner during the 21st century by traditional religious martyrs, scorners, and false prophets requires an empathetic heart. For example, there is an International pressure being placed upon the Iranian government in hopes of preventing the enslaved Iranian citizens from being stoned to death. The Iranian citizens are held captive by their own government to not have the freedom of religion as we in America have it. Never once in history has the Iranian government taken heed to international pressure concerning their religious beliefs. Traditional religious leaders of that country unwaveringly believe God requires of them to execute and kill their citizens by stoning them to death if they as sinners are accused or caught committing adultery. While the American government hypocritically works to oversee the faulted system of a government overseas, its own systems stands in need of improvement in that same area of throwing stones at its tax paying citizens.

The traditional religious leaders of the American government are under pressure by activists and liberals who goes beyond religion to define equality and fairness. Although the American laws have made it unmistakably clear, that the government has always recognized and preserved marriage as a legal union of one man and one woman, in 1996 President Bill Clinton signed a marriage definition act called (DOMA=Defense of Marriage Act), and made it into law. Within the Defense of Marriage Act, marriages are classified to be legally viewed either as a first or second class of marriage. The federal government created new fair reform that acknowledged the American citizens' complaints, comments, questions and concerns towards the traditional marriage laws. The new modifications of DOMA; made alterations to the traditional standards for the eligibility of a married couple. Simultaneously, as DOMA made improvements for the sake of fairness and justice, the perception of the Word of God concerning traditional marriage caused some Christians to excuse DOMA and others to disapprove it. Those who approve it believe that DOMA is the beginning settlement to the long term dispute of traditional desolation and division in America. Some of them believe that the abomination (HATRED) of desolation (HOPELESSNESS) within events of today's generation relates to the prophecy of Daniel. They believe that the occurrences of abomination (Hatred) within the hearts of the 21st century religious martyrs are guilty of elevating an idolatrous altar of hatred and loathing for and against the weak and simple babes in Christ, upon the sacred altar of mankind's marriage to Christ; by being partially fair and partially bias unto and against them in an ungodly manner as worldly masters on

9

earth. Meanwhile, those who they accuse; also accuse them of doing the same thing as they charge DOMA of given the conscience (sense of right and wrong) of mankind over to idolatry.

Under this new form of government the standards of who can receive benefits provided by the federal government programs are based upon the sexuality of a couple. In other words, the government signifies only the traditional married householders are eligible to be recipients of federal assistance in most states. After 2004, when the first US state allowed same sex marriage, the marriage definition DOMA became a fortified gateway for the open debate which gay activists and liberals use to declare the federal government of America as unconstitutional. This only adds to the continuous debate of the Separation of Church and State in the form of America's legislative government.

Such daring debates stir up the vain acts of an emotional anger, which causes the inner-spirit of people to inappropriately behave as if they believe they have an adequate reason as Christians to pledge and devote to violence and hateful actions. The spreading of hatred as a religious attribute befits the unprofitable traits of false ministries. Haters, whom uses religion as an excuse to despise men; vehemently generates hatred to support and protect their own religiously sown characteristics and vengeful mindset which desires to have dominion on earth as rulers. The religious ideas of those who consider themselves to be superior are use to having the ability and legal authority to rule over other human beings. Those who promise to dedicate their hearts onto the traditional ideological and theoretical oppositions that are provided and are shown all throughout history are the seducers, gainsayers, and men-pleasers of the 21st century. Their hostile attitudes are recorded for the future generations to observe and preserve, as an old mark of the Old World's historical records.

In the past, the futile acts of violence in America once provided the majority of religious martyrs and scorners a false sense of having an everlasting source of a god fearing security boost; against the minority class. In the mist of them making it legal to take vengeance against whosoever they religiously despise, they showed indeed the measure and dedication of their disapprovals against others. The integrity of their philosophical religious values led their hearts to commend and praise the hostile actions that encrypt an incomprehensible price that goes beyond man's understanding of agape love. This is a common occurrence that still happens during their search for the Spirit of Righteousness and Truth. Only the Anointed Power of the Holy Ghost can reconvert their hostile hearts from seeking the vengeance of destruction, which doesn't match the peaceable and loving heart of the Lord; Jesus Christ. The virtue of their traditional religious standards signifies the debt of their own persuasive divisions, which exists today as a well known religious veneration and belief that is supported by the oldest and most respected of all denominational religions of the world. For this cause, many may see that the oldness of the letter doesn't make old doctrines holier or profitable.

In order to consummate the membership of a person to a false prophet's denominational religion, the new members are required to be willing to uphold the traditional religious desires of the Sect of the Pharisees as a religious respect, which encourages their hostile attitudes to deny God; by denying that their spiritual engagement with the Holy Spirit which lives within all whom are created by God. Traditional religious scorners and martyrs of men whom support the ideas of the false prophets' hostile definition of agape love falsely teach people to believe in the lie of the Adversary which indicates that they as despisers and haters of certain kinds of sinners shall receive the Kingdom of Heaven.

Such vain and unproductive practices religiously makes people think of being spiteful or malicious. The ideas of the false prophets also encourages people to use the Lord's name in a religious way of making a definite show of the flesh unto themselves and unto all others of their superiority in an attempt to prove that their vengeful religion stands for righteousness, although it does not. They believe that indeed they are doers of the Lord's Words, and being malicious is their way of making a defense for themselves on the behalf of supporting their traditional religion. This is just insane, and such persons are incompetent or irresponsible for their actions, because of their own ignorance or psychiatric disorder.

The Fruit of the Spirit of God proves what's acceptable unto the Lord, but the hypocrites of today's society are basing their religious relationship with the Lord God upon their inability to be free thinkers. Due to them having a complete lack of reason or foresight in causing chaos and confusion, they are of the world and the Lord has hid the truth from them. Their inadequate understandings of the Fruit of the Spirit of Righteousness and Truth are taught unto them as a false form of knowledge, which is provided unto them by other blind religious leaders of the world whom also are set apart from gaining an understanding of the Lord's heavenly truth. The heavenly truth indicates that all mankind who believes on the Lord are apart of the same Holy Root of the First Fruit of Jesus Christ. (Amen!)

The hearts of many are misled into building their faith upon the weak foundation of destructive lies and confusion, while the minds of them think; God is a partial God. As a result thereof; the manmade houses of the gods on earth reflectively encounter a chain reaction where the majority of the world electively creates or adds unconstructive criticisms into their religious political values. Within the hearts of a massive multitude of people who are misled to yield their hearts towards hatred, are the keen desires which represent the irrational barriers between religious politicians. Cunningly these people exercise unfairness during their trials and tribulations as they carryon with the desire to have lordship on earth and excuse their own selfish overly-excessive needs to live imprudently by the wisdom of this world in a despotic and discriminatory way, while in vain they gloat in their worldly glory.

Ignorance has been proven by the Fruit of the Spirit of God, to not be the work of God. The knowledge of the Holy Spirit makes manifest and brings awareness unto the saints of every society and origin of people, whom seeks for the Kingdom of Heaven. Meanwhile, the undeniable heavenly truths reflectively are shown as the consequence and end result of every unproductive infertility that is residing within the legalized manmade laws of the land. The indisputable truth of the Holy Spirit reveals how the unlawful traditional laws of the land place a person or a group of people into bondage, and forcefully coerces them to live through either a psychological or physical state of poverty. In so much of a desire of mankind, this isn't done by the will or by the works of the Spirit of God. Obviously, such unfair laws were originally thought-up and made to serve as the support hose for the heartless supremacists whose common interests and likenesses consist of the same old worldly desires, which men used centuries ago to make themselves outwardly appear to be more holy than thou. In so doing they have kept, maintained, and upheld the tyrannous measure of the Pharaoh of Egypt whose religious dictatorship reigned against the will of Moses, the will of God, and against the will of the minority, and inferior groups of people.

The unfair standards and principles of the traditional religious tyrants' perception of the Word of God in the beginning caused a broad spread of discrimination to occur all throughout the world. The act of bigotry has influenced the religious intolerances and has lessened the hearts of men to desire to unite as One Body in Christ with every sort of mankind who confesses Jesus as their Lord and Savior. The act of hatred smeared the faith of the inferior and the superior class of people before and after the life, death, and resurrection of Jesus Christ. Therefore, as one generation pass unto the next the inferior and superior class of people have gradually became tarnished, spotted, and blemished by the tyrannous traditional religious teachings which lacks heavenly wisdom and spiritual truth, because hatred causes the heart of mankind to be filled with much deception and confusion.

The oppressors' traditional religious teachings completely demands and desires for all church going people of every creed and of all denominational religions within today's society to devote their hearts to simultaneously fight vigorously one against another, and to stand together equally yoked against every idea of legally changing any governing law of the land that is dogmatically written. This sort of vain fighting to them seems to be God's definition of a good fight of faith. In the singleness of the spiritual eye of Christianity, the point of views and values of the oppressor's ethnic code of religious beliefs are revealed as a drawn up petition or doctrine which religious men uses to systematically lift the voice of their opinions against the love, mercy, and grace of God.

They fail to understand that because of God's love, everyone who believes on the Lord is protected by God's mercy. The Lord's mercy keeps us from receiving the wrath of God which we all may deserve, and his grace blesses us with things we don't deserve. This is the true definition of the Compassion of Christ, which false teachers have not the power to obtain.

The system of traditional religious believers is based upon their inadequate study and lack of heavenly knowledge concerning faith and morals. As they fear what the do not understand, they also preach against what they fear without seeking for knowledge to get an understanding. As they preach boastfully against what they do not understand, the sworn duty of them lives by the unwarranted and arrogant viewpoints and opinions of either a despot authoritative person or the despot instructions and guidelines of a religious tenet or theory. These sorts of ideological views, beliefs, and opinions require and seduce people to refuse to open their hearts and minds to the spiritual side of the Gospel of Jesus Christ. Like a scorner or a martyr whom are willing to die for their religion, the despots spiritually dare not to change their old dictatorial way of thinking. We all should serve the Lord in newness of spirit and not in the oldness of the letter in hopes of putting away the desires of the flesh, because the desires of the flesh waits patiently to destroy the holiest of holy; concerning the Gospel of Jesus Christ.(Romans 6:2, 6,7:6)

The despot religious rulers of the world prefer to count slackness against the faith of a person or a group of people. While acting out of vengeance, these cruel religious rulers traditionally refuses to accept the true fullness of the Gospel of Christ which indicates how God provides hope for all to consume as a reproved approach towards bring unity unto one of another for the edification of the Body of Christ. Instead of working on uniting together as one Body of Christ, the loyalty of the despots count slackness against all whom they are religiously trained to despise to make themselves appear to be superior rulers. Under such provisions and stipulations the hearts of them causes divisions to hang every religious quarter of their own impious minds. Traditionally, people such as these are tutored and trained to believe on the religious percept which works to prevent or disallow the true nature of God's agape love and compassion of Christ from being the key foundation of man's truest focus within the walls of the world's most respected traditional religious denominations; by which man makes written doctrinaires and laws for. God's gift of love, freedom, and compassion for all people should not only be mentioned within the fullness of every governed constitution made by man, but it also should include the righteous sense of fairness, equality, and justice for the inferior race of the lowly peoples during the reformation of democracy. Unfortunately this is not clearly glorified by the historical governed constitutions created by man, because it takes away their power to have dominion.

(Prov.13:12)The conclusions of such unholy laws and policies created by man defers, hangs, and suspends the faith and the hopefulness of the hearts of many people by seducing the hearts of them to give way to the earthy judgments, opinions, wishes, and evil sensations of the flesh; that loves to hate, envy, strife, and commit all sorts of other evil acts against people of all ages including elders and children. Such sins are also made against God and reduce the remorseful hearts from desiring to repent, because subjectively they have no shame in wrong doings (2Cor.7:1-12). When one inwardly understands to do right, but is forcefully coerced to abide by another law like the unlawful commandments of men; they break the covenant which the Lord personalized by writing his laws in their individual hearts. (Heb.8:10-13)

Romans10:11 "For the scriptures
saith, Whosoever believeth on him
shall not be ashamed."

Before waking up out of the life of ignorance which blinds, confines, and imprisons the conscience of an individual babe or a group of people with worldly religious lies; the hearts of the people are weighed down by the world's burdening perceptions that inwardly causes an individual to wrestle against flesh and blood while warring against the earthy principality and powers of worldly men. The world's traditional religious images and ideas indeed work to keep all mankind under bondage. The worldly are unwise to understand the truth about the loving will of God. The truth from time to time becomes buried or clouded unto them by their traditional religious deceptions, which provokes anger and feeds mankind the earthy desire and fleshly sensations that comes from the sown seeds of hatred. The desires of the flesh turn the spiritual heart of mankind to provokingly hate or to despise their neighbors who openly confess their sin. For example; some gray-haired elders who are misled to think more of themselves than they ought, sits within certain religious organizations and coerce the youth to believe that an elderly person have no sin or hasn't ever sinned a day of their lives. In so doing they kill the religious enthusiasm of the youth by requiring of them to do what they themselves cannot; like live without sinning.

The Word of God is true, but after it has perversely been subverted by traditional religious men to befit the traditional religious realm of the world, the lies within the world's sense of what thus saith the Lord thy God, traditionally deludes the original meaning of the Word of God and turns the image of the incorruptible God to appear to be monstrously corrupt. It's a known fact to all mankind, that a half truth is still a lie. It's traditional for men who make themselves apostles of Christ to use fair words and well put together speeches to half way explain the intentional love, mercy, and grace of the Lord and Savior. The Word of God doesn't lie, but the words of man makes God appear to be a liar, because without knowing God; the words of men cannot indeed teach the Word of God to the full extent of meanings. Again, I the messenger and author of Discerning Perceptive indeed say; "A partial truth is still a lie."

In most cases through confusion many people believe that God contradicts himself, although he really does not. What causes them to think he does is the fact that they've been tutored and coerced to believe in the false projections, which indicates God to be an all powerful partially bias monstrous God, who desires to send all sinners to Hell. This made-up image of God is what the false Apostles' hearts fear, and they teach all mankind to share that same worldly fear.

The fear of Satan is led by the dark spirit of Condemnation and not by the Spirit of Righteousness. (1John3:17-21) The spirit of Condemnation comes to destroy the Spirit of Man, but the power of the Lord's Spirit of Righteousness comes to revive and save all condemned hearts. People need to understand that when the comforter comes within the Spirit of Righteousness it adds unto them a godly sorrow that leads them towards righteous repentance. The character of righteous repentance doesn't burden the devoted makeup of the heart of anyone with grief nor misery, but it brings them the compassion of Christ's love, peace, and joy during their temporal time period on earth. It is the nature of the spirit of Condemnation to kill and bring the heart of the weak to be burdened by the sufferings of worldly sorrows, despair, grief, and misery.

> Romans11:11 "I say then, Have they stumbled that they should fall? God forbid: but rather through their fall salvation is come unto the Gentiles, for to provoke them to jealousy."
> Romans11:12 "Now if the fall of them be the riches of the world, and the diminishing of them the

riches of the Gentiles; how much more their fulness?"
Romans11:13 "For I speak to you Gentiles, inasmuch as I am the apostle of the Gentiles, I magnify mine office:"
Romans11:14 "If by any means I may provoke to emulation them which are my flesh, and might save some of them."

(Merriam Webster School Dictionary: definition of Emulation is that it means to eagerly desire to equal or excel & cause a rival against)

Romans11:15 "For if the casting away of them be the reconciling of the world, what shall the receiving of them be, but life from the dead?"
Romans11:16 "For if the firstfruit be holy, the lump is also holy: and if the root be holy, so are the branches."(Romans9:11-21)

(Gal.1:7/2Cor.11:14) For instance, the accursed world's traditional religious concept of the Word of God is that sinners shall not receive the Kingdom of Heaven, but they fail to spiritually teach that the significance of the anointed message of the Word of God is to deliver all sinners out of the temptations of the world and that the Lord desires that none should perish. Meanwhile, they believe they are alive in Christ, although their faith is full of dead works which profits them nothing. They cast away and revile people whom God created; as if they believe life is granted unto mankind from the dead works of casting away a person who desires to know God. The dead works of their flesh works to satisfy their own religious desire to have dominion over the faith of all whom they religiously believe in casting away during their traditional religious pursuit of having an excessive relation with God.

All thanks goes to God that the anointed message of the Holy Scriptures is filled with his heavenly wisdom, which converts and wipes out the vain formation of such traditional religions' mental images from the dark hearted imaginations of men. It is by the teachings of the anointed, which prevents the same old vain discriminatory imaginations from reentering the hearts of God's chosen people through their faith on the Lord. The anointed wisdom of God allows the blind to see and understand how the traditional misinterpreted messages of their tutors of past times boastfully cast away people which God foreknew before the law of sin was introduced unto them.(Rom.1:18-32/11:1-2/Eph. 4:17-18)

HATH NOT THE POTTER POWER OVER THE CLAY? (ROMANS9:21-23)

Because God concluded that all humans fall short to sin, he sent his only begotten Son in the form of the flesh; to teach all mankind how to live in this world with sin, because he knew all shall fall short to sin. Meanwhile, traditional religious church's teaches men to live in denial of being sinners. Whosoever says they have no sin is a liar and the truth isn't in them. It is by the teachings of the Holy Ghost that the chosen few learns how to live with sin without being hypocritical towards others and without being deceitful nor deceived. Be not deceived this doesn't mean God is the Father of sin, therefore the Gospel of Jesus Christ teaches us how not to indulge ourselves to the practice of sin. (Romans6)

The Holy Ghost makes intercession to the Spirit of Man as to reveal and mediate unto all believers exactly how to properly use the spiritual gifts of God that are freely given unto us by God, so that everyone of us may gain strength in faith; to confess the Son of God as our Lord and Saviour. It is by the Lord's mercy and grace through our faith on the Lord, that anyone of us shall be delivered out of the temptations of the world for the true arbitration of God. After receiving the Holy Ghost and strength in faith, we individually are provided a unique escape route of liberation as a spiritual defensive comfort within the Word of God, which rescues us from being consumed by the psychological traps of traditional religious bondage.

Deliverance unto us is a blessing which enables us to understand our spiritual abilities to be obedient unto God; knowing that death is the last enemy which the Lord shall destroy for us all. Death symbolically represents anything that causes us misery and worldly sorrows; including anger, hatred, envy, jealousy etc., because all are enmity against God and leads all whose hearts yields to such acts and emotions to destruction and death. (St.Luke12:10/St.Matt.12:30-32/St.Mark3:28-29) Only if we are not a nonbeliever of the power of the blood of Jesus or if we do not blaspheme against the Holy Ghost does the Power of God forgive us of our trespasses, and the Power of God also gives unto us the power to forgive one of another; without us accusing another living soul.

(2Cor.11:15/Rom.2:1-13)Meanwhile, instead of exhorting God's gift which is the gift of knowledge of the Holy Ghost for all goodness sake by testifying and preaching that it is Christ whom was ordained by God to be the Judge of the quick and the dead; traditional religious scornful men hypocritically makes themselves an apostle and live under the old law in the same way of the Pharisees, Sadducees, and scribes as judges themselves. They do so as if Christ's birth, life, death, and resurrection were for nothing. (St. Matt.23:1-4/Acts10:42-48/2Tim.4:1-5)

Falsely and imprudently traditional religious people preach and teach one of another how to use the Word of God as a cloak of maliciousness as they judge the Word of God and compare one of another by the unreasonable partitions made under their own traditional religious laws and concept of the Holy Scriptures. Christ contained and placed limits or restrictions against the traditional religions' unreasonable partitions, as he walked in the flesh. (St. Matt.16:5-12) Therefore we all should beware of the doctrine of traditional religions which profits man nothing. The Gospel of Jesus Christ describe the fears and unreasonable sacrifices that are traced back to traditional religions to be divisible from the Fruit of the Spirit of Righteousness, just as the Holy Spirit identifies or make manifest of the false teachings within the statures of traditional religion that are likened that of the one who creates enmity against God.

Christ requires for all to keep in remembrance of the Commandments of the Word of God of the Old Testament, but within limits as of a learning process thereof; for the sake of us spiritually transitioning ourselves from the Old Covenant to the New. The New Covenant consist of all which we all have heard since the beginning..."God is Love." So we are commanded by God to "Love Thy Neighbor as Thy Love thyself". Some are unwise to know and understand who their neighbors are. (St.Luke10:25-36)Their neighbors consist of domestic strangers and good Samaritans alike, whether the people are foreign or are un-foreign. (Eph.5:29-33) No man truly hates his own flesh, but is often misled to hate their family, brethren, and neighbors alike.

The unreasonable judges of the idol minded traditional religious church ministries during the 21st century still prefer for its members and every civilian of their local community to convert and turn their conscience over to desire to do whatsoever ungodly things that binds them to traditionally preach and teach one of another to practice pretending to be God. This sort of vain idol worship makes them all commit to the same classical errors of the Pharisees' tradition. Their reprobate minds are coerced into thinking more of themselves than they ought. Therefore, they religiously make themselves outwardly appear holy in so much that they are physically accepted in the eyes of men as to befit themselves to sit in Moses seat; like the scribes and the Pharisee once were implicit to believe the best way for them to serve God was by exercising lordship over others by exercising authority upon them as ministers and not as servants. (St.Matt.23:1-19, 23-37/St.Mark10:35-45) While they cunningly teach the Lord's babes to desire having the judging powers which belongs only to God, their abominable and detestable

21

messages binds heavy burdens on their shoulders by making the babes feel grievous to be born. Some burdens holds so much weight against the faith of the weak and simple until it causes them to disbelieve on the power of the God and in vain wonder if God created them just to send them to Hell.

Even a blind man can see how the tutors of such hypocritical religious orders live in sin and preach the Word of God to save themselves, but will not lift one figure to move the burdens they place on the consciences of others as to revive them from the dead works of bondage with the inspiring Word of God. It's like they glory in the flesh of the simple and the weak babes in Christ as a sacrificial ritual, to make their selves feel good about accusing others while putting down their dignity. The burden of their accusations falsely tells the simple and weak to do what they cannot do; as an unreasonable sacrifice or service.

These traditional religious tutors without fear publically proclaim their ministry is the righteous ministry of the Lord, but they follow Satan's constructive methods which places political politics into the foundation of their love for their ministry. Their dissimulated love desires to have an overly excessive outlook on life, which falsely labels a perfect servant of God as someone who devotes their conscience to live under the evil thoughts of a denominational religious leadership which practices yielding their hearts to despise their neighbors. These religious organized groups have followed the world's evilly revised perceptions of the New Commandment for centuries, and their followers clearly define love within the curse of the Old Law. Such love in the end is a vain useless key to the Kingdom of Heaven. Yes, even the Old Law said, "GOD IS LOVE.", but after it has been twisted into hate; love is turned into the darkness of night and is as hard and feel as cold as a stone. As we live under Christ's New Covenant, and it is prudent for us all to know and understand that everyone who lives without the fullness of God's LOVE do not know God nor do they possess "THE KEY TO THE KINGDOM OF HEAVEN."

Hypocritically, it's commonly known for traditional religious leaders to teach their members that they ought to do what they themselves cannot do. Without having a clear conscience unto God, they seductively preach unto the simple and the weak to practice the acts of despising their neighbors like Satan despise every living soul that God made. They also teach their members to always rely on their eyes physically seeing an engrave image of God, which resembles the prosperity of a rich man. Symbolically, the engrave image of a rich man religiously represents whom false apostles believes has the favor of being on Christ right-hand side. Meanwhile, the outer appearance of prosperity which their physical eyes see; keeps their focus not on the Lord, but on being busy bodies that deal in worldly matters. This method defines and supports the point of their religious accusations which they make against sinners of all ages, nationality, sex, or religious creed unto God. Either they don't know or they fail to understand that those who confess Jesus as their Lord and Saviour are angles of God. Some are weaker than others, but all fall short to sin in some form or fashion. Most denominational religions teach people to not believe that those whom they religiously despise and accuse unto God are created from the Pure Root of the First Fruit of Jesus Christ.

Like during the first battle in heaven, Satan's jealousy on earth is over the Power of God and it sets a spark to the flare of warring here on earth. Satan's form of jealousy on earth works to coerce God's Angles to think the righteous image of God is equivalent to the malicious and unfair commandments of traditional religious men. Satan is a liar and was a liar since the beginning. His teachings during the 21st century are revealingly seen to be in accordance with the perception of the religious warfare of the men who makes unrighteous judgments against other men of God, by making an insufficient attempt to measure someone's sin; as if they themselves have no sin. They brutally beat those who they find with sin and persecute them with traditional vain philosophies and words of deceit for the ordinances of their own impure perceptions of God's love. They think God requires of them to insult and cause misery and injury to whosoever they love to despise.

They preach to the simple and weak spirits to do the things that they themselves can't do, only to make their selves outwardly appear to be God's chosen people. They boastfully preach corruptibly like ravening ravishers over the Lord's Sheep in a desperate attempt to inwardly seize, control, and confine the consciences of the babes' purest love, by trying to remove the Spirit of hope and faith on the Power of God from the hearts and minds of them. The fair words and well put together speeches of the false prophets takeaway the denote meanings of what the Lord says he'd do by, for, and through his almighty love, mercy, and grace which delivers and saves all who believe on him.

As Satan's children work to take the comforting power of the Holy Spirit away from all whom they despise, they publically praise and speak well as a liar by stating that they don't lie against the Holy Ghost. Hypocritically, they think they are in sink with the Holy Spirit of God as they devote their hearts to daily worship the father who teaches them to love as a despiser and a hater of men. Although they preach and profess that they believe that they are edifying the Lord through their deeds, they spiritually fail to attempt to revive the spirit of those who they've seductively coerced to disbelieve on the power of God. They fail to teach them that God has the power to deliver them out of every situation they maybe in. God himself is keeping hid from such ministries of the one truth of the Gospel of Jesus Christ, because the truth is hidden from the world. They who are of the world perceive not the righteous ordinance of God, and they that are blind shall lead the blind into the ditch. False leaders and followers fails to teach the weak and the simple babes in Christ that Jesus has already paid the ultimate price to redeem all of them which believes on the power of him. Due to false doctrine, the weak and simple are susceptible to be misled by the blind who iodize earthy things rather than having their Spirit encouraged with confidence to have great expectations through faith on the Redeemer.

A Spiritual Restoration is evolving amongst all whom are declared as the most despised within the world. As the most despised gain the Lord's favor to receive heavenly knowledge to clearly understand what the spiritual image of his New Commandment looks and feels like, they are enabled by the Holy Ghost to associate their own inner childlike purest spirits with the Greatest of All Commandment which is the same commandment we've all heard since the beginning. The Lord commands the most despised to Love the oppressors, and choose none of their evil ways.

After gaining such knowledge, the spiritual revival of the conscience of one's moral mindset has an effect on one's thoughts, which causes an individual to stop and think; "(WWCD?) What Would Christ Do?" Without hypocrisy this moral thought becomes an automatic part of their mindset during Every Situation! This extra thought leads the Lord's people to reevaluate and self examine their selves by the comparison of the Spirit of Christ, for the sake of edifying the entire Body of Christ without spots and blemishes. Through the singleness of the eye, they also are revealingly seen by the three whom bare a greater witness in heaven than the three witnesses in earth. The three in heaven occupy their minds to spiritually be opened to heavenly wisdom as their hearts desire to follow Christ. They indeed separate themselves from other doctrines, which once may have blindly misled them to do evil things, including spiritually beating a person's Spirit of Hope of being redeemed to death. All glory is to God for sending his son whom may save all by manifesting unto all that any doctrine or denomination which beats a person's spirit to death without reviving or resurrecting them indeed are a vain religion and such religious pride is vanity and is unseemly.

The stratagems of Satan's coercions affects people today the same as it affected man in the beginning, like during the days of Adam and Eve. Satan still uses his knowledge of the Word of God to seduce the seekers of the Lord's ministry into committing their faith to disbelieve that the most despised shall be redeemed. Like Eve, there still are the existence of those of them during the 21st century whom are willing to yield their hearts to Satan's unwise and overly excessive desire to either be like

God; knowing good and evil, or to be the judge of the Word of God as if they are God; the One True Judge. These people are susceptible of being tricked by Satan's cunningly disguised stratagems, which cloaks, covers, and conceals the Lord's truth. Just like Satan coerced Eve into tricking Adam into disbelieving the Word of God, and doing what God commanded them both to not do; Satan is coercing people of today's society into being covetous. Those whom are tricked by the wiles of Satan, selfishly and ruthlessly are indeed working to imprison the conscience of others by tricking them into desiring vain glory.

THE HISTORICAL CONVERSION OF THE OLD LAW INTO CHRISTIANITY AND THE CONVERSION OF ESCHATOLOGY: The ideological lessons of the end of the World.

Certain traditional religious denominations subconsciously teach its members to yield their hearts to believe that imminence is equivalent to immediacy although it's not. Yet many construes the two as one of the same, rather than to set them apart to see that imminence is firmly fixed in place as the primary basis for steadfastness and dogged persistence concerning all whom lives in eager expectation of Christ's return. Some who preach the gospel hangs the end of the world concept threateningly over one's head in hope of saving some by showing the immediate importance of one's faith.

(Acts 17) In faith, Apostle Paul who is the author of 1Thessalonians wrote an Epistle to provide confirmed guidance to the Church at Thessalonica and all nearby churches (Acts 5:17-30) and to excite their faithfulness and piety in all goodness and holiness. Only a few months after the first letter; probably approximately about A.D.51; he also write the 2Thessalonians from Athens to commend and speak well of their faith and charity (**love**). The second letter of Apostle Paul which is defined in the King James version; set the record straight and rectifies the people's mistake in judging that the Day of Judgment was at hand.

The letter includes: 1:3-12 which gave the people the commendation or the approval for patience in persecution; 2:1-12 gave them an explanation regarding future events; 2:13-3:15 appeal strongly to

26

steadfastness, prayer, and industry; and finally it includes in 3:16-18 where Apostle Paul provided an ending prayer of blessings with salutation which also compliments and express the Lord's goodwill as he reached the closing stages of warning all against idleness.

Satan's deliberation of the Holy Scriptures goes against the evidence of what the Fruit of the Spirit signifies unto man, and his forethoughts rectify the mirror image and reflection of his own kind of worthless qualities which transfigure and change the denote meaning of godliness. As an end result of his construed suggestions, eschatology is formed. Eschatology is a branch of theology or religious beliefs on a doctrine that concern the ultimate or final destination of the human race including the Second Coming or the Last Judgment; "The Book of Revelation."

Instead of the members of these denominational religious groups and organizations edifying the entire body of Christ; they are forsaking their own mercy as they enviously covet and grasp after Satan's theory of a modest or an inconspicuous nature of humility. Their philosophical religious theories are originally begotten out of anger and greed, which electrically transfers into jealousy, vengeance, and strife. They hypocritically love the idea of themselves having a closer relationship with the Lord than everybody else. They are tricked into covering the Lord's Word of Truth with lies. In such cases, Satan tricks many into disbelieving that there is no dissimulation in love, and through their disbelief they revere hatred as a substitution of LOVE like ravening wolves. They act as if they believe they are required by God to serve the acts of injustice against one of another or against those who they religiously are trained to despise, despite of them hearing the preaching of the Gospel which states that all who confess Jesus as their Lord and Savior shall be redeemed by the Redeemer. The iniquities of various sorts of religious denominations works against the entire human race and against God by tricking and keeping the hearts and minds of the weak and simple babes in Christ living in doubt as to make one to have a lack of trust on the Power of God. The iniquities of various sorts of denominational religions seductively tempt all to believe on false perceptions and old wives fables concerning the Doctrine of Jesus

Christ, which tempts and seduces the members of the Body of Christ to be unholy servants of sin instead of making them servants to righteousness unto the holiness of Christ.(Romans6:19-22)

Without love and compassion people are made impoverished and destitute of the Lord's Truth. They seek to equip themselves with physical knowledge of the Holy Bible as tutors and scholars, but they are ever learning and never able to come to the knowledge of the spiritual truth. (2Tim.3:7-17) Their corrupt minds are reprobate concerning the faith. They memorize The Names of the 5 books of Moses and mark the religious rituals done on the Day of the Pentecost, with the desire to emulate the Holy Ghost. They may emulate the outer appearance of what the scriptures physically describes the Holy Ghost looks like, but the teachings of Holy Ghost is an inner spiritual experience which the powers thereof cannot be premeditated nor faked.

With all devotional respect being given unto the physical appearance of all who are in unity and on one accord in one religious place or another (Acts2), Christians today desires to recapture the spiritual atmosphere of The Day of the Pentecost. As a traditional ritual, many false prophets and false teachers think they have captured the fullness of Christ. They attempt to make themselves appear to have been blessed by God with the gift of the Holy Ghost, but inwardly they know the Holy Ghost have not yet come unto them. Therefore they pretend to speak the Word of God in an unknown tongue as if the Spirit gives them utterance. (St.Matt.23)The purpose of all their works are to be seen by man, because they think more of themselves than they ought.

After the Day of the Pentecost, Christ made it clear unto all to learn and understand the will and way of God; so that they may have the stability to be encouraged to stop practicing the things which goes against the will of God. It is unwise for anyone to dare speak the Word of God in an unknown tongue or in another language without there being an interpreter present. Since speaking in tongues are for a sign to them that believe not, (Deut.10:12-22/Eph.5:17/Roman12/1Peter1:13-17) without an interpreter a person can possibly be putting on a show that serves no purpose except for the purpose of seducing the heart of the weak and simple to be set upon false hope. (1Cor.12:31, 14:22-40)

The real ministry of Christ Church was build upon the solid rock of the Word of God, which teaches the reason for Christ's birth, life, death, and resurrection is to save all who believes on him, but due to the cause of false brethren who crept in as unawares to spy out the Free Spirit which we have in Christ Jesus; we must stand firmly together as did the chosen Apostles at the churches of Galatia against those whom haven't the spiritual sense to completely understand neither the Old Law nor the New. (Gal.1:1-2, 2:1-6) They are religiously taught to use the Holy Scriptures in the same old ordinance of the prince of the world which is why educated scholars like to think they can work their way into Heaven. Therefore, so that they might bring the weak and simple into bondage they like to boast that they may appear to rule the religious realm by the vote of the majority. It is the desire of the prince of the world who prefers for people to vehemently misuse certain scriptures to view his preference of defining and judging the Word of God as a judge and not a doer. By the bowels of their own bellies they confirm their own desires towards devoting their reverence and respect of God on idolatry as non-compassionate tyrannous religious tyrants. Through their unbelief of the Power of God, their work is enmity against the Spirit of God.

Certain traditional religious perceptions of what thus saith the Lord thy God encourages people to be inspired and aroused by the evil intentions of Satan in the area of desiring to humiliate all of humanity by speaking down on their dignity and accusing them unto God as unworthy. Such inspirational worldly wisdom indeed works as the spot and blemish of the flesh of all who yield their hearts to believe in Satan's perceptions of the Word of God. In today's society many churches are poorly orchestrated and are destitute of the Holy Truth. They place all of their efforts into condemning and imprisoning the consciences of people who confess Jesus Christ as their Lord and Saviour, by burdening their hearts into believing that the Lord left them with no hope of ever being delivered out the worldly things that tempts them to sin. During their vain and greedy efforts of being saved, they work not as servants of God whom uses the Word of God to help others, but they work diligently as servants of Satan's whom only think they are saving themselves by attempting to send all who they religious despise to hell.

Most religious discouragements such as these normally come from religious people who think more of themselves than they ought. Their evil way of living is in accordance to what they believe thus saith the Lord thy God requires and commands of them. Their intentions indeed are proven by the fruits they bear to be deluded and deceived by their overly excessive desire to be God. Had they heard the Gospel of Christ and believed, they would've grown in the Word of God to know and understand that the false perceptions of what thus saith the Lord thy God; brings about foolish and unlearned questions. These questions feeds the spirit too gender strife and religiously make people consider that men-pleasers, seducers, and gainsayers are systematically and precisely living righteous during their daily walk of life. Those who consider such either don't know or don't understand that they aren't worshipping in accordance with the righteous way of the Lord.

Traditionally, they seek to enthuse and excite God's people into believing in their sort of religious venerations and ideological images of God, which is an animated creation of Satan's description of God's image. Satan describes himself unto mankind as God and through his coerced dictatorship he dogmatically describes God unto the entire human race as an unfair and monstrous God. Through jealousy, Satan's description of how the spirit of mankind should simulate the image of God; beguiles all whose character and moral virtues seeks to equal the simulation of an oppressor. Indeed they suggest that oppressing the spirit of others is to them as a righteous simulation of the love, mercy, and grace of Jesus Christ; the Lord God Almighty. For centuries, Satan has seduced many to be ignorant of the Lord's New Law of Righteousness, which proves the spiritual contents of what is reasonably good, godly, holy and acceptable unto God. (Romans 10)

Like that old-time religious practice of the Pharisees, Sadducees, and the Scribe, the traditional religious martyrs of today's society are falsely teaching God's people to believe that God purposely wants the Gospel of Jesus Christ to be evilly preached. Therefore, they preach the gospel in the way which encourages people to fully devote their hearts into vengefully protecting the deprived traditional religious rituals which lacks good sense, empathy, and agape love. These traditional beliefs and rituals instinctively and automatically are keeping the hearts and minds of a massive majority of religious people bound by hatred. These false teachers are unwilling to humbly co-exist in this world as peace makers, with whosoever they may fear; due to their own lack of understanding of what makes them distinctively different. They live without the human intervention of agape love, and they separate themselves from the Spirit of God during their violent times spent ridiculing, persecuting, and crucifying one of another on earth.

The unlawfulness of one's heart prunes and disengages their ability to receive the Lord's heavenly wisdom. The Holy Spirit allows all who believes on the Lord the ability to clearly understand the Spirit of his holiness, which is defined within the Holy Scriptures. Chaotically, indeed lawlessness or the lack of self-control makes people vulnerable of being easily misled or tricked into upholding the fleshly desires, which supports religious boastings of an ungodly pride. Like most scorners who boast, the spirits within them are filled with the characteristics of hatred and unrighteous judgments. In exchange for making religious claims of having the rite to have dominion and supremacy over others, their religious mayhem in return converted their hearts to desire the type of empowerment which is designed to attempt to control and restrain all Christian citizens' on earth. Indeed false teachers work steadfastly, in hopes of converting the purest and most content heart **(the heart of a child)** into desirously being discontent in unbelief and unhappiness.

The weak and simple babes in Christ are cunningly seduced by the vain philosophies and theoretical conclusions of the false prophets, whom release their fear of God through a religious expression of hatred. While they use the Lord's name in vain, they minister lies against the Lord's ordain Commandment of Love. As they lie in efforts to protect their coerced religious reasons for attempting to justify their misuse of the Word of God as a cloak of maliciousness, they also lie against the Lord's Holy Spirit of Righteousness and Truth. Since the beginning of sin, this has been the way Satan seduce people into thinking that despising sinners and spreading hatred is equivalent to the Lord's way of righteousness.

(Ex.12:15, 18; 13:1-10/Lev.2:11)Corruptibly Satan uses the Word of God to distort and beguile the hearts of Christian believers by misrepresenting unto them the grace of God's unconditional love for the devilish kind of love that is conditional. All who are seduced by the religious culture of Satan resides among the living in a dissimulation of love in an orderly but anarchy fashion. In such case, chaos is formed within the hearts of these men in despite of their desire to know and love God. Through chaos, many are forcefully influenced to eat the meats that are presented unto them by the false teachings of the leaven of the Pharisees and the Sadducees in despite of their pure hearts desiring to keep the feast with the unleavened bread of sincerity and truth. (St.Matt.16:11/1Cor.5:6-8)

"WAKE UP!"

As Christians of the 21st century we must awake out of sleep and wisely understand that our good fight of faith is an inward fight against the wiles of Satan. The stratagems of Satan encourages the entire human race to become discouraged and this depression comes between and separate the spiritual faith which religious people have on the Redeemer; Jesus Christ. Jesus is the One whom has the power, the will, the good pleasures, and the love to save even the most despised human being. Satan's religious perception of the Word of Truth deludes the Lord's Heavenly Truth with lies and misleads the heart of God's people into seeking to find the wars that are best fought in an outwardly fight against flesh and blood. Therefore, religious people create reasons to war with one of another.

It is up to us to study the Word of God and through our private studies the Holy Spirit within the Holy Scriptures converts our worldly way of thinking into desiring to resist or restrain ourselves from the temptations of the world which Satan cunningly presents unto us as a gift. His deluded version of a gift curses us but blesses him as we are tricked into seeking too gain and maintain MONEY & CONTROLING POWERS of authority either over religious dominance or through a monarchy government. After comparing spiritual things with spiritual, through our personal studies of the Word of God; we all can agree that Anarchy and chaos during today's generation is still found all throughout the embracement of every arisen broaden traditional religious organization which practice enmity, bigotry, intolerance, and every sort of prejudice act.

The Holy Ghost teaches us through the Holy Scriptures that there's no dissimulation in love, but false teachers religiously teach people to verbally and physically seek to persecute, belittle, and crucify the spiritual dignity of the weak and simple babes whom are in Christ. The error of a religious person whom seeks to defile and condemn the conscience of another living soul, forsakes their own mercy and does so to justify their debased and despoiled reasons of why they maliciously use the Word of God to discriminate. After comparing spiritual things with spiritual, the Fruit of the Spirit revealing proves that at some point in the religious livelihood of the human race the pure hearts of the most respected of all religious leaders are corruptibly tempted to desire to be equal to God.

Many were called by God, and a few are chosen. Therefore, the fakers falsely judge the characteristics of the Power of the Lord God and incorrectly show favoritism for and/or against the simple and weak. Such judgments have spoiled mankind since the first sin was committed, and misleads their hearts astray from the One True Doctrine of Jesus Christ subliminally. By the whelm of a religious impulse coming from the insensitive and non-compassionate scornful hearts of false prophets, the weakest of all pure hearts tends to unwarrantedly suffer by the hands of the corrupt teachers whom teach men to follow after the corrupt traditional religious image of God. Such false tutors disbelieve the Lord shall save the most despised of them. In an involuntary and unintentional manner of behaving disorderly in a boisterous way, the members who are misled by false prophets are religiously trained by the traditional corruptions which incorrectly define the godly essence of the Lord's love. The 21st century unawares who are destitute of the Lord's heavenly wisdom and spiritual truth take great pride in keeping their faith on the conduct of false ministries.

It is wise for us all to get some heavenly understanding on how Satan tricks a person or a group of people into engaging in an unethical fight to give you an idea about his support for the value or importance of the old religious code of principles and standards; so that we may learn to fight for our own Salvation in fear and trembling of the Lord. Religious fighters are violently fighting for nothing, because Christ fought meekly in a firm manner against such fighting's, and he by grace and through faith won the war against religion when he died upon the Cross. With this source of knowledge it is important for us all too individually grow in the Spirit of meekness unto God.

As we true Christians spiritually grow as a united front unto the edification of Christ, the Holy Spirit enables us to spiritually compare and identify the difference between the desire of Satan from the good will and good pleasure of God. Upon recognizing our own individual faults and failings, the Spirit of God converts us from devoting our hearts and minds to the veil traditional religious way of thinking; concerning how we spiritually praise, worship, and serve him so that we may desire to learn and understand how to do what Jesus would do. No, we cannot change our past wrongs, but we can reproach the evil likeness of our sown dead works and deeds; in hopes of preventing ourselves from committing the same said errors. Unlike the most extreme negative critics of the 21st century whom uses religion to belittle others under the false hopes of lifting up themselves above us all, we may shed our fears from wrongfully thinking that we should suffer persecution for the Cross of Christ upon Judgment Day.

34

A person whose heart desire to follow after the inhumane errors and inaccuracies of the religious ideological and biblical perceptions of the founding forefathers of the sect of the Pharisees and Sadducees also is always ready and eager to steadfastly defend the depth of their traditional religion's ordinance of hatefulness. The gruesome depth of their malice is exposed of by the Fruit of the Spirit of God, which manifests their worldly ideas and religious definitions of what holiness signifies. Their definition is as vain as the fruit of their iniquities which they religiously sow into the field.

Indeed the iniquity of their false teachings work the works of unfruitfulness by which profits them nothing on a daily basis. All throughout false teachers' traditional religious history their distasteful and offensive religious judgments revealingly have made all sinners at some point either think or believe that God doesn't love them enough to save them out of bondage. Their false preaching is an example of how the Pharisees and Sadducees mentally persecuted the entire human race back in the days when the law of the Pharisees and Sadducees ruled the religious realm. During the 21st century, their place of self-righteousness continues to bring about injustices and doubtful disputations against God and against the conscience of mankind. When in doubt the consciences of many waver in the faith of the Gospel of Jesus Christ. With all obscurity and darkness in their hearts, the false teachers add and subtract from the Word of God in an attempt to prove that their perception which judge the Word of God is accurate, perfect, and true. All false prophets who know not God preach and urge God's people to believe that God desire to send sinners to hell instead of advising all to have faith and believe that God would rather deliver all believers from the temptations of the world in hopes of saving some or all from sin.

> Proverbs6:16 "These six things doth the Lord hate: yea, seven are an abomination unto him."
>
> Proverbs6:17 "A proud look, a lying tongue, and hands that shed innocent blood,"
>
> Proverbs6:18 "An heart that deviseth wicked imaginations, feet that be swift in running to mischief,"
>
> Proverbs6:19 "A false witness that speaketh lies, and he that soweth discord among brethren."

A partial truth is a religious lie, and traditional religious false teachers are well known for preaching blasphemously against the Holy Ghost. The strength of such hideous ministries residing in today's society are sowing the insignificant seed of the Pharisees and Sadducees' old laws and customs that are banned by Christ, because such religions are in lack of agreement with the New Commandments of the sound Doctrine of Jesus Christ. These sorts of dreadful religions are identified by the fruit that they bear as they command people to abide by the repugnant and vile biblical messages which mostly pertain to the makeup of the traditional religious memorandums and dogmatic doctrines that sway people to have an ungodly fear instead of the righteous fear of the Lord.

The traditional religious memorandums of most church organizations includes the usual sacred preliminaries that goes with the organizing of a dogmatic traditional religious missionary, which permits all false prophets to continue to make every effort under the oldness of its letters; to control the minds of the people through the use of traditional religions' vain philosophies and deceptive words. The vainness of the false prophets' dictatorial religious words of deceit are contemptuously overbearing as their words impose their own ill-willed opinions into the minds of the simple, because they compel the weak and simple babes to discord a lack of agreement with the Lord's will in a domineering manner. These authoritarians are regarded suspiciously by the Lord's ordained enthrone of supreme virtue and value of agape love which exalts, glorify, and predestine the saints to reprove the overbearing words, will, and ways of the false prophets and take the task of the holy acts of reprimanding, reproaching, and gently rebuking all evil with boldness.

The leaders of every false ministry are perfectly trained in misusing the Word of God and are religiously described as traditional religious martyrs of men. In a senseless attempt of recruiting more members, the false ministers of this generation whom makes themselves an apostle of God; indeed tries to justify the doctrine of the Pharisees and Sadducees subconsciously as unawares. Of course they proclaim their ministry is equivalent to the ministry of Jesus Christ, but their teachings intermix with doctrines that aren't of the Lord. Traditionally their main beliefs involve them In upholding the old insignificant and irrelevant procedures and standards which the old-time religion of the world was built upon.

> **St. Luke14:11 "For whosoever exalteth himself shall be abased; and he that humbleth himself shall be exalted."**

Within these particular denominational religions' repulsive and disgusting usage or display of the Holy Bible Text, their missionaries work to uphold the vileness of their own bellies as they work to spread jealousy and hatred abroad. Indeed their nasty religious contemptibility and negligence works to edify the agenda of their own traditions. Even the missionaries of the most respected denominational religions of the world commit their hearts to the vain acts of falsely accusing, and making miserable the lives of redeemed sinners who confess that their faith is on the Lord. The ministers who exalt themselves configure and demand unreasonable requests that burden the total loyalty of the purest of hearts, by making the spirit of the purest of hearts; feel grievous of being born. The most respected religion of the world requires for all to idle the religious things of the traditional religious realm; including idling the desire of gaining and maintaining world domination.

(St. Matt.20:25-28/St. Matt.23/St. Mark10:41-45) Such religious idling excludes being a loyal servant of the One God whom seeks unselfishly for spiritual reconciliation through the permanent unwavering easement of contentment and peace from all as God requires, because God gave no man the power to mix the old with the new without housing both. Under such circumstances the piece that was taken out of the new agreeth not with the old. (St.Lk.5:36) Therefore, the vain battle between flesh and blood within such religions persists to exist, because like new wine the New Commandments of the New Testament must be put into the perspective of a new bottle. The new bottle clearly signifies the renewing of the mind which converts from comparing the physical aspect of things towards comparing spiritual with spiritual by which the Holy Ghost teaches. (1 Cor.2/1John2:27-29)

The firm unyielding spoiled religious principle rules and ordinances of the blemished leading missionary's of the Pharisees are still ruling a majority of religious congregations within the religious realm during the 21st century. These religious regulations supports the irrational traditional presumptuous religious theories that traditionally place a yoke of bondage around the necks of all whom believes on the religious decree which falsely charges God's love, mercy, and grace of being worthless or unable to redeem all sinners who confess Jesus Christ as their Lord and Saviour. Such religious code of laws also overly exerts the leaders of such missionaries which belittles and put down the dignity of others. In fact, they end up subconsciously condemning the spiritual conscience of all who they religiously ridicule and deride.

The leaders and members of such false religions are coerced to think more of their selves than they ought too. Blasphemously they glory in the flesh of those whom are weakened by their ideological gains of vain glory, and they misuse the Word of God to vigorously fight to sustain the conscience of the simple which they coerce into possessing an ungodly fear of the Lord. As they gloat and take pride in causing another living soul agony and misery, the gloom of their religion builds the characterized stature, rank, and status of the Sect of the Pharisees' whose religion continues the doubtful disputations. With envy in their hearts they senselessly fight vehemently to condemn the simple and weak during a delusional attempt of either upholding or bring back honor unto themselves. Meanwhile, they fervently stand firm on their traditional religions' unconvincing debates which they zealously stand up for as to defend.

Meanwhile, their religious conscience seeks vengeance which works to restrain or imprison the minds of all which they think the Holy Scripture secretively classifies unto them as unsaved, worthless, and hellhound children of Satan. In every aspect of way, traditional religions such as this; mentally abuses the free spirit of a person or a group of people to enslave and control their minds. Through trickery and twisted froward and perverse words, the tutors of such religion misuses the Word to bind the hearts of the simple babes to desire to have what they cannot or to do what they cannot. Disastrously they create resentment, jealousy, envy, and strife which falsely promote the old traditional religion to be better than the new, when in spirituality such bitter offense restores autocracy, monocracy, despotism, and dictatorship for the malnourished spirits who thinks tyranny and authoritarianism makes them equally yoked with God. The father of these religions has not the nurturing nature of Christ; only destruction. Blinded by the words of a liar, such persons fail to see that the father which they traditionally serve cause conflict and confusion against the spiritual conscience of all born again Christians whom may or may not clearly understand how mankind uses the wiles of Satan to control their minds.

No longer should we born again Christians continue giving gainsayers and men pleasers the pleasure of feeling empowered to keep us in mental bondage, because the Lord freed us all from the obligation of paying the Pharisees' psychological debt in spite of the numerous amounts of traditional religious organizations of the 21st century which still subconsciously idolize the old method of coercion. Desirously, the religious gainsayers and men pleasures acquire for their church members to attain the psychosomatic religious impulse of the Sect of the Pharisees' old-time religion as a reverential respect. Simultaneously, Satan coerces all Christian believers to devote their faith on the traditional religious point of views that resides under the irrational ideas that chastise the purest of hearts into desiring to chase after the vain glory of men.

(Gen.2:15-17) As Christians reach out their individual hands and partake of the fruit from the un-forbidden tree of knowledge, they grasp their knowledge from the worldly hands of false teachers, gainsayers, men pleasers, and seducers of men, whom traditionally have sought to find religious authority, control, and superiority. Indeed they are susceptible of being tricked into using the wiles' of Satan which deludes the true concept of the Lord's love, mercy, and grace. These sorts of people seek the Holy Scriptures in hopes of finding confirmation to prove that the irrational and unreasonable theoretical traditional religious advocates, activists, believers, and campaigners who promote and support absolutism or totalitarianism are placed above the rest, and they also believe they are at the right hand of God. Instead of seeking for the Kingdom of God by faith; they seek the scriptures by the works of the law, because they seek to be justified by the works of the law. Due to the irrelevant circumstances, such persons goes to church as a religious ritual and live as scorning fools for men, and this very act is enmity against the will of God.(Gal.2:16-21)

Romans 3:5 "But if our unrighteousness commend the righteousness of God, what shall we say? Is God unrighteous who taketh vengeance? (I speak as a man)"

(Philippians 3) Who dare desire for all members of a religious organization to feel obligated to devote their total loyalty towards paying the same psychosomatic debt of bondage as the hypocrites of the Old Law? As false traditional religious teachers of the 21st century diligently beseech for religious dominance over the consciences of an entire nation or race of people, they make themselves a transgressor whom inwardly desires to rule tyrannously over people as religious dictators, and they misuse the Word of God to boast of their selves.

Boastfully they think they've gained bragging rights to the throne of lordship on earth and in heaven. Therefore, they sing their own praise and toot their own horn with overconfidence, so that their religion physically is viewed and regarded throughout the entire world as the highest rank in Christ. Spiritually, this type of traditional religious ritual turns a weak person's heart towards desiring to adore the unspeakable sin which no traditional religion cares to make mention of during the 21st century, because all traditional religions fall short towards acknowledging the Holy Truth of the same said abominations which carries the same old psychosomatic sinful religious pride within their own transgressions. They have eyes, but cannot see. They have ears, but cannot hear. Therefore, they speak without a full understanding.

THE DOUBLE STANDARD PREACHERS: Who dares to blaspheme against the Holy Ghost?

The charge of every religion that coerces the members to have the same said overly excessive desire for a relation with the Lord cost the price of every willing soul which yields and desire to rule tyrannously and gain lordship over others. To become a devoted member of such a high ranking traditional religious organization, cost more than what their bragging rights are worth. They are forever learning, but never comes to acknowledge the true fact that they cannot neither save themselves nor make themselves happy by bring misery unto others as a religious ritual. When hopelessness and desolation intercedes the hearts of religious people, their main aspiration over turns their own religious faith and works for Satan's false ideological perception that goes against the Lord's truth concerning holiness. Their misinterpretation of the scriptures misleadingly concludes and authorizes certain Christian believers within the religious realm to believe they have religious rights to a dominating type of affect over the lives of others. With having dominion on their hearts and minds they preach the Key to the Kingdom of God as to place grief and burdening upon the hearts of every ear who hears their way of preaching. They misuse the Key to the kingdom of God to coerce people to think that there is no heaven or that they are hell bound with a one-way trip ticket and no way out.

Such religious subjugations place the yoke of bondage around the necks of all who places their trust, faith, and belief on the unfairness and unreasonable lustful ideological standards which every traditional religious government of today's society operates under; to enhance the false pretense of being made up of an equal and fair governing body of Saints and Christians. The One True Gospel of Jesus Christ not only tells the story of how Christ was born, died, and resurrected on the 3rd day, but it also identifies how the traditional religious realm's controlling factors and the wiles of Satan's wickedness twains together and encourages all constituent partners, fellow members, and citizens to revere after the cruel old leaven of malice of men.

During the 21st century, religious people still love to hide their jealousy and hatred in the same mannerism as the religious sect of the Pharisees and Sadducees as they dogmatically dictate their usage of the Word of God. Physically they practice worshipping a partially bias image of God under an imperfect religious governing policy or rule of law. Religious people worships and idol these laws which supports the inadequately set political standards of false religions' hypocritical principle

42

expectations of the living. Those whom make themselves apostles of Christ use forward perverse words in the form of their own double mindedness, while making false accusations against mankind unto God and visa versa; they also use forward perverse words against God unto mankind as they sermonize the Word of God by preaching double standards.

Two wrongs don't make a right. For example, the orthodox religion within the original origin of every human civilization inhabits those who religiously continue the path of the ancestors whom expected the fate of a certain race or particular group of people to be viewed for all eternity as insufficient. They disbelieve the Lord and Savior has the desire to use his power to convert the old thoughts of them to equal the renewed Spirit of the Lord. Therefore, those whom are religiously accused by the orthodox religions of the world are corruptibly coerced to believe that they are destined too suffer persecutions by the hands of all Christians during the entirety of their physical life, because the faith and superiority of all the lords of the lands desire to work indeed through the orthodox Christian religious memorandums of injustice and laws of iniquity unto their physical death. Throughout all of that which the most despised are tricked to believe, they also through doubtful disputations of the traditional messages of the orthodox religions do believe that they shall burn and Hellfire is their fate. In such belief resides no hope, which is what Christ's birth, life, death, and resurrection blessed all oppressed individuals to obtain. A none-believer is a blasphemer against the Holy Ghost, in which case, a none-believer shall not be saved. The Lord blesses all who are hears and doers of his Word, Amen!

The double minded standards of an orthodox religious martyrs' way of thinking of themselves in comparison to how they feel ill-willed towards others, makes it very difficult for them to recognize the errors of the old traditional religious trend that they respectfully value as the most supreme religious way of life. In other words, they fail to understand that what they label and hold onto as an established belief especially in religion as orthodox; measures up to the same standards that creates

43

condemnation instead of convictions against all societies of every walk of life. Their ill-will sets forth an unfair balance of rules and laws for only them to gain an unfair advantage in the world among the living. The unfairness of their religious rules and laws makes every deed of theirs' dead, because without hearing the voice of the Lord they preach controversially as to make a debate out of their traditional religious moral values. Insomuch of all that they do; they hinder their own spiritual prosperity and think they are totally doing right as they receive worldly rewards, but they can't justify their wrong doings. Their ideal purpose of setting up unfair rules and laws is acceptable only in their eyes, because to them they see Christianity to mean that no other living soul equally deserves to be treatment by the same token of fairness under the heavens as they.

With envy and strife in their hearts, they are blind and their perception of the Holy Scriptures clarifies unto them as they commend themselves by themselves; to yield their hearts to the idea of slanderously ridiculing those who they judge and choose to despise in a condemned demeaning way. Meanwhile, they fail to understand what the scriptures means concerning uniting themselves to every part of the Body of Jesus Christ. The error of their perception is due to their blind eyes and deafened ears which disallow them from clearly seeing that all who believes Jesus is their Lord and Savior are of the same Holy Root of the First Fruit of Jesus Christ. Neither have they understood that the message within the Holy Scriptures meant for them to humble themselves with the lowliest of spirit with every living soul which confess Jesus as their Lord and Saviour. Instead of entreating the Spirit of God unto others with a gentle reproof and with a meekness of spirit, they ferociously engage themselves to entreat the ungodly spirits unto others with roughness, which is not easy to be received by any man no matter how strong the beneficiary may be in the Word of God. Upon Judgment Day the leaders and followers of the religious sect of old traditions will stand alone and give an account for what they did and said during their life time.

The innocent babies that are born or added into the world's irreligious society are traditionally taught by false tutors to believe that they and their loved ones surely will not be saved by God, if they possess a distinguished unsatisfactory marking of a religiously despised stereotypical image that the leaders and followers of the religious sect of the old-leaven of malice solidifies; as a religious belief which authorizes them to harass, injure, and persecute the weak and simple babes of Christ under the inquiry of the traditional religion's philosophical spoiled theories that are created by non-compassionate religious men. According to such religious societies, those who possess a despised stereotypical image shouldn't ever expect to be treated equal amongst them. Such teaching brings not humility unto the Lord but great shame of disloyalty. Indeed they are of an unfair and off balanced society of people whom the Lord knew wouldn't ever give the weak and simple babes a fair chance at receiving the Holy Truth or a fair chance at succeeding their true purpose in life. Therefore, he left unto the entire world of people of every Nation; the comfort of The Comforter.

The religious malice of the world constantly causes confusion which creates division and wars. Meanwhile; the principle standard and value of the Pharisees and Sadducees dictatorial religious procedures are traditionally carried out by and for the immoral sanity and corrupt judgments of the religious world. The Pharisees' overbearing traditional religious policies goes well with the traditions of the religious martyrs of the 21st century who desires to continue seeking vengeance unto God, because they believe that there's retribution and justice in the traditional religious act of downing the dignity of others, in hopes of redeeming themselves for whatsoever it is that they lack; as they religiously work to fulfill the desire of the flesh. With Satan's very own angry obscurity and triviality being the foundational build of the world's most oldest and respected religious congregations, traditional religious martyrs of the 21st century simultaneously preach to make worthless of the weak and simple babes in Christ whom desire to worship the Lord.

If a spiritual man is of God then who are they whom religiously practice despising their neighbors and strangers alike? Who are they whom demand an ungodly fear and reverential respect of all persons whom they religiously desire to rule tyrannously over? Do they really think that having dominion over people will increase their chances at fooling God into believing that their self-made image of Christianity is more compatible to the will and desire of him than those whom they slanderously dictate the Word of God too? Who are they whom pull the wool over the eyes of the weak and simple babes of Christ by pretending to physical serve the Lord, while indeed they work their iniquities clearly by mocking God? Who are they who indeed are an enemy against God?

The foundation of the 21st century religious Sect of the Pharisees and Sadducees falsely claims their religion is identical to the Lord's Church, while working to maintain dominion over the life stock of human-beings as if we are a soulless herd of cattle. They falsely preach that God gave them the authority and power to have dominion over people, when the true fact is that God gave mankind the authority to reign with dominion over the fish of the sea, the fowl of the air, the cattle of the land and every creeping thing that creep upon the earth. While in search of controlling powers certain religious organizations mammon as they uphold the religious aspect of capitalism and slavery.

An Evolutionary Spiritual Change is Evolving & it's Time to Stop Trying to Bully Our Way into Heaven

In America which is grounded upon indivisible liberty and justice for all, the Christians think that the purpose of every American is to fight for religious superiority, but the 21st century American Muslims is working to build a loving environment with all people of all faith. Could it be possible that the clash of the Religious Titans of the 21st century whom are guilty for causing a desolated environment are being sought together not unto the death of one of another, but for the sake of redemption. Citizens all over America are seeking to provide an open comprehension of what godliness signify in the viewing of creating and maintaining world peace in the religious realm of life. Some are rebellious against the idea of Christians and Muslims uniting in peace, because they fear what they can't see nor understand.

The vision of unity as one body wasn't meant to be foreseen by the false Christians who are sticking to the vain idea of fighting for their religion by the misusage of political powers, because using tyranny to fight for their religion is all they've ever desired to know. Many traditional religious leaders of the 21st century organize or gather themselves together and call themselves an Assembly of God, but they are the ones who say and do not what they say. Unfortunately, their main focus as an assembly is centered on detecting the subtle distinguished differences of a person or a group of people to detest, despise, and hate; as a religious ritual.

The ministries of these false prophets commonly use the power of coercion in efforts of either recruiting more unto themselves to make increase the number of their members or they make use of that same said power of coercion to prevent as many as possible from uniting together as one body of faithful servants of God under the Heavens. Although the Bible text says, "All fall short to sin," they refuse to believe that the meaning of the word "ALL" includes them as well as all who they religiously are trained to despise and hate. Instead of admitting the truth of their faults and failings, they as sinners would rather confess not their faults unto one of another as the Lord instructs; for the edification of the Body of Christ or the Church of Christ. They'd rather assemble together and pretend to not have sin. Maybe they think that if they work hard enough, they can trick God into allowing their sin to entering their sin into the Kingdom of Heaven. Or maybe their lack of heavenly knowledge causes them to be too shame to confess the truth of their faults for the edification of the Body of Christ.

All false prophets fail to steadfast in the faith on the Lord as stern believers on the Power of God. They disbelieve that the will of God has the desiring power to forgive and save all sinners except those who lie against the Holy Ghost. Therefore, indeed do false teachers build churches and organize themselves together as a religious group of liars against the power of the Holy Ghost. In false hope of saving themselves, they willingly harass and injure all distinguished sinners and speak evil against them. Indeed they hope to retain favor in the Lord, while their evil speaking harass and injure others. Religiously they work to prevent other sinners who honestly confess of their sin, as to hinder all who confess of their sin from believing on the Lord who is the Lord of all lords and is the only one who can save and redeem them.

The New Law is established unto us by faith to deliver those of us who are puffed up and have not mourned for those fornicators among us whom we know might be taken away from us. Since some of us have not yet purged out the old leaven of hatred and malice from our religious hearts and minds so that we may be made whole with a renewed mindset, we allow ourselves to commend and encourage each others to glory in the flesh of the fornicators and deliver such sinners among us unto Satan for the destruction of the flesh. This ought not to be so, because the Lord forbids. (1Cor.5:1-13, 8:1-13)

In much regards to what they truly represent as an assembly of traditional religious men, false apostles curse themselves and are obligated to do the whole law, which the blood of Jesus Christ set the entire human race free from the obligations of. The Powers within God's gift of everlasting life delivers all who are misled by the destructive preaching of false prophets, to prevent the weak and simple babes from being overwhelmed by the principle standards of the Old Law. Being overwhelmed by a massive force liken that of a baptism, but yet is filled with condemnation; many of the new members of the false prophets' congregations are easily tempted by the vain traditional religious philosophies and idolized words of deceits, which distorts their mindsets to simultaneously believe on the past generations' vain beliefs which encourages them to disbelieve on the power of the Lord's love.

> **Romans12:3 "For I say through the grace given unto me, to every man that is among you, not to think of himself more highly than he ought to think: but to think soberly according as God hath dealt to every man the measure of faith."**

Without heavenly knowledge every endeavoring attempt made by false prophets to simulate the true image of the Lord is a loss cause and is a worthless effort on their behalf. As a false teacher seek the scriptures for physical evidence of their traditional religions' perceptiveness and discernment of the Lord's denote truth, they cunningly are misled by Satan who desires for them to rule tyrannously over all others whom are spiritual seekers of the Kingdom of Heaven. Therefore, Satan religiously trains false tutors to use the Word of God to despise and hate sinners. The hearts of such unawares are lead by Satan's desire to mislead and hinder God's people. (2Peter2:12-14/Jude10, 12) These false tutors are the spots and blemishes of the flesh of the weak and simple babes. They originally seek to use the Word of God as a stumbling block, which works to overthrow the spiritual Power of Faith; which the Lord God freely gives to all whom believes on him.

Therefore, these despisers of men reluctantly forsake their own mercy through hypocrisy, divisions, and deceits. Subconsciously, the unawares delude the denote meanings of the Lord's ordained ordinance of law. Out of the fretful fear that they should be persecuted by the Cross of Christ, they entangle themselves to preach as hypocrites do. They do all they possibly can to make their selves physically appear to have the physical makeup of Christ's character. Inwardly they are ravening wolves, evilly working in the flesh; seeking to physically advantage the appearance of their religion by compromising their own image to befit with all that which relates to their religious false preachers' negotiated ideas. This they think works for them within the Gospel of Jesus Christ as they selfishly devour the dignity of others. They work with no compassion nor remorse or shame. With this being rooted in their hearts to do, they worship and practice the physical image of what the traditional religious world assumingly think resembles the Lord's righteous act of humility.

When Christ walked the earth in the form of the flesh, his walk didn't consist of accusing people whom sought to kill him to his Father; like does the false prophets before and after him. As he walked his straight and narrow righteous path; the men-pleasers, gainsayers, and despisers of men religiously accused him of not being worthy to call himself the Son of God. They were like those of the 21st century who religiously accuse those whom believes on the power of him of not being worthy of God's love, mercy, and grace up to the end of their physical lifetime on earth. Any religion which accuses those who confess their faith on the Lord to be the children of Satan, are one of the same as those which religiously encouraged the people during the life of Christ to fight for the traditional religious venerations of mankind, which aren't proven by the Pure Root of the First Fruit of Jesus to be consistent with the spiritual image of Christ.

Many are called by the Lord to preach about the blessings of the gospel, in hopes of converting a person or a group of people whose hearts are condemned and lack the spiritual understandings of the Lord's purpose for their life. The few who are chosen by the Lord to preach the Gospel goes about from place to place trying to awaken religious enthusiasm as an Evangelist, and they desire not to condemn the spirit of another living soul as they preach to convert the condemned hearted into true Christians.

Most of those whom were voted into political office to over see the world's affairs prior to the moderate generation of the 21st century were not chosen by God to preach the Gospel of Jesus Christ, but they are educated men who preach from other doctrines which are reversed of the Doctrine of Jesus Christ. The method of their education as religious tutors works to awaken their pupil's and citizens of all nations to submit to a despotic form of religious enthusiasm, which couldn't prevail over the Lord's will to bring them closer to understand the powerful will of God's love mercy and grace which forgives all sinners who doesn't commit the unforgivable sin. The people who are taught by educated men of the world are more easily seduced by Gain-Sayers and men-pleasers to be equally excited as their tutors, regarding them being vengeful, spiteful, and greedy, but patients is a virtue for all who endure them.

For example, after 30 years of being ruled by an oppressive government in Egypt under the leadership of President Hosni Mubarak, in 2011 A.D the peaceful movement of the Egyptian citizens finally received the sign of Jonas. They received hope of being free; when President Mubarak resigned on February 11, 2011. It is not for certain upon his immediate resignation whether or not the repressive government would immediately change Egypt into a democratic state, but one thing is for certain; the peaceful movement of tens of thousand peaceful Egyptian protestors is one step closer at making it happen. It is inevitable for the Will of God to prevail in every corner of the earth in the terms of saying that every knee of all walks of life shall confess Jesus is Lord. Patience is a virtue, and everything that the followers have declared to be worth waiting for is also worth peacefully fighting for even if it means to be physically killed by the military. While waiting for the Lord to convert and redeem all who are misled by Satan's warriors, the true soldiers of Christ place their hope in making righteous judgments. Through the acts of a righteous movement they meekly are walking in the way of Christ as lovers of all mankind and as peace makers. Even the Egyptian's military turned and sided for peace over war.

True Christians know that all dictators and oppressors are misled to serve the Lord with their lips, and their deceived hearts are led to do the things which cause destructions and wars; not peace. Their dictating hearts are far from the Lord. The oppressors of the 21st century like

President Hosni Mubarak are unawares who subconsciously worship the prince of the world and their wisdoms cunningly trick others to seek to fulfill Satan's desire to sit in Moses' seat. What it means to be like Christ to them is to be worshipped by the simple and weak spirits whom are despised by their dictatorial traditional religious venerations and rituals. The unawares indeed devour the Lord's inspirational Word of God.

As many educated traditional religious men, women, and children unwisely practice what they preach, they do so without humbling themselves with the lowliest of spirit to have empathy for all others. Their lack of the Lord's Heavenly Wisdom keeps them from being submissive unto God concerning them having obedience unto the Lord's New Commandment of Love, because their spirit fails to understand the simplicity of who it is that they really are serving. Therefore, they love to smite the faces of others. When such persons don't know the difference between good and evil or right and wrong, they are unwilling and reluctant to change because of what another person of their own religious faith may say against them.

It is prudent for all religious venerators to understand that whosoever they accuse and religiously manipulate to deny the Lord as their personal Savior, are psychologically susceptible to be beguiled by their own idolized religious display of distasteful malicious preaching. Their preaching's hypocritically influences whosoever they religiously despise to either disbelieve in God or to believe God hates them, as if his purpose of creating them is simply to send them to hell.(Prov.22:5,6-11/Ex.20:12/Col.3:20-25/Eph.6:1-12)

The Holy Truth

If Christ's babes aren't properly feed the bread of life, their faith on the Lord will become malnourished. Those whom are infected with religions' malnourishments are traditionally taunted by the intent of false apostles' traditional religious venerations which is where false teachers, gainsayer, and men-pleasers hide their truest of all seductive intentions. The purpose of their intentions is religiously devoting their hearts to do unjustified harm against whosoever they religiously despise. A malnourished spirit is tainted with famine for the provision and satisfaction of traditional religious people whose enjoyment of taunting the simple and weak babes in Christ has always been willingly done by and for the sake of them satisfying the mischievousness, hatred, and malice within themselves. Therefore, it is prudent for all parents to instill their children with the righteous fear of the Lord. (Ps.34, 111:10/Prov.1:7-19)

> **Proverbs15:33 "The fear of the Lord is the instruction of wisdom; and before honour is humility."**
>
> **Proverbs8:11 "For wisdom is better than rubies; and all the things that may be desired are not to be compared to it."**
>
> **Proverbs8:13 "The fear of the Lord is to hate evil: pride, and arrogancy, and the evil way, and the froward mouth, do I hate."**

If Christ's babes who thirst after righteousness are properly feed the bread of life; they shall not go hungry nor thirst anymore, because the bread and water that the Lord gives unto them will be in them always. The righteousness of Christ didn't accuse anyone to his Father during his daily walk in the flesh, although he knew that they sought to kill him to satisfy the malice of a religious belief or veneration. Today ungodly men still desire to send people straight to hell on a witch's broom for the sake of fulfilling their own devotional feeling of religious reverences.

(2Cor.10:8-18) False Apostles tends to study the Holy Scripture for one reason, and that reason is for the sake of evaluating and comparing themselves by themselves; as one compares themselves to others. Simultaneously, they commend themselves amongst themselves as to boast of the Lord's labor as if to claim it is they whom redeem sinners. Within all that they do to prove to themselves that they are better followers of Christ than all whom they think are worthless, they can't indeed serve the Lord of Host, because their deeds are vanity and their hearts contains much vexatiousness. When they walk the earth after the form of the flesh, they seduce others into thinking they are Christ's new chosen apostles. Meanwhile, they seduce the weak to refuse to live under the wholesomeness of the Lord's New Covenant of Love, because they themselves virtuously are unaware that they are living under the Old Covenant, which doesn't require for man to reach God by first going through Christ. In their eyes, they view themselves to have a full connection to God or they visualize themselves as if they are God.

The entire human race is presently living under the New Covenant and we all are instructed by the Lord to follow the good Spirit of Christ. The men whom are deluded and are destitute of the truth are coerced by the Prince of the World to feel obligated to stone people to death, as if they can do the whole law of the Old Covenant. Listed below are just a few short word phrases, which are commonly spoken of by people whom religiously have been seduced into being men pleasers, despisers of men, and gainsayers as they give reasons for fighting for their covetous religion.

MOST POPULAR QUOTATIONS WHICH ARE PROVIDED BY THE ADVOCATES WHO SUPPORTS RELIGIOUS HATE CRIMES

> A) "It's my family's church."
> B) "It's my constitutional right."
> C) "It's the tradition of my people, church, or country."

The agendas and traditional differences and customs which the religious belief of one religious nation has given unto the entire world to believe in have prearranged an impractical explanation unto the belief of all traditional religious world leaders. All who willingly upholds a superstitious and illogical but realistic reason for misusing the biblical term of Christ's Holy War are following the delusional discrepancy of Satan's definition of a holy war; like the Pakistani and Ukraine leaders.

Satan being their father provides for them to fulfill the nature of their flesh, and the worldly hearted people within the religious realm dictates the traditional religious excuse for others to fight deliriously by the nature of the flesh, while shedding the blood of the weak and simple babes in Christ. Finally, a new day is dawning and the leaders of the United Nations during the year 2010 and 2011 A.D. are repenting from seeking such prosperity under such unreasonable religious notions.

"QUESTION" Is the Constitution of the United States of America a denote perception of the Holy Bible

Is it written in the Constitution of the United States of America or somewhere in a historical legal book of the land of what the holy truth clearly signify or is there a law of the land that clearly explains what the Lord means for all who has an ear to hear and to understand concerning the holy message within the One True Gospel of Jesus Christ? Is it possible that the constitutional law of the land reveals the hidden secrets which indicates who are to be saved by the Lord and who are hell bound? Does the written constitutional law of the land define, suggest, or elaborate on which religious group or which religious ministry has rightfully divided the Anointed Truth? Or is the laws of the land just another form of doctrine that consists of many derived ideas from a group which privilege themselves to misuse the law of the land to give themselves and their off springs all the legal authority and civil liberties on earth?

Since people are trained to work their way into heaven, automatically many think that Jesus owe them something like an employer owes an employee who works for a pay check or how a slave works for a slave master for food, cloths, shelter/housing. Since those who think Jesus owes them something are causing the world's alienated legal system to be on bad terms with it's civilians, like the laws which acknowledges the grievous ideological differences between the Separation of Church and State; maybe it is wise for someone to stand bold on the Word of God in America and let them all know that Jesus Christ has paid the ultimate price for all who believes of him to be saved by grace; so that they all may have their empty and deluded laws replenished and restored to revive the peoples faith on the Power of the Lord.

Some people are stiff neck worshippers of God. They feel as if God is indebted to them and owe them salvation, and they misinterpret their spiritual freedom and their human rights with their own personalized privileges which seduce the spirit of them to think they have the Lord's permission to traditionally choose to discriminatively do and say whatsoever they are accustomed to evilly do and say. Oftentimes traditional religious people view their spiritual freedom in a religious way of fighting in vain for their right to serve the Lord. They do not use their liberty to serve the Lord as a privilege. They subconsciously think they've earned the right to use the law of the land maliciously. Therefore, this is from whence their boasting comes from.

Satan has beguiled the world through his trickery and has convinced many to believe that certain people on earth whom confess that they trust and believe on Jesus; should be reviled, rescinded, withdrawn, or revoked by the laws of the land from having equal civil liberties to serve the Lord in Spirit and Truth. The creational envious engrave image of Satan's law have misled many of his followers to believe that, "Having the privilege to serve and worship the Lord on earth, is lesser important than it is to fight for a traditional religious belief or custom." Therefore, the delusions created by Satan insanely create many wars of fascinations and obsessions all throughout the ages of time, even unto this present day of age. Meanwhile, many have died free-willingly because they chose to fight for their traditional religious civil, human, and constitutional rights. Instead of them hating the sin and loving the sinner, the oppressors in the world do the opposite.

The promise and the glorious gifts of God that are freely given unto God's people, came unto all by the price of the shedding of the Blood of Jesus. After the ultimate price has been paid, no man can regenerate or redevelop the price the Lord paid.

Galatians 2:18 "For if I build again the things which I destroy, I make myself a transgressor."

Galatians 2:19 "For I through the law am dead to the law, that I might live unto God."

Galatians 2:20 "I am crucified with Christ: nevertheless I live; yet not I, but Christ liveth in me: and the life which I now live in the flesh I live by the faith of the Son of God, who loved me, and gave himself for me."

All are descendents of those that were brought out of the land of Egypt. Unfortunately, a half truth builds a trail of deceptions, and the liar has built a trial of trickery and dishonesty since the first lie distorted the minds of mankind. His deceptive lies which are not to be trusted have kept many from serving the Lord in Spirit and in Truth with all of their hearts. The lies of Satan's are set within the worldly idea of men's religious rights which are rooted deeply into the engraved image of their idol worshipping minds whereby many define the Lord's righteousness by the bowels of their own bellies.

For instance, the beguiled ones don't believe in allowing certain individual sinners the opportunity to praise the Lord. The lies of Satan cause the mindset of them to worship the Lord with their lips for the sake of themselves being commended by others who believe in the same such traditional belief. Therefore, the sown seeds of these peoples are rooted into taking great pride in being commended by men, as if they think their arrogance is powerful enough to open and close the gates of heaven and hell for or against whosoever they religiously choose to despise or love.

Like those whom biblically lived under the doctrine of the Pharisees and the Scribes; the leaders of such ministries today desires for more of God's people to become unreasonable judges of their own selves and of others, and they use their fruitless terminology of the Doctrine of Jesus Christ to convince themselves to think more of themselves than they ought. Upon the same judgment they may judge their neighbors and strangers by, whether it is of belief or disbelief; it shall be mete back to them again.

Of course it's clearly understood by the saints that the reasons why such persons of these types of ministries are the judgers of the Word of God instead of doers, is simply because that cunning Adversary has taken the Word of God and have changed the incorruptible appearance of God into a corruptible and forcefully coerced image unto them (St.Matt18:6). It is by the reflection of the Adversary does the scorners and martyrs of the 21st century do worship the likeness of their hearts by worshiping the Lord with their lips; like the worldly worshippers reverence a traditional ritual, belief, or custom. The leaders of such ministries expects for all members to abide or put up with their false teachings for the sake of keeping the mindsets of themselves encouraged in upholding the unreasonable regulations and rules of the old laws of the Old Covenant.

Without reproving the intent of their own hearts, they without empathy desire to not be in this world without being applauded, highly praised, commended or seen of by men of an orthodox religion as they compare themselves with themselves. As a result thereof, the world has been coerced to implement or execute the ordinance of the Pharisees, Sadducees, and the Scribe's judgments into the written form of governing laws of the land. These laws govern tyrannously over whosoever is habitually despised by the followers of the Old-Time Religious Law. Unfailingly people trust and depend on providing physical evidence to prove to themselves and others that their vain traditional religious philosophies and words of deceit hold the righteous key of the biblical truth. Therefore, it is prudent that we continue to privately pray for understanding as we obey God and privately study the Word of God for ourselves.

The unfair and unjust laws of the land provide the sinister minded citizens of the world with a tool of physical guidance. For centuries the ominous parts of such laws befits the empty desires of the misled traditional religious missionaries whom wants to use the law of the land as a traditional religious ritual of violence. Meanwhile, they constantly commend one another, as if one man commending another proves unto them that they are profiting the gain of their own salvation by despotically working their way into heaven (Matt.16:26). Therefore, God sent Jesus whom left the world the remembrance of his "Walk". His walk included his Trials & Tribulations and the Power of his Word. The world was left with all of these as an example for all who believe on him to follow his steps.

(THE WORD WAS GOD AND GOD IS LOVE!)

The Lord's examples which he left are viewed as spiritual evidence for the spiritual minded to know and understand how to follow his meekness, kindness, gentleness, and above all his love. Regardless of the name of the missionaries on earth, if they're doing harm unto the faith of others who confess Jesus as their Lord and Savior; then they are working not for Christ but against Christ. The Comfort of the Lord blesses the spiritual minded with the wisdom to accept the ability to spiritually see life through the singleness of the eye, and to humbly understand the love, mercy, and grace of the Lord is the only right path for all to follow.

Meanwhile, the worldly anticipates a different path for their selves to follow. While duplicating their own judgmental ideas of the Word of God, they place conditions upon God's unconditional love. Their own emulated psychological interpretations of their physical appearance religiously simulate the way they see and judge the Word of God. They fall short towards perceiving the spiritual aspect of the Lord's daily walk of life, because they are too focused on the things that concern the world; like traditional marriage. Ironically, the heterosexual community of the world has turned their backs on their own views of traditional marriage as they fight enthusiastically to keep it holy.

Traditional religious marriages have lost its flavor in the account of the worldly heterosexual community who presently are encouraging themselves into committing adultery which increases the only exemption which the Lord gives unto mankind for a placement of a written divorcement. The <u>unconverted</u> heterosexual community also makes a mockery of God as they give unto themselves honor and glory as hypocrites for using the Word of God as a decoy to justify their wrong. They intertwine themselves together with <u>true Christians</u>, whom have repented of such justifications. Their deceptive hearts divide the true meaning and purpose of Christ's established church and cause division to persist among the heterosexual community as they cheer on the acts of conceiving and birthing children out of wedlock; either naturally or by using test-tubes known as stem cell inseminations. Such interactions between true Christians and the worldly heterosexual community delude the true message of Christ.

For instance, the worldly heterosexuals hide themselves behind religion to protection themselves as they commend themselves, all while they fight to keep the traditional marriage between a man and woman traditional. Hypocritically, they think more of themselves than they ought all while they themselves mock God. They tend to think they can advantage themselves by affiliating with true Christians while pointing their fingers at a gay couple for doing the same things as they. Those whom mock God whether gay or straight need someone to tell them that being gods on earth or being lords of the law of the land doesn't make a person God. Maybe then they'll stop seeking for their wrongs to be justified by Christ and accept the fact that two wrongs don't make a right. (Gal.2:17/1John3:8-16)

True Christians are spiritual and holy. They beseech for all to anticipate the psychological and spiritual aspect of Jesus examples during their daily walks of life, as they themselves receive persecution. They live in hopes of all being inwardly converted by the Lord's spiritual gifts, which the Fruit of the Spirit provides and manifests unto all who believes on him; in hopes that all may receive the exact same spiritual things which the Holy Ghost signify and reveal is the righteous image of Christ's holiness.

The holiest Power of God's Love is what makes the spirit of the true Christians' righteous judgments pure, longsuffering, and kind. Without judging anyone; a spiritual person rightfully may judge the situation, circumstance, and the surrounding acts of events which troubles a great multitude, because they with empathy sympathetically understands that it wouldn't be very wise of them to blasphemously judge the conscience of the living nor the dead.

On the other hand, worldly people are religiously misguided to believe in the things that are understood by the bowels of their own bellies. The bowels of their bellies concludes the reason why some of the most religious people worship the Lord inaccurately in the accordance of their own systematic irreligious methods and vain desirous usage of the Word of God. They religiously treasure the ideological idea of themselves remaining in harmony with the majority voters whom uses their liberty to viciously rule the world. Seductively, the worldly methods of preaching the Word of God subverts the heart of many people to desire to do what they either should not or cannot do; under the New Law of Christ. Simultaneously, certain malnourished ministries religiously misjudge the Word of God to falsely teach and trick the weak and simple babes who desire to follow Christ into having either very little hope or no faith at all on being saved by the Blood of Jesus. They do all that they can to put a person down, and they do nothing at all to help revive them out of their infirmities.

Wisely, spiritual people desire not to mock God, but it's traditional for religious men to mock God as they train and commend their selves to stay encouraged in the dead deed of ridiculing others. Spiritual people understand that all people who proclaims they are authorized by the Word of God to judge men's consciences are a liar, whom blasphemes against the Holy Ghost (Eccl.8:8/St.Matt.7). All of us are unique, but none of us are perfect. Through the singleness of the eye the spiritual ones refuse to judge any man, because everyone of us may subconsciously stumble over the diversified traditional religious concept of the Word of God and non of us are given the power by God to know nor to confine the Spirit of another person's conscience. The choice to judge one of another isn't apart of the desiring nature of a true Christian.

Men who practice misusing the Word of God to judge other men interact evilly as a mediator of a vain religion, because the vanity of their hearts causes them to intercede against God and against God's peoples as if they have dominion over the peoples' faith. They know not what the scriptures said to Elias, how he made intercession to God against Israel due to his jealousy for the Lord of hosts.(1Kings19:10, 14) Nor can they understand what said the answer of God unto Elias about his jealousy for the Lord God of hosts(1Kings19:18), because their hearts are dark, their ears are deafened, and their eyes are blinded for seeking righteousness as if it were to be received by the works of the law and not by faith.(Romans9:21-33,11:8, & 11:16)

> **Romans11:8 "(According as it is written, God hath given them the spirit of slumber, eyes that they should not see, and ears that they should not hear;) unto this day."**

At this present time there is a remnant according to the election of grace. (Deut.32:21) As it is written, Moses said, "I will provoke you to jealousy by them who are no people and by a foolish nation I will anger you." As it is written, the last shall be first and the first shall be last. The godly factoring of this being known is one of the many things that make the false teachers jealous. Moses' Laws were given to them of the old time, because they didn't have what we the people of the New Testament have today; "FAITH!"

Provoking jealousy isn't an acquired option for the Evangelists and ministers of the One True Gospel of Jesus Christ during the 21st century, but there are some who unlawfully make themselves apostles of Christ. They provokingly teach the heart to anger through jealousy, and they seduce God's people to become jealous despisers of men by using the Word of God to smite the faces of other members of the Body of Christ. They believe that the measures of such religious techniques will work in their religious favor. In reality their religious practices doesn't revive the Spirit of Faith, because it condemns the conscience of mankind.

Without heavenly knowledge, these men think their stratagems will first condemn and then save the hearers of their religious words. All thanks and glory is to God for making himself spiritually clear to the entire populated world by instructing us to believe in the truth, which states that you can't fight evil with evil. Men who think they are doing a good deed while fighting evil with evil are actually destitute of the Holy Truth. They are the provokers of those who are spiritually weak. They may easily coerce the weak and simple babes into becoming hearers and doers of their words under their false commandments, but it doesn't make nor mean they are right for doing so.

It has been boastfully said by many manmade apostles of the 21st century when they offend other believers of the Son of God that it isn't they who condemn the hearers of their religious messages. All puffed up they say, "It is the Word of the Lord of host, which condemns those of them who are offended." Satan was a liar in the beginning and shall continue to lie against the Holy Truth for evermore. These false apostles are blind and can't see that within the New Testament, the inspiring Word of God doesn't enforce jealousy in no way form or fashion. The things which cause a heart to feel condemned, angry, and jealous are the provoking concept of what the Prince of the World saith thus saith the Lord thy God. God is greater than any condemned heart (1John3:16-24).

1Cor.1:19 "For it is written, I will destroy the wisdom of the wise, and will bring to nothing the understanding of the prudent."

1Cor.1:20 "Where is the wise? where is the scribe? where is the disputer of this world? hath not God made foolish the wisdom of this world?"

1Cor.1:21 "For after that in wisdom of God the world by wisdom knew not God, it pleased God by the foolishness of preaching to save them that believe."

1Cor.1:25 "Because the foolishness of God is wiser than men; and the weakness of God is stronger than men."

1Cor.1:27 "But God hath chosen the foolish things of the world to confound the wise; and God hath chosen the weak things of the world to confound the things which are mighty;"

1Cor.1:28 "And base things of the world, and things which are despised, hath God chosen, yea, and things which are not, to bring to nought things that are:" (Rom.4:13-18)

Yes; God is a jealous God, but before he allow the stumbling blocks of these ignorant manmade missionaries to cause his people to die for the reconciliation of the world, he concluded all in unbelief that he might have mercy upon all. In fact, when Jesus was crucified on the Cross, he asked his Father in prayer to forgive all of them because he understood that they knew not what they were doing. Having empathy without faulting or accusing anyone to the Lord is the righteous act of God and is also the godly act of God's chosen ministers, Evangelists, Bishops, apostles, and brethren etc.

Romans11:17 "And if some of the branches be broken off, and thou, being a wild olive tree, wert graffed in among them, and with them partakest of the root and fatness of the olive tree;"

Romans11:18 "Boast not against the branches. But if thou boast, thou bearest not the root, but the root thee." (Romans9:21)

Romans11:19 "Thou wilt say then, The branches were broken off, that I might be graffed in."

Romans11:20 "Well; because of unbelief they are broken off, and thou standest by faith. Be not highminded, but fear:"

Romans11:21 "For if God spared not the natural branches, take heed lest (afraid) he also spare not thee."

(Rom.4:13-18/St. Matt.23:13) The ambitiousness of every Church that emulously strives to equal or excel another, simultaneously promotes an ungodly emulation of iniquity and wickedness against man and against God. Such ministries that have a lacking of fairness and injustice are promoters of a shameful injustice indeed. No man is perfect, because both the worldly and the spiritual minded falls short to sin. The spiritual minded wisely walks by faith, while worldly people imprudently walk by sight. It is by the law that the worldly prefers to physically live in war, during their everyday efforts of making their traditional religion appear to be of a higher caliber than any other. This is their desirable quality of making peace for their selves, but it is by faith that the spiritually minded prefers to spiritually walk while living in spiritual peace with themselves and amongst all others. Under the Old Law the people are susceptible to become men-pleasers, gainsayers, and seducers of men. Confusedly they easily entangle the livelihood of the Lord's spirituality with their worldly traditional religion, while trying to translate or orally explain the Word of God in the way which befits their own vain traditional religious beliefs, rituals, and expectations.(1Cor.8:4-9)

1Cor.8:10 "For if any man see thee which hast knowledge sit at meat in the idol's temple, shall not the conscience of him which is weak be emboldened to eat those things which are offered to idols;"

1Cor.8:12 "But when ye sin so against the brethren, and wound their weak conscience, ye sin against Christ."

1Cor.8:13 "Wherefore, if meat make my brother to offend, I will eat no

flesh while the world standeth, lest
I make my brother to offend."

THE LIFE PURPOSE OF THE AUTHOR GLORY

The author of Discerning Perceptive, whose sure name is Sister Glory
Sanders Thompson spiritually recognize, acknowledge, and compare the
spoiled disfigured traditional interpretations of the Word of God by the
spiritual things which were revealingly given unto her to comprehend by
the Anointed in a dream; to privately make more people aware of their
every situation. After spiritually receiving from the Anointed that which
she could not obtain from man, she uses that form of knowledge to
vitally bring out the true perceptive meanings of most traditional
religions whose traditional teachings insinuates or suggests that in order
for her or any other living soul to prove themselves to be saved by the
Blood of Jesus, they must fervently perform whatsoever sort of
unreasonable sacrificial rituals or impossible tasks that preferably befits
the impoverished traditional misguided interpretations of the Word of
God.

In much of her version of what thus saith the Lord thy God, the men
pleasures, despisers, and gainsayers are exposed of and are uncovered.
As an old-time favorite saying of the author, "Show me your fruit and I'll
tell you of what Tree you're from." Seductively and inaccurately the
false prophets, gainsayers, and men-pleasers desires to unreasonably
define the responsibility of Sister Glory. She's a vital member and an
attached branch of the Lord's Church, but many disturbingly prefer for
her to deny God and take sides with one worldly organization or
another so that they may conclusively dictate and judge her; as to
suggest how she ought to be traditionally classified as either just or
unjust in accordance to one profane understanding of the Doctrine of
Christ or another. (1Cor.8:5-9/Phil.2:11)

Traditional religious martyrs are using all sorts of persuasive guile words
in their fair speeches and conversations one with another, while their

dead deeds works against God's babes and elders of all ages. They've worked fervently indeed to convince or to sway the author of Discerning Perceptive and a massive majority of others into believing in keeping the traditional religion of the world's evil ways of spreading shameful injustice.

Sister Glory stated that although traditional religion wants her to believe that her past sin places a split between her and the other parts of the Body of Christ, the Anointed has already brought unto her the Fruit of the Spirit of God and delivered her out of the temptations of the world. It is prudent for her to know and understand the Holy Truth of the subjections of her own life and her eyes are opened to understand that a sin is a sin. The Lord has removed her Key to the Kingdom of Heaven from the hands of all of her adversaries whom traditionally worship religion as a reverence of respect of worldly matters and placed the knowledge of the Tree of Life concerning her salvation into her hands where it belongs. As a peace maker and a servant of God, Sister Glory dedicates the duration of her life on earth edifying Christ as she righteously fight meekly on a daily basis for her own Salvation.

The last enemy to be destroyed in her life is death, and death was destroyed upon the Lord removing the doubt of her not ever being saved from her heart. Meanwhile, the Holy Spirit remains alive and builds her confidence on the power of her redeemer Jesus Christ. With the Key to the Kingdom of Heaven in her hands she properly desires to use the Word of God to edify Christ by reviving the Spirit of every condemned heart, which reads or hears of her written perceptive of the Word of God. May God Bless the Hearers and doers of his Words, Amen!

THE WORD WAS SENT TO SAVE ALL

Although the pure hearted babes in Christ subconsciously maybe coerced into worshipping Satan under the corrupt minded tutorship of false apostles, the hearts of them that doesn't yield to the oppressor's ways are not reprobate. In due season by faith, they shall spiritually be equipped and blessed by the merciful loving spirit of the Holy Ghost to be revived from the vileness of vain words of religious men which kills the goodness and godly spirit within all of mankind.

For instance, the word of a false apostle speaks against the consciences of the Spirit of God and a God fearing man, but the Holy Ghost is the bread of life that lives within the inner consciences of all who believes on Jesus. The Lord's bread of life nourishes their souls and revives their Spirit from traditional religions' depth and from the bowels of abomination, hatred, condemnation, the Lord's disapprovals, worldly burdens, and from every oppressive wall of bondage.

There are those who know the truth, but are yet spiritually divided against themselves, because the hearts of them yields to the ways of the oppressor and they with that form of knowledge still chooses to stay under the instructions of worldly tutors where they themselves yearn to be praised by men. They choose to side with the voters of a majority for the sake of fitting in with men pleasers, gainsayers and despisers of men whose spiritual minds are persuade to do unto others the same immoral things as the false prophets beguilingly does unto them; by using traditional religion as their source of reasons to "Discriminate."

Customarily, false apostles and false prophets cause inconveniences to the goodness and godliness of the purest of all spirits. They use fair words and well put together speeches to preserve their own inner consciences while making others think of themselves to be unsaved, because they themselves are seduced to yield to the errors of the ageless religious empire on earth. In the matter of course of action, they change the glory of the incorruptible God into an image made likened to the traditional criticism of corruptible religious men. (Romans 1:23, 25)

In other words, when the "Faith" of the simple ones who spiritually believes that the Lord's heavenly powers have the ability to save all from sin is repeatedly taunted, weakened, or inflicted with foolish religious doubtful disputations; it causes the spirit of them to suffer distress, misery, and persecution and their hearts becomes condemned and ship wrecked. Irritatingly, the depth of the hypocrites' traditional religious follies curses and encourages the simple and weak babes to replace their beliefs on the Lord with disbelief, which cuts off or casts out their spiritual faith on Christ. (Act 27/2Cor.11:15-33/1Tim1:18-20, 3:9)

The Holy Spirit reveals that due to one's lack of heavenly wisdom, they also lack the ability to boldly trust the instincts of their inner godly consciences. Doubt causes the best of them to become confused and waver in faith. The doubtful traditional disputations of false ministries impose and enforce burdens upon the hearts of the simple and weak babes, and it causes or tricks people who want very much to have a close relationship with God to covet against the Lord by casting worldly sorrows upon one of another. Such acts likened of this committed by any person or any religious denomination, fails to edify or glorify God. (1Tim.2:1-8)

After receiving an understanding of how worldly sorrows worketh death (2Corinthians 7:8-12), a person who doesn't totally desire to idol worship or devote their hearts to the vileness of traditional religion can with a clear conscience spiritually grow towards the holiest desires of their hearts and choose to rather treat the tyrant leaders and followers of traditional religion the way that they themselves desire for the tyrants to respectfully treat them, which is good and fair. Indeed this is as a reasonable sacrifice and service done by them unto God. When someone faithfully endures much and suffers long for God without desiring to cause another living soul pain, agony, grief, or worldly sorrows; they no longer are confound to the traditional religious laws of bondage, which may have once caused them to inwardly be burdened to do that which works death to the spirit of themselves and to others.

After reproaching the traditional religious acts that are committed by religious people whom believes in casting out sinners, the weak and simple babes in Christ are made into strong ministers of God who knows that casting out sinners is a wrongful act, and they fearlessly feels not ashamed for renouncing their loyalty to religions which practice casting out sinners as a traditional ritual. The strong ministers of God are enabled by the holy gifts of the Lord's love, mercy, and grace to wisely discern and cast out the sin which lies within the traditional religious methods of men whom misconstrues the Lord's ordinance of righteousness by confusing or misinterpreting the works of casting out God's people with casting out Satan.

Only God's chosen ministers are capable of reproaching such vain traditional religious acts without hypocritically casting out a single individual sinner who is not guilty of committing the unforgivable sin. Only a chosen minister of God is capable of rebuking Satan and convicting the Spirit of Man without judging or causing the spirit of anyone to feel condemn. A true servant of God can preach the gospel of Jesus Christ without blaspheming against the Spirit of the Holy Ghost like religious hypocrites, because for their love of the Lord and Savior Jesus Christ and by righteous judgments; their preaching is made perfect. The preaching of them may convict the spirit of man to revive, restore, and resurrect their faith on the Lord, but they do not condemn man by killing or destroying their faith like false teacher and false ministers of God does.

> **1John4:1** "Beloved, believe not every spirit, but try the spirits whether they are of God: because many false prophets are gone out into the world."
>
> **1John4:2** "Hereby know ye the Spirit of God: Every spirit that confesseth that Jesus Christ is come in the flesh is of God:"

(1John4:3-11/1John5:1-11) The Saints mostly observe God's chosen Ministers, Bishops, and Evangelists as they properly take a firm reproach on using the Word of God to rebuke the works of evil. Those whom are chosen by God self examine everything with a pure conscience, and they preach the Gospel of Christ so well that no traditional religious blame can hold them down nor retain or confine the clarity of their holy messages. Unlike false prophets, the one's whom are chosen by God; are rightfully blessed by the Divine power of Heavenly Wisdom to accurately use the Word of God to convict and revive the spiritual faith of mankind. The few whom are chosen by God the Father, the Son, and the Holy Ghost are given heavenly insight of God's heavenly Wisdom; to understand the Anointed teachings which provides true evidence of the intent and the true purpose of the Spirit of God's love. (St. Matt.12:1-17/Romans16:17)

The almighty intent of God's love is predestined to prevail on earth against all evil works of men, and God's love is an ordained award of honor that is granted unto those of us whom are obedient to God's Greatest Commandment. Obedience to the Commandments of God, gives the promise of life everlasting to all sinners who believe on the Lord. With that knowledge we can discern the difference and the intent of the spirits which the Word of God prepares, trains, and instructs us to try (try in the reference of testing the spirit) in 1John4:1. Having Heavenly knowledge enables us all to identify the spirit of traditional religious false apostles from the peculiar spiritual people whom God chooses. Meanwhile, the Fruit of the Spirit of God manifests or makes known of the spiritual things which the anointed teaches.

As Jesus suffered the persecutions of this world, he taught the Word of God without verbally abusing anyone whom was spiritually weakened by worldly traditional religious insight of the laws of the land. Although there are two differential groups of citizens of the land, both the religious group and spiritual group of persons suffer the same persecutions of this world. For example, we all are forcefully obligated to pay taxes in a discriminating or an unfair manner, because the law of the land is made likened to corruptible men and is partially biased.

Like his Father, Jesus knew that all fall short to sin. Yet, he graciously walked up right to show the Christians, Saints, Sinners, Jews, and

Gentiles worldwide; exactly how to be a fool for him and not a fool for man. The walk of Christ represents what true Christianity signifies in the eye of his Father. He committed himself to his Father to do only that which the Father instructed him to do (1peter 2:21-24). He preached to teach all who has an ear to hear; how they are free from the bondage of the world's vain ideas and imaginations. The vain ideas and imaginations of the worldly resemble the dictators' scheming thoughts of mankind which order for all mankind to follow the Pharisees' religious doctrine.

For instance, the vain hearts of the world believes in upholding the traditional religious ideas and imaginations that are associated to the Pharisees doctrine that contributes mostly to the overly excessive ideas of sex. The unwarranted sexual elements, characteristics, and attributes of their religious definition of the word lascivious provide a great subtraction to and change the meaning of the Word of God. It is traditional for all beguiled religions of the world to tyrannously miscalculate the Lord's purpose and add worldly burdens to the conscience of every society of people while demanding for all to worship the Lord in a cruel but traditional unrighteous way.

Any law that approves and encourages it's citizens to commence or initiate the violent acts of hatred and prejudice hostility against one or another, like the main principles of the Pharisees Doctrine; then they are made liable to cause religious people to talk right and walk wrong although their hearts know what is spiritually right. Therefore, when people pledge their allegiance to a flag or any other idolized image like the power of money and riches or even their ancestors' traditional religious ways, God approves his chosen people to give to the idolaters and the rulers what belongs to them and give to Christ what belongs to Christ. Those who are obedient to the perfection of heavenly understanding to this commandment will not leave this world owing man nothing where love is concern. A spiritual person who is a discerner of the spirit can relate their understandings of this spiritual factor of truth by rightfully dividing the Holy Scripture in the Book of St. Matthew 22:15-32 and St. Mark 12:24-25. While self examining ourselves by comparing spiritual things with spiritual, in concern of evaluating our life's purpose with the spiritual purpose residing within Jesus' parables; we all are set free by the Holy truth.

Meanwhile, religious people solely think these passages are limited to things of a physical genre which they possess in the world. Under the leadership of idolaters many people are solely mislead to believe that they have a greater chance at religiously gaining redemption, authority, and respect by, for, and through the pursuit of controlling money and power during the days of their lives on earth. They too are spoiled and are tutored to obey the traditions of men and the rudiments of the world and not Christ. To conclude the old religion's respective value of having money requires one to understand that it brings them a false sense of empowerment under the New Covenant especially concerning them giving and receiving the praise of men (Gal.3:3/Colo.2:6-10). Many church houses are greatly established upon praising, commending, and glorying the ones whose tithes and offerings are of the greatest amount in value in comparison to all other members.(St. Matt.23:23) This is disgraceful and ought not to be so.

St. Matt.22:21 "Render therefore unto Caesar the things which are Caesar's; and unto God the things that are God's"

St. Mark12:9 "What shall the lord of the vineyard do? he will come and destroy the husbandmen, and will give the vineyard unto others."

St. Mark12:10 "And have ye not read this scripture; The stone which the builders rejected is become the head of the corner:"

St. Mark12:11 "This was the Lord's doing, and it is marvellous in our eyes?"

St. Mark12:12 "And they sought to lay hold of him, but feared the people: for they knew that he had spoken the parable against them: and they left him, and they went their way."

St. Mark12:16 "And they brought it. And he saith unto them, Whose is this image and superscription? And they said unto him, Caesar's."

St. Mark12:17 "And Jesus answering said unto them, Render to Caesar the things that are Caesar's, and to God the things that are God's. And they marveled at him."

St. Mark12:24 "And Jesus answering said unto them, Do ye not therefore err, because ye know not the scriptures, neither the power of God?"

THE STRONG CAN LEARN FROM THE WEAK AND VISA VERSA

(St. Matt.10:26-28/St.Lk.12:4-5) Since the gay community has been vehemently trained by the world which resents them to have an ungodly fear of God, they know that they are among the most unloved in the world. In all that they do, their devoted concept of following Jesus Christ's greatest Commandment inspires them to love those who violently look down on them with disgust. Their entrusted act of faith in this area spiritually represents and resembles the true image and concept of God's greatest Commandment of Love more so than the traditional religious concept of the worldly heterosexual community. This theory is contemplated by the factoring of how the gays are compared to the good Samaritans of God whom are inwardly capable of humbly working with and helping the spiteful religious heterosexuals whom greatly despise them, in despite of the awful and evil way the same said heterosexuals who are bone of their bone and flesh of their flesh may mistreat them.

> **St. Matt.7:12 "Therefore all things whatsoever ye would that men should do to you, do ye even so to them: for this is the law and the prophets."**

(Gen.1)The heterosexuals didn't create gay people; God did, but the heterosexuals have argued for centuries that God didn't create gay people. Their interpretation of the Word of God perceives that gay people are created by Satan. Within the gay's imperfections and faults, the hearts of some of them are converted and they are transformed as born again Christians, and they too like the straight community are instructed by the Lord to uphold the Word of God during their everyday walk of life as peace makers amongst all whom vehemently hates and despise them. Only in accordance with the traditional teachings of religious warfare and feuding does the heterosexual community believe that they are pardoned by God while they fight for their religious throne on earth against the gay community. Without the power to judge the conscience of any man, they forsake their own mercy during their dispute. It is pardoned for man to hate the sin and love the sinner, but most heterosexuals' within the religious community oftentimes can't determine the difference between good and evil and for this cause, they vehemently choose to fight for their religious rights to hate the entirety of a homosexual. According to them a homo cannot be reformed by the

Lord nor can they be inserted back into the protection of the Holy Spirit of God. Stereotypically they view Christianity in the way of the worldly, who suggests people are born sinners and shall die as sinners.

By the traditional religious wars within the religious realm of life, men are taught to religiously hate gays, in spite of the Word of God acknowledging that all that believe on the Lord are saved. By the faith of an individual rather gay or straight, the Lord blesses all through his mercy and grace to reset the minds of them free from thinking that a person's sin is unforgivable in the eye of the Lord. With the Lord all things are possible, like leaving a proper guide for the gays who desire to know God to follow. The power of God is powerful enough to deliver all who believes on his only begotten Son out of the temptations of sin. (Prov.6:16-19) Abomination is any and everything which gives an offense to the Lord like a (Prov.11:20) perverse heart, (Prov.12:22) lying lips, and (Ps.66:18) vain prayers. All of these are included in the abomination of desolation. (Matt.24:1-15/Dan.9:27)

Worldly men are guilty of thinking God is a monstrous and an unforgivable God. While lying against the attributes and characteristics of the Holy Ghost, they themselves disable themselves from receiving the heavenly power of authority to find the same said hope of deliverance which he promises to give unto Israel as well as all other servants of God who diligently seekers to find the Kingdom of Heaven and all who wants to be delivered out of the things which tempts their spirit to sin against God. Just as the gays can learn a thing or two from the heterosexual community as apart of the Body of Christ, the Lord knows the heterosexuals can also learn a thing or two from the gays; like humbling themselves to perverse speaking men without choosing any of the oppressors' ways. They also can learn how to love their neighbors as they love themselves knowing that all have faults and failings. (AN AGAPE KIND OF LOVE REQUIRES NO REPENTANCE!)

Of course through unbelief, most traditional religious martyrs accepts the unproven opinion of men who worships men instead of accepting the true anointed teachings of the Holy Ghost, because they are trained and religiously are tutored by the high Priesthood whom historically exalts themselves by belittling, humiliating, or abasing people in making others feel hopelessly unworthy. (St. Luke 14:11/St. Matt.23:12) They love to misuse the Word of God to dispute against the spiritual belief of a sinner who believes on the Lord to save and redeem them.

(Gen.1:1-4/St.John1:1:17, 18-20) The truth is the light, and the light is Christ. There has been no darkness in the Light of Christ since God separated the light from the darkness in the beginning. (St.Luke6:41-49) Therefore, every religious person or organized group of people which speaks evil and spreads hatred against their own family members, neighbors, and strangers alike; must stop and reconsider rebuking the repulsiveness of their own hearts before trying to help remove the mote out of their brethren's eye (James1:14-26/2Peter2:10-16/Jude9). The repulsiveness of their hearts symbolizes the shameful immovable beam of their own iniquities, which they've adapted through their own vain religious beliefs. Such rebuking can neither be done <u>by</u> nor <u>for</u> men whom fight evil with evil or against flesh and blood, because the inquired firm meek reproach of the Lord is done <u>for</u> and <u>by</u> the Holy Ghost; to recompense and justify the faith of **all** people as **ONE** <u>Body of</u> <u>Christ</u>. There are many parts that makeup the body and the Lord didn't exclude any person created by God. (St. Luke3:1-14, 15-20)

THE TRADITIONAL RELIGIOUS MISSIONARIES OF HATE

The Word of God teaches that it is by faith that the spiritually minded men shall live, and no man can judge the Spirit nor retain it (Eccl.8:8). Although the despaired hearts suffers persecution, they yet are comforted by the Comforter Jesus Christ; knowing that he loves them in spite of their sin. One day the traditional religious heterosexual community will awake out of sleep and realize that there are no new things going on underneath the sun. When they awake, they will understand the fullness of God and regret wasting so many years of their lives hating their own relatives and others whom they didn't know; for nothing more than just to support their own unholy traditional religious beliefs which identifiably helps Satan to spread hatred and create a desolated environment.(2Cor.7:8-10)

Just as it was yesterday there are people today who believe on the Son of God, who are protected by the Word of God by their faith. The key to the Kingdom of God is the work of faith, and not the works of the law. Although the worldly think they can judge the conscience of the gay community and can judge the Divine law of God, God didn't give anyone the powers to do so. Those who judge the Lord's law aren't doers of the law, but are judgers. (St.Matt7:21/James1:20-25) The traditional religious realm of the world has dictated the Word of God for many centuries. This has been done for and by the worldly as they hid themselves behind the Word of God by depriving the godly meanings from the Holy Scriptures to justify the evils that are embedded or sown into their own hearts, which loves to strife and hate their family members, neighbors, and strangers alike.

The Word of God is true, but after it has been subverted by the supremacy of mankind to befit the traditional religious realm of the world for so long; the world's concept deludes the original meanings of the Word of God and turns the image of the incorruptible love of God to appear to be a corrupt form of hatred that comes from a monstrous God. It's a known fact unto all mankind that a half truth is still a lie. It's traditional for men to make themselves apostles of Christ, and use fair words and well put together speeches which half way explains the full intent of the Lord and Savior. The Word of God doesn't lie, but the words of man makes God appear to be a liar; by not teaching the Word to the full extent of meanings. Again I say that a partial truth is still a lie!

Questions

What are the common consequential reasons for the heterosexuals to hate the gays?

Is it because God made Adam and Eve and not Adam and Steve?

Or is their primary reason for having hatred in their hearts is because the Prince of the world have coerced the martyrs and scorners to use the old method of traditional religion to trick their own kindred into thinking that God instructs for the gays to be hated by them under the New Covenant of Jesus Christ?

ANSWER

Well, the right answers lies somewhere within the fact that gays can be married wheresoever's the reproved law of the land allows, during the 21st century. Once upon a dream not too many years ago, the religious people of the land which now allow gay marriage, fought vigorously to keep the idea of gay marriage unconstitutional. The term unconstitutional in the English language was purposely setup in America's legal system to biblically define an ungodly circumstance or act of events for the past, present, and future elected Supreme Court Judges to use as a standard method of either preventing or approving certain inalienable rights of the people to be granted. The valued decision of a Supreme Court Judge depends on the vain double-minded discretion of a nation of haters and despisers of men. The term ungodly has the power to convince a person to feel justified as a hater when spoken very highly of in an unjustified manner by many orthodox religions who knows not God under the New Covenant of Jesus Christ. They use God's name in vain by exhorting their self as they individually glory in the misery of another man's flesh by persecuting those whom they've been trained to religiously despise or hate. (St. Matt.5:10-24)

While resorting to such undignified measures of hatred, it is traditional for religious men to oftentimes proclaim themselves to be a better quality of Christians than those whom they are use to discriminating against and are comfortable persecuting. The inward state of them honestly believes that they are justified in their conservative religious deeds of making ravening railings as religious haters of men. The wisdom of this world stands on Satan's vain desire to produce division through the contradictable religious ideas that brings forth confusion. Whether right or wrong the Fruit of the Spirit proves that in the hearts of most members without the consent of any law, they deceitfully would mentally and physically give themselves to one of another in marriage.

> **St. Matt.22:30 "For in the resurrection they are neither marry, nor are given in marriage, but are as the angels of God in heaven."**

In hopes of preventing unrighteous judgments, all who confess Jesus Christ as their Lord and Savior must also consider that upon Judgment Day each individual will receive their righteous judgment of God according to their works. Whether their works as missionaries were good in mastering agape love or evil in mastering the veil acts of hate, all must stand alone and be judged. Before that day comes, the gays and the straights are in grave need to get it together as one body, because there is none other body except the Body of Christ.

By the measure of faith the author's worst case scenario is and always has been the same. "People aren't born sinners," says Sister Glory. "But all are born into sin. If the Holy Bible is right, then a whole lot of people are living bibliographically wrong."

It really is sad to hear people say that they believe that a person who is on familiar terms with a natural born gay person, is a natural born sinner. Such of a notion only provides evidence that they don't understand the things presented before them concerning the teachings of the Holy Spirit. To say a person is a natural born sinner is just as bad as saying God is a liar, so then reside the great debate of what is the truth. Some people believe that being gay is a matter of choice, and others firmly believe they are born gay and theses two conflicting ideas always will forever cause people to be at odds.

Sister Glory suggests that it's predictable for certain gays to renounce, abandon, and give up totally on their sexuality for a reason which goes beyond the commonly known factor of trying to fit in. Often times a gay person who seeks for righteousness actually does find the Lord God. After being converted by the Spirit of the Holy Ghost, they will always remain to not be accepted by society due to the stereotypically misjudgments of traditional religious men of the world. They need to know and understand that they aren't what society says they are, because they are righteously approved of before God.

The worst case scenario of situations like this is commonly all the same. After misplacing their faith in men for so long, a person's convertible heart gets crushed and they most likely are coerced to reject or disavow as to deny the traditional religious beliefs and theories of all orthodox religions. Why would a person want to go into a place where people think they are garbage? Unfortunately often times with their minds made up or affixed on rejecting all orthodox religions they are susceptible to also miss out on being apart of a true ministry of God which is set apart from the world and is blessed by the anointed which teaches its members to practice loving all people without hating any.

Unlike the house of man, all sinners who believe on the Lord are welcomed to enter the House of God. After being exposed to the preaching which resides within a true House of God, the sinners learn to rebuke the sin factors of their life and yet remain as a member thereof. With a reprobate heart within the houses which are built by mans hands resides all kinds of people of different walks of life whom are known for being troublemakers and busy bodies. Instead of making peace with the Lord and giving him praise for sending the sinners to worship the Lord with them, they'd rather war amongst themselves to prevent sinners from entering the house which they respect. They claim the building where they worship to be their house as of a property of ownership, and the rule of their political ordinances within the material building consists of them being totally in control of who they allow too enter in, who may stay in, and who may not enter thereof.

Since Jesus denies the traditional practice of hatred, both the gay and straight communities which worship together are truly blessed. They both are required by God to have a mustard seed size amount of hope of being redeemed, and by faith they all may individually be united as a unit of One Body in Christ for the edification of the Church of God. As a reasonable sacrifice made by all children of God, maybe someday all will humbly come together and renounce the traditional religious methods of spreading hatred and stop burdening their own hearts with the concerns and matters of the world. This reasonable sacrifice is made available by God the Father, the Son, and the Holy Ghost for all whom are baptized into the death of Jesus Christ. Therefore, we all should stop serving sin so that our sin might be forgiven and destroyed. We are the children of God whom are planted together in the likeness of Christ's death and in the likeness of his resurrection also. (St. Matt.28:18-20/Romans6)

THE LORD'S METHOD OF PURIFICATION IS A SPIRITUAL PROCESS OF A CONTRITE SPIRIT (Titus3:1-8)

No man can cleanse his own heart (Prov.20:9). Although the world brings their own traditional religious concepts of what thus saith the Lord thy God into their manmade congregational house of worship, the children of God understands that a spiritual change mortifies the deeds of an individual or a group by making them spiritually knowledgeable of which spirit to follow. The intent of the Spirit of God does not authorize anyone of us to judge one of another, but it empowers all of us who believes on the Son of God with the Holy gift to spiritually identify which spirit we individually possess; so that while we diligently seek for the Kingdom of Heaven we can sustain ourselves to follow after the holiest of Holy. This heavenly gift advantages us to easily choose to do the works and will of God as a reasonable sacrifice, while edifying the Lord in the form of a reasonable service. A worthy praise such as this is above and beyond the dead deeds of every idol work and religious practice of men.

The Fruit of the Spirit shows the same light of truth unto all mankind alike, and the Word of God says repeatedly, "HE WHO HAS AN EAR, LET HIM HEAR." Unfortunately, some people are too occupied stirring in the worldly matters of another man's business or the business of this world to hear the Word of God. They don't understand that the Holy Spirit of Truth convicts the heart to revive the Spirit of man; not to condemn it like the worldly doctrines of religious men and false apostles' teachings does. When the Spirit of Truth is involved, the inner spirit of the convicted heart of men can reproach the dead deeds of their own flesh and become sorrowful enough to desire to live in love, peace, joy, and happiness; without hating another living soul. This is the spiritual simulation of a born again Christian, who possesses a godly sorrow. The religious coerced words of mankind that are filled with worldly wisdom may cause the condemned hearts of mankind to continue condemning the consciences of others, but God is greater than a condemned conscience. (2Cor.7:6-16)

2Corinthians7:8 "For though I made you sorry with a letter, I do not repent, though I did repent: for I perceive that the same epistle hath made you sorry, though it were but for a season."

2Corinthians7:9 "Now I rejoice, not that ye were made sorry, but that ye sorrowed for repentance: for ye were made sorry after a godly manner, that ye might receive damage by us in nothing."

2Corinthians7:10 "For godly sorrow worketh repentance to salvation not to be repented of: but the

sorrow of the world worketh
death."

Be not deceived by those leaders who support violence while using the
Lord's name in vain. They know not God nor do they honor God in the
presents of you, but they do cause shame and deny his calling upon
their life. The spiritual process of a born again Christian keeps God's
children from turning into a reprobate person. A reprobate person is
like a scorner, who thinks they are righteous because of the cleanness
and the correctness of their outer parts and their inward part is full of
wickedness and ravening. All scorners' ravening hearts are full of evil
rage, desolation, and despair. These are the evil fruits which they
devote their hearts too, as they covet to make merchandise of the weak
and simple babes in Christ. The scorners are the spots and blemishes
that feed on the flesh of the weak and simple babes in Christ, and places
stumbling blocks at their feet. Through covetousness with feigned and
soothsaying words traditional religious martyrs makes merchandise of
them for the sake of money, wealth, and other things which pertains to
their religion's pernicious ways of gaining worldly profits within the
religious realm, by maliciously condemning the purest of hearts.
(Titus 1:11-16/2Peter 2:1-2, 2:13)

There's a grave difference in a man's weakness and a man's wickedness.
A scorner is unwise and unlearned to understand which is which, and
the ignorant traditional accusations they make unto God against the
weak are made of a curse unto them and the followers of them, because
their vain accusations aren't in compliance with the Divine Order of
God. Without heavenly knowledge neither the martyrs nor scorners can
obtain heavenly wisdom nor can they receive heavenly understand to
know that the will of God is to love God first and to love one's self with
the same measure of love for strangers and their neighbors in despite of
one's differences.

Romans13:10 "Love worketh no ill will to his neighbour: therefore love is the fulfilling of the law."

St. John13:34 "A new commandment I give unto you, That ye love one another; as I have loved you, that ye also love one another."

St. John13:35 "By this shall all men know that ye are my disciples, if ye have love to another."

Although religious people know that they all have faults, they yet tend to find it easier to subject to the vileness of despising others who confess their faults and imperfections. The love of God causes a person to be longsuffering and kind to all others, but a scorner is deceived and is doomed to damnation as they pick and choose who to give their love too and who to despise or hate. All of God's children shall obtain his heavenly wisdom to identify with the Lord God's Divine Order of Law, which co-asides with his natural nurturing nature of cleansing a person's heart through his spiritual purification process.

Ps.34:14 "Depart from evil, and do good; seek peace, and pursue it."

Ps.34:15 "The eyes of the LORD are upon the righteous, and his ears are open unto their cry."

Ps.34:16 "The face of the LORD are against them that do evil, to cut off the remembrance of them from the earth."

Ps.34:17 "The righteous cry, and the LORD hearth, and delivereth them out of all of their troubles."

Ps.34:18 "The LORD is nigh unto them that are of a broken heart; and saveth such as be of a contrite spirit."

Ps.35:19 "Many are the afflictions of the righteous: but the LORD delivereth him out of them all."

Ps.51:17 "The sacrifices of God are a broken spirit: a broken and a contrite heart, O God, thou wilt not despise."

The purification process is the works of the inner Spirit and not of the flesh, but the religious martyrs of the world believe in working their way into heaven. (Titus 3:1-8) It is by the Spirit we live and by the flesh we die. Therefore; the Lord's purification process converts our hearts into being of a Contrite or Sorrowful Spirit. This process frees us inwardly from judging others, and it frees our consciences from the unrighteous judgments of our outer appearance that are made against us by the world. The Lord's purification process rebukes us from hating, despising, envying, strife, and committing all sorts of evil acts against ourselves and against one of another; by causing us to be humbled by the shameful injustices of our own fleshly deeds. The Spirit of God converts us to do the works of the Lord, which leads us to repentance and redemption.

DIVISION IN THE CHURCH

We aren't created by the hands of man nor are we molded by man's hands, but if we are mentally and spiritually placed under the corruptible principalities and powers of man's unlawfully religious dictatorship too long; we may become reprobate for the sake of one religion vs. another. (2Cor.13:5/Colo.2:8) Being reprobate for the sake of up holding the acts of such hypocrisy gives God no glory. The Spirit of God's unity is indisputable, but the world tends to use the Word of God hypocritically to cause disputes to surface between the principalities and powers of one religion against another. Hypocritically, those who speaks evil of others dignities does the same things. (Gal.3:3-5, 9-10)

For example, the Iranian government calls an adulteress an evil woman, and they makes it legal for the government to put her to death upon capture. Evil, is the act of being unforgiving and murdering the adulteress. Without empathy and compassion the hearts of them forgives her not, and the standard value of the Iranian government pardons themselves from the sin of a murderous reprobate minded group of people whom are fighting vengefully to redeem their selves by violently showing their disapproval of adultery.

As a simpler example of one church vs. another, in America certain religious organizations doesn't believe in using musical instruments during worship service and they speak evil of the dignity of those which does. They believe that it's impossible for anyone who uses musical instruments during worship service to worship the Lord with all of their hearts. They twist the Word of God to befit their own understandings of the scriptures. They sarcastically question the legitimacy of a person's disability to physically place a harp, piano, drum, etc into their hearts. They fail to see the spiritual adventures of one who passionately plays a musical instrument for the Lord. Therefore, they criticize and dispute against a person's ability to physically worship the Lord in Spirit and in Truth with all of their heart and soul, while using musical instruments. (Deut.11:13/St. John4:21-26)

They themselves proclaim that they worship and serve the Lord in spirit and truth during their everyday walk of life, but they yet disbelieve that it's possible that a person can praise the Lord with all of their hearts in songs and hymns while playing or listening to musical instruments. Hypocritically, while congregating and ministering outside of the walls of their congregation, they listen to music on CD's mp-3 players, I-Pods, I-Phones, and even on the radio on a daily basis.

Listening and playing musical instruments outside the walls of their congregational house seems to keep them spiritually inclined as they sing spiritual hymns alone with a musical tune. They excuse themselves to embrace the sounds of musical instruments by claiming that their daily walk of life is different on the outside the walls of their congregation than it is when they congregate in a building where they worship and praise the Lord. Hypocritically, they think that worshipping the Lord within the walls of a church house/building that is built by the hands of man is different from worshipping the Lord while grocery shopping, riding in their automobiles, air planes, trains, or even relaxing at home amongst their invited company or guests. What makes the acts of them hypocritical is the fact that the Word of God doesn't discriminate. God requires everyone to worship the Lord daily in the same way no matter where they are.

Other religious organizations believe it's a sin when religious practices are compelled by someone who believes in praying indirectly to God through a man like a Pope whose grand role in the religious realm of the Priesthood is to be like a mediator between man and God. Hypocritically, while despising and speaking evil of the dignity of such religions; they themselves does the dame thing. They individually pray for the sick, poor, weak, and the incarcerated, etc. upon request as if they too think they are mediators between man and God.

In most cases they try to justify their reasons of doing the same things by acknowledging that their perception of the Holy Scriptures indicates that they ought not to believe that the Lord hears a sinners' prayer. Those whom pray should understand that Jesus Christ is the mediator between them and God. Therefore, they should pray in faith with an understanding heart that in order to get to the Father they must first go through the Son.

As one religious organization disagrees with the tactics of the religious practices of another church, their speeches speaks evil of one of another's dignity. Such acts allow desolation, dissimulation, conflict, confusion, and anger to separate these dictators from possessing the agape love of God. They speak evil of the dignities of one of another because they are coerced to think one religious group is closer to God than the other, while proclaiming their own insidious religious doctrine or pernicious religious ways are of the Doctrine of Christ. In reality every doctrine which speaks against God's ordinances are falsified doctrines of the world. The trueness of God's ordinances goes beyond the physical structuring of Christ Church, which worldly men try to imitate or duplicate. In fact, the ordinance of God is supernatural. It takes a down to earth type of person who privately studies the Word of God to show themselves approved unto God to understand the grace and mercy of his ways.

The Word of the Lord states that upon this Rock I build my Church and the gates of Hell shall not prevail against it. The Rock isn't the physical image of Christ's Church, but it is the spiritual image of Christ's inner spirit. The Lord's Adversary has beguiled men to believe in simulating or reproducing the physical structuring of Christ's church, which Christ founded or established on the Day of the Pentecost unto every origin of people around the world.

Oh, I've heard certain religious people say that if a person doesn't speak in tongue in reference of how it was done on the day of the Pentecost that the individual person is not saved by the Blood of Jesus. The perception of such a notion has lingered for centuries and has brought about unanswered questions and confusion unto many.

Speaking in tongue for every dialect of the world to hear and understand the same exact things at one time has only been done once and is an impossible task to duplicate. When the Lord fulfilled the works of his Father he needed not an interpreter, but yet he was able to be heard and understood by every different origin of people around the world whom all spoke a different language. What Christ did concerning speaking in tongue is now given unto mankind as a gift. Those whom think other wise may as well insanely stand at the cliff of the Red sea holding a staff and attempt to part the sea. Man must wake up and learn to understand that they weren't called to do what Moses, Christ, and others were called to do. Simultaneously, they also must understand that they were not called to speak to a multitude of people from different dialects to where all can comprehend what they say as it was done on the day of the Pentecost (Acts 2/1Cor.14). If their sanity is in tact maybe they will also conclude that with great powers comes also great responsibility. In other words, those who receive the gift to speak in tongue also should pray that they may interpret what they say.

THE DIFFERENT PERCEPTION OF ONE'S OPINON OF THE ANONINTED TEACHINGS OF THE HOLY GHOST

To explain the difference within the interpreted notion of one religious person from the perception given by another concerning the same said biblical passage is like playing the telephone game. When a group of people plays the telephone game, they form a circle and start a secret within that circle to see if the word or phrase used to begin the secret will end the same way as it began. The rules of this game are simple. The first person of the circle starts the secret, and shares it with whosoever is closest in a whisper; so that no other within the circle can hear what is being whispered. That person then speaks softly the word or phrase they heard or think they heard onto the next person. The game ends when the whispering returns to the starter of the circle. When the secret returns to the starter, nine times out of ten something about the secret fails to be the same.

An educated person is for ever learning, but knows nothing. A wise person understands that what happened on the day of the Pentecost was God's way of establishing the Gospel of Jesus Christ unto all people from multiple nations in one place at one time. This elaborates on the fact that faith comes by hearing the Word of God.

The telephone game is like the game Satan play's when causing confusion. Causing bewilderment is the greatest way for him to win souls. His followers which plays his deceptive telephone game fails to simulate Christ's love, mercy, and grace, and they think they have it all worked out as they condemn those whom they religiously despise. Satan's followers think that their act of love is of Christ's perfect love, and some even think their love is greater than Christ's.

Within another fine example of one religion vs. another, some religious organizations serve the Lord's Supper every Sabbath Day of the month, and another may serve the Lord's Supper only once a month. The one which serves the Lord's Supper every Sabbath religiously believe that in doing so they are working closer to the Doctrine of Christ than the others. Again, controversy and conflict exist between them. In this instance, God gets no glory, because when one religion fights against another in concerns of arguing that one is closer to God or to the Doctrine of Jesus Christ than the other; such debating causes the Spirit of both the oppressors and the oppressed to be jealous, angry, envious, strife, hateful, desolated, divided, and confused. Behind these emotions are not the works of godliness nor righteousness, and none of these indeed edify, exhort, nor give God glory. To conclude this matter; it is wise for all people to stop competing against one of another for the Lord's love, because such competiveness brings about hostility and is enmity against God.

After men's hearts yields to these kinds of conflicting inner spiritual emotions, they no longer are inclined with the law of God. Although they have the intent to do righteousness indeed, their hearts are full of ungodliness (Rom.8:6-8). In reality, this kind of fighting isn't man against man, but it is Satan against God. Satan may have fooled the world into thinking the Holy war is fought best when such religious men humiliates the dignity of others or when they encourage themselves to shed the blood of others, but the Holy War is the inner war of the Spirit of every individual who desires to do righteous unto the Lord.

In the mist of such warring the Spirit of Man also inwardly wrestles against the jurisdictions of hierarchy by which worldly leaders pick and choose the area and the range which legal authority extends a chain of command between the church and the state. The extended chain of command between church and state routinely pertains to the ranks of power as of an angle of the third of the nine orders of angels in the traditional Christian hierarchy, which traditionally consists of religious men's legal authority and legal ability to enforce laws or pronounce legal judgments. The actuality of a spiritual fight over principalities and powers constructively consists of an inner spiritual war within the individual heart of the babes and elders of all ages, who desires to know which spirit to rebuke and repent of. They mainly desire to control all spirits whether good or evil which enters into their own hearts so that they may have no guilt but a free and clear conscience unto the Lord of Host.

If ministers use or misuse the Lord's name in vain to draw a babe's heart to become filled with hatred, envy, strife, grief, misery and such liken unto these; they do so not by the Spirit of God but by the lust of the flesh. (Gal.5:16-21)   God is love and so are the works of his Spirit. (Gal.5:22-26)   Traditional religious doctrines of false ministers are contrary to the One True Gospel of Jesus Christ. They vengefully teach through the eyes of the world and not through the singleness of the spiritual eye, which is the heart of the Man who is spiritually created in the image of God.   False apostles' religious doctrines and commandments religiously twain together with their sinful fleshly desires which yearns to draw or induce others to submit their consciences to believe in their vengeful religious doctrines and commandments over the Doctrine of Jesus Christ. They trick men into disobeying the Lord's Greatest of all Commandments. This is the prince of the world's method of protecting or marking his territory.

Just as the Lord reign on the just, he also reigns on the unjust. But many orthodox religions of the world have deluded the truth of the Holy Scriptures with an evil perception of the Word of God, which separates the godly spirit of all who are traditionally trained by the wisdom of the world to have an ungodly fear of the Lord God. The Orthodox religions of the world have for centuries beguiled many to live in unbelief of who the Lord is and of whom he says they are. According to the true Word of God, a non-believer is ineligible to receive the Kingdom of Heaven. A nonbeliever hasn't the faith to believe that Jesus has the power to save those whom confess him as their Lord and Savior. Meanwhile, many orthodox religions declare a nonbeliever to be all of whom are religiously despised by the dictating leadership of their orthodox religion. Therefore, it is clearly noted that most followers of orthodox religions are afraid that they themselves will be persecuted by the Cross of Christ. That's why they are coerced into thinking that they may gain a closeness with the Lord by conjoining their uncertain and wavering faith which despises others under the orthodox religious leadership of the past, and that's also why they for centuries have religiously accused other Christian believers of being either unsaved or worshippers of the Devil.

Ironically, everyone who spends their entire lives speaking evil on the dignity of whosoever they love to hate, looks down on, and despise; does so basically because in doing so they hope of having themselves grafted into the Book of Life. They are the Spots and Blemishes of the flesh of all whom they hinder from loving, worshipping, and serving the Lord's Divine ordinance of Love. In the Spirit of Righteousness and Truth, God will have mercy on whosoever he chooses to have mercy, and according to the Holy Scripture; the Lord chooses to have mercy on those whom are despised the most of all.

Oh how I pity those who religiously are trained to double-mindedly believe that they are the most despised, because they deceive themselves as they mercilessly and maliciously use the Word of God to hinder those whom they religiously despise the most of all.

> Romans8:20 "For the creature was made subject (focused) to vanity, not willingly, but by reason of him who hath subject (focused) the same in hope,"
>
> Romans8:21 "Because the creature itself also shall be delivered from

the bondage of corruption into the
glorious liberty (freedom) of the
children of God."

SATAN

Many false religions believe that Michael; the Archangel and the Devil
are one of the same. Evidently, they don't study the Holy Scriptures to
show themselves approved unto God (Dan.10:13/Jude 9). As the first of
the Chief Princes within the Old Testament, Michael was described as
the guardian of the Jewish people in their hostile act of antagonism to
heathenism.   Heathenism is defined as an offensive term that
deliberately insults an unconverted member of a people or nation that
does not acknowledge the God of the Heavens and earth which is made
mentioned within the Holy Bible.   In Dan.10:21 Michael was also
described as the Prince of Israel.

Even unto the New Testament was Michael mentioned in Rev.12:7,
which states he fought in heaven against the dragon. Even though the
Holy Scriptures explains that the Lord's adversary lost the first battle in
heaven, it is also written that Michael's desire was to contend,
challenge, compete, and argue with the devil whom accused, charged,
and blamed the strict Protestant Christians' denominational faith for
seducing God's people into wanting to have their own system or
organization that charged people before God day and night (Rev.12:10).
During Michael's run of competition against the Devil, he dared not to
bring against Moses a railing or slanderous accusation unto God. He
properly used the Word of God and said to the Devil, "The Lord rebuke
thee". (Jude8-23/2Peter2:10-18/2Peter1:2-10)   In conclusion of false
religion's inaccuracies of the Word of God, those whom are misled must
understand that Satan cannot rebuke Satan.

This is a fine example of how Satan coerces people on earth to believe
that his traditional irreligious concept of the Word of God is true. His
beguiled words, imprecisely teach his followers to represent the wrong

nature of God while thinking or believing more of them-selves than they ought as if they are better than others. They are tricked into having a proud attitude while provoking those whom they belittle to become angry. The wile of Satan turns the pure hearts of mankind into being unjust judges, whom believe they are working righteously above the rest. Therefore, they feel justified while lifting themselves up at the expense of putting down others. Publically, they rejoice in provoking the simple and weak babes in Christ to anger, although they know that a heart that is consumed with anger is an evil heart indeed.

Satan knows that an irate person is commonly known for giving in to an evil act out of anger. In such cases, the provokers of anger receive a boost to their evilly implied morale after causing the weak and simple babes in Christ to become angry. While causing a heart to become angry, they wittingly believe that the angered simple and weak babes in Christ are of the world and are their enemies. Having enemies in the world encourages them to think that they can relate to the Holy Scriptures which suggests that the weak and simple babes are of the world and that the world knows not God and will hate those of them that do. These provokers say they know God, but they take great pride in making the simple and weak appear to hate them; by publically doing and saying ungodly things against them. As the reactions of the babes are drawn by anger to retaliate, the provokers then disguise themselves to be innocent and pure. Meanwhile, they publically target the captured image of the provoked babes' angry reactions to make the falsehood of their own religious appearance to be harmless and innocent in the process so that the theoretical imagination of themselves being hated by the world (babes) more believable. The liars believe in their own lies, and goes beyond intervention to physically prove their lies are the truth.

After boastfully creating so many enemies, surely they have not read nor understood that a proud heart is what the Lord despises. (St. Luke16:13-15/St. Luke18:1-18) Satan also coerces those whom follow him to publically charge others unto God in efforts to make those whom they publically humiliate to also think lesser of them-selves. Such acts which causes shame and embarrassment upon another living soul, provokes the hearts of the simple and weak babes in Christ to desire to be on the wrong-side of the tracks which satisfies the image of Satan's own self-made key of destruction. The main key purpose of the wile of Satan's efforts is to enter into the Body of Christ by any means necessary. His perverse words falsely sway people to follow after the spirit of him. They think that their pernicious and malicious traditional religious way of life perfectly fits the keyhole to the gateway to the Kingdom of Heaven, but it doesn't. (Rom.8:18-25/Jude10/2peter2:12-13/2Peter3:9-14)

God the Father sent the world a gentle or friendly reproof which rebuke and reprimand any and every emulation of Satan's religious teachings with seriousness. God the Father sent his Son who was made or birth into the world in the form of the flesh to a virgin woman known as **Mother Mary** (Ps.132:11/Luke1:26-32/Acts1:14) whom was made or birth into the world of people, who lived under the old law. By choice, Christ sacrificed himself to be born to live and to die in the form of the flesh by the old law; to renew the old law and save all who believes he is the Lord and Savior which was prophesied to come. Jesus Christ sacrificed himself to save all from the errors of Satan's insidious religion's malicious ways, which dangerously misleads and seduces the hearts of all who subconsciously are tricked into worshiping the prince of the world's fabricated messages of the Word of God. Insomuch of all of which Jesus did, he established the New Testament.

Unintentionally, many people of the 21st century passionately follow the true character and evil intentions of Satan, because they've been traditionally given over to the ignorance of the Prince of the world; without privately studying the Holy Scriptures for their own selves. Satan's cunning falsehood makes it impractical for a person to know and understand that they are following the hostile antagonisms of his mendacity which triggers the false perceptions unto others whom convincingly believes that certain deceitful traditional religions are not to ever be made void. Satan convincingly sways their hearts to worship the enmity that works against the Lord's truth. The works of animosity is also against the works of God. The works of Satan seduces the hearts of many to unintentionally yield to the one unforgivable sin which completely lies against the Holy Ghost and this sin misleads people to BLASPHEME against the Holy Ghost.

The Lord walked holy and beloved through the bowels of his Father's mercy and grace as he kindly humbled himself with the inspiring mind of meekness. His love also suffered long while he destroyed the bondage of the adoption of Satan's traditional religious laws of the land, but traditional religious peoples still love to use Satan's perception to persecute each others with. The Lord suffered long in order to redeem the hearts and minds of all sinners and persecutors who strongly believe in God, but yet misuses religion to torment, oppress, and bully others. God is not a partial God and the love, mercy, and grace of God even provides an escape route for the oppressors. It is they who love to force all to live as the conservatives. These corrupt conservatives are abound and abundantly filled with the knowledge of sin but have no good sense of righteousness or faith. The Lord redeem the hearts and minds of all whom knows, trust, and believe on him; so that we all may receive the adoption of sons. (Rom.3:17-28/Gal.4) Knowing good and evil is of a curse, for all whom walk by sight and not by faith.

It is prudent to know that the law of the Lord is summed up in one word, LOVE. (Prov.10:12/Gal.5:22/2Tim.1:7/1John4:7-8) Love heals a multitude of wounds and covers a multitude of sins regardless of the kind of wound or the size thereof. Without receiving the whole truth, which leads all mankind spiritually into Redemption and Salvation; Satan's Spirit of Condemnation works on killing the glory of the Lord's godliness by any means necessary. The world's murderous religious acts of antagonism befit the intent of the Lord's Adversary. Satan and the spirit of him are enmity against the spirit of all mankind alike, and there's no exception for anyone who religiously uses the Lord's name in vain concerning the Lord having no respect for such person's.

DO YOU UNDERSTAND WHAT FEARS TO FEAR OR DO YOU FEAR WHAT'S NOT UNDERSTOOD?

This Spiritual and Holy War isn't man against man, but it is Satan against God. Satan is in the mist of the inner substance of all things which causes divisions and wars. The contents of the works of Satan are made up of the evil elements, which the Lord and his chosen disciples preached against amongst the entire religious world; by advising and instructing all ears to hear the Word of God and by telling all mankind to not be drawn or seduced into the things which causes people to despise and hate one another.

(Gen.3) Satan beguiled Eve in the beginning to desire to take pleasure in evil. The principalities and powers of Satan misled her godly conscience the same way as he misleads people today. Today he cunningly causes people to separate themselves from the Spirit of God by coercing them to yield or commit their hearts to consider the aspect of being as gods in the world by engaging themselves evilly to be against others. Meanwhile he disguises and hides his true feelings, thoughts, or intentions from the minds of his subconscious followers' religious beliefs, practices, outlooks, and ways of life. The ways of Satan's condemning spirit place burdens on the hearts of all hearts which yields to the dark side of his tempting spirits that causes anger, envy, strife, and the feelings of hopelessness; to fulfill the desires of his spirit of Condemnation. The religious followers' of Satan are well known for doing all they can to condemn the spirit of man, but they fail to lift one finger to revive or save any.

The spirit of Satan's spirits is made of many allegiances, and they work together to cause desolation, wars, and destruction. The evil spirits of Satan create iniquity and enmity, which attempts to restrain Gods children from obtaining the holiness of Christ. The evil substances of Satan's destructive spirits twain with traditional religious men's desire to be commended by God causes people to have an overly excessive desire to be as powerful as God, but God gives to no man the power to neither judge nor retain the spirit of another man's conscience. Nor does man have power in the day of death. There's no liberation, deliverance, discharge or release of service given unto anyone who think they can save either themselves or another living soul by protecting or preserving the evil spirit within this spiritual war. (Eccl.8:8-17) Evil can not rebuke evil. The spirit of Satan cunningly causes the conscience of the purest of hearts to be weakened by his tricky religious words. He conjures up wars between men as to cause them to grievously fight amongst themselves and against each others by misusing the Word of God as a cloak of maliciousness against every living soul.

Satan hasn't a Soul and his ungodly jealousy and animosity which sparked his interest to start the first war in heaven is now misleading man to attempt to soul win over Jesus. His stratagem is to trick a person into believing that the things which make wars also will make peace for all religious members who willingly uses the tools of his religious wiles to mentally and physically fight in his war against God with the vehement desire to win. Satan's followers religiously think that if they successfully use the Word of God to condemn the conscience of another man by tricking them into believing that they have no hope of being redeemed from the bondage of sin; that their traditional religious hostile deeds will indeed bring those whom they oppose, oppress, and condemn unto repentance.

As hypocrites, Satan's followers worship the false images of God's character, because they all are tricked to personally misperceive the statue and desires of the bowels of Satan to be pure, holy and acceptable unto the Lord. His followers have been trained up to confusingly describe their essential pathway to be the trueness of God's Devine order of law. The wiles of Satan dissimulates, disguises, and hides the idea of God's love with hate; to advance his own appearance of light, which falsely appears to be the image of the light of Christ.

(St. Luke24:1-9) The followers of another doctrine, which isn't after the Doctrine of Jesus Christ are perplexed and bewildered as they desire to be commended by God for their dead deeds of injustices, and they don't understand that God's promise of ever lasting life are promised not to the swift who seek amongst the dead law for God's promise of everlasting life, but it is promised to the sown seeds of Abraham, all Jews and Gentiles whom all are sown the seed of life everlasting through the righteousness of faith. (Rom.4:2-4, 13-18/Gal.3:10-18)

Everlasting life remains today to be the same promise of the Old, but is made new with the New Testament. God's Word is true and he told Adam that in the day that he eats of the tree of knowledge of good and evil, he surely would die. On that day which he did eat thereof, God feared that mankind would also put forth his hand, take and eat from the tree of life and live forever and put them out of the Garden of Eden. In translation to the scriptures, as it is written in the beginning when mankind were removed from the garden of Eden after the first sin entered the world, men now must under the New Testament put forth their hands and take also of the tree of life to learn, know, understand, and do that of the New Commandments' of the Lord; in order to be righteously led by the Fruit of the Spirit unto repentance, redemption, and salvation. God knew that without being enabled to partake of the Tree of Life, men shall perish under the bondage of the Serpents' religious laws that are in the world. So he placed at the east of the garden of Eden Chĕr-ū-bĭms, and a flaming sword which turned every way, to keep the way of the tree of life, not to prevent man from obtaining life everlasting from the tree of life but to keep the tree of life sacred and holy forever. The Tree of Life is obtainable through Heavenly Wisdom, and she is more precious than rubies.

THE DAY THE LORD CALLS ME HOME

Satan's followers and false prophets strive about words as hypocrites, which spiritually profits them nothing. Upon the Day of Judgment it's going to be every MAN for them-selves. Sister Glory says, "I personally will love having the ability to say unto the Lord God, that as a witness on earth that I have fought my good fight of faith while working out my own salvation in fear and trembling of him." She carried on to express how after being born again that she dared not to hinder or forsaken her own mercy by falsely preaching unto God's people to subvert, undermine, or threaten the desire of anyone to want to do that which they cannot do, because the Holy Scriptures inspires her to strive to not be a hypocrite.

With a clear conscience she dared not to forsaken her own mercy by accusing railing accusations against those who preached unto her to do what they themselves weren't able to do. In the mist of all of her doing she spiritually identifies with the Spirit of God which lives within her. Free-willingly she wrote her perception of the One True Gospel of Jesus Christ to the best of her ability and prayed that the Lord would restore the goodness of God's love, mercy, and grace unto all whose hearts maybe condemned by the false preaching of false prophets. She stated that without a doubt she's a firm believer of the Power of the Kingdom of Heaven, and she desires not to blaspheme against the teachings of the Holy Ghost.

Without lying against the truth or burdening her conscience with religious men's matter of expressing their unreasonable definition of what Christianity means to them, she by the grace of God without shame nor worries am speaking boldly of how she rebuked the evil spirit of those of them who tried to draw her into the religious misunderstandings of a false prophets' concept of the Word of God. Upon Judgment Day she believes that she will boldly be able to stand before God and say that she has been taught by the Anointed and in return of receiving his Heavenly Wisdom, she can explain unto him of how she strived as his servant to teach others the ways of his righteous judgment which led the hearers towards repentance and not unto boastful pride. In confidence, she suffice the desire of her content soul which is satisfied in all things that she's done in the spirit unto the Lord, without yielding her heart to be hindered by the burdens of this world.

1Cor.4:4 "For I know nothing by myself yet am I not hereby justified: but he that judgeth me is the Lord."

1Cor.4:5 "Therefore judge nothing before the time, until the Lord come, who both will bring to light the hidden things of darkness, and will make manifest the counsels of the hearts: and then shall every man have praise of God."

1Cor.4:6 "And these things, brethren, I have in a figure transferred to myself and to Ă-pŏl´-lŏs for your sakes; that ye might learn in us not to think of men above that which is written, that no one of you be puffed up for one against another."

No man has the right or the power to neither judge nor retain the spirit of anyone on earth whether they are dead or alive, because whether a person is dead or alive; all are the Lord's (Rom.6:8/2Tim.2:11). Those who think their religion's vain judgments against men are pardoned from the wrath of God; can think again! They too must accept full responsibility upon the Day of Judgment as they profess unto the Lord God the foundation and ground work of their laboring, which subversively weakens the hearers of their religious concepts of the Word of God; by making the weak feel grievous of been born. This sort of laboring is made manifest by the Spirit of God, and is made known of what sort of work such persons have chosen to build as to add unto the foundation that is already laid by Jesus Christ. Whether good or evil every man shall receive his reward according to his own labor. (1Cor.3)

> Ps.95:10 "Forty year was I grieved with this generation, and said, It is a people that do err in their heart, and they have not known my ways:"
>
> Ps.95:11 "Unto whom I sware in my wrath that they should not enter into my rest."

People can feel their inner spirit wrestling against the Will of God and against his Good Pleasures, as they hear and understand the truth but yet repeat the malicious preaching's of false prophets who love to cause anguish and vehement grief as to condemn the conscience of another person's faith on the Power of God. Having heavenly wisdom means to gain the knowledge to understand the differences between God's good will and way, from Satan's desire to will his own type of pernicious way through the use of his evil subversive words of the wrong kind. Heavenly wisdom helps those of us who believes on the Son of God to protect ourselves from the pernicious ways of Satan with the Amour of God which is provided by the Comfort of the Holy Ghost.

Those who privately study the Holy Scriptures to show their selves approved unto God are the true seekers of the Kingdom of Heaven, and those who privately and publically study the Holy Scriptures to justify their wrong; shall not find justification for the wrong which they do. Meanwhile, the Holy Spirit prevents the false prophets from controlling and causing the conscience of men to feel grievance of being born; by commanding all to restrain or control the inner spirits within their own hearts from desiring to discriminate or envy the oppressors (Prov.3:20-35). Discriminators are spiritual fulfillers of the beguiler's desires, which mentally and physically sow the seeds of suppression and spreads grief, hatred, and other worldly sorrows. Such dead deeds likened to these, reside within the hearts of most traditional religious martyrs and scorners alike.

As a born again Christian the author says, "I don't believe I'm neither better nor worse than any other living soul, because God created man equally. I believe that what JESUS has done for me to strengthen my faith and to bring me to know and understand his Heavenly Words of Wisdom; is of his Will and of his Good Pleasures. I also believe that what he has done for me to free me from bondage is the same as he'd do for all others who desires to diligently seek to know and understand the image of the Lord in a holy, unique, and adequate way. There's no sin too big for God.

> 2Tim.2:12 "If we suffer, we shall also reign with him: if we deny him, he also will deny us:"
>
> 2Tim.2:13 "If we believe not, yet he abideth faithful: he cannot deny himself."

A SEEKER OF SPIRITUAL KNOWLEGDE WILL FIND HEAVEN'S WISDOM

Scorners can't see the wrong of their own methods as they are seduced and tricked by Satan to defile their selves. Knowing a scorner cannot tell their right hand from their left, isn't a reasonable validation which gives justification to Christian citizen of any sort of religious denomination the underlying principle or right to hate and despise them, and yet most denominations which house people who desires to be Christians; tends to spread hatred against the blind with passion. Again the word of God says there is no justification in wrong doing.

To make things worse, Satan sends out his children into the world to seduce traditional religious men into forsaking their own mercy by making unrighteous judgments of others. They curse their selves by cursing all whom don't desire to follow after their vain religious methods, because they themselves fail to do what they claim others ought to do. Their intentions maybe to defend their theoretical religious beliefs and to avenge God, but the desires of their hearts works the Vail of Fears, which for centuries have misled the hearts of mankind unto death, destruction, and despair.

The highly encouraged standing point of Satan's evil Vail of Fears includes the idea of a "Kill or be killed" principle mentality which resides within most religious martyrs' livelihood, because they are trained by the wiles of Satan to believe in an evil "Do or Die" deceptive religious concept, which profits man nothing. The impurity of Satan's notion of the Word of God swindles the hearts of so many people to be foolishly jealous of all levelheaded homosapiens who speaks the truth.

(homosapiens means humanity [New Latin Species name, from Latin homo "man" + "sapiens "wise, intelligent"])

His followers' lewd desirous hearts enthusiastically have for centuries been willing to put down the dignity of others in false hope of saving themselves from the persecutions of Jesus Christ. Indeed they fulfill the evil desire of Satan who coerces them into believing that wickedness delivers those of them that are given to it. (Job14:1-5/Ps.53/Rom.3:7-9, 10-12; 3:19, 20-31)

Those who believe that salvation will come unto them if they successfully do the deeds of the law also are encouraged to be puffed up with pride as they boast of their physical accomplishments. They act like they think they can save themselves from the temptations of the world without the help of the Lord. After observing their works and analyzing their ways, they indeed appear to be mentally hypnotized. They indeed covet to have an overly excessive relationship with the Lord of Host as if they are placed under an evil spell, which makes them think that the evil things that they do and say against the dignity of others; are done for the better good of all of humanity.

For example, a minister may provide a more personal traditional religious outlook towards the Holy Scriptures by personalizing the Word lascivious. For the better good of all humanity, they use different philosophies to articulate the word "Lasciviousness" within the Holy Scriptures pacifically to define the fleshly desires of the homosexual community. It's like misusing the word black in the English language to thoroughly define all Afro-Americans as sinister or evil, while the word white thoroughly defines all Caucasians as pure, good, and innocent. The motive of such sermons commonly scrutinizes and deludes all to believe God has forsaken and abandoned all gays, and wants them to revile them like they did the earlier victims of the AIDS virus because everyone assumed the aids virus was a homosexual disease.

In actuality, the correct perceptive measure of the acts of lasciviousness isn't partial, prejudice, nor bias; because it also pertains to whatsoever is the lewd wantonness of the heterosexual community as well. Certain ministers would rather not admit that the lewd wantonness of their ministry causes them to have an overly excessive desire or wantonness to have a closer relationship to God than the gay community. Two wrongs don't make a right, and the fact of the matter is simple; except they recognize and admit their faults they shall continue to divide themselves and none will ever repent of their acts of lasciviousness. (Jude4/2Peter2:10-16/St.Mark7:20-23/Eph.4:19-32/Gal.5:19-26)

After Satan enters God's domain which is the conscience of men's spiritual minds, his corrupt tactics twists the denote meaning of God's predestined ordinance of law and creates unto the hearts of mankind an illusion to faithfully rely on. This always has been Satan's way to deter men's hearts from acknowledging another person's God given spiritual-right to obey the Greatest Commandment of God and live in Righteousness and Truth; without lying against the truth. The Righteous Truth may hurt like a dog sometimes, but it sets the faithful soul of all whom trust on the Lord's Anointed teachings free from the yokes of bondage that are created by the wiles of Satan. Satan and his followers evilly implies that the substances which works within their dead deeds of evil thoughts and opinions ought to be viewed and forced upon all mankind, even though the Fruit of the Spirit of God proves how such speaking religiously transfigure and change the appearance of their deceptive works and evil acts into an illusion of great religious beauty, but in reality their works are a misapprehension of magnificence done against God.

All thanks and glory is to God for not leaving any of us to be ignorant enough to continue viewing the evil devotional perspective of the Word of God as a religious way of righteousness. The dead deeds of traditional religious men are made obvious by the Fruit of the Spirit of God to co-aside with Satan's malicious and forwardly perverse way of misusing the Word of God unfairly and improperly against the weak and simple. By their own understandings of the Word of God, they give God no glory. Their congregational ministry befits their own occasional fleshly desires to have others put out of the assembling of God.

(Prov.8:21-36) God created man with Wisdom being his daily delight, and with God and Wisdom being together as one; they made mankind to possess the awareness and the conscience of God. Meanwhile, Satan is determined to destroy man's relationship with God, through an unethical defined sense of right and wrong which is of his own condemnable spirit. He desires to misdirect as many people as possible, by preventing them from understanding the fact that the Lord's Spiritual Truth resides in the Spirit of Love.

In so doing, the Prince of the world causes religious people to inwardly commit sins against the depth of the Lord's righteousness by creating an illusion of a religious battle for all and against all. Many people are convinced that they are vehemently obligated by God the Father, the Son, and the Holy Ghost; to fight vigorously amongst their selves in this age old religious warfare. Satan's vain despotic religious acts misrepresents the value of God's love for all mankind; especially those who follow his despotic ways, because they are coerced to think they know God well enough to judge the depth of his love, mercy, and grace. Therefore, they preach of who shall ascend or descend either into heaven or into hell as if they can raise Christ again or can bring him down from Heaven. The ordinance of those who follows the wiles of Satan are made manifest by the Holy Ghost to not be in accordance with the heavenly understandings of the anointed teachings' that are proven by the Fruit of the Spirit of God.

It's by the unrighteous judgment of their hearts and of the false and unclear things which they believe in that causes their hearts do give way unto false teachers' who trains them to religiously look for physical signs of hope in the ways of war.

> Romans8:24 "For we are saved by hope: but hope that is seen is not hope: for what a man seeth. Why doth he yet hope for?"

Many are misled to believe in the evidence which their eyes can see. If their physical eyes could see through the stratagems of Satan's followers who presents unto them a malicious way of judging the Word of God, they would willingly stop killing the godliness of their own hearts as well as the hearts of the weak and simple babes in Christ. Save yourselves from yourselves, you hypocrites. You maliciously judge the outer appearance of mankind by comparing physical things with physical. Satan knows that you will easily believe in what you physically see through the world's eyes of scientific and political religious theories which are tools. These tools originally were given unto you by God to edify Christ with, but traditional religious martyrs and scorners have coerced you to use the aspect of science, religion, and politics together to devour one of another instead.

After being cunningly coerced by the wiles of Satan, men are known for using science, religion, and politics against the goodness of God's Will and Good Pleasure. The Holy Ghost has made manifest that man have been misusing the Lord's gifts to support the makeup of their political theories, which sways them from having faith in the righteous order of God's Divine ordinance and Law of Love. Their faith resides within their own peculiar religious set of boundaries, limitations, and restrictions that surrounds their comprehension level of the Lord's limitless and unconstrained Law of love. After the knowledge of science, politics, and religion are twined together against the spiritual side of the Lord's Tree of Life, Satan knows that he has found away of giving God's people reasons of not obeying and trusting on the Lord. Subconsciously, many are placing boundaries around God's love, mercy, and grace to support the evil traditional religious elements which befit Satan's purpose.

While Satan's delusional dissimulations of the Spirit of God's love deprive men from doing the Will of God and of his Good Pleasure, the Spirit of God's love still prevails in the hearts of all whom are chosen of God; to boldly choose for their individual selves to withstand against the traditional evil tactics of worldly wisdom. For the sake of reproving themselves, those who renounce their membership from among the type of traditional religions that uphold Satan's evil tactics also rebukes the things which are of Satan's desire. It is of Satan's desire to cause them to have a lack of hope as he misleads them to walk despotically through the path of disparity, dissimilarity, and inequality. Without equality being apart of their spiritual sight, Satan praises, commends, and entrust his children's obedience will carry-out his ill-willed form of rage by the help of his ungodly spirits that upholds iniquity.

Satan religiously use the emotional resemblance of God's jealousy to inflict an ungodly fear, rage, and anger against mankind and to coerce more people into emotionally thinking that they are reconciled by God as they choose to believe on the evil ways of traditional religion. It is it is traditional for religious people to define an unjustifiable accusation against the Lord's spiritual topic of reconciliation and repentance. Satan coerces these people to believe on the deceptive idea which concludes their theoretical religious point of views that regulates the notion that the actual religious act of seeking for vengeance will reconcile them with the Lord. His ideas seduce those who revere the circumstantial standards that religiously surround the ill mannered reasoning for the despots' to uphold the religious practices of inciting ill-willed behaviors towards. Such unforgiving behaviors relatively modify the evil traditional religious ideas of men who think they have hope of receiving remission of their sin through the vain practices of despotism. Again I say, "If the Holy Spirit is right, then a whole lot of people are living bibliographically wrong."

God's wisdom has past the test of time, in spite of the religious world's scientific political affairs. The power of the glory, which comes from God's all loving and all merciful grace is instilled in the conscience of all of God's people. The works of Satan's workers hinders Heaven's Wisdom from being viewed spiritually on earth by and through the carnality of men's hearts and minds. Carnal-minded individuals are well known by the fruits they bare, and their occupations are defined within their deeds. By their own understandings and through their dead deeds, they work the evil works of the substance of things which ought not to be hoped for; like religiously hoping that God would have all whom they religiously despise to perish so that they themselves may take pride in all of their religious boastings.

Their works are proven by the Fruit of the Spirit to work worldly sorrows, and the Holy Scriptures says that worldly sorrows worketh death. All of Satan's children desire to be viewed as gods while they rule despotically and tyrannously over God's babes and elders of all ages without spiritually receiving God's knowledge of righteous judgment through the New Commandment. For this cause, many aren't able to view the heavenly truth, which enables us to understand that the balance of God's love, mercy, and grace is upon all sinners in hopes that we all may repent.

Heavenly Wisdom is a spiritual being, and she resides on the right hand of God. She instructs us all to believe in things we cannot physically see such as the substance of the things hoped for, which are the evidence of unseen things. Heavenly Wisdom provides us with things like the very insight of God who issues out the knowledgeable Fruit of Righteousness for us to see ourselves equally with all others through the singleness of the eye. Wisdom instructs us to humble ourselves to live as equals to one another without the unwarranted and unjustifiable desire to despise any kind of man for their faults. (Proverbs)

A person who has obtained Heavenly knowledge can stand on confidence without wavering like a leaf in the wind to all sorts of doctrines like a hypocrite. As we all are fighting our own battles individually to work out our own Salvations, (Ph.2:12-15) God requires the same things out of all us today as he did of those in the beginning. He requires for us to be selfless and love others as we love ourselves. God requires for all of his children to follow after the likeness and the Compassion of Christ, regardless of the common stereotypical disposition or the natural attitudes which the wiles of Satan seduces people to trespass against them with. The children of God knows and understands that the worldly mind-set is concerned with dealing in the temperament things that are apart of worldly matters. Therefore, they are able to look over the ignorant attitudes of those who don't know God.

Every individual church which doesn't show or illustrate the Compassion of Christ blasphemously is ministers of hate. Christ is urging all Christians whom he made strong to help the weakened and simple babes to understand that the reason why they should not believe in following ministers of hate is because within the training of those whom are ministers of hate; resides the existence and zeal of loathing. Detestation is carried over unto the congregational members of these ministries as a misleading constitutional continuation, which makes ever act of their perseverance and persistence legally done in vain. They may receive worldly riches, but they would lack heavenly rewards.

(Job28:18, Prov.8:11) The precious gift of the Lord's Heavenly Wisdom changes the spiritual mind fold of all who retains her, from the corrupt state of being haters and despisers of men; into the incorruptible state of being honorable and humbled men and women of God. The gift of God's power of life is defined within itself. It convicts and revives the dead spirit of mankind back to life. Without Heavenly Wisdom there are people of this old world who still call themselves men of God, although their deeds aren't godly deeds. God is love and his powers shouldn't be misused to hate anyone with. (St. Matt.7:15-23)

A SIN...A SINNER...AND THE ENEMY

A sinner sways in their words and in their ways. They use God's Word as a cloak of maliciousness, while speaking out about things that they don't understand. Their lips loosely speak of love and grace, but they use love as an excuse while their non-compassionate grace and unloving finesse are made manifest to not be the works of God. These people don't seem to understand the grave difference between a person's sin from a person who chooses to sin.

A converted person recognizes their own sin is the cause of them being separated from God. Being converted is what causes a man to adapt or equip their spiritual mindset with the Armor of God; not to intentionally misuse the Power of God to do evil works, but to defend their selves as to defeat the evil works that deceptively waits to lure them to sin during their temporary time period on earth.

The enemy Is seen by the saints overseeing a group a people, who creates wars in hopes of religiously creating or making their own form of deceptive peace on earth through wars and rumors of wars. The enemy seduces people to vigorously fight with vehement passion for the thrill of making or creating a temporal kind of peace for themselves. Through the falsehood of their intentions they have for centuries deceived many into believing in a falsified type of godly love for God which is a conditional kind of love that befits Satan's conditional standards.

The enemy is trying to gather more lost sheep's to join his flock. The weak and simple babes in Christ are in for a battle for their lives, and all are in need to know and understand that the Key to the Kingdom of heaven is placed in their hands, so they'll desire to learn how to use that key and stop giving their key to the men of the world who haven't the power to retain the spirit of their conscience. They really need to beware of traditional religions which have been known for trying to retain the Spirit of mankind by placing a yoke of bondage on their shoulders or around their necks. The babes whom stumbles and fall to such bondages symbolically are like Atlas; a Greek mythological character of a Titan, who was forced by Zeus to support the heavens by holding the pressure of the world on his shoulders. A memorable picture of Atlas is of him holding the whole world on his shoulders as a punishment.

In hopes of sparing a babe in Christ from death and from worldly sorrows, the author of Discerning Perceptive writes to mentally and spiritually survive or revive those of you who are beguiled and placed in a state of misery which is equivalent to the state of bondage which lacks hope of being delivered or saved. As a strong servant of God she and many others are required to compassionately and properly prepare the weak and simple babes of Christ to withstand against the wiles of Satan with the nurturing teachings of the Anointed. She knows and properly understands that a person whom is weak in the Spirit may obtain the knowledge of God by someone whom is strong in the Spirit of God. She personally can relate to this factor, because she remembers all of the strong souls which individually made a major impact in her life.

When she was lost without hope, the Lord sent her his love, mercy, and grace so that the comfort of the Comforter, which delivered her from bondage; could make her internally strong where she was spiritually weak. Therefore, she now has a willing desire to help all others who like her at some point or another during their life time may either be oppressed by the oppressor or through the endurance of discrimination have been exposed to the feelings of having the weight of the world on their shoulders.

The physicians of the world medically and scientifically calls a person's feeling of distress or stress; a mental disorder or mental disability, but the Lord's cure for depression and stress comes by hearing the Word of God. The mental stability of many have been properly maintained and restored with peace, by them being obedient and having faith on the Lord; without taking expensive medications. Of course Christ used medicine to heal the sick whether it was in the form of him using his spit and clay (St.John9:6) or by the anointing of oil concerning the elders (James5:14-15). It is prudent for all to understand that it's not a sin to take medication from their physician for their sickness, but it is a sin to unwisely put their faith in the medicine and not on the Power of the Lord who blesses the medicine with his healing powers. Simultaneously, all must accept the fact that medicines aren't going to stop the Lord from calling anyone home. When it's our time to physically die, it's our time to die. The Lord makes no mistakes and he doesn't contradict himself.

You babes need to know and understand that Christ died to save you all, and nothing on earth shall prevail against his true purpose and intent for establishing his Church upon a Rock. With great powers come also great responsibilities. The key to the Kingdom of God is heavenly wisdom (the Holy Ghost) which all of the children of God are predestined to possess. Those of you who obtain her are advantaged to uphold an understandable knowledge of the Power of God. Instead of giving your power over to the dogmatic disbelievers of the Blood of Jesus and the doubters of the Power of God's ability to either save your soul or to save the souls of the most despised, be strong in the faith as servants of God and he'll see you through troubled times. When your faith on the Power of God is strengthened, desire to teach all who ears hears the Word of God of how to properly and rightfully use their heavenly gifts of wisdom and knowledge; to teach others how to walk meekly amongst all mankind alike without desiring vain glory of men and please stay away from desiring vengeance.

In fact, it is customary for traditional religions to target the base of a man's sin while defining and confining a sinner's conscience within the habitual institutional religious law of the land and within the traditional principles of the world's traditional religious customs and beliefs. A sinner is held back from pursuing the Lord's Will under traditional religions' standardized stipulations, terms, and consequential expressions of righteousness and truth. The provisions, legal clauses, and written contracts of world's traditional religions states that certain conditions must be met by its members and these stipulations are provided or supplied unto traditional religious followers by the wisdom of this world. Instead of these sinners being trained up to **fight the good fight of faith**, they are trained to **fight a bad fight for faith**, because they are coerced to fear the fears of this world, which fills them with the substances of Satan's wisdom that are tangible to the physical reality of things that can be seen, touched, and physically felt.

Satan tricks and misleads the earthy superior race of people to disbelieve in the essential meaning of the New Commandments which Christ has spiritually written in the hearts of mankind. Through trickery, his unchanging general ideas of what the Lord's sacred parables and holy words means or says; gives them an inhumane desire to the yield their hearts to commence worldly misery, sorrows, pain, and destruction. They honestly don't know that in Christ there's no fear in love. Therefore, the deeds of them worketh an ungodly fear into the world unto all whom they inflict with grief and misery. The compassionate Spirit of Christ specifies a godly fear, which is spiritually led by the essence of the Righteous Spirit of God. The essence of Christ's love and compassion gives those who follow after Christ recompense or compensation in the form of redemption in return of their obedience unto God. (Gal.3:13/4:5)

In most cases the physical sins of a person is judged by those who traditionally view religion on the same accordance with the sect of the Pharisees. They feed on the weak and condemn them as sinners by maliciously misusing the Word of God as their defense, while claiming to possess religious magisterial authority. As they minister their own perception of the Word of God, they strip the love, mercy, and grace of God from the Spirit of Hope, which is written and is freely given unto the hearts of all mankind alike within the New Commandment of the New Testament(1Cor.2:4-16). Satan's workers are the inheritors of the world who continues to build the Kingdom of his own, by using the Word of God reversibly from what the Spirit of God clearly signifies. The true purpose of the Word is to uplift and edify all sinners and transform them into Saints by which they may worship together as One Body in

Christ so that none should perish, but corrupt traditional religious martyrs uses the Word to separate themselves from others in hopes of saving themselves by using the Word to vanquish, revile, or subdue others who they are beguiled to believe God desires to perish. (1John1)

There are reprobate minded men, women and children of all ages who are blinded by Satan's lies, and they can't spiritually see the hypocritical standards which are hiding within their worldly physical religious battles and wars. The standards of these religious reprobates have the peoples vengefully battling one of another and it consist of the teachings of hatred, envy, strife, jealousy, greed, anger etc. These standards are enmity against God and his people. Satan's main objective is to cause mankind to disobey the Word of God. His method in doing so includes the fulfillment of his evil will to destroy the Spirit of God and win a large number of souls, by deluding the denote meaning and purpose of the Word which God sent out into the world full of grace and truth; so that he could destroy what the good Lord God built. (St. John1:1-17)

Although the leaders of all sorts of irreligious traditional earthy political congregations may say that they don't dispute the Word of God, in reality they really do. Their desire to dispute the Word of God is formed or sown within the spirit of them by the earthy sensations of this world, and as their flesh war against the spirit; the spirit of them are made manifest by the spiritual teachings of the Holy Ghost to be enmity (an enemy) against God.

A SERIOUS MESSENGERS' NOTE FOR ALL CHRISTIANS OF ALL FAITH!

After the end of the world prophesy has been unveiled unto all of mankind, the Lord himself balances out the false traditional religious teachings of the end of the world prophesy and clarifies that it he who is the destroyer of death. (1Cor.15:26) All of God's little ones whom humbly obey the Lord's Commandments do so without arrogance and boastful pride. In love, they choose to do right not because righteousness is defined within the spirit of them in the same mannerism of a traditional form of a religious veneration or in the form of an irreligious respect of making grievances, complaints, accusations,

117

or criticisms against others. God's little ones are unlike those who revere a majority of the world's most popular traditional religions' vain admirations. Humbly, their desire to do right includes the spiritual unselfish consciences of themselves knowing God loves them and they are privileged to value the gift of the Lord's promise of everlasting life. Such knowledge brings them unto the unity of agape love. Therefore, they spiritually without boastful pride receive pleasures on earth as it is in heaven. They don't waste their valuable time presenting an argument as to defend one religion or another, because they are spiritual and not religious. Being of a religious body that fight for religious purposes glorifies one man's opinion against another, but in so doing God receives very little to no glory at all.

God's little ones' desire of living righteously includes the desire of them living in peace with the Spirit of the Lord growing within their godly spiritual consciences (Eph.4:1-15). This is where and how all babes are strengthen and molded by the Potter Maker to grow up and be God's strong servants. Before most true Christians (A.K.A The Saints) gained the power to be spiritually healed from the old traditional religious realm's perverse idea of having an ill-willed kind of love against others, they too at some point; hypocritically devoted their hearts towards making another person's heart partially unwilling to fully open up to the Lord's agape love. After the Comforter came unto them, they as followers of Christ were converted and they began to trust on the Lord God, and all whom believes on him knows that righteousness is done through agape love which is neither partial nor bias. Ten times out of ten, when you enter a congregation where the Lord allows you to witness the ill-will of the elders, bishops, deacons etc, whom are unwilling to open up to the Lord's agape love unto you, you need not to worry, but say your peace and leave. If you stay under their tutorship too long, you will open yourself up to be susceptible of being hindered by their murderous presumptuous ways.

Therefore in the process of making righteous judgments towards the actual acts and events which surrounds the circumstances of the lives of all whom may or may not spiritually agree with the Holy Spirit of God's

Will and Good Pleasures, the true Christians are taught by the Anointed to not judge any man. Instead of entrusting our own judgments on the defilements of any traditional religious preference of judging the Spirit of another person, we as soldiers for Christ prudently are urged to make righteous judgments within every known event and circumstance of our lives with empathy. While doing so, we humble ourselves as an equal unto all others through the mercy and grace of God; by comparing spiritual things with spiritual. Remember, those who don't love you are coerced by Satan to not love you. Therefore, don't give into the evil spirit of anger. Just pray for them and give it over to God, because only he can save them.

We all have heard that when you know to do right and do it not, then to him it is sin. So choose to do the right thing as you hear the voice of the Lord and follow the godliness and the holiest desires of your hearts. The Lord knows and understands your problems and hears your righteous cry. The Lord didn't leave you to be ignorant my friends. You know that if you choose to do wrong by making unrighteous judgments against another living soul, wrong shall return back to you again.

Like the reapers of the field, we shall individually reap what we individually sow and also reap the works of another man's labor. Therefore, we ought not to desire to remove the growing weeds of the field which God has made, because as imperfect persons ourselves; the vanity of our own hearts will also pull up the wheat. "Let go and Let God do what you cannot!"

What dooms you to damnation isn't what the worldly religions suggest or think of you, because they are sinners too. We all fall short to sin, but damnation follows after wrongful ideas leads you to believe that worldly religious people are right for being hateful and spiteful towards you, when they are spiritually wrong. The Fruit of the Spirit proves what is righteous, but traditional religion often times teaches people by the destituteness or the lacking of the Holy Truth. Being evil spoken of, isn't the same as being evil. They spoke evil of Jesus Christ, and Christ wasn't evil at all. Many believed he was the Prince of Satan, so more than likely the world will believe the same about you. You're not greater than the Lord so you can't expect to get better treatment from the religious rulers of the world than he did. Without adding nor subtracting or lying against the truth, according to the Word of God; Condemnation is defined in St. John3:19-21.

> **St. John3:19 "And this is the condemnation, that light is come into the world, and men loved darkness rather than light, because their deeds were evil."**

Spiritually we can self examine and identify our own wrongful deeds to either be good or to have a bad reputation. The Fruit of the Spirit of Righteousness and Truth manifest or make known to us whenever the wrongful deeds of our flesh desire to be superior over others; of what spirit to follow. The Fruit of the Spirit makes it obviously clear for us to understand and see how seductively our godly spirits can be misled to morally be abandoned, if and when we decide to discriminate as to condemn the spirit of others. The vain hearts of mankind which yields to the act of showing favoritism for or against someone supports an ungodly act that lacks godly morals and good sense. After self examining ourselves, we may thoroughly evaluate the Holy Spirit in search of the Holy Truth to reassure ourselves of which Spirit we are required by God to follow.

Godly morals don't confine a person's mind to strictly stay on the course of the moral virtues of sex, because there are so many more heavenly standards for our minds to freely give reverence too. For example, patience is a virtue, and the Lord's godly morals may cause a person to patiently wait before having sex or decide to not to have sex at all, but godly morals also includes the moral values which equals the value of being as holy as possible. Godly morals are neither bias nor prejudice. God isn't a partial God, so why do so many religious men think his Son was sent here to condemn sinners; instead of saving them all?

When a person obtains the feelings of a godly sorrow for goodness sake, they are equipped with the predestined holy power to identify the difference between good and evil. The great power of godly sorrows allows God's people to see the wrongs that they personally have done by themselves unto themselves and unto others; not for the sake of upholding their own religious way of despising and speaking evil of the dignities of others, but to admit or confess our faults to one of another for the edification of the Body of Christ. Upon receiving a godly sorrow, true repentance shall follow. Godly sorrows makes men's hearts feel happy and sad simultaneously. Simultaneously, it also can make you feel the agape love of the Lord and the hatred of men. At the same time joyful and sad as you go through agony and pain. Godly sorrows, strengthens the faith of God's peoples to be on the Lord side. This is all apart of the Lord's plans to provide unto his children his spiritual knowledge, while strengthening the faith of their conscience to believe on him.

Repentance is a spiritual process where the Lord converts the hearts of all mankind away from the poor quality and underprivileged state of being condemned and from being so easily coerced or tricked by those who relligiously accepts the traditional false ministries' theoretical discernments and deprived concepts of the Word of God over the Lord's uplifting and spiritual teachings of the Anointed Truth. The true teachings of the Gospel of Jesus Christ work to unite and unify all people of one faith. False teachers and false ministries believe in dividing the faith of the people by the multiple bases of an age old tradition. Since the Holy Scriptures explains to all who has an ear to hear that it is of God's will for all to believe that his all powerful love, mercy, and grace is come to save all whose faith is on Jesus Christ, then by all means; stop and think why certain ministers fight against this truth! It's like Satan's followers completely are deluded mentally to war against the predestined comforting spiritual teachings of the Holy Ghost, which implies that Christ came into the world that he may save all sinners from sin.

The sorrows of the world makes you grievous of being born by making you think there is no hope of you or no hope for someone you know and love; of being saved by the Blood of Jesus Christ. Such sorrows are promoted and supported by false witnesses on earth. You'll know them by the fruits they bare. Their fruits simulate the spirit of their hearts through their works. In vain their dead deeds works to fulfill the fruit of the dark spirit, which command of your obedience to desire to **disbelieve** that the Lord's love, mercy, and grace **is able to save you all**; including you oppressors who are subconsciously coerced to religiously despise others.

YOU BELONG TO WHOSOVER YOU SERVE (St.Matt.5)

Stop giving away your God given rights and powers of the Lord's Holy gift of glory, and stop denying the truth of yourself. You have heard, the truth will set you free; so why lie against the truth (St. John8:32). If you are prejudice, then confess your fault unto one of another. Come together in the righteous name of Jesus and pray that God will show you the light of your own life, which maybe hiding under or behind a bushel of lies. The Lord will make it easier for you to hear and understand his Word and see yourself in the way of Christ if you'd take a moment and yield your hearts to the receiving of his glory.

You are who you are, not because of the choices you've made. You are who you are, not because of what or who religious people and men-pleasers may believe you are. You are who you are, not because of who your parents, grandparents, and siblings are. You are who you are, because God created you in his image and likeness to be a Child of God! You cannot serve God and mammon.

THEORETICAL CONCLUSION

Be very wise and reprove the evil deeds of your own flesh, and do so as gently as a dove without beating yourself up. After reproving your own ways, spiritually repent and be blessed. Go out and tell the World what God did and is still doing for you. Help others to understand all that you know of concerning the Power of God. Remember, there is no pretense in true repentance. If we as One Body in Christ can't spiritually see our own individual faults, we will not confess of our individual sins. Neither will we be able to edify Christ as One Body nor repent. Nor can we help our brothers and sisters to remove the mote out of their eyes, with a beam left in our own eye. Faith comes by hearing the Word of God. "May God bless all hears, and the doers of his Word. Amen!"

Ephesians5:6 "Let no man deceive you with vain words: for because of these things cometh the wrath of God upon the children of disobedience."

Ephesians5:7 "Be not ye therefore partakers with them."

Ephesians5:11 "And have no fellowship with the unfruitful works of darkness, but rather reprove them."

Ephesians5:13 "But all things that are reproved are made manifest by the light: for whatsoever doth make manifest is light."

Ephesians5:14 "Wherefore he saith, Awake thou that sleepest, and arise from the dead, and Christ shall give thee light."

CHAPTER 2 ALL WHO SIN AGAINST A PERSON ALSO SIN'S AGAINST GOD

Every Saint Has a Past, and Every Sinner Has a Future through Christ Jesus

> St. Matt.7:3 "And why beholdest thou the mote that is in thy brother's eye, but considerest not the beam that is in thine own eye?"
>
> St. Matt.7:4 "Or how wilt thou say to thy brother, Let me pull out the mote out of thine eye; and, behold, a beam is in thine own eye?"
>
> St. Matt.7:5 "Thou hypocrite, first cast out the beam out of thine own eye; and then shalt thou see clearly to cast out the mote out of thy brother's eye."

A skilled discriminating heart mentally recognizes whatsoever things that are deeply sown and rooted within it. It's by the choice of the discriminator to carry on with their traditional religion's evil intent to torment and ridicule those whom are religiously marked with the things which they are traditionally trained to believe keeps men from receiving God's love, mercy, and grace. It's also by the choice of the discriminator to either stay or to renounce such religions. Those who choose to carryon living with godly intentions by spiritually reproving or disapproving their own traditional religion's discriminatory thoughts with the intent and desire to remove or cast off the dead works of their own flesh; keeps themselves from causing themselves and others confusion, afflicting, pain, and sufferings.

Many times the sown and rooted prejudice seed overwhelm the discriminating hearts of mankind. With no remorse, such persons mercilessly devote themselves to embrace free willingly to the prevailing despotic customs, principles, and standards of an idolized traditional way of worshiping the Lord. The unrighteousness of their traditional way of worshiping, gives unto them a false sense of power and control over others; as they seek to have dominion and follow after their manmade religiously derive false doctrines of ungodly traditional religious laws. Their religious laws take or replace the original origin or denote meaning of partial passages from the Holy Bible text to befit the occasion of the Adversary. Therefore, the minds of skilled discriminators are deluded to think they are worshipping God with all of their hearts and might, as they egotistically devote themselves to idol worship the false sense of power and pride thereof.

As the discernment of their worldly hearts looks down on others with great contempt, they commend themselves to be godly although they spread hatred against others. Life to these worldly leaders and blind followers of men is like the basic skills of mathematics. To them, the key to happiness and success on earth is all about being apart of the controlling factor, which suggests that righteousness resides under the rule that states that the vote of the majority defines righteousness as in the form of a massive agreement over the vote of the minority.

Those who are desirous of being apart of the blind leaders controlling factors are known to become unwilling to stand up for what's right, because they want to be recognized as a member of the world's controlling party, clique, or group of people (St. Matt.15:9-14). The thrill of possessing controlling powers over others seems to overwhelm or over power their idol hearts with pleasure. They honestly can't comprehend the difference between good and bad. Therefore, their ideas and desires to have dominion over others are vexed and are full of vanity.

Often when given or placed in a position of authority in a controlling environment, they choose to make a difference distinctively between whosoever may have a distinguished quality or mark; to either express their hatred or favoritism for or against them. Peoples whom loves to despise others would rather give honor and glory unto themselves and be glorified by men for successfully humiliating another living soul, instead of humbling themselves and glorying God and being glorified by God. The evil deeds of their prejudice hostility and animosity aren't the wrought of God, because God isn't a partial God or a hater of men. He's a hater of enmity and is a just and equal God to all mankind, but for many centuries; partially biased people have perpetrated their corruptibly bias deeds to be of God. They are like wolves in sheep clothing. Although their outer part appears to be clean, their inward parts are full of ravening and wickedness. (St. Matt.15:16-20)

St. Luke11:34 "The light of the body is the eye: therefore when thine eye is single, thy whole body also is full of light: but when thine eye is evil, thy body also is full of darkness."

1Cor.6:19 "What? know ye not that your body is the temple of the Holy Ghost which is in you, which ye have of God, and ye are not your own?"

1Cor.6:20 "For ye are bought with a price: therefore glorify God in your body, and in your spirit, which are God's."

St. Luke11:35 "Take heed therefore that the light which is in thee be not darkness."

The spirits that works in the children of <u>disobedience</u> has not yet so learned Christ, and they irreverently blaspheme against the Holy Ghost, while subconsciously preaching against the Power of God. The Power of God is superior to all other natural and supernatural forces, which makes the heart of man sick. (Act. 10:38/St. Luke 4:18-19)

> **Ps.13:12 "HOPE deferred maketh the heart sick: but when the desire cometh, it is a tree of life."**

Even though Christ <u>predisposed</u> of the unjust tyrannous traditional religious worldly ordinances of laws, which were represented by the governmental authorities of the <u>Pharisees</u>, <u>Sadducees</u>, and the scribes, many of the standards and principles that are related to or is regulated with their traditional religion and worldly ordinances still exist in today's society of the 21st century. Many today say they refuse to stray away from the teachings of the Old Time traditions of religion. During the life of Christ he exposed the worldly <u>malicious</u> things residing within the doctrines of men's traditional religious laws. He clarified the <u>malice</u> within men's worldly religious laws are <u>enmity</u> against God. Those who sought to kill him by their <u>obedience</u> to the old law, refused to believe on him and many didn't know him.

(Prov.8:13/16:6-8/1Cor.15:22-26&27-28/2Tim.1:1-10/Rom.8:6-7/St. Matt.5:19-24/7:18-29). Just like those of the past, many today don't know him and they yet still believe that as they work the works of iniquity, they are doing God's works. They also fail to yield their hearts to his <u>predestined</u> ordered law of love, by not keeping the unity of the Spirit of God in the bond of peace (Eph.4:3). Instead they are full of ravening and violence as they speak with strife in their hearts as froward and perverse men.

ARE THE LAWS AROUND THE WORLD MADE UPON THE SPIRIT OF TRUTH OR THE SPIRIT OF ERROR?

While comparing spiritual things with spiritual, the worldly laws of the land are seen clearly with the singleness of the heart by all the Saints; to be distinctive from the teachings of the Holy Ghost. Since the beginning of sin, worldly men have survived the world with sown seeds of deception; which covers up their own hidden agendas as they walk in the vanity of their own hearts and minds (Eph.2 & 4). The unjust tyrannous traditional religious orders of law are more discreet than others, because of the oldness of their hidden agendas there of, which chokes the truth and deludes the minds of many to believe in its false pretense of being spiritually supportive and equally treats all man kind alike.

Many historians have produced scholarly historical studies of past events, which are arranged chronologically in order of dated times without a godly analysis or spiritual interpretation; to tell a story of the worlds' history. The Saints and the author of Discerning Perceptive use these chronicles to spiritually study and understand how the laws of the land were despotically established. In choosing to study the Holy Scriptures to show approvals unto God; the Holy Spirit makes manifest unto us of the dead historical deeds made by people who left a foot print in the history of the world, while revealing unto us how the biblical despotic governments spiritually deprived the religious lives of a great multitude.

The historian's resourceful findings within the studies of the world's history have been spiritually compared and self examined by the teachings of the Anointed. Clearly with the help of a godly analysis or spiritual interpretation, the most admirable findings of the author's studies reveal the prime foundation and the root or sources of men's despotic governments' traces back to an earthy sensation known as greed. For the desire to have rule over money and the powers thereof, men have concluded their joys of life here on earth; comes from receiving whatsoever values thereof that money may bring. The earthy desire of gaining such joy by gaining and maintaining worldly possessions cause the hearts of many to become <u>avaricious</u> (greedy) with a strong desire to gain control and keep money, even if their ways of doing so would cost them their very souls. While promoting their greed as an <u>avaricious</u> religious ritual, they count slackness against the poor. (2Peter3:9/James5:1-3/Phil.4:11)

> **1Tim.6:9 "But they that will be rich fall into temptation and a snare, and into many foolish and hurtful lusts, which, drown men in destruction and perdition."**
>
> **1Tim.6:10 "For the love of money is the root of all evil: which while some coveted after, they have erred from the faith, and pierced themselves through with many sorrows."**

The actions of the despot legends mentioned in the resourcefully written chronicles of many history books are revealed by the Anointed to have ruled <u>abusively</u>, <u>oppressively</u> and <u>tyrannously</u>. The core of their personality traits were shown through their dead deeds, which resemble the fleshly characteristics of <u>envy</u>, <u>strife</u>, and hatred and is <u>enmity</u> against God. Their evil deeds stressed the absence or deficiency of restraint and often of discrimination, as they vainly desired to gain and maintain political controlling powers, wealth, and even worldly possessions especially for what belongs to another. After gaining many worldly possessions, they even desired to possess the devotional consciences of other men whom mindsets were/are devoted by grace through faith unto God. (Ex. Libyan leader Moammar Gadhafi)

Democracy

The origin of Democracy and its political influences have been studied by historians who recorded its time line of being developed as early as 600 B.C., in ancient Greece. The Greek city-states and the ancient Athens despised the act of dictatorship, and they criticized it to be the worst form of government to live under or to support. Therefore, the Athenian's democracy evolved into a <u>Direct Democracy</u> for the people to meet in one place to make the laws for their community.

Ironically only the Athenian male citizens during the ancient times were given legal permission or the rights, privileges, and favors; to permanently serve within the Athenian's assembly, where the act of deliberating on policies and making them into the Athenian's self governed laws were done. This is how <u>despotism</u> **(the idea to rule by a despot: TYRANNY)** is practiced, and was the developing foundation of the world's traditional religious laws within all the lands. In other words, despotism was practiced within the church of them and became the core of their traditional religious conduct which dealt with worldly matters. The laws that were passed by the Athenian's male citizens are revealed and proven by the Fruit of the Spirit to have represented how the males commended themselves throughout the development of their own governmental controlling system.

During the ancient times the Athenian slaves and women were like the oppressed children of God today, and they used the spiritual gifts that God gave them as religious tools to morally wrestle against the principalities and powers of the Athenians' governing system that controlled their entire way of life; for the sake of keeping an inner peace within themselves while coping with the many different forces of iniquities. Like Satan's stratagems, the governing system of the Athenian's laid down dissimulated religious laws against the holy truth and acted as if God hated the slaves and women, either because of the differences of their physical appearances or physical sin. In other words the Athenians were taught to believe that God was a partial God, and the male citizens believed they were pardoned by God for their ongoing sinful desire to have the dominion to command or demand others to abide by their ways of living. Maybe these men misinterpreted a chapter out of the Holy Bible text which convinced them to desire more than what the Lord promised unto them (St. Matt.20).

They commended themselves to be above all others and they reigned despotically against other citizens of their community who physically differed from them by either race or sex. After seeing how the Athenian male citizens commended themselves to be closer to God than all others citizens, the Anointed teachings of the Holy Ghost helps the author and a few other chosen ones to spiritually compare and discern the workers of good and bad without judging anyone of the past or the present. The Lord made it obvious for all who believes on him to see the similarities of the ancient Athenian's governing law as well as many other laws which relates to or regulates with the teachings of the Pharisees, Sadducees, and scribe. Heavenly Wisdom has spiritually noted certain similar governing factors of the doctrines of the Pharisees, Sadducees, and the scribes' doubtful disputations of the truth have exceedingly transferred along onto the laws of the 21st century. These laws beget turmoil, havoc, and confusion unto this newest generation of people, including the Americans, but not excluding the non-Americans, Jews, or the Gentiles.

2Cor.10:12 "For we dare not make ourselves of the number, or compare ourselves with some that commend themselves: but they measuring themselves by themselves, and comparing themselves among themselves, are not wise."

2Cor.10:18 "For not he that commendeth himself is approved, but whom the Lord commendeth."

131

Every existing society on earth at some point of time have, disallowed equal civil or human rights to certain people upon the massive vote of the majority of worldly authority figurers whose biased voting's are based on the authenticity of their perception of traditional religion. By the earlier form of voting policies into law, discrimination was made a legal form of governing policy for all religions of every society.

In most cases, historian scholars have concluded within their historical notes of the exclusions of certain peoples' arbitrary and hereditary class distinctions and privileges being properly represented during the earlier composing of manmade governing laws of all the lands. History reveals that when the historical legendary authority figures of the world deliberated on rules and policies that concerned the entire community's interests, these dictators had hoped of providing the best ware fare unto their selves.

While obscuring the Word of God unto many civilized people, whom the law may have classified as an uncivilized society of people; the law makers formulated an unclear expression of what the Word of God says the laws of the land ought to do unto the poor. By the law of the land many civilizations received a bad verdict, because they had poor representation within their own community. Many civilized populations were crafted by worldly law abiding authority figures and lawmakers, whom either weren't able to understand or didn't care about the distress made by them unto those whom their laws oppressed.

For example, the ancient Athenian male citizens ruled despotically as governing officials, whom had dominion over all the slaves and the women. Although the slaves and women made up a large part of the Athenian's population and did most of the work within the community, they weren't treated fairly. They were told what to do, what to think, and how to feel. The male citizens failed to restrain themselves from discriminating against them at the voting poles. They misused their authoritative sense of empowerment, and legally they immorally bind their own vain hearts to vote in the ways which upheld the evil driven forces of malevolence in their lawmaking deliberations.

As a spiritual analysis is now being made by Sister Glory concerning the truth, she has learned that the historian scholars noted the findings of no division between the ancient Athenians' legislative and executive branches of government. In spite of, she believes that the historians didn't have evidence to prove neither the Athenian's government nor any government likened unto theirs were or is in compliance with the ordinance of God. Many people today are led to believe that such laws likened unto the ancient Athenians legislative and executive branches are established on the Word of God, because of the long length of time in which they lasted without a protest. After giving a thorough spiritual analysis Sister Glory declares that the truth lies in the judgment of the Spirit of Righteousness and Truth, which reveals that when the children of God are oppressed; they wrestle inwardly against the evils that attempt to confine the Spirit of God that lives within them.

For centuries the historians failed to clearly interpret the inward divisions of the slaves and women, who were forced by the tyrannous laws of the Athenians to keep silent and not express their opinions. Without the rights to share or to have an opinion would oppress the mightiest of men. Since they couldn't voice their opinions, it's fair to say this was the main reason why there were no findings of divisions noted within their legislative and executive branches of government. The ancient and modern Americans were also noted to have prospered on the notion of silencing the lambs of God by the usage of the same legislative and executive governing principles and standards of the Ancient Athenians.

The term or phrase, "See No Evil, Hear No Evil, Speak No Evil, and Knows No Evil," can relate solely to the surrounding circumstances and events, which conclude a worldly understanding to the false religious concept of why a government believes in creating desolation. Making a desolated environment is the best way for the despots to increase in power and make peace for themselves against all others. They routinely used evil to create a desolated environment against the women and slaves so that they themselves would receive a false sense of honor, admiration, and loyalty from them. For centuries the oppressed were trained to remain silent.

<u>The word democracy comes from two Greek</u> words; "<u>Demos</u>" which <u>originally</u> means "<u>people</u>" and the word "<u>Kratos</u>" which means "<u>rule</u>" or "<u>authority</u>." Biblically, Demas was the name of a governor of the people who deserted Apostle Paul for the love of this world (Philem.24/Col.4:14/2Tim.4:10). The published historical studies of many historian scholars, after being spiritually analyzed and interpreted by the teachings of the Holy Ghost; reveals to the author a reasonable reason of why politicians and lovers of this world followed Demas's ideological theories, which gives special importance or prominence to emphasize the unconverted vain idea of men that think democracy is…, "The idea to rule the people by law."

A WELL KNOWN FAMOUS AMERICAN QUOTER

32nd President of the United States of America: FRANKLIN D. ROOSEVELT

> **"Never in the history of the world has a nation lost its democracy by a successful struggle to defend its democracy."**

The biography of the person quoted above is in the world Book Encyclopedia

THE BIBLE TEACHES US HOW TO MAKE RIGHTOUS JUDGEMENTS

The many religious biblical translations of the Holy Bible changes the holy style of a person's labor, but God's Holy style is unchanging regardless of the different definitions and conversion of language. Within all dramatic trends of translated bibles floating all around the world, many scholars have determined to agree with most certainty; that the Gospel originated in Palestine as early as A.D.60-100. The Authorized King James Version is the bible of choice for the author of Discerning Perceptive. In America which is the birth place of the author,

134

this bible was noted by scholars to have been carefully revised and compared to the original Greek. With the same previous spiritual translations thereof, the King James Version bears the stamp of apostolic or prophetic authority.

According to spiritual annalists and scholars who translated scriptures from the original Greek doctrine, in the land of Galilee approximately around A.D.32 while Jesus was teaching the Word of God; the Holy Ghost was not yet given. So as Jesus spoke of the Spirit, he himself was not yet glorified. Therefore; there were divisions between the people because of him. He spoke of the spirit while saying, that those that believe on him would receive the Holy Ghost (St. Matt.1:18-25/St. Mark3:1-4/St. John7:38-43/Roman8:24). Although the Gospel of Jesus Christ says that Jesus came into the world that he might save some, many denominations fails to properly teach that **all** who believes on the Lord are the ones whom Christ collectively preached to be the ones whom he came to save. Instead, they judge the Word of God by falsely preaching by the spirit of Condemnation unto the people as to kill their spirit; in false hopes of retaining the minds of them from receiving the Spirit of Hope of being saved.

Jesus spoke boldly against doers of unrighteous judgments. He said unto all men to follow him and judge not to the appearance, but judge righteous judgment of all people. Instead of committing unrighteous judgments on or against another, he instructs for all men to righteously judge the one truth of the Gospel of Jesus Christ, which says that Jesus came into the world to save all from sin. To judge righteous judgment of our neighbors is believed by many to be easier to do in comparison to righteously judging strangers, but the Lord requires us to righteously judge both our neighbors as well as strangers. (St. John7:24) He testified and bared records of himself to judge no man, but he judges righteous judgment of man by his Father's word, which his Father had taught him to speak of unto the world. (St. John8:12-18) Within the Lord's righteous judgment resides heavenly wisdom, which understands the circumstances and events that surround the acts of every imperfect soul created in the form of the flesh by God the Father, the Son, and the Holy Ghost.

Approximately A.D.34 the Lord left the world with a Comforter, known as the Holy Ghost, and no man can reach the Father except through the Son.(St. John5:20-27) Before he was taken up and a cloud received him out of the sight of the men in Galilee, (St. Matt.28:10 & 18-20/Acts1:11)whom looked up steadfastly firmly in belief toward heaven as he went up, he gave commandments unto his chosen Apostles through the Holy Ghost to go and teach all nations, baptizing them in the name of the Father, the Son, and the Holy Ghost. (Rom.6:3-4/St. Mark16:15-20/St. John20:20-23/Rev.22:13)

This was the beginning stage of the Lord's evolutionary way of changing the spiritual hearts of men. He evolved and aroused the inner spirits of men, women, and children worldwide; in spite of all the misinterpretations made by the past and present despot generations concerning the Word of God. The few that are chosen of God, have the knowledge to exhort the Lord and the righteous understanding to persuasively influence mankind to break away from the covetousness of worldly men's vengefully false dialect and perceptions of the Lord's Word of Truth.

As the people of the world continue to covet after the traditional religious teachings of worldly men who commend themselves and calls themselves servants and freemen's of the Lord, the unfruitful fruits of their dead deeds are spiritually compared by the Fruit of the Spirit of God; which identifies them as ravening wolves in sheep's clothing. (St. John5:19/8:34-38/1Cor.7:20-24) The natural religious ravening spirit of their carnal minds, desires to tamper in the business of another man's matter and the matters of the world, as to associate, falsely claim, and accuse certain Christians to be hell bound. While doing so, they tend to unwisely "Kill the Faith of the Christians whom they religiously believe are disconnected from receiving the Word of God."

Before any child of God ever knew of men's tyrannous religious laws, their faith was predestined by God and not by man to be completely

136

focused on the Lord. But after being introduced to the tyrannous religious commandments of men's law, many children yield their faithful hearts to defer the beginning era of their pure hearted childhood. Therefore, their faith under the dictated commandments of traditional religious tutors of men is tricked, tainted, and spoiled by traditional vain religious philosophies and words of deceit. Like the leading conscience of those who are misled into believing that the Key to the Kingdom of Heaven resides in upholding the tyrannous traditions of a religion which religiously cuts off the pure hearted babes, many are seduced into believing that the weak and simple babes are ungodly and have a lacking in religious faith on the Lord and shall not be saved.

Many are called and the few that are chosen by God may temporarily be misled to lack religious faith at some point or another, but as a child of God; they still are favored by God to spiritually hold onto their spiritual faith on the Lord. This is rarely mentioned in many traditional religious houses, because they themselves religiously preach falsely. They don't believe that those, whom they are trained to religiously despise, are the ones the Lord instructs for them to reconcile with. A hater of men doesn't know God, and they shall not receive the Kingdom of Heaven. They'll be too busy receiving and commending themselves by themselves, and amongst themselves to spiritually hear the voice of the Lord.

This is why they today idolize traditional religious laws more than God. Through their traditional religious eyes and ears they cannot understand the Lord's parables being broken down to a simple form which states sweet and bitter waters can't flow from the same fountain. They are busy trying to make an exception or a clause to the Lord's Word of Truth as a judge so that they may give themselves permission to continue praising themselves. When man made a fountain which has two separate jots to join two separate spouts, they assume their bitter sweet fountain proves the parable of the Lord is fraudulent, because they disbelieve that the Word of God shall save those who they religiously despise, hate, and discriminate against.

They forsake their own mercy, because they doubt that the Power of God is powerful enough to save the least of them. The Lord is the Holy Root of the First Fruit which created all mankind. All this doubting should not be, but it is so. Those who lack faith in the Power of the Lord's ability to save the least of men and the most despised men on earth, also have doubt of themselves being saved by the Power of God. Through worldly sorrows many religious people manipulates the Word of God and create grief, agony, pain, and sufferings against others, because they religiously fear that they themselves might be persecuted by the Cross of Christ.

The perceptions of the Word of God being viewed by worldly analysis and carnally minded people, suggests that it is righteous for them to religiously use the Word of God as a cloak of maliciousness; to physically attack and persecute those whose outer appearance appeals to their religion's unsanctioned reasoning's for humiliating and making unrighteous judgments against them. They believe that godliness consists in the abundance of the things they possess, as if their worldly wealthy possessions are of a sign that dictates the prosperity of their conscience towards God's love (St. Luke12:15). If what they preach is true to them, then they believe that entering the Kingdom of Heaven is easier for the rich than it is for the poor. Also their wealthy possessions are viewed by them as a sign of approval sent by God from heaven. According to the hypocritical judgment of such false apostles and pretenders, a person's wealth symbolically means that God has made it easier for a camel to enter through the eye of a needle, than for a poor man to enter into the Kingdom of Heaven. This false commencement of the Word of God ought not to be insinuated, but traditional religious men think that a poor man is poor because God is punishing them. The worldly seduces the weakened spirit of mankind to believe that righteousness lies in the ability of men with money being highly praised by others, although this kind of idol worship gives God neither glory nor praise.

For centuries, traditional religious dictators and idealists have been setting up false ministries which have misled people to love God with their lips through words, but not through their hearts and souls. Through their deeds they think they are worshipping the Lord God, as their own hindrances of loving everybody obstructs the progress of them from edifying the Body of Christ. (1John3:11 & 4:12-13 & 16-21) Throughout the years, the Holy Ghost has brought comfort and hope to all who have kept the faith on the Lord God, Jesus Christ; who died to save **All** believers from the sins of this world.

1John4:4 "Ye are of God, little children, and have overcome them: because greater is he that is in you, than he that is in the world."

1John4:5 "They are of the world: therefore speak they of the world, and the world hearth them."

1John4:6 "We are of God: he that knoweth God heareth us; he that is not of God heareth not us. Hereby know we the spirit of truth, and the spirit of error."

Ps.94:20 "Shall the throne of iniquity have fellowship with thee, which frameth mischief by a law?"

Ps.94:21 "They gather themselves together against the soul of the righteous, and condemn the innocent blood."

Ps.94:22 "But the Lord is my defence; and my God is the rock of my refuge."

THE VISIONS AND PROPHECY OF DANIEL RETURNS

The Christians of the 21st century A.D. includes the Dalai Lama who is the spiritual leader of the Tibetan people. These people are living witnesses of how the Holy Ghost has expanded over into the American lands to create a spiritual evolutionary change against the American peoples' old ways of thinking. The old American way of thinking once caused most Americans to falsely judge and condemn each others and also falsely accuse and judge peoples of other countries. The Holy Ghost is massively converting the hearts of all believers of Jesus Christ within every society into desiring reformed laws, which edifies and exhorts the Lord.

This inevitable spiritual change provides all believers with a fulfilled heart of heavenly wisdom to understand that on the Day of Judgment, we all must stand alone before God to be judged. More hearts are constantly taking heed to the Holy Ghost's teachings. Regardless to whether they believe on him or not, every head shall bow unto the Lord. All individuals shall be held liable for the way in which they individually work on working out their own Salvations; in fear and trembling of the Lord of Host. More misinformed hearts now realize they do have hope of their names being written in the Book of Life, and by faith; their names are written.

Despotism has been recognized as the primary foundation of America's traditional religious ways of living, and it created the beginning structuring of all manmade governments; especially within the walls of the most religious countries. It also left behind an evil legacy of genocide for those of us during the 21st century to reprove, reproach, rebuke, and repent of. While giving us advice, encouragement, and warnings concerning living with hypocrisy and deceit; the Holy Ghost strongly urge us all to appeal to God. In so doing, the Holy Ghost strengthens us all to stand bold and earnestly speak the sound Word of God as it should be spoken; without blasphemously condemning the Spirit of God which resides within the conscience of another persons' spirit. Such empowerment is unlike the blasphemous condemning spiritual teachings of many traditional religions which lies against the Holy Truth and brings doubtful disputations and railing accusations against the enabling Power of the Holy Ghost's ability to save all whom believes on the Son of God from sin.

Unfortunately, there are a great number of seducers, gainsayer, and men-pleasers that are imprudent or unwise to do that in which the Word of God requires, because they've fallen in subjection to the teachings of Satan. Unwisely their teachings seduce the minds of the simple and weak babes in Christ who seeks to understand the anointed teachings of the Holy Ghost. The simple and the weak are seduced by the hearing of traditional false interpretations of the Word of God, which makes them impaired or unwilling to stand boldly for God and have compassion for one of another. (Ps.94:11-16, 59:1-2, 26:9-12) These types of Christians are tricked by the wiles of Satan to minister and support worldly ministries which judge God's law and teach God's people to live in fear of being dominated, exploited, subjugated, reviled and kicked out of the assembling of the religious world that was built by man's hands centuries ago.

All whose hearts falls in subjection unto the beguile teachings of Satan as to devote their ideas and focus their hearts' complete loyalty towards serving the evil spirits of him, can't indeed understand nor believe that Jesus Christ shall provide comfort and hope and redemption unto the ones whom they traditionally label as the least expected to enter into the Kingdom of Heaven. Such doubtful disputations of the truth exist in men's imaginations, because certain traditional religions trains the minds of men in accordance of how the unawares label or brand God's people in equivalence to the unrighteous judgments that they themselves unwisely make against the Word of God and against mankind.

The Fruitful Spirit of Righteousness and Truth authorizes and empowers all who believes on the Son of God with the ability to test the Spirit of all religious Kings, Parliaments, and every organized religious organization to determine or spiritually analysis the purpose of their main objectives;

141

by searching spiritually for the presence of the Fruit of the Holy Spirit. When a person has the presence of the Holy Spirit reflectively comparing and spiritually demonstrating the goodness of God's Good Will and Good Pleasures, indeed their way of life proves their love for God is genuine and valid. Those whom solely entrusts and calls upon the traditional religious rulings of despotism, ironically changes the original course of righteousness, peace, and justice. While in pursuit of happiness for themselves, they do so by discouraging all whom seeks to understand the Lord's Anointed teachings of the Holy Ghost as to cause them to disbelieve on the Holy Ghost Power thereof.

Although the tyrannous religious leaders and followers of the world are forcefully and cunningly coercing many into believing in some sort of worldly traditional misinterpreted idea or misguided impression of certain messages that are falsely derived from the Holy Bible text, the Lord's Spirit intercedes their spirit through the Word of Truth and makes reasonable references to clearly explain why the tyrants classifies and categorize themselves as the most despised people within all the lands. It is traditional for religious men's despotic or cruel nature to activate and stimulate their warring nature. It is by the warring nature of mankind that Satan gives them reasons to subject their spirits and intertwine their selves in a preexisting violent or hostile war. The tyrants' old misinterpreted ideas and misguided impression of certain derived passages from the Holy Bible text gives false reasons unto people who revere the religious realm as to why and how they are suppose to war.

After spiritually analyzing the intent of the hearts of those who are inspired and loves to elaborate on the misinterpreted message of the Word of God that causes them to conceitedly suggests that they are the holiest ones on earth or are the only ones whom the Lord came into the world to save, a child of God can easily humble themselves to not argue with them; knowing clearly that God desires not for any to perish. Boastful religious suggestions like these are found to be absurd and meaningless. Those who imply such false claims misguidedly claim to be Christians with their lips and their hearts are far from upholding Christ's consecrated Spirit of love. After spiritually judging against one's religious hostilities which are filled with vengeance and violence, those who are filled with the Holy Ghost recognizes that such person's discriminatory actions indeed honors the despotic ideas of a secular and unholy religion which may or may not be ancestral.

The leading role of foolish men irrationally either causes or continues to entice and persuade all others through duress by coercing people into viewing or thinking that the roles of their despot position upholds the righteous expectation of God within the religious realm, although they as oppressors possess an impure heart. Meanwhile, an irreligious traditional act of violence throughout history paves the way for them to think they may reach the Kingdom of Heaven through the idea of being involved in a religious competition with other congregations.

History has revealed the religious intentions of certain peoples whose roles in life are that of a Commandeering Chief, King, and members of a religious Parliament or legislative body which have invoked the hearts of others to pursue a worldly form of jealousy, anger, envy, hate, and strife. Although these types of traditional religious people are viewed by many witnesses on earth as the most acceptable part of the Body of Christ because of their high rank positions, the greater witness in heaven recognizably observes how they and the world's most prestigious traditional religious martyrs within all the lands rejects the knowledgeable Power of God.

Even the false leaders and followers of the most prominent of all religions on earth abuse and oppress all whom they religiously despise. The tendency of their efforts are an attempt to restrain the consciences of men as a cultist type of traditional religion which is well known by a historic influential arranged political document, policy, principle, standard, and/or a revered condition that they are adapted too within this religious realm.

The people of the world today whom follow after the pre-existing evil custom-made traditional religions of the world, places boundaries and yokes of bondage around the necks of the corresponding philosophical religious theories of how Christ requires for his chosen few to teach, preach, and live. They also display their own traditional religious kind of love in an attempt to pass religious strife off as an agape love of God. Like a brick wall, the traditional religions' insensitive kind of love surrounds the heart and faith of each committed member and seduces more people to devote their faith in worldly matters. Such seductions prevent the hearts of them from receiving the godly ability to fully love all mankind.

By mercy and grace through faith; the Holy Ghost teaches everyone the same way, but the comprehension level of everyone is different. The Holy Ghost teaches the weak and the simple how to adopt and adjust their spiritual minds to live in love and in peace with the lords of the land whom uses perverse words against them; without compromising their spiritual belief on the Power of God. They do so with ease as they recognize that Jesus is the Lord of lords and is the Lord and Savior of all mankind.

Although the seducers' abusive and oppressive religiously modified environmental conditions may attempt to cause the weak and the simple babes in Christ to live in spiritual despair, the Lord intervenes and redirects the steps of their despaired hearts to still obey his greatest of all Commandments. The Holy Spirit directs them to continue loving the seducers, in spite of how badly they are persecuted by them. The Holy Spirit strengthens the faith of the weak and the simple, who loves God and teaches them to also love their selves and love all others; including those who may use froward and perverse words against them. They are taught by the anointed to love the perverse speakers without entangling their own hearts to be drawn into the temperament evil ways of Satan, and in the end; those evil characteristics that brings <u>death</u> unto the loving and forgiving Spirit of mankind is destroyed. The last enemy being death will be destroyed! (Heb.2:14)The reign of desolation and despair is bound on earth to die as it is in heaven. Therefore, to the saved; Satan has no strong hold and no powers!

Instead of subjecting their hearts to vehemently despise or hate those who use perverse words against them, God empowers the feeble and simple babes as he directs their steps just as he empowered Jesus Christ. In fact, God enables the weak to walk amongst all seducers of evil, without cursing anyone whom falsely accuses them of not being a child of God. The same God, whom freed the slaves of Egypt, left an example for all believers through the day of the Lord's Passover; to be against the habitations of physical and mental slavery thereafter. (Exodus 11:1/12:1-14/St.Luke 9:1-6/9:23-27/9:49-62/St.John 6:1-6/6:25-33) The Lord's set examples feed and fill all believers with the Lord's bread of life, which endures unto everlasting life.

> **Exodus 23:9 "Also thou shalt not oppress a stranger: for ye know the heart of a stranger, seeing ye were strangers in the land of Egypt."**

After the majority of peoples of the world have been physically and psychologically strengthened to resist the weakened traditional religious form of despotism made known unto man, we ourselves during the 21st century are not as susceptible of being easily persuaded by the coercions and tricks of religious false teachers. Most of us, whom have been delivered by God after being tricked by the Devil for so long; now knows and understands that Satan is predestined to be loosed out of the prison of our minds. It is by faith that we live. Simultaneously, we are well aware that he shall go out to deceive the nations which are located in the four quarters of the earth. Therefore we must maintain our faith and be strong for the weak whom are easily beguiled into surrendering their hearts to a life of misery. Satan desires for our faith to have a lack of hope of ever being delivered out of the traditional religious predicaments which vainly suggests, reassures, guarantees, and tempts the simple to believe that they either are not or shall not be saved by the blood of Jesus, but the anointed teachings of the Holy Ghost has taught us to know better.

AMERICAN CHRISTIAN'S HISTORICAL START OF RECONSTRUCTION BETWEEN A.D. 1865-1877

Before slavery was abolished many blacks followed black leaders like Frederick Douglass of New York, who wanted to fight in the Civil War to end slavery. Many were rejected from being allowed to enlist in the Union Army, because back then the US Constitution recognized and supported slavery. The white business owners, sharecroppers, and plantation owners had threatened to not support the Union. They feared that if they supported the Union, they would lose the loyal support of the Border States which strongly were committed to slavery.

It was a strenuous process during the Reconstruction time period, and due to much controversial conflicts; eleven states had withdrawn from the Union which restored relations with the Confederate states after their defeat. This was one of many challenges which Lincoln had to face. His Reconstruction Plan was laid out for all to see in Dec. 1863. Within his plan, in hopes of getting the support of the Confederate states to back the Union; he offered a pardon to every Southerner who took an oath to support the Union. In his deal of a proposal, if 10% of a state's voters who voted in the presidential election in 1860 took the oath to support the Union; then that particular state could form a new government and adopt a new constitution which forbade, prohibited, and made slavery illegal.

The non-dictating white Christians within the country believed they had needed and found a competent Christian leader named Abraham Lincoln, who was wise enough to assist the country in moving forward towards black freedom. On Jan. 1, 1863, he issued the country with the Emancipation Proclamation, and in 1865 he pressed the 13th Amendment all the way through Congress, which abolished slavery throughout the nation. The people of Congress proposed the 13th Amendment to the US Constitution, and created the Freedmen's Bureau; to protect the interests of the Southern blacks. The Southern blacks didn't have an education, because the Southern laws had banned them from getting schooling. Not only did the Freedmen's Bureau obtain jobs and set up hospitals for the Southern blacks, but it also acquired schools for the Southern blacks. Meanwhile, Lincoln's written Emancipation Proclamation also made known of his decision to use black troops. He offered the blacks their freedom, if they help to fight in the Civil War that began in 1861. After the war was won the reconstruction of the country's government was on its way towards reformed changes.

Before the earlier Southern blacks were given citizenship in America, they and their white American sympathetic supporters were being murdered by the Ku-Klux-Klan because killing them appeared to be the best way for them to keep the blacks from exercising their rights to be protected. The Klan was a secret white organization that was founded in Tennessee approximately around 1865-1866. During those days the interests of the Republican Party were divided into two main groups; the *Radicals* and the *Moderates*. The ideas which divided the interests of these two groups still persist to exist in the 21st Century. As and end result, the Party which now controls the Republic Party are known as the Tea Party.

When the Southern blacks were given citizenship, Senator Charles Summer of Massachusetts and Representative Thaddeus Stevens of Pennsylvania were the leaders of the Radicals in Congress. They wanted the Southern Republicans to be loyal to the Union and maintain control thereof. The Moderates controlled the Republican Party, under the rule which states that the majority ruled. Both the Radical and the Moderate Republicans agreed that the rights of the blacks needed to be provided greater protection by those of them who had the power of authority to grant it unto them in Congress. Within all of their disagreements, this one agreement proves just how powerful the Holy Spirit is and always has been. The Holy Sprit made an Oxymoron out of the ideas of all the hypocrites, by revealing unto to all of them that cruel kindness are a combination of contradictory words. Those who believe in such incongruous words also believe that they can make sweet water come from a bitter fountain.

On April 9, 1865 the Civil war ended, and reported; President Lincoln was assassinated a few days later by John Wilkes Booth. Then Vice President Andrew Johnson became the 17th President of the United States of America as a result thereof. In the month of May President Johnson publicized his personalized Reconstruction Plan, which was dissimilar to President Lincoln's. His plan gave the Southern states the authority to determine what kind of role their blacks should have in the process of Reconstruction. His plan didn't offer blacks a role in the government Reconstruction; instead it did the opposite of what President Lincoln's Reconstruction plan offered. He created the Black Code law which forced the blacks to sign a work contract which made it mandatory for them to work at a job for a year. Meanwhile, another Black Code of law gave employers permission to whip the black workers, and another Black Code of law allowed states to jail unemployed blacks and work their children like slaves. In other words the white Southern sharecroppers, business owners, and plantation owners were given legal authority to use the Black Codes to retain total control over the blacks in the South.

Since he originally was from the Klan State of Tennessee, the moderate Republicans which also supported President Lincoln's Reconstructive Plan; depended on Lincoln's Vice President to attract Southern support to the Union which was designed to provide protection for the Southern blacks. Unfortunately, Johnson inconspicuously didn't have the same interests. During the summer and fall of 1865, when Congress was taking a break; Johnson attempted to help a large number of newly elected Southern Confederate officials who opposed the idea of Congress giving protection to the blacks. When the Republicans returned to Congress in Dec., they refused to accommodate any of Johnson's newly elected Southern Confederates.

President Johnson opposed every idea of allowing the federal government to protect the rights of the blacks, but protecting their rights were one of the major interests of the Republicans who were in Congress. In 1866 when Congress proceeded and passed the Civil Rights Act which assured a range of legal rights to the former black slaves, President Johnson vetoed it. Since both the Moderate and Radical Republicans specified that Congress ought to be the ones to validate an agreed Reconstruction Policy and not Johnson, they resubmitted the Civil Rights Act and Congress past it. The Civil Rights Act is now known as the first major law in U.S. history to be approved over a President's veto. To add more strength behind the Civil Rights Act, the 14th Amendment was pressed through Congress and added to the Constitution. It gave the blacks' citizenship. The elected officials of Congress, who followed the accomplished path of Abraham Lincoln, declared that none of the defeated Southern states could rejoin the Union unless; they supported the 14th Amendment.

In 1865 the new Black Code laws of President Johnson was structured all throughout the South. His new reconstructed governments pardoned all Southern whites; except for the main Confederate persons in charge and the rich Confederate devotees. Nowhere did he offer the blacks a role in the process of his Reconstruction plan. Let's not forget that under President Lincoln's plan, the governments had to abolish slavery and promise loyalty to the oath of the nation by abolishing slavery in order to qualify for readmission to the Union.

After receiving a spiritual analysis, it is believed that the spiritual Christians within the American colonies had to put forth the effort to step out on faith and resist the tyranny of cruel kindness and escape the bonds of such wrathful worldly despotic ordinance of laws. The earlier American Christians were like the slaves of Egypt written in Exodus who were tempted into being unbelieving of God's ability to save and set them free from such bondage. As a unit of many members they realized that their faith on the Lord without works was dead. So they united their faith on the Lord as one body and meekly fought for peace. From them begot all sorts of freedom fighting organizations like the human and civil rights agencies. The warfare of these Agencies weren't brawling in the sense of stirring up the members to want to be commended or glorified by men. The earlier Christians who made up these American agencies fought not because they were inspired by money or because they desired to shed another person's blood. They meekly fought for peace, because they refused to instigate more anger unto the desires of those who were motivated by antagonism. They in meekness of spirit humbled themselves as children of peace and followed the path of Christ, until their time on earth ended.

It is historically noted that some of the earlier foreigners and pilgrims that settled in the new lands of the North America region were more spiritual than others. Although they were of the same nationality, they evidently were spiritually divided by the mystical spirits of good and evil, because they fought amongst their selves in the process of establishing the foundation to the earlier American laws. Together the most spiritual ones boldly stood on the spiritual principalities of the Word of God and fought a good fight of faith, because they wanted to see, feel, and taste freedom for themselves and for all others who sought to be set free from the evil bondages of the old world order of laws; like the old tyrannical laws of Great Britain. As the good spirit of them fought for equality, the others fought against it. This explains the identifiable spiritual era of the first American colonists who sailed to the New Lands, and it also explains the different point of views of the separated political parties of today's 21st century generation.

THE MODERNIZATION OF THE 1900'S-2011

Not too many years ago in the mid 1900's after the Civil Rights Movement was won, certain members of the Ku-Klux-Klan publically professed that their members sought to possess power in the political office. Some of them took off their hoods and put on police uniforms and others put on suits and ties. It is highly believed that the Klan successfully managed to run and win many political campaigns over the extension of several years in America afterwards. Hypothetically speaking, if the Klan did periodically rule politically in Congress they must have lost most of their conservative political clout to the more liberal minded Republicans and Democrats, after spending too many years misusing the American laws to discriminate against all moderate American citizens or because of their greed and love of money.

All of a sudden from out of nowhere, the repressive ideas of the old Republic Party were revived and once again certain American people sought to possess political powers. During the year of A.D. 2010 the Republic Party was on bad terms among themselves and this is why they once again historically were divided into two groups; the Republic Party and the Tea-Party Republicans. The Tea-Party replicated many of the old conservative Americans' ideas and they resisted the moderate Republicans of the 21st century. The open-minded moderate Republicans are recognized as born again liberal mined Christians, whose reformed tolerant mindsets desires to honor God by being more considerate to the best common interests of all races of Americans. The conservative leaders and followers of the Tea Party accused the liberal Republicans of being too weak to defeat their all time political sworn enemies, the Democrats. Instead of having two parties, America now has three; the Republic, Democratic, and Tea Party.

As history repeats itself; it is prudent to consider the hearts of a majority of the original American ancestors who desired to transform the Natives/Indians and other indentured servants over to their ideology biblical theories and perceptions of what thus saith the Lord thy God, while keeping in mind of there being One God, One Christ, and One Lord for all mankind to worship and serve, and these three are one. Unfortunately, the hearts of many earlier American ancestors were in error, because they desired to have dominion over the Natives and all other indentured servants as they misinterpreted what thus saith the Lord thy God concerning the Spirit of Righteousness and Truth.

> **Prov.23:7 "For as he thinketh in his heart, so is he: Eat and drink, saith he to thee; but his heart is not with thee."**

St. Luke6:45 "A good man out of the good treasure of his heart bringth forth that which is good; and an evil man out of the evil treasure of his heart bringth forth that which is evil: for the abundance of the heart his mouth speaketh."

THEORATICAL CONCLUSION

Every Saint Has a Past, and Every Sinner Has a Future. Therefore, when a person concludes their selves to be more than what they are, it's absurd. Every Church is called out and is set apart from the world. The Word isn't for a Saint who needs no repentance, but it is for the sinners. The Lord didn't come to call the righteous, but the sinners to repentance. (St.Luke15:1-7/St.Matt.9:9-13/St.Luke5:27-35)

Repent Sinners Repent!

May God Bless the Hears and Doers of His Word! Amen!

CHAPTER 3 SPIRITUALLY ANNUALIZED INTERPRETATIONS OF HISTORY

> Ecclesiastes3:15 "That which hath been is now; and that which is to be hath already been; and God requireth that which is past."

HOW MANY CHURCHES ARE SET UP UNDER THE TRADITIONAL IDEAS, WHICH PROMOTES RELIGIOUS WARFARES AGAINST THE WILL OF GOD? (2 Tim.2 & 3)

The search for this answer should be the least of your concern, because it brings about more strife and not peace. There is no edification being given to God by whosoever chooses to not avoid foolish and unlearned questions. The will of God is to save sinners by convicting your spirit and reviving your faith on the Lord. Therefore, my main agenda is not to provoke God by provoking someone to anger, but my gentleness unto all implies an inherent or habitual tendency, which the Holy Ghost applies unto to me to teach patients towards the things of the past and present as well as the future. There's nothing new going on underneath the Sun.

> Gal.6:1 "Brethren, if a man be overtaken in a fault, ye which are spiritual, restore such an one in the spirit of meekness; considering thyself, lest thou also be tempted."

As a servant and a friend of the Lord, my steps are diligently guided to instruct traditional religious followers who may have an understanding of a form of godliness, but denies the Power of God thereof; to stop opposing and contradicting themselves to be occupied with bitter hostility and warfare. I write my discerning perception of the Word of God to encourage all readers. It is neither by my will nor by the will of any other man, but by faith and through God's all merciful love and grace that all lost sheep's shall receive the meek teachings and heavenly knowledge of the Anointed. By faith, after receiving the heavenly riches of truth, perhaps God will give his sheep's repentance to the acknowledgement of the truth and cause them to turn their ears away from old wives' fables. An old wives' fable is a man made parable which causes people to be ever learning, but never able to come to the knowledge of the Lord's truth. Upon traditional religious men acknowledging the truth of themselves being captives of the devil's snare, their desires may convert and change towards them reproaching, reproving, and rebuking the evils that lurks and lingers within them as to renew the heart of their own evil mindset; in hopes of recovering themselves out of the snare of the Devil. (Gal.6:1-6)

Just as "Jan-nes and Jam-bres" opposed and contradicted Moses, so men of corrupt minds oppose the author of Discerning Perceptive; by persecuting and accusing her of being reprobate and good for nothing concerning the faith. Again it is not a concern of the author to strife over such worldly matters of another man's business, because she's confident that the power of the Holy Ghost shall make manifest of every foolish act and idea of their folly which lacks good sense, heavenly wisdom, and properly guided spiritual foresight.

> **2Tim.3:12 "Yea, and all that will live godly in Christ Jesus shall suffer persecution."**

Within the land of the free and the home of the brave, the reprobate idea to rule despotically and to have dominion over others still exists during the 21st century. Nobody in the USA within this new generation is born with these desires, but many are trained up under the structuring of the old traditional religion's despotic environmental conditions and circumstantial standards, and such tutoring coerces many Americans to believe that the religious acts of despotism will bring unto them the Lord's promise of Deliverance from all evil. They are unlearned to know and understand that the acts of wickedness shall **NOT** deliver anyone who is given to it as one renders evil for evil. The sentence or judgment men makes against an evil work is not executed speedily.

Therefore, the reprobate minded hearts of these sons of men are indeed working without hearing the voice of the Lord advising and directing them to humble their selves to understand that their violent acts of vanity are enmity against the will and good pleasures of God. We all are constantly warned and urged all throughout the Holy scriptures to learn and understand the Lord's righteous truth which indicates, proves, and points-out the ill will or unjustified reasons why the hearts of most reprobate minded people are desirers of vain glory and are fully set to do evil. It is the Anointed which teaches all of us who hears the proper display of the Word of God, to desire not to glory in the flesh of the weak and simple, nor to love smiting their faces by misusing religion to justify an evilly given motive which supports the traditional religious efforts of the no good rascals who are glorying in the flesh of the weak.

The Lord directs the steps of all who believes on him and blesses such persons with the ability to discern the spirit. The ability to differentiate a true servant of God from the false ones through understanding the practice of righteous judgments consists of judging the circumstances of a person or a group of people instead of judging the persons who have sin. With an understanding heart a true servant of God knows that due to certain circumstances we all are at risk of being susceptible at some point or another to sin. It is by the beguiling methods of the false prophets whose traditional religious ways of misusing the Word of God as a cloak of maliciousness that causes many people to enticingly be coerced to yield their hearts to the evil principles and standards, which disgracefully expresses their own poor confidence of God's ability to save all sinners whom confess that they believe on the Son of God. Satan works to trick us all by his wrongful purpose and intent, which misleads us to condemn a man who maybe poor in heart but desires to be pure in spirit. (Eccl.7:12-25, 8:8-17)

The traditional despotic political religious environment of mankind is like a premeditated murderer, which plots and waits to kill the godly spirit of mankind; by seducing them to live with an ungodly fear as an unbeliever. Traditional religious martyrs and scorners are commonly known for worshipping their families' age old religious form of despotism, which misleads the heart of many to religiously entrust and commend the Pharisees' traditional acts of vanity. Every religious community that promotes warfare as a righteous veneration for its members to devote their hearts to overturn, reverse, and delude the denote meaning of the Word of God in the process thereof; by distorting the minds of all whom the Holy Scriptures clearly implicates the Lord's love, mercy, and grace is for. Traditional religious martyrs' deluded message of the Word of God suggestively insinuates that the grace of God's love and mercy are against the unjust as if God is a monstrous God whom commands of these traditional religious men to also be monstrous towards one of another on earth. The unclean and foul acts of men against men are enmity against the will and good pleasure of God's grace.

WHEN THE ENEMY IS NEAR

The enemy was near when the desire to have dominion over others rose up in the hearts of the first American settlers. The godly intent of the Founding Forefathers' hearts were over taken and overwhelmed with evil intentions, which stimulated the mindset of most of them to seek to legally develop unlawful or unfair governing laws against the conscience of the freeborn and the slaves; to encourage them to act in accordance of revering and obeying them. When the primary goals of their officially authorized follies conjoined with the traditional religious principalities

157

and powers of their own bellies, it desolates the heart of every community within every state of the United States. Upon searching for the Holy Truth, the Holy Ghost prevails and causes people to desire to reproach and evaluate the ideological theory of the intent of the governing body which the first American settlers used as a legal system to serve and protect themselves from despotism.

The base structuring of the American laws of the land ended up making many of its own earlier settlers, as well as the citizens of today whom know the Lord and understands the differences between good and evil; feel ashamed of the maximum approval ratings that mostly support the old despotic nature of the autocratic, oppressive, and domineering forms of America's original traditionally admired dogma known as the Constitutional Laws. The American law during today's generation still convertibly contains partially bias intentions for and against certain citizens which controversially is responsible for a law known as "The Separation of Church and State." Unfortunately, the configuring of such laws are full of deceptive words that upholds many worldly truths that dishonestly defines and spreads abroad the known "if" factor, which sets and leads the standardized conditional ways and reasons why the yesterday's divided American homogeneous who were identical and the heterogeneous who are a diverse societies; to hate one of another.

In vain the hypocrites say they love God the Father, the Son, and Holy Spirit, but they yet hate their own brethren in Christ. In such cases, the hypocrites decides to religiously practice what they preach as to grant permission unto themselves in a vain traditional religious attempt; to restrict the devotional faith, confidence, and self assurance another person or group of people may have concerning their own individual personal relationship with the Lord. Meanwhile, they themselves think that they shall personally receive the blessing of God's promise of everlasting life through his son's love, mercy, and grace.

Every traditional religion which supports despotism has led all Christians towards clearly seeing and understanding how the earlier formation of the infamous legendary laws of bondage and wickedness reflectively changes the incorruptible image of God. Despotism is supported by false ministries which mentally lays the blame on or condemns the blameless hearted. Instead of translating the new letters or the Epistles that are written by Jesus' chosen Apostles in the righteous perspective, which implies that the grace of the Lord God is upon all who believes on the Son of God; the false ministers of the world adds and subtract from the main objective of these Epistles. In so doing, they dictate to the minds of all whom they consume to control in a creative desolate religious environment. In their vigorous and diligent effort of making unrighteous judgments against another person, their bias hearts idol worship the false images that persuasively teach the civilized and compassionate humanitarian societies how to mercilessly and sadistically uphold their aggressive faith on the physical things of the world. Such teachings divide the Spirit of God's people during today's generation the same way as it did during times past. The Fruit of the Spirit of God proves that righteousness resides unto all whom diligently seeks to find the Holy Truth. Therefore, there's no need for none to put down the dignity of a sinner who enthusiastically make inquiries about God. It is inevitable for those whom are called to get to know and understand that the fullness of God's love, mercy, and grace is for all mankind including the unjust. (Ps.19:13/1Cor.1:1-8/1Thess.3:1-13/1Thess.5:23)

Philippians2:13 "For it is God which worketh in you both to will and to do of his good pleasure."

Philippians2:14 "Do all things without murmurings and disputings:"

Philippians2:15 "That ye may be blameless and harmless, the sons of God, without rebuke, in the midst of a crooked and perverse nation,

among whom ye shine as lights in
the world:"

The time to learn love is now and as compassionate people of Christ, we must have more compassion to empathize with other peoples' circumstances as we would of our own. The power of the Holy Ghost identifiably strengthens us with confidence in the Word of God, to recognize and reprove certain dead acts that we ourselves and others may either mistakably approve of or are burdened by. Although Christ was born, lived, died, and resurrected on the 3rd day to save use from sin, which we all fall short to, many of us are unwilling to stand boldly on the anointed teachings of the Holy Ghost and defend ourselves against the words of religious men whose perception of the Word of God sways our hearts to live in skepticism and doubt of the ability and the Power of God.

We as true Christians publically proclaim unto the entire Universe that the Anointed teaches us what man cannot, and such teachings brings deliverance and Salvation; unlike the teachings of traditional religious men who limits their faith upon the Spirit of Condemnation. Without a doubt, the Anointed teaches us to believe that life eternal is the final destination unto all who believes and obey the Lord God, because the last enemy that shall be destroyed in our lives is death. Death symbolically represents the spirits of anger, envy, strife, jealousy, and hatred etc. It also signifies the Christian faith of receiving eternal life in Heaven.

As children of God, we all believe that we have the mercy of the Lord on our side; working for us and not against us. As we perceive the Word of God, we are to remember and preserve the things of our past; to spiritually compare and properly identify which fight belongs to us and which fight goes against us as we work on working out our own salvations in fear and trembling of the Lord. Understanding such ground rules and orders, spiritually converts our hearts from believing in carrying over Satan's dissimulated kind of love unto our children, because Satan's desolated love creates conflicting chaos and confusion within the individual mindsets of many of our counter parts. Without judging those whom take par in bringing misery and worldly sorrows unto themselves or others, we believe we are being delivered by God out of certain circumstances and situations which have placed many burdens upon the necks of our parents, grandparents, and past ancestors.

TWO WRONGS DON'T MAKE A RIGHT

In the case of making righteous judgments without judging any man, we as born again Christians of the 21st century are wise to recognize that we ought to empathize with one of another; knowing that the same tyrannous religious perspectives which causes us and our grandparents to suffer; are similar to the created dissimulations of the Word of God which distorted the faith of the earlier Christians of every nation around the world.

The world is exposed to the unreasonable judgments and tyrannous religious nature of an oppressive society of people. Theoretically speaking, the resourceful root and unreliable wavering faith of every person who supports the abusive and tyrannous reign of religious laws are victims of the Prince of the world, and his long reign of terror was prematurely formed and forcefully developed in the hearts of a long line of descendants all around the whole world.(St.John12:28-41)

I'm remorseful to say that when the ancient children of God were tutored under the spoiled dictating leadership of Kings and Parliaments, the despotic religious idea to rule as a majority over the minority evolved within the hearts of many. Meanwhile, the earlier American Christian settlers requested and wished to alter any repressive rule of law that were publically put in place to govern domestically against the godly spirit of them, because they preferred for the laws of the land to match the godly desires of their hearts. Unfortunately for them, the desire to create wars and rumors of wars increased in the hearts of the unbelievers among them. The unbelievers voted against the righteous judgments of the first American Christians' desire to make peace. Over

161

the years some of the world's most powerful positions of political offices were overtaken by tyrants whom eagerly desired to be tormentors at their own discretions. Although we during the 21st century are greatly aware of how the works of the old despotic religious laws terrorized and mentally oppressed the Christian ancestors, many of us are beguiled to still desire to use despotism as a religious tool against one another.

Two wrongs don't make a right. For instance, instead of preserving the old law and make new reformed laws, many whom were/are called by God to replace a despot leaders' political position of power were/are coerced by Satan into believing in twinning the old ill-omened worldly laws with the new compassionate Law of Christ. Ill-fatedly, they are tricked into having an overly excessive relation with the Lord. Unfortunately, their hearts are turned into having a selfish over egotistical intent to spare their own revolting traditional religious venerations under the New Covenant of Christ. The old doesn't agree with the new, but after the mixture of the Old law with the New law have preexisted in the world for so long; it threatens and frightens mankind so severely that many people are now misled into thinking that neither they nor any man dead or alive can stand and reproach the evils within the today's generation of distorted religious sayings. The fact of the matter is, not too many are wise enough to understand the difference between the Spirit of God from the distorted spirits of the evil adversary. Therefore, they tremble at the sound of the hearing of the Word of God in a different perspective than that in which they are traditionally use too.

Instead of receiving strength in faith they are discouraged. Their wickedness or sin isn't what causes their hearts to be discouraged; it's their lack of honor which lacks the desire to understand God's Heavenly Wisdom. Therefore, they are accustomed to honor men who have held a religious position of office by the vote of a majority. The highest honored traditional religious scorners of the world may appear to be unapproachable through the singleness of the negative eye of those who view God in the form of a threat, but through the singleness of the eye of a spiritual-being and by the wisdom of God; man can by grace reproach and rebuke what many think is unapproachable. Maybe if they knew that there's no justification in wrong doing, they may stop fighting evil with evil and stand boldly for righteous changes.

While traditional religious martyrs and haters of men confusingly use their old age traditional religious code of unethical acts of deliverances in an attempt to rescue those who they religiously despise from captivity, hardship, or world domination, they attempt to do so by either doing evil things against a person/persons or by being evil towards those whom they religiously look down on. Meanwhile, they simultaneously transfer the concept of their own bowels that are filled with negative energy and aggressive false perceptions of the Word of God, which works against God and condemn the hearts of God's people whom are forced to put up with a legal but unlawful bond of religious insecurities.

Such seducers and men pleasers intimidate the members of the Household of God, like the old time oppressive American slave masters once used the Word of God to terrorize and coerce their indentured servants. In so doing, many are swayed to believe in either mocking God or worshiping the image which fills the bowls of another man's belly whom has perceived God to be their God with their lips. With their hearts being far from God, their perceptions of the Word God are unlike the perceptions of the true Saints of the Body of Christ. As they preach to encourage themselves to believe on God, they also preach to discourage all others from believing on the Power of God's ability to save them all from the oppressive temptations of the world. Within the structuring and the making of the first American governing laws of the land, such worshiping explains and answers the questions of how and why man worship man and not God.

During the 21st century, the most religious people with no remorse still believe in worshiping the old desolated religions. Without desiring to lift one figure to revive any, they are accustomed to using the old tactics of traditional religion to mark and make a person feel sad and spiritually abandoned by God. As a supremacy group of religious people, the most religious also believe in using such tactics to completely dominate and oppress all unfamiliar persons, newcomers, and outsiders whom are unaccustomed to their traditional creed of religion. Their main objective is to religiously think of ways of how to control the religious realm by creating and promoting a desolated environment that's filled with chaos, conflict, and confusion. During their life-time on earth, they follow the old desolate traditions of their ancestors. Today the religious influence to reign with the same strenuous religious intent and purpose as the Pharaoh during the Old Testament in the land of Egypt still exists. If we the people knew not the heart of a stranger being strangers ourselves of one of another's heritage and creed, we'd easily be likened of those world leaders and despot rulers of the Old Testament who religiously failed to seek understanding and became gainsayers, men-pleasers, and despisers of men. Fortunately for us, we are enabled by the Holy Ghost to recognize as strangers ourselves of the similar pain and suffering as well as other similarities we have with foreigners and unfamiliar people of other societies. Therefore, we desire not to have dominion by the number to rule despotically over any.

The authenticities of America's despotic religious laws are as real as the hearts that formed it. Many generations have passed away and every generation afterwards have reproduced the cruelty of the same old despotic and vindictive religious rule of laws that were brought in and fully formed the malicious desirers of the flesh. The American laws of the 21st century which suggests and advises the majority to religiously practice bitter hostility against the minority, only motivates the hearts of them to believe in religiously resenting, hating, and to rail against one of another.

Such laws gives a full form of tyranny unto the hearts of the citizens whom religiously idolize the ideological religious theories, principles, standards, practices, and beliefs that have prolonged and extended the old traditions of the representative assemblies from Great Britain since the late 1400's. This vivid time frame is brilliantly estimated between the time America historians declared Christopher Columbus discovering

America and goes throughout and beyond the early 1600's which oversees the time period when Americans formed the assembly of the House of Congress. Flamboyantly, tyranny transformed and distorted the true intent of the first American born again Christians whom were of the first 13 American colonies, into desiring vain glory.

The velocity or rate in which the earlier American settlers transferred their beliefs and standards into the US House of Congress and every equivalent part of the US House of Representative, indicates the structured powers of the laws for all 50 US States are determined by the factoring ideas that beguiles many men to believe that the older despotic laws are better by age. (St. Matt.20:25-28) The American despot leaders of today's society continue to desire to rule tyrannously. Subconsciously, they surpass, outshine, and overly exceed their own life's value. Their main-worth or chief importance unto God is to be a minister unto all (St.Mk.10:44), not as a humbled servant of all; like Christ whom gave his life as a ransom for all, but these tyrants wants to minister unto all as a god, lord, and master. This is where the conflict of spiritual interests has set many apart from the lord of Host and apart from the Body of Christ.

The conflicting spirit of ascendancy within the tyrants' traditional religious trend of causing despair is twisted with the unfulfilling demeaning substance which seeks to revive, restore, and complete their hearts with the essence of an earthy desire to have world domination. The oppressor uses such a tormenting tool of defense against God to seduce others into hearing the religious autocrats' false ministries, which coerces many to abide by America's traditional religious terms, principles, standards, and conditions that deludes their minds into thinking that they have the Lord's authority as rich gods and lords of the land to have dominion over all others (St. Matt.20:25-28, 22:28-32/St. Mk.10:42-45, 12:23-27). This overly excessive desire ought not to be the contention or strife of men after Christ freed all of us from such bondage, but such strife in reality does still exist.

St Mark10:42 "But Jesus called them to him, and saith unto them, Ye know that they which are accounted to rule over the Gentiles exercise lordship over them; and their great ones exercised authority upon them."

St. Mark10:43 "But so shall it not be among you: but whosever will be great among you, shall be your minister:"

St. Mark10:44 "And whosoever of you will be the chiefest, shall be servant of all."

St. Mark10:45 "For even the Son of man came not to be ministered unto, but to minister, and to give his life a ransom for many."

Theoretically speaking, the American Christians of the first 13 colonies desired not to be followers of a despot leadership in America as that of Great Britain. They were forcefully coerced into accepting the religious terms, principles, standards, and conditions of certain domestic American dictators; whose hearts creatively integrated assertions and theories that were legally made with the intentional aim to go against all Christian residents who didn't support the interior design of despotism. By the vote of a majority, one party ruled in favor of preventing a Christian or a Christian group from having the right of authority in America to publically make any objections of any kind against any American proposal which created a domestic desolated environment.

Today certain integrated laws of the despot leaders of the past have not yet been reformed. They are being publically reproved, reproached, and validly contested by and for all who have birth rights to possess equal citizenship in America. These American citizens represent all Americans whom are denied equality by the religious American despot leaders of the world. It is unfortunate that the today's tyrants still seeks to have dominion over all whom are denied or have ever been denied equality in the United States. These tyrants believe they are obligated to yield their hearts to various religiously coerced assertions, theories, and aims which still constitutes and represents the world's non-compassionate legal but unlawful rights of authority; that displays inequality and iniquity against certain American citizens of the 21st century. The despots of the 21st century recognize that the Constitution of United States has granted all American citizens the freedom of religion, but the tyrants prefer to misuse their liberty as an occasion to the flesh by reason to war. (Gal.5:13)

Every person, which supports an unfair or unbalanced institution or government whether foreign or domestic tends to commend and speak well of a worldly belligerent governing systematic body of theoretical religious concepts. They are eagerly spoiling and destroying the godly spirit within themselves for the sake of upholding an unrighteous religious fight. It is common for them to follow leaders whom misjudge the Word of God and misjudge the Lord's intentional plan of reviving and reconciling the godly spirit of hope unto all believers of the Son of God. Instead of them bringing unity as a people of God with love being their motivation without dissimulation and hatred, the follows a belligerent governing system brings division unto the people of God; by boosting them up to be loyal subjects to the spirit of greed through the law of death and war.

Many countries besides the USA, during the 21st century still are lead covetously after the old traditional religious doctrines of laws which are supported by scorners whom hate the resourceful knowledge that comes from Heavenly Wisdom. The lost souls of all scorners place their hope of being God's chosen people within the foundations of all sorts of religious laws, which distorts order and creates wars and rumors of wars imprudently. Some Christians conclude the leaders and followers of such laws are mentally insane, but the creators of such laws are not insane at all. They are manipulated by hypocrites whom misjudge what is right. (St. Luke12:56-59)

The war makers of the world who misinterpret the spiritual messages within the Holy Bible are misled to think they are not of the world, but are the children of God whom are warned by the Lord God to expect to be called crazy and to also expect to be hated by the world, which also hated and persecuted Christ. Meanwhile, those whom are oppressed by the war makers of the world believe the holy message of the Holy Scriptures redirects the hearts of them to understand that the oppressors are the ones whom are of the world and those whom follow the ways of the oppressor are also of the world. The hearts of those whom are delivered out of oppression are redirected by the Spirit of God to understand the reason why they were oppressed by the world is because the oppressors of the world don't know God nor do they understand God.(St.John15:7-27/17:1-26)

In most cases the scorners and haters of men in return rejoice over such accusations, because they interpret being called an oppressor an honorable name to be called in the religious realm. They suggest unto themselves as oppressors, to rejoice through such persecutions because it is appointed by them to uphold the oppressive acts of discrimination as apart of a religious ritual of their own kind. They admire thinking of themselves being hated by those whom they use the Word of God in vain against, as they accuse and persecute people for the Lord's name sake. Without knowing God the Father or the Son, they think that they can use the Holy Scriptures to prove their misinterpreted outlook of themselves to be the doers of the Lord's Word. Just as the Lord answered Judas whom asked him in St.John14:8-20, 21-24 how will he manifest himself unto them and not unto the world. (23) The Lord's answer suggests that if a man loves the Lord then that man will keep or continue maintaining the Lord's words.

After privately studying the Holy Scriptures, a Christian may see a bigger picture than that which has been generated by the religious oppressive men of the world concerning the Word of God. The eyes of those whom are opened by the Holy Ghost can clearly see how it is that while envying with strife in their hearts, the traditional religious oppressors of all societies maliciously misuse the Word of God to attempt to attest or prove that they are receiving persecution from worldly people whom they say persecutes them in the name of the Lord in an in vain way. The tendency of the oppressors' religion is seen as they try to confirm to the weak and simple babes that their repressive and unstable illogical biblical concept of the Word of God proves that they are right for smiting the faces of those whom they religiously oppress.   They manipulate the Word of God and label those whom they oppress to be evil and worldly, while labeling their selves to be innocent and pure. This is how they seduce many to believe in the unification of their presumptuous reasons for thinking that they are right for using the Word of God as a cloak of maliciousness against others.

The Holy Scriptures is self-explanatory in St.John15:18-22/16:1-4 where the Lord explains the enmity of the world. The Fruit of the Spirit of God proves how it is that the oppressors twist the Word of God and use their lips to worship him by their own definition of thinking they are suffering from persecution as Christ also suffered.   According to them the afflictions which they undergo are created by those whom they despise. Therefore, they cunningly claim they are being persecuted by sinners of the world for worshiping the Lord. In spirituality, they forsake their own mercy and cause death upon their own selves as they evilly reap what they evilly have sown. In such cases, they may feel like they are being persecuted by the world, but in reality they are being self examined by the Spirit of the Holy Ghost, which convicts and revive the godly spirit of the least and the worst (the just and the unjust) alike. As they submit evil against evil, they themselves think they are making a reasonable sacrifice unto God concerning the root cause of their sufferings. Meanwhile, they promote their wages of war as religious venerators unto the whole world so that they may convince others to think their religiously grounded discriminatory or undemocratic deeds are pardoned by God.

Without seeking for the truth which lies within the clear meaning of godliness, many are tricked by their aggressively asserted hostile and unrighteous religious beliefs, which sway many to think that they as the oppressors of the world are working the Lord's way of Righteousness. They have deafened ears which cannot hear and blind eyes which cannot see; that they are their own worst enemy. Their creative images of a holy war gives them reasons to believe in killing the spiritual faith of the innocent and shedding their blood in honor of fighting for an ideological traditional religious concept of a holy war.

The intentions of those whom today still religiously desires to reign tyrannously, relates solely to the historical traditional religious dictators' show of willingness and readiness to fight for the traditional ideological religious notions, theories, and ideas; that causes them to think the worst of others. With a false sense of contentment, they unjustly judge the physical characteristics of an individual, group, or ones' culture. Their ill willed acts of aggressions are relatively known during the 21st century as, "HATE CRIMES". Like the Sect of the Pharisees and Sadducees; the despot leaders' hearts today leads them to commit the acts of iniquity, which offends against a person's dignity or self respect as to persecute, injure, humiliate, and insult their very being. They do so by religiously suggesting positive hatred is to be bestowed upon them privately and openly, as if they are avengers of God. Vengeance is mine saith the Lord, but traditional religious despotic men ears are deaf and they cannot hear the voice of the Lord.

They like to use the Lord's name in vain and blaspheme against the Holy Ghost, while publically and privately proclaiming their unjustifiable hateful acts of enmity are justified by God. The despots' religious hostile acts of enmity condemns the spirit of babes and elders of all ages alike unto death, by causing the weak and simple to have a lack faith on the Lord God's ability to save them from the sin which supports the unfairness's written in the governing laws that defines the thoughts of the religious realm of all the land.

The despotic leaders of the world think their condemned religion's hostile acts of antagonisms that suggest the clash of temperaments and leads to hostility saves the conscience of the weak and simple babes in Christ; like the Spirit of Righteousness does. Therefore, they vehemently fight to protect their religious beliefs. In reality, the Spirit of Righteousness convicts the spirit of the weak and simple babes in Christ, not to condemn their spirit like traditional religions does, but it spiritually revive the conscience of them by nurturing the Spirit of God which lives in all of them unto life everlasting. God is greater than any condemned heart.

SINNERS WHO SIN WITHOUT THE LAW SHALL PERISH IN THEIR OWN CORRUPTION (Rom.2:11-12/2Peter2:1-12)

The despots fail to refrain themselves from desiring to oppress and discriminate against others who confess of their sin, because most of those who confess their sin possess subtle differences and fine distinctions which are easily detected by traditional religious despisers of men. In the end, these despisers treasures up unto themselves wrath against the day of wrath and revelation of the righteous judgment of God, without knowing nor understanding that it is they whom the Words of Truth says despise the riches of God's goodness and forbearance of longsuffering. Their unforgiving and untamed corrupt hearts fail to repent of their own trespasses and transgressions against others.

Subconsciously, they are tricked by the prince of the world to think they are obeying the law of Christ, but they yet obeys the law of unrighteousness, indignation, and wrath. It is the goodness of God's love mercy and grace that deliver all forms of hearts which seeks for glory, honor, and immortality with the Lord's sweetness and eternal life. God sent the Holy Ghost to teach humility to all believers by humbling them to patiently continue in well doing; in spite of all who brings railing accusation against them before God. (Romans 1:16-18/2:1-12/1Cor.9:20-21/2Cor.11:12-15/2Peter2:10-12). All who continues to obey the laws of unrighteous judgments and the unjust and unworthy commandments

171

of men are superior in the world by number, but the efforts of their works are brought to nothing.

> **Proverbs3:31 "Envy thou not the oppressor, and choose none of his ways."**

Many religious oppressors love to work the works of iniquity and commits vengeful acts of abomination through their hearts of hatred for people. As it is written: because the hearts of the false brethren unawares brought damnable heresies into Christ's Church to change the Gospel of Christ, still during the 21st century the remaining functions of their aftermath comes in privately to spy out the freedom and gifts of the Lord's true prophets, ministers, and servants. The unawares hatred for others causes them to forsaken their own mercy.

Many are bewitched into committing their trust and devoting their faith unto the false oppositions of science, old wives' fables, and vain babblings of genealogies which minister questions, rather than edifying the Lord. False brethren's often make notions about their traditional religion's ideas as to associate despair and tribulation to the faith of all whose ears may hear of their religiously given oppositions. The dejection which comes between ones' mental stability to understand the difference between worldly wisdom and the Lord's heavenly wisdom; brings about misery concerning the all loving and merciful Body of Christ and all of his holiness and godliness. The false teachers are called to uphold the pernicious and injurious ways of speaking evil of the dignities of God's incorruptible Spirit of Righteousness and Truth. Their wretchedness also speaks evil of the dignities of others, while making their own understandings of the Word of God appear to be more virtuous and wiser. They are the Spots and Blemishes of the flesh of all who they despise.

The method within the religious realm being provided by the Prince of The World, places the minds of whosoever are despised by such religious persons to live in an oppressive state of bondage, because the Prince of the World cunningly coerces all traditional religious believers into not obeying Jesus Christ. The false ministries that are manmade, supports organizations which deludes men's minds to desire to despise one of another, in spite of the manifested evidence proven by the Fruit of the Spirit of God which verifies and identifies such ministries indeed are the workers of the flesh and are not the workers of the Spirit.

The most disturbing part of living as a born again Christian for the author of Discerning Perceptive, is being able to see how the members of certain organizations are so hung up on idolizing the physical signs of certain things that were done on the Day of the Pentecost to the point of them misleading themselves to think their idol ways of worshiping in a congregational house will eventually get them into the Kingdom of Heaven; by association. As they practice imitating the physical things done on that day, she view them to be likened of those mentioned by the Prophet Ē-sâí-as, also known as Isaiah in the New Testament; whom says they honor the Lord with their lips, but their hearts are far from him. The hypocrites preach blasphemously unto them within these congregational houses against the Holy Ghost, by teaching them to honor the commandments of men. (St.Mark7:6-13)

It saddens Sister Glory's heart to witness this, because she knows that the simple and weak babes whom are bewitched by false ministries are susceptible to subject their hearts to the lies which chokes the true light of Christ, and place a yoke of bondage around their necks. They are compelled to feel obligated to do unreasonable things that are required of them under the tutorship of false ministries. All who worships such mockery are ridiculously manipulated to work the unsuitable acts of a hypocritical imitation of the Divine ordinance of God, but they are tricked into believing that they are righteously being led the way towards earning their salvation. The blind leaders of them are placing themselves in the Lord's field of righteousness, either by honoring the coerced works of their own religion's ideological concept of the Lord's law or by the hearing of a false teacher's integrated assertions, theories, and aims that constitutes a religious insincere imitation of faith. (Gal.1:3-8 & 3:1-8/Rom.10:17/Rom.11:1-15)

> Gal.3:11 "But that no man is justified by the law in the sight of God, it is evident: for the just live by faith."
>
> Gal.3:12 "And the law is not of faith: but, The man that doeth them shall live in them."
>
> Gal.3:13 "Christ has redeemed us from the curse of the law, being made a curse for us: for it is written, Cursed is every one that hangeth on a tree."
>
> Gal.3:14 "That the blessing of Abraham might come on the Gentiles through Jesus Christ; that we might receive the promise of the Spirit through faith."

WHO KNOWS THE HEART OF GOD TO DISCERN HIS PEOPLE?

Discriminators and prejudice workers, works are for nothing. Their works aren't the works of God, but are enmity against God and their acts of iniquities doesn't please him. It's impossible for the workers of these works to overthrow the Will of God, but they yet still try. The righteous Will of God is marked by his greatest of all commandment ...LOVE. A prejudice heart mocks God's love by turning the significance of his love into political dissimulations of love; as to fulfill the earthy sensations of discrimination, which hides behind unjust laws that are commanded by man and puts on a false appearance of righteousness.

All glory and praise goes to God, because as one generation pass onto the next and the traditional religious teachings of dissimulations and divisions which once completely separated, distorted, and divided the entire United Nations finally are all slowly fading away. The existence of discrimination still resides within the hearts of many scorners and it legally persists to exist within all religious governing laws of the land during this generation in spite of the Lord's oppositions, warnings, and pleas, but the scorners no longer have the same image of authority and controlling influence of power today as they once had when America was first established.

The fading away of the USA's traditional religious political dissimulations of love and inequality symbolically represents the rising numbers of those who are denouncing and condemning the Nations' traditional political reign of religious terror. For centuries the doers of iniquity have falsely ministered traditional religions' deliberate intentions of doing unjustified harm towards others for the satisfaction of mentally enslaving the minority while vainly using the name of Jesus. It is prudent to understand such religions are dogma and are characterized by an imperfect established opinion of the Doctrine of Christ. Most ideological ideas and opinions that were set forth from the Holy Bible concerning faith and morals have misled people into committing their hearts to be ill willed, mean, and spiteful.

For this cause, more people throughout the years have sought to find God on their own without being hindered by the dictatorial unwarranted and arrogant point of views and opinions of a dogmatized denominational religion of any sort. It is commonly known for a believer who seeks for the Key to the Kingdom of God to find the Anointed teachings of the Holy Ghost, which instructs all believes to privately study the Word of God and show their selves approved unto God. After being rescued from mental bondage by the Comforter, a person may free-willing choose to yield their hearts to the anointing

175

teachings of the Holy Ghost over the seductive teachings and commandments of men's dogmatic religious beliefs.

Let's be clear, with Satan being the most beguiling creature on earth it's impossible for anyone to determine the difference between truths and lies without help from the Lord. For example, the assertive religious doctrinaires of the world and commandments of men are contemptuously overbearing towards others like a dictatorial regime, which imposes one's will or opinions on others. The radical leaders of some of the most moderate minded people like the Libyans, Americans, Christians, Muslims, etc. are characterized as a dictatorial whom is unduly and offensively positive in laying down principles as a disposition for all to follow abstract theories; in framing religious and non-religious laws or policies.

In such cases; the legal but unlawful doctrinaires of the world resemble a community or government in which one person possesses unlimited power under an autocratic rule, in a domineering manner. Autocracy affects citizens all around the world by publically proclaiming that the faith of its members which coordinates such rules and policies are in God, but the fruits which they bear single handedly denies the Power of God's ability to save all sinners thereof. In other words, men are coerced through the laws of the land to think they are saviors of themselves as antichrists, whom denies that Jesus is the Christ.

> 1John2:27 "But the anointing which ye have received of him abideth in you, and ye need not that any man teach you: but as the same anointing teacheth you of all things, and is truth, and is no lie, and even as it hath taught you, ye shall abide in him."

They which have received an anointing from the Holy One, no longer desire to judge the Word of God but rather accept knowing the Holy Truth to understand that; **"No Lie is of the Truth."** With an understanding heart, many Americans and non Americans today have so learned how to refuse the profane and old wives' fables, as the Anointed teaches and instructs all to twain together towards godliness instead of following the lies which hides behind the forceful opinions of traditional religious orders of the world; especially those that leads our hearts towards enmity.

The Lord directs our steps towards gaining heavenly wisdom to understand that a godly man knows that everyone that doeth righteousness is born of him, and an ungodly man hates their brethren and abides in death. This death being mentioned pertains to the wisdom of the world, which directs the hearts of mankind to suffer the grief's and sorrows of the world. Ungodly men are of the world and they bare the fruit of death which arouses peoples desire to commit unrighteous judgments against God. As they falsely profess that they have neither faults nor failings or no sin, their selfish desires to have an excessive relationship and closeness with the Lord causes them to pretend to be what they are not..."Perfect!"

It is by the power of the Anointed One, which purifies all who believes on the Lord. The powers within the Lord's purification process allows all who accepts Christ as their Lord and Savor with the ability to recognize the difference between being a spiritual person of God from being a religious man of the world, without desiring to judge or hate whosoever are spiritually discerned. A discerner of spirits is commonly someone who is capable of recognizing the scornful hearted that are filled with hate and rage from the prudent hearted whose hearts are filled with sympathetic love and peace. The few of us who makes proper spiritual discernments of the Spirit of an individual don't react like the false brethrens, whom spiritually are discerned religious hypocrites. Whatsoever judgments are made by a hypocrite relates to the false judgments that they make on themselves, and they love judging the Word of God for the sake of thinking they have the authority to judge

177

the conscience of another person's heart. (St. Matt.7) I say again my friends, God didn't give any man the power to judge the conscience of another person's Spirit.

Those of us, who would rather properly use the Word of God as a tool to identify which spirit is presented unto us whether good are bad; are wise to use God's gift of knowledge to sensibly choose the righteous things to do and have a clear conscience unto God in doing so. With the Lord controlling and leading our hearts, we would rather suffer ourselves for the sake of righteousness and truth rather than to cause spiritual despair, grief, and misery unto the spiritual conscience of others; whom confess Jesus as their Lord and Saviour.

The gift's and tools of the Lord and Savior, if used properly by and for those of us who seeks for redemption; shall deliver us all out of the temptations and sufferings of the world. Instead of restoring and reviving the faith of those whom may suffer worldly sorrows, religious dictators and false apostles are well known for preaching the Word of God in a correspondent way to condemn their faith. The false apostle's religious methods are similar to the ways of the Lord's adversary. Their evil ways of oppression, changes the denote meaning of the Word of the God. While paraphrasing or rephrasing the meaning of the Word of the God, to condemn a person; they state that if the Lord said it, than it has got to be the truth. Unfortunately, the religious dictators and false apostles don't know the intent of the Lord's Word.

Those of us who privately study to show ourselves approved unto the Lord, are able to recognize that we are molded by the Potter Maker who makes it possible for us to present a full picture to the false apostles' religious dictatorial jesters, by being a correspondent for the Lord; through confirming not only what the Lord said, but also what the Lord did within our reports. Without being a hypocrite, we hope that we may revive the conscience of those who are misled into having a lack of hope by religious dictators, who tell lies against the holy truth.

Within the process of accepting the Lord's truth, a child of God undoubtedly gains the common sense to discern good and evil. The

Lord's Heavenly Knowledge and <u>Wisdom</u> brings clarity and redemption to the soul of his servants by revealing the **Fruit of the Spirit** of Righteousness and truth unto them. The Fruit of the Spirit helps all believers to clearly understand the intent of the Word of God as we individually **hope** to be redeemed by Christ. We all can identify with the Word to recognize that Christ comforts and strengthens our faith and purify our inner spirits individually, at his own discretion thereof. There are no two persons alike. Therefore, we all as One Body in Christ; are blessed differently at a different proportion at the discretion of the Lord.

The signified advantage of receiving the zeal to hear, see, and do the works of the Lord as good Samaritans, is having the spirit and the desire to be as forgiving as he is. Knowing that Christ is "LOVE", helps us all to control the things within our individual selves that profits us nothing; so that we may become fervent in desiring to not subject our hearts to despise or hate another living soul. To the Hell with being angry, envious, and filled with the desire to strife, because Hell is where these things will lead a person. Life is too short to waste on things which profits man nothing. The Lord's truth does not lie against the Holy Ghost, but corrupt minded men do so all the time. He didn't hate any man, and neither should we.

THEORETICAL CONCLUSION

Whosoever believes that they know exactly who on earth shall or shall not receive the grace and mercy of the Lord, also preach that they know exactly who are going to Heaven and Hell. As they read the Holy Scriptures, they judge the Word of God by the same mannerisms in which they choose to despise and judge people. It is strongly suggested by their religious leaders that it's sacrificial for them to mistreat whosoever they religiously choose to despise. Those who make themselves an apostle of Christ are unfit to manage their own affairs or to behave safely in a state of freedom. They think those whom they despise the most of all are the least to receive the Kingdom of Heaven. Therefore, they accuse people of being worthless and unworthy of God's love mercy and grace. This sort of ministry of men fits the navigated religious occasions and character of Satan's beginning characterized intentions of converting his corrupt teachings into the religious world's dogmatized ideological theories and religious concept of what thus saith the Lord thy God; to increase his stratagems of dividing or separating the spirit of man from God. This is the tactical measures of Satan's plan for the sake of religiously conquering the spiritual war fields of perverse disputing of men.

Many have not yet understood that regardless of all of their doing; without charity their works is for nothing. Vengefully for the Lord they stand as bold as a sand castle residing near an ocean's shore, but is knocked down by the One Truth which was indicated in the beginning and will remain until the end. The Holy Truth encourages all people to stop judging one of another, because on Judgment Day **God is the One True Judge.**

CHAPTER 4 STOP PLAYING THE BLAME GAME!

(PHILIPPIANS 3:1-9, 10-21)

As the Fruit of the Spirit proves what is righteous, certain individual political laws of dissimulations are made manifest for and by the Spirit; as the reason or cause of many men's spiritual divisions and despairs. Such politics are apart of the daily walks of those who follows the desires of the world's desolated laws that are not of the ordinance of God's Law of Love. Certain political issues are designed to fulfill the inner earthy sensational urge of mankind which envy and strife, while desiring to rule despotically. Those who use traditional religion to envy and strife, fails to prevail against the peaceable and lovable teachings of the Holy Ghost, because these traditional religious things deceives men to fear death and feel grievous of being born.

Most of the 21st century American offspring's sole purpose in life; isn't to seek vengeance for their deliverance through despotism and suppression like the oppressor **(SATAN)** who desires for all traditional religious people to do as apart of his trained religious practice. Within the repression of religion, traditional religious followers' attitudes range from mild objection to bitter hostility or warfare. This implies that they religiously give recognition and gratitude to a hostile or threatening force in their hearts, as they search the Holy Scriptures in a positive effort to encourage others to believe on the affect of their vengeful faith on the Lord.

Today more people spiritually seek for redemption from the oppressor's pre-existing despotic unfair laws of the land. Therefore, they are putting forth the effort to reform the traditional unjust laws as peace makers; to reconcile their inner consciences with the Lord. This has been the war of the world for ages, because most of the past majority of rulers, gods, and lords of the world have always refused to use their political position in office to bring spiritual peace into the life of their community, state, and country by reforming the unfair and unreasonable ideas within the original laws that were made.

The religious despot of the first 13 American colonies preferred to be called the Supremacists of power, and they established a governing controlling system, which ironically confined, restrained, and imprisoned the godly spirits of a great multitude. Theoretically, their self-made religiously grounded terminal governing systems gave them physical and temporal dominion over all other classes of people, especially over those of a different race, sex, sexual orientation, and religion within their newly established settled country. The responsibility of America developing a despot government wasn't the fault of the ancestors of the first 13 American colonies, but it was the beguiler Satan who had tricked many of them into believing that despotism would lead them to the promise land of the Lord.

Like the earlier subverted Christians, we during today's generation must spiritually learn how to adapt and deal with the inner spiritual fighting's and wars, which were developed in the beginning by the prince of the world. Just as he cunningly coerced Eve into judging the Word of God, that old Adversary still persist to attempt to spiritually coerce God's people today to be reprobate minded by using the tools of his stratagems to mentally separate all pure things which God made. Satan's simulations of the Word of God separates all who are bone of the Lord's bone and flesh of the Lord's flesh. He makes the nonreligious people who originally are believers of the Son of God religiously appear to be impure. The wiles of his stratagems suggests that if a believer doesn't idol worship traditional religion as the majority choose to do, then it is righteous for the majority to consider them as Anti-Christ. Within all of Satan's deceptions and deceits, his teachings are clearly made manifest by the Holy Spirit to be of the opposite of everything that is of God's Will and Good Pleasures.

Godliness is contentment, but the devil cunningly fills God's people's heads with his dogmatized delusional opinions and ideas, which are of the substance of circumstances that concerns the religious world. Satan redirects their hearts to idol worship the world's religious position of office, by making the world's traditional idolized religious faith to be equivalent to that of his own overly excessive desire; to be like God. He was a liar since the beginning, and all who believes in his lies, are susceptible towards escalading the evilness of his oppressive behavior to desire to gain, regain, or maintain men's religious attention to look towards the destitute desire of being commended, rewarded, and favored through and by the eyes of other religious men.

After receiving the anointing wisdom, which comes from heaven and not from this religious world; we must stand bold on the Word of God and spiritually fight that same good fight of faith as our anointed ancestors once had too for our own salvation. In so doing we must boldly fight unlike certain religious followers, whose bitter hostility enforces their vengeful dialect to seek to find deliverance through their display of coercing one sort of people to despise another. As we fight for our souls with the Lord directing our steps, we too shall overthrow evil with kindness; as our spiritual battles replicates the good walk of Jesus Christ like our spiritual ancestors' whose love and kindness has taught us how the Lord prevailed against all evil when they meekly and patiently walked before us.

We the spiritual people of the United States of America during the 21st century, coherently understands our spiritual battle is not of a religious or physical war concerning our faith on the Lord. America is the most diversified Nation throughout all the lands. As we submit to the serenity of our prayers and accept the things we cannot change and change the things we can, Satan uses our physical differences of appearance and our multiple differences of opinions against us; to advantage himself. Meanwhile, Christ's Spirit of Righteousness and Truth has expanded our spiritual mindsets as born again Christians and fills our hearts with the power of God's heavenly wisdom, which expresses the understood loving Will of God and his Good Pleasures.

As we fight for our own salvation, our deeds of godliness revere the agape love we have for one of another. While edifying the entire body of Christ, our godly deeds are seen by the spiritual eyes and heard by the spiritual ears of the citizens of every country around the world; including by the citizens in the Middle East. As we pray and preach about peace being an inevitable act of God for all people, our spirituality seems to threaten the Middle Easterners' supreme legislative body which religiously regulates and creates wars and rumors of wars amongst its citizens in a delusional effort to avenge God, as if they have not heard that God avenges himself.

The religious despot leaders of the Middle East; are like all others who desire to physically kill themselves while killing all whom may oppose and challenge their unreasonable grounds of supporting the traditional religious martyrs' vengeful dialect of fighting a Holy War through the shedding of blood. Like all other religious parliaments which men assembled in the past, the 21st centuries' despotic religious martyrs' supreme legislative government of the Middle East; no longer have the same influential powers over the mindset of the citizens as they once had. The Fruit of the Spirit of God has proven to all citizens on earth what the Heavenly Father's godly ordinance of law consists of. With an understanding heart more people of every region of the world including the USA are renouncing and denouncing their faith from all tyrannous religions, which either ruled despotically for or against their ancestors. They today are meekly revealing their lack of interests in killing themselves or others under the unfair dogmatized religious order of laws of the land.

Historians and religious annalists have concluded all throughout the world's history of how and why people were separated by clicks and groups of all sorts, but this separation was of mans' own doing; like the Southern state vs. the Northern colonists within the USA before, during, and after slavery was abolished. Some people apparently shares different point of views concerning their own presence or existence in the world, as to affiliate and compare their selves with who they think they are; against whom they believe Christ wants them to be. Meanwhile, others associate themselves in accordance with the makings of their own written contract, which legally regulates and constitutes their ancestors' religiously old perceptions of the Holy Scriptures.

All nationalities were noted by historians to have vigorously fought amongst their selves before they gradually learned how to spiritually separate the evil wrath of their own emotional differences, and unite together as one united-front; for the sake of gaining their independence. The zealous desire of the oppressed Christians of today's society, is to teach all who has an ear to hear the Word of God; that peace comes to the peacemakers and there's no way a religious nor nonreligious person who may attempt to reproach this teaching can confusingly deny the Lord's Words of truth of this spiritual matter of fact; except they be reprobate.

Although we the people of the United States during today's generation are not bound under the laws of another country as our ancestors were, we are yet still divided against ourselves. Therefore, the Holy Spirit empowers us during the 21st century to continue our focus on reforming any remaining unjust American laws, to diminish the things which keep us from equally viewing ourselves to be of One Body under the Heavens.

In other words, as the Holy Ghost manifest the fleshly desires which lies behind the deeds of certain dogmatic American laws that our hearts discern, we've spiritually grown to recognize that now it is high time for us to awake out of the worlds' ignorance and stand bold and fight meekly to get away from and rebuke such laws of bondage. Our desire to do so is not for the sake of gaining lordship or to have dominion over others, but we desire to do so for our freely given spiritual independence; so that we and our children can depart from the unwarranted tyrannous dominions of the religious despot leaders of the world, who falsely promotes worldly gain is godliness. Rebuking evil is a fair spiritual way of escaping the destructive despot leaders of the world, whom for centuries have denied granting equality to whosoever their traditional religious realm has always despised.

> **Genesis3:4 "And the serpent said unto the woman, Ye shall not surely die:"**

Genesis3:5 "For God doth know that in the day ye eat thereof, then your eyes shall be opened, and ye shall be as gods, knowing good and evil."

After the oppressor in the beginning deceived Eve into believing that God was hindering her and Adam from being as gods, he used the same oppressive method against the entire human race during the 21st century to deceive men into blaming Eve for Adams disobedience. Women for centuries are virtuously compared by traditional religious men to be a Jezebel, as if God's gift to men is made to be men's weakness instead of their strengths. Many fail to understand that the oppressor isn't identified to be neither man nor woman, but is the serpent himself. Satan's stratagem is to deceive as many as he cunningly can into believing that his oppressive tools are to be viewed as the tool of righteousness, while he mislead men's hearts to follow his oppressive ways.

Those who desire to put down the dignity of others are religious fault seekers who are greatly distorting the godly image of God in the presence of the living witnesses of God, within the House of God.(1John5:6-11) The desire to seek to find fault, isn't the way of reconciling anything with anyone during today's wicked generation. (1John5:18, Gal.1:4) In fact, the act of faulting a person or a group of people only weakens the moral fiber and spiritual character of both the ones whom are known as religious fault seekers and those whom their religion accuses of being unworthy to receive God's love, mercy, and grace.

Traditional religious fault seekers are inclined to criticize the legitimacy of the spiritual complaints made against the true mannerism of their religion's defective legal statures and achievements in creating a desolated environment. Their dissimulation of agape love promotes their religions' false position and defected rank to have full religious authority to be non-empathetic, as they subvert the Word of God to variously declare their display of inequality has been and should continue to be viewed by all citizens as the righteous way for the world.

From the heart their mouths speaks on the position of their religious stance for love, peace, equality, freedom, and justice. As dissimulators, who hide their fears of being persecuted by the Cross of Christ; they also deludes the Lord's truth and speak to magnify their own appearance of what they religiously think true Christianity signifies. Meanwhile, their hearts leads their actions to use their traditional religion to publically suggest that their religious faith which discriminates against the faith of all sorts of spiritual activists; should remain as apart of the world's legal governing controlling system.

While thinking more of themselves than they ought, religious fault seekers desires to continue using the stratagem of their traditional religious orders, which for centuries have misinterpreted and misrepresented the denote meaning of God's love for all sinners. To keep their unjust laws of the land intertwined together with their pursuit to destroy what spiritual peace, equality, freedom, and justice for all clearly signifies unto all others whom they religiously despise, they use traditional religion to urge the world leaders to refuse to change the world's olden governing systems. By their religious desire to continue to make unrighteous judgments of God's law of love; they define agape love to be partially biased as they represent the characterized conditional love of their own traditional religious law.

In order for such persons to equally love themselves and others unto God's holiest of meaning, requires a change of heart on their behalf through repentance of their ideological perceptions and traditional religious definitions of God's love, which indeed is maliciously displayed by them. Morally their traditional values indeed must be spiritually reproached, reproved, and rebuked free willingly by them. Not only is this conviction of their conscience a reasonable sacrifice, but this must be done in order for them to stop blaspheming against the Holy Ghost as despisers of men.

This spiritual process of a change of heart; isn't of man's own doing, but it is the Lord's. Man can fake a lot of things, but they can't fake the Holy Ghost. In order for anyone to uphold the trueness of their love for God, they must also love their brethrens, neighbors, and strangers unconditionally as they love themselves and God. (St. Matt.22:37-40) The spiritual act of reconciliation or the desire to reconcile comes upon all hearts which desire to receive a sympathetic understanding of the surrounding acts and events, which leads a person to humbly seek to understand the faulted actions of their own unruly behavior; in order for true repentance to follow.

> 2Tim.4:2 "Preach the word; be instant in season, out of season; reprove, rebuke, exhort with all long-suffering and doctrine."
>
> 2Tim.4:3 "For the time will come when they will not endure sound doctrine; but after their own lusts shall they heap to themselves teachers, having itching ears;"
>
> 2Tim.4:4 "And they shall turn away their ears from the truth, and shall be turned unto fables."

THE CLARITY OF CALAMITY RESIDES WITHIN ITS DEFINITION

1). State of deep distress or misery caused by major misfortunes or loss

2). an extra ordinarily grave event marked by great loss and lasting distress and affliction.

3). (IT'S A DISASTER)

Proverbs17:5 "Whosoever mocketh the poor reproacheth his Maker: and he that is glad at calamities shall not be unpunished."

Proverbs14:31 "He that oppresseth the poor reproacheth his Maker: but he that honoureth him hath mercy on the poor."

Whether truth or fable, for centuries historians have claimed that Christopher Columbus discovered America, but the analysis have also noted that he was greeted by the Indians whom were already settled in the North America Region. Christopher and his people were called pilgrims whom traveled as wanderers unto this foreign land. This land once upon a time symbolically represented a shrine or a holy place, and they as devotees and ardent followers of one of another; called the Native Americans "Indians", because Christopher Columbus thought they had arrived in India.

Although the Natives were already settled in the North American region of the world, American historians noted that the Natives had migrated to North America from Asia by crossing a glacier between Siberia and Alaska called the Siberia Bridge between 30,000 and 40,000 years ago. This conclusion today still deflects the beliefs of the Native American Indian's being an originated origin of people in the North American region, but it doesn't stop the elder Native American martyrs from believing America is the origin of their peoples' heritage.

The indigenous people known as the Native American Indians believe they originated in the North American region of the world, and history reveals in peace the Indians lived as free as the sparrows and the fowls of the air, until 1492 when their free ways of living were permanently distorted and forever affected upon the arrival of the European boats or ships which wandered unto their homeland. American history reveals that when Spanish men expelled from those European ships, they settled in the Southwest region of the US and in Mexico. Some of them traveled to Florida, and to the Caribbean Islands, and to South America to live. Amongst those groups of people, were some God-fearing people who were noted by the historians to be Spanish Missionaries.

They religiously wanted people of all origins to convert to their preference of religious beliefs to be equally yoked to their beliefs. Therefore, they physically and psychologically worked on converting the Natives and their personal indenture servants into believing in their revised religious ideas, beliefs, and customs. Many Spanish men used the worldly power of coercion to forcefully beguile the Indians into being more like Europeans, but a rose is still a rose and the Indian culture still lives on in America during the 21st century.

As ardent followers of a particular religion, the earlier American colonists enslaved the Indians by forcing them to work in mines and on large farms known as plantations. The Indians were forced to undergo extremely harsh working conditions, which are noted by the historians to have been the cause of thousands of the Indians to die. The Indians were worked to death. The Indians were viewed by the settlers to be strangers and vise versa, the Indians viewed the white settlers to be the strangers, who had journeyed to their un-foreign lands and sacred places; for their own religious and nonreligious reasons.

Money being the root of all evil also became the main source of the earlier Spanish men's historical reign of terror. Spain ended up gaining great wealth in the gold mines, which the Indians were enslaved to mine thereof under the tyrannous dictatorship of the Spanish men's laws, which supported the Spanish men's sole intentions of gaining and maintaining the control and powers of authority; to settle and create the first American colonies for themselves.

After other different regions of the world that consist of different origin of people saw how Spain's country grew wealthy, their hearts turned to also desired to want a piece of the American Pie. They became zealous to form colonies of their own in America as well. Their intentions later became recognized as the beginning reason why so many people devoted their hearts upon using religion to gain and maintain control and power within the American land. Many ongoing historical American battles and wars are the end result thereof.

(1Cor.15:47-51) In spite of all the physical warring, the longest reign of wars for all people is that which lies within the battles of Spiritual Wars. All Spiritual Wars consists of spiritual divisions that evenly separated ones' religion from ones' spirituality, during biblical times and these divisions still exist today. It arouses people to fight amongst themselves inwardly, while fighting for their human and civil rights as free-spirited individuals. Both the spiritual and religious minded people all over the world are in need to know and need to be made well aware of how the combining of certain pre-existing tyrannous governing laws of the land still twains together with the Word of God, and causes despair and misery unto them as a threatening force, which works toward opposing their God given rights to believe that through the blood of Jesus; they may obtain Salvation. During the fight for freedom, justice, and peace on earth, the traditional religious people indeed are fighting for their salvation by fighting for their religion, but the Spiritual people are keeping their fight more on a basic level; as they work on working out their salvation in the way in which the Lord instructs.

While fighting for a religion, mostly all citizens of every Nation of the world are governed and misled to believe in corruptibly using the commandments of traditional religious men and the Commandment of God together, instead of voiding the commandments of men. They twin them together as if putting them together will help in reconstructing or bring balance into their single party rule, which the commandments of men dictated and legally established into law; to support their own moral governing standards and religious point of views. Not all citizens on earth believe that the law of the land fairly compares to the Word of God. There are many men, women, and children who have grown to be known as spiritual activists, whom disagree with any and every sort of religious doctrine of mankind that doesn't agree with the Lord's greatest of all commandment of the New Testament.

THEORETICAL CONCLUSION

Out of vengeance, the Blame Game only increases a person's heart to anger, and then leads all other evil and unrighteous spirits to enter in and delude the godly spirit of righteousness. Playing the Blame Game is an act or event which keeps one from forgiving and truly repenting and reconciling. There's an engrave difference of how an understanding heart seeks to identify the acts and events, which causes misery and grief; from one who bluntly seeks to accuse a person or a group of people thereof. An understanding heart which seeks to identify such actions; commonly seeks to find a peaceful solution or resolution as a reasonable sacrifice unto God, but without understanding; many hearts maybe seduced to seek for revenge through rage.

CHAPTER 5 THE LAW IS GOOD IF A MAN USES IT LAWFULLY, SO BEWARE OF COVETOUSNESS

(1Tim.1:6-16)

Hypocrites judge not what is right, instead they go with the adversary and in all of his ways they are lead to think as they follow him that they shall be delivered from him. Their beguiled minds think they are following the magistrate of the righteousness of Christ as they depart and go with the adversary to the magistrate of the old law. Therefore, they misleadingly are coerced into fearing to give diligence to the Lord's way of thinking. They do so because they're religiously coerced to fear man whom will hale them to the judge and the judgment of them will deliver them to the officer, and the officer will cast them into prison. (St. Luke12:56-59/St. Matt.6:25/1Peter5:7) The wiles of Satan covet the hearts of men to follow the adversary whom they falsely think can kill their body and soul.

Citizens of all Nations during the 21st century, whom are the offspring's of the ancestors who spiritually knew God and fought the good fight of faith against the supporters of despotism, were taught to also stand up and fight against the old traditional laws of bondage. By faith, they are keeping a good conscience unto God as the blood of Jesus purges their consciences from the old laws' dead works; as servants of the Living God.

By the love, mercy, and grace of God; the citizens of this evil generation today are blessed to witness the Power of the Lord delivering them out from the laws of transgressions and death, which unlawfully still tricks and forcefully coerces many whom are spiritually weak into completely devoting their total loyalty to either a person, group, or an idolized religion that causes destruction without understanding the Lord's new law of love which is filled with mercy and grace. By the terms of such unlawful laws, mankind are turned into the Spots and Blemishes of the flesh, which causes the inner spirits of the weak and simple babes' in Christ to be divided against their inner selves. (Roms.4:14-16, 6:9-19, 7:6-13/Heb.2:14-18, 9:8-9-14)

The inner spiritual wars within the heart of God's children are a replica of all other spiritual wars. The inner spiritual wars are a battle against principalities and powers and not against flesh and blood. Those who know not to do right unto others tend to do wrong, and they make the Spirit of God out to be uncompassionate and full of rage as they claim to be servants of God. They may not be vampires, but they are blood seekers. Meanwhile, God requires all of mankind to individually reach out their hands, where the Kingdom of Heaven resides and partake of the Tree of Wisdom (LIFE) to gain a spiritual understanding of how to work on working out their own salvation. This form of knowledge is more precious to the Spirit of Man than gold and rubies. (Prov.8:11/Job28:12-28)

(Tim.1:9-20) Without empathy of the Lord's law and without understanding from whence comes the law that is made for the lawless, disobedient, ungodly, sinners, for the unholy and profane, and for the murders of fathers and mothers etc.; the desire to rule or dominate continues to seduce the hearts of the weak with the old traditional techniques of the earlier traditional religious ancestors' methods that are provided by, through, and for the upholding of the adoption of the old tyrannous governing laws of the land.

Without empathy, the followers of such tyrannous laws are taught to believe that Christians ought to be spiteful and greedy while they live in pursuit of receiving praise of men. Such praising brings them to a deluded place in their hearts which they think defines peace, joy, and happiness. They virtuously enjoy taking pride in causing misery to others, and they are physically and spiritually incapable of living in peace as they war with others, because they as hypocrites believe in living without reconciling their consciences with the Lord. (St. Luke12:56-59)

Having no empathy makes a non-compassionate person feel powerfully happy when causing others to suffer. Many Americans and non-Americans of the 21st century, hypocritically think they are religiously right as they vengefully stand against the idea of reforming certain tyrannous governing laws. The laws which they obligate themselves to fight for, unlawfully governs and physically oversees the entire body of God's people on earth as to control, direct, or strongly influence their consciences to also believe it is righteous to minister the Lord's law unlawfully.

The unlawful laws which works against the ordinance of God's love, hinders and/or prevents the tyrants and lords of the land from being willing to give all citizens on earth; including the unjust, the same equal human and civil rights as that which they themselves possess. Individually, the majority disbelieves on the Power of the Lord, because they think they religiously know of the unknown measure of the stature of the fullness of Christ. Therefore, the laws and commandments of men that are enmity against God, misleads the tyrants to unfairly work against having unity within their faith through their destitute knowledge of the Spirit of the Son of God.

As they lie and wait to deceive, they indulge and openly admit their sole religious intention is to satisfy their preexisting traditions of world order; which for centuries are historically noted for taking away certain free spirited peoples' freedom to legally be treated fairly on earth. They'd rather judge the Word of God maliciously against the consciences of all whom their religion ridiculously despise, because they think such vengeful usage of the Word of God is proper and gives them the power and authority to retain the spirit of others. This for centuries has been Satan's way to keep the spirit of others obligated to be employed as devotees of their vain religious affairs, which uses religion to spiritually destroy one's faith or hope of being saved by the blood of Jesus. (2Cor.3:9-12, 5:12-21/Gal.6:8-16)

Such unlawful and unjust laws were and still are vainly made for and by the people whom loves to despise others, for the sake of placing themselves up on a pedestal. Such persons, in vain use their traditional religious interpretations and venerations vehemently to strongly stand up impassionedly for their own desires to keep certain tyrannous manmade rules of laws and religious politics in tact. As they uphold such order, they discriminate against certain people who the Holy Ghost made manifest are the ones the Lord's law is made for and not against. The act of using the law of the land to religiously discriminate has been the world's way of trying to prevent the tyranny within all sorts of manmade governments from being incriminated as an abuse of power. Every tyrannous government which people have laid the blame on is predestined to change, but Satan fears that such repentance which is a change for peace; would discontinue his followers and children's arbitrary and despotic religious controlling power of authority.

THOSE WHO CATCH FISHES ARE FISHERMENS, BUT JESUS CHRIST MAKES FISHERS OF MEN (Mark1:16-17)

For centuries the vigorously cruel and oppressive governments have physically dominated the majority of all minorities' state of minds, through the insensitive commands of the despot leaders; whose made-up rules and laws are marked by the rule of tyranny that is written and rooted within the oppressed hearts of their traditional religion. As an example, in March A.D. 2010; several American news reporters reported the desolated trend of totalitarianism and cruelty within the traditions of religious organizations had struck again. The reporters stated that in Denver, CO an innocent toddler was disallowed the privilege and the right to hear the teachings of the Word of God as an enrolled student of a Catholic school. The Archdiocese, which is contrary or different from the sound doctrine of Jesus Christ, says that the school legally has the right to discriminate against any student whose parents are disobedient to the Catholic teachings.

In this particular case it was reported, that the parents of this toddler were lesbians. Ironically, on May 14th A.D. 2007 approximately 3years prior, the state of Colorado was made the 10th state to allow gays to adopt a child who resided in the community as an orphan. This ruling was a permanent established rule of law either through statute or case law. This bill of law is recognized as the House Bill 1330. It is strongly believed that the Lord's inevitable revolutionary love and compassion reformed the legislative law within the state of CO, but the Catholic church members fought to try to prevent this bill from becoming law, because of their religious faith. The Catholic's Archdiocese refuses to allow it's free spirited members to accept the things that they cannot change like an innocent child being excepted in their school, and it disallows them to change the things that they had all powers to change; like protecting little boys from being molested by men whom called themselves Priests of God. Therefore, the liberty of the Catholic members appears to be coerced and imprisoned under a doctrine other than the Doctrine of Jesus Christ.

The local and National news broadcasting service within the US reported a certain Catholic priest had refused to speak to the media about his decision of denying the child's enrollment, but he later admitted his decision was due to the school's traditional religious policy. His admittance and all other remarks were publically displayed to be viewed via the internet blog page http://www.fatherbillsblog.com. On this blog page, the readers can see for themselves how the priest willingly went into details about his own interpretation of the Word of God, to justify his decision to protect the faith of his priest hood.

The readers are advised by the author of Discerning Perceptive to see also the Holy Scriptures which indicates the story of Moses and the Israelites, which were mentioned on this blog page. Unfortunately, a person may be misled into unfairly comparing the trusting faith of the Christians of today's generation with the Israelites whom lacked having faith, if they read this blog without spiritually comparing spiritual things with spiritual things. Don't be so easily convinced into unfairly disregarding the newness of the spiritual heart and the faith of the Christians of the 21st century, whom may appear to be compared to the fleshpots of the Israelites by the writer of this page. After recognizing this fact, consider the unfair comparison of the blog which used the oldness of the letter of a biblical story; in an attempt to philosophically justify an unreasonable dispute of why the priesthood today denied an innocent child.

After checking the most recent modern religious polls, the Catholic Church and many others likened to its teachings are at a record high of people renouncing their memberships. The Christians of the 21st century whom stood on the Word of God and protested against the Catholic's Archdiocese stood firm and spiritually reprimanded the ordinance and regulation of the Catholics' Archdiocese; by rebuking its evilly implied rules and policies. As they continue to imply their kindly intent to obey the Lords' greatest commandment that hangs all the law and the prophets, they bring awareness unto the Priests and compare the fortitude of the religious faith of the Catholic Priesthood with the anointed teachings of the Holy Ghost. (St. Matt.22:37-40/2Tim2:18-26)

The reborn Catholic and non-Catholic Christians of today's society are making it known to the entire world that they are against the Catholics' Archdiocese policy of despotism, and they are doing so with the lack of harshness. With a stern and sharp reproving, they are expressing the Lord's disapproval of all false religions which fails to equally represent the anointed teachings of God's love, mercy, and grace unto all mankind alike; in hopes of saving some. After being tutored under the vain philosophies and words of deceit for so long, many priests and most of their members are now spoiled minded men who cause chaos and confusion among their inherited congregation. Many religious people think God gives them the power to judge the Word and the consciences of the two lesbians, as they verbally charge and accuse all gays of pulling a publicity stunt. They speak as if the entire gay community collaborated together with the adopting parents of the child, before the two decided to pursue the enrollment attempt.

Satan would like to continue manipulating the circumstances of the unfruitful religious acts and events between this present generations' state of affairs like he previously did during past generations. He'd like to make the physical appearance of the majority of church going people of the 21st century to appear to be the Righteous Ones, but the Fruit of the Spirit of God proves most of their hearts fails to comply to the Lord's greatest of all commandment. Even though they may preach about peace and love, they too fall short to sin against peace and love. They may talk right, but they walk wrong.

The Fruit of the Spirit of God has made manifest of the divisions between the despising policies and procedures of all manmade churches. For centuries such policies and procedures have been unchallenged as it desecrates its followers by corrupting the purity and perfection of God's love. The way of life of the old religious organizations which used discrimination to setup their religious standards and policies still continues, because religious people whose hearts are far from God refuses to be humbled; to accept the purest of heart. The pure hearted kindergartener who was denied enrollment at the Catholic school is a prime example.

Instead of being Fishers of men, Satan has coerced his followers to concentrate on being fishermen. Unlike a fisherman, those who are Fishers of men; don't catch fishes with the intent to devour them nor do they throw fishes back into the sea. Fishers of Men are blessed by the Lord to take in every catch; not to consume nor devour, but to care for and love. The fishes that are caught by a fisherman are picked over for the slaughter. Some are thrown back into the sea, if they aren't of the preferred size or are the right preference of species which a fisherman may fish for.

In other words, Satan gives man reasons to hate and despise others, but God gives man reasons to love every part of the Body of Christ, including the parts which count slackness against people as fishermen's do. Manmade traditional religions are slaves to sin, and such religious persons of the 21st century who continues to physically compare their previous lives in an association with the Pharisees' old interpreted reasons to vengefully defend their discerned religious beliefs are slaves thereof.

Their blind eyes and deafened ears fails to understand that hypocritically the tyranny within their own hearts supports ungodly laws, which causes distress and despair upon free spirited individuals of all nationality, sex, religion, and creed by simply keeping people divided;

against the Lord's Will and of his good pleasure. For the love of religion, men who despise men seeks to be justified by Christ (Gal.2), but they fail to fully understand that Christ is not the minister of sin, and his greatest Commandment unto them is to be done without dissimulation.

Although the unfairness of manmade laws advances the old traditional religious believers' point of views, concerning their own religious philosophical teachings, principles, and ideas of defining the life value of a born again Christian's characterized moral virtues; they unrightfully misjudge the stature of their own character and unworthiness as judgers of the Word of God and not as doers. By the desires of their own bellies, the supporters of despotism and tyrannous laws religiously think they are justified by Christ. As they seek for justification in their known methods of accusing others while excusing themselves, they are found sinners of blasphemy, who are liars against the Holy Ghost.

During their every day walk of life, the religious ones whom are taught to despise others in a vengeful manner seems to desire to prevent whosoever they despise from gaining the Lord's heavenly knowledge. Maybe they are afraid that if the ones who they despise receive the Lord's heavenly knowledge, that they'd use that knowledge to reproach, reprove, and rebuke the evil spirits within the unfair manmade laws of the land.

Although the reign of tyranny within the governing law's intentions are clearly made to teach people how to desire to have dominion through lordship and how to despise each other, the Holy Ghost teachings within the house of God's temple is made not by man's hands and is manifesting the truth of the One True Gospel of Jesus Christ. The Holy Ghost's teachings makes clear to the senses and minds of all believers of the Lord; that neither the old laws or religious politics have the power to separate the love one has for God; nor the love God has for all mankind. The love God has for mankind is predestined to simulate the love man has for each other and visa versa, and it is inevitable for God's love to universally prevail above all. The Holy Ghost in meekness instructs those who oppose themselves or possibly are living in error of uncertainty to perhaps reflect hope unto them that God will give them repentance to the acknowledging of the truth; so that they may recover themselves out of the snare of the devil.

Certain people can't understand the difference between their right hand and their left, but God loves them all the same. It isn't God who desires to send any to hell. That's the desire of Satan. God desires remains to be the same today as it was during the days of Moses and Jonas. He requires for all to go through an inevitable spiritual process which leads all of mankind unto **Repentance and Reconciliation.** He requires for all to know that he loves them, and he still during the 21st century sends out his chosen people whom hearts desires to properly use Christ's Word of Truth amongst a multitude; to cry out to his people about the changes that are required of all believers, without hypocritically misusing the Word of God. In so doing as true ministers of God, they spiritually destroys the ungodly spirit within the hearts of the lost, and revives the godly spirit within all who believes on the Lord; in hopes of saving some or all who has an ear to hear and understand.

THE FATHER REWARDS OPENLY (ST. MATT.6)

Along the Atlantic Coast, history reveals the first13 American colonies were established by the English settlers. Although the English settlers were not divided by their nationality, they were divided by their desires and purposes. Some were in a bind by a written contract to serve another person as an indentured servant. They desired to gain their freedom, but many died as an oppressed slave. Just because they died as an oppressed slave doesn't mean their faith on the Lord was in vain, because it was the Lord who walked with them during their physical life time and provided them with an inner peace in spite of how bad they suffered persecution. It was the Lord who sent out his eleven disciples to teach all nations to observe all things which Jesus commanded. (Ex.20/Malachi4:4/St. Matt.28:16), and after doing so there were no nation of people which went unlearned. Nothing new goes on under the sun, and during those days all who knew to do right and did it committed sin.

Many old English travelers, whose exceptional roles in American History are religiously commended by their own kindred; viewed themselves as the most supreme over all other authority figures. They wanted to gain riches and wealth in their newly found homeland and did gain riches and wealth. Meanwhile, there were other old English travelers who wanted the basics in life such as their own land, and they gained their own land. Like the Spanish men, the English settlers were noted by historians to have been made up of religious missionaries who also wanted to practice their own religion in their own way.

Whether their way agreed with the Lord's way or not, they and the Spanish men were persuade to believe in their own understandings of who, what, and which of their own common factors of character mostly related to the Holy Scriptures, and they fixated the beginning of their traditional dealings upon those particular religious beliefs. According to their beliefs they were authorized by God to exploit whosoever and whatsoever their traditional religion desired to honor, dishonor, and represent. By the desires of their own circumstances, they desired to do just as their hearts were coerced to religiously do. For the sake of honoring despotism, their committed hearts dictated the Word of God to befit their ungodly ordinances and rule of laws; to befit their every situation, circumstance, and occasion.

Many centuries and generations later, it became traditional for a majority of people to think that the desires of their hearts which craves to have an overly excessive relationship with God were incorruptible and imperishable, as they served the Lord God with the continuous desire to cause the minds of a multitude to suffer a great loss of hope and faith on the Lord's ability to deliver them out of the temptations of this world. During this generation the religious hypocrites through their evilly sown traditional religious deeds, still continue to cause others a lasting state of distress or misery; by casting worldly afflictions to be bestowed upon them. Such afflictions bring forth worldly sorrows that work unto death, and not godly sorrows unto repentance and life everlasting.

For instance, certain people are well known for their religious venerations and beliefs in using the Lord's name in vain while cursing individuals with religious VOODOO through their evil speaking of the dignities of others. Just as some religious people believe in good luck and bad luck, there are those who religiously believe in good curses and bad curses. Their religion over looks the spiritual factor that the Lord's blessings being a heavenly reward; is given to all who passes his tests of trials and tribulations.

Some even go beyond the call of luck and pray to God to curse the ones they are religiously taught to despise. They devote their whole livelihood towards making it religiously legal for worldly crafted governments to use certain traditional religious vain philosophies and words of deceit, to delude the denote or clear meaning of the Lord's righteous truth; for the sake of upholding the superior laws of the lands' well governed traditional religious acts of discrimination. Many of them are religiously encouraged to kill the free spiritual faith of God within God's people as they despise and desire to see certain sinners suffer.

Then there are those who are known for taking part in religiously governing politically elevated evil traditional religious beliefs and rituals, in hopes of legally persecuting and causing more misery, agony, pain, sufferings, and worldly sorrows. Within all that they do, they deny their faith to be Voodoo workers whom believes in cursing others, because they too fail to realize that the intent of their hearts desire to do the works that aren't of the Father in Heaven, but is the works of the Adversary. Most of these people religiously go regularly to their houses of God, which are made by men's hands; as a venerating traditional ritual. They falsely claim themselves to be apart of a congregation which praise God the Father, the Son, and the Holy Spirit and then they return home to raise all kinds of hell.

Non-worshippers of Voodoo refuses to devote the heart of their spiritual faith to such religious witchcraft, and they are greatly aware of how such persons loves to rejoice in another man's misery and take credit in the cause of a person's despair. Therefore, it is easier for all believers on the Lord to recognize and witness voodoo workers who publically surrenders their religious faith to the very distasteful and shameful acts of injustices. In Jesus name, voodoo worshippers use the Lord's name in vain to bring desolation and not peace.

In fact, in despite of the numerous amounts of religious people pretending to be Christians within the state of Mississippi, the Magnolia state was yet voted the most religious state by a new Gallup Poll, which calculated and declared the Magnolia State to be the most religious state of the USA, during the year of 2009. The editor-in-chief of the Gallup poll and others like him unwisely concluded such speculations to be true after simply interviewing approximately 355,334 people throughout every state with one particular question, **"Is religion an important part of your daily life?"**

After doing so the Gallup researchers' calculations indicated 85% of their chosen Mississippians answered yes, and they apparently declared that since Mississippi's yes percentage rate were higher than all other states, then their poll ratings was enough physical evidence for them to publically proclaim Mississippi to be the most religious over all others. Some Mississippians took pride in the acceptance of such religious praise, without truly knowing or understanding the basics of what the Mississippians who voted yes; religiously teach or believe. Other Mississippians, whose faith on the Lord are neither idol nor religious; don't desire to boast on the result of such polls, because they are spiritual and would rather be commended by God and not man.

ALL HISTORICAL ACTS OF VANITY ARE INEVITABLY CONVERTING INTO REDEMPTION THROUGH LOVE, REPENTANCE, & RECONCILIATION

In 1607, whether truth or fable; the first English settlement was established in James Town, Pennsylvania. In 1619 the residents of James Town established a self government, and during that same year the people of James Town witnessed the first arrivals of African people who were captured, stolen, and kidnapped by white men who were employed by the Englishmen. These white men without remorse took the Africans from their mothers' bosoms out of the lands of Africa. They were brought into James Town as slaves, indentured servants, and devotees to fear; to revere and serve all the English settlers and every white man alive. These African slaves were forced and retained to serve the rest of their life time in the Englishmen's hostile and tyrannous environment, as workers on their farms and plantations.

Since the ordinance of the Englishmen's governing law defined kidnapping as an unlawful act of forcefully carrying a "<u>person</u>" away against their will, the Englishmen used the wisdom of this world to subvert the laws to be as discerningly deceitful as the composers of it. The law makers persuade and coerced the English Christian settlers to religiously and legally believe the Africans weren't humans but were wild beasts. The false image by which the Englishmen's law defined the entire African's nationality, seduced many white Christians to be susceptible towards supporting the composers of the unlawful acts of injustices, which were legally committed against all humans of the nonwhite American race.

Although a chosen few of the English settlers inwardly disagreed with their colony's self made tyrannous governing laws, they were too weak by number to stand against the lawmakers without being put outside of the protection of their own colony. Their own creed who spitefully despised all Africans also despised all who rebelled against their legally formed tyrannously established governing laws that were suppose to have been made for the protection of the entire English colonists.

The English men were permitted by law to travel by ships to Africa to hunt and capture as many Africans as their ships could carry and bring them back to the American colonists. They physically bound them with chains, ropes, iron bracelets, and cuffs by their wrists, necks, and ankles at gun-point. They caged them like wild-beasts, and transported them as products to be sold under the Englishmen's made up laws of the land.

Meanwhile, the despot tyrants, delegates, and the entire American English settlers were waiting for the arrival of these captured slaves so they could practice psychologically binding and retaining them religiously, mentally, emotionally, socially, and physically into believing that their dark skin color was of a curse from God, and God made them to be less than human. The main objective of the earlier American practices were done to uphold the first American Englishmen's despotic traditional religious belief which suggested that they were chosen by God to be revered as masters on earth. Therefore, they preached unworthily of God's love, mercy, and grace unto the African American ancestors to make them think all blacks were undeserving of God's love, mercy, and grace. Although all supremacists on earth heard about Moses being called by God to free the slaves in Egypt, they yet desired to live like the Pharaoh. During the 21st century, the white American's rebirth of the religious practice of demanding such reverence are the dreams of the KKK's who has conjoined secretively together amongst a few true white Christians and make the rent of the main Christians' objective and characteristics in the reformed American political view of life of an inferior quality. (St. Mark2/St. Matt.9)

Like the taming of a wild beast, the earlier white American supremacists brutally enslaved the Africans' bodies and minds in efforts to control and kill their inner spirits; in an attempt of them making it impossible for their free-spirited African heritage to be remembered nor revivable once destroyed, so that the niggers couldn't passed down their free-spirited thoughts of living to their off springs. Fortunately, the whites were divided, because not all of them believed in the earlier Americans' desolated religious translations of the Word of God, and they bought their African slaves as to protect them from their tyrant counter parts.

The supremacists of controlling powers and delegates to the USA's Constitution were misled into using the technique of despotism to forcefully influence and control the mindset and the conduct of the entire inferior African American race, as their laws repetitively from one generation unto the next; used coercive words of deceit which destroys the Christian moral statures and fiber of their own kindred. During the days when American slavery was legal, the judicial writ empowered officers to carry-out unrighteous judgments and unreasonable punishments under the unjust laws of the American colonies against the good will of the African American slaves and all other indentured servants, whom weren't of the white Americans' origin, religion, sex, or creed; including the white Muslims and Jews. The Judicial writ officers' job was to establish a punishable legal system and procedure, which the majority of settlers agreed with; to psychologically dispose the thoughts of running away from the minds of the African slaves as to subdue, vanquish, and conquer the minds of all; to prevent them from think of ever escaping all over again. Being free from such bondage was just a dream for all who died as slaves.

For example; when the African American ancestors were caught trying to escape or run-away from their slave masters, they were brutally beaten and their families were sold like a product under the supremacists' self governed law. If they had any kinship or reproduced into an extended family, they too would be sold and separated from their immediate family for the rest of their lives by the supremacists of power as apart of their punishment. Often when they were put to death, they were publically executed, tortured, hung, burned, beaten, skinned alive, beheaded, castrated, and crucified. The supremacists made up irrational reasons and excuses for one of another, as their hearts yielded to commit to such unlawful but legal unjust acts of such horrific magnitude in a public forum of demonstration. One reason was to strike fear into the hearts of the other Africans who were forced by them to bare witness of the white Supremacists' powerful governing laws, and the debt of their reasoning was excusable upon their denote misunderstandings of the Lord's New Covenant.

Since a divided group was recognized by the earlier Americans to be of a religious sign of weakness, they silenced their own kindred whom disagreed with their tyrannous religious rule of laws. To keep them from publically protesting, the white supremacists made all white American protesters or activists appear to be the weak link of their society. A "Nigger Lover" is the labeled name of disgrace which the earlier American peace activists were called. It was a unique form of verbal and psychological abuse which the supremacists commended as they deliberately placed all white American activists outside of the protection of their own law, which was originated to protect all whites.

Ironically, it was commonly known for the earlier white supremacists to disown their own kindred for whatsoever irrational reason they desired. Consequently, such extreme conditions caused the earlier American Activists to secure their own safety from the distorted laws which originally were proclaimed to have been designed to protect them. To prevent themselves from being tortured along side of the niggers, they themselves pledged to remain silent to save themselves. They knew that they were safe as long as they all pretended to stand up for the tyrannous policies and laws of their community. Hypocritically, their silence saved them from being tortured, but it helped to influence the tyrants to continue onto the next stage of discrimination which appears to have no end.

The earlier white Activists agreed to commend the unfair rules of their manmade governing laws, which put the fear of God in their hearts just as much as it did to the slaves. Such laws tamed the spirit of the black community into believing their owners were gods, and today that type of defined display of fear is biblically understood to be of an ungodly fear and the desolated behavior of such slave owners are recognized to have not been and never will be the act of godliness under the New Testament.

They even used this type of ungodly fear as a form of religious veneration for the freed blacks to submit too. Most slave owners either failed to understand or disbelieved that when the Son of God sent his chosen Apostles out into the world to teach the whole world of the One True Gospel, his Apostles successfully managed to teach the One True Gospel to every corner of the earth. This means that even the people in Africa were reached and became blessed to receive the Anointed spiritual knowledge which gives life.

Due to the slave masters' worldly desires to receive worldly rewards, they failed to comprehend that the Africans' and the Native American's free Spirit was and still are of God. This form of knowledge was and is still freely given by God. They were afraid that if God was for the Africans, Indians, and any other origin of people who they despised, that they themselves would be persecuted by the Cross of Christ. Therefore, they worshiped vigorously to prevent themselves from being persecuted by the Cross of Christ. They did not understand how the falseness of their technique which worked fears also worked death to be bestowed unto them-selves as they served the Lord God through the evil deeds of placing an earthy fear unto others.

As the slave masters exercised unfair or tyrannous dominion over the African American ancestors, they became desirous to be looked upon by the entire African race as if they were gods. They religiously practiced being godly missionaries through the physical factors of appearing to be god like, but their hearts were far from being holy. While using the Holy Bible text inaccurately, they ministered unto the Africans in the well known blasphemous manners like cult religions still do under the sun during the 21st century. Such a like ministries befit the old traditional self governed laws of the land. The earlier established cultists and religious venerators still exist in today's orchestrated political campaigns and skillfully are organizing evilly filled traditional religious congregations.

The whites and blacks as well as all other races who are true reborn Christians can spiritually empathize with the lost; without neither blaming nor accusing anyone unto God, because they spiritually understand the things which cause their neighbors and strangers to live in error. By the grace of God they desire not to render evil for evil or railing against railing, but they desire to serve the Lord with the intent of preaching reconciliation and repentance. As they reproach, reprove, and rebuke the ungodly intent of the world, they surrender their hearts as a part of the Body of Christ; for the edification of the entire Body of Christ.

> 2TIM.1:7 "But God hath not given us the spirit of fear; but of power, and of love, and of a sound mind."

THE FALSENESS OF LOVE BETWEEN A SLAVE MASTER & AN OBEDIENT SERVANT... IS SIMILAR TO DEVIL WORSHIP

One cult is another man's religion. The old world were heedful to consider believing that any other religion compared to their own were worshipers of the Devil, but the coercions of their assumptions came from their own religious veneration and lack of understanding the Word of God; which is relevant to their own reasons as to why they edify one culture over another. Meanwhile, the martyrs and scorners are well known for displaying their ill-will upon their lack of understanding. As they reap division among themselves, they demonize all other origins of God's people instead of uniting themselves together as one body of different origins and edify the Lord.

As a firm illustration of such acts, it has been historically noted of how they taught the Word of God in their own formal religious veneration for themselves to be regarded as gods by all indentured servants whom they captured or enslaved. They desired for their captured slaves to have reverential respect for their religion due to their own devotion of making their philosophical religious theories sacred by their own religious customs and associations there of. Like the biblical leaders of the sect of the Pharisees; traditional religious followers today are devoted to the despot doctrine of their ancestors, because they find the handing down of such dictatorial religious information, customs, beliefs, and practices from one generation to another; impressive by reason of its age.

The spiritual people of today's society reconsiders and understands that the ways of the old world's religion were distorted, when the African American slaves and all other indentured servants didn't voluntarily comply with their slave masters' religious teachings. Although the Fruit of the Spirit proved the slaves were filled with godliness, they were yet still brutalized and punished by the hands of men who perpetrated themselves to appear to be God. Therefore, to physically protect themselves and their families from the sorrows of the world, the slaves decided to defer their own spiritual beliefs in the presence of the white

American supremacists. Ironically, some blacks and nonwhites were coerced by Satan to fight evil with evil and railing against railing, but others of them found Jesus through faith, and desired to continue fighting evil with kindness until the time of their life on earth was over.

Historically, many black slaves yielded to the Englishmen's theoretical religious wishful opinions. Although the free born Africans were constantly coerced into revering the whites in the manner of respecting or admiring the supremacists' cult religion, they deeply admired their own heritage, opinions, and preferences which didn't co-aside with the white supremacists of power where godly love is concerned. Therefore, they secretly passed down their unconditional loving African heritage to the best of their ability onto their off springs.

Unfortunately, all African American ancestors were kept from legally recording the history of their people, and most African Americans today suffers from the loss of memory of their family tree. After being separated and scattered abroad, many have adapted to the single parent style of house holds; where the parents today are coerced to believe in the independent duty of rearing up their children in broken homes. In despite of their lack of physical remembrance of their African ancestors, many today are still blessed to be comforted by the Comforter; to live as freemen by the Fruit of the Spirit of God.

The supremacists' traditional cult teachings suggestively demanded and required for the African slaves to show the white masters who hindered them that they had courteous and respectful regards for their religious principles, ideas, theories, and beliefs. As a physical gesture to show respect, the cultists trained the African slaves of all ages to bow their heads or bodies in submission upon greeting a white person whether the white person were younger or older than they. Once upon a time not too long ago black elder men were ordered to say yes sir to all whites even to the white preschool children. In the old days the words Sir and Madame were apart of the African American Negro's daily language.

Although the words signifies unto all Americans during the 21st century as a courtesy title equivalent to Mrs. for married women, and Mr. for men these words are viewed as a toner of respect amongst the entire North America community. Many even violently persecutes and ridicule children who chooses not to say yes sir and yes madam upon answering a grown up. These children are frowned upon as if they either are children of the devil or are the devil's advocates.

Even the minds of the parents of these poor children are delusional as they fail to acknowledge their child is a little person with feelings. If a little person, who has a mental view point on logic, don't feel as if they are being respected by their elders; why should they be persecuted and forced to give reverential respect unto the extremists whose radical behaviors gives them no respect? Although the words Sir and Madam are acknowledged in the English language as a courtesy title, many extremists fail to acknowledge the true fact that respect must be earned. Therefore, in the State of MS the entire African America community fails to consider this factoring towards their own children. After they have been spoiled by the vain philosophy, which suggests for them to believe that a child is disrespectful to their elders, if they fail to use sir and madam; either upon greeting or upon answering a yes and no question. As a spokesman for the children, ask yourself, "What's so disrespectful about answering yes and no to a yes and no question?" If you answered NOTHING, then start helping the youth to stop thinking they are criminals in the eyes of the Lord!

During the early-mid 1900's the elders of the American black community still revered the practice of their African ancestors' physical gestured behaviors of the bowing of the head in regards of showing respect to the whites upon greeting. They remembered being taught as a child to not look directly into the eyes of any white person upon greeting or while conversing. Since it was a long term crime and punishable by the white men's law for the blacks to look into the eyes of a white person, when they conversed with them during the days of slavery; most African American elders during the late 1900's still lived in fear and bowed their heads as a sign of respect upon greeting and conversing with white people. Although slavery was abolished, racial discrimination still persisted during the late 1900's in a major way against the entire black community. Therefore, most black elders during the mid and late 1900's were still afraid of the whites; especially in the Southern Hemisphere of North America.

It is spiritually believed by many spiritual people that the very rare eye to eye contact which was made between black people (whether bond or free) and a white person during the days of slavery, weakened the evil spirit of the oppressor. Through the eyes of the blacks, a white Christian could see through the oppressors' lie and would understand that black people did too have a soul and weren't wild beasts. Although the Supremacists denied seeing a soul within the heart of the blacks, the very rare eye to eye contact strengthened the slaves to believe they were their masters' equal as a human being. This caused the slave masters to simultaneously become filled with anger and fear of the blacks. Therefore, the whites became more determined to make their own race feel it was essentially necessary for them to carry on with the tradition of having the blacks revere them, even after slavery was abolished. Through the vain display of constituting the unreasonable laws, which discriminate against the entire black community; the white oppressors fought vigorously to maintain their religious traditions and beliefs.

It was the Lord whom ordained and commanded all to come together on earth as brethren of one Body in Christ, and with an understanding and compassionate heart, both the whites and the blacks gradually became more loving, kind, and caring towards one of another. During slavery, the human-side of the African people was easily seen within their eyes by many slave masters who believed on Jesus Christ. For the born again white Christians, it was like looking into the eyes of an innocent child. In other words within the eyes of all mankind their spiritual heart and soul speaks. Whether a person's heart and soul is filled with madness, sadness, misery, and pain or with godly love, joy, peace, and happiness others could virtuously hear whatsoever their heart and soul says aloud through the expressions of their eyes.

The despot white American ancestors and non American leaders ruled despotically to have dominion over the blacks with insecurities, because they were afraid that they would lose their control in power over the blacks if their white Christian brethrens and sisters' spiritual eye connected with the spiritual heart of the slaves. Their whole rivalry was against this sort of spiritual connection, because they knew that the godly spirit lives in all mankind alike and is more than a conquer. The Lord's holy power delivers all mankind out of the temptations of the world, which works the deadly deeds of hatred and despair and makes intercessions to their spirit; to desire to do the righteous deeds of God and gives life through love over death and hate.

The black American ancestors like the Native American Indians, were forcefully coerced under the yokes of bondage to believe that they were not the white man's equal. They like Eve were taught this by the cunning words and the perverse teachings of the beguiled concept of Satan, whose teaching is enmity against God and blasphemes against the teachings of the Holy Ghost.

Acting as gods or lords of the American land, the white cultists ministered unto the Africans to fear them and to love them with the tenderness of feelings; like African slaves revered their grandparents. The Holy Bible and its contents for centuries have been exploited by cult religious people whom made use of the scriptures unfairly in their attempt to gain their own advantage in the world. This ought not to have been done, but it was and still is being done. The laws of the land were configured to have similar formations of the Word of God, but it was rebellious against the ordained order of the law of God and against God's greatest commandment "LOVE." There's no dissimulation in love.

After one generation past unto the next, the memory of the Africans' heritage and their spiritual beliefs in the hearts of most African Americans today have slowly faded away, and the false simulation of love has grown in their hearts. The falseness of love has seduced many to vengefully fight for the Lord in the same mannerism as their oppressors. The Lord's Love has became a religious word which feels more like hate, and this is the master key to Devil worshiping within all sorts of traditional religious congregations today.

REDEEMING THE HEART AND SOUL OF AMERICA

As the spectators of the African origin were forced to watch the brutal murdering of their own people (strangers, friends, family, and close relatives) by the white supremacists without the legal ability to help their brethren, they grew to understand that the theoretical implicit agreements of the original American colonists' self governed laws had put them outside of the laws' protection.

The laws of the supremacists of power were composed and broken down into two parts implicating that if a person were born outside of the purebred white race, then their dignities were to be evil-spoke of and regarded by the vote of the majority of whites as impure, negligible, worthless, and distasteful. In the beginning of the building of the Church within the American Nation, only the white male property owners' political votes were counted in the building of the American's governing laws. In other words the laws implied absolute proscription against the Africans' origin by the white supremacists. The ordinance and power of the white supremacists insinuated to the illegitimate opinions, emotional attitudes, and unrighteous judgments of the traditional religious orders that ironically labels the Africans and all other origin of people as evil beings.

As one generation past unto the next the original Americans off springs composed more laws, which clearly revealed that they expected for the Africans to continue to be obedient toward their selfishly composed order of laws. Such delusions helped the white oppressors to gain and maintain a false sense of godly powers, as far as the earthy sensation of controlling powers is concerned. Therefore, the primary fleshly or earthy sensation of man's law has been resourcefully traced back to the root of all evil, the power of MONEY!

Meanwhile, the teachings of the Holy Ghost, which still exist today entered the hearts of certain white oppressors and converted their

215

hearts to become born again Christians and gave them and their off springs the Lord's heavenly wisdom to understand the difference between good and evil. They renounced themselves from being a participant of the evil acts of creating a desolated environment after realizing that the creator of a desolate environment causes additional divisions to come between them and God.

Instead of hurting the blacks they secretly helped them. Some even helped to shelter the runaway slaves in their own homes and on their private properties. When the other white rivalry found them defending or helping the blacks, they persecuted these white Christians by calling them nigger lovers to degrade them amongst their own origin and nationality of people. As a punishment these white Christians were also placed outside of the protection of the original law of the land with the blacks.

With a clear conscience of not frustrating the love of God, the white reborn Christians continued doing what they'd believed God's Spirit of Righteousness and Truth required and commanded them to do, and so did their conflicting rivalry. While fulfilling the desire to love God first, the rebirth of the spirit within the true white Christians turned from hating their counter parts and they started loving their neighbors as they loved their-selves. As the beginning era of the inevitable change of heart evolved, the rebirth of those Christians fought a good spiritual fight for the rest of their physical lives, against the principalities and powers of the bondage of this world. For every generation before, during, and after that point of time, were many redeemable events made by the American reborn Christians, in efforts of reproving and restoring hope and grace back into the heart of the American law.

1Tim.1:6 "From which some having swerved having turned aside unto vain jangling;"

1Tim.1:7 "Desiring to be teachers of the law; understanding neither what they say, nor whereof they affirm."

1Tim.1:8 "But we know that the law is good, if a man use it lawfully;"

(Romans14:14-19,22,23/2TIM.3:1-9)

> Titus1:10 "For there are many unruly and vain talkers and deceivers, specially they of the circumcision:"
>
> Titus1:11 "Whose mouths must be stopped, who subvert whole houses, teaching things which they ought not, for filthy lucre's (MONETARY GAIN/PPROFIT) sake."
>
> Titus1:15 "Unto the pure all things are pure: but unto them that are defiled and unbelieving is nothing pure; but even their mind and conscience is defiled."
>
> Titus1:16 "They profess that they know God; but in works they deny him, being abominable, and disobedient, and unto every good work reprobate."

The following definitions are in accordance to the Merriam Webster Dictionary.

The creation of–Cracy; like in the end of the word democracy, resides within the social and political clash of powers which separates the lower, middle, and upper class of people. The most illogical thing for any person who is born and raised in the USA to do, is to fight for what the English language stands for without knowing what transpired in the creating of the language. During the 14th century the word <u>hierarchy</u> was used in reference to determine or to describe the ranks or orders of angels. In Greek the word has two separate elements hieros and archos. Hieros means "Holy, sacred", and archos means "leader, ruler." Another definite but often vague awareness of these words was and still is used to determine and to describe a form of government administered by some sort of priesthood.

Hierarchy has expanded and is long-drawn-out from the ancient religious realm's usage into describing a government as the traditional religious people of the 21st century in America are using it to religiously deter, define, and describe the religious classifications of different groups of people. Gradually the intent of its transferred meaning which was once an honorable definition has changed to the arrangement of traditional religious objects, elements, and values in graduated series, which continually judge and sort people by sarcastic and stereotypical grades, classes, or intervals. Religious people has turn to old wives' fables and things which doesn't edify the entire Body of Christ, but brings about unclear answers towards centuries of questions; to either include or exclude one sort of people from another. Like their ancestors' prior religious venerations they today work to either omit or allow certain people entry to their particular defined religious congregations whose principle beliefs and standards fits that of both traditional religion and earthy political progression and development. The rank of order of angels are now being misrepresented as to what the rank of self religious men of the world have theoretically determined amongst themselves to describe themselves incoherently without making sense. Their misinterpretation represents how they have confused themselves to be at the rank of the highest of all angels.

In America, <u>Anarchy</u> means: a state of lawlessness, confusion, or disorders. This form of democracy was described by the white American slave owners as to have the absence, suspension or break down in governments' law and order. An anarchy government is now described by the American people of the 21st century as a chaotic form of government that's made up of a society of individuals who have no government and enjoys complete freedom.

Ironically, in Greek anarchicia is the written term used for Anarchy and it means to rule, but the original Americans' expectation of this type of government was that it was made up of absolute chaos, lawlessness, and disorder. Its original meaning has been deluded by the vain philosophies and distorted definition within the deceptive English language, which has seduced most American people into believing that Anarchy stresses the absence of government and creates chaos which involve the absences of law, order, and rule.

Hypocritically while promoting slavery, the earlier Americans' creative form of knowledge of an Anarchy Government; displayed the beginning spreading era and formation of despotism amongst every citizen within the United States of America. The intellect of many earlier American settlers and the American founding forefathers reacted to their life's purpose as if they were unaware of the spiritual truth which proves that before they or anyone else were ever introduced to any form of law, they all were once pure hearted individuals. Like a child, before they were introduced to the Old Law, which their religion is based upon; there were no philosophical theories of any sorts present within the spirit of them. Without the law, all were apart of the same society which was made up of individuals who enjoyed complete freedom. As it is written; "Unto the pure all things are pure: but unto them that are defiled and unbelieving, nothing is pure." Nothing is pure to the defiled and unbelieving, because even their minds and consciences are defiled. (Titus 1:15-16) In fact, those whose minds are defiled will disbelieve that the contents of the Holy Bible text is properly arranged; to honor those whom traditional religions bountifully degrade, humiliate, bring shame upon, and debase.

Monarchy is a government that has a hereditary chief of the State with life tenure, residency, permanent status, and authority varying the rights to hold a position from normal too absolute power. In other words, Monarchy is the undivided or absolute rule by the hereditary of one person, as of a dictatorship or autocracy. Before Christ, a Monarchy government was as of a religious ritual under the leadership of the forefathers of Saul, and the leaders among the Israelites after Joseph's death. This spasmodic leadership was passed onto Saul by judges who in vain acted out of vengeance to deliver unto the Israelites a religious governing law. While living under the excessive control and power of the oppressing dictatorship of the Pharaoh's governed laws, the oppressed are forced to think, feel, and believe in the ways instructed by Pharaoh's laws. The entire traditional religious realm has oppressed the minds of the innocent and the blameless to incoherently think or believe that the Jews killed Christ, and no where do they truthfully preach the entirety of that truth which reveal that Christ died by the hands of the law. Instead, it is taught as a traditional ritual that the Jewish people crucified Jesus Christ. A half truth is a lie. To bring complete balance to the righteous way of life for all mankind, the One True Gospel must be told inclusively to fulfill the comprehension level of every believing heart of the New Covenant of Jesus Christ.

Proverbs28:9 "He that turneth away his ear from the law, even his prayer shall be abomination."

1Corithians9:21 "To them that are without law, as without law, (being not without law to God, but under the law to Christ,) that I might gain them that are without."

1Corithians9:22 "To the weak became I as weak, that I might gain the weak: I am made all things to all men, that I might by all means save some."

1Corithians9:23 "And this I do for the gospel's sake, that I might be partaker thereof with you."

THE SEPEREATION OF CHURCH & STATE

After Christ's resurrection, during the Middle Ages (A.D. 400's to the 1500's) the ancient Roman's taught Christianity. Christianity qualified all men are equal before God, and a <u>Roman Statesman name Cicero</u> had a saying which added to the universal law of reason, and his saying remains as a binding explanation on all men and governments everywhere. He says that men have natural rights which every state must respect. Therefore, when ever a state attempts to demand complete, total, or unqualified loyalty from its citizens, the demands of the state then conflicts with the spirit of Christianity. Therefore, because Christians must obey God and his New Commandments; Christianity taught that no state can demand total loyalty from its citizens.

During the middle ages, all Romans' who spiritually believed on the Lord also believed that they were citizens of two Kingdoms; one on earth and the other in Heaven. This belief still exists in the American lands. The revelation of the ancient Roman Christians' thoughts, converted their spiritual faith to consider that they could preserve freedom for themselves on earth from the despotic laws of the land, by standing up as <u>peacemakers.</u> In their every attempt to seek diligently for the Kingdom of Heaven, the Fruit of the Spirit proves the Holy Ghost filled the hearts of them with the knowledge of the Lord's righteous way of reforming the despotic laws of the land. The only righteous way the minority of peacemakers who truly believe that they are citizens on earth and in Heaven have ever succeeded in reforming any unfair law, is and always has been by coming together as one electoral body of Christian church members; whose over all desires were not to be commended or praised by men, but to exhort and edify the entire body of Christ without desiring to glory in the flesh of others.

222

As they obeyed the despotic laws of the land, the ancient Roman Christians gently and meekly reproached the dead deeds of the despots' law, which they all were coerced to honor, respect, and revere. They rebuked the evils within the earliest known oppressors' distinctive cause of creating a desolated environment, by spiritually evaluating the aftermath or the end result of the barrenness of the hearts of the privileged lawmakers; whose hearts during their time in power on earth sinfully possessed many hidden chauvinism or prejudices.

It is prudent to understand that not everyone in America who says they are Christians will uphold the Greatest Commandment of God. The works of those who refuse or fail to uphold the Greatest Commandment of God are vain and useless. The true anointed American Christians of the 21st century are like the ancient Roman Christians; we dare not to condemn any prejudicing hearted extremist or activist whether they maybe natural born Americans or non-Americans, but we do condemn their actions. We'd rather work diligently to bring such religious terrorists unto the Lord's heavenly knowledge of the Holy Truth in hopes of changing their bigoted dogmatic hearts, by helping them to spiritually understand that the sin of their own narrow minded fleshly desires seductively increases the vain desires of their traditional religion's primary agendas, which plots and make plans to spread hatred, confusion, and war; not love, empathy, compassion, and peace.

Like false prophets, there are fake Christians and phony Christian ministers who would rather desire to condemn the hearts and the works of those whom they traditionally are trained to despise; in hopes of redeeming the malicious transgressions of their indecent formulations of a religious ministry. Instead of them doing what Jesus would do as true Christians, they do the opposite. They are of the world and they believe that they need to apply "Just Laws" and rules to resolve their traditional religions' social and personal disputes. In order to apply Just Laws and rules they must first classify and uphold the accurate truth and the right form of righteousness, while disallowing the false and the wrong. The blind leaders and followers of false prophets always fail to consider the importance of not living in vain with hatred and spite in their hearts. Unto them it's a tick for tack world. In other words they do unto others whatsoever things others do unto them. They love those who love them and hate those who hate them.

There is not one wise false prophet neither alive nor dead that understands that in order to enforce a Just Law inquires for "the truth" and "the right" must be made clear and obvious from the fabrication and the falsehood of a religious life. The just and the right, must be discernible from the wrong in order for the "Just Law" to befit every living soul under the sun who has a personal right and a valued relationship with the Lord. Therefore, the social responsibilities of a Just Law is to support fairness for all citizens under the sun in love; just as the Law of Christ is justly and fair unto all angles in Heaven and earth, because the souls of all sinners who lives under the sun are at stake.

For the souls of the few who understands that being under the Law to Christ means to abide by the Golden Rule which implies in St. Matt7:12 "Therefore all things whatsoever you would that men should do to you, do ye even so to them: for this is the law and the prophets."; shall receive a heavenly reward. The universal truth of what this basically means is that the one objective moral standard to the Golden Rule; is written in all of our hearts (Rom.2:15). As it is written, we are given a standard law of evaluation, as a godly tool which we can use to assess our own actions, and base our response on whether or not we would want those same actions which we commit; to be done to us.

As far as creating a governing system where enforcing a Just Law on earth is concerned, the task for the chosen becomes quit simple for all whom spiritually have the ability to discern the just and the right from the wrong. The simplicity of what truth really is resides within the hidden secrets of the Lord's parables which explain the just and right way of forming and maintaining a governing system for all. The Famous Question was asked by Pontius Pilate the sixth Roman procurator of Judaea in St. John18:29-38. He asked Jesus, "What is Truth?" (St. John8:31-32)The Holy Truth which defines what truth is makes the truth obtainable. Jesus said unto the Jews who believed of him, "And ye shall know the truth, and the truth shall make you free." It is reasonable now to say that the truth is knowable and this form of knowledge points out that there is more than enough evidence of truth provided and proven by the Fruit of the Spirit of God all within and around about the entire universe. Pontius's governed administration was of an arbitrary form of government. He was appointed the position in A.D.25-6 during the 12th year of Tiberius. In Luke 13:1-5 after Jesus was told of the slaughter of certain Galileans whose blood Pilate had mingled with his sacrifices, the Lord and Savior spoke to Pilate on the connection between sin and calamity. Although most Americans reluctantly states that the Jews killed Jesus, the indebt story of his death written in the King James version of the Holy Bible includes in detail that Jesus suffered, and died under the Roman's 6th procurator of Judaea; Pontius Pilate. Jesus Christ received a brutal death by law just as he prophesied would happen. (St.Matt.20:17-19)

The radicals and bigoted groups within the American society, ranges out from among hiding within the ministry of Baptist, Catholic, Methodist, Jehovah Witness, Pentecostal, the Church of Christ, Buddhism, Muslim, Protestant, Evangelical Lutheran, Presbyterian, the Church of God, etc. Ironically, hypocrites occupy and make a home in whatsoever religion that their familiar hearts have claimed themselves to be partial Christians of. Unfortunately, the proclamation of their theoretical assertions, religious allegations, and their biblical ideological declarative speeches includes persecuting and insulting other constituent members of the affiliated church which they inhabit. Those whom are insulted and persecuted by the misinformed traditional religious bigots, radicals, and extremists are commonly the main ones' whom the anointed teach righteousness and truth unto, because the anointed is known for teaching what man cannot; like peace and love.

Those who are the chosen possessors of the Spirit of Christ are appointed by God to stand bold on the foundation of God's love for all mankind. Meanwhile, the Fruit of the Spirit of Christ makes their love for God equivalently broadened in a balance of an equal portion which is made manifest unto even the bigoted radical religious societies. The greatness of their nurturing spiritual nature in life is love, and they love all of mankind especially those who religiously oppress and suppress them. In spite of how bad the oppressing hypocritical bigots may persecute them, they with a pure and forgiving heart love them too.

As deceitful as they are the extremists and radicals claims to be Christians, but they have neither the will nor the desire to humble themselves as an equal unto all who confess Jesus as their Lord and Saviour, nor are they willing to humble themselves unto all who believes that the people of the world are all One Nation under God. They fail to refrain themselves from fighting over God's name. Regardless of the name, there's only One God in heaven for all to serve. It's like they fail to see that a Rose is still a Rose no matter what name it is given to it. Only the different origin of a seed changes the name of a flower, and God created man not Satan. The Christians who walk after love, peace, and understanding while in pursuit of Happiness are followers of the original Rose which saves all from sin. Many call themselves Christians, but their defiled hearts walk after hate, war, and confusion while in pursuit of Happiness. The origin of their originality beguiles them to think that they can fulfill their own destiny by warring and working their own way into heaven. According to the creator of righteous judgments, the person who preaches and teaches like wise, dedicates their hearts to the spreading of abomination (hatred) against others. Those who think they can work their way or pay their way into heaven, gives unto themselves a false sense and an unreasonable illogical way of thinking of themselves as the actual doers of the righteous works of the Lord and Savior. They are like Satan who lies against the truth and wait to deceive.

THERE'S DESCENT PEOPLE LIVING DURING INDESCENT TIMES

Despite of the evils that one society has been embedded to think of itself or of another, the Fruit of the Spirit proves that not all people who makeup one particular society are completely evil. It's common for the innocent one's who are born and raised in such societies to be declared by worldly religious people as evil, but in reality the innocent one's are simply misunderstood. It takes the agenda of an empathetic person to understand that just as eager as the anti-social people are to worship the things that they do which creates cruelty within this malicious world, there also exist eager people who humble themselves to the idea of having a pro-social behavior towards the entire human race. Those who humbles themselves are working diligently to restore the lost whom the dogmatic image of the narrow minded radical Islamic community have coerced into believing that their unjustified dutiful acts of killing innocent bystanders and civilians are religiously justified.

The 21st century's traditional religious revolutionaries, within the dogmatic anti-social American society; are a group of narrow minded people whose greatest sin is their hatred for every human being who diligently seeks to form a peace on earth as it is in heaven. It is prudent for everyone in the entire universe to clearly understand that these haters who calls themselves American Christians does not qualify to give account for the self-made image of all individual Americans. In fact, the haters make their home in America to inhabit the support of the old American ideological laws which reduce and place the peace making American Christians under absolute despotisms. If a group of Christians support the customary acts of discriminating against those who are an affiliated member of their own religion, what more can others expect for such groups to do unto them that are not apart of their church. Under such strenuous circumstances, the evils within every radical group works to convince people to believe that they all are justified in wrongfully murdering the spiritual goodness of God's love, mercy, and grace through the hostile acts of warring against each other.

Therefore, they arrogantly spread a worldly fear unto the minds of the weak and simple babes in Christ. Bogusly, the false prophets of anti-social groups and illogical religious communities consist of radical extremists who are willing to fight indecently for their traditional religious beliefs. The foul course or pathway of their indecent desire to fight are due to their ignorance, which thirst to convince others to think that one sort of misconstrued traditional religion is better than another sort of lewd traditional religion. They claim themselves to be above all, and they play the traditional role of the oppressor who convinces many citizens today like Eve who was convinced in the beginning; to believe in viewing the tormentor's ideas as the most logical representative of the Word of God. A tormentor only represents themselves.

The eyes of the Saints residing within every corner of the earth can clearly see the leaders and followers of despotism within every society of every nation; even within their own. The Saints may view such leaders and followers as the slave masters who desire lordship and dominion during the 21st century. The overall desires of the hearts of a majority of the citizens of every nation seeks to find peace, freedom, and equality from the despotic governments and leaders like Al-Qaeda, Osama Bin-Laden, the radical anti-social American Christians, and all other extremists during this generation.

A seeker for the Kingdom of God can't find rest by devoting their faith unto false ministries which causes damage to its own members. False ministers are ignorant of their traditional religion's negligence, which creates reasons for people to have a lack of consideration for others. As long as such extremists continue living as terrorists amongst their own people, the may not ever find pureness within anything, because unto the defiled; nothing is pure. Due to the defiled hearted, such ministries refuse to preach the One True Gospel which edifies every part of the Body of Christ, because they disbelieve in conjoining together as One Nation under God indivisible with liberty and justice for all. The tarnished religious messages of all terrorists are one of the same. They all individually claim their belief in religious despotism is of God. The flawed meanings behind the despots' personified religious messages, are unclear and does not compare to the message of Christ's chosen Apostles, because the significant purpose of the dictating false messengers' hearts are distorted and bewildered.

1Corithians9:25 "And every man that striveth for the mastery is temperate in all things. Now they

do it to obtain a corruptible crown;
but we an incorruptible."

1Corithians9:26 "I therefore so run,
not as uncertainly; so fight I, not as
one that beateth the air:"

1Corithians9:27 "But I keep under
my body, and bring it into
subjection: lest that by any means,
when I have preached to others, I
myself should be a castaway."

There are corrupted members residing within all kinds of earthy
denominational religions all throughout every corner of the world. The
Holy Bible defines them as the children of the wicked one. They
religiously claim their selves to be Christians and God fearing people,
but they fight vulgarly to revile and over throw others who spiritually
profess and confess Jesus is Lord. They are misled by Satan to think they
have the authority to gather up people whom confess Jesus is Lord, and
they falsely accuse them unto God and convincingly misjudge unto
themselves that those whom they lay blame upon are the tares of the
field, which are made mentioned in the Book of St. Matthew Chapter
13.

St. Matthew 10:27 "What I tell you
in darkness, that speak ye in light:
and what ye hear in the ear , that
preach ye upon the housetops."

St. Matthew 10:28 "And fear not
them which kill the body, but are
not able to kill the soul: but rather
fear him which is able to destroy
both soul and body in hell."

Instead of doing their best to make peace amongst themselves for the sake of obeying the Lord's Commandment and grow up together with those whom they point fingers at and unrightfully blame, they serve the purpose of their father; Satan who desires for them to root up and root out the ones which they falsely accuse unto God. In their minds they believe they are fighting on the right side or the right hand of God. They falsely preach to the weak and simple in a boastful pride like manner, because they are overly confident that they are righteously following the New Commandment of God in a holy war, but they are not. Since the beginning of sin, Satan has beguiled his children to serve him until the angles in heaven come and gather out of the Kingdom all things that offend, and also gather them which do iniquity in the time of harvest, which is the end of the world. (Joel 3:10-13/St. Matt.13:36-43/Rev.14:13-20/Rev.19:19-21). The hearts of these dictating religious tyrants choose to teach their denominational religious members to devote their hearts on making unreasonable traditional sacrifices as a way of proving unto themselves that they are worshipping God. They preach and command the people of their ministry to be divided against their selves; by demanding for them to do what they themselves cannot. While tricking them into fearing individuals within the religious world, they distort the spirit of agape love with the evil spirits of envy, jealousy, and strife. As the dictating false apostles yearn to be commended and glorified by men, they praise the vain philosophies and words of deceits which becomes the cap of the motivational crown of the evil personality of every leading radical extremist of a lewd religion like Al-Qaeda and all other anti-Islamic American Christians whom are evilly provoked by a social phobia of some sort. Fearing what they don't understand, the anti-Islamic American Christians are appear to be provoked by anger to desire to carryout the evil acts of discrimination against all American Muslims.

A sin is a sin, and the sin of Al-Qaeda and the anti-Islamic American Christians share great similarities. For instance, both use unrighteous judgments against their own native people as well as against people who are strangers unto them, and both forsake their own mercy in the process. As one generation passes unto the next, the Holy Ghost persuasively has prevailed at the renewing of the minds of many to recognize the traditional religious curses which linger amongst their particular society of people. The Power of the Holy Ghost simultaneously is transforming and rehabilitating the minds of the anti-Islamic Americans, the American Christians, and the American Muslims; by giving them the ability to understand the vainness of exactly what they were traditionally taught and religiously trained to fear about one of another's position in the religious realm. Through an understanding heart, all sides now can clearly see that the oppressor among them is not fully representing the personal arbitrary side of their inward oppressed spiritual qualities and state of being a loving and peaceable people. With a sympathetic understanding they are realizing more and more during the 21st century that they cannot be controlled nor defined by any form of hereditary despotic law.

In other words, every Christian in America and those all around the world along with the Muslims are continuously emerging out of the old traditional mindset of bondage which for centuries has brought about wars and confusions between them. As the goodness of God's love mercy and grace comes out and comfort the spirit of all societies, the Power of the Holy Ghost simultaneously transforms and rehabilitates the God fearing Muslims of Islam and the God fearing American Christians; to want to work together as One Nation under the One True God, who created everything that is made.

(St. Matt.12:33-37/Gal.5:22-26/Col.3:12-17)The Fruit of the Spirit which all children of God reap and sow are proven to be that which is acceptable unto God. From out of the mouth, their hearts speaks of an unconditional love that goes beyond the unconstitutional views made by the single focus of the physical eyes of man. During the intervention of stopping the liars' tongue, the True Ordinance of God's Commandment being written in the hearts of God's children; exceeds the conditions of a religious love, and their love for God is evenly given onto all of mankind by the intercession of the Holy Spirit, which mediates unto the spirits of all who believes on the Lord and Saviour. As the gift of the Holy Spirit reveals who they serve, the Fruit of the Spirit of them indeed does prove what is acceptable unto God. Together as one Body in Christ, they've grown from being weary and are made manifest with the spiritual strength and heavenly wisdom to refuse to yield their hearts to the commandments of men. With humility, grace, and a clear conscience unto God; they are humanly capable of defining the nature of their born again behavior as a pro-socialist who loves all unlike the anti-socialists who are professional religious despisers of men.

The First Fruit of the spiritual Power of the Holy Ghost proves unto all believers, that the human race are not diverse and dissimilar because of their distinguished subtle differences like their nationality, race, sex, sexual orientation nor any other sin of the sinful flesh. As the power of this acceptable holy knowledge puts an end to the ancient aged old discriminating emotional desires of who were trained up by their ancestors to be destitute of the holy truth; the Holy Ghost Powers are putting an end to their rioting hearts and is charging and accusing all whose continuous efforts dwells on inflating despair. No two people are exactly alike, and the human race is indifferent due to the intent of their hearts. After the ancient aged old vain philosophies and the deceptive words of the Kings, parliaments, and the false prophets of the world have misjudged the Word of God for so long, the faith of most churches today are built upon corrupt religions in stony and non-fertile places. They are known by the fruits they bear. As they use the Word of God to falsely judge the conscious consciences of their neighbors and strangers alike, they fail to understand that God gave no man the power to judge the conscience of another man's spirit. While falsely accusing themselves of being without sin, they falsely accuse others of not being saved by the Blood of Jesus. Although the ears of the false prophets may hear the mouths of all whom they accuse unto God saying, that they too believe on the Lord Jesus Christ to save them, undoubtedly through unbelief; the false prophets continues to preach condemnation against the Holy Ghost by lying against the holy truth, which states that all who confess they believe on the Lord; shall be saved.

During the 21st century the people are converting and are opening up their hearts, minds, and church doors to all sinners. The liberal Muslim community and the liberal American Christians are hoping to bring understanding of their chosen missionary unto each others. Those among them who are lost, lacks the understanding of why on earth do the liberals fight for peace as a unit of one with every nation; are like those who represents the more consecutive way of thinking the worst of one of another. They think negative of every idea of creating a peaceful environment, because of what the conservative side of their communities have said and done against each others in the traditions of past times. Within the USA more people are also opening up their hearts, minds, and Church houses to all sinners. The liberal Christians invitingly are welcoming the liberal Muslims, and the liberal Muslims are invitingly welcoming the liberal Christians. Overall it's the duty of the liberals of both societies who believes in worshiping a fair nonbiased God.

As unequally yoke as most individual religious groups may compare themselves to be from one of another, they religiously are equally yoke concerning the universal Golden Rule written in St. Matt.7:12. Therefore, as all universally believe that God is love, they too must stand bold upon their faith against their own conservative counter parts whose faith spreads the disease of hatred abroad their own kind. In order for a peaceable change to come out and redirect the old rioting world ordinances, an inward change must first come from within and redevelop the hearts of an entire civilization.

Is there a civilization on the face of the earth which resembles the Lord's set example of love? Who may be able to prove that they've learned how to peacefully coexist amongst their selves without creating a desolated environment among themselves or against others? Peace and love must first be mastered within the heart of a society of people, before one society can properly draw themselves close to others of a different nationality. America has came mighty close to fitting the Gospel of Jesus Christ's set description of a peaceful Nation of different nationalities, but a fair governed united nation of One Body hasn't yet been established. The entire governing society cannot comply within the universal Golden rule which completely supports the intervention of a "Just Law" for and by the people who also suffers for the same reasons as the forefathers who hid behind a dissimulated form of conditional love.

The outline of what causes the despaired hearts within the 21st century are retraced back to groups like the anti-Islamic American Christians whose Christianity are spiritually congested by a disease known as Islamic-phobia, and their religious theoretical conclusions of the human race are much different from the pro-social American Christians. Meanwhile, in a stage of balancing out the era of wrongful thinking, the lewd religious martyrs mix their ideas through the political affairs and concerns which oversee the liberal Muslims which makes them afraid of their conservative counter parts like Al-Qaeda and Osama Ben-Laden. These two are positioning themselves in the religious world as worldly men that lie and wait to destroy the liberal mindset of every religious society which has found a sympathetic understanding of Muslims; like unfairly displaying false judgments on the Indonesians and the innocent American Muslims with the murderous anti-Islamic groups from Saudi Arabia, Taliban and Afghanistan, and Pakistan. People like Al-Qaeda and Osama Ben-Laden has coerced their own society of people to fear them and biblically think they are obligated by an old despotic religious law to fight vigorously against flesh and blood in a religious war. Simultaneously, we the liberal Christians of the world do hope the conservative groups may open up their hearts and minds to understand that they are beguiled by the unreasonable and irrational idea that God under the New Covenant of Jesus Christ; gives them a non-judgment permissive, liberal, and lenient authority to rule tyrannously with dominion over others. Our job in this is to pray and hope that God will continue providing the slackers whom lives amongst us and lacks compassion and shame, with an understanding heart of his holiness; so that their hearts like ours maybe filled with remorse.

IT'S KARMA THAT PLACES AN UNGODLY FEAR INTO THE HEARTS OF THOSE WHO SERVE GOD AND MAMMON (St. Matt.6:22-24)

Universally there's a law known as The Circle of Life Law that concludes the faith of all to believe that for every action, there's a reaction. A change is coming to the long term disadvantaged circumstances of the traditional religious believers, who inherited the traditional religious customs of the ancient despot leaders and followers' oppressive beliefs that they today may revere. As a matter of fact, there's as an up rise in the number of peoples renouncing their religious faith from the traditions of such autocrats during the 21st century. Historically, there's a traceable heroic trend of individual spiritual candidates who have emerged out of the traditional desolated environment of the world and sought to tell all the offspring's within their generation of exactly what the anointed teaches unto them; concerning the One True Gospel of Jesus Christ.

(St. Matt.10/St. Luke9)These heroic servants of the Lord's, started preaching immediately after the Lord's twelve Apostles went out into the world and preached unto all nations, baptizing people in the name of the Father, the Son, and of the Holy Ghost. (Roman.6:3-4/St.Matt28:19-20/Rev.22:13) Without ceasing, the Lord's Word's were spoken and the lost sheep's of the house of Israel heard them saying, "The Kingdom of heaven is at hand." Out of the many lost sheep's that have heard the preaching of the Kingdom of God, only a few were called upon by the Word of Jesus. Their hearts weren't reprobate, and their ears weren't deafened to understand the truth. The few who are chosen and are given the power of the twelve disciples of Jesus Christ, does not incite nor provoke rage and war, but they motivate love, understanding, and peace on earth as it is in heaven. With that power they too practice going out from house to house and city to city preaching the Kingdom of God. The Lord gave them the power and the authority over the devils to cast out unclean spirits. Not as a poltergeist or a spellbound exorcism, but casting out unclean spirits are done by spiritually self examining and comparing our individual self with the fruit of the Spirit of God. By the nurturing nature of spiritually comparing ourselves, we speak life unto ourselves through the proper usage of the Word of God by faith and remove the things about us that worketh death unto our souls.

Like Apostle Paul; a Roman Statesman named Cicero and the 16th President of the United States of America whose sure name was Abraham Lincoln, continuously provided the basic motivational pattern of teaching spiritual peace and justice. Even long after the departure of their physical lives on earth, their spiritual teachings of Christ lives on. Most conservatives and misguided traditional religious Americans and non-Americans of the 21st century knows not God nor none of the three individuals mentioned, but they are religiously trained by the reverence of the ancient churches which seeks dominion; to charge peace makers unto God. One reason for them blaming and falsely accusing the peacemakers unto God is to incite a holy war against them, in hopes of descending God from heaven. (St. Matt3:16-17/Lk3:21-23/St. John1:32-33)

Like Apostle Paul, Abraham Lincoln changed the law of despotisms for ever. After he campaigned for peace as an electoral body of one and won the Presidential seat by the vote of a majority, the constitutional right for all people living in America changed the political governing rule of America's most irrational despotic laws forever. When he ran for office, he campaigned for political fairness and equality. He suggested for all white Americans to understand the error in the dead deed of being brute slave masters of black people. In all fairness the season of slavery changed along with the converted hearts of a majority whom agreed to abolish slavery. That's how the 16th United States Presidential election was won, and that's what started the beginning era within America History where equality was worth voting for.

During his time in office as the USA's 16th President, between March 1861 and his assassination in April 1865 he elaborated on Cicero's spiritual perception of the universal law of reasoning in his own special way. With the understanding of the Lord's purpose, his spirit and the spirit of many white Americans converted before, during, and after his

236

campaign trail. The beginning era of the USA's reformed governing laws legally changed as the citizens grew to believe they all were one nation under God. Through the unity of one faith and one belief of One God, the white American voters were enabled by the prevailing standards of the Spirit of the Holy Ghost to vote for a change of policy and rule of law which strengthened the faith of both the whites and the blacks and all others who are of a different religion, nationality, sex, and creed.

In 1892 the American Nation adopted the Pledge of Allegiance which was composed by Francis Bellamy, as an oath of loyalty to the USA's national flag and to the republic American government. Within it all, the American people with the Lord, converted the Monarchy form of government into a Republic Governing body. The word republic also refers to a country which has an elective form of government. During the 19th century in America, the entire idea of the expressed word "republic" is linked with the perception of a Democratic Republic, where the voting aged American citizens of all races as a whole; may exercise powers over their elected leaders through lobbying, and other unjust processes besides the inclusion of a fair election.

The down side for the American citizens, whom expect the American militants to help other countries to have a fair voting system in place, is recognizing that their own system is manipulated by the liberty of the rich lobbying overseers. If a USA President is elected with a group of stinking rich deceptive lobbyists, lobbying monies for their campaign to gain more votes; in the end the President's control in powers for certainty will be coerced. All glory is to God that the 44th President of the United States of America declined most of every lobbyists' offer of supporting his campaign, because as a circle of life the lobbyists again would've gain the gratitude of karma which receives the credit for the guilt of the beguiled whose lack of humility afterwards is forcefully taken away from the elected one's modesty; as a service fee to the lobbyists. Money is the root of all evil that resides within such a government. It is common for all to know and understand that the voters of a Democratic-Republic government have some control over their government.

For example, in America if the voters are not pleased with the performance of their elected leaders, they can either place a rule in order where the President can be voted out as of an impeachment or the citizens can refuse to re-elect that same leader. Hypocritically with that form of knowledge, both the religious tyrant leaders and the Christian peacemakers by all means are at war amongst themselves. They use the influential side of their debating characteristics to incite more votes by exploiting their favorite candidates' interests. Either they desire to love the most despised and the lowly and desire to use their position in power to create peace for them or they yearn to hate and mistreat the most despised and lowly minority groups. In such case, instead of peace; they work to create war against them.

Such campaign stratagems are identical to the same purpose of President Lincoln's campaign promises, which includes the entirety of all who either will vote for or against the incitement of peace, freedom, equality, and justice for all. This has been done through the invention of two American parties who historically are separated by the logic of their interests. A house that is divided against itself will not stand, and the Republic Party, whom loves to incite peace for themselves which befit their interests of being characterized as the supreme race of people in America over all other races in the beginning creating a desolated environment. As times have changed so have their interests.

Now that the voices of the American minorities have been heard crying out to God for peace, justice, equality, and freedom most of the conservative rebellious republic voters of the 21st century have taken it upon themselves to accuse the liberal minority for inciting a riot. The moderate Republicans and moderate Democrats fear that their political opponents, the liberals; will do unto them the same bad evilly implied hideous things which they have done. The narrow minds of the conservatives are misled to think that they must rule and have physical and religious dominion over the minority until the Lord returns from the heavens on a cloud. Through an unreasonable fear, the conservative rebellious traditional religious republicans and democrats are inciting more fears unto the hearts of their extended moderate counterparts.

The moderate Americans are seen to be those who desire peace and equality for all races, but are coerced into being afraid of loosing their souls and political powers to their opponents; the liberals. The faith of them is tossed to and fro wavers like a leaf in the wind.

They don't see the liberals as a peaceable God fearing group of people, instead; they see them as demons who are trying to change the ordinance of their faith. The Holy Truth reveals who and what the liberals really are unto God as it makes public the path which they've walked all throughout American History. Even the lost can see the Holy Truth which makes known unto them that the liberal groups in America and in all other countries have fought and continues to peacefully fight for the human and civil rights of themselves and others. Simultaneously, the blind and deaf can only see and hear of the path which the majority groups have walked all throughout World History, which includes them using violence to free themselves from despotism as well as to forcefully influence others to be overly whelmed by the laws of despotism.. All ears which hear the Holy Truth can understand how the majority of moderate groups have fought to keep, and maintain human and civil rights in the land of the free and the home of the brave all to their selves. During the private sector of their lives, the majority of the most American moderate society has traditionally refused to equally share the benefits of being an extended American family with all other races which either legally migrated or were born in America.

Most conservative groups in the USA are misleading their off-springs to sociably think that the minority will unlawfully use the legal system to give themselves the right to war against them within the governing aspect of life. In reality, to conclude the spiritual aspect of it all; the minority only have used the legal system to reform the laws which for centuries have kept them from being treated as an equal in America. Evidently, the minority realizes that two wrongs don't make a right. But in order to surpass the things which we as Americans fear, we all are required to seek for the Holy Truth in every predictable and unpredictable matter. There's no lie residing in the Holy Truth.

The idea of the Romans' during the Middle Ages, referred to the theoretical idea "That a government which governs least, governs best." To keep balance of this theory, during the 21st century the preexisting republic and democratic republic governments attempts to maintain the old regulations of the old Monarchy government. Some people think that by keeping monarchy in play during the newer generation of today's society will preserve certain particular freedoms and equality for the gene pool of a certain particular heritage of people. During the 21st century the American governing laws still acknowledge a separation in Church and State, but due to an imperfect system; the ideas of the Church and State always managed to intertwine together and cause an endless degree of chaos, conflict, and confusion. The twinning of the two causes worldly sorrows and misery, because the Law of the Lord being new; doesn't agree with the old.

DOES "-CRACY" DRIVE PEOPLE CRAZY OR IS ITS TERMS JUST MISUNDERSTOOD?

> **1Corinthians9:25 "And every man that striveth for the mastery is temperate in all things. Now they do it to obtain a corruptible crown; buy we an incorruptible crown."**

-Cracy is the word that means the state of having a combined form of government. It is prudent for all to understand that the beginning formation of the laws of the American land was dogmatically composed by the vexations of the worldly hearts which desired both, earthy rewards and heavenly rewards. The doctrinaire of manmade laws which befitted the vexed hearts of the composers was made without the empathetic compassion of the Holy Ghost. The worldly leaders whom composed the foundation of the laws of the land for profit were being excessively and offensively positive in laying down delusional principles to express the opinions of a dictator or an authoritative hereditary clique. Their laws proposed many carnal-minded dispositions as a final written settlement for all to follow, although their deluded religious principles and theories were unclear and difficult to understand.

It is evident that the final settled written legal document of the earlier composed laws of the all the lands consists of irrational religious theories and principles that are surrounded by the religious realm's legal but unlawful words and phrases that befit the traditional religious concept of classifying one kind of idea that suggests for all law abiding citizens on earth to believe that the laws' original composers' theories are identical of the Lord's Divine order of righteousness and truth. Scriptures from the Holy Bible text were deprived and placed into manmade laws to help support the despot men-pleasers, Gain Sayers, and the subverted who coerces or tricks many people into believing their irreligiously composed laws and ideas supports the grounds of holiness and aren't defective. While undermining the independent value of the spiritual morals, allegiance, or faith of all of God's citizens on earth, the laws of the land were composed by people who ironically thought God gave them the authority to compare and judge their composed religious laws by their own corrupt perceptions of the written scriptures of the Holy Bible text; to forcefully beguile many into being easily coerced into following or compromising with the old traditional religious realms' idea of maintaining a new world order.

Without spiritually analyzing spiritual things, the main intent of the despot leaders of the 21st century, is to make the old traditional religious laws appear to be godly and righteous. Within their empty ideas of reality, resides an unrighteous and untruthful idea of promoting goodness through the acts of being evil. As a figure of speech, the defense of their political views of promoting goodness through the acts of being evil towards a majority of Americans are of a metaphor or an simile of the quality of what goodness consist of. Regardless of the symbolic image of their views, they place their well orchestrated ministries under false pretense which deludes the godly acts of the Lord God's righteous judgments which appear to be without love, mercy, grace, and understanding. This sort of deluded view also was the leading formation of the earlier unawares' composed religion, which later was transferred unto many members which started up all sorts of different congregations. The old abstract theories of mankind, gradually have became the frame work of the composed laws and policies, which forcefully impose the will and opinions of the wicked one who since the beginning of sin, has sought to hold complete autocratic and oppressive control as the Prince of the world. In a domineering manner, the old religions' dictatorial stereotypes suppresses the browbeaten and broken inner-spirits of the oppressed, and such domination symbolize the overbearing infrastructure of the old unreasonable religious beliefs which false prophets and false ministers are coerced and beguiled to teach men to believe in. Such tyrannous religions request for all to make an unreasonable sacrifice of their selves and be unbelieving of the upright integrity of the Lord. Through unbelief their lies against the Holy Ghost are an abomination, which changes the righteous and holy view of God's Divine ordinance of law and this is an unforgivable sin.

For centuries, this chain of evil genocide has been pursued by the Holy Ghost for all mankind alike; to spiritually change the evil methods of the prior composed manmade laws thereof, and to stop the liar's tongue. The main reason for the up rise of hostility within the desolated environment of the traditional religious martyrs of the world is due to them refusing to renounce the tyranny within their traditional religious beliefs. Tyranny is the spot and the blemish of their evil religious ways of suppressing and oppressing other citizens of God under the heavens. While commending and edifying their selves, they misuse the Word of God to kill the spiritual hearts of those which are oppressed by their religion. It is not good for these martyrs to traditionally worship religion as an idol god. They have neither compassion nor remorse in their hearts due to their traditional diverse different perception of what the holiest of holy signifies. This explains their religious reasoning's for having such a profound feeling of disapproval of others. They live under the tutoring of religions which use the Word of God to give themselves reasons to cause strife. They religiously work to befit the interpretations of the more subtil creature than any beast of the field which God has made; "Satan." Satan's followers have misled the minds of the simple and weak since the first sin was committed upon the earth, and the oldness of his spoiled methods makes it harder for the human race to distinguish or understand him than any other beast of the field which God had made.

Meanwhile, those who eat of the tree of life gains an understanding and a compassionate heart, and they are spiritually strengthened to be more confident to step out on faith to publically make known of what their faith in God personally means to them; instead of following the leadership of a dictator. They stand boldly on the Word of God as they oppose the tyrannous methods and beliefs of the earlier religious composers of the governing laws of the land. They oppose the teachings of the religious martyrs of the old traditional religious way of living, because they are aware that religious martyrs misjudge them and misjudge the law of God.

The traditional religious martyrs are dogmatically willing to die while defending their double-minded customary faith; like the ruler of Libya name Moammar Gadhafi. For example, so they say in A.D. 2011, country by country the world consisted of billions of protestors who were rising up against the despotisms of their own government. There was a recording shown on all the news broadcasting channels of Libyan civilians undergoing an airstrike by their own military, and other videos revealed a massive group of unarmed protestors being shot by the police as they gather in the streets.

In America the army and police haven't been sent out to kill any of the thousands of peaceful American protesters in Madison, WI, but symbolically speaking; the American law of the state seemed too had been unfairly used against them, as it was carefully orchestrated to hold the American protestors hostage in the form of a threat; while a police warrant was issued to capture and hold the 14 democrat members who were accused of leaving the state to stall Wisconsin Gov. Scott Walker's controversial budget bill. Publically it was said, that if they didn't return and vote on the measure of Gov. Scott Walker's proposal; a layoff notice would be sent out to 1,500 public employees. Whether the layoff is a threat or a promise, more than likely, if the Governor get enough votes a majority of the 1,500 employees are guaranteed under Gov. Walker's proposal to loose their American right to compromise as American workers. It isn't proven, but it is honestly believed; that a majority of the 1,500 employees are apart of the peaceful protest which disapproves of Gov. Walker's proposal, because it breeches their support of the American workers' Union Rights.

The religious martyrs are blemished and spoiled by the imperfect vain traditional religious philosophies and words of deceits, which gives them an illogical sense of sincerity or naturalness concerning them having a religious conviction within the beliefs of their own bellies. Their religious faith causes them to physically fight against any given liberal-minded person of peace, because they think the intentions of the liberal-minded are enemies against God or enemies against them. In reality the liberals are against any form of despotism; whether foreign or domestic. They are apart of a moderate society whom are not in favor of the conditional standards and principles of the despotic traditional religious stipulations of the 21st century nor do they agree with the past dictatorial religious beliefs of the world.

As the martyrs defend their religious beliefs, they automatically suggest that all that is not in agreement with their religions' tyrannous ways are evil and/or are devil worshipers. The martyrs suggest that a hypocrite and a blasphemer against the Holy Ghost, is every liberal-minded person who renounces the tyranny of their unreasonable traditional religious beliefs or customs. The expertise training of the religious martyrs of the 21st century proposes that a person should be willing to sufferer for the cause of whatsoever they as a martyr believe. A martyr also thinks that if a person abandon, relinquish, renounce, or give up on the traditional religious faith of a martyr and still profess publically that they believe that they are working for God, their rejection of a martyrs' faith, custom, and belief is evident enough for them to religiously say that they are a hypocrite.

According to the old wives' fables and religious doctrines of the despotic martyrs, all who disbelieve in the tradition religious martyrs' seductive motive for vengefully fighting for the Lord God are of the world, and all who believes in violently fighting with diligence from the heart for their religion; shall be saved. The irony of these religious martyrs, who still support the old world order of religious laws, is how their contradiction in terms can't grasp the true concept of the Word of God, which was sent into the world by God to save all who believes on his only begotten Son. Therefore, because of their own insincerities, they will never follow after the Lord's loving and forgiving examples, because the truth of God's Divine Order of Law is hidden from these particular religious martyrs' carnal minds.

THEORETICAL CONCLUSION

In spite of the continuous existence of America's unlawful laws of evil genocides, the ideas of a majority of American peace makers, during today's generation have become as ONE electoral Body in Christ. No longer does the majority rule the world tyrannously, because no longer are the mindsets of the minority are set to remain silent. No longer are the minority spiritually divided against themselves, because the coercions of many past circumstantial acts and historical events haven't the control in powers as it once had. More Americans are now directing their attention towards the same mysterious flaws of the oldness of the manmade letters which spread hatred abroad; for the sake of reproving, reproaching, and rebuking such flaws.

The Saints are marching into the 21st century life style, and they are spiritually armed with the ability to compare the spiritual things of God with the spiritual things which they find residing within the manmade laws of all the lands. After being led deeply into a desolated environment for so long, many minds are turned reprobate and are comfortable living by the spirit of bondage and disobedience. Meanwhile, others acknowledge their religious rights to freely believe that they are freed from the yokes of bondage or the obligation of saving themselves under the terms of the sect of the Pharisees law and the Old Law of Moses. They understand that Jesus Christ paid the ultimate price which released them from the obligation of working their way into Heaven. After being freed by the anointing teachings of the Holy Ghost, the true discerners of the Spirit, spiritually recognizes their religious liberties exceeds beyond that which the descendants of the earlier despotic society are willing to allow. In America the Christians recognize their freedoms are respectfully defined as the freedom of choice; in their pursuit of happiness on earthy. By faith, those who truly recognize their liberties are more spiritually strengthened and are cautious to not eagerly or impatiently vote for that which inwardly disagrees with the new spiritual Commandments of God that are written in their individual hearts. In every aspect of life, the Lord's children are watchful as they rebuke the evils of their own hearts which envy, strife, and spread hatred. They survive in the state of being an agape lover of men, knowing that all fall short to sin; without accusing another live soul unto God or desiring to cause any to suffer.

The Fruit of the Spirit of Righteousness is manifesting the end of the works of the flesh unto the whole world, and the living witnesses; humbly understands why they as the Saints of this present day of age must humble themselves more with an understanding heart of the true factoring nature of life, which concludes no man alive lives without sin. With that knowledge all are urged to patiently learn to live without speaking down on another person's dignity like the false prophets of the world and the manmade ministers who hypocritically talk down on people and yet do the same things. It's time to reconcile and repent unto the Lord.

Chapter 7 YES WE CAN!

"All things are possible though Christ Jesus"

Many traditional religions practically disbelieve in intermixing one sort of denominational relationship with another sort. It's unlawful to them for people who believe that God's only begotten Son died on the Cross and paid the ultimate price to save them from sin to twain together with someone outside of their denomination. In spite of them sharing common interests in the Lord, such practices unto them are religiously prohibited. It's not for certain whether or not the losers of the 2009 U.S.A Presidential election or a certain 2009 American beauty pageant participant yet understands why they seem to have gained less votes of the majority. It is evident that they attempted to defend the American traditional martyr's ideas and concepts of what is good for this generation. Many dogmatic American politicians act like the regular citizens of America have not yet perceived an understanding of the errors of what the American traditional religious martyrs inhumanely does or says to the Spirit of mankind, because they still are defending the old perverse disputing of endless genealogies. Such disputing between mankind minister unanswered questions; rather than endowing godly edifications one of another by their common interests for the better good in faith. (1Tim.1:4) Some regular American citizens actually are misled to think that they will make it to heaven for assertively standing up for their ancestors' religious quests and beliefs, and others think they will inherit the Kingdom of Heaven, because of what their last names are.

Although a religious person during the 21st century is able to recite scriptures by the oldness of its letter, it's not for certain if they understand whereof they affirm their interpreted beliefs. Some martyrs affirm their interpretations of the Holy Scriptures on the traditions which they are accustomed thereof. Therefore, the hearts of a majority of all countrymen of every nation during the 21st century are pledging resistance against every sort of misguided martyr's ideological concept of the Holy Scriptures. The true Christians who desire to resist the temptations of the old scorners of men are able to boldly confess the truth of man's imperfections as imperfect persons themselves. In so doing, they desire not to be commended by man; but by the Lord God, and they desire to not have worldly lordship or dominion over any man. They desire to live in love and in peace with all mankind with a clear conscience unto the Lord God.

Within the traditional religious realm not only do the religious martyrs, men-pleasers, gainsayers, and the subverted; speaks evilly without compassion against the dignities of others, but they've attempted to continue the Sadducee's, Pharisees', and Scribes' regulated political policies or traditional religious teachings to rule tyrannously and to have dominion over whom they speak evil of. The traditional religious martyrs whom can't affirm their interpreted religious beliefs, lacks the desire to restrain themselves from such dishonorable roles, because they fail to understand that their laws and traditional religious teachings are what led certain Jews to crucify the Lord and Savor; Christ Jesus.

All who desire to obtain the Tree of Life by the fear of God seeks for Heavenly Wisdom! Every seeker of Wisdom finds her, and she advises them individually to not envy the oppressor and to not choose any of his ways. (Prov.3:25-35) The heart of those who find her and humble themselves unto her are converted to be like a child to their mother, and gains the Lord's heavenly understandings which explains the rarely understood story of the crucifixion of Jesus Christ. Wisdom also clarifies in plain words which hand the Kingdom of God exists in.

As the "Anointed One" teaches what man cannot, the seekers of heavenly Wisdom gain the spiritual understandings of God's significant purpose of sending Christ into the world, which was to save all from the same evil sin that was committed by the people of past generations as well as today's generation. Due to the sin of unbelief on the Power of God and the sin of Blasphemy against the Holy Ghost, Christ died to save all who are placed into a state of bondage. He didn't die to make anyone feel obligated to live in an ungodly fear of the Power of God under the religious law of the Pharisees and Sadducees. He decided to die in order to kill and stop those laws which coercively corrupt the mindset of those who religiously beseech to physically kill those of them who the old law religiously despises.

Jesus understood the fullness of the mercy and grace of God the Father. (Ex.32/Deut.4:20/Deut.9/Ps.106:45-46/Jonah3:9-10) Even the Lord God repented of the very thought of allowing the heat of his wrath to increase to the point of considering to destroy his people who corrupt themselves. In accordance to the multitude depth of his mercy, he also require unto all under the New Law for all who believes on him to also repent of the old traditional religious law of the Jews which once coerced people to persecute, crucify, and kill one of another. Such acts within today's society symbolically represent how the martyrs still use the same old law which mistreats and misjudge the Body of Christ.

Although the followers of Christ are set apart from the Old Testament by the New Testament, the simulations of the traditions of the old religious law still exists in the hearts of traditional religious people of the 21st century. Their God forsaken way of worshipping, resembles the Pharisee and the Sadducees of past time; as a pattern of a perfect replication. Like those of the past, they today have not the power to kill the Soul of Jesus Christ which lives in the sinners of all whom are hated by the followers of the Old Law.

Americans and non-Americans alike, who deny the heavenly truth tends to divide people up as to separate; by using religion and politics to demonize and persecute citizens of their own country as well as other countrymen whom also are flesh of their flesh. Like the despot leaders of foreign countries during the 21st century, the American despot leaders don't totally agree with a majority of the American citizens' social and religious outlooks of life. Like the Taliban and Pakistan leaders, certain American despots' perception of the Holy Scriptures leads them to think the Spirit of God is leading them to viciously fight an unholy war and this unsanctioned thought has filled their hearts with vengeance, while the desires of their own bellies influence them to afflict pain and sufferings against their neighbors and strangers alike.

Certain people of the world will not ever understand which vexed hearted manmade laws lacks godly compassion or heavenly understanding, and they desire to continue striving vengefully as religious scorners. They are unwilling to step out on faith to hear and do the true instructions of the Lord God's Greatest Commandment. Instead, they'd rather rebuke the voice of the Lord God, which says there's no dissimulation in love. God tells them to do well, but if doing good means they must humble themselves to be as weak as the weakest person they meet or to renounce their dictating traditional religious rituals and beliefs; they'd rather die, because they are coerced to think their salvation is given unto them through their religion. Therefore, in their minds they think their religion is what they are fighting for and they are willing to die for the Lord. They religiously search for reasons to injure or condemn a person who publically rebukes or renounces their despot traditional religious ways of thinking. They desire to hinder all others who desire to be set free from their religiously claimed livelihood. In so doing, they actually think that they indeed are persecuting others the same way in which the Lord God works when he convicts the spirit of all whom are born again. In reality, they don't convict the Spirit of any man to revive them in the way of the Lord, but they do indeed condemn them.

For the love of God, many who have been oppressed by the old traditional religious rule of laws; are humbly converting into an empathetic group of forgiving hearts. Most American citizens today recognizes how they spiritually joined together in a fair attempt to use the presidential election of 2008 to break away from the past despot religious politics, but they still are facing those of them whose theoretical tyrannous ideas requests for some to abusively misuse the powers of America's legislative governing system unlawfully. The American people are not ignorant, and they are very aware of how the politically religious rich lobbyists intervenes with the pure intentions of the today's establishments, which originally were designed to help the people on Wall Street and Main Street.

Through the eyes of many Main Street Christians, the money hungry lobbyists are thought to be all who use the wisdom of the world to redesign the innocent laws of God to incorporate the agendas of the original worldly despots. The 21st century despots of the world are defined by them to be those who are accustomed to connecting their business mindset with religion in a dictatorial way. The Main Street Christians views the acts of them to be evilly incorporated, as they see them despotically attempting to run the big business industries for the sake of gaining and maintaining control and powers psychologically and economically; to have dominion over all other citizens. Certain rich lobbyists in America are compared to the scribes and the Pharisees by many citizens on Main Street, who compares spiritual things with spiritual. Within the comparison thereof, the poor Christians on Main Street are witnessing how the rich American lobbyists live as hypocrites and sit in the synagogues of Wall Street; as if the streets of Wall Street represents unto them to be Moses' seat. Regardless of the defense made by the rich lobbyists' who claims their techniques are rooted under Capitalism, the works which they do in comparison to the Spirit; are believed by many Main Street Christians to be intentionally done to psychologically undermine the greatest majority of all minorities. Meanwhile, they believe that the rich lobbyists are working to redesign the laws of the land to broaden their rich appearances to be pure hearted. On the political stand point of life, many Main Street voters think that the rich lobbyists are helping themselves to the richest dreams made in America, while disregarding them on Main Street as if they and their Christian families are unworthy to obtain righteous judgments under their manmade laws.

The rich American despotic religious rulers have subconsciously advertised themselves to be in agreement as far as them politically using unreasonable premium costs and outrageous interest rates to make themselves richer and the poor poorer. Their reformations of the original American's order of law have led many middle class American citizens into bankruptcy. Many big banks and insurance companies are run by tyrannous people who desire to disallow the small business owners and individual seniors and children of all nationalities an affordable interest rate or a fair and reasonably priced consumer policy. In such case they make it impossible for most to either sell or buy their products and services. Some may call such acts free enterprise in America, but others call it Capitalism. (See also the 2009 Rated R movie called "CAPITALISM A LOVE STORY.") Of course you may find some humor in it, but be not deceived; the principle part of narration of the story given by Michael Moore is real. Within this film you'll find that he investigates the money-making meltdown and the bailouts of confidential and private financial institutions. During the time of a crisis, some people feel like they must laugh to keep from crying. While watching this movie for yourself, consider this factor while being entertained.

The despot leaders of America know that all American citizens depends on banks and insurance companies to survive during their daily walk of life, and much evidence has been revealed to conclude that they have misused that form of knowledge to help the big business industry; to corruptibly turn their fair consumer policies into another form of unfair political lobbyism against the consumers on Main Street. The evidence of the stratagems that has been presented by and through lobbyism, have convinced many who have been scammed by an entrepreneur business in America, which follows the ordinances of certain corrupt laws to legally make an illegal pyramid; to conclude that many CEO's within some of America's most prestigious Insurance Companies and banks are guilty of doing the same things against the American middle and low class consumers who makes between or under $40 thousand to a $100 thousand or less annually.

Despite of all the individual complaints that are made by the American citizens who have suffered at the hands of certain of these big business industries over the last past decade, the rich American despot political leaders of these corrupt organizations are able to hide behind certain made-up laws of the land, which unlawfully made the big banks and insurance companies' tyrannous policies legal. Meanwhile, the American despot authoritarians make all citizens who complain about being treated unfairly by such legal but unlawful policies of such big businesses; appear to be at fault of their own disadvantages.

WHAT DRIVES THE TEA PARTY MEMBERS in A.D. 2010?

The Tea Party members are a group of Republicans who reportedly accused the original Republicans for being too liberal. If they are too liberal, then ask yourself; who are these people who supports the despotic American laws of the land that makes it legal for the Insurance Companies to drop the middle and low class American tax paying citizens' insurance coverage's; if they have a pre-existing health condition. If that's called being too liberal then what is the new definition of being conservative? How else can an American citizen receive heath care in America if the manipulated authorities' within America's government are coerced ironically by greedy lobbyists, whose hands are in the tea pot of money laundering insurance companies? How do they live with themselves, knowing that their greed for power and money deflect and turn aside the life of newborn babies who were born in America with a birth defect or medical issue?

Maybe those who politically work without compassion for the people, are in love with money and also loves the ideological pleasures of what having money may bring unto them more than they love God. Such persons could care less about the American Dream or the children's birth defects and medical issues. Therefore, the question still stands. Who are they who have improperly used the laws of the land to manipulate and corrupt the medical system? Fortunately, the innocent babies who can't speak nor fight for their own hereditary and arbitrary issues have God in heaven on their side. During the 21st century, it is highly believed that God sent his Word of Truth with a clear understanding through the hearts of his servants and Saints of all nations whose mouths speaks to spiritually advise, warn, and urge all people to vote and practice doing the things which brings peace, justice, liberty, and equality unto them by a gentle reproof.

THE FIGHT OF THE RESISTANCE IS INJUSTICE INDEED

The Lord's freedom, justice, and peace are the universal moral fibers of a successful society. As Satan coerce his warriors to believe that their confrontational fighting and slaughtering is justified as a manner of fighting a resistance, God is making ways for the Holy Spirit to reveal unto all during the year A.D. 2010 of the wiles of Satan. As an illustration, the Palestinians' government which has been accused of seeking to slaughter the Israelis is declared by many Christians to not be a fight of the resistance as the government has proclaimed, but it is injustice indeed. Everyone around the world wants to live free of despotism, but not all are free.

The key message of the messenger within this matter is simple. In order for the Americans to solemnly or soberly say or teach unto the Palestinians and the Israelis how to end their conflicting wars of terror, they must first recognize, identify, and stop the inner-fighting that presently goes on among their selves. The talk of peace coming from America must be easily received and given from within the American government unto all American citizens equally in order for the talk of peace from American leaders to hold a solid factor of meaning. (St. Matt.7:1-6)

The joy of helping those who cannot defend nor help themselves affects all classes of people and of every race. It's not yet fully understood why so many American voters are so naïve. Often, they are tossed to and fro by every sort of doctrine that doesn't co-aside with the Doctrine of Christ. Maybe the reason being is associated with the unconverted vain hearts of those who are willing to politically vote for the same biased traditional religious interests which either creates new or supports the old preexisting malicious policies and laws. Was it not made obvious who support laws that manipulate the liberties of the American justice system, when the congressional seat of the House of Congress was on a standstill predicament after the November election of 2010? Those whose hearts bleed with greed are desirous to protect the profound unreasonable performances of the big business industries which illogically threatens the entire secure economic stature of the American Nation.

The insight of Medicaid and Medicare is designed to help pay for the medical expenses of the poor working class American population, but ironically the nature of the original American base of Capitalism is rooted into two parts. One part the original entrepreneurial mindset determines "How much money can the government or an individual make off of poor American citizens," and the other part determines "How much money can the lobbying political representatives of the government or an individual industrialist save for themselves; by cheating the poor working class Americans who are in financial need." This is neither a black nor white issue nor a gay and straight issue, but it is an issue about good vs. evil; concerning the ideas of the rich Americans vs. the poor.

The end result of despotisms within the beginning structuring of the American government wasn't thoroughly thought through, and the miscalculations thereof has caused a massive majority of Caucasian Americans to become equally poor to the descendants of the inhabited African American slaves. Like a chain reaction of American despotism and greed, most white children and senior citizens in the 21st century are suffering right along with every other race of people. The traditional slavery motto in America states that "If man doesn't work, man doesn't eat." The poor American workers may work hard from sun up until sun down and hold two jobs for the rest of their lives, but in the end of their lifetime on earth they find themselves to be forever learning to build a franchise for the 1-5% of rich Americans, but never able to own one for their selves. This is the final result of most working class Americans, whose ancestors historically are noted for fighting for the riches of this world. Some use the term of investment as a route out of poverty, but after certain politicians corrupted the investment market; the illegal pyramid was politically masked.

More American people have awakened out of sleep during the 21st century and many recognize how the spirit within the Republican Party is dividing between its own members. Most traditional religious martyrs likes to follow the original American way of politicizes life instead of prioritizing life. Although certain filthy rich republicans preach about helping those who are in need, their actions are made manifest by the Fruit of the Spirit to be selfish. Their spirit does not co-aside with the practice of the modern born again American Christians' faith. The desires of the modern day Christians who preach about helping the needy, actual does help them without allowing greed to conquer the intent of their hearts.

THIS IS NOT PRESIDENT OBAMA'S WAR! THIS IS THE POLITICAL AMERICAN'S WARRING AGAINST THEIRSELVES!

In 2009 A.D, Barak Obama became the first black biracial elected Democratic American President. This man was unanimously elected the 44th President of the USA, and he inherited a political nation which indivisibly sarcastically speaking, was dividedly failing and falling apart economically and socially. Victoriously, President Obama won the election by more than 10 million extra votes than that of the Republic supporters who filled the campaign trail with the unethical past ideas which helped approximately 1-5% of wealthy Americans in gaining and maintaining control in money and power byway of using the same technique and methods which drove the American economy into debt. Evidently, 90-95% of the voting American population were uninspired by the hearts of the Republic Party members. Controversially the interests of the Republicans were against the interests of over 10 million civilians who publically stood against the Republicans' traditional methods. These civilians voted for the candidate who was supported the all time American Dream of Unity, Peace, and Justice for All! For this cause, many Republic voters turned into Obama supports at the 2008 Presidential election voting poll.

The Republic Party confessed publically during their entire campaign on live TV, that they thrived to uphold the same standards which many voting Americans believed had domestically controlled the American population and foreign citizens for the last failing decade. The Obama supporters were a group of American people of every race and of all sorts of denominational religions known in America. They united as one unit under the heavens; in an attempt to over turn the American Nations' legendary views of democracy. The election was won by the maximum number of supporters who chose to reproach the evil legacy of genocide head-on. The response to the winning number of electors who voted for President Obama wasn't as a display of racial despair or a radical notion, but it was done by the American people as a public display of desiring righteous order to be distributed unto all Americans in the terms of fairness and truth. In the end of it all the racial barrier for the white American Presidency was destroyed by a unique strategy of "a rich man verse poor man" during the era when the poor sought for a political refuge which made sense.

Although some people may come unto the knowledge of God they still desire to keep unlawful and unjust rules of laws in tact. The Lord God however will continue to gracefully protect his own just as he always has. President Obama maybe doing the best he can to reform the detectable despotic American laws which causes desolation, but he's not God. Americans should stop overly expecting President Barak Obama to perform and do that which only God can. He can't change the hearts and minds of his opponents, but he can stand up for what he and his supporters believe in. Over all, everyone who is totally against despotism has a voice and they have the right and it is their duty under the Declaration of Independence to use their voices as a tool in efforts to toss out such Un-American, non-patriotic, and unconstitutional regimes and make available new safeguards for their present and future security. Although we Americans may confess that our faith is on the Lord we all should pray that the main desires of our government leaders is to allow God to use them to do well by and for all American citizens (the Unjust Sinners & the Just Saints). Like all whom are born again Christians whose sins are forgiven, President Obama is just a man who's trying to make a spiritual change for all American citizens. We know that with God all things are possible, but without him; man can't do anything alone.

Apparently President Obama is wise enough to understand, that any house which is divided against it's self shall not stand. Many Americans saw him live on CNN News after winning the election, entering a plea to all whom maybe against him to stand with him during this challenging moment of America's new history; to help him to help the entire American population out of an economic recession, which resembled America's historical Great Depression. He spoke openly and clearly to the Republic Party members who willingly divided themselves. One side of them appeared to the American people on Main Street to be of a more traditional conservative sect and the other side a more moderate or liberal sect, but yet all were of the same Republic Party.

Some may ask why the Republic Party separated. They seemed too had been doing better as one body rather than two separate bodies as they attempted to separate the interests of the American people whom President Obama represented during his campaign. Within all that the Republic Party did, in A.D. 2010 right before the Americans' General Election for the House of Representative took par in November, apparently it was very possible for all the regular voters on Main Street to understand how the Republic Party members who attempted to divide the Democrats, ended up creating chaos and division among themselves. Some may distinguish themselves as being conservative Republicans and others, as moderate or liberal Republicans. The entire nation can see how the interests of certain Tea Party Republicans who were made up of a group of conservatives disagree with the moderate and more liberal minded American citizens.

President Elect Barak Obama spoke clearly with great sincerity during his presidential campaign, without being either hypocritical or ignorant of the conflicting truths concerning the American issues and struggles of the 21st century. He refused to lie against the truth of the hereditary and arbitrary issues of his own life struggles, which most conservatives stereotypically attempted to use to distort his image as a natural born biracial American citizen. He spoke very diligently from time to time about how he and his family managed to survive during the times when the dream of there ever being an Afro-American President; was viewed as an ideal joke. He constructively spoke about desiring to be an American leader of peace and change.

He professed publically in hopes of guiding all Americans and other countrymen, as one whole unit out of a life of vile misery and grief. His opponents hypocritically attempted to speak evil of his dignity to delude his character in hopes of making the interests of his moral fiber physically appear to be viewed by the public which voted him into the Presidential office as non-patriotic. In vain they used his spiritual nurtured nature, birth rights, and even his birth name against him; to insinuate to the American voters that he is unworthy to be the 44th U.S.A. President.

A win is a win, and all we can do is pray to live to see the day when ignorance on earth fails completely at continuing on distorting the true nature of God's plan, so that all of mankind can be once and for all united together in love as One Body in Christ unto God. It is believed by the faith of true Christians that God's grace and mercy shall fulfill the Law of Christ. The Law of Christ is fulfilled in one word, "Love." We true Christians do believe that the probability of there someday being peace on earth is higher and is closer than what the average man may think. Therefore, we place our faith in the unseen things which all chosen prophets of God had hoped for, like hoping for all races to live in harmony, humility, and in peace without shame being enforced. Desiring to live together in liberty while in pursuit of happiness is the ultimate evidence of the Fruit of the Spirit residing in America, which proves that we know the true will of God and it also proves that God is the main provider of justice. In America God is the only one whom true Christians serve as they believe the Power of God can and will provide fair Justice for all citizens alike. (Romans 3:19-28, 5:1-11, 8:24-25, Rom.12/Heb.11:1-6)

During the 21st century, we as American Christians desire not to have the USA government or any other government to take complete control over the spiritual conscience of our faith on the Lord. We do however, desire for the USA government to step up and protect us from being overtaken or taken advantage of; by our own domestic laws, which gives superiority to the Big Business Industries' insensitive governing procedures that have irrationally placed us indivisibly under bondage.

Every average American citizen is forced to comply with an irrational and unreasonable unjust rule of law in some form or fashion. Such laws requires for us to make irrational sacrifices against ourselves and against our own family. The head of every middle and poor class household in America are forced to decide on whether to spend their last dime on food, shelter, or medication to survive. Unfortunately, certain legal but unlawful American laws have placed most of us in a disadvantage. Apparently, our level of education is the most important key to our prosperity, but it has no prospering effect on the truth of our dilemma. Many of the highly educated middle class of the 21st century are twice as poor as the educated lower class citizens. Since the American economic situation over the last past decade have allowed the big businesses to generate and add higher interest rates on mortgage loans, and make extremely high medical insurance expenses to our barely surviving households, even the middle class who makes One-hundred-thousand dollars annually; are loosing their houses and some are surviving daily from church food banks like poor people. Now of course the ignorance of many Republicans have made light of the subject by mocking the poor. Some try to justify their wrong by stating sarcastically that the poor Americans think a rich person is someone who makes One-Hundred-Thousand dollars a year. In other words they use sarcasm to manipulate the middle class to vote in their favor. Most rich lobbyist appears to be out of touch with the middle class's financial situations. Certain politicians who support the rich lobbyist on Wall Street were observed making light of the middle class's financial situations. Maybe they cunningly are tricked into believing that the middle class community thinks that it's normal for an individual who makes $100-thousand annually to stand in a can-good donation line as a recipient thereof along with the householders who are making less than $20-thousand annually.

Since the rich lobbyists of the big business industry are refusing to make their invested products and services affordable for the average American families' budgets, the middle class American people are crying out to the leaders of the US government by which God is the head thereof. In prayer, they ask the Lord to provide the average middle and low class citizens with their needed products and services at an affordable rate. As an American citizen and a redeemed soldier of the Lord; some people personally believe that the righteous way of life ought to remain and should increasingly consist of them having the freedom of choice, but resisters disagree. The resisters would rather continue following the pathway of the despot traditional religious dictators of the past. They verbally proclaim the scriptures within the Holy Bible suggests that the freedom of choice in America ought to only support those of them who are traditionally considered under their religious point of view; as higher in class or rank as they irreligiously belittle the less-fortunate. For the greed of money, many are convinced to believe that the rich are the highest in rank over all other classes of people.

As soon as the Presidential election was over, a certain group of Americans whom voted against President Obama made it publically known that they were hoping for him to fail at providing relief for the American people on Main Street as the 44th President of the United States of America. Therefore, many citizens on Main Street have criticized certain politicians which vowed to agree with the group which hoped Obama should fail, for choosing to politicize President Obama's potential vow to the American citizens. He promised to work towards removing the powers of inequality from the hands of the big businesses; in efforts to help promote financial freedom to all high, middle, and low class citizens fairly. Maybe, those who politicized his intentions feared that they themselves on Wall Street would suffer persecution by the governing laws which President Obama promised the American citizens that he'd work on reforming.

Meanwhile the Democrat Party members became more focused on prioritizing life rather than politicizing it. The people, who still hope to see President Obama fail; hypocritically aren't patriotic enough to understand the severity of their desires also includes the failure of the USA as a whole. (9) Nine months after being sworn into the United States Presidential office, President Obama was named the Nobel Peace Prize laureate as a sign of honor, and this angered many of the conservative Americans for some reason unknown. An example of his definition of fairness consists of him trying to reverse the tax curse where Uncle Sam normally takes more from the poor and lesser from the rich.

(Eph.5:8-11)The Fruit of the Spirit proves what is righteous unto God, and the evident of righteousness makes it very obvious for all to see and understand the true character of the Lord's love for all humanity; by the identity of his compassionate Holy Spirit. To the same token, all of God's children can clearly see the observable goodness of mankind meekly fighting the evil that exists within the present despotic American laws; in the same mannerism as they clearly saw those peace makers in the Middle East peacefully protesting in hope of gaining freedom from an uncivilized legal but unlawful regime during A.D. 2010-2011.

As easy as it is for them to see the evils within the uncivilized regime in the Middle East, they also can see the double-minded rich conservative authoritarian leaders of America; demanding an unreasonable compromise from the rich liberal minded moderate American representatives of the US government. Their demands consist of them feverishly desiring to have complete economic control of money and power, during a recession. An unfair compromise was placed on the table by those of them, which requested for a tax break to be granted to the rich, while demanding for the poor and middle working class American citizens to take a pay cut during an economic recession crisis; for the sake of recovering and balancing out the budget. Some suggests that since they are not able to see pass the worldly glamour of life due to their own wealth, maybe this is their logical way of giving a legal but criminal mandate to their political theory of fairness within their own definition of what social justice and equality means. Is it possible that their political fight for social justice through "CAPITALISM" overly exceeds the Universal American Dream?

The perception of many moderate American Christians, view the rich conservative American despots; pledging their allegiance to uphold a democracy which only supports their desire to make it legal for themselves to have better opportunities. The conservative Americans are charged by a great majority of minorities for protecting and conserving the rich lobbyists' income brackets during a recession, while simultaneously making life more miserable for the poor and middle class Americans. Most Americans are aware of the despot leaders who are willing to protect the wealthy even though their way of protecting them first bankrupted the low and middle class American householders before bankrupting the entire American economy as a whole.

Simultaneously, the rich authoritarian conservative leaders in America are heard boasting of their worldly riches. It is highly believed that the boastful pride of them causes them to react arrogantly. The response of their egotistical behavior is believed to also maybe the leading reason why they conceitedly consider themselves to be among the first of importance on earth by rank, as if being rich American despots makes a person greater than every other ethnic group in America. Mostly every idea of compromise which they've presented to the media thus-so-far has been viewed by the general public as a threat against the working class citizens on Main Street. Their threats had caused insecurity to enter the hearts and minds of a great multitude of American citizens, whom believe they are being demoralized by the despots; who have debased them by the same despoiled ideas which ran the United States into a depression in the 1900's.

During the recession of the 21st century, certain leaders are accused of hoping to maintain the interests of only 1-5% of Americans. The word is circulating that they are willing to throw the working class citizens on Main Street outside of the protection of the American laws in the process. Of course the conservatives in Congress haven't admitted to doing so. Certain deliberated policies which they propose either are misunderstood or is misrepresented, because to many their proposals sound almost like they are actually pushing the people on Main Street under a bus. As the American citizens on Main Street feel dishonored and mistreated like second class citizens by certain politicians who appears to them to fully represent the rich lobbyists on Wall Street, they bear in mind how the working class American citizens throughout history have been desecrated although they are the main source of America's prosperity. Unfortunately, for the elder citizens on Main Street who has followed the American rule of laws all of their lives, the good quality and character of them are forcefully coerced into thinking that they have worked all of their lives for nothing. Their saved retirement funds which include Social Security benefits are deteriorating. Therefore, a majority of Americans believe they are standing in the mist of a domestic war not because of racism, but because of greedy politicians and rich lobbyists who are in the House of Congress; working against the interests of their very survival.

In the eyes of a great mass of Americans, the ideas of the conservatives are double-minded, and they view the circumstances of most of the rich authoritative American leaders debasing them. Everyone can clearly see certain politicians attempting to stop every legislative proposal of the first bi-racial African American President of the United States of America, which not only is designed to help provide jobs for the jobless but is also designed to aid the needy in the mist of the recovery stage of the preexisting failing economy which he inherited.

The foundation of their language which many heard them speak of at Town Hall meetings and at public conferences was the very cause of the perceptive outlooks of themselves being viewed by the people on Main Street to have a wantonness desire to be revered and feared simultaneously. The American despotic leaders seemed to have perfected the old-time motto: "It's my way or the highway." The highway symbolically stood for a brutal punishment to every American householder which President Obama's proposal was designed to protect.

The citizens of America, who once thought the domestic war in America between the Republican and Democratic Party was racially motivated as a cultural war finally can identify the true source of the domestic wars in America; is due to greed. Greed is the root of all evil as in the accordance to the holy truth written within the Holy Scriptures from the Holy Bible text. It is highly believed that the American Dream has become corrupt by the fraudulent idea which suggests that some government regulations that the Democratic Party throughout the years pushed forward to preserve personal freedom and equality to the needy; aren't necessary. These suggestions are possibly the reason why there was a birth of a new political Party in 2010 A.D. After seeing how certain American Republican leaders have led the House of Congress more liberally than the despotic Republican ancestors along side of President Obama, a different group of Republicans (Tea Party members) regrouped and electively replaced several liberals in the House of Representative on November 02, 2010. Whether truth or fable; during their campaign, several members of the Tea Party accused the prior Republicans within the House of Congress who President Obama initially was sworn into the White House to work with to fix the deficit; of not being conservative enough. The impression or imprint which they made on many citizens on Main Street concerning this matter appeared to be confrontational against them and not conciliatory.

Some may profess that they see the same good vs. evil mentality of the Tea Party members' spirit, which has significant resemblance with the evil vs. good mentality of the old-fashioned Republicans of the 1800's; by comparing spiritual things with spiritual. The Tea Party members repeatedly were blamed for holding the American people on Main Street hostage As they riot in the daytime, they were observed by all Americans through the lens of the news media; displaying their passionate unreasonable methods of compromise with the liberal moderate Republican representatives who also were against the liberal Democrats. The greatest disagreement within their plans to repair the American deficit consist of them desiring to do whatever they could to prevent 1-5% of rich lobbyists from making the same finical sacrifices as they required the other 95-99% of working class American households.

Through the lens of the news media, many recognize President Obama's interventional theory of fairness displaying the major factoring of what is equal and fair to the credentials of all individual American households, whether Republic, Democrat, or undecided. His deliberate act which intervene the age old American dispute of equality was believed to perhaps had been premeditated and predestined, because many have waited for the Lord to send another strong messenger in the Commandeering Chief's position; to defend the oppressed citizens against the irony of the domestic despot leaders' devoted acts of insincerity. His speeches coherently countered the unfair economic trend of injustices. It is obvious that greed in the late 1900's-2008 had kept this country facing an unreasonable debt problem, which is now identified as an irrational and totally impossible arrangement for the United States to have ever been placed into the predicament thereof.

In order to prevent a great depression from being added unto an already undesirable consequence of a failing economy, the people needed President Obama to immediately use his economical and spiritual senses to stabilize the USA's currency and debt flow. Before his term in office began, the unemployment rating had already risen to approximately a 6% total increase and as a ripple effect; a 3% increase was added after he became the President. Everyone who thought that the increase would immediately stop rising upon him being elected as the President of America learned that in reality they'd all have to patiently wait out the ripple effect of a major financial shockwave, which was triggered by numerous political decisions that included the political idea of relocating many major American factory jobs overseas; like Emerson Electric Co., Caterpillar, Whirlpool, and many more.

WHY DID AMERICA'S MOST POPULAR BUSINESSES MOVE OUT OF THE USA: _IF A MAN DON'T WORK, A MAN DON'T EAT=CAPITALISM_

Prior to President Obama's term in office, several rich lobbyists who owned a big business were offered a relief from paying import and export taxes on their products and goods, if they agreed to relocate their businesses over-seas. The purpose of this business proposal suggested that the American people on Main Street wanted to help rebuild certain countries overseas, but the American people on Main Street didn't suggest this proposal nor did they have an equal vote on such said issue. Instead, they hoped that their elected representatives and present Commandeering Chief would make reasonable choices on their behalf. The issue was suggestively proposed by the rich lobbyists of Wall Street, whom had powerful influence over Congress. They were the only ones in America who could profit from such a decree. Not only were the big business owners offered an opportunity to personally make more and save more American dollars, but under this particular tax free law the rich lobbyists were advantaged to also avoid the American Job Union Laws; regarding them having to deal less with the problem of paying foreign workers the America's minimum wage rate nor did they have to give raises to the foreign employees. Without the protection of the Union Laws, the American employers' over-seas could violate all sorts of American labor laws. Some may describe such work as a modern day form of a slave drive. Once Congress passed this law, the American rich lobbyists who owned the American big business industry were offered the opportunity to keep away from abiding by the American Union workers' Law. They didn't have to provide the foreign workers with medical insurance and other benefits and amenities. The American government during the 20th century had removed fairness from the adored quality of its established civil way of functioning and convertibly influenced foreigners overseas to work harder for lesser pay than the American citizens. Another advantage they would have upon agreeing to transferring the American jobs to the countries overseas, is having the ability to still sell there merchandise to the American citizens for the same common pre-existing sales price or at a higher rate; without having to pay export and import taxes.

A person can have all the book sense in the world, but without street smarts (aka Common Sense) they are unwise. A person who has common sense knows that nothing plus nothing leaves nothing. A person who has very little book sense understands that this is the universal mathematical rule of law. Common sense tells all who are in touch with the economic crisis, that the government can't collect federal taxes to the wages of those thousands of unemployed American workers who lost their jobs which moved overseas, because nothing plus nothing leaves nothing. Common sense tells all who are in touch with the economic crisis that when the import and export tax law was converted and all major industrial jobs became obsolete in America, that the government needed to have immediately refigured a constructive way to bring stability to the cash flow of the Treasury Department, but such firmness wasn't simultaneously implied. Not only was the US Treasury department still suitably inclined to support the less fortunate, which started to increase as unemployment increased, but it also unduly had to help the rich lobbyists on Wall Street to pay 1 million $dollar bonuses to at least 70 CEO's who already were given a tax break during President W. Bush's administration. Without sufficient funds being collected by the Treasury Department to balance out that which was distributed, a wise person don't have to be a graduate from Harvard University to know that sooner or later the federal government would go broke.

The rich lobbyists, who supports the Republic Party point of view concerning Capitalism between 2004-2008 appears to have had it all figured out, but their carelessness has disrupting the prosperous economic flow of common sense in America. Within certain political views concerning Capitalism during this time frame, also came many decisions made against America's valued economic values concerning equality. Some politicians believe that it was President Clinton who passed the bill on the behalf of the Big Businesses for the rich lobbyists, and others believe President George W. Bush was the one. Instead of playing the blame game, the common sense of most American people during President Obama's term in office believe that all leaders in Congress should be more interested in ending the bill rather than playing the blame game. The Citizens on Main Street practically are tired of listening to all of the political squabbling concerning who did what in the past. Until such abusive laws end all who have common sense are wise to recognize that the American government is sponsoring a massive economy lose, and they also are wise to know that those who refuse to end such laws are supporting domestic despotism in America.

Later In 2011, state by state; the actions of certain Republic Governors started supporting the same principle purposes of the mentioned bill to the big business owners within their state, by simply removing the control of the Workers' Union from the working class American citizens. These Governors claimed their main goal for doing so, was to balance out their states' budget. Maybe the sense to them believes that taking away the power of equality from the peasants on Main Street will save America economically. As the citizens publically marched to these individual state capitals' to peacefully protest, like in Madison, WI; certain Republic Governors publically suggested for President Barak Obama to not intervene in their state's proposal. In fact, someone concluded that he had enough on his plate to deal with and needed not to get involved in their matters. Whether or not President Obama will intervene is still in question. Lord knows, many people on Main Street hopes he and the leaders in Washington, DC does.

Although it was never guaranteed by President Obama, that the unemployment problem would be resolved over night during his campaign, his stimulus packages and the cost cutting measures which he used to boost the economy as soon as he took office; must have had a positive affect on the failing economy, because according to CNN News; the rippling effect of an unstable economy was stabilized at approximately a 9% high unemployment rate for the first 2 years of his presidential time in office. Remind you, the unemployment rate was already at a 6% high upon him being sworn into office and constantly rose as a ripple effect. Approximately in the later part of the month of Feb. or early part of March in 2011, the government reported the unemployment poll revealed a major decrease from the 9% stabilized unemployment rate Reportedly, it was the most improved rate than it had ever been in the last past two years. Unfortunately, due to over 300 super-cells, Tornadoes, floods, and many other natural disasters occurring in the USA during President Obama's term in office, which consistently destroyed the foundation of many industrial jobs and small businesses over and over again; the unemployment rate once again started to increase. As the biblical sign of the end of the world grows stronger, certain blind politicians continues to focus on criticizing

President Obama as if he has the power to stop the course of natural disasters along with the manmade economic disasters. Meanwhile, the money in the Federal Reserve continues to decrease. Again I say, "NOTHING PLUS NOTHING LEAVES NOTHING!

It is highly believed by the author of Discerning Perceptive that if President Obama and his Democratic team along with the original Republicans in the House of Congress, would come together and seek to find wise ways of reducing insufficient tax-free funds and products from being imported and exported; they more than likely will stop the unbalance of cash flow which corrupts the US Treasury Department and will start rebuilding America's economy. It's time to "Do the right thing."

In reality this may never happen during President Obama's first presidential term in office. There are too many Tea Party members in the House of Congress working against him and against the people on Main Street. They act as if they are working for the rich lobbyists. The author isn't claiming to be a psychic, but she believes that until this particular problem is resolved, a crash in the economy will always threaten the American working class citizens, and the American economy will always be intimidated and panicky. In relation to all of what has been observed through the news media, President Obama has been seen politically relating with big business owners of other countries. He appears to be inviting big business owners to establish their companies in the United States, in hopes of them hiring American workers.

Since the American Workers' Union are threatened by individual Republican Governors within certain States to be abolished, maybe President Obama's plan will work and will eventually reverse the American lobbyists' greedy curse all the same. Without the Worker's Union in tact, company owners from other countries may see a great business deal in the USA after all. Just as American Big Business owners were influenced to employ workers over seas, maybe the Big Business owners of other countries will be enticed to bring their business to

America and employ us; so that we maybe able to go out and reboot our economy through selling and purchasing products that we make for them.

BELIEVE IT OR NOT

Approximately between One Point Nine-Trillion & Two-Trillion Dollars was reportedly stored up by the big business leaders of America and after it was detected, on Dec.15, 2010; President Obama asked the American Big Business leaders on CNN News to consider using that money to start hiring workers on Main Street.   Hypocritically, the Republicans who knew of this secret stash; were doing nothing with it and didn't mention the money until after President Obama spoke of it publically.   With their defense up, they in return accused President Obama of trying to direct the government into telling them what to do with the money. Nobody knows what the future may bring especially in regards to the rich refusing to use that money to hire new employees, but we all can hope for the best. As the bombshell was dropped on how much money they've managed to save during a recession, many lives were made miserable on Main Street.

This money could've been used to help rebuild the failing economy, if they simply would've used it wisely. The key word is **WISELY**! Many Republican leaders professed publically that they would rather hold or save the money, because they doubted the economy would get better. In reality it appears to too many Americans that they were working twice as hard to make a better life for no one except for themselves. Although they maybe all for themselves, God is for us all.

If they were saving the money for rainy days, because they doubted the American economy would get better, it is reasonable for the American patrons and all other citizens to conclude that they all are weak spirited Representatives of the United States. It is written in the Holy Bible, that a true Christian walks by faith and not by sight. So those who walk by sight and not by faith responsively lacks hope. Faith without works is dead.   Most witnesses of the Holy Truth refused to cross out the possibility that these Representatives were working on hindering the economy for the sake of politicizing their position against the Democratic President Barak Obama. Neither could any person of the Christian faith deny the possibility that these Representatives had more faith in their own works than they did on the Lord; except they be reprobate. To conclude this theory, let facts be submitted to a candid world. Only when a person believes in what they do, will they have no doubt in having a successful outcome. What do you, the reader believe? "Do you think they prefer doing nothing at all, except to wait patiently to deceive or do you think they were saving that money for rainy days?"

As a concerned tax paying USA citizen, the author has a few unanswered questions for them. ["How long have they had One Point Nine-Trillion Dollars saved for rainy days?" With the economy facing over a Trillion dollar deficient, did they not know that we were going through a storm while they were waiting for the rain?" As they complain about President Obama's successful methods which stimulated stability to an unstable economy which he inherited, what are they doing with so much money secretively saved up and where did they get it from?]

The Trillions of dollars may not personally mean anything to the rich lobbyists during this economic crisis, because unlike the middle working class American citizens; they are wealthy and suffers not and lacks for nothing regardless of how bad the economy maybe. They are set for life. The hardcore decisions which the rich American lobbyists have clearly made in the past have hurt the American economy, and they today are willing to make those same choices with no regrets. With them knowing that their way causes destruction, they make them-selves look like they are a heartless group of people. For the rich American lobbyists to see the Main Street citizens suffering, while sitting back on all of that money and do absolutely nothing except hinder the growth of the economy; is absurd.

As a none rich American who don't have a couple of trillions of dollars stored away for rainy days, the opinion of the author of Discerning Perceptive concludes that for the next 2 years of a tax break for the rich, we all ought not to fool ourselves and worry about what matters to the rich concerning taxes. We ought to be happy and count our blessings, because if the Republicans could control it all; we the people on Main Street may would've been issued a tax increase instead of a tax break for the up coming year of 2011, and we all know that we couldn't afford for that to happen!

THE WISDOM OF GOD IS IN YOU TO MAKE RIGHTEOUS JUDGEMENTS (1KINGS3:16-28)

These people must be delusional if they think that they can convince a majority of wise American people like you on Main Street, who have suffered the most of all under their care; into believing that President Barak Obama and the liberal-minded Democrats are the cause of your continuance of sufferings. Some have said to you that if President Obama and the Democrats were more demanding and stuck to his guns without budging or giving in to the Tea Party Republicans, you would receive immediate relief during this economic struggling time. Maybe they don't realize that America's democracy in Congress is run by the vote of the majority and not by the tough voice of one. If the majority would've voted during the November 2010 election like they did at the 2008 Presidential election, maybe the Tea Party members wouldn't ever have obtained the most number of votes in the House of Representative to block every proposal made by Barak Obama and the other liberals in Congress.

Although some Americans are coerced into thinking that President Obama is a weak President, the wise ones understands it isn't he who's responsible for their suffering. They understand that they are suffering due to greedy politicians, and it is they who refuse to assist you and your families with a job or with a Workers' Union during this economic crisis. The wise are able to understand who are held accountable.

In fact, the proposals which those who caused the American people to suffer; demands the government to either reduce or cut the funds from the households of those whom are incapable of surviving on their fixed monthly income. For instance the SSI recipients no longer receive an annual pay increase known as a cost of living increase. Although the cost of living has skyrocketed, they were forced to take an annual pay cut. The SSI recipients pay for their own Medicare insurance out of their fixed income budgets which cost over $100 dollars a month. The poor Americans make less than $1,000.00 a month in SSI benefits. Their living expense is beyond their income. In some states if they make over $1,000 dollars a month, they are automatically disqualified to receive government assistance from the Dept. of Human Services (DHS) for food stamps also known as EBT and Medicaid; health insurance. The cost for their food, medicine, gas, utilities, housing, etc. overly-exceeds their income, and the Republicans are fighting in the House of Congress against themselves and against the liberal-minded Democrats to per-say that they want to reduce the very little assistance which these people presently receive? Hypothetically speaking, if the Republicans deny the needy or continue adding unfair negotiations against them, at the voting polls during the upcoming 2012 election; the needy will more than likely also deny them. This befits the ideological statement about them which suggest that they were fighting against themselves.

The rich lobbyists strategized in opposition against President Obama, whom was forced into negotiating and settling an awkward deal, with a majority of politicians who were representing the ideas of the rich lobbyists within the new House of Representative. In order to end the old Bush's tax law for the upcoming year of 2011 and create a new tax law, the strategy of President Obama was consistently proposed to financially secure the people on Main Street with a no tax increase law and provide them economic security by other means. The strategy of the rich lobbyists' representatives was to keep them-selves in a winning position concerning this matter. The concerns and the interests of the rich lobbyists and the Tea Party Republicans ironically appeared to be one of the same in the eyes of many, as they labor to resolve the economic crisis by taking more money from the less fortunate citizens on Main Street and little to none from the rich.

The Tea Party Republicans twinned together with those whom portray themselves to be of a more moderate and liberal mind. With their

275

minds on their money and their money on their minds, together they are susceptible to agree amongst themselves to only agree with the moderate liberal-minded Democrats and President Obama, whom made a proposal which offered to give the Americans on Main Street a tax relief in 2011, if President Obama and the Democrats in return would agree to the irrational terms or demands which they the Republicans; presented on the behalf of the clandestine rich American lobbyists; who mainly wants to continue receiving a tax-break. Need I remind you, they already were relieved from paying import and export taxes to the Federal Government?

Some politicians responsively reacts within the eyes of the public as if they think they have gained the ability to keep misleading and deceiving the simple and the weak minded who may would have believed the sky was falling if they heard it on a news network called "Bamboozled News". Fool me once shame on you said a wise man. Fool me twice, shame on me. The sly news political analysts of a News broadcasting company had tricked some simple minded people on Main Street into thinking that the tendency of President Obama's proposal was indistinguishable from that of a socialist. Inwardly, the desires of most of them were trained to despise a socialist. Simultaneously they've been observed by the public, speaking evilly against President Obama for signing a tax bill that they say was indistinguishable from the law that was previously made by President Bush. The maturity level of them were seen striving to corruptibly convert the image of his proposal of balancing the budget. The judgment of their efforts made it difficult for certain citizens on Main Street to differentiate the complaints of his proposal from the complaints that were made against President Bush's tax law. For example; before the tax proposal was past into law, the works of the Republicans demanded for President Obama to include a continuation of the Bush's tax-break for the rich in his proposal or they'd refuse to agree to pass it into law. His proposal also included giving an extension to the receivers of unemployment federal funds. They made it well known to America; that **if** the proposal wasn't passed into law with their terms included; he'd suffer the consequence of watching the citizens on Main Street who were dealing with foreclosures and lost their jobs which moved overseas or filled bankrupt on Main Street suffer from a tax increase without employment and without unemployment support from the federal government.

Like the two harlot women mentioned in 1Kings3:16-28, the three parties in the House of Congress are all claiming to stand for the same body; the American body. Two of these parties are Republic and the other one is made up of Democrats. The difference between the three is seen through their actions. Whether their actions are good or evil, God gave mankind the same spiritual sense, which he gave King Solomon; to determine for them-selves when righteous Judgments are or are not being made by either group; concerning the claims made by each individual party's extensive sense of sincerity. The sincerity of their intentions reveals each party's true colors. Religiously speaking of mankind in general, President Lincoln said it best, but as a paraphrase thereof; "There's no such thing as pure good and pure evil." Neither group is perfect. There's one group seen standing up for the entire American body of citizens, and another group is seen speaking in the terms of personally standing for a particular set of people. Can you distinguish the difference between which is which?

Even a blind man can symbolically see whether or not the deeds and unique bowel of either party symbolize a true prioritized love for all Americans or a politicized love for worldly mastery or for the love of money. Like a battered black American man once said, "Can we all just get along?" A sympathetic person, who is spiritually inclined, can spiritually see and compare the resemblance of President Obama's compassionate reactions towards his love for the people on Main Street, to the compassionate reaction of love which the real mother in 1Kings3:26 had for her living child. You also can discern how God has blessed you to have a sympathetic understanding heart to make righteous judgment, so that you too may discern between good and bad politics.

We the Christian people of the United States of America can clearly see which politician is politically choosing righteously, because the Lord didn't leave us to be ignorant. The judgments of the world have a good and evil side towards the way people view how the Commandeering Chief, President Obama, patiently and carefully has publically approached every situation presented unto him. Some people judge him by comparing what he says and do with how they personally feel within the debt of their own bellies. He publically profess that he wants to make a mends to the concerns of all Americans. As we take it upon ourselves to use the Holy Scriptures to determine which spirit we are following within ours own hearts, we need to continue supporting the most righteous ones; knowing that none of us are perfect and we all are liable to make mistakes. Without agape love, the deeds and works of any person or group are done in vain and are not worth anything. Therefore we must support the politicians who we individually think possess the real biological mother's love for all mankind which also sufficiently represents the love of Christ.

WHICH PARTY DO YOU THINK REPRESENT THE LOVE OF CHRIST IN AMERICA?

In reality, many people believe that the preference of the Republican Party were inclined to hold the American citizens on Main Street hostage against the true intentions of President Obama's plan of bring financial relief unto them during the recession. Within the cloud of smoke, some Americans on Main Street are led to believe that the Tea Party Republicans in the House of Representative are looking out for their best interests. The general public is well aware of the Tea Party members and the Republican members in Congress who openly admitted that they were unwilling to agree as a majority, on anything presented by President Obama concerning a plan which involved balancing the budget; unless he also agrees to some sort of irrational term of their party. It is typical that a massive number of voting Americans can make inquiries among themselves to whether or not they believe that the members of the New Tea Party Republicans, who controlled the House of Representative; displays the character of the lying harlot lady in the Book of 1King3:26 whom told the King, "Let the child be neither mine nor thine, but divide it." The jester symbolically represents the ideological method of reverse psychology, which many believe the Republicans used; in an attempt to politically cause division between President Obama and the people on Main Street.

Sarcastically speaking, many accept as truth; the idea that by threatening to use the well-being of the citizens on Main Street as a human shield in the line of defense against President Obama, the Republicans were enabled to get President Obama to surrender to certain of their irrational terms. In a certain sense; in a twisted and warped way if a person didn't know and understand the full story behind certain laws that were signed by President Obama, they maybe susceptible to be misled to stereotypically view him in the same disapproving way as they've viewed the 43rd President of the USA. If the truth be told, President Obama is like a solider of war waving a white flag on the battlefield, when out numbered or defeated by the US House of Representative. Unfortunately, the battlefield for him is on American soil in the US House of Representative.

If an agreement on the new tax bill would not have been made by the deadline meant the bill would've been killed, and an automatic tax increase would have been given to all Americans. Everyone knew that a tax increase would destroy, demolish, and devastate the lives of all working class Americans and leave them shipwreck.

Whether the Tea Party members know it or not, many freethinking American citizens have accused them of politicizing their position in office. They point the fingers at the Tea Party members for making the delusional terms of their own made-up negotiated alterations within President Obama's tax proposal appear to be purely made-up by President Obama, after they sarcastically speaking had twisted his arm and pent his back up against the wall. The freethinkers believe the Republicans' revision of President Obama's tax proposal, is identical to President Bush's previous outlook; concerning the rich being granted a tax-break. The determined difference which they expressively see between his tax proposal and President Bush's old tax law is that President Obama's proposal embraced a tax break for the citizens of

Main Street, and Bush's did not. Bush's tax law only gave a tax-break to the rich. Theoretically speaking, the rich got richer under the Bush tax law and the middle and low class Americans were made poorer. The same thing is expected to persist during President Obama's term of office, due to the alterations which the Tea Party made to his proposal.

Let's take a close look at the Book of 1Kings3 and spiritually compare the King to the political rulers of the United States. There were two prostitute women standing before the judgment of King Solomon concerning which one was the biological mother of a child, which they both claimed. During the sign of a threat on the child's life, ask yourself what was the motive behind the **will** of the biological mother; when she decided to give her child to the psychopath lying harlot woman who claimed the baby was her own. Do you see how the real mother's bowels yearned upon her son? For this cause, with no strings attached; she made a painful decision which a corrupt-minded person may conclude proves to them that she didn't love her son. Some of you are like the lying harlot who psychopathically seems to lack a sense of social and moral obligation. Therefore, some of you may think that some sort of personal gain should've been sought by criminal acts, without feeling guilty. You think the woman should have fought the powerful King for her child or died trying to get the child back.

The evidence provided by the Fruit of the Spirit proves that the bowels of those who lacks the ability to spiritually recognize the nurturing nature of what sacrifice sufficiently means under the New Covenant of Jesus Christ would rather have someone to die or to have the child to die, so that neither would have a child. Like the radicals within all communities, some of you think shedding your own blood or the blood of anther is sacrificial unto God and it is the only way you think you and others can prove your love unto God. Misery loves company!

In relating to the same principle acts of the lying harlot woman, the principle idea that states, "Either things will go my way or no way"; is your M.O. and also is the ideal illusion of the politically viewed reaction of a certain political Party in the House of Congress during the 21st

century. All voting American citizens can righteously judge the actions of those who are suppose to be their governing representatives, by comparing whether or not if they are supporting their economic issues and personal concerns with the tax law, unemployment insurance, minimum wage laws, old age pensions, health insurance, civil rights laws, and aid to education etc; to per-say who they think seem to not be doing things in the way in which led them to vote them into office. After analyzing the acts of the primary elected representatives of the USA, a person may see that some politicians prefer things to go their own way or no way at all, instead of the way in which makes more moral sense.

Some Americans think that because President Obama desires for the cycle of discord and suspicion between the Republican and Democratic Party members to end; he makes himself a weak and unworthy President of the USA. In the regards of the thoughts of other Americans who are not dumbfounded to the Power of God nor suffers from a short attention span concerning the actions behind his motives, they have taken it upon themselves to consider the true unique circumstances in which he faces that places the heart of him in the same predicament which consists of the same principle threat as the real mother in 1Kings3. For this cause, they believe that Fruit of the Spirit proves that his choice didn't make him weak nor unworthy, but it made him humble and wise. To conclude the Americans' cycle of discord and suspicion, the Word of God settles the thoughts of every individual individually with this, "President Obama is weak to those who think he is weak, and he is strong to those who think he is strong, because whatsoever a man thinks; to them shall it be. Like the Republican Tea Party, he is thought of as a Hero in the minds of some Americans and a villain in the minds of others.

Some who misinterprets the Holy Scriptures may pass false judgments without spiritually recognizing that the lady who stood up for her helpless and innocent child's life, would rather suffer herself; than to see her son harmed or killed. After evaluating the Fruit of the Spirit of God presented within the point of this particular story, God will bless a blind person to clearly understand that King Solomon was wise to know that the real mother wouldn't desire to have her son killed just so that she and the liar could share parts of his dead body, and the desire of the one who requested for this to be so is absurd. Instead of allowing the King to take a sword and divide her son in half and share his dead body between the two of them, the real mother would rather go through life lacking the ability of being able to legally nurture her son in her own bosom, as long as she knew that her son would yet still be unharmed.

Just as all of God's people of Israel saw the wisdom of God working in King Solomon after they heard of the righteous judgment which he had made concerning the two women in the Book of 1King3:27-28, the children of God in American also may see the wisdom of God working in President Barak Obama as he made a righteous judgment to balance out the circumstance of his priority. Many understand that he righteously discerned what was placed upon him concerning him living up to his vow to protect the American people as the 44th President of the United States of America from foreign or domestic despotism, as they witnessed him distribute a momentary tax-break across the border unto all Americans; the rich and poor including his friends and foes alike, just so that he could help the helpless Americans on Main Street to the best of his limited ability.

Ideologically speaking, any politician who has a clear perception of reality concerning the 21st century political affairs but lacks the godly sense of social and moral obligation, tends to lie against the truth to receive personal gain by committing criminal acts against the innocent without marked feelings of guilt; are mentally ill. The best descriptive words known unto the author within the English language, which helps her to understand the characteristics of such persons' state of mind and also explains her perception of their way of thinking, are the words "Psychotic Reverse Political Psychologist Syndrome." They spiritually are destitute of the Holy Truth and know not the way of the Lord. Therefore, they are known for reversing the Holy Truth and corrupting the incorruptible image of God, by claiming the defective things that causes grief, misery, and worldly sorrows unto the weak and simple babes in Christ are good and pure. Psychologically, they reverse the Doctrine of Jesus Christ for their own distorted pleasures and create wars and not peace.

Let the truth be submitted to a candid world, historical changes to America's reformed democracy were made throughout the years by the countrymen who were convinced by the Spirit of God to believe that their acts of reforming the US Government's regulations of this society for this economy were/are necessary for the spiritual growth within the American society. The reformed government regulations like Human and Civil Rights were acknowledged by the most predominant religious sect in America (CHRISTAINITY) as godly and righteous acts which preserve personal freedom and equality for all Americans. Such reformed laws also have been proven through America's history to have improved the welfare of this country every since the desire of peace and equality was first established within the heart and soul of America. The Fruit of the Spirit of God proves to all people of Christian faith that the old biased laws of America changed because the Lord ordained the hearts of Americans to change after the Christians learned the difference between hate and hope.

The political presentations that are presented to the American public of the 21st century, makes the general public think that the Republicans want to do-away with the principle standards of such government regulations. The appearance of the most dominant Republicans within their own presentations unto the general American public, arguably has convinced many to assume that they have an all or nothing attitude towards stripping the Human and Civil Rights of the American society from as many pre-established laws that were declared all throughout history to be reformed. It is highly believed that the Republicans, who ruled the House of Representative in 2010-2012 by the massive numbered votes of a majority; are financially prepared by rich lobbyist to block the freedoms and equality from the American middle and lower class citizens without feeling guilty. The middle and lower class citizens are recognizing how certain political decisions of the government are forcing them to settle with having very little to no funds to survive on within this current economy.

The American people are use to politicians lying to them throughout their campaign about what they stand for. They are use to them lying, to get voted into a political position and do the total opposite of what they claimed they would during their campaign. Therefore, most citizens feel that there's no logical reason why they should waste their time at the voting polls. After witnessing the reverse factor of such truth, it is fair to say that most of the 21st century politicians say what they mean and mean what they say concerning such factors. The outwardly shown approach of their intentions either is for or is against; helping the needy organizations that provide assistance to the general public. Unfortunately, under the circumstance of there being lesser voters, those who say within their campaign that they are against the moral values of the general public; are winning political grounds.

For instance, while working on preventing the rich from the patriotic task of paying taxes to help boost the economy, says many Americans; "Certain politicians are weakening the Public Education System." In America everyone knows that IT COST TO BE THE BOSS. Many are now worried that if the Republicans succeed at taking funds away from the children of the general public, only the rich kids will be able to afford to receive an education in America. Apprehensively, they worry that the future generation more than likely are not going to be governed by individuals who are being mentally trained to have a sense of social and moral obligation, because for the greed of money is the root of all evil. Many believe that if the government continues to frustrate the lives of the children who are apart of the general public, the future educated rulers of America would not be able to rationally relate to the logical problems of the upcoming generation on Main Street, because they will be totally out of touch with the experiences of the general publics' future point of views. Today many are forced to educate the American children in public schools with lesser funds, and a majority of them think that the Republicans who have politically fought and won the fight to reduce or totally eliminate such funds; are playing with the future economic life of this country like playing a game of roulette. Many people believe that such reactions of certain particular politicians indeed, resemble the desires of the lying harlot lady who preferred for the King to kill the child so that neither of them would have a living child.

Hypothetically speaking, the terms and conditions of the Republic and Tea Party members' proposal gave President Obama's heart the grounds to yearn for the helpless working class and poor Americans on Main Street. The spirit of him reveals indeed that he shared a common interest with the Americans on Main Street. His reactions towards the circumstance of such situations suggest to the people on Main Street, that he sympathetically understood the pain which the terms of the government prior to him entering the Presidential office had caused them. Many Christians believe that his compassionate heart have an agape love for all American citizens. Therefore, the expectations of him being more than a one term President of the United States of America isn't a clear-cut but his chances are high.

Of course there is some creative challengers who are inquiring his chances of winning the 2012 election are slim to none, and they base their inconclusive thoughts on a disputable internet daily poll. Insufficiently, the internet's voting poll stereotypically suggests that the same equal number of Americans voters of the 2008 Presidential election who has no internet assess to vote on line; have fallen out of favor with him? Just to prove a point, count on one hand and ask yourself how many people you know of; that is voting daily on this online voting poll.

In reality, it is highly probable that the majority of Americans who aren't easily fooled by the deceptions are willing to forgive him and reconcile with him at the voting poll in 2012 for not being perfect. In fact, none who aren't mentally ill expects for him to be perfect, and they understand the reason why he passed certain laws which are similar to President Bush's. They are wise to recognize that he was forcefully coerced into giving the 5% of wealthy Americans a momentary tax-break, only to in return; protect the people on Main Street from encountering further sufferings from more irrational works of political afflictions for as long as he possibly can under the circumstances of him having a limited source of political influence.

America has accomplished many successful things in a short time period under the leadership of the Commandeering Chief; President Barak Obama, like stabilizing the economy, lessoning the unemployment rate, and finding and killing the world terrorist; Osama Bin Laden in spite of him lacking political support in Congress from the House of Representatives. The short attention span of a large number of Americans which are coerced to suffer from <u>Psychotic Reverse Political Psychologist Syndrome</u>" will vote against him in 2012, but it's not a definite fact that their votes against him will be enough to make him a one term President.

Some elected governing officials strive for mastery by politically deliberating and mandating governing policies into laws to befit the desires of their own bellies. Historically, this political method has always been devised to exploit fear into the hearts of all; who such governing officials despise. The despotic hearts of the supreme authority figures since the beginning of sin, have strived to physically present illusions which convinces others to believe that their defined repressive factors of life that <u>cruelly</u> suggests and expresses their own exploitive definition of the quality of fairness, equality, and justice; is the righteous path for all citizens to follow. This method is identical to the despotic rich American lobbyists' way of keeping themselves rich and the poor people poor. Since this has been the true nature of most rich despots on earth for so long, the heart of their trade mark have had plenty of time to manipulate the laws of the land so that the designed works of the law of the land would set them and their future representatives in a political position to keep supporting their defective definition of fairness, equality, and justice; for all to obey.

IF THE 44th PRESIDENT OF THE USA FAILS WHAT SHALL BECOME OF AMERICA

One of the main things which President Obama's opponents hope he fails at during his presidency, is making a fair balance of the tax laws among the owners of the Big Business Industry and the employees thereof. Maybe the despotic rich lobbyists' fear being equally added to the American law, which for decades have only been applied to the working Low and Middle class American citizens' traditional American motto that says, "The more one makes the more Uncle Sam takes."

When President Obama alerted the rich that his objective was to stop the government from issuing more unreasonable taxes against the Main Street Americans, the despotic rich lobbyists became very attentive and ready to act hastily against him! Of course he knew that because of their hostility and lack of sympathy for the less fortunate, he would have to work twice as hard at making a fair balance of the tax laws. Meanwhile, the citizens of God prayed twice as hard to the God who is in Heaven, to prevent the working Middle and Low class American citizens from having their taxes raised at the end of the Bush's tax law before A.D. 2011. Prayer works!

In other words, the Big Picture of what fairness represents unto God is truly established by Christ, and some think that the current Republic Party members who won the Nov. 2010 election calls such ideas of fairness a sign of socialism by definition. Was Christ a Socialist? Apparently, socialism isn't viewed by all Americans the same way. Unfortunately, for all American citizens who disagree with the traditional tyrannical policies of America, the believers of such oppressive laws are still winning political elections to run the country.

President Barak Obama; publically informed all American citizens in his own words in a unique way of his political perception. For instance, he notified all Americans that in order for him to extend unemployment befits up to 15 months to the citizens on Main Street and prevent those of them which were already being taxed beyond their income, he was forced by the Republicans which controlled the negotiating table in the

House of Representative to also extend a tax cut to the 5% rich population for the next two years. It was plainly confirmed by the Tea Party Republicans that he had to agree before the Bush tax law ended at the end of the year of 2010 A.D., in order to stop an unwarranted tax increase to overwhelm the Main Street citizens.

DOMESTICALLY AMERICANS ARE HELD HOSTAGE BY WHOM & FOR WHAT?

For this cause, President Barak Obama publically described the conditionings of the Republicans who were voted into the House of Representative as hostage takers who had placed 95% of Americans on Main Street into a hostage situation against him. I have a hypothetical question for you readers. "Could you image a group of rebels going into a town armed with live ammunition to free their people who were being used as human shields by the enemy?" If so, then you can understand President Obama's political perspective.

To give an illustration of what the people were faced with to the best of his ability, he attempted to explain how things looked through his eyes concerning this particular matter. He suggestively implicated to the American people on Main Street that the elected Republicans' negotiating stratagems, resembled to him to be a threat against the best wellbeing of the unemployed people on Main Street, whom were unemployed due to no fault of their own. Before allowing the wellbeing of 95% of Americans to be further harmed by the so called hostage takers, whom many believe desires to mandate a governing policy or law to befit the desires of a tyrannous group and also are accused of striving for mastery; President Obama publically made known to all Americans of his intent to compromise with the Tea Party Republicans concerning his tax relief plan.

It was once said, that a wise King takes advice from his council, but always follow his heart. In order to keep his promise unto the working Low and Middle class Americans on Main Street, who elected him two years prior; President Obama decided to follow his heart and include the low 1-5% of the wealthy Americans in his tax-break proposal for the

288

upcoming 2011 year. Maybe he and a great number of those who voted for the Tea Party member in the 2010 Nov. election, thought that the Tea Party members would help the country to recover from this economic crisis without taking away the one thing that the American people had left; their dignity.

He knew that he had to find an immediate middle-ground and compromise with the Tea Party members who controlled the House of Representative, so that he could provide a better living for 95% of the Americans whose wellbeing and dignity were threatened by a tax increase and unemployment cuts. In reality, he realized that if he didn't compromise with the Republicans before the era of the Bush's tax law ended and the new 2011 year begins; 95% of Americans which he was electively representing would immediately be hit with a higher tax bracket. He knew none could financially afford such a hit during the recession.

In other words, the significance of passing a new tax bill before 2010 ended was important to all middle and low income working Americans. It was the only thing that would stop everyone on Main Street from paying higher taxes and from loosing their only source of income which pays for food, shelter, cloths, medical expenses, and other necessities. The House of Senate had already preapproved the passing of President Obama's first tax proposal as it was, but the House of Representative since then was under the new leadership of the Tea Party Republicans. They had threatened to stop the passing of President Obama's tax proposal, which also included an extension of unemployment benefits for the people on Main Street for the up coming year of 2011.

At approximately two weeks prior to the New Year of 2011, the pressure was on. Certain members of President Obama's Administration had detected that the Republics included a few more extra unwarranted clauses to the new proposal. Some even became worried that if these unwarranted clauses which were included in the proposal should so happen to be signed by President Obama and passes into law; it would cause more misery to the American people on Main Street in the long run and the Republicans could use it to cause him to be entrapped in a politic battle, which they doubted he could win upon the next election.

Meanwhile, President Obama stood firm against everyone who refused to see the urgent need for him to agree to pass the Republicans' converted version of his proposal. Although the Republicans' renewed terms within Obama's proposal didn't contain everything that the people on Main Street and those who counseled President Obama had hoped for, Obama knew that it contained some positive things which would immediately provide financial relief for 95% of Americans.

Wisely, he enhanced the idea of doing something to help most Americans vs. doing nothing at all. He acknowledged that doing nothing at all would cause an immediate catastrophic end to the recession and create another economic depression to the American economy. In other words, he stood firm. The practical belief of a Christian leadership suggests for all to worry not about what tomorrow may bring, because tomorrow isn't promised to any man. If the Lord furnish the birds with what they are in need of, according to the Christian faith; the Lord would also provide for all of his people with what they are in need of.

Politically, President Obama's outlook on life clearly backed up his defensive position as the President of United States of America, whom promised to protect the people from being held hostage from domestic and foreign terrorists. The observation of his methods viewed throughout the mainstream media appeared too had been concentrated more so on prioritizing the life of a majority number of Americans, while the observers outlook of his domestic opponents debating's; appears to politicize his life and the life of all Main Street Americans. In the end, the new proposition was announced to had been approved or passed by the House of Representative and awaited for President Obama's written signature by a reporter on the "Up To The Minute News" on Dec. 17th, 2010. The change which President Obama mentioned during his campaign trial was slowly being met one day at a time.

He articulated unto the American people of his rationale motive for agreeing to the Republican's unfair deal. The media later revealed certain Republicans criticizing him for making a rational decision to include the American citizens with an understanding to the position of his Presidential status. They charged him for agreeing to their proposition which gave the rich a tax break, and they accused him of being no better than President Bush concerning the matter. Maybe they didn't realize that within the definition of despotism, the citizens on Main Street could analysis the circumstances of the political acts and events that were circulating around and about them. They really didn't need anyone to devise a lie for them to believe, because they knew the truth. Maybe they assumed the Americans aren't smart enough to see through the illusions of their smoke and mirrors. The people on Main Street aren't dumb. They saw the despotic acts of the new Republic Party, creatively politicizing a plan to use against President Obama with all of their fair words and well put together speeches. Most of them on Main Street did feel victimized by all whose intent was to hold them hostage, to subdue their political plan to uphold the interest of the rich lobbyist.

WITHOUT A DOUBT THE PAST AMERICAN DOMESTIC TAX LAWS HAVE BEEN UNFAIR TO THE MINORITY AMERICANS FOR AT LEAST A CENTURY

In the same reference of fairness, the old American despot laws for years have issued tax breaks onto the foreigners, who became legal residents of the United States of America. Approximately between the mid 1980's-1990's, Americans had started to notice an increase in Asians and Chinese people opening up more wigs, nails, and clothing stores in America. They received help from the American government, which distributed unto them money that came from the vault which collectively took money from the poor working American tax payers. The poor American citizens even observed many naturalized Mexicans whom were granted the equal rights to become citizens in America, receiving tax breaks. The wisest migrating foreigners are seen taking their fair share of the American pie and investing into owning hotels and other America businesses.

The most advanced minds of a migrating group of people were the Arabs who came to America within the 20th-21st century. They came with a plan to live peacefully in the land of the free and the home of the brave. When they searched the street which they had heard were paved with gold, they sought to own as many gas stations as they possibly could. In the end, the Arabs have cashed in on their American dream and have received a piece of the America pie within almost every state of the United States of America. When the oil price increase changed from 99 cents per gallon for regular gas, to $3.00-plus per gallon, the Arabs both over seas and domestic were positioned in place to have the best of both worlds. Not only were they allowed tax breaks in America, but it isn't against the law for them to refuse to recycle their American dollars which they collect and earn; back into the American economy. They could easily send money back to their families in their original home lands or they can easily send money to their governing leaders. In so all that which is done, the rich Americans became richer and the poor Americans became poorer.

The fate of the American nation predictably has turned out very similar to what the original tyrannous slave masters wanted, but by a twist of fate; all whom once were slaves are now able to work freely for themselves. The Native Americans have become the proud owners of casinos, and they strongly believe in giving back to their community. For instance, they build daycare and school houses for their youth.

The African Americans have become the proud business owners of all sorts of different articulating things as strong ministers of God. They've jumped over the stereotypical barriers as athletes, musicians, dancers, song and book writers, movie actors, and directors etc. On the downside of their prosperity, most of them lack either the intellect or the heart to give back to the struggling communities which they emerged from. Maybe, they are discouraged to reinvest back to their own community because of the unfair entangled involvement of the despot American government or maybe they lack the sense of compassion to care about their community after they escape. Therefore, the poor African American community remains poor while all other American origin of people gets richer. Not everyone can see the irony of greed and disgrace which still exists thereof, but a discerner of the Spirit can clearly see the trait of evil's fate; lying and waiting to deceive.

THE LACK OF FAITH & THE UNGODLY IRRELIGIOUS HOPE OF FAILURE

As the first African American biracial President's courageous courage affected the financial affairs of Wall Street in a positive way in efforts of bringing some relief to the investors of Main Street; his intellectual boldness took a stand for equality and justice for all American citizens. This disturbed the rich American population whom were willing to lobby against him by all means. Their cynical plan to play the racial card of despair against him back fired due to him being both of an African and a white origin American.

The rich resistance on Wall Street believes the obligation of their rights and duty is to enhance the American citizens' hearts into fearing almost every proposal made by President Obama, and they purposely used his constitutional power of authority as the 44th President of the United States against him. Some even vulgarly suggested that America should fear the possibility of him using his political office for the American Muslims to overthrow the American Christians. Every unreasonable measure of disloyalty that they used against his loyal allegiance to this Nation are constantly failing, because they are unwisely drawing conclusions against him that are too far fetched for anyone in their right minds to believe. While President Obama is continuing to use his God given constitutional power of authority to stabilize America's unstable economic problems which he inherited, his opponents may call his economic decisions unconstitutional, but they can't deny the positive confirmation of the increase of job markets that rose up after his first 2 years of office.

The Americans were kept in the loop by the greatest of all News broadcasting systems and services of the 21st century like twitter and face book. They were very aware of the rich lobbyists not using their money to help mend the broken economy. Instead, they were noted for bragging about spending millions to falsely advertise against President Obama's plans to reboot the economy. They in false-hope, desired to make his plans physically appear unto the American citizens on Main Street to be of an Anti-Christ, non-patriotic, and unconstitutional. Ironically, in the mist of all of their fears of President Obama, their own presumptuous ways exposed their claims against him unto the entire world; to be a lie.

After the truths of Obama's intentions worked as planned, he bailed out the GMC Automobile Industry, which is the foundation of America's prosperity. GMC was on the verge of going out of business, due to the illegitimate and irresponsible decisions made by the rich lobbyists and the Big Bankers, long before President Obama's term in office started. The rich lobbyists slanderously stated that GMC should've filed bankruptcy and everyone knew that if they would've filed for bankruptcy, in the end they would've distorted their respected American name brand.

The irresponsible money handlers on Wall Street had placed a great burden on the entire American country, and their actions of greed caused the people on Main Street to lose stability to the point of them no longer being able to afford to purchase foods and medicines; more less a new car. Even the middle class were losing their homes to the Big Bankers' high interest rates under the law of foreclosure. As the truth of the rich lobbyists were gradually being exposed; they attempted to create other lies for the people on Main Street to redirect their attentions too, but they exposed themselves to be up to no good as they made a public display of their every false accusation. Everything that goes on in the dark comes to the light.

Some of President Obama's opponents publically profess that they hope he fails to make international peace with the other American Allies, and they hope he'd fail to mend the broken economy, which he inherited as a new leader of the American Nation. They hope that he fails to help make the American lands a more greener country after he proposed to create more green jobs for the American citizens through the act of making America a more Earth Smart Nation. They knew that if he successfully bailed out the GMC Automobile Company, concerning the things he promised during his campaign he could kill two birds with one stone, because GMC was going green by making energy efficient vehicles.

After stabilizing the high unemployment rate at 9% for the first 2 years of his presidency, he desired to also make the United States of American a more productive greener Nation. Thus so far the automobile industry has transformed and are solely depending more so on creating productive solar energy and electric power engines for newer model vehicles over the old age gas and oil base motors.

Although President Obama was not overly eager to approve offshore oil drilling, he never excluded the possibility of drilling for oil on American soil. Maybe someday Americans will restart drilling for oil on American soil so that the economy may revive itself instead of depending on purchasing oil from other countries of the world, unless they decide to discontinue using it for Earth Smart reasons, which may include the fact that technology has advanced all of humanity to use more solar and other natural energy sources instead of gas and oil.

THEORETICAL CONCLUSION

The American and non American Christians of today's generation are more understandable, loving, and peaceable towards one of another; in comparison to our conflicting incompatible past ancestors who were unable to get alone and coexist. Although we are uncomplicated and simple people, we are yet a long way from being safe from the latest terrorist attacks and murderous attempts of the enemy who kills the godly spirit of mankind. There's some good and bad inside of us all. While we the American people of the 21st century are expecting our destruction to come from a terrorist attack from over-seas, we are out of focus on the fact that our destruction is coming from within our own domestic country through the laws of despotism that are created by American political tyrants.

The choice to continue upholding grudges for the wrongs of past occurrences between one countryman and another are verbally influenced and is dictated by the hearts of those who uses their maneuvering influences to manipulate or control the governing laws of their own homeland against their own citizens. Many American and non-American despots are slowly being inwardly converted by the teachings of the Holy Ghost.

Certain despot leaders of other countries like <u>Mahmoud</u> <u>Ahmadinejad</u>; the Iranian President, presently desire to make cursing charges against the leadership of The United States of America concerning the 911 attack. While the agendas of his peoples desires to be set free from his tyrannous government, he'd rather for the citizens of his country to religiously dwell on worldly matters with the spirit of envy and strife in his heart. Such spirits settles and enslaves the minds of many and seduces them to not possess a forgiving heart. As such person's mock God, their own heresies are made manifest by the Holy Spirit to be enmity as an enemy against man and God.

As the Holy Ghost works to restore love, joy, peace, and faith within the heart of all mankind alike, the unbelievers are being reproached, reproved, and rebuked daily, not by the works or will of men, but by the

Holy Ghost which never ceases to exist; as it continues to teach truthfully without deceit and hypocrisy unto every generation.

It is fair to say that the goodness of the Lord's new purpose for all of humanity is to love God, self, and all others as one loves themselves. Love will conquer all evil concepts that are creating rationalization to spread abroad within every traditional religious understanding, which worldly men may have concerning the Lord's Spirit of Righteousness and Truth. Within the hearts of most traditional religious Americans and non-American church houses of the 21st century; reside false ministers, who still desire to congregate oppressively in absolute chaos. The greatest success of these false ministers and phony Christians are to promote a legal but unlawful partition which divides God's children one from the other not for the edification of the church, but for the earthy desire to have mastery on earth or dominion over others. Satan creates chaos, confusion, and war; not peace.

CHAPTER 8 HATRED IS THE ENEMY & IS AN ABOMINATION

Whether the laws were structured by a chain of Commandeering Chiefs of a hierarchy group or organized in the form of an anarchy or monarchy government, the beginning structuring of every manmade governing law in the world that have brought forth the sown seed of hatred throughout the terms of chaos and confusion; are enmity against God. The evil spirit of condemnation did not just distort the earlier formations of the American language and laws, but it also misrepresented the formation of all other manmade tyrannous laws which causes many authoritarian leaders around the world to still resort to unequally dividing the freedoms of its own citizens.

The religious act of spreading hatred is a detestable thing and that is what Satan does. Spreading hatred is the act of abomination because hatred is a strong aversion like that of Ahab for Macaiah, which gives offence (1King22:8, 39-40, 51-53). Hatred has divided all Nations by insinuating some were greater than others, and that God didn't love those which traditional religions' unchanged laws are designed to despise. Hatred is the legacy of many manmade laws' evil genocide, which vexes the greedy hearts of people who desire to be worshipped like gods on earth.

Without humbling themselves as a reasonable sacrifice unto God to obtain the spiritual gift of inner peace as true servants, the despotic leaders of the lands stresses their religiously given mental stereotypical images against whomever the founding forefathers and the earlier citizens had religious defined to be incapable or unsuitable to receive the legal associations of certain human rights and civil equitable. They've changed the image of our incorruptible God into a corruptible God, by using Satan's cunning methods of teaching what thus saith the Lord thy God.

The past despotic rulers and leaders whom composed the laws of the land, have passed down their corrupt teachings which judges the Word of God onto their own off springs. Today, their off springs honor their vain teachings and devote their hearts in desiring to continue to have those whom they religiously despise the most of all; placed outside of the protection of every manmade religious law known to man, as if their faith during today's generation also desires for God to place whosoever they've been taught to religiously despise outside of his love, mercy, and grace. They prefer to think that they religiously can make peace by creating war. Like their father, they hope that peace would come to them if they continue placing those who possess any markings which they religiously despise, outside of the protection of the lands' legal formation of law. Since we now are required by God to live under the New Covenant of Christ, war makers are religiously living in error. Their religious act of vengeance is not love nor is it godly, but they think it is. Although the manmade laws of the land may speak of equality, they make it impossible for equality to be granted to all man kind alike.

This undesirable religious chemistry continues to cause people during the 21st century to have a lacking in harmony or congruity together, because the majority whom rule the world in reality and truth; are traditional religious people who refuse to change the unfairness of their out dated corrupt laws of the land. Instead of abolition the old way of thinking as born again Christians, they religiously prefer to mend, twain, and mix the old leaven of their old religious covenant and laws with the Lord's New Covenant and New Commandment of the New Testament. The Lord's new solution to fastening and praying which fixes the old problems in today's reformed society isn't given unto the world by the Lord for religious people to take unprofitable advantage of, as their overly excessive desire to either be God or to have a relationship with God causes them to use the Word of God as a cloak of maliciousness. It is unprofitable for any man of the world to twine their old traditional religious imperfect concept of God's law of love unto the pure minds of those who are with the renewed rational meaning of God's beginning intention of ever creating his fondest image of the human race in his likeness. The bottom line is this: The twining of traditional religion doesn't agree with Christ's church. Instead of preserving the old law, like preserving old wine; knowing that the old don't agree with the new, traditional religious martyrs' would rather work to constrain, retain, and confine the spirit of mankind and condemn many unto death.

LET FREEDOM RING

When two or more people encounter one with another and they can't agree, normally confusion and chaos fill their conversations and it makes the goodness of their words lack godly values and/or godly qualities. It has been written that the natural man can't comprehend the Spirit of God, because they are spiritually discerned. The things that are of the Spirit of God, to them are foolishness. (1Cor.2:14) Therefore, the spiritual change which the Word of God speaks of is disputed by them in all areas of life, and the disputing will one day cease to exit in the hearts which truly are spiritually changed.

> **1Cor.8:5 "For though there be that are called gods, whether in heaven or in earth, (as there be gods many, and lords many,)."**
>
> **1Cor.8:6 "But to us there is but one God, the Father, of whom are all things, and we in him; and one Lord Jesus Christ, by whom are all things, and we by him."**
>
> **1Cor.8:7 "Howbeit there is not in every man that knowledge: for some with conscience of the idol unto this hour eat it as a thing offered unto an idol; and their conscience being weak is defiled."**

The image of God being written in all men's hearts tells us all what is good and evil. Having the moral values of God is what keeps us from joining hostile gangs whose primary objective in life is to reign with terror and to have dominion over others, as killers and murderers of the Spirit of Hope. The Spirit of Christ prevents children from being born fatherless even if the biological parent is dead or is AWOL (absent without leave). The Holy Spirit protects people from the barrier of the worldly stereotypical persuasions, which segregate and isolate people due to their different race, sex, sexual orientation, size, shapes, religions, nationalities, creed, origin, and social outlooks. The Spirit of Christ protects those who believe on him from the unwarranted acts of injustice by keeping all believers spiritually inclined on one accord with God's Divine order of law. All praise is to the Almighty God for setting our hearts free from the bondage of this world. In spite of our differences, we all are "Free at last, free at last, thank God Almighty. We're free at last!"

> Gal.6:7 "Be not deceived God is not mocked: for whatsoever a man soweth, that shall he also reap."
>
> Gal.6:8 "For he that soweth to his flesh shall of the flesh reap corruption; but he that soweth to the Spirit shall of the Spirit reap life everlasting."   (St. Matt.7:2&7:9-12/18:23-35)

THE SPIRIT OF GOD VS WORLDLY RELIGIOUS CLASSIFICATIONS OF SCIENTOLOGY

Stereotypically speaking, if skinny people are classified by the majority of the world to be sexy and more beautiful then thicker people, then its understandable why thicker people are more pruned and falsely coerced to be willing to sicken or starve themselves to be skinny. In some cases, being over weight has turned into a medical issue, which scientifically is concluded by man to be the technical cause of ones' physical death. In spite of such health issue being scientifically proven, it is the Spirit of God which gives all believers of the Son of God an inner peace and comfort, while leading them to gain the sense of godly contentment with knowing that in order to descend into heaven one must physically die in a spiritual content state of mind. After all as it is written, "contentment is godliness."

It is very common for a person who is classified by the majority of the world to be misled by the condemning spirit of insecurity. Some who are bound by the spirit of insecurity becomes more willing to inflict pain unto their selves if they thought going through pain would reverse their insecurities. For example, some surgically suffer their bodies under radiation or even a knife to remove the unwarranted worldly form of chastising in the punishing spectrum of being called fat. Most times after successfully having their fat surgically removed such persons still aren't content with themselves, because they've search for love and joy through receiving acceptance in the wrong hands (MAN HANDS); by attempting to satisfy those who falsely teach them to believe in things which places burden on their weakened hearts.

(St.John1:9-11/3:19/9:11)This is condemnation; anything taught which doesn't save a condemned spirit, but places more burdens on an individual's condemned heart. No yoke of bondage can revive nor save the possessor of a condemned spirit from the evil condemning spirits of insecurity. Instead, it makes them more susceptible to have a lack of confidence. As it condemns the goodness of an individual's inner spirit, it removes, destroys or kills the honorable spirit of godly contentment from their hearts. What does this mean? Does this mean that it's a sin to use science to identify the truth with others? Heavens no! This means that the evidence of science cannot be misused to replace the faith mankind have on the Lord.

The spirits of those who are misled by the common evil teachings of condemnation are tempted to stray away from the greatest ordinance of God. They are misled to live a life of misery, sorrow, worry, and grief, because they are discontent, displeased, and dissatisfied unto God with their own life in reference of their size or outer appearance. They are blinded by an ungodly deceptive image of their selves, which disables them from clearly seeing just how beautiful they really are. In other words; they maybe deceived to believe that they have a weight problem, but in reality it is the worldly society who has a problem with their weight.

Obesity has been proclaimed to be causing a National Security problem within the USA military recruiting department, but yet the FDA for years had legally allowed steroids to be administered in almost every type of poultry, fruit, and vegetable which Americans eat, without making it legal for the steroids to be properly labeled as an ingredient for the consumers to have a right to choose whether to consume it or not. Steroid users and doctors have always known that one of many side-affects of steroids is that it causes weight gain. During the year 2010 the FDA has legally proposed to put forth the effort to reduce the administering of salt in processed foods, because of all of the scientific evidence of salt causing some of the same medical problems for people as do the weight gain issue. Such as the higher risks of heart attacks etc. After the lack of labeling of steroids on food products had caused many American consumers to speak out, the American consumers are now able to find poultry and other foods labeled with the words "All Natural" written on certain packages, which means no steroids were applied or indigested by the cattle or whatsoever eatable product inside.

Medically speaking, all who are naturally born will die of something someday. Whether physical death comes by a fatal accident, a senseless murder, or the technical terms of obesity, cancer, heart attach, lupus, kidney disease, lime disease or any other medical term of a natural or unnatural cause. All bodies must return back to the dust in which it comes from. Ashes to ashes dust to dust and the spirit shall return to the Lord in Heaven. The soul will go to the Lord's ordained resting place until the return of Christ, and everyone born in the world has a soul which is given by grace to each individual. As we live in fear and trembling of the Lord, and fight during our days on earth to

303

individually gain our own Salvation; peace and contentment comes and fills our condemned hearts. God's children know and understand that the Lord God is greater than a condemned heart.

It is only when the weak and simple babes of all ages yields their hearts to Satan's perverse perceptive of the Word of God do they give him the power to delude their hearts to be inexplicably irrational, as they seek or hunt for reasons to be ill willed towards others for reasons that seem unaccountable or self defeating, but yet appeals to the required religious traditions of mankind. Such seekers devotes their hearts to deliberately and dogmatically behave in a way that seems contrary to good sense by the interests of their own bellies, which appeals to their earthy and fleshly sensations in the seductive fashion of idling religious doctrines that have no basis in facts.

Such likened doctrines requires for people to make unreasonable sacrifices that are unlikely to be carried out after the performance of Baptism, because of the unprofitable and unreasonable requirements that religiously are filled with the commandments of men; for newly baptized members to devote their hearts too. Simultaneously, the stratagems of the adversary transfigures a defective simulation of God's love and present a false image of God's goodness indeed, and also change the appearance of God's spiritual image of peace, joy, and happiness within the minds of God's children. His false simulation of love, holiness, and godliness to men on earth is contrary to what the image of God's love, mercy, and grace signifies and this is proven by the Fruit of the Spirit; not by men. The false apostles of the world truly misrepresent the Lord's comprehensible meaning of how to make reasonable sacrifices unto the Lord and what reasonable sacrifices to him plainly means. The Wiles of Satan causes the heart of those which yields to his way of thinking to desire to seek to be commended by traditional religious men, who idol worship Satan's irrational reasons to hate.

The advantage of acquiring an open mind to prioritize moral values unto every individual American House hold requires the growth of heavenly knowledge to spiritually understand all individual's different personality traits. In the sense of gaining respective spiritual profits of this magnitude God blesses his children from being susceptible, vulnerable, or easily influenced to yield to the discriminating stratagems of Satan. They are susceptible to accept the physical things that they can't change without burdening their hearts to envy and strife. They spiritually are capable of changing the things which the power of God allows them to change, but the most challenging thing for everyone is accepting things which they cannot change. Therefore, corruptibly the people who don't know God continues to war among themselves because they can't change the hearts of those who ironically support the traditional laws of despotisms.

Although God's children are traditionally misjudged by the world in the same manner which the hearts of the misguided orthodox religious world dutifully judges the Word of God, their free spirits lives in love and in peace with a clear conscience unto the Lord God. They understand that their love for God is the truth seeker. The knowledge which they find allows them to understand that Satan's devices works to draw their inner spirit away from being satisfied, happy, and thankful unto God. With that form of knowledge they empathize instead of judging all who can't find the inner peace of God. With this heavenly knowledge the children of God fasten and pray unto God to fix or mend the broken hearted, who religiously are trained to hate them. The children of God during today's religious society are recognized indeed treating all who maybe oppressed by people who are near and dear to their hearts as well as those who are far from the Lord with meekness, gentleness, kindness, and love. Many people live a stressful life until death as they worry about the matters the world, although God requires of all who believes on the Lord God to live worry free. God ordained all of his people and instructs all not to fret, so don't worry; be happy!

Often, people worry about things they have no control of, like dying. Through the power of coercion, the pure and simple hearted are sent out as the Lord's sheep amongst the wolves. The ravening wolves create a false reason for them to worry about how to prevent themselves from dying from certain things which they have no control of. For instance, nonsmokers are dying of colon, lung, and other types of cancers. Skinny people young and old are dying of heart attaches, and most religious physicians are singing a song of a different order. The tune which they sing relates to dietary supplements and surgical practices which place emphasis on the outer beauty of those who are afflicted with worldly pain and sufferings. Due to them having a college degree, many would rather live oppressively under the thought of themselves having the ability to cheat death or the ability to be accepted by the world. The stress of them normally comes from worrying about how they are going to pay the bill for cosmetic and medical surgeries or how embarrassed they may feel to be incapable of keeping up with the life style of the Smith's and Jones's as the perseverance of their efforts to keep up with the expectations of the religious worldly society's definition of prosperity, success, and perfection distort the godliness of their hearts.

> 1Tim.6:5 "Perverse disputings of men of corrupt minds, and destitute of the truth, supposing that gain is godliness: from such withdraw thyself."

In vain the believers of the lies of Satan began to worship and praise his false images and ideas of beauty, because it provides them with a false sense of hope of gaining love and peace from the majority of a society which hypocritically condemns their own selves as Judges. It is commonly known after a person has physically suffered the persecutions of the world to try to fit in with the persecutors in an attempt to gain their acceptance, later they become inwardly torn from the true fact that no matter what they do to fit in they still remain misunderstood in the end to be undesirable and unacceptable in the eyes of those who judge them in the beginning.

THE INCOMPATENT WAY IN WHICH THE OCCULTISTS AND FALSE TEACHERS USE AN OXYMORON TO PREACH THE WORD OF GOD

Being inwardly torn is a good thing, only when it leads a person to godly repentance, but being inwardly torn is a bad thing when it leads a person to worldly sorrows by those who use fair words and well put together speeches which cause death of another man's faith on the Power of God. The Fruit of the Spirit provides evidence of the promise of life everlasting, which is made available unto all believers on the Son of God by the Comforter; Jesus Christ, but the un-forbidden fruit of the world provides insecurity unto death through grief and misery. Godly sorrow leads a person to spiritually see how to restore their faith on the Power of God when they suffer grief and worldly sorrows, and this spiritual sight does not come by the wisdom of men or by the prince of this world. (1Cor.2:5/2Cor.4:7, 5:1)

During the early 1900's, an occultist group of white American supremacists used a combination of contradictory words and taught their kindred to believe that their pureblood race of people were chosen by God to be supernatural beings. Some weren't purebloods but were able to trick all others into believing they were, because their skin color looked similar. They were seduced to lie about their mixed race, because they wanted to also be apart of the occultist assembly of superior Americans, who were in power. The occultists and supremacists all concluded their race were of the most pure, beautiful, intelligent, and supreme of all humanity. They were religiously trained to be against interracial relationships, and in the making of another life they religiously disapproved of mixing their blood stream with any other race of people. The religious occultists' defined oxymoron image of themselves seduced their offspring to judge themselves to be physically and spiritually perfect in the eyes of God.

Hypocritically, many pureblood white men raped a countless number of women whom weren't of their race, heritage, or culture. In some cases, those who weren't true to the pureblood religion of their white race; used the corrupt works of intimidation to carry on as if they were true

307

representatives of the true white American Christians religious belief of God. Meanwhile, they hid the truth of their rapist obsessions from their wives, family members, and friends. On the other hand there were those rare few true white American Christians who were real followers of Christ. With despotism being a major apart of the legal system in those days which they were obligated by the law of the land to obey; it much harder for them to walk like Christ, but with Christ it was not impossible for them to do so. They didn't agree to the vain religious beliefs of the white supremacy, and they made no difference between them and those who weren't of their race. Some of these Christians voluntarily helped the African slaves to escape to freedom and others of them free willingly involved themselves to have interracial relationships.

See also, the Wikipedia free online encyclopedia which defines the Aryan race at (http://en.wikipedia.org/wiki/Aryan_race). The author of Discerning Perceptive perceives the definition of the Aryan race as a hypothetical ethnic type of people. She also gathers this concept from the reference of the Merriam Webster Dictionary and other history books. She says that because the Aryan race is evilly spoken of by the world which defines the entire Aryan race to be evil, doesn't mean that all Aryans were/are evil. She believes there are good and bad people in every race of people all around the world.

The author of Discerning Perceptive believes that the racially implied ideology of extremists like Adolf Hitler was derived from the original speakers of Indo-European languages. The perception of the author of Discerning Perceptive suggests that the superior tyrannical rulers' and descendants of the oppressors of the Aryan Race used a combination of inconsistent words to sway people to think or believe that this derived racial ideology represented a distinctive race or sub-race of the larger Caucasian race, and like a catch phrase their ideology were extended onto all races world wide. For centuries, white people were feared worldwide by all other races of people. An anointed person with good sense, who studies the source of American despotism; can understand how the misusage of the English language or any other language can corrupt the pure mind of a child to be misguided by philosophical words of lies and deceits. The recorded American history was duly noted by historians, whose historical studies revealed the classification of the original Aryan race; was a group of extremist white people.

The inventive theory of the Aryan race of white people was described as those whose blonde hair and blue eyes historically and originally represented an unbiased ethnic group. This also explains why many households' hangs a picture of the image of a pail footed and blue eyed Jesus on the interior wall of their homes.

Later a combination of contradictory words were added to the definition of the Aryan race, and these words were misused to structure political racism in American as did the Nazi and neo-Nazi's ideological concept which predominantly was made by the racial philosophy of Adolf Hitler. The Aryan race's racial theory also became a model for scientific and stereotypical racism in America. That's one of many reasons why the 21st century American generation is still faced with some of the same principle type of Radical Racism. For example, there is an untold and foreseen American story being made, concerning the Anti-Islamic Americans who states that the Radical-Islam is spreading in the USA.

The Muslims Next Door: (in reference to chapter 6 a sin is a sin)

The theory of the radical Anti-Islamic Americans during the 21st century reflects the same stereotypical assumption of the past American despots. This is influencing many American citizens to believe that all American Muslims are a hostile and murderous type of people. Repulsively the analogy of their ideas relates to the same stereotypical theory of the occultist Nazis and the racist white Americans from the early 1900's who corrupt the incorrupt image of a peaceful and unbiased ethnic group of people. The deeds of these American radicals who are known for using the same said oxymoron which generated political racism by Adolf Hitler in the earlier 1900's, is targeting the innocent American Muslim community in hopes of either rebuilding the type of unfair American government which has been destroyed or to alert the United States Civil Defense Team of a possible security threat.

Many white American Christians and African American Christians think these people feel threatened because America finally has a bi-racial African American Christian President who confessed to the nation that he once had a relationship with the American Muslim religion. If the true anti-Islamic Americans succeed at restructuring political racism in America, in the next upcoming presidential election, the occultists may possibly coerce enough Americans to vote for more laws of despotism against all American Muslims for the future generation to reform.

Like all other past despot laws which were portrayed to be created to protect all Americans, the new laws which supports despotism will eventually hurt those who voted in favor of the law more than the ones who the law is portrayed to be against. It is fair to say that the prosperous Christians worldwide must put on the whole armor of God to rebuke the evil wiles of Satan during their last days on earth like their souls depend on it, because it does.

Overwhelmingly, different measures of occultism have the radicals believing that they are obligated by God to use their political powers to rule over and retain the spirit of others. They think of themselves to have a godly supernatural source of power giving them the authority to rule unfairly and have dominion over others. Therefore, they think that having dominion over others will create a balance to the belief of them being of an unbiased ethnic classification, although they're actions are biased and prejudiced. The incompetent way, in which the occultists and false teachers use an oxymoron to preach the Word of God places more coals in the fiery fire of the hearts of the 21st century's extreme radical groups, whose religious theories are shared and fueled with the same principle factors as that of the radical Adolf Hitler.

These religious people are known for using (oxymoron) a combination of contradictory words to seduce every nationality of American Christians to <u>fear all peaceful and loving American Muslims</u>. For instance, they are seen in the news media using the factors of an oxymoron in a desperate attempt to prove there is an abundance of truth in their theoretical irreligious point of views which have coerced them to religiously believe that the innocent American Muslim community is a part of or have interest in being apart of the radical Islam, which seeks to kill all white Americans. Maybe they are not aware that there are white and black Muslims and they all want peace.

Ironically, the incompetent theory of the entire African American community desiring to kill all white Americans began after the first slave ship brought the first group of Africans slave to America. The wiles of the earlier radical American slave masters thought that if they could created a scary image of the African slaves unto all who populated the first 13 American colonies, the true white American Christians would even become willing to persecute, torment, and kill them. Therefore, the supremacists told the white Christians that if they didn't agree to such worldly immoral nature, the Africans whom they breaded like animals would rise up against every white American household. As an end result almost every person of the first 13 American colonies, out of fear; refused to resist the evil temptation of their new world order. They agreed to use the powers of evil to keep complete control of the entire African race of people through the same corrupt measures of despotism which they themselves escaped from. Therefore, they created a desolated environment for all minority groups like the African Americans born in America.

To end the created stratagem of such fear factors requires and understanding heart of the Holy Ghost, which is enabled by God to sort out the truth from the lies. American Christians today whom are endowed with Heavenly wisdom aren't afraid to admit that they acknowledge God is the same today, yesterday, and forevermore. Unfortunately, certain beguiled people today either don't know or don't care to know how the Fruit of the Spirit make manifest unto the innocent minds who the Lord favors, with the sight to spiritually see and understand how the bogus impressions and false ideas of Christianity were sown and rooted throughout history or during today's generation. These counterfeit Christians are false worshipers of God and they work fervently at causing wars and not peace, because their blind eyes worship, revere, and praise the ideology of occultism, which segregates people instead of uniting them.

Once upon a time not too many years ago, African Americans were delivered out of slavery and were given the legal right to have a religion. Of course there were several different forms of denominational religions in America. Although all of America's pre-existed religions had different beliefs, they all claimed to believe in God the Father, the Son, and the Holy Ghost; except the white American Atheists.

Since American religion was forced upon all African slaves in America under the tutorship of occultism by many false tutors of Christ, some of them turned completely away from God and became atheists who believed there was no God, and they refused to believe in anything associated with the American occultists' oxymoron definition of God being a partial and monstrous. Therefore, they believed in fighting for freedom, but disbelieved in fighting for or against any debatable American religion.

Some Africans during the slavery days lived in America fearing nothing, because they had grown to understand that the Devil couldn't do nothing worst to them than that which he had already done. They knew and believed on the righteous order of God which they and their people had spiritually grown to know and worshipped all of their lives in Africa, and they disbelieved that the oppressive white Americans who were willing to kill their bodies could also kill their souls. They weren't afraid of death, although they knew that the white Americans law guaranteed them that they would die by their hands. Others lived in fear of the entire white community and they feared everything associated to the white Americans' culture including their despotic religious laws, which granted the whites' permission to murder the Africans if they refused to comply or disallowed the white American slave masters' religious oxymoron definition of a monstrous God to retain their spirit as a controlling factor.

Therefore; after gaining the legal right to learn to read the English language, some African Americans gradually started studying and believing in the Koran. The Koran is a book composed of writings that contained revelations made to Muhammad by Allah. The revelations of the Koran are similar to the revelations of the Holy Bible; but not identical. Therefore, the desires of the African American Muslims sought for refuge from the white American oppressors in Allah and those of them which were converted in Christ contained the desires of the Christians who sought to find protection in Christ. They all had one thing in common. They all wanted to live or have peace on earth as it is in Heaven, but there were and still are radicals within the religion of both the Christian and the Muslim societies insinuating for one to be against the other as sworn enemies.

After studying how religious cultists who claimed to be Christians, religiously protest as they mistreated and misjudged the African slaves, an open liberal minded person can understand why some African Americans have chosen to believe in the revelations of Allah as the sole deity and Muhammad as his prophet. Maybe they believe in Allah mainly because they think they have seen the characteristics of the Spirit of God working in their favor according to the directives of Allah more so than commands of the blonde haired blue eyed Americans, who they believe enslaved and degraded the entire African American community under the dictating tutorship of the earlier white Americans' false ministers of God.

All are enabled by the spiritual teachings of the Anointed Spirit of God; to comprehend the difference between good and evil. In many areas religious people all throughout history saw more evil than good coming from the despot slave masters who suppose to have been followers and servants of Christ. The goodness of God's character which the slaves' offspring knew thereof was deferred by false teachers, who completely corrupted the image of God's character by claiming the blonde hair blue eyed devils who pretended to be followers of Christ were of a split resemblance of the Lord God's image. Apparently, before the first slave ship arrived in America; the true Christians were few and Satan's allegiance were many. Today, by the power of the Holy Ghost; the table seems to have turned and the last are now first and the first are now last. In other words, it was hard back in the slavery days for an African American and their offspring to find a white American Christian who were willing to walk in the Holy way of Christ. Today, Christians and Muslims of all races are not hard to find in America. On a serious note, many American ancestors were convinced to believe that the white false Christians were using a false religion and a false god to control them. This belief still exists as a major rule of thumb for those who have experienced the rebirth of Christ in their hearts, which constitutes and define a true born again Christian.

The thorough American despots of the 21st Century are not separated by race. The race of them are conjoined at the hip of their greedy hearts as they use fair words and well put together speeches to depict the theoretical conclusions of the vain desires of their own bellies. Historically, they are well known for using vengeance to violently fight fervently for their irreligious beliefs. The American despots and false religious teachers of the 21st Century are working fervently to expand their allegiance by averting or avoiding the true concept of why certain African American leaders were historically noted for violently walking vengefully among the white Americans. They also avoid explaining how the Holy Ghost converted most of those leaders' hearts and/or how spiritual changes were made by these once vengeful leaders before their term of life on earth was over. Therefore, as the despots teach African American history, they speak to insinuate a riot without clearly explaining what led certain African American leaders to seek vengeance. Nor do they explain how the Holy Spirit worked good works for, by, and through all who spiritually changed; so that all nationalities of Americans are now enabled to live in peace and in love as friends of God.

The truth is, there is and always have been false teachers and radicals existing in all religious denominations. The theories of the religious radicals have transferred from one generation unto the next. For example; the white American ancestors were coerced into killing black people for religious purposes and for self satisfaction, and the aftermath of such disorders caused the African American ancestors to start fighting back. There were a group of African American ancestors who were willing to fight evil with evil in the sense of them possessing a kill or be killed spirit. Later, the Christians all over the world can recognize that it was the power of God who turned them into peace making Civil Rights Activists in America (See also the Malcolm X movie featuring Denzel Washington). The African Americans only wanted the whites to stop killing them and treat them fair and equal. Even the radical whites' peaceable counter-partners desired to live in love with all Americans regardless of their differences. Therefore, historical pictures reveal whites and blacks marching peacefully together for the same cause. Within due time, as the seasons changed; so did the white Americans' overall view on Civil and Human Rights. The liberal-minded blacks and whites overthrew the conservatives and learned to live in peace with one of another thereafter.

After all that has been done, the existence of using a combination of contradicting words to place fear in the hearts all nationalities of Americans against all American Muslims; still remains during the 21st Century. Certain public officials and private citizens are guilty of claiming that the radical Islam is spreading in the US. Meanwhile, they claim that their purpose for suggesting such offensive slanders against all American Muslims, which today makes up a large portion of the black community; is because they are seeking to secure the United States present and future generation from a terrorist attack, which they think may come from the in house American Muslim denomination.

The American Muslim community has taken offense to such remarks made against them, but they peacefully continue living their daily lives as a group of peaceful and prosperous working class American citizens; without rioting against their accusers. They refuse to give in to the occultists' stereotypical scenarios that are theoretically brought up against them, even though they are being targeted by violent American believers of such a religious oxymoron.

Occultism, the study of supernatural powers; has always been a powerful worldly tool of Satan's since the first time he himself used it to coerce man to commit the first sin in the world. It is possible that due to the vain beliefs of the occultists during slavery, the mentalities of some Americans during today's generation are divided. For instance the rich are divided against the poor and the lighter-skinned blacks are mentally divided against the dark skin tone blacks. Concerning the divided nature of the African Americans, manipulatively the hearts of them are distorted because of the false idea which suggests that the lighter skin toned African Americans bloodline were better than the dark skinned, because the lighter skinned tone African Americans had traces of the Caucasian DNA flowing through their blood stream. It's a matter of thinking who has good hair and bad hair. The culturally indorsed theory of the Caucasians' bloodline was pure and made it impossible for such persons to be filled with impurities were suggested by white occultists like Adolph Hitler centuries ago. The actions of those who promotes this false theory is throwing more coal in the fire in the aspect of dividing the African race during today's generation, because in return of using a combination of inconsistent words that contradicts the truth; the prejudice hearted have turned the theory of the old made-up ideology of the white supremacy into a reversed trend of intimidation. The proud dark skin toned African Americans are standing up for what they believe in.

Meanwhile, the godly spirit of the lighter and the darker skin tone African Americans are continuing to overcome such falseness with the help of God, while such distorted premature irreligious teachings continues to attempt to bind their consciences. They are comforted by the Comforter of the Holy Ghost to know the difference between right and wrong. They recognized God as the potter-maker of all mankind, and they are gradually becoming content living in their own skin. In fact bi-racial relations between blacks and whites have increased, because the thorn which once pierced their sides has been removed.

Today certain American neighborhoods still live under the false impressions that were given unto their ancestors. The formations of different American gangs are color blind. It is believed by many that the gang members of today's society have been psychologically trained to kill each others by the coercions of the past traditions of the world's irreligious unlawful laws of the land. The East side, vs. the West side, and the North side vs. South side, the straight vs. gay, white vs. non-whites, the rich vs. the poor etc., as if one area or a certain clique of people are better than others. These derived ideologies have seduced gang members and hereditary cliques to mentally and spiritually live in error against the will of God.

Although Americans are separated by their differences in opinions, social out looks, pay rates, nationalities, origins, sex, creeds, religions, races, etc.; free willingly they must meekly continue to fight the good fight of faith to win the spiritual fight of peace within their selves for their selves, as they struggle to live in harmony together with the oppressors in lands or territories which the Lord God blessed all to possess. All of God's people were delivered out of the Land of Egypt. Therefore, all should stop trying to take the credit for one's own accomplishments or achievements and learn to share and share alike. In so doing, all would lack the desire to rob, shoot, and kill over what another person owns.

FAITH WITHOUT WORKS IS DEAD AND WORKS WITHOUT AGAPE LOVE IS DESTRUCTIVE!

There are no justifications in wrong doings according to the Word of God. Men who follow after the stratagems of Satan, supports the wrongful acts of vileness by any means necessary; even to the point of claiming their vile acts to be godly acts. Therefore, it is traditional for certain despicable religious practices which cling to their proposed evil deeds to corrupt the conscience of their mines. They enhance themselves in the continual act of repeating Satan's historical hidden agendas, which are to sow the seeds of evil comprehension and misunderstandings of the goodness of God's grace that resides in the Lord's Spirit of Righteousness and Spirit of Truth.

Ironically all official governing bodies whether Republic, Democratic, or Democratic-Republican have almost total control over the lives of the people on earth. For centuries, by the vote of a majority and by the

317

consent of the voting people, such governing bodies have governed as a Totalitarian or oppressive Government. Fortunately, Christ died to prevent any form of government from taking complete control of the spirit of any man, woman or child which God created. Civil and Human Rights Activists have been fighting a good fight of faith vigorously for years in America, while patiently waiting for the unfair and abusive methods and misusage of political powers within the local, state, and federal forms of governments to end. They are able to spiritually recognize and connect the idolatrous altar that was erected by the Israelites under Antiochus Epiphanes to the principle abomination of desolation during today's' generation that describes the signs of the approaching destructions that were spoke of by Jesus Christ. (1Macc.1:54;6:7/Dan.9:27;11:31;12:11)

In order to change the unfair governed laws, the heart of the people's intentions first must change from the old mindset of one sort of people legally being treated better or worst than others concerning religious humanity towards serving the Lord. The story of President Lincoln winning the presidential election is a fine illustration of how the old American laws couldn't change without the spiritual hearts of the American people changing their mindset; concerning the tyrannous irreligious ideological ordinance within the government's display of God's love.

The American's form of democracy was intentionally made for the people and by the people, as the 16th President of the United States; Abraham Lincoln once said. Therefore, it is the right and the duty of the people of every generation to mark the things of the past and understand which laws promotes despotism and hatred through a dissimulation of love. This responsibility should be done for the people by the choice of the people and not by force, so that all of God's children in American can sort out whatsoever kind of reformations are necessary within their individual lives.

In Congress, July 4, 1776 the unanimous Declaration of the thirteen United States of America, also known as The Declaration of

Independence, suggests that it is the right and the duty of the American people to throw off the design of any governing laws which reduces us as individual American citizens; to be under absolute Despotism. This includes the throwing off our own domestic laws, which supports despotism. In so choosing to throw off such governing laws, we the people of the United States are to provide new safeguards for our future security as a united front; not as a divided border.

This document during the year 2010 A.D. is still viewed by many Americans as one of the primary foundations of democracy. It doesn't constrain, hinder, or confine any American from altering the former systems' totalitarian, despotic, and cruel government as many think it does, but it conspicuously gives consent to all American citizens to make necessary modifications in efforts to prevent the acts of repeated injuries and usurpations to be done against us by any sort of foreign despotic laws within the territorial governing lands; including our own domestic laws. The legal problems of today's society in protecting the old governed unalienable rights of all American citizens whom are endowed or gifted to possess certain unalienable rights by the creator of mankind; is the same today as it was when the manmade laws were first composed, because one sort or group still believe in the racial ideology of the Aryan Race.

For instance, some Americans' perception of the wordings within the Declaration of Independence strictly relates only towards the interests and to the common good heritage of the original Americans' warring ideological ways of maintaining National security from other despotic Nations. In 2010 A.D a Republican politician of one of the state of the United States; signed an immigration bill, and made it legal for the police officers to determine a person's immigration status if they form a **reasonable suspicion** that someone is an illegal immigrant. It may not be safe to give out this person's political position or real name in Discerning Perceptive, because the author maybe infringement of this person's right's, but the local news media reported that this politician commanded for the police officers to start approaching the citizens of the state in which she represented and requested all whom were

319

approached by the officers to show them proof of their citizenship. All American Hispanics were warned through social networks like Face-Book and Twitter and by well known News Medias which reported that they are pruned to be shaken down if they visited the state in which she presided over. Although the idea of this regulator may have been to **protect** the USA citizens, her immigration laws appeared too so many to **mandate racial profile**. Meanwhile the Republic Party publically announced that they desired for the US Military to be ordered to arrive in her state to help protect the boarder.

This protective measure within the United States has always been regarded by the US State Representative as the responsibility and duty of (ICE) the US Immigration Custom Patrol. Ironically, when President Obama took office and appointed more Latino Americans whom weren't strangers to the oppressive conduct of the past USA Republic and Democratic governed leaders against their origin of people; to serve in a high political positions during his Presidency, the idea of the states having the power to do the job of the ICE became a National issue.

This state is the boarder of New Mexico and it is reportedly where illegal immigrates have been known to illegally cross over into the United States or central America even with America placing armed US Boarder Patrollers to secure the boarder. The Hispanic Americans were born and raised in America. Over 90% of Hispanics have dark skin and most of these Spanish speaking people publically professed that they felt violated and insulted by this new Immigration Law. The regulator of the law publically announced that she will have the police officers trained in recognizing an illegal immigrant living amongst the other Hispanic American citizens. Hypocritically her public description of providing police training consists of the officers being trained to listen for a Hispanic's accent. Ironically, the accent in which they were trained to listen for also is the way the Hispanic Americans pronounce their words. She proposed that their accent is an ideal indicator or a sign of probable cause for the police force to use as an acceptable reason for stopping all Hispanics and questioning their place of origin.

The Hispanic Americans correspondingly agreed through social networking, that they thought she had picked a way of making racial profiling legal. During the 21st century the Hispanic Americans are the descendants of their legalized Hispanic American parents and grandparents. Therefore, their thoughts concerning themselves being racially profiled by the American laws of the land were reasonable. Naturally, the 21st century Hispanic American generation has a Hispanic accent. The controversy within this law, consist of the consciences of the highly populated Hispanic police officers which inwardly concludes this particular immigration law to them were unconstitutional. The law forces them to enforce the acts of what their hearts define as legalized discrimination against themselves. This new immigration law requires of them to do a job performance, which they weren't emotionally or physically trained to do and the principles within this law goes against the conscience of their desire and will. Again, any house divided against its' self shall not stand. Such stress can cause a person to lose their sanity. This new measure of immigration law attracted another administrator of the southern state. This regulator publically stated that he also wanted to make it illegal for the police officers in the south to do the same things towards reducing and eliminating illegal immigrants from the USA.

Meanwhile, others are more open minded to validly declare and carefully draw up an undisputable formulation of the wordings within the Declaration of Independence, which specifies the certainty of the doctrine also pertains to the voting rights and duty of every American person; who wrestles inwardly against the principalities and powers of a legal system that legally abuse and oppress them as citizens under absolute despotism and reduces them as if they are less than human. The Hispanic Americans fairly understands the difference between following Christ and following Satan. They wisely understand the common facts and differences of how followers of Satan indeed use the Word of God as a cloak of maliciousness to condemn the spirit of others. They also fully understands that they as followers of Christ indeed are required by God to use the Gospel of Jesus Christ to convict the spirit of those who oppress them in hopes of not condemning any, but to revive and save some.

All Americans have the rights and the duty to use their voting powers to either reform or abolish any old despotic local, state, and federal law; to institute a new or updated Government which brings peace, justice, and equality to every citizen for the sake of reassembling the unreasonable despotic laws in hopes of making the laws more reasonable or tolerable unto every citizen of the United States of America in despite of their differences.

Although both formulating viewable sides are correct, some political authority figures within the United States during the 21st century remains devoted to the United States Governments long established law of 1781 known as the Articles of Confederation, which the 13 original states agreeably established. Many American citizens of today's generation fail to understand that The Articles of Confederation which served as the basic law of the United States in 1781 was abandoned eight years later and was replaced by the Constitution of the United States in 1789. Absurdly the Articles of Confederation is the document which religious martyrs of the 21st century believe should go unchanged. As luck would have it, the Declaration of Independence suggests that mankind can stop suffering by righting their wrong; by ending the unfair forms of laws, which many tyrants traditionally are accustomed.

Quote from Declaration of Independence:

> **"Mankind are more disposed to suffer, while evils are sufferable, than to right themselves by abolishing the tyrannous forms of law which they are accustomed."**

Unwise the despot American leaders of today's generation indeed, are traditionally more disposed or liable to suffer and endure evil, rather than to vote bills into law which can easily be designed to befit the renewed mind set of America's born again Christians. The born again

American Christians of the 21st century, who are putting forth the effort to abolish the old dissembled American laws which discriminates; are being taunted and bullied by those who religiously and politically are hiding behind the old American religious perception of the Holy Bible which places an ungodly fear into the hearts of all citizens. Those who desire to use the power of the old despotic American law in today's society knows that the tyranny of the old American laws were designed to control and support the leadership of the present and future American despotic discriminators' state of mind which traditional religious persons are accustomed.

THEORETICAL CONCLUSION

Life, liberty, and the pursuit of Happiness have been religiously dictated by a traditional religious form of order for certain religious people who don't believe in providing equal equitable unto all mankind alike, because of their indifferent religious beliefs, opinions, and social out looks of life which seduces them to think more of themselves than they ought. Their traditional religions' broadly perceived conceptions of the Word of God make them desire to be worshipped, praised, and commended by men. All those whose alienated spiritual rights are given to them by God and not by man nor by any manmade law, does realize that they as peace makers; aren't warring against flesh and blood as they war against the principalities and powers of the despotic manmade traditional religious laws.

In peace they yet live amongst traditional religious martyrs as believers on the Son of God, and they are enticed by the wisdom of God to love all mankind without being enticed by the wisdom of men who desires to envy and strife. Although changes have been made within the reformation of the American structured laws, by every past and present generation; there are more changes to come according to the wisdom which comes from above. These changes do not include an addition to an already dead law, but are the deaths of such laws through the act of them being renewed.

According to the 3rd paragraph of the Declaration of Independence, it may become necessary for the American people to right themselves; by dissolving, abolishing, or throwing off the political bands which have connected them mentally with an unlawful law of despotism. In so doing requires a person to first give a decent respect to the circumstances and opinions of all American citizens. This has to be done by every American citizen in order for anyone one of us to verify or declare that despotism is the main cause which impels us during today's generation. Therefore, we all must learn to agree to disagree by speaking against tyranny while defending ourselves against the political bands which inwardly causes our spirit to separate from that which mediates our personal relationship with God.

CHAPTER 9 THE START OF THE OLD & NEW REBELLIOUS REVOLUTION

> Romans11:20 "Well; because of unbelief they were broken off, and thou standest by faith. Be not high minded, but fear."
>
> Romans11:21 "For if God spared not the natural branches, take heed lest (afraid) he also spare not thee."
>
> Romans11:23 "And they also, if they abide not still in unbelief, shall be graffed in: for God is able to graff them in again."

THE DIFFERENCE BETWEEN THE SPIRITUAL TRUTH AND BIBLICAL FABLES

There have been many fables told by American historians in efforts to honor and respect the deeds of some ancient despot rulers and their supporters of despotism, as to associate their worldly deeds and rewards in their completions and accomplishments of gaining wealth and control of power under traditional religious beliefs and practices. As an example of such accomplishments "The Willie Lynch Letter" to the early Americans during the early stage of rehabilitating slaves who were born free in Africa or were born slaves on American plantations. Within the historians' determination and efforts made to tell the stories of past American history are two truths, which went undetected or untold by many historian scholars.

One untold truth is that the Root of all transformed evil acts committed by the ancestors of the first thirteen American colonies was due to their greed of controlling money and powers. Many men today religiously believes, the possessive value of money and power is a gift from God and that it would bring loyalty and grace unto the outer appearance of them and their off springs in the future.

For example, it was reported by most news broadcasting systems that the SEC legally protested against Goldman Sachs Inc. in April 2010, for making a bet against its own mortgage investors, whom they failed to inform that their investment was a major meltdown in the Housing Market waiting to happen. While they mislead others, they themselves are coerced into desiring to possess the root of all evil. Certain men like to delude the true concept of having heavenly love, joy, and peace within their hearts with that the same evil of the past which still exist amongst the infected hearts of certain business owners and CEO's of the Big Business industries including the bankers.

The Second truth is similar to the first, which also has gone untold. The second truth is associated to the worlds' emulations of God, which evolves around the vengeful acts of ones' own religious jealousy. During the 21st century, the world's emulations of God are like that which the past despot rulers had for God in a sense of religious people being taught to have an overly excessive desire to be God or gods. This evil generation yet still describes other men whom are appointed by men to be equal to the "Holy Father". Within the traditional religious realm of Priesthood also dwell many religious members whom view, revere, and praise religious leaders like Popes, Pastors, Bishops, Protestant Ministers, etc. These members believe that these men are the holiest and are incapable of sinning.

The beginning eras of such religious beliefs started centuries ago and religious men-pleasers, gainsayers, despisers of men, and traditional religious teachers maliciously past their vain religious philosophies down unto the off springs of every generation afterwards until this evil generation. They today use traditional religion to advise and coerce people to customarily pursue the same religious vain objective vows of empowerment which were traditionally taught unto them to indicate or specify their defined religion's faith.

327

The mental emulations which religious men have of the Lord God's character have been manipulated and misunderstood to be equally compared to the world's motivated religious form of jealousy and vengeance. The Holy Ghost teaches all to mark and remember the things which they were taught in the past. Therefore, the leaders and followers of every future generation may choose for themselves to either accept or not accept despotism as their continuous pathway of rationalizing or reasoning with themselves to fight for or against all others; in an attempt to either be commended by the gods on earth or by the despot leaderships of the world. Many desire to justify or uphold the evil traditional religious legacy within this generation's spiritually renewed group, because people today are still coerced into believing that good comes from the acts of evil.(Rom.11:11, 14, 21)

Many historians have failed to tell the spiritual side of the historical stories, which expresses the ungodliness of the oppressive worldly hearts, who gained earthy control in powers. Nor did they reveal the benefits of the godly gains received by both the oppressors and the oppressed, which teaches all whom gains heavenly knowledge to have empathy for each other.

JEALOUSY

Ironically, due to the lack of wisdom and the lack of restraint of discrimination many despot rulers today believe that the measured height and depth of faith within their own vain hearts are of a friend of the Lord, but bias behaviors of the unwise produces enmity against God and leads people to also submit to the vain acts of worldly jealousy. The jealousy within the religious realm on earth prefers to put people outside of the Lord's amour of protection.

As such religious persons believe their traditional religion equally compares to the godly jealousy which God possesses for his creation (all of mankind), they are all unaware that they are yielding their hearts to ministries which be full of leaders whom either doesn't know or don't care to know; that the Lord God desire to not have anyone to perish. Therefore, the desire to afflict an immeasurable amount of pain and suffering arises and lives within their proud religious hearts. For this reason do their puffed up hearts cause them to be non-compassionate as they use the Word of God as a cloak of maliciousness to fight against the weak and simple babes in Christ, while boastfully they glory in the flesh of the weak and simple.

> Romans3:8 "And not rather, (as we be slanderously reported, and as some affirm that we say,) Let us do evil, that good may come? Whose damnation is just."

> Romans3:9 "What then? are we better than they? No, in no wise: for we have before proved both Jews and Gentiles, that they are all under sin:"

> Romans6:1 "What shall we say then? Shall we continue in sin, that grace may abound?"

> Romans6:2 "God forbid. How shall we, that are dead to sin, live any longer therein?"

> Romans3:26 "To declare, I say, at this time his righteousness: that he might be just, and the justifier of him which believeth in Jesus."

> Romans3:27 "Where is boasting then? It is excluded. By what law? of what works? Nay: but by the law of faith."

They work by the law to fulfill the vain desires of their own bellies, which over excessively wants to be viewed as powerful as God. (Romans 3:9-25) Their vain idea of praising the Lord in the Spirit of Truth and Righteousness with all of their heart and soul misleads them to believe that the more torturous they become towards other sinners who may be weak in spirit; the more satisfied and well pleased God would be of them. (Rom.3:8) Therefore, they are more motivated by the flaws of their own praise of casting out sinners, than they are too save any. They fail to understand that the jealousy which God has for mankind is bounded in his love, mercy, and grace, so that he uses his jealousy not to condemn mankind but to save. Thus to say; God's mercy causes himself to repent of the evil that he said that he would do unto mankind, although man may deserve it. Simultaneously, God's grace provides mankind with the goodness of forgiveness which none deserve. (Colo.3:12-15/Eph4:7-13/1Cor.12/2Cor.9-11/Romans 5)

As the vain hearted spread hatred abroad, they claim to possess the fullness of Christ, because they believe their simulations of jealousy equals to that of God's. The worldly form of absurd jealousy adds to the despot's greed of possessing control and powers, and it causes many hearts to desire to have an excessive relationship with God while lacking the Knowledge of God and the Compassion of Christ. In so doing; their religious intentions to degrade, persecute, humiliate, and to abandon the goodness of God's love, mercy, and grace grows rapidly from one generation unto the next. Many people are coerced to desire to cast away others who also are flesh of their flesh, because of their subtle differences in nationality, religion, sex, race, sexual orientation, origin, etc.

> Jonah3:9 "Who can tell if God will turn and repent, and turn away from his fierce anger, that we perish not?

Jonah3:10 "And God saw their works, that they turned from their evil way; and God repented of the evil, that he had said that he would do unto them; and he did it not."

THE BELIEFS OF UNBELIEVERS

As the despots live in unbelief; they fail to believe that all men are equally created by the same Holy Root of the First Fruit of Christ, and they are puffed up in the traditional makeup and characteristics of religion and traditional religious laws of the land. Like busybodies they boast of their religious differences and pledge allegiance and their loyalty to be against other believers of the Son of God. Publically they profess that their religious faith requires of them to desire for others to be broken off from among them and from God's grace. They preach as if God gave them the power to judge the conscience of another man's spirit as their misuse of the Word of God condemns the Spirit of Man.

Therefore, they believe God has predestined them to break others off from receiving godly love, mercy, and grace within their religious form of manmade political laws. Every tyrannous law of despotism made by man are proven by the Fruit of the Spirit of God to be built upon the sincerity of the world's love for God as the conditions of religious orders simulates the desolated love which befits the ordinance of Satan.

(2Cor.8:7-8/8:9-14) The believers of such rule of laws fail to be humbled with all lowliness and meekness in Spirit. Nor do they desire to be longsuffering unto the weak and simple. They live in fear of being punished severely by God for being longsuffering and forbearing. Therefore, they hide behind a religious dissimulation of love; because they've been hindered to think that it's an unforgivable sin to affiliate with another sinner. They create a dissimulation of love to revere for others to keep them on bad terms. Instead of being endeavoring to keep the unity of the Spirit of God in the bond of peace, they create chaos, conflict, wars, and rumors of wars (Eph.4:1-3, 4-7, 8-12, and 13-15).

As men judge other men, they profess publically that others whom the Word of God says are of their flesh are not of their flesh, and they proclaim that those whom they believe aren't of their flesh are incapable of obtaining God's love, mercy, and grace. Since the past despotic rulers believed that they themselves were the only chosen ones on earth who were endowed by God with certain unalienable liberties and rights, they chose to derive their just powers through, from, and by the consent of all manmade governments. They made policies into laws to suit themselves and their off springs that they taught to also believe are superiorly gifted by God as the supreme rulers over all other races of people through their natural heritage. Their traditional religion teaches them to also believe that the same certain unalienable liberties and rights which the law of the land granted their ancestors, are automatically given to them as an inheritance. As they religiously and traditionally proclaim they have the same religious liberties and rights to reign with dominion over others within today's society, they themselves see faults within their traditional religious way of thinking. •

Consequently, many religious people today desire not to repent, because they are afraid to change. Therefore, by the will and desire of their own traditional religious belief they fight to not reform the tyrannous manmade laws of the land, which arouses their religious hearts to discriminate. They are unlike those who are of their same heritage, whose renewed minds now believe the Lord identifies two classes of citizens of two kingdoms; one in heaven and the other on earth.

They are vigorously busy working on recovering the abnormal old laws, because they disapprove of the recently reformed laws which gives equal fairness to all citizens on earth so that inequality can be revived to persist as a normal form of government. What the Lord binds on earth is bound in heaven, and whatsoever the Lord shalt loose on earth shall be loosed in heaven. (St. Matt.16:19/St. Luke13:11-27) Simultaneously, whatsoever Satan bound on earth the Lord shall loose on earth just as he loosed in Heaven!

> St. Luke13:16 "And ought not this woman, being a daughter of Abraham, whom Satan hath bound, lo, these eighteen years, be loosed from this bond on the Sabbath day?"

Men today who maliciously judge other men lives in unbelief of the Power of God, and like the past religious despot leaders they too fail to understand that all people are apart of the same Holy Root of the First Fruit of the Body of Christ. The despots are the same today as they were yesterday and will be the same forever more. They prefer to have others broken off from receiving equality under the governing body of the world's law, which they falsely claims to equally distribute legal authority; concerning all citizens on earth an unbiased measure of civil and human rights. Many religious leaders during the 21st century prefers to give consent to the government to discriminate and hate people more so during the worst recession known to man. While jobs are lacking due to big and small businesses going out of business, traditional religious people who are employed by the government have converted to a level of firing good workers, because they can legally discriminate against them to compensate the baring of their own employment; as they blame their reason of misusing the political law of the land for discriminations on religious basis.

They too prefer to have people broken off from God's love, mercy, and grace like a broken branch from a tree, in hope of they themselves might receive God's favor and be grafted or united in (Gal.6:12-16). This results from the false teachings of Satan. (Gen.1) Satan presents himself to them as an angle of light, but there is great darkness in his light which God separated in the beginning. As the worldly desire to have a relationship with the Lord, they are tempted by greed to overturn the goodness of God's grace; by not being zealously willing to gather the lost flock with or for God. Only the Lord's chosen ministers and apostles meekly work to reproach all concedes of discrimination, to help the people as a whole to recognize that God is love. If the Fruit of the Spirit proves that they aren't with God, then they are conceitedly working against God. (St. Matt.12:22-30, 31-39)

THE WORLD SEEKS FOR A SIGN TO COME FROM HEAVEN (St. Matt.12:35-41)

The sign of the Prophet Jonas shows the sign of empathy, rehabilitation, and above all love, but the worldly are cursed and the sign of Jonas is hidden from them by God. They are blinded by the light within Satan's deluded darkness. Submitting to the spirit of empathy mistakenly is viewed as a sign of weakness and is frowned upon as a sign of disgrace unto those of them whom refuse to identify with the true character of the Lord's love and compassion. Those who are misguided by hatred, fails to compare their own love to the Spirit of Christ, so that they too may yield their hearts to the Compassion of Christ for the sake of restraining their own hearts from hating and despising.

For case in point, it is believed by many that a terrorist name Bin Laden was threatened by the desire of his own people during the USA President Obama's term in office. Bin Laden's people desired to be redeemed from his old unwarranted tyrannous laws, which distorts peace and equality within their governed form of democracy. He very much so was threatened by the United States President Obama's compassionate desire to create peace in the Middle East and he dreaded all of his liberal success as a peace maker. Making peace frightened and forced Bin Laden into loosing his strong hold in the recruiting department for new terrorists. One thing for sure, Bin Laden can't fight if he didn't have a group who would be willing to fight with him or for him.

In fact, the desire to create peace by way of putting the Lord's meekness into action; has wisely become the new modern day American desire. Christian believers have wanted to bring peace and prosperity into the Middle East for ages, and the new modern day desire of the moderate liberal Americans' interests in uniting as Christians and Muslims alike; jeopardized Bin Laden's safety and security within his own establishment. He knew that his own people inwardly desired to be set free from his irreligious reasons of demanding for them to give their complete loyalty to him and his country's historical violent control in power. He had them all living in fear of his terrorist ability as a political dictator, because he liked to slaughter, persecute, and kill whosoever publically rebelled and rose up against him and his irreligious beliefs like Hitler; the radical white supremacy did in Germany. Before Bin Laden was found and killed by American soldiers in Pakistan, he lived to see the day when the Holy Spirit made manifest the Power of God unto the citizens of his country through the numerous peaceful protests, which rose against his infuriated militants. He may have thought that it was impossible for him to be defeated but it was inevitable, because nothing on earth shall prevail against the will of God. God's will is for all of mankind to live in peace and love one another and edify the Lord Jesus Christ.

In another instance to explain a godly form of rehabilitation and a great state of new reform that has easily been distinguished in America, President Barak Obama nominated a Hispanic lady name Judge Sonia Sotomayor for Supreme Court Justice; to replace Justice David Souter on the Supreme Court. Within his idea of nominating the best candidate for the position, he considered all qualified possible persons' experience and background history of making fair decisions as a judge in the court of law. Debaters against his decision publically requested for Judge Sotomayor to explain her motives towards a statement which they claimed she made concerning her empathetic thoughts about a Hispanic woman judge being more experienced than a white male judge. They publically announced in the news media that they were concerned to know if they could trust her at making fair decisions with empathetic understanding for all mankind as the newly selected Supreme Court Judge.

Judge Sotomayor didn't completely make a full public response towards the debaters at first. The words which some chose to express their disapproval of her nomination falsely charged her of a hate crime. Many Americans who watched it unfold in the media thought that some politicians tried to keep hate alive by insinuating that her claim and statement proved to them that she was a racist against white Americans. Later after Judge Sotomayor stood on the ground of truth, and empathized with those who accused her; she clearly explained how her statement wasn't racial but was factual, and in the end the American people saw through the lens of the media of how her accusers publically withdrew from claiming that her comment was racial. Maybe they withdrew because they couldn't lie against the truth of her responses. The truth hurts sometime, but it always set the righteous free.

Her answers unto the public for making such of a statement appeared to have elaborated around the factual aim which all Americans with good sense understood to be filled with historical truth. All can relatively per-say that the white American males haven't ever been placed in the same unfair political situations as other nonwhite Americans in the sense of them not ever being legally oppressed and discriminated against by the domestic American governing laws of the land. In other words, within her publically made answer which was broadcasted through the news media, she seemed too had sympathetically compared her own personal experiences with America's historical background concerning Democracy. In so doing her explanation convinced most Americans to believe that her educational back ground in law helps her to compassionately be drawn to desire to execute fair legal judgments by; using common sense with much empathy, she literally appeared to understand the broad rage of fairness' which could be legally made by her as the Supreme Judge within the American law towards people of different origins within the United States. This was another godly form of rehabilitation in America's reformed laws, which works for the better of good to end the long reigned history of racial discrimination. Be not deceived, the author doesn't think racial discrimination is dead, but she does believe that it has a greater likelihood of decreasing in value by people like Judge Sotomayor, who are willing to legally use their political powers properly; to do right unto all Americans.

Now if President Obama fully intend to succeed at making peace and prosperity as his common interests which also is the common interests of the majority of the American citizens, the author believes he must continue to defy the odds of himself failing at the hands of those who are inclined to motivate racial discrimination, by speaking truthfully with the intent to reconcile and unify as many American people as he can without making justifications for the past wrongs that were done against a great multitude of Americans. In so doing, the author believes that he will with the help of the Lord; silence the tongues of the present American despots who yet are still beguiled into being against domestic equality, justice, and peace for all Americans. The desires of the American despots will always revert to the works of the old man, which the bible text states; their minds needs to be renewed, because they don't have the mind of Christ. The job of the haters is to hate, and the job of the Christians is to love.

The truth will set all people free from iniquity, and all saints saw President Obama working well with others, like Nancy Pelosi whom humbled themselves to meekly reveal the hidden corruptions and to fight for peace and prosperity with truth being their weapon. Together they succeeded at breaking the yoke of bondage around the necks of a great multitude of American politicians and regular citizens by providing truth to the table, but their opponents still desired to create war. Many are hoping to see the day when their opponents will stop using illogical reasons to keep fight against them and allow the truth to set them all free from the desire of hating and causing confusion. The 44th American President Barak Obama and all who voted him into office has a peaceful desire to repair the USA's relations as Christians with the Muslim Nation, but the spirits of their debaters and religious martyrs which resides within the company thereof; are against making peace.

337

On a similar but nonrelated issue, as recent as January 2, 2011; the eyes of the world were set upon a deadly church blast in Alexandria, Egypt. It was reported by the CNN News media that the Muslims and Christians lived together in peace there and no one could explain why a person would set off a bomb at the Christians' congregational site. According to a forensic test, the homemade explosive device contained nails and ball-bearings. Reportedly in the official Middle East News, the explosion wounded nearly 100 and killed at least 21 people in this church region. It was reported by the State-Run Nile TV that this caused Governor "Adil Labib to stress constant worry and tightened up security to guard the churches.

In the land of Egypt; according to a pre-established population poll, which provides the populace stats concerning the inhabitants of religious Copts or Coptic Christians that are adherent of an Egyptian sect. of Christianity and the Muslims; the Christians make up 9% and 90% of the Egyptians' population are Muslims. The alleged bomber was a suicide bomber. This person's devised plan, which did cause fatal damage to many innocent peoples; imply the mind of ignorance of the Prince of the world which beguiles the life purposes of his follower to be misled to a suicidal end.

As Satan coerces many to place blame, in A.D. February 2011; tens of thousand Egyptians' Christians and Muslims in Cairo publically protested together against Egypt's regime government. Judging by their circumstances, all they wanted from their government is democracy, which includes humanity, liberty, and dignity. Reluctantly, the Egyptian Vice President Omar Suleiman stated to the media that Egypt was not ready for democracy, and he pledged a constitutional reform. The media announced that the Egyptians dismissed President Hosni Mubarak's embattled regime's government pledges of constitutional reforms, and they want him to step down. Once again, the Holy Spirit made manifest that it is inevitable for all countries to break free from laws which govern despotically. The author believes that the sign of Jonah includes the factored belief that together we all must stand for righteousness and truth, but if we are divided by violent behaviors under despotism, we shall truly fall.

> Romans10:5 "For Moses describeth the righteousness which is of the law, That the man which doeth those things shall live by them."

> Romans10:6 "But the righteousness which is of faith speaketh on this wise, Say not in thine heart, Who shall ascend into heaven? (That is, to bring Christ down from above.)"

> Romans10:7 "Or, Who shall descend into the deep? (That is, to bring up Christ again from the dead.)"

> Romans10:8 "But what saith it? The word is nigh thee, even in thy mouth, and In thy heart: that is, the word of faith, which we preach,"

THE UNTOUCHABLE SUBJECT ABOUT DISCRIMINATING AGAINST THE GAYS

As another example of a sign of Jonah's empathy, certain phony Christians and certain fake Civil Rights Activists are opposing gay people equal civil rights of employment etc. Like hypocrites to their own cause, they base their decision to discriminate against the gay population on the charity of a traditional religious law of the land, which is like the foundation of a sand castle. When a wave of pure and natural waters being the pureness of the Lords Words of Truth beats against the judgment of such traditional religious establishments, the Holy Truth

339

breaks it down until it falls apart. There's no dissimulation in LOVE, and God is LOVE!

In general, the religious laws of the land are made up of many members, like a beach of sand by which the Lord is strengthening and is giving true portions of heavenly gifts and understandings unto at his own discretion. As a result thereof, the foundation and the beliefs of the law of the land are like a divided house. Any house which is divided against its' self shall not stand. The solid foundation of the Word of God is a rock of faith (St. Matt.7:24-27), which withstands the storms of deception and the hands of time.

TRADITIONAL RELIGION'S CARNAL MINDS DO NOT PURGE NOR PURIFY THE SPIRIT

The lustful desires of those who has forsakenly lured peoples' hearts into speaking evil of the dignity of God's love, mercy, and grace unto others in false hopes of deliver themselves unto God as clean, innocent, and pure; by blaming and charging railing accusations against whosoever they religiously are trained to despise also forsaken the assembly of themselves. They tend to do so without having the compassion of Christ and without having mercy for the spirit of others. In the spiritual sense, this is one of many examples which demonstrate how men deny the good will of God by subconsciously denying God and the Power of God thereof. (St.Matt.10:32-42)

Since hypocrites and unawares have wavered like a leaf in the wind for so long, their off springs and pupils also have grown to prefer to hinder others rather than to reprove themselves and edify Christ. If that's not a hypocrite than what is? Hypocritically, many traditional religious martyrs of different denominations share the same common interests as judges of the Word of God. They desire to fight evil with kindness and goodness, but in spirituality they subconsciously fight evil with evil. Two wrongs don't make a right!

Unfortunately; it is traditional for a religious group to think that their worldly given reasons for vengefully upholding the acts of retaliation is

340

acceptable unto God, because they believe they are defending some sort of religious ideological concept or theory that has been past down to them. They are unaware that such religious ideas are filled with generational curses. Regrettably, they create for themselves a false sense of inner peace through the acts of vengeance especially when they think they are religiously offending the defined concept and spirituality or moral values of others who confess Jesus Christ as their Lord and Savior. By the deeds of the law, there shall no flesh be justified, because by the law is the knowledge of sin and the law is not of faith, but is the wage of death (Acts 13:9/Romans 3:20/6:19-23/7:5-13/8:3/Gal.3:12). These prior examples are fine examples of how many traditional religions orchestrates their outer appearance to resemble that of God, but their hearts are far from him. Believers of the old traditional religious law must do the whole law in order to be true to the contents of its traditional religious nature. That's like man trying to fit a camel through the eye of a needle. Not only is this impossible, but it's not the will of God's predictable truth.

The problem reborn Christians tends to have against the deeds of the old traditional religious believers is how religious people follow after the old covenant, which isn't established by faith; but by works. The orchestrated style of the old traditional religious believers, works to destroy the faith Christians have on the Lord; by suggesting that if they as a born again Christians don't work their way into Heaven the same way as traditional religion teaches; then they shall not be saved.

Under the New Law of the Spirit of Life which is established by faith, grace comes unto the Spirit of born again Christians by faith and not by the works of any rebellious religious law of mankind. The inward ravening's within traditional religions are rebellious and are enmity against the love, mercy, and grace of God. Although traditional religions have tyrannously ruled the world for so long and the despot members thereof have adopted the name of Jesus and misuses his name to call themselves religious Christians, every true born again Christian of the past and present are connected to the Heavenly Father through Christ under the law of the Spirit of Life. These spiritual Christians aren't idol worshipers of any religion, because inwardly they serve the Lord.

Most spiritual Christians of the 21st Century, view traditional religion as being of a curse of itself and unto mankind alike, because they spiritually believe there is no condemnation to all whom are in Christ Jesus. To them this means, the law of the Spirit of life in Christ has made those after Christ free from the traditional law of sin and death (Romans 8). Although the law of the Spirit of Life has freed all whom believes on Jesus from the yoke of bondage of the traditional world order of law, traditional religious followers and leaders still exist today as if they do not know Christ.

Through their lack of knowledge they still preach against the Spirit of Righteousness as if they do not believe that they are the followers of the unawares, whom the Holy Bible speaks of. They are without the fruit of faith in the law of Christ. (Gal.2:3-8/2Cor.11:20) If they hear the Lord's spiritual truth being told in a way in which their religion does not discern or understand, the religious martyrs and scorners still wouldn't comprehend that Christ disapproves of the methods of every religion which presumes to preach against the dignity of those who confess Jesus is their Lord and Savior; including there own. (2Cor.4:3-10) Be not deceived, speaking down on the dignity of others isn't the same as speaking truthfully against sin.

The Fruit of the Spirit is the Truth, and every man is a lie; concerning the traditional religious speeches which don't edify Christ in the way in which he instructs his chosen ministers to use the Word of God to edify or build up one of another in the faith. Instead of using the Word of God for the edification of the Body of Christ knowing that we all fall short to sin, traditional religious martyrs idol worship the principles and standards of traditional religion and uses the Word of God destructively by tearing down a person's faith. (2Cor.5:14-15)Realistically thinking, some people just don't get it. They don't know how to edify others whom confess Jesus as their Lord and Saviour without rebuilding that which Jesus Christ destroyed.

Traditional religious believers may attend worship service at a church every Sunday or Sabbath's Day, but they can't seem to see how it's possible that it is they who fit the characteristics of the disturbing corrupt images of false teachers and false prophets; described all throughout the Holy Bible text. Like Satan transformed himself into an angle of light, traditional religious worshippers are the main ones who are transforming themselves into an apostle of Christ, but their ministry is of the opposite of Christ. (2Cor.11:10-21)

For example, Christ gave himself up for us all as a ransom; that he might redeem all from iniquity, injustices, sin, and evil; whereas false apostles use traditional religion to hold the weak and simple as a ransom that they might save themselves or receive glory of men as they glory in the faults and failings of others. Glorying in the flesh of others is the traditional religious way of them redeeming themselves, by making their religious selves appears unto the unlearned to be of the Redeemer. Satan liberates people's minds and tricks them into thinking that the glory of gaining the world is equivalent to being redeemed by God. In such case gaining the glory of the world to them is worth loosing their souls (St.Matt4:1-11/Deut.6:16/Ex.17:1-7). While speaking and using perverse words of hatred and malice which the wisdom of the world religiously teaches them, the signification of their voice religiously condemns the spirit of the babes in Christ; instead of edifying the church by that which the Holy Ghost teaches. (1Cor.2:13, 14:9-23, 2Cor.12:19-21)

Christ's work of righteousness purifies unto himself a peculiar people who are zealous of doing good works by faith, for all who are waiting patiently for his coming or return. But false apostles work to purify themselves as they desire to have an excessive relationship with the Lord God. Their excessive self righteous attitude is too great of boastings to be capable of providing heavenly knowledge concerning the righteous sacrifices man ought to make such as humbling themselves with the character of meekness, which is a reasonable and acceptable sacrifice in the eyes of the Lord. Although their lips speaks of walking in meekness as a humbled servant unto all within the world, they fail to do so themselves, because their vain hearts leads their deeds to be evil. They don't lift one finger to gather the least of Gods little ones. Instead they work against the image of God's grace to spread hatred and cause the least of many of God's sheep to be scattered and not gathered. (St. Luke11:23)

In other words, the law and works of traditional religious people can not purify the heart of mankind, because they themselves fail to love one's neighbor as one loves their self. In that indifference or discrepancy traditional religion misleads people to subconsciously be weakened to the flesh which reveres hostility and leaves a bad feeling which is enmity against God. That's why God sent his own Son in the likeness of the sinful flesh, and by his merciful love for sinners; Christ condemned sin in the flesh. So then that the righteousness of the law of the Spirit of Life might be fulfilled in all who walk not after the flesh, because the flesh of traditional religious followers and leaders lusts against the Spirit which deters a person from doing that which fulfills the law of The Spirit of Life..."LOVE". Although Christ condemned sin in the flesh, traditional religious followers still work by the spirits of condemnation as if they can revive the dead.

Those who practice the traditional religious form of what they preach, commits to the evil works of the flesh, which hinders the spiritual growth of the Lord's Spirit of Righteousness and Truth; by spreading hatred and confusion to come unto traditional religious members for all of them to receive vain glory through envy and strife (Phil.2:3). Religiously, it's a traditional ritual to provoke many to anger and be envious. Their carnal minds aren't focused on the law of God, and neither indeed can they please God in the flesh. (Rom.8/2Cor.10/Gal.5)

The law of the Spirit of Life is fulfilled in one word ...**LOVE**, which is a reasonable sacrifice unto the Lord. While the Lord requires all to do that which is reasonable, false apostles requires all people to do that which is unreasonable such as being prejudice, partially bias, and hypocritical blasphemers against the Holy Ghost, while making it impossible for anyone who follows their coerced religious despotic methods to fulfill the law of the Spirit of Life. They are too busy doing the whole Law of Moses, which is established by works and not by faith, and such works are an unreasonable sacrifice for anybody to accept, bear, or put up with.

Jude4 "For there were certain men crept in unawares, who were before of old ordained too this condemnation, ungodly men, turning the grace of our God into lasciviousness (excessive wantonness), and denying the only Lord God, and our Lord Jesus Christ."(2Peter2:2&7-10)

Jude9 "Yet Michael the archangel, when contending with the devil he disputed about the body of Moses, durst not bring against him a railing accusation, but said, The Lord rebuke thee."(2Peter2:11)

Jude10 "But these speak evil of those things which they know not: but what they know naturally, as brute beasts, in those things they corrupt themselves."(2Peter2:12)

Jude11 "Woe unto them for they have gone in the way of Cain, and ran greedily after the error of Balaam for reward, and perished in the gainsaying of Core."(Jude 14–25/2Peter2:13)

Although the chosen Apostles of Jesus Christ ministered unto all the Churches of God to flee from evil and abolish the enmity of their own fleshly hearts, which leads them to be in disbelief of the goodness of the Power of God; the despots prefers to use the enmity of their fleshly desires to make war through the dissimulation of their love for God by fighting against the will of God through their fighting against others. It is high time for all religions to awake out of sleep and realize that there's no dissimulation in love.

> St. John15:2 "Every branch in me that bearth not fruit he taketh away: and every branch that bearth fruit, he purgeth it, that it may bring forth more fruit."
>
> Romans11:23 "And they also, if they abide not still in unbelief, shall be graffed in: for God is able to graff them in again."

THE FRUIT OF THE SPIRIT OF GOD USES REVERSE PSYCHOLOGY TO SPIRITUALLY REVERSE THE RELIGIOUS TREND OF WORLDLY LABORING

Yes it's true; we all individually shall reap what we sow, but it's also accurate to believe that we as individuals shall reap the works of another man's labor as it is written. The source of their boasting comes from the tradition of their unbelief in the Lord's ability to deliver certain sinners out of evil temptatluns at his own measure of debt. Further more, they boast mostly because they don't understand the difference between a person's weaknesses from their wickedness. The godly ones who God is able to deliver are traditionally viewed by religion to not be godly at all, and this frustrates the grace of God, as they desire to receive life from the dead works of their boasting. Can any man receive life from dead works or from the teachings which are of the dead? God forbid! (Romans 8:6-8/James 3:13-18/4:4-5)

Boastings comes from the tradition of religious believers who either denies or aren't subject to know and understand that the Holy Root created all mankind which spiritually means he made all apart of the body of Christ. Yes, it's true of what traditional religious people say, "Nobody is born a Sinner." But they religiously forsaken their own mercy by speaking about things they know nothing about. They use they study of science and other worldly materials and tools to delude the truth of their own fate. Unbelievers don't believe the Holy Root of the First Fruit created every branch. Therefore, the boasting of certain straight branches desires not to live equally with the gays. Everything that God made crooked only he can make straight, but traditional religion fails to consider the fullness of God's works (Ecc.1:15, 7:13, 7:25-29). Without Heavenly Wisdom they fear what they don't understand, because the wisdom of the Prince of the world has influenced them to become over wise in knowing nothing at all of the Power of God. If they knew the Power of God then they would not desire to foolishly destroy themselves by judging others to fulfill the whole duty of the laws and commandments of religious men as men pleasers. (Eccl.12:13-14, St. Matt.10:26-28)

Inappropriately, many people today are divided and are spiritually attached to something other than the Spirit of God. The Spirit of God spreads the goodness of the Fruit of the Spirit unto all sinners alike, and as touching as the elect of God, all believers of the Son of God are beloved for the father's sakes. If we are forgiven by the elect of God's grace, then the Son of man also has the power to do the same. Holding on to grudges and being spiteful towards certain sinners out of ones' own desire to vengefully honor the Lord in the accordance of the reputations of traditional religious believers or to be vengeful because of how someone wrongs them is neither righteous nor godly. In fact, grudges only open the doorway for more evil spirits to enter in and consume the conscience of one's mind to be enmity (ex. carnal minded, envious, hateful, and full of strife etc.) against God, by which no man

347

can find peace within such because all are evil. (St. Matt12:30-45/St. Luke11:19-26)

> **1Cor.10:13 "There hath no temptation taken you but such as is common to man: but God is faithful, who will not suffer you to be tempted above that ye are able; but will with the temptation also make a way to escape, that ye may be able to bear it."**

The key elements of overcoming the madness, is by being humbled enough to desire to seek for heavenly wisdom and understanding of the Lord God with a loving, compassionate, and forgiving heart, knowing that all sins of sinners are forgivable; except the sin of unbelieving in the Power of God who sent his son to save all sinners from sin. Another unforgivable sin is the sin of those who blasphemes against the Holy Ghost by denying the righteous truth of the intent of the Holy Ghost's power is willing, capable, and able to bring all unto the knowledge of God.

Neither of the chosen Apostles of God by any means was ordered by the Mes-si-as whom is called Christ, to provoke any man by either of these types of unforgivable sins which promote an ungodly jealousy. Instead, by grace he humbled them to teach all others to humble themselves and strive worthily as an equal to all mankind (1Cor.9:14-23/1Cor.10:30-33), to reproach and reprove the equality of God unto all, because through the fall of them Salvation comes to provoke all to an acceptable godly jealousy, which leads the hearts of them all to true repentance (Romans11:14&15/Romans9:16-27). Since tomorrow's not promised to any man, the best time to repent and reconcile is the present, because tomorrow maybe too late.

Romans11:29 "For the gifts of and calling of God are without repentance."

Romans11:30 "For as ye in times past have not believed God, yet have now obtained mercy through their unbelief."

Romans11:31 "Even so have these also now not believed, that through your mercy they also may obtain mercy."

Romans11:32 "For God hath concluded them all in unbelief, that he might have mercy upon all."

LIFE EXPERIENCES ARE MANIFESTING BY THE HOLY GHOST

The emulators of traditional religious greed, continuously deludes the mind set of men of all nations, and their destructions have become a legendary lesson for the whole world to see, as the aftermath or the end result of their unlawful and evil deeds unfolds. A few may learn faster than the majority of others from their present and past experiences of life, but if they desire to change for the better or for the sake of goodness, they first must self examine themselves with the Fruit of the Spirit of God and stop comparing themselves by the sown seeds of religious men.

They must desire to change their ways of thinking in order to change their evil ways of living; so that they may live with a clear conscience unto God, but many religious scorners never change. Due to the unchanged mindset of the majority of them, the links within traditional religions' misguided and delusional chains of the worlds' false concepts of God's Divine and ordain order of law have legally persisted throughout the world from one generation onto the next. As the inevitable new spiritual revolutionary change evolves throughout the American land, one city and state at a time; more people who are subtle to hate one of another are living congruently in love and peace without deceit with one another. The scorners hate to see peace being made, but they haven't the power to prevent what God has predestined. They believe God hears their vain prayers as they repeatedly have asked the Lord to prevent equality from being granted to those whom they religiously despise, and they haven't yet figured out why their prayers goes unanswered.

St. Matt.16:18 "And I say also unto thee, That thou art Peter, and upon this Rock I will build my church; and the gates of hell shall not prevail against it."

Gal.6:10 "As we have therefore opportunity, let us do good unto all men, especially unto them who are of the household of faith

Ephesians2:19 "Now therefore ye are no more strangers and foreigners, but fellow citizens with the saints, and of the household of God;"

1Tim.6:12 "Fight the good fight of faith, lay hold on eternal life, whereunto thou art also called, and hast professed a good profession before many witnesses."

1Tim.6:17 "Charge them that are rich in this world, that they be not

highminded, nor trust in uncertain
riches, but in the living God, who
giveth us richly all things to enjoy;"

1Tim.6:18 "That they do good, that
they be rich in good works, ready to
distribute, willing to communicate;"

1Tim.6:19 "Laying up in store for
themselves a good foundation
against the time to come, that they
may lay hold on eternal life."

As imperfect as the people of the world maybe, the worldly laws of
democracy are constantly being reproached, reproved, and rebuked by
God fearing people today the same as it were during earlier generations.
God's peoples are working through the One True teachings of the
Gospel of Jesus Christ and by the power of the Holy Ghost, while
reforming the laws of despotism. They preach, practice, and work
against despotism not in a coercing manner like religious people does by
using profane and old wives' fables and vain babblings as one religious
body of persons opposes another, but God's people are doing so in a
persuasive manner; which sincerely teaches all mankind alike through
one's own oppressive life experiences and by the Word of God. They do
not teach the Lord's way of righteous order with the intent for man to
involve themselves as a busy body in another man's matter, but they
teach for all mankind to learn how to be more spiritually involved with
ones' own matters. (1Timothy1:18-19, 1Timothy4:7, 6:20-21/1Cor5:1-
7&6:20/1Peter1:18-19-23)

The world today, are living witnesses of the inevitable prophesy of the
prophets of Jesus Christ. All throughout the nations, the Fruit of Spirit
of God is spiritually purging the hearts of the American people and all
other people of foreign and un-foreign lands to come together as one
body of peace makers. The Fruit of the Spirit of God gives all believers
the righteous powers to get rid of the sinful desires within themselves,

which causes their hearts to vigorously desire to repeat the forbidden religious conduct of walking in the vanity of their minds. (Eph.2:1-10) The mind of a spiritual Christian understands that the minds of the founding forefathers and other ancestors once religiously reigned treacherously against others who are flesh of their flesh and bone of their bone. (Eph.4:1-12, 5:23-33)

The Lord's Heavenly Wisdom manifests unto the spiritual Christians of how the despot rulers of the worldly hearts are darkened and how this cause their understandings to be alienated or diverted from the life of Christ. For this cause, the hearts of the despots are misled to lack, lose, or be unable to find the feelings of love as they give themselves over unto lasciviousness or excessive wantonness to be gods; to work all uncleanness with greediness. Within such acts of alienations come the acts of violence, which seduces them to devote their hearts to discriminate. (Eph.4:13-32)

Such religious martyrs fail to understand that all sinners are perfectly made, because God created man and woman equally in his image and likeness. Therefore, all are apart of the Body of Christ; with Christ being the Head and the Savior of every member of his body. As the God head of the body, Christ being not the Lord God of sin; nourishes and cherishes the body for all of mankind to strengthen the growth and the effectual working in them by the measure of every holy part of himself to make increase of the body unto the edifying of itself in love, by letting not the ignorance that is in sinners continue to cunningly tricks them into being bitter, wrathful, angry, and evil speakers. (Colo.3:12-17, Titus3:2-3)

As a Spiritual Christian I believe the power of the Holy Ghost is given to all who believes on the Lord and all falls short to sin. Of course God is not the Father of sin, but he is the Father who gives mankind the Power to forgive all who sin. Within the American lands resides some God fearing people of different origins, race, and religious back grounds and they are coming together on one accord with their faith on the Power of God, while acknowledging the same said purpose of the Power of God is for all people foreign and un-foreign; including the gays. Without being partial or bias as Spiritual Christians a few of us desire to live in peace and in love with all others without dissimulation, and the image of our desire simulates our spiritual strength, growth, and Christian faith. We agree in Christ as one with the Lord. As we meekly pursue equal justice and peace for all mankind through godly love, traditional religious martyrs implore and pray that we being the spiritual Christians that we are; would beg the differ of our faith, because it's traditional for them to hide the quality or the state of themselves being evilly compelled under their own traditional false appearance of being good that simulates the heart of them treating gays evilly for the account of what they describe is done for a good traditional religious purpose or reason.

The traditional religious martyrs believe God wants them to separate themselves from others whom are flesh of their flesh and indeed they cast people out of the assembling of men, due to their weaknesses and subtle differences. They'd rather continue warring after the flesh, and spreading hatred for the sake of honoring their traditional religious teaching, which is the sown source of their childish understandings. It is easier for them to cast out other believers of the Son of God, rather than to say unto them all, "Arise and walk" because they don't have that form of knowledge to spiritually explain to anyone of how to Arise and walk. (1Cor.8:1-7, 8-13/Romans1:21-32) Therefore, it is traditional to find one sort of religious congregation separating themselves from members of another sort of congregation, in despite of them confessing their faith is on the Son of God.

In spite of the ordinances of traditional religion, the Holy Ghost is still teaching the Saints how to live and treat all others in the flesh, without being a hypocrite. The Saints today still choose to live undivided as one body in Christ for the true edification of Jesus Christ. They surrender their faith in hopes of restoring the godly desire of being spiritually saved, knowing that God freed all of mankind of every nation from the yoke of bondage, which beguiled Eve through subtlety and inwardly caused her to suffer worldly sorrows. More Americans today are privately and publically devoting their faith as one body in Christ; in the manner of following after the Lord's path of righteousness, which is not evil but is good.

(1Cor.12:8-14, 12:22-28/1Cor.14:1) Unlike Christ, no man is without sin; therefore God gave mankind grace according to the measure of the gift of Christ, which also is the gift of his glory for all of mankind to profit withal (together). By the effectual working of the power of God, Apostle Paul, like the saints today, was made a minister to bring all mankind towards understanding what is the fellowship of the mystery of God's predestined order of law, and to strengthen the hearers of God's words with the ability to compare and comprehend what is the breadeth, the length, the depth, and the height of the love of God, which also is in Christ Jesus. All believers are blessed to know and understand that none of these things neither any creature which God has made; can separate themselves nor any man, woman, or child from the love of God (Rom.8:33-39), but this mystery is hidden from unbelievers. Eph.3:7-16-21, 4:7-8/1Cor.12:1-7)

After spiritually comparing the boldness and knowledge of the present ministers, bishops, and other teachers with the Word of God, the Saints of Jesus Christ can see how some are coerced to preach another gospel with a puffed up attitude and all can see how their boastful patterns are identical to that which the unawares preached during biblical times upon the establishment of Christ's Church. Some preach as if they honestly believe that because they have a college degree in ministry or a title of some sort with their names, that only they are given the gift of praise to minister the Word of God. The ministers whom God chose, understands how these types of teachings cause insecurity and doubt in the faith which men has on God's ability to save all from sin. The unawares have been passing down the unrighteous worldly knowledge of their own bellies through traditional religious teachings for many centuries, and those who stay under traditional religious vain philosophies too long, turns into scorners who refuse the Word of the Wise. (Prov.13:1/Gal.3:3-13/Col.1:25-29/Col.2:8-15)

PUFFED UP AND TEMPORAL LOVE IS CONDITIONAL, BUT GODLY LOVE IS GENTLE, EVERLASTING, AND IS SENT INTO THIS WORLD TO EDIFY GOD

According to the puffed up ministers of the world, they are given unalienable rights by God to administer what they describe to be tough love, but in spirituality they place dissimulations on love and claim to be Soul Winners for Jesus as they condemn the weak and restrain the simple from believing that they are saved by the blood of Jesus. Puffed up they are as they think they can compare the Word of God with the physical sin of a sinner and determine who will not be saved by the One True Judge upon Judgment Day (Romans10:6-12) as if they think they know the mercy and grace of the Lord well enough to judge the Spirit of God. They preach to the weak about how they must physically work their way into heaven, as if the Lord hasn't paid the price already.

Due to the birth, life, death, and resurrection of Jesus Christ, more worshippers today are recognized by the fruit they bare. As the saints of Jesus Christ spiritually preach and practice the Word of God like Apostle Paul did during biblical times (Acts8:1-3/9:3-5/CH.22 & 23); after the Lord showed him his weakness and wickedness, they can now identify the false apostles of Jesus Christ whom preach and practice like Paul did before he heard the voice of the Lord speaking to him.

By and for the love for God, the image of God is edified as the saints dare not to defile themselves by using the word of God as a cloke of maliciousness to restrain or condemn the faith of others. Nor do they commend themselves by themselves, because they'd rather be commended by the Lord God. They use the Word of God appropriately with a pure conscience, to bring all others to the knowledge of the Spirit of God and to strengthen others' faith without corrupting the image of God (1Cor.8:1-3). Apostle Paul, Timothy, and Simon Peter preached much about the discernment of the lying vanities, which shipwrecked the faith of many churches of Christ during biblical times (1Timothy1:19, 3:9/2Cor11:25), and during today's generation the saints are preaching the same.

A larger majority of Americans today are boldly professing their beliefs publically with a clear conscience and without being ashamed of preaching the One True Gospel of Jesus Christ and without fearing the worldly fears of being slaughtered by the religious kingdoms of the world for believing that although profess themselves to be nonreligious, they are still saved by the blood of Christ. Meanwhile traditional religious martyrs are being put to shame by the One True Gospel of Christ so bad that they out of shame are lying against the truth of their traditional conduct and evil deeds, as they deny the abusive legal methods used by them against others.

For example, the militants' forms of abuse of powers are used as a form of torture towards prisoners and citizens alike regardless if they maybe free or bond. These techniques are being reproached and reproved by the intellectuals of the Holy Ghost, and those who are found guilty of such acts are denying the existence of such forms of abuse. The Saints speak to revive the unbelievers' faith into believing that whatsoever God promise he'd do for one, he'd do for all who believes on the Son of God, so that they all may hear and learn the error of man's boastful glorying in the flesh and to know how not to defile themselves by being puffed up like blasphemers, who refuses to humble themselves to feel and understand the godly sorrows of the weak in spirit.

As humble servants of mankind and as a friend to the Lord and Savior, the Saints mourn for those who are weak, instead of delivering the weak and simple unto Satan by the subtle teachings of traditional religion, which destructively kills the faith of the Lord from the heart of mankind alike. As the Saints walk in the flesh they live by the Spirit of God, so that the spirit of them is strong and wise enough to convert the weak and simple from being unbelievers that they may lead them to believe that they too are saved.(1Timothy1:15-20/1Cor5:5-13)

The Son of God has given them an understanding heart to know him, his will and of his good pleasures, and the goodness of the Fruit of the Spirit of God has proven to them how to convert from that which is evil. More Americans today are desirous to keep themselves from idols and deceivers of the Anti-Christ who confess not that Jesus Christ has come in the flesh to save all from sin. They flee from all who are sought out to kill their faith in the Lord God, because they spiritually understands that it is by faith man lives and an unbeliever brings damnation onto them selves.

FREE THINKERS ARE SAINTS TOO

1Cor.2:12 "Now we have received, not the spirit of the world, but the spirit which is of God; that we might know the things that are freely given to us of God."

> **1Cor.2:13 "Which things we also speak, not in the words which man's wisdom teacheth, but which the Holy Ghost teacheth; comparing spiritual things with spiritual."**

Most orthodox American and non American religions are guilty of sowing the seed of the un-forbidden fruit of knowledge without also partaking of the fruit of the Tree of Life. They are well known to be partially biased as they coerce people to be busybodies in the matters of the world, and also coerce people to not believe that God's love, mercy, and grace are capable of saving all mankind alike by the blood of Jesus. These orthodox traditional religions' have taught men that it is good to be evil, even if their evil ways cause others to harden their hearts from desiring to know God. They derive certain passages from the Holy Bible text and use the goodness of its context to befit the religious principles and theories that are destitute of the wholesome truth of God.

Although these religious organizations or congregations are called orthodox, their teachings are viewed by many to be unorthodox and are evil spoken of. Most unorthodox religious practices and beliefs are contrary to what is acceptable unto God and promotes the same religious law which crucified Jesus Christ as a ritual of righteous order. For this causes some people to turn into an atheist. Many unorthodox religious concepts of the Word of God are hypocritical where godly love is concerned, especially in the manner of its described characteristics which distributes hate as a simulation of God's Holy love.

The faith of an atheist is atheistically strong, and they are unwilling to accept the evidence of Revelation. Nor do they accept their life's spiritual experiences. Instead of accepting or acknowledging the spiritual things which they experience in life in the way in which the Holy Spirit manifests it to been seen, they rationalize with the occurrences of supernatural things to physically attempt to provide a logical explanation which separates one's faith on the Power of God, in efforts to make the spiritual experiences of life incredible or unworthy of believing. They act just like a lawyer in the world who works to provide physical evidence in the court of law to prove his/her case to the judge and jury.

The saints' or spiritual Christians' faith on the Lord is strong and sturdy, and they do not desire to worship the Lord under the dictatorship of an orthodox traditional religion. They exercise their God given rights to serve the Lord God with a clear conscience. Free willingly they accept the spiritual evidence of revelation and the way of righteousness, which are proven unto them by the Fruit of the Spirit of God. They receive wisdom and strength through God's love mercy and grace, and by faith they grow to understand the One True Gospel of Jesus Christ from their spiritual experiences.

We being saints spiritually believe on God the Father, the Son, and the Holy Ghost. Although we profess ourselves to be freethinkers like an Atheist, we solely express our belief in the One True Gospel of Jesus Christ without being bound by the bondage of the expectations of religion. In other words, we don't believe that anyone is obligated to under the New Testament to follow the path of men-pleasers, gainsayers, and subverters of the Word of God who may stand up at an alter of a synagogue or a congregation and commend themselves to be ministers of God as they scourge themselves as a thorn in the side of the members and visitors alike by causing a widespread or great afflictions.

As a follower of Christ, we refuse to be either an Atheist or believers of any traditional unorthodox religion which are apart of the teachings of vain glory, because we desire and prefer to be taught by the anointed teaching of the Holy Ghost instead of man's wisdom. We don't believe it's necessary nor required by God for any man to feel obligated to follow the stereotypical religious thoughts of any other besides that which is peacefully instilled in our hearts by the anointed teachings of the Holy Ghost.

It's not coincidental that the free spirited individuals of the 21st century are standing on the Word of God as we fight the good fight of faith for equality for all mankind. It's a tough job, but somebody got to do it, because a large number of civil rights members aren't strong enough to fight a good fight of faith for equality for all mankind without feeling ashamed, abashed, and confused; due to their devotion to traditional religion. Hypocritically, these particular civil rights activists' preach about love, and simultaneously the spirit of hate coerces them to yield their hearts to discriminate against the civil and moral rights of all persons.

St. Matt.10:16 "Behold, I send you forth as sheep in the mist of wolves: be ye therefore wise as serpents, and harmless as doves."

The free spirited martyrs of the 21st century are like the old traditional religious martyrs, but they don't commend themselves like religious martyrs do. They are spiritual and who would rather die before denying their knowledge of the fullness of Christ. Unlike a scorner, they are opened minded to the wise. They understand why their spiritual liberty is unlawfully judged by another man's conscience, especially of an unorthodox traditional religion, which lives by the commandments of men (Romans14:14/1Cor.10:29-33). In spite of the unorthodox judgments made against them, they choose not to offend nor judge any who persecutes them. Their hearts remains focused on spiritually preaching the Word of God to revive man's faith from the unorthodox teachings into believing in the power of God. The quality of their spiritual preaching is for all who has an ear to hear the Word of God. They teach their spiritual perception of the Word of God, which warns all people to flee from traditional religious idolatries that consist of the commandments of men, especially if they recognize the commandments of men killing the Lord's Spirit of Hope/Faith of receiving salvation from their hearts. They also teach all to believe on the Son of God and of his powers to save them from sin regardless if they are gay or straight.

While the traditional religious teachings of many churches of today's society still coerce people to subject or submit to the idolized quality or state of being preeminent with superiority over one of another other, the spiritual Saints of Jesus Christ adapt themselves to the prevailing standards of such traditional religious teachings by using the gifted powers of the Holy Ghost, which enables all believers of the Son of God with the holy ability to humble themselves to live in contentment. As One Body in Christ, those of us who humble ourselves to live in contentment with the satisfaction of gaining godliness over the growing religious desire to give ourselves over to lasciviousness are truly blessed with the ability to empathize with the religious oppressors and the oppressed during our everyday walk of life. With an empathetic heart we are more established to do just as the Lord required of the first church in the Book of Acts.

In so doing, they today acknowledge and glorify the Lord whom is preeminent over all. After gaining the ability to sympathetically understand the fullness of God, any sinner who confesses their beliefs on the Son of God also acknowledges that they also desire to make a fair show unto God in the flesh. With that knowledge, they as humble servants for all mankind and a friend of God prefer to be strong for the weak and simple, by confessing their own sins one to the other and edify one another while edifying God. They are prudent to believe that as children of God they are also inquired as sinners who are saved by the blood of Jesus to walk in truth, which is the light and there's no darkness in the light of Christ. According to the New Commandment, which is written in the hearts of all mankind alike; this is an acceptable and reasonable sacrifice unto God. All masters on earth are given the godly ability to spiritually evolve and maintain a true democracy for all people to live without partiality and hypocrisy if they so desire to do so, while desiring to support and use fair laws as one electoral body in Christ. The shame of traditional religious martyrs causes them to do the opposite, because they disbelieve they are sinners after they are baptized in the name of the Father, the Son, and of the Holy Ghost, and they are unwise to understand the meaning of walking in truth.

Those who desire to continue to live under traditional religion's democracy are spoiled by the vain principalities and powers of the wicked one, who lives in high places and loves to instruct and govern all others to live by the great deceptions and heresies of the vain teachings and commandments of men. Deceptively, many of them think more of themselves than they ought, and hypocritically they desire to support the usage of their traditional religion's unlawful laws, which requires others to be and do things that they themselves cannot do. Such as, being an unbeliever of the power of God's ability to keep his promise unto all mankind by the blood of Jesus. Also under their tyrannous traditional religion, they practice the powers of coercing, which seductively suggest, for the members and nonmembers of traditional religion to be unbelieving of the Lord's ability to deliver all and save all from the yokes of bondage which are of the temptations of this world.

POLITICALLY DIRECT

Despotism, under the power of coercing, convertibly transformed into worldly laws by a governing controlling system created by the first generation of idealists whom desires were to form their own religion and to become rich and powerful. For them and by them, democracy was subversively formed. Although democracy was designed to do good and not to do bad, the partially bias the intervention of greed entered in and created false images within the hearts and minds of the earlier generation of all nations including the settlers of the United Nations. Their greed caused many to believe that they themselves were advocates of supremacy over all human races. Meanwhile, many were forcefully coerced to believe in the supremacists' unlawful religious doctrines, which implies that those who were first in rank, power, and influence possesses the Severity of God's greatest quality of being supreme (St. Matt.20:7-16). This idea causes national confusion and worldly wars to break out.

> St. Matt.19:30 "But many that are first shall be last; and the last shall be first."

Although the American founding fathers distrusted the Athenian's version of a Direct Democracy, they were appeased and impressed enough to conciliate or make peace with the Athenian male citizens' persuasive measures; to rule by the vote of the majority as the supremacists over the distinguished inferior and lower class American citizens which were made up of slaves and women. The men who wrote the Constitution of the United States feared that a Direct Democracy would give too much power to all whom they considered to be the lower class and that it would lead up to a disorderly crowd within the lower class community. Therefore they decided to change or adjust their own democracy and established a Republic form of Democracy to fit their own desires of usage. They decided to divide and authorize powers between the Federal governments from the State, to regulate a particular controlling system of partiality, which would honor their beginning interests of being recognized as preeminent over all others who were peculiar, abnormal, or unusual people to them.

They also took precautionary measures and divided the powers of the Federal Government between the legislative, executive, and judicial branches. As an additive, they took in an extra precautionary measure which included a President to be elected in by an electoral colleague or an organized body of persons having common interests or duties instead of by the direct vote of the people, which use to legally but unlawfully exclude slaves, women, and non land owners. The electoral method of a president is a simulation of the Athenian male citizen's way of being politically correct. Although the Americans weren't exact in all things done by the Athenians when formally composing the law of the land for and by the American people, they used the Athenian's tyrannous general concept of gaining and maintaining control, money, and power.

It is very much understood that long before America existed the ancient Romans were engaged in their own political democracy. They emphasized that political powers were to be brought into existence, and the Romans set their democracy up on firm basis by the consent of the people. Approximately 600 B.C. when democracy began to develop in ancient Greece, a Roman statesman name Cicero; stressed his belief that men have natural rights. His idea later became a recognizable universal law of reasoning for many to not fully submit their conscience to the Romans' despotic ways of living. His belief being equally yoked with the Spirit of God capsized the idea that all men are created equally in the image and in the likeness of God. More reborn Christians later desired to be treated as an equal, while other born again Christians desired to treat all men fairly. This evolved into a spiritual evolutionary change, by which all sorts of religious people from then until the 21st century are still changing into the spiritual desire of walking and living after the example of the life of Christ. Cicero, bound the spirit of all men, including politicians and governmental officials, and encouraged them to live with a clear conscience by loving and treating all men alike regardless of their faults, flaws, failings, and distinguished subtle differences.

BEING BIBLICALLY DIRECT OR HEAVENLY SENT

Also during the middle ages around 400A.D. and 1500 A.D. the up rise of Christianity also known today as the spiritual teachings of the Holy Ghost, reformed the mind set of believers and nonbelievers alike. Christianity caused all men to acknowledge the same religious belief which indicates that all men are equal before God. Although not all men believe in the Lord God, they all fear him all the same. (Romans 14:11)

Christians in the middle ages were noted by historians to have stressed their belief that Christians are citizens of two kingdoms, one on earth and the other in heaven (1Cor.15:47/Phil.3:20). The concerns of the middle age Christians were validly intact as they argued against worldly politics by stating no state can request nor demand absolute loyalty from its citizens, due to the prescriptive righteous order of God's law, which command men to consciously obey God as he works in men both to will and to do of his good pleasure (Philippians 2:12-13/St. John10:25-38/1John5:3-12). Today in 2008-2010 A.D., Christians still use this method to work out their own salvation in fear of the Lord.

During the middle Ages, the argument of the worldly desirers of the flesh, being composed of integral parts within the man made political governing body, united together and formed a feudal court system to protect the worldly peoples' rights to pledge their loyalty and service to one of another. The carnal minded kings, councils, representatives, assemblies, and modern parliaments etc. rejected the Christians' teaching for the occasion of fulfilling the earthy desires of their own bellies, by composing together an unreasonable but rationalized case against the One True Gospel of Jesus Christ. Their case clearly indicated and implied unto the citizens on earth that they have undisputable rights as superiors and fulfillers of earthy controlling powers. They rationally argued that the heritage of their undisputable rights as superiors of society, whom reigned with dominion over all others should also be recognized by the law of the land to also have lordship over all others including Christians. In other words the Christians were demanded by them to respectfully acknowledge their logical

364

explanations against the supernatural perception the Christians had of the Holy Truth. Therefore, they implied for all Christians to pledge complete loyalty unto them.

FEUDALISM

Feudalism expanded from the feudal courts and it became a major controlling factor by the constitutional form of government during the mid-evil times. The composed laws of feudalism placed Western Europe under a social, economic, and political system; by which it legalized vassals to hold land on conditions of giving military and other services to the land owners who were called the lord of the land. After this was legally done in return for protection, the lords of the land were forcibly obligated by law to agree to turn over the use of their land. In other words, man was taught or coerced to live in debt with one another where love is concerned. (Rom.12:8-10/13:8, 10)

> 2Cor.9:7 "Every man according as he purposeth in his heart, so let him give; not grudgingly, or of necessity: for God loveth a cheerful giver."
>
> 1Peter4:9 "Use hospitality one to another without grudging."

This legal act translated into the minds of earlier societies as it does today. As one neighbor defaults their concerns towards helping another, such laws inappropriately causes people to be misled to believe that there is a price to pay where love is concerned. The old phrase, "I'll scratch your back if you scratch mine," is a good scenario to explain how one's own misguided intention of the heart can easily be misled by the unwarranted frustrations of feeling obligated to help another out of troubling times and situations. The frustrating feeling of being kind and loving to another lacks the genuine character of godliness, because it seduces people to give grudgingly. Therefore, they constantly and confusingly frustrate the grace of God's love to become unbalanced by debt, as if there's a debt to pay in order to retain love.

Spiritually speaking; there is no debt to be paid where love is concerned, because Jesus Christ paid that debt along time ago. To love, honor, respect, and protect people under this type of law is worthless and spiritually profits man nothing. Feudalism only designed a legal form of doctrine for the people to be subordinated to live up to the dictates of a leader of more than one ruling system of governing laws. It made the people live inferior to the system's authorities and of its controlling powers. The tyrannous methods of political control of power still existed in America during the year 2008-2009 A.D., but it is being morally analyzed and reformed by the consent of the people as a whole unit under democratic leadership with the assistance of the Republican Party in the USA.

Although there was a wedge between the Christian's belief and the worldly men's belief concerning of whom one should be loyal too, either to God or to one another, the earlier Christians survived by cooperating together to lay out a foundation for the world's future forms of constitutional governments.

For instance, in 1215 King John was forced by English nobles to approve a historical document called the Magna Carta, which became a symbolic representative form of liberty (freedom). After many hundreds of years passed in 1628 the Parliament passed the Petition of Right, to stop King Charles I from collecting taxes without having the Parliament's consent. King Charles refused to cooperate. He didn't approve of the limits of royal power, and in 1642 the Civil War broke out. Approximately seven years later King Charles I was beheaded and the Puritans had composed commonwealth, which was/is a political unit, whose intentions were of the common good of all the people.

The Parliament supremacy was established by the English revolution in 1688. A philosopher name John Locke concluded the main purpose of the government was to protect the lives, liberties, and property of the people. In 1689 Parliament passed the Bill of Rights to stand up for the people basic civil rights. After all of those years of many legal successes, modern democracy still didn't exist. In 1918 for the first time, all men were permitted to vote. Eleven years later in A.D.1929, women were permitted the right to vote on policies made into laws for the first time. Other countries like Spain also dealt with the lacking of democracy for years. The French Revolution in 1789 promoted the idea of liberty and equality. This caused the King to be restricted of certain powers, but it didn't make French a democracy.

As another illustration of how the earlier Christians laid out a foundation for the world's future forms of constitutional governments, prior to King Charles I, during the 1300's -1500's the term democracy and many reformed ideas of what democracy clearly signified, was spiritually shown after the Cultural Reawakening called the Renaissance. This was when the people were noted to have started to require from rulers more expansions of liberty or freedoms, which went beyond the prior traditional despotic freedoms where dominion had been exercised. The Spirit of Christianity originated the conscience of all kinds of folks, to help with the infirmities of the hearts of many, and elevated the people's democratic political views and beliefs in the broad spread of brotherhood and love between all men alike; regardless of ones differences (Romans 8:26). Christianity helped individuals during the 1500's to find religious expressions in the Protestant Reformation of individuals' conscience. In fact, a leader of the Protestant Reformation whose surname was Martin Luther in the 1500's opposed the Roman Catholic Churches beliefs in men being the intermediaries, between God and man. Meanwhile, the Protestant Churches during 1500's were developed. Some were noted by historian scholars to have practiced the congregational form of government, which clearly was built up to be suitable to a democratic structure within the churches.

1Tim.2:5 "For there is one God, and one mediator between God and men, the man Christ Jesus."

367

1Tim.2:6 "Who gave himself a ransom for all, to be testified in due time."

Although the Protestant Church and the Roman Catholic Church differed religiously, as far as the belief in the Mediator, they both agreed to counterbalance their differences to defend each others right to resist absolute monarchy. Together they argued against Monarchy and by the Fruit of the Spirit they provided spiritual evidence which proves that earthy rulers gain their political power from the consent of the people. They themselves refused to devote the conscience of their minds, to the rulers of this world. They stood boldly against the wiles of Satan for the sake of devoting their complete loyalty to God and not to the fears of the traditional religious teaching of condemnation that was lead up by rulers of the world, which places the yoke of bondage on their necks.

Historian scholars have noted the experiences and the purposes of the English Revolution of 1688, the American Revolution in 1775, and the French Revolution in 1789, were the actual acts or events, which surround the physical circumstances that triggered the spiritual war within the hearts of a great multitude of the people, and how balance was made by the people for the people who sought for political and spiritual freedom. They desired to be protected from being forced to live under the adverse conditions of the governments of the world, which ruled tyrannously. The people strongly urged governments to promote the spiritual idea of love, peace, justice, liberty, and equality for all mankind as either a written or unwritten law of human rights. The British colonies in North America in July 4, 1776 had representatives who assembled and vividly spoke out on their adopted reasons for declaring their independence from Great Britain. Their deeds were apart of an inevitable evolutionary chain reaction of God's predestined order of Law, which is constantly evolving to fulfill the American Dream of love, peace and prosperity. It is by faith that the American Dream lives, and some day the hearts of all mankind alike will live without desiring to be apart of Satan's despised heresies and deceits, which leads men to hate one another.

FAMOUS QUOTES MADE BY FAMOUS PEOPLE CONCERNING DEMOCRACY

> FRANKLIN D. ROOSEVELT="Never in the history of the world has a nation lost its democracy by a successful struggle to defend its democracy."

> ABRAHAM LINCOLN="As I would not be a slave, so I would not be a master. This expresses my idea of democracy. Whatever differs from this, to the extent of the difference, is no democracy."

> ALBERT EINSTEIN="My political ideal is democracy. Everyone should be respected as an individual, but no one idolized."

> ROBERT MAYNARD HUTCHINS="Democracy . . . is the only form of government that is founded on the dignity of man, not the dignity of some men, of rich men, of educated men or white men, but of all men."

If the worldly and the Christians during the old-times could work together to keep from being targeted by a monarchy form of government within and beyond the walls of the House of God, surely we today can spiritually stand up for the same things to prevent ourselves from being forced or tricked into pledging our loyalty to the pandemonium allegiance of anarchy, chaos, and mayhem which continues to demonize the lives of our today's generation beyond the walls of the House of God and unto the walls of the governing laws of man that were made by man's hands. The key of preventing ourselves from being over taken by disorder and turmoil is by understanding the foundation of what the word "anarchy" actually means. Within the original grammar of the Greek language in which we've deprived the meaning (to rule) from its correct origin and transferred an unlawful volume of it's meaning within the English word to speak thereof to mean lawlessness. After a combination of contradictory or incongruous words of the English language, the original idea of anarchy has be deluded into having a new meaning which links to the idea of people living in chaos <u>without</u> rules or laws. The original American principle concept of anarchy is an Oxymoron in the English language. For example, [Late Greek oxymoros "pointedly foolish", from Greek oxys "sharp, keen" + moros "foolish"]

Pro-choice is a superb spiritual and acceptable sacrificial way in which certain liberal activists may choose to praise and edify one of another as they edify God. By choice they individually humble themselves to be viewed as an equal to the weakest link amongst the living in hopes of gaining and maintaining PEACE, and PEACE has been freely given to all men by God as an unalienable Right. Pro-Choice is a modernized method, which Christians of the 21st Century use to deliver the original message of God's Divine Ordinance while promoting peace, equality, and prosperity across all nations. Pro-Choice Christians unfolds the truth which indicates, "No man has the power to judge another mans' conscience, nor the authority to demand for a person or a group of people to give their complete loyalty to the ideas of any other besides that which they've solely received from the Anointed teachings of God.

Manmade laws of today's society, still holds onto the evil flaws of the prejudice hearts of past time rulers, and it reaches out against those whose subtle differences and characters have a distinctive quality, in which the supremacists of power, during the ancient times despised the most. The evil unjust and unlawful laws of the world promotes the legalizations for all who don't carry the despised distinguished markings and influence most whom does carry the markings to lie against the truth and pretend not to be carriers or sinners. Meanwhile, the law pressures people to deny the truth of themselves and the weight of the world pressures such persons to hypocritically spread hatred, envy, and strife, and do all sorts of ungodly acts against those who confess or are caught flirting with sin.

Equality means equal opportunity and is written in America's Declaration of Independence to befit all Americans, but the tyrant lawmakers and extreme radicals have historically used an oxymoron like that mentioned in chapter 8 to define an unbiased ethnic code of honor to them-selves as they portray to all other races, that equality mentioned in the earlier legal documents of the United States of America; only represents their derived racial ideology of equality. The vain principle and standards of their racial ideology is used in the same manner as the oxymoron of the Aryan Race was used. While sculpturing an American occultism form of religion, the extreme radicals used a combination of contradictory words to structure political racism in Nazi and neo-Nazi; by the racial ideology of Adolf Hitler.

Insomuch of doing, they have made the law of the land in America to place stumbling blocks in the way of certain citizens, by changing the meaning of what justice, fairness, and righteousness implies. The followers of the tyrannous laws of the land are like the followers of the sect of the Pharisees, they are totally exact in their physical appearance, but their hearts are far away from serving the Lord in righteousness and in truth. Equality from a tyrant's point of view is sanctioned by their vain authoritative approval.

Pro-choice is the ideal proven factor of faith amongst the Saints that suggests that all men are created equally by God to have a right to live in absolute proscription to God within their own spiritual conscience, without being forced to give absolute loyalty to the ideas of another man's religious beliefs. While engaged in a personal relationship with God the Father, the Son, and the Holy Ghost; the spirit of pro-choice activists understands that they must give an account for their own actions upon the day of judgment unto God whether good or bad, and with a clear conscience they choose to live and let live without defiling their own genuine consciences nor the consciences of others. (Acts 23:1/24:16/Romans 13:5)

371

> 1Peter2:19 "For this is
> thanksworthy, if a man for
> conscience toward God endure
> grief, suffering wrongfully."

> 1Peter2:20 "For what glory is it, if,
> when ye be buffeted for your faults,
> ye shall take it patiently? but if,
> when ye do well, and suffer for it,
> ye take it patiently, this is
> acceptable with God."

> 1Peter4:14 "If ye be reproached for
> the name of Christ, happy are ye;
> for the spirit of glory and of God
> resteth upon you: on their part he is
> evil spoken of, but on your part he
> is glorified."

On the other hand, worldly politicians and traditional religious cultists have defined Pro-choice by their own religious definitions and psychological ideas which imply different restrictions and limitations to be placed onto the lives of individuals whom they oppress. They do so as if they believe they can and/or must give an account to the Lord God for the actions of others upon the Day of Judgment. In the mist of all their doings, the anger within their own hearts vengefully leads the deeds of their flesh to cause misery and hatred to be spread abroad the lives of many people. It's time for change and the change doesn't come by man but by the Spirit of the Holy Ghost.

> 1Peter4:15 "But let none of you
> suffer as a murderer, or as a thief,

or as an evildoer, or as a busybody in other men's matters."

1Timothy5:13 "And withal (together) they learn to be idle, wandering about from house to house; and not only idle, but tattlers also and busybodies, speaking things which they ought not."

1Thessalonians3:11 "Now God himself and our Father, and our Lord Jesus Christ, direct our way unto you."

1Thessalonians3:12 "And the Lord make you to increase and abound in love one towards another, and towards all men, even as we do toward you:"

1Thessalonians3:13 "To the end he may stablish your hearts unblameable in holiness before God, even our Father, at the coming of our Lord Jesus Christ with all his saints."

THEORETICAL CONCLUSION (Romans9:13-18)

(1Cor.8/1Cor9:11-13/Lev.6:16, 26) Not every educated man that has the worldly knowledge of a scholar have the sense of right and wrong or are knowledgeable of what an idol is, nor are they aware of which idol thing is considered to be weak and defiled in the spiritual eye. (Titus1:10-15/1Cor.9:21-27/2Tim.2:1-14) Unto the pure all things are pure, but unto them that are defiled and unbelieving is nothing pure; but even their minds and conscience is defiled. Any men who strive for mastery, yet he is not crowned except he strives lawfully.

There were false prophets also among the people who entered in as unawares unto the chosen Apostles of God while the chosen ones were worshipping and ministering the Word of God as instructed of them by the Lord Jesus Christ. Today during the 21st century there shall be false teachers among us privately and subconsciously bringing in damnable heresies, even denying the Lord that brought them, and bring upon themselves swift destruction. They are the spots and blemish of your flesh and many of you shall follow the pernicious, destructive, and spiteful ways of these unawares' traditional reasons and motives of whom their way of truth shall be evilly spoken of.

> **1Peter3:8-9 "Finally, be ye all of one mind having compassion one of another, love as brethren, be pitiful, be courteous not rendering evil for evil, or railing for railing, but contrariwise blessing; knowing that ye are thereunto called, that ye should inherit a blessing."**

> **1Tim.1:15 "This is a faithful saying, and worthy of all acceptation, that Christ Jesus came into the world to save sinners; of whom I am chief."**

1Tim.1:16 "How be it for this cause I obtained mercy, that in me first Jesus Christ might shew forth all longsuffering, for a pattern to them which should hereafter believe on him to life everlasting."

> Col.4:1 "Masters, give unto your servant that which is just and equal; knowing that ye also have a Master in Heaven." (1Peter 2)

The laws of the land being composed by man aren't in compliance with the Commandments of GOD. As a personal opinion, if the laws of the land would have made it illegal for man to hate or to spread hatred, then the followers of the laws of the land would be susceptible to gain an inner balance of world peace. Since the manmade law of all Nations or Kingdoms under the heavens is made up like the Doctrine of the Pharisees and Sadducees, they are hypocrisy. In the beginning when man first made laws, it was developed by the vexation of their hearts. Its foundation was built upon the desires of their own bellies to be gods. The bases of the manmade laws were built by the founding forefathers consented and approved theoretical ideas and concepts of right and wrong. The laws of the land became a legal form of a religious doctrine, which the composers used to judge and to discriminate against all who weren't of their common heritage.

THROUGH THE FAITH OF THOSE WHOM THE LORD MOLDS, PEACE IS BROUGHT FORTH WITHIN THE WORKS OF REFORMED LAWS.

> Acts7:35 "This Moses whom they refused, saying, Who made thee a ruler and a judge? the same did God send to be a ruler and a deliverer by the hand of the angel which appeared to him in the bush."

Acts7:36 "He brought them out, after that he had shewed wonders and signs in the land of Egypt, and in the Red sea, and in the wilderness forty years."

Acts7:37 "This is that Moses, which said unto the children of Israel, A prophet shall the Lord your God raise up unto you of your brethren, like unto me; him shall ye hear."

Acts7:38 "This is he, that was in the church in the wilderness with the angel which spake to him in the mount Sī'-nă, and with our fathers: who received the lively oracles to give unto us:"

Acts7:39 "To whom our fathers would nor obey, but trust him from them, and in their hearts turned back again into Egypt,"

Acts7:40 "Saying unto Aaron, Make us gods to go before us; for as for this Moses, which brought us out of the land of Egypt, we wot not what is become of him."

In the American lands, the elderly and the young during the 21st century; recognizes the 14th American President, Abraham Lincoln; as the Greater Emancipator, because he wrote the Emancipation Proclamation, which abolished slavery and freed the black slaves in America. Regardless of how many Presidents which the American people have had, it is amazing how the names of some don't just automatically pop up in the minds of the entire American population quit like that one named,

"Good Old Abraham Lincoln." During the time of his life he was as of a voice of one out of the voices of many white supremacists whose hearts repented, and reaped the labors of other men who worked before him. (Dan.2:1-3, 4:5-7/St. John4:34-38)

He was converted into an abolitionist (a free spirited thinker of God), and meekly fought against the political standards of the white supremacy whom believed black people were wild beasts and were without a soul. During those good old days, a black man living in America wasn't legally considered to be a MAN at all. They weren't legally permitted to read, write, nor do arithmetic. Centuries later, the term "I AM A MAN" became a universal cry for and by the blacks derived from the earlier Africans which lived in America.

The American peoples' political views of democracy as we know it today, are politically divided into two separate organizations; the Democratic and Republic party. Not all white peoples shared the same views with the white supremacy laws during the days of slavery, because the vote of the white abolitionists out voted the white Supremacists when Lincoln was elected the United States 14th President, and during those days blacks weren't allowed to vote. The reformations of the American laws that preexisted before today weren't made by blacks, but were made by all whom spiritually supports the earlier Americans who sought to recreate the laws to make it equivalently relevant to the spirit of the people, for the people, and by the people so that all mankind can be granted equal equitable.

American History and African-Americans' History both reveals how and why the Supremacists traditionally viewed black peoples to be nothing more than a piece of materialistic property, which they kidnapped out of the lands of Africa to sell, purchase, and to own as a product. As Abraham ran for the United States President's candidacy, he was scorned by many rebellious white supremacists that deemed it to be unlawful to take away another man's personal property. Of course they were reflecting their ideas as slave owners, who were unwilling to be forced by any law to free their slaves. Although Lincoln preferred himself to be a white Supremacist, he referred to describe democracy as a government of the people, by the people, and for the people including the blacks. Other white Supremacists of the Republican Party many times openly argued that the Constitution of the United States wasn't intentionally speaking about blacks where it states, that all men are created equal.

Due to the strong hold of the white supremacists' republic political views on democracy during those days, Lincoln knew that his run for the President position of the United States was threatened by those who idolized political greed and prejudices. He therefore was noted for saying that he agreed along with the white supremacists' inherited views on equality, but he agreed not as a slave master but as an abolitionist.

When his opposing counter parts heard this, they disgracefully accused and mocked him due to his own proclaimed position as an abolitionist, by labeling him as a "Nigger Lover". This name was a low form and disgraceful name to be called during his days. As a token of remembrance, Lincoln's face was placed in the opposite direction on a copper coin known as a penny. The value of a penny at the time was of the lowest value known as American money. Its worth is valued at one cent, but ironically the value of a penny is now worth more than the coins which are no longer made out of pure gold or silver. Based on the comparison of purity between that of a copper penny, and of all other coins which now contains the metal which is added in the silver coins during the process of making of them, the value of copper is worth more. "The Last shall be First and the First shall be the last." Not just in the physical sense, but also in the Spiritual sense of life everlasting.

As a white reborn Christian, President Lincoln defended his role as a white supremacist by stating that he didn't think the American Constitution of the United States was referring to the men, women, and children of the African American's community where it reads, "All men are created equal," but he strongly stood firm on his spiritual beliefs which led him to desire to give compensation to the blacks in return for their sufferings. He showed through his actions that the quality or state of his mind was focused on making reformation, repentance, and reconciliation for hopes of gaining redemption. During much studies of American history this side of the story is rarely mentioned or is uniquely disguised behind the world's interpretation; which speaks evil of Lincoln's dignity, but the truth is the light and all things done in the dark are being brought to the light.

Today many blacks and whites believe that Lincoln contradicted himself, because they fail to humble themselves to understand the trials of his troubling tribulations. Like all ministers of God; Lincoln was made a minister according to the dispensation of God, which was given in season to him to pass down for all others after him to follow and fulfill the Word of God. Just because he didn't read off the Holy Scriptures every time he spoke or carried the title of a Rev., deacon, or Pastor, etc.; in front of his name, doesn't take away the fact that when he preached the gospel; he also practiced what he preached. By faith he set a system of rules for ordering affairs within the law of the land, which was designed to persist for as long as it benefitted the sole purpose and intent of his heart, which constitutes the righteous order of the gospel of Christ without charge. Therefore as a freeman of God, who was free from all men, he willingly made himself a servant unto all Americans whether free or bond. (1Cor.9:1-27/Colo.1:25-29)

This was and is a major aspect of the earlier American characteristic, which clearly explains a major segment of America's unresolved livelihood. Within all of the belittling and downsizing that the historians spoke against concerning the good white Samaritans which existed in the United States of America before slavery was abolished, many historian scholars have over exaggerated, distorted, and changed the true appearance of the godly compassion of the original American settlers; only to criticize and pass false judgment upon them by accusing and labeling them to be viewed as a group of cold hearted devils. If historians would've included the true details of how the original loving hearted Americans Christians really were, it would've logically explained to the future generation of the true cause of Lincoln's depressed state

380

of mind, which is incorrectly taught unto us to be due to the lack of sanity. In spirituality, he possibly felt the oppressors' terrors of emotional despair, which attacked him from all sides (2Cor.6:3-18, 11:23). After comparing spiritual things with spiritual, all can plainly see how easy it have been for men to misjudge another for their faults. Unfortunately the carnality of a judgers' mindset prevents them from understanding why God forbid them to judge any man at all.

After comparing spiritual things with spiritual, the Holy Ghost reveals how Lincoln spiritually did the same things which we the people of the United States of America during 2009 A.D. does when we are faced with the evilest things of the world which works to condemn and kill us. President Lincoln had to wrestle against the principalities and powers of the world as he worked to abolish slavery. He even suggested having all the black slaves set free from the yokes of bondage of the white American supremacists' laws with the option of having them shipped out to reside in a different land or territory so they could be free to live and create their own self government. By choice, Abraham Lincoln abused not his power in the gospel during his elected time on earth as The United States 14th President.

Within this new generation of the 21st century, many white Americans are unfairly marked by bad memories that consist of the white American race being described as a torturous body of people. "Go back to Africa Nigger!" is a phrase most black Americans from the age of 35+plus, can remember being personally said unto them in-between the late 1960's thru the early 1980's. The free black Americans respectfully know that there were two sides to this historical story. They without boastful pride believe that the private white abolitionists who defended them, were not totally insulted, when the blacks responds to the cruel paraphrase went on to say in return; to the bad reputation of their white despotic counter parts and prejudice family members, that they have remained living in the United States of American since the first slave ship sailed in.

This sort of conflict of interest led up to many years of arguments and much division within the whites' religious community where godliness and love is concerned. For many years the white supremacists forced the blacks to go to their church houses every Sunday, especially in the Southern part of the United States. Within their church they taught their black slaves how they ought to religiously worship God as Christians, which included how to live in tyranny and in fear of the white community as if the white men were their GOD.

It is deeply believed by many elderly American abolitionists that the time and season of their awakening after receiving the Lord's truth, would occur before their physical deaths. Meanwhile, they as living witnesses accredits Jesus after seeing how the Lord God has directed their steps and lead them straight through their trials and tribulations in the righteousness of the Lord's preferred sense of righteous order. Therefore, they have no reason to doubt that the Lord will make away for them to live and see all the things which the Father promised.

Spiritual things are seen by all who live in love. Such persons are led by the Spirit of God to believe that the Lord hears their cry, and answers their prayers as he has promised. Those who suffer persecutions and are ridiculed for the confession of their sin may not know that they are all freed from the bondage of the old law if they remain to be tutored under the leadership of false teachers. In much regards, their spiritual minds of the lost when the hearts of them are led under the tutorship of God's chosen minister, the desires of them should be stirred towards independently gaining peace and freedom instead of them feeling obligated to do the whole Law of Moses.

When the lost are found receiving spiritual tutoring by a chosen minister of God, their hearts are guided to rightfully understand of which law they are taught. So regardless if it is the Law of Moses or of some other law that works against the New Commandment of the Lord, they are made aware by the fruit of the Spirit of what is permissible for their hearts to yield too. The followers of the laws which support the tradition of men's religious engagements are well known for creating desolation, misery, division, and warfare. The permissible creation of the Greatest Commandment of the Lord bears the opposite result thereof. Even a baby can understand the differences.

With faith on the Lord all sinners are bound to confess their sin, but due to false teachers of the Lord's ministry; those who are rightfully lead up by the Spirit of the Lord to confess of their sin are ridiculed by the despisers of men, gainsayers, and seducers in the world. Even the most prudent men alive love to talk with a forward and perverse tongue, which yearns to gossip whispers, and make complaints against others. We all shall spiritually know them by the fruits they bare. They may smile in our faces and through their good words and fair speeches stab us in our backs, but vengeance isn't ours to fight for; it's the Lord's fight and he is fighting for us all. AMEN!

The goodness within the Lord's chosen ministers encourages us to pray not for the riches of the world which could be lost, stolen, or shall someday be given over to decay; like the price value of an American dollar has decayed over the years to a failing economy. The Lord's chosen ministers are encouraged to pray for heavenly rewards instead of the temporary things like money or the things money may buy, because as earthy things perishes to the point of almost being worthless to the possessors thereof; so will the faith of the possessors thereof shall perish.

As an illustration of what a worshiper of worldly riches and money maybe capable of, simply seek out the true story of the American man who crashed an airplane into an American IRS building and killed himself and others. Within the search, ask yourself what was the state of his mindset. Of course no man alive may ever know for sure, but many speculations may cause a person to think that he acted out of madness or frustration, due to his person experience involving a failing American economy.

The spirit of some Americans who may suffer economic failings may either turn to ask for government assistance or plea to be excused for making extreme decisions under extreme circumstances. Who honestly knows what a person is going through as they deal with a great lose of riches during a recession? After the value of money has lost its stamina and no longer reigns with enough power to support the needs of an American working family's living expenses, the American Dream to them over seas in other countries may appear now to be an American nightmare. The goodness within spiritual men desires to pray for the heavenly treasurers, which no other man on earth can take away from them; like having a peace of mind while living through much Hell on earth. Like farmers and like the ants, the spiritual peoples know when it's time to plow, plant and harvest.

For example, those Americans who stood against Abraham Lincoln; the USA's 14th President, wanted to make the blacks think like the majority of American white supremacy Christians and the white supremacists were coerced to think that all blacks were hellhound. His opponents resorted to such religious teachings, because they were overall against allowing all other religious white voters who lifted up their voices against despotism to vote for Abraham Lincoln.

It is highly believed by the author of Discerning Perceptive who gives respectful regards to the Lord of lords, the King of kings, and the Master of all masters; that the circumstance of the American way of living a divided life exists because during the process of forming America many spiritual-minded white Americans acknowledged their faith on the Lord and proclaimed publically that they disbelieved in the domineering mindset of the non-compassionate masters in earth. As an end result Sister Glory believes that later, these peace making individuals became known as the Democratic Party.

The main focus of the American Democrats' political agenda seems to have always been to satisfy the spiritual law which Jesus Christ reestablished and written in their hearts. The Law of Christ is accredited in America for creating domestic peace for all citizens who differ in various ways. American History reveals many peaceable Democratic members who have fought passionately against the non-compassionate ideal law makers who during times past and present desires to run a country under total absolutism or totalitarianism to have dominion over other human beings.

Indeed totalitarianism enhances the minds of non-compassionate men whose greedy hearts and minds convincingly twains together with their passionate desire to have complete control of authority and dominion in a physical unholy war. As their hateful hearts search the world over to find a way to have the final say-so in the political aspect of life in concern of them making a way for themselves to physically prosper, they willingly misuse their political powers to draw themselves physically closer to a legal but yet unlawful remedy which persuasively enforces their slavery mentality.

There's a little good and bad in everyone, and there's no-one who's better than the Lord. Therefore, the American Republic and Democratic Party are all urged to give in account of their intent for acting out in the political field of life. As members of a higher Party than the one on earth all Americans are in deep need to understand who they are serving. All throughout history many members of both parties has suggested that they have at some point felt that it was the duty of their ancestors and now is their offspring's inherited duty; to stay unmoved as a group of opinionated individuals.

The ideal aspect for the Republic members is to convert the rich Democrats to think that complete despotism within the American traditional religious laws of the land should be supported by every generation even after understanding the first despotic legal system in America brought forth destructions, divisions, and wars through arrogance and boastful pride. Meanwhile, the ideal aspect of the Democratic members is to remind the rich whom weren't born with a silver spoon in their mouths of the unfair things they once suffered as law abiding citizens under the unfair laws of the Republic Party before they became rich with worldly possessions.

The Lord giveth to the deserving and the undeserving alike because he's a just God, and the Lord shall taketh away. Destruction may end up being the worst case scenario for both American Parties if the two can't learn to co-exist as servants of God. The Lord has the Power to take away all that man have and to leave them with nothing if he so chooses to do so, as an ordinance of humbling everyone. Every knee shall bend and every tongue must confess Jesus is Lord.

SATAN MEANT TO DO EVIL IN OXFORD, MS BUT GOD MADE ALL THINGS AND PREDESTINED FOR ALL TO DO GOOD

As an illustration, I was baptized at a young age at my dad's family church, in my home town of Oxford, MS. This church has deep roots in America's History, which runs deep within the South. I must say that this church's history within the community of Oxford, MS in Lafayette Co. astonishes me more so than any other church's histories which I've visited during my life time.

Some Americans and immigrants who seek to find a close connection with the Lord, travels to faraway lands that are written in the Holy Bible to see where the Lord ministered unto the people before he was crucified, but I found closeness with the Lord as a diligent seeker of righteousness and truth in my own back yard. Without going outside the USA, I've learned that my family's primary church home miraculously was the first ever black origin church established in Oxford, MS in A.D. 1865. The Town of Oxford, MS is well known as the home of a famous author whose sure name is William Falkner.

History reveals how in A.D. 1865 the original white citizens of Oxford, MS decided to give the blacks, whom they owned and coerced to participate in their church's faith; a church building of their own to worship God in the same mannerism as that of their white missionary. In those days the whites took their black slaves to their church. Upon receiving their own church, the blacks agreed to name it after the whites' Church. Therefore the blacks named their given church, "The Philadelphia Missionary Baptist Church."

The natural attachment which I have with this church goes back to my childhood, when I use to watch my granddad; Enoch Sanders, whom was called by the Lord to be a deacon. My granddad was born in 1909, and the Lord blessed me to learn much from him during my early childhood as a pure hearted babe in Christ. Being raised up on his farm, he strongly believed in bring up his grandchildren and all other children of the neighborhood in the way in which they ought to go. He strongly believed that in doing so, if a child grows up and strays away from the spiritually righteous things of God they'll return back to the righteous form of God's knowledge again. Throughout the years of my many different experiences, by the Spirit of God dwelling within me; I'd like to share what I've spiritually analyzed after I've seen the consistencies of the Lords' spiritual gifts evolving into reality before my very eyes. Therefore, with great caution I do not tell this spiritual story with the devilish intent to fault any man, dead or alive.

For the true purpose of implying a greater or superficial likelihood of truth, I the author of Discerning Perceptive do imply as a discerner of the Spirit; say that I believe that it was the Power of God that unified the blacks and the whites where I was born and raised. The hypothesis of my personal spiritual insights and theories were spiritually analyzed as I personally researched the historical background of the first established black originated church in Oxford, MS. The Philadelphia Missionary Baptist Church was the beginning root of my expanded lifelong spiritual journey.

Although my theory isn't something that I can prove, the Fruit of the Spirit proves what is righteous unto me and it is by faith that I believe that the Fruit of the Spirit proved in A.D. 1865 unto the residents of Oxford, MS whom were poor in spirit, that they were ordained by God to peacefully co-exist. It's not a secret of how things were for the blacks in the south during those days. At the time the blacks were controlled by the whites, and they were considered as the most despised residents. The Spirit of God clearly brought in an inevitable revolutionary change to the entire Lafayette Co. Community. The Power of God convicted the weak and made them to be strong in the Spirit.

To the same token, I truly believe that God enabled the original white Christians of the Philadelphia Baptist Church in Oxford, MS to be spiritually guided by the teachings of the Holy Ghost, and the teachings of the Holy Ghost directed their hearts to endure great persecutions from their own kindred and strangers alike. After the white Christians of the original Philadelphia Baptist Church were converted from the oppressor's old way of thinking, their hearts desired to stop teasing, bullying, and tormenting the black citizens of the Lafayette Co. community; only to fulfill the Law of Christ, which is fulfilled in one word..."Love." Love is the bond of perfectness. (Colo.3:11-17/Phil.4:7/1Cor.14:26/1Cor.10:31)

The Holy Ghost strengthened the spirit of those of them who prayed in faith unto the Lord for understanding, and upon receiving a sincere empathetic answer to their prayers; they were called out from the world by the Lord to stand bold against their own family members who continued in the world as followers of the oppressor. When Christ called out the Church's of God in Oxford, MS in 1865, the white residents and visitors of all walks of life were ordained to sincerely reveal unto their kindred of what the Spirit of God personally had shown them; in hopes of them saving some of their loved ones from the oppressor.

(St.Matt.10:34-40) After many locals came forth and told their kindred and strangers of their personal and sympathetic insights of the inspiring Word of God, division and wars broke out within their homes, jobs, and church houses. The spirit of the oppressor didn't like being exposed of by the Lord's Law of Love, and for this caused the eyes of many white citizens of Oxford to see their enemies residing in their own household. Like during the biblical days, many white Christians were reviled and cast outside of the protection of the law of the land. They were reviled and were treated similar to how people whom has AIDS are mistreated. Many whites religiously became rebellious to every prospective part of the new governed law of the Lord, and out of fear of being persecuted for the Cross of Christ; they constrained those who were spiritually converted to be cut off from the Body of Christ. Nothing new goes on underneath the sun. This was the religious way of the Pharisees during biblical days when Jesus walked the earth. Those whom rebelled against equality and fairness basically found it hard to accept the holy truth, and they remained in fear of what they didn't understand, and they didn't understand the characteristics of God. Meanwhile there were a variety of blacks whom secretively felt equally the same way about the rebellious whites.

After comparing spiritual things with spiritual, I've personally concluded that the Lord converted the hearts of the white ancestors of Oxford, MS; who were called out by God to embrace the Holy Truth. It was they whom decided to agree amongst themselves to set up a missionary similar to their own and gave it to the free black slaves within the entire Lafayette, Co. community. Upon issuing the blacks a missionary of their own; the white Christians taught the blacks of the ordinances of their church, which befitted the original white members of the Philadelphia Baptist Church's traditional perception of Christianity. With the customary introductions that go with organizing a church, the black members proceeded satisfactorily upon a proposal that the church be named Philadelphia Missionary Baptist Church after the original Philadelphia Baptist Church. I believe what Satan meant to do evil, appears to reflect on men being trained up to worship men, but God meant for it to be done for good. Therefore, both the black and white residents of Lafayette County in Oxford, MS were set free from the burdens of despotism and all were able to worship the Lord in Spirit and Truth without being forced to fight against the principalities and powers of the Lord.

In spirituality, this historical church's story reveals the beginning era of a traditional religious end of Satan coercing the citizens of Oxford, MS to hate one of another. In 1865 the blacks gained their religious freedoms to start thinking as freemen's of God and not as religious slaves, whom were forced to go to their masters' church out of fear of what man may or may not do unto them. After being tutored by the vain philosophies and words of deceits for so long, many are still spoiled by the spots and blemishes of that old-fashioned southern style traditional religious root thereof.

Approximately a hundred years ago, harmony was expected by those who spiritually believed a change would come, and many today believes that a righteous change has came for the entire Oxford, MS community. Many are enduringly still evolving into One Body in Christ, in spite of them being apart of different ethnic groups and religions. After very close observations have been made concerning the present situations and circumstances among the citizens of Oxford, MS; it is made perfectly clear to many that the born again Christian citizens who peacefully coexists during the 21st century, still haven't fully broken the insecure chain of their ancestors' oppressive past doings.

Of course there are many visual positive improvements being seen, but there still is a strong inner appearance and a negative vibe which spiritually is associated with despotism within the town. Even after a hundred years has past, the Holy Spirit is still making changes against the oppressive methods which have circulated and hovered around and about the citizens of Oxford. The spiritual core of the entire populations' living quarters is at a higher standard of expectations concerning the residents living in peace and in love with one of another as one united Body in Christ during the 21st century.

Even the students and staff of The University of Mississippi during the year of 2010 sought to find closure from the old pride of the schools' oppressive mascot "The Rebel". The Rebel represents a slave master mentality which modifies the oppressive success and unity of the Old town of Oxford, MS. By the vote of a majority, the Ole Miss Campus students and staff voted in hopes of putting in the form of an order of agreement or a new decree; a complete end to the era of the preexisting Rebel's symbolic state of oppression. The Rebel's repressive attitude lingers over the enduring stamina of the entire Oxford, MS/Lafayette Co. Community. Instead of keeping the Rebel Mascot, which frustrates the success of the students and staff whom were forced to bear the excruciating prolonged hardship of racism, they voted in hopes of doing away with the traditional Rebel mascot.

In the face of desolation from one generation onto the next; the ravagers gloatingly took great pride in the negative aftereffects of the Rebels pastime, and peoples of all nationalities finally came together at the University of Mississippi in Oxford, MS and agreed to vote as a unit of one body to change or replace the Rebel mascot for one which has no tidings to what the Ole Man Rebel represents. Many desired not to change the Rebel mascot and a selective few oppressors publically chanted "The South shall rise again!" as if they couldn't perceive the truth. The truth is... the South hasn't fallen. The South has become respectfully setup to have higher expectations of its residents and visitors for the sake of the children whom are the south's future leaders.

The children who are bountifully expected to graduate from either the City of Oxford High School or the Lafayette County High school systems never neither owned a slave nor were born into slavery. Therefore, to conclude the contents of this matter, many believe that it's time for the grown ups to stop suppressing the growth of this present generation over the mistakes made by the ancestors of the past. In order to move forward, the adults of this community must stop the old methods of degrading the youth whom are the future leaders of the Town of Oxford and have higher expectations of their morale.

COMSEC IS KNOWN AS THE STUDY OF CRYPTOGRAPHY

During the 21st century some lily-livered fainthearted peoples are still living by the old tyrannous teachings of their ancestors as they speak with that old-time spineless master vs. slave mentality. They are treacherous because their hearts are evil and they are made even more dangerously empowered when they twain together with the **worldly Richie rich**. The **worldly Richie rich** no longer hide the terrors of their racially prejudiced hearts behind religion, because the root of their evil and prejudiced tendencies hides totally behind their greed for money and controlling powers thereof. They've been coerced by Satan to think that the earthy value of money brings unto those who possesses it; heavenly peace and joy on earth. In reality, those who are filled with worldly riches are not excused from the spiritual sicknesses of the world, which causes misery, grief, worldly sorrows, destruction, and death.

The biggest threat within every society consist the twining ideas of two tyrants; the **Richie rich** group and **despising haters of men**. The ideas of the worldly Richie rich consist of them gaining and maintaining monetary powers by all means necessary. None of these would be ever willing to give to the poor. The source of their ideological battles relates to them making the poor poorer and the rich richer. Through the power of coercion, the haters of men are men-pleasers who hide their prejudice intentions behind the ideas of the conservative Richie rich. If undetected, such racists are like a lizard known as a chameleon; they can easily adapt to the bias tendencies and predispositions of the Richie rich and hide their true colors in the process. Meanwhile, all whom the impersonators offend are blinded by the intent of the worldly Richie rich standard principles of life which elaborates on a rich man vs. a poor man mentality and this prevents those whom they offend from really noticing their truest of all commitment is founded on racism. In fact, if accepted by the worldly Richie Rich population, which comes in a diversified race of people, their prejudice double-minded tendencies eventually causes the Richie Rich leaders of the world to be divided amongst them-selves in the act of a double cross.

Certain chauvinistic lifestyles within the personality traits of the olden religious establishments that exist during the 21st century are worse than others. The dogmatists of every society has forsaken their own mercy by tampering with things which they don't understand; like man's gift of free will, which is freely given unto every individual by God free willingly. The bigoted hearts of men exists all over the world, and they discriminate against those who they religiously are taught to hate in a very diplomatic and discreet way. Of course they neither refuse money from consumers whom they may hate, nor do they refuse to give themselves illogical reasons to excuse themselves for doing something evil unto those whom they inwardly love to hate.

Therefore, a tyrant business owner may indeed bully certain customers and employees whom they personally and religiously despise. Their intimidating behavior may even make the despised ones to feel so uncomfortable and so unwelcomed doing business for or with their organizations' unfair tendencies and bias predispositions; to the point of the oppressed ones voluntarily choosing to either quit working for or with the company. Therefore, the reviled are pressured into not ever reconsidering to return to these particular establishments either after their first visit or after making their first business deal.

There are many private organizations and church houses which makes no difference in the way they help people whom without a doubt are in need. They realize that the needy come in all forms, shapes, and sizes within every nationality, but some olden natured authority figured institutions lurks all around the world, and provides a discomfort in the atmosphere within their establishments against certain people. They run a high masquerade of unfairness and inequality which is covered under a full secret code.

Like the study of <u>cryptography,</u> their codes are difficult to comprehend. The functional art of cryptography Is the ideal of a baseball coach rubbing his cheeks, chin, or forehead; to sign for the batter to swing or for a runner to run. If the coach's secret codes are detected by an imposture or by the opposing team, he simply changes the sign to throw the one who cracked the code off track, but he never changes his plan of intent.

This same method maybe applied in a public institution like a restaurant, as a creative masquerade or cover up for one employee to sign for the cook to know when a food critique or a heath inspector is present. If prejudices reside in the heart of the cook or if discrimination ever becomes the resourceful reason for the usage of such secret coding within any establishment for whatever reason; the end results for the hated and despised customer, consumer, or employee could be catastrophic. The hated residents which live all throughout America are very aware of which establishments they ought not to go, concerning the hearts of a chauvinistic or bigoted tyrannous business institution.

In despite of all the things which may reflect, reproduce, and be a sign of negativity, the most positive side of life for Sister Glory who was born and raised in Oxford, MS resides in all things made by God, including the things that the Lord reveals unto her to know and understand; like how well the blacks and whites of Oxford, MS are <u>equally</u> and fairly treated. In order for other Mississippians whom suffers the same said fate of racism requires a balanced insight of how equally willing all race of peoples in the Southern State of Mississippi are willing to congregate together in the House of God in spite of ones' past faults and failings.

Someone once asked, If the Lord is for Sister Glory then who can be against her? Well, the clear answer to that question is everyone and anyone who has been brought up under the old dictated tyrannous unfair law which the new Law of God voided and renewed. The denote meaning and the direct messages within the Old Covenant concerning the Word of God instructs people to misuse the Word as a cloak of maliciousness. Therefore, non-converted martyrs whose defiled hearts yields to every evil aspect of thinking, accepts such wisdom of malice to work to kill the godly spirit within her. They dishonor and corrupt the Word of God as they refuse to believe the Lord gave her the authority to rightfully use the Word of God in the form of edifying Christ. As she boldly stands to defend, protect, and guard herself from their malevolence, she boldly stands against the wiles of the enemy. Therefore, corruptibly they still use the unrighteous desire of the world to make her suffer persecutions and harassments by the authority figures of the old religious dictated laws of distorted religious men. With the Lord being for her, no man can stand against her. She isn't greater than the Lord is, therefore she knows to expect to go through the same things as he; concerning her being treated cruelly. She has made a pack to speak of deliverance unto as many churches worldwide as she possibly can, to bring salvation back to the Lord's ministry.

She believes that she is ordained by God to shine a little light on the things which she recognize are of the works of God. Therefore, the Power of the Lord humbles her to do so. Meanwhile, out of the woodworks come the haters with vengeance on their hearts and minds. Within her overall view of her life, she let's no man take neither the credit nor the blame for her success nor for her faults or failings by accusing anyone unto God. She understands that whosoever is accredited for the works of God receives vain glory and praise of men. In such instances; God gets no glory, because in the mist of accrediting one man or another for what the Lord does, the endorser thereof gives no honor, glory, and thanks in true reverence unto God! Therefore, she stands and waits to be commended by God instead of waiting to receive praise from men. Meanwhile, she dedicates the duration of her life on earth, evangelizing and edifying the entire Body of Christ with the intent to bring honor and glory unto all who confess Jesus Christ as their Lord and Savior.

After many evil generations have passed unto another, the Christians who despise the unfair laws of mankind during the year of 2008-2010 are constantly seen rising up against the formatted law of the earlier American founding Foretathers. As the inner spirits of mankind emerge together with the same soaring holy desire to work compassionately for the Lord, indeed they do show their good works through their faith and trust on the Lord God. Such persons are helping to reform the hearts and minds of many to be on the Lord and not on the world. The Spirit of God intercede the Spirit of Man and converts their hearts into passing on their commitment to worship and honor the Lord with all of their hearts, might, and soul. Indeed, the Spirit within them is well-known for worshipping the holy acts of God through the cares of Civil and Human Right's Advocates and supporters. They are a group of peaceable abolitionists who are in favor of abolishing the financial, physical, and mental stages of slavery and every evil works of the spirit that is controlled by the prince of the world. The Prince of the world has tricked those of them whose domineering thoughts works against God's grace within their desire to rule the world.

The peaceable abolitionists indeed are working to end discrimination, by encouraging more and more people to not lose their souls to the evil spirit of hate. The spiritual love which a Civil and Human Right's activist commonly demonstrates indeed doesn't save a soul, but it does discourage prejudice peoples from forfeiting their Salvation. They discourage the hypocrites who allow the spirit of hatred to pile up within their hearts. In so doing they help to prevent others from destroying their devotional loyal love for God. From time to time certain people will claim themselves to be for the Lord, but they hypocritically command for other people to follow the old tyrannous way of life to hate their brother. Hating is the principle movement which God's peaceable love was designed to endure and stand against.

Throughout USA history the Civil and Human Right organizations were made up of many spiritual minded supporters who upheld the Lord's spiritual characteristics. They secretly and publically have worked together as servants of Christ to help reform the old governing laws for all American citizens. Indeed the reformed laws which freed the African American slaves also provided hope unto other future Americans who were being added into the legal protection of the law. Gracefully ever family who migrated and every person who is freeborn in America desires to have the same equal amount of rights to work, learn, and live under the United States written Constitution of Common Factors. Without desiring vain glory, all Americans are in need of the basic things that are biblically based on providing every human being with equality, liberty, justice, peace, and above all ...LOVE.

Even after the American Civil War was won and the black Americans were legally freed from slavery; they weren't treated as an equal to the white Americans. For Instance, many older southern ex-black farmers in the United States who still are alive today, remembers when the white farmers could receive government funds to purchase tractors and other farming utilities and tools; without having to give up their whole life savings or their rights to any of their properties, but the law required for the black farmers to surrender all of their personal and private possessions and properties in order to get government funding. After they had worked as slaves and fought for their freedom in the Civil War to gain the ability to purchase their own land, inequity indeed is what the American law gave unto them in return.

I come from a poor family. We didn't have much, but the Lord's been good to us. "My granddad was a sharecropper," said Sister Glory, as she shared a very personal story that her dad and granddad shared with her when she was a little girl. She declared that many life long learned lessons of a struggling African American sharecropper's family helped her humble herself to spiritually understand the humility of God's peace making character, which resides within the Spirit of her as well. The most recognizable lessons that she learned concerning her receiving agape love joy and peace, were taught through the expressions of much pain, and suffering. No matter how hard a sharecropper may have worked according to her dad or how much more crops they as farmers produced each year to settle their debt with the plantation owner; the owners would always claim they were still in debt. For the winter months the plantation owners would offer her granddad a Christmas loan a token of appreciation of his strong commitment to work out his dept as a sharecropper. Many people look at debt being a sin, but credit has been a great sin since the beginning. That's why God instructs us all today to pay our debts as we go, and owe man nothing where love is concerned. Being indebt where love is concerned isn't like credit card debt, where you can file bankrupt and clear out the debt. Being indebt where love is concerned requires spiritual growth and change.

The unreasonable American laws of the land place a person in debt at the birth of a new born baby. It once was normal for a midwife to perform childbirth, but during today's generation most people frown upon the very notion of such. Although giving birth is a natural right for all women, in America a woman must sign a hospital contract and first agree to pay the expenses of whatsoever it may cost; regardless if she can afford to pay the balance thereof or not. In other words, a baby is born in debt, and upon leaving this world they too shall die in debt. Being in debt is the new American way of life. Hypocritically speaking, a person must pay a physician to pronounce them to be dead upon their death.

The plantation where her dad was raised and spoke of during most of his adult lifetime was located in Batesville, MS in the 1940's. He remembered how the owner of that plantation claimed he had ownership of every black family which inhabited and worked his field. Apparently the plantation owner refused to acknowledge slavery was abolished and he had forbidden them to move off of his farm land, because he claimed that every black person who shared crops with him; owed him crops. The plantation owner actually knew that the survival of his old plantation solely depended on the black workers who worked his fields. In other words, this plantation owner failed method of keeping the blacks in financial debt was designed to keep the African Americans in slavery through trickery. It had gotten so bad that most blacks would wait for the sun to go down to load up all of their personal property into a motor vehicle and move away undetected by the plantation owner at night.

The story of the day that her granddad moved the entire family off of that old plantation was like a clip taken from a horror movie. Enoch Sanders put all of his faith on the Lord. Although he knew that the plantation owner had threatened to do harm to everyone whom had fled the plantation if he ever catches them, Enoch Sanders boldly started moving in broad daylight. Without wavering in faith, he believed that the truth would set them free. Slavery was over and no black family had to live on the plantation where they shared crops with the owner. But the truth which the plantation owner believed in was built upon a bunch of lies. The plantation owner called the police in hopes of stopping them from moving, but to the owners' surprise the white police officer who responded on the scene explained that he couldn't stop the blacks from leaving, because slavery was abolished.

Later, the test of the black farmers' faith included them managing their own farm land without receiving help from the unfair despotic American laws of the land. Therefore; by God's merciful grace, emerged different non-profit organizations that sprung up among the American society to help the poor farmers in America regardless of their nationality. As an updated experience of what the black farm land owners had to experience after being delivered out of the bondage of such plantations

See also on Google Web Search; 2010 A.D. Shirley Sherrod, a former African American USDA official, who isn't the racists which a particular News carrier falsely reported her to be. Open your hearts and minds to explore farther than this website to gain an understanding.

THE NEW AMERICAN/CIVIL RIGHTS SOCIETY OF THE 21ST CENTURY IS REAPING THE WORKS OF THE OLD MAN'S LABOR

One of the reasons as to why organizations like the Gorillas, Black Panthers, and the NAACP etc. formed was to fight for the rights of the poor so that they too would be treated fair and equal under the Constitution of the United States during the earlier years. Although some white folks walked peacefully with the blacks (like with Martin Luther King Jr.), others like the KKK marched to war against the entire black community and visa versa. Even if there were some open-minded organizations which allowed whites to organize with the blacks during the earlier 1900's concerning the Civil Rights movement; other organizations did not. They did not because most Americans had a great lack of trust, confidence, and faith on the reliance of a person of the white community intertwining with the black community.

A lack of trust was implanted and rooted into the hearts of every nationality in every corner of the earth by the unawares, and the core of their insecurities slit their inner spirits in half. Its like one half of them desired for the Lord to deliver them and to change their situations, but their other half was filled with doubt of such deliverance would make things better for them. The nature of their doubt is understandable, but it doesn't justify the wrongful teachings of those of them who traditionally are taught to have a lack of hope of being saved by God.

It is strongly believed that God knew all about the troubles of the oppressed and he heard the righteous crying, "Father, Father", and he forbade the gates of hell to prevail against the workers of the Lord, after hearing their cries. The ideas of such believers suggests that God converted the hearts of many oppressors as well as the oppressed and gave unto them the righteous faith, to believe that they could be delivered by him from the mental stresses and evils of the world. Simultaneously, there were many whites who fought peacefully with the blacks, and together their faith was on the Lord and not on the differences of a person's nationality. After walking together with the Lord, many decades later; every nationality consists of people today whom are led up by the Anointed teachings of the Holy Ghost. Without desiring vain glory, they dedicate their hearts to promote the Divine Order of God onto one of another and not just onto themselves.

All who believes that the Lord lives in everything created by God are working out their own Salvation with their faith on the Lord. During the time period of the campaign of the 44th USA President election, most of the people who voted for Barak Obama desired for the unreasonable laws of our American governed country to change in the principle form of refining certain policies that were shaped and created by both (the 42nd & 43rd USA Presidents) President Bush's administrations. Many people concurred that they believed that such laws created by them allowed private insurance companies and big bankers to corrupt our economy's normal way of life by making unreasonable policies against the working class tax paying middle and low class Americans.

It is rightfully believed that a standard refining of certain policies may provide a fairer distribution of earned wages and bring a sense of fairness unto other economic sources like providing a better form of health insurance for the poor as well as for the people on Main Street. A standard refining may even offer a better business relationship between the banks and the American consumers, without unfairly forcing the working class and tax paying American citizens to become consumers of either of them; especially during a recession.

It is absurd to force a person to give what they don't have to spare, but it is highly believed that the American government through President Bush's administration, coerced many American politicians in Congress to support a regime or government which forces the poor to pay an extra expense known as high interest rates. High interest rates technically added to the poor laborers of America an overly-exalted cost of living, because like the rich; the poor and middle class Americans have always been capable of investing in purchasing a home. Like the historical debt of the black American sharecroppers, the American people who lives and works on Main Street during the 21st century aren't given a fair deal in the matter of becoming debt free. You can't squeeze blood out of a turnip nor can you legally feed your children when the cost of living overly exceeds your income during the time when the economy has collapsed. As a domino effect, it was believed by most Americans that the middle working class American citizens lost their 20th century homes as a result thereof. On the opposite side, it is believed that the middle class Americans of the 21st century lost their homes because they made poor choices in investing their hard earned money in buying or purchasing a home after the high interest rates had increased.

To the same token, the people on Main Street are hoping that the government will soon pass a new reformed insurance bill which would return the "Power of Choice" back to the working American families of all races. Unfortunately the interest of the controlling Republic Party for the past eight years withdrew the power of choice from the hands of the poor stockholders on Main Street who is also coerced to pay into a failing 401-K retirement system. If they save their own money at home, they wouldn't have to worry about paying back any extra expenses or increased interest rate on every dollar they borrow from their own savings. Upon the middle class loosing their jobs during a recession, they also lost their retirement funds. Simultaneously, the ways of the Bush Administrations gave assurance to the big business owners and BIG insurance companies and insecurities unto all other Americans. The

Bush Administration allowed big business owners to setup in-house rules and policies, which prevented the stockholders on Main Street from being able to privately assemble and vote amongst the design of certain rules and policies. Meanwhile, the rules and policies of the insurance companies in America were perfectly made up against those on Main Street.

For that reason, the consumers on Main Street rose up against the unreasonable rules and clauses within the Bush Administrative policies that were designed to allow the insurance companies to decline coverage for every American citizen who has a pre-existing health condition. Such powers ought not to have been given to the assembly of any major American insurance corporation, but it was; and now that power is rebuked and criticized sharply by the people on Main Street. Therefore, the new idea of President Barak Obama administration appears to desire to modify the Bush's philosophies while offering the people on Main Street security over insecurities. Such suggestive modifications include a more reasonable sacrifice of the rich to appease unto all other Americans who live in the middle class and poverty bracket, and only a few who are financially rich are willing to make the indicated sacrifices that are proposed.

Of course it is highly believed that Satan is also working to once again magnify his created image of an illusion of a war. Ironically, the private insurance supporters are entwined together with the same political people who have the authority to sign many tyrannous insurance policies into law; for the present private insurance companies that have full control and the power to deny providing help to the poor, and refuse to cover any persons with a pre-existing health problem.

The democratic reformers of these laws are slanderously confronted by members of the Republic Party with speculations of a future added tax which they claim will be bestowed upon the American tax payers if the government passes a reformed insurance law. The irony of such speculations in a certain sense is viewed by both the democratic and republic voters in America as a threat made by the government against the government, because if the Republic and Democratic Party doesn't compromise the issues of bettering America before the laws of the Bush administration ends, all American's will end up paying higher taxes in the up coming year of 2011. It's not a secret that only 1-5% of Americans can afford paying more taxes.

The views of most average Americans sees the factors of how higher insurance premiums and interest rates are like an increase of taxes, which many poor Americans can't afford to pay. The rich lobbyists' corrupt methods of using politics to empower themselves, have made it harder for the average American workers to make a decent profit of earned income to support their families. Although the selfish rich lobbyists makes themselves richer, the reformed insurance laws of the New America of the 21st century; will hopefully be developed by both the Republic and Democratic Party members to make it easier for the average working American family to survive off of minimum wage.

MAN CANNOT MODIFY AN EVIL MANMADE LAW EXCEPT BY COMPLETELY ILLIMINATING THAT LAW, AND MAKE A NEW LAW WHICH IS GOOD

Within all the warnings and pleas made by the legislative local and state administrators to the republic lobbyists of congress during the entire 20th century before President Barak Obama took office; they still were willing to up hold an old governing policy, which doesn't agree with the new American generation. The political rich lobbyists may refuse to reform or change any old local, state, or federal law by getting rid of the old oppressive laws all together, because some of their representatives publically proclaim that they believe that such reformations of any old law is unconstitutional. They are more so willing to either add to or take away from laws which supports despotism, but they are more resistant to kill the law of despotism and create a reformed law to replace it. They accept despotism over the brand of America's democracy.

After Obama entered the White House, the political republics publically shared their own distorted American point of views of him on every media broadcasting system known in America. He publically was called

403

a socialist by those who refused to co-aside with the new reformed laws that he and most of the American people agreed upon during his presidential campaign. After being elected by the people by more than 10 million extra votes than his opponent, he made proposals to Congress that changed the intent and the purpose of the old laws for a massive number of American citizens whom felt that they had been misrepresented for the last past eight years by the previous political representatives of Congress. He stood boldly to uphold the Americans who had been oppressed and beguiled by the rich and powerful lobbyists of Wall Street.

For this cause, he made major suggestions on the simplest political issues that were prepared crookedly by the richest Americans who led the entire country into a financial debt before he took office. Although the legacy of the 20th Century United States presidential candidate's campaign successfully made the rich Americans richer and the poor Americans poorer as promised by the American despots, the entire USA was placed at financial odds with other countries. The USA ended up in debt before President Obama became the 44th President of the United States of America. By Nov. 2010 the employment poll showed the American economy had stabilized after President Obama's 2nd year in office.

Since the republicans decided to modify certain evil laws by keeping the old out dated local, state, and federal laws in place during the time when the American people greatly needed reformed laws to take par, the American citizens were forced to be in a domestic war with their own government. This war was designed by Wall Street lobbyists whom greedily desired to permanently take complete tyrannous control over the financial freedoms and stabilities of every American household.

President Obama's campaign slogan about change converted the American citizens to decide to use their voting rights, which is defined within the Declaration of Independence as their required American duty. They voted to incriminate the political form of lobbyism, which always pursues the same things or demonstrates the same principle of abuses and usurpations as did the history of a certain King of Great Britain whose repeated injuries and usurpations had in an indirect purpose or aim to establish absolute tyranny. After making their final plea to the accused party they publically protested against the accused party. The politically correct form of lobbyism is truly designed to reduce the people on Main Street and the poor American citizens; under absolute Despotism. The rich lobbyists of this generation are believed to be like the old republic supremacists who once were in power but lost the Presidency to President Abraham Lincoln. Many Americans suggestively think that the rich lobbyists of the 21st century are like the republic supremacists who campaigned against President Abraham Lincoln regarding them refusing to carry out the full potential of America's democracy equally unto all branded classes of Americans. The Americans whom scrutinize the rich American lobbyists of the 21st century believe that America's democracy wasn't just for the wealthy, but it was also for the poor who helped in making the rich Americans rich. To prove that the rich were made rich by the poor and that most Americans believe that democracy is for all Americans, let us submit to an honest world that history reveals how many American activist groups were formed and fought for equal rights to be issued by the American government for all American citizens.

The blind leaders and followers of the USA's lawmakers of despotism claim that they don't understand the main sources or reasons why there exist the talks of a possible future tax increase for **only** the rich being mentioned by President Obama. Some argue that a tax cut for the rich will produce revenue. Maybe part of President Obama's reason for desiring to tax the rich is because history has revealed that enforcing tax increase on the poor Americans helped to boost the economy many times before in the past, and maybe common sense tells him that it makes more sense to tax the rich whom can afford to pay taxes instead of taxing the poor during the time of a 21st century economy melt down. Or maybe he speaks about taxing only the rich because the desire for a reformation of the old insurance law is requested by most struggling Americans whom are making less than $200-thousand or $45-thousand a year. With different individual state officials ridding the Job Union

Laws which were designed to help the working class Americans, his opponents are losing grounds to say that taxing big business owners will cause them a problem with providing their workers with civil benefits like health insurance and other bonuses, because without the Union they no longer are obligated by law to provide such things to their workers.

Therefore the citizens, who support President Obama and other reformed political leaders, can clearly understand that a future tax increase under the Obama's administration for **the rich is very necessary.** In the process thereof many Americans hope that the idea of taxing only the rich is well thought-out, because the old laws which gave the rich a tax break while increasing the taxes on the poor; failed to build a strong economy. Some even think that since a strong economic system wasn't set in place for the growth of the misrepresented 21st century American generation whom were forced to co-exist with the preexisting despotic local, state, and federal laws; the entire country was led into an economic disaster. America's economic failure was felt worldwide before the Obama's new ideal government reformation of the health insurance laws took affect.

The ditch, which the blind American leaders had led many American companies into before Barak Obama was elected the 44th President of the United States of America; were bailed out of debt under President Obama's leadership. Upon President Obama proposal to do so, many despotic leaders claimed that his bailout method would not only fail, but they claimed it would sink the American deficit deeper in debt. After the Bailout method worked and the businesses like the GMC Automobile Industry repaid what they borrowed from the government, the ears of blind leaders and followers who stood against him reforming the governing laws of the American lands became deaf of the truth as they claim that President Obama's bailout methods were not responsible for the success of America not falling into another great depression, which is exactly where America was headed upon his first day in office as the 44th President of the United States of America.

CAN ANY MAN CHANGE ANYTHING THAT IS CREATED BY AND FOR GOD?

God Forbid! When man attempt to change things, their vexed hearts commonly desire to make changes without knowing the works of the Lord. Without knowing which way they ought to go, they neither can see nor hear the voice of the Lord who directs the steps of men towards receiving the gift of life, which is filled with the Lord's purest and heavenliest of Wisdom. Why man must suffer themselves to fulfill the law of **sin**, when the Lord opens the gateway to Heaven for **all** to come in? God's gifts gives men the **Power to Forgive**, and provides them with the ability to **rebuke** the **darkened spirit** out of **self first**, then requires them to minister onto others, so that all could hold the **KEY** to the **KINGDOM OF HEAVEN**. The Key contains **"THE LORD'S HEAVENLY WISDOM and his WISDOM is at HAND."**

All Americans who believe on the Son of God knows there is only One Salvation, One Lord, One God, One Christ, and One Heaven, but the world has divided Salvation into having numerous names. They've also managed to make numerous changes to the character of God's name by dividing themselves through the endless acts of discrimination instead of uniting together as one Body in Christ. There isn't a name made-up by man that can change what lies within neither the name of Salvation nor in the name of the Lord God; Jesus Christ, and the Holy Ghost. Oh what a wonderful web we weave for our selves, but thanks to God's love mercy and grace, this web can't hold any man down if they desire to change (repent). Except a man be born again, he shall not enter into the Kingdom of God.

Without heavenly wisdom many people fails to realize that the HOLY BIBLE speaks to all who hears and fears God, because the Holy Ghost teach all believers on the Son of God of exactly how to recognize and rebuke all evil spirits from entering into ones' heart; by first rebuking that which resides in ones' own heart. This is a spiritual process and not a physical practice as traditional religious people may suggestively think, feel, and believe that it is. It's common for false tutors to think that they know who hears and fears the Lord, and they'll include themselves as hearers and doers of the Lord's words in efforts to exclude others without thoroughly and diligently self examining themselves; to seek for righteousness within the intent of their own desires and deeds. Therefore, by their own desires, they as good for nothing reprobates and unwise scorners indeed delude their minds to think righteousness consist of edifying God through the task or force of causing division.

Any man who thinks he knows anything knows he knows nothing. Therefore, with the lack of knowledge thereof; false teachers falsely accuse others of not being saved by the Blood of Jesus and falsely excuse themselves as they contradict and misjudge the Word of God. This sin isn't only a sin against men; which is forgivable, but this sin is also a sin against the Holy Ghost, which is an unforgivable sin. This sin is the one many ministers dare not to publically discuss, because they are guilty themselves of being judgers of the law of God and not doers. They think they are worshipping God, while they preach falsely as hypocrites and blasphemers of the Holy Ghost.

Sure the Holy Scriptures mentions what's not allowed to enterer into the Kingdom of God, but a partial truth is still a lie. The Holy Scriptures also mentions how the Spirit of God makes intercessions for the spirit of man, with the power to deliver all believers on the Son; out of the temptations of the world. Those who either lack understandings of what this mean or are have doubt in the Lord's ability to save all from sin are commonly the main ones who minister falsely unto the weak and simple babes in Christ, by seducing the minds of the simple and the weak to share their same said doubtful disputations and conflicts of interests on the true Power of God.

The hearts of all who diligently seeks for the Lord's heavenly knowledge finds the wisdom to understand that being born again is to convert to the holiest way of thinking, and this kind of knowledge causes a godly spirit known as a godly sorrow to enter the hearts of all who believes on the Son of God to find Heaven's Wisdom. When the Lord's Wisdom comes unto a person who believes on God, she brings them knowledge.

She also begets unto their hearts a godly sorrow. Due to the godly sorrows of their hearts, Wisdom does come in and strengthen the inner godliness which lives in all mankind and provides for them the ability to spiritually see the light, which God sent into the world so that the Spirit of the Son of God might save them from sin. Jesus is the light of the world, and this light being of the Lord begets the desire of the Lord, to shine in the inner spirit of all who posses his Wisdom. To trend meekly and lowly without boastful pride, is what the Lord God has always required of his servants and friends since the beginning of time, because boastful pride works men's deeds to be full of indignity, humiliation, disgrace, and shame.

When a person humbles themselves to the humility of other men's saneness, lucidness, rationality or the lack thereof, and convert themselves to desire not to humiliate and ridicule others as false ministers of God may have done unto them, they possess the Lord's Wisdom to understand that yielding their hearts to vengeance will only revive their old man's vengeful desires. Be not deceived, God is not mocked. Their old man if misguided or malnourished, are liable to return unto them and worsen the state of their minds to be more of poorer quality than it ever was before. In such of a case, vengeance may possibly take control of their temporal or earthy hearts. Some people are worse than others as they reset their hearts and minds on worldly matters, especially after the Lord delivers them from such mental bondage.

In their fair words and well put together speeches false ministers of God religiously preach on a daily base in agreement with how their traditional religion have taught them to physically fight evil with evil, in false hopes of them winning a religious war. Without Wisdom being their daily delight, they fail to understand that the Holy War is the Lord's and it isn't a physical war but a spiritual one. Like the cheers of a cheerleading squad, the leading cheers of the members of their congregation roar "Let's Go Fight Win" as they riot in the daytime. Their sermons cheers on their team of followers to fight grudgingly and war until the Lord calls them home, because they believe that they will be

409

winners in the end. Without peace, it's impossible for a house to fulfill the true valued quality of a home on earth as it is in Heaven. You can't fight evil with evil according to the Wisdom of Heaven.

The people who fail to be lowly and humble themselves are known as scorners, and a scorner isn't willing to neither learn nor understand that without being lowly, they'll end up desiring vain glory; only for the sake of seeking vengeance. Neither will they know that the spirit of vengeance brings the angry aggressions of the worst kind into their hearts and this causes them to desire to fight evilly. Free willingly they must desire to refuse to allow any sort of evil spirit to enter into their hearts and be born again. If the zeal of them desire to be converted, the Lord will deliver them out of the carnal mindsets of the traditional religious beliefs that are well orchestrated by the portrayal of worldly men.

This spiritual process isn't done by man alone, because all spiritual gifts of God are given by the grace of God according to the Anointed teachings of the Holy Ghost, but one must want to change in order for such of a spiritual change to come. It's like an adult regaining the innocent mind fold of their childhood. Ooh, can you believe in how sweet and pure all grown ups once were before they became grown ups? Every grown up who are assisted by the teaching of the Anointed can remember their childhood, and if they humble themselves they will be able to spiritually see how much they've changed. Through the eyes of an innocent child all things are pure. A child doesn't accuse anyone of being impure, but they can learn to do so under the leadership of a defile minded adult, which sees nothing to be pure. The Word indicates that whosoever shall not receive the kingdom of God as a little child, he shall not enter therein (St. Matt.19:13-24/St.Mark10:15-27). All things are made for him and by him, and all things are made pure according to teachings of the Anointed.

By the Lord's mercy and grace, all who believe on him are enabled to spiritually understand the dangers of the evil spirits which enters their own hearts, and seduce them to make wrongful judgments against others by the religious doubtful disputations of their own bellies. Every heart which yields to the evil spirits of Satan at some point or another are susceptible of being misled into following the same teachings of the heartless laws which seduced the people whom lived in accordance with the old traditional laws of the Pharisees and Sadducees during biblical times. Most Christians today are aware of how the same said heartless religious teachings of the past generations worked against God and they don't desire to rebuild what the Lord destroyed. They are aware that the despotic teachings of the unawares are still privately creeping into Christ's church during the 21st century and is persecuting all who desires to worship and follow "The Christ." The unawares of the 21st century indeed are persecuting Christians in the same tempting mannerism as the Jewish biblical manmade laws of the land once taught men how to sought and persecute Jesus Christ when he walk the face of the earth in the form of the flesh.

God demands and deserves to receive all honors, glory, edification, praise, and thanks; for delivering all who believes on his Son out of the corrupt things of this world. The things of the world tempts people into being mentally enslaved as an unbeliever, and seduces the minds of them to covet after the world's doubtful disputations which causes a religious person to work enmity against those who believe on the Lord's ability to save all mankind from sin. A none-believer despises imperfect men who confess Jesus Christ as their Lord and Savor. In unbelief of the Power of God, it is common for a despiser to blaspheme against the Holy Ghost. They do so while restraining themselves from believing or desiring to know what the Lord promised he'd do for all mankind, because unlike the Lord God; a despiser of men loves to count the physical views of slackness against those whom they despise.

Many traditional religious people choose to fight for their Salvation without desiring to restrain their hearts from discriminating, and from out of their hearts their mouths speaks. Without having the Lord's spiritual aspiration to restrain from desiring vain glory, the words and deeds of a discriminator degrades others and causes misery, grief, and worldly shame and sorrows to be present unto whosoever they despise

411

while edifying their own selves. A despiser is commonly known for improperly using the physicality of traditional religion to mentally form applications of ideas and principles to regulate or normalize their dead deeds to outwardly appear to be a normal religious standard for them to follow, but their hearts are evil. They boast proudly of their religious beliefs, while physically stirring up confusion and chaos in the lives of another man's spirit. They do so as if their traditional religious reasons of causing chaos are acceptable and are pardon by God.

Since no man has the power to judge the conscience of another man's spirit, the Lord's Spirit of Righteousness and Truth makes manifest unto all of his followers, brethrens, servants, friends etc. of the selfish and overly excessive and unreasonable deeds of their flesh, and then his Spirit within them comes alive unto the conscience of them to revive them consciously to know the Lord. This is a spiritual change not a physical change, but without heavenly Wisdom; man can't discern their left hand from their right. Imprudently they discern only what they physically see and they miss seeing the evidence provided by the Fruit of the Spirit. As the Spirit of the Lord walks with them and direct their steps, their spiritual minds devise the way in which they ought to go, because by the Spirit they also can manifest clearly the difference between good and evil. The Spirit of God helps his peoples to understand the difference between the works of the world and the works of the Spirit of God. The Spirit of God desires for all to receive him whether they work is by their walk of faith or if their work is under a dead law, because the Lord God is for the Just and the Unjust. In other words, God is not a partial God nor is he a bias or prejudice God. With him all things are possible, and without him man can't do anything.

During today's generation, most traditional religious congregations require the head of their congregation to be appointed, and the appointees normally seek to choose a person who possesses a college degree in a scholastic major of ministry. Unfortunately, most of these degree-holding educated people are taught by man on how to administer the Word of God, and those who desire to sit in Moses seat are willing to administer the Word in the preference of how the

412

members of a religious congregation are trained up on. In other words, these ministers are easily influenced to preach the Word of God in the way in which the congregational members desires, more so than the way the Anointed desires for the Word of God to be taught. In such instances, many appointee scholars seek to fulfill their own desires to sit in Moses' seat.

On many occasions, their educational level makes them as wise as the Wisest of men of the world, but they spiritually knows nothing of neither The old nor the New Law, except what they are taught through a text book which is derived from another man's understandings of the Holy Scriptures. Without privately studying the Word and patiently waiting to receive Heavenly knowledge from the Anointed teachings of the Holy Ghost, they yet follow the worldly concept and take the Old law and mend it with a new patch from the new law.

God warned all who follows the dead law that they must do the whole law; because the Lord God foreknew that the Old law is of a curse within itself. Without heavenly Wisdom, whatsoever the carnal and double-minded ministers may truly think, sees, say, and do under the New Testament of Jesus Christ; they subconsciously regulate Satan's dead deeds, which come from the desires of their own bellies to be gods and lords of their ministry. Their devotion to their ministry is apart of an unrighteous faith on the Son of God.

Being delivered by the Lord comes not by the law or by the will of man. It is by the faith of all who believes on the Son of God that they shall receive the glorious gift to interpret righteous judgments. Every minister who pledge their allegiance to doubtful disputation as an unbeliever of the Lord's ability to save all sinners (all, except blasphemers against the Holy Ghost whom commits the unforgivable sin), fails to discern the quality and the purpose of their own inner spiritual intentions as a self-made minister of God. Without admitting the truth of their own self-centered intentions, there's no way that they can discern the intentions of others without making wrongfully judgments against them.

A self-made minister of God fail to humble themselves to open up their hearts and minds to receive the Fruit of the Spirit, which is only received by a born again Christian who truly believes of the power of the Son of God. Only a receiver of the Fruit of the Spirit can obtain the knowledge of God to discern good from evil in making righteous judgments. The inevitable Gift which God gives to all mankind is the freedom to choose the route of their life, and all will surely reap what they've individually sown just the same as we all individually reap the works of another man's labor (St. John4:32-38). If we sow well we shall reap well, and if we sow bad we shall reap the bad which we've sown. It is by the power of the anointed teachings of the Holy Ghost, which provides evidence of the spiritual comfort that covers all sins of mankind without causing any man to suffer worldly sorrows, despair, and persecutions while delivering them out of the temptations of the world.

HYPOCRISY/BLASPHEMY=False teachers teaching others to do what they themselves cannot, while lying against the Power of the Holy Ghost

The Word of God isn't hypocrisy being taught nor does it teach men to blaspheme against the Holy Ghost. What the Lord tells man to do isn't hypocrisy nor does the Lord say unto men to blaspheme against the Holy Ghost, but the teachings of the Lord tells all of mankind to make reasonable sacrifices. Those that follow after the canceled traditional religions are false apostles, bishops, ministers, pastors, and false servants of God, etc. Their ministry consists of the commandments of men, which teach other men to do and say things that they themselves can't do.

The Lord knows that not one good thing will come out of trying to do something you know you can't do. If child of God is unhappily married to another person who doesn't know the Lord, the godly spirit of the one who loves the Lord may try to make the best out of their marriage, but if the one they are married too hasn't the desire to work on their marriage problems they are logically bound to divorce. It takes two to make the marriage work. Nine times out of ten, if the Lord isn't the chief head thereof, the marriage will be filled with hidden adultery and eventually will end in a divorce by the consent of the one who knows the Lord. A spiritual person who co-asides with their inner spiritual faith on the Lord's ability to save them, commonly uses such factual grievances of a divorcee of an adulterous marriage as a relevant motive for them to also renounce their membership of a religious organization. They spiritually realize that they aren't married the worldly religion of hypocritical men, but are married to the Lord God who is the Lord of the Heavens and the earth.

All things are possible with God, as long as it's apart of the Lord's plan and of his will and good pleasures. The hypocrisies of the world consist of the unfair and unreasonable sacrifices religious men are seduced into desiring to make as they are made apostles of, for, and by men. They worship as if they don't believe the Lord has paid the ultimate price through his death to graciously dispose of the theoretical beliefs in stoning a person to death like that of the old law. They fail to understand that the old law is for their learning of the new testimonies made by Christ within the New Testament, which influences mankind to stop denying truth and reframe from despising men who confess Jesus as their Lord and Savor.

Satan desire to doom mankind by seducing them into using the Old Law to work evilly, but God meant for the principles and standards of the old law to be properly used for Good. The new patch which false tutors use to mend the Old Law is their way of misusing the Lord's words as a cloak of maliciousness, which substitutes the physical stones that were used under the Old Law to spiritually condemn or stone a sinner to death. These religious followers refuse to acknowledge that under the New Commandment, God sent the Word to convict and revive the Spirit of all sinners not to condemn them unto death, but to reform them unto life everlasting.

When the evil spirit of earthy and fleshly desires enters Christ's Church, (the church mentioned here is in reference to the hearts of the people) it formulates an evilly aspire desire among the people who goes out and seeks to fight against flesh and blood in an unreasonable sacrificial pattern in the remembrance of Christ's sacrifice. The evil spirit coerces people to think they have logical reasons to vengefully fight a holy war with an ideal reference of defending some sort of religious belief.

It is by the grace of God that the Holy Spirit reveals the wiles of the worldly, which indeed works to unite with the children of God by pending their backs up against a wall with a no-way-out scenario. When the Lord's angles are cornered on every side, the weak and simple ones are easily influenced to react like a frightened cat that's cornered by many malicious and ferocious bull dogs. The merciful Lord empathizes with the reasons why some of his peoples' hearts deters to a kill or be killed mentality, and he strengthens them to be more than a conquer by enabling them with the power to endure pain and afflictions knowing that an evil person may kill their body but not the soul.

The evil mentality of the worldly hindered many oppressed blacks who survived the era of history, when the white Supremacists desired to expose the entire African American population to be of a brute beast. Only the Lord could stop the madness and with Wisdom by his side, he knew that whatsoever that a man think of themselves or others by the vexations of their own hearts, that shall it be; at least to the thoughts of them. Those who thinks they know everything, yet knows nothing at all. In other words, whosoever think they are right while belittling others are right in their own eyes. (Lev.26:6/Isa.48:18/Ps.119:165/Rom.8:6) With the Lord knowing the heart of the oppressed black Americans during slavery, he urged people of all races to resist the things of the world which tempted them to forsaken their own mercy. A peaceful walk is walked with the Lord.

(Rom.10:15, 12:18, 14:19, 15:13/Matt.5:9/Prov.12:20, 16:7) Since peace comes unto peacemakers, the Spirit of God deters the hearts of those who serve the Lord to not walk by sight; but by faith. The descriptive traditional religious sarcastic stereotypical character of the world, evilly rely on misjudging the conscience of a person. They are well known for claiming a person to be inhumane and unworthy of God's love and their claims are made manifest by the Holy Ghost to be the judgment of a liar. Men are not soulless brute beasts, but are living souls whom God created and love.

On the contrary, the inhumane acts of men come unto those whose hearts worships without the restraint of discrimination. By the desires of their own bellies they are misled to a kill or be killed mentality, which increases more within many whom vehemently feels determined to prove their vain religious thoughts are true and holy through the vain acts of vengefully causing a mental disorder to widely spread amongst a great multitude. The Lord himself instructs all who believe on him to discontinue fearing the hearts of the earthy and to stop working with such vengeance in their hearts, because vengeance is the Lord's. Through an earthy fear, man does the works of Satan.

Despite of those who chose to criticize the NAACP in the 21st century by falsely accusing them to be of a group of racists black people, the NAACP was first established in 1909 in a white woman's house with her consent and support. Therefore, the critics misjudge the characterized intent and purpose of the Lord; whom was and still is the chief head of this organization. In order to prove this organization is on the opposite side of racism, let facts be submitted to a candid world. The NAACP grew by the grace of God into a group of whites, blacks and a combination of people of all other races. They've fought together for years and successfully have changed the traditional religious concept of the martyrs who sought to humiliate, brutally beat, and kill them. The religious concept of the martyrs' idea of a spiritual war pertained to those of them which followed the Sect. of the Pharisees and Sadducees' religious doctrine and loved seeking to shed the blood of whoever they opposed. The history of the NAACP members reveals how they tread peacefully, while spreading the true concept of godliness which signifies their reverential respect of all mankind, to the point of them requesting for equality and civil rights in America to be given to all Americans in spite of their different race, religion, sex, nationality, and social out looks of life.

417

Now concerning the unbalanced measure of religious faith during the 21st Century, many of these members yet falls short to uphold the true meaning of godliness when they face questions of genealogy especially where sexual orientation is concerned. Meanwhile, their Christian counter partners who take heed to the message of the Word of God; avoids such questions, because they are wise to know that "No man is perfect!" Without blaspheming against the Holy Ghost they fight for righteousness to be distributed fairly through democracy unto everyone. Meanwhile, their ideas of creating peace through the proper use of democracy for all mankind are fought against vigorously by all who religiously oppose their ideas. The opponents of them disbelieve that God desires for man to harmonize in agreement for such peace on earth. They think the peaceful followers and leaders of such organizations are deceived by Satan, and they warn themselves to beware of them; in hopes of stopping such faith from being apart of their religion.

Let's let facts be submitted to a candid world. The elders of the 21st century remember when the white supremacists called black women and little girls, "Gales" and the black men "Boys". Many stories have been told in a downside term of the racial name callings, especially after many black Americans were imprisoned under the unfair law of the land for peacefully protesting for their rights so that they lawfully could be treated under the law as "a Man". In the South, many black men during the Civil Rights Movement marched together peacefully while holding signs that read "I AM A MAN" as a peaceful demonstration. They were brutally attacked by police dogs and white police officers who were unlawfully but legally trained to hunt and devour them.

Many reformed black and white Christians during today's generation have sought for peace together and have been enabled by the Fruit of the Spirit which resides in their hearts to see beyond the physical aspect of their oppressed life story. They can spiritually recognize that the evil names which were/are offensively used to do evil unto them could not and cannot prevail against the works of God. They are spiritually converted into new creatures that can see their life story through the singleness of the eye. They say that the evilly used slurs were spoken to demoralize and undermine their confidence on the Lord's ability to bring them comfort and peace on earth, but they as born again Christians tells the story in a righteous and forgiving way, which edifies the entire Body of Christ without blaming or accusing any man unto God.

For instance, during the era when discrimination was smiled upon as a form of democracy, the victims and enemies of such democracy tells a unified story of how most legal voters of the southern states once used a vogue evil fashion to identify or to describe the African American people's heritage. Due to the old-time white southern voters strong southern accent of the English Language, which was very poorly pronounced and improperly stated; the distasteful name which they called the African Americans had a rougher edged sound.

Upon them being called a gale or a boy, they were enabled by the Spirit of God to read between the lines to recognize that they finally were given the identity of a human being. Gale and boy, was recognized as an adequate name of a person and not a wild beast. After carefully pondering over the actual definition of the repulsive names, they noticed that the meaning behind the unpleasant reformed names had changed. They were disassociated from the apes and monkeys' population, to the rightful inhabitant of a human-being. They believe that their loving character had the Power of God, which instilled into God's white children the desire to move the blacks from being viewed as soulless wild beasts; into a new reformed outlook which classifies all black Americans individually as a person whom are born with a soul.

For this cause, the born again Christians of every race with a clear conscious gives all glory, honor, and thanks to God because as one Body in Christ; they are enabled to end the desolated love of mankind which separates mankind from God. Both races which once were totally divided are now seen working side-by-side together on one accord as the Lord directs their steps. Through the love mercy and grace of God, the elders of all races can clearly see how Jesus worked it out for them to make it through the dark trials and tribulations of life together. The works of them are not in vain.

THERE'S NO FOOL LIKE AN OLD FOOL AND YES IT'S A SIN TO CALL AN INDIVIDUAL PERSON A FOOL

Be not deceived, some elders are not converted and they still are training their children and grandchildren into desiring to use their freedom for the occasion of rioting in the daytime for all to see. The Fruit of the Spirit proves what is righteous and it provide evidence that not all whites were/are racists against the blacks and visa versa. Meanwhile the Fruit of the Spirit of God also is proving that not all are concerted or strongly rooted in the Word. Through the form of retaliation, the weak-willed are unwisely influenced to call out racial slurring names. These families may someday take heed to the Power of God and stop using racially implied names all together. Like all others whom have grown to know and love God they may wisely understood that vengeance wasn't for them to pursue; vengeance is the Lord. After gaining that form of knowledge by faith they too may discontinue following the evil spirit of Satan.

In fact, the unawares irony are found seducing a portion of the black community who are known for calling themselves during the 21st Century by the disgraceful name "NIGGER or NIGGA" and the lack of knowledge of some whites calls themselves "RED NECKS". The ill-mannered side of both ill-bred groups is how they justify the wrong of making mockery of such name calling, as if they don't see anything wrong with calling themselves these names, but are easily offended if a person of a different race calls them by the names which they now ignorantly calls themselves.

Ironically the spiritual-minded people of all races, who morally lived through the time-period when discrimination was smiled upon as a revered form of America's democracy essentially sought and found refuge in the Word of God. The elders of the African American community remember how they were looked upon as a group of demigods by the whites. In Greek mythology demigods or daemons were acquainted with an evil spirit. To add pain to misery they were discouraged, depressed, and dispirited when a white man called them "Gales and Boys", but many of them concludes that such names was like a heavenly sign of both races making major spiritual progress!

What this mean is in despite of the southern accent of the English language and the vogue terms which the white supremacists unlawfully but legally used against the entire black community during the earlier years of the 1900's, many elderly African American Christians of the 21st century says that they are honored to have lived through that era, because they believe that the Holy Spirit taught them during their youth to stay positive thought the storm. With the Lord on their side, they refused to teach their children and grandchildren to yield their hearts to the disheartened evil spirits, which are an enmity against the Spirit of God. Spiritually they mention of how grateful they are to God for converting more whites to realize that they are people with souls too. To be called a gale and a boy during their later years of life; they said sounded much better than being called by the name of an animal or treated like one.

Many southern whites and blacks, who spiritually are connected with the Lord and lived through those days, boldly fought a good fight of faith against the principalities and powers of the Prince of the world. Today they are rejoicing in peace and in love, because they believe that the Lord survived them to receive a righteous order of blessings throughout the trials and tribulations of their obedient life. After meekly fighting for a better life for themselves and for their off-springs, they say they are blessed to see a change has come.

1Cor.15:8 "And that, he was seen of James; then of all the apostles."

1Cor.15:9 "For I am the least of the apostles, that am not meet to be called an apostle, because I persecuted the Church of God."

1Cor.15:10 "But by the grace of God I am what I am: and his grace which was bestowed upon me was not in vain; but I labored more abundantly than they all: yet not I, but the grace of God which was with me."

1Cor.15:11 "Therefore whether it were I or they, so we preach, and so ye believed."

1Cor.15:12 "Now if Christ be preached that he rose from the dead, how say some among you that there is no resurrection of the dead?"

1Cor.15:13 "But if there be no resurrection of the dead, then is Christ not risen:"

1Cor.15:14 "And if Christ be not risen, then is our preaching vain, and your faith is also vain."

Those who differ from the earlier composers of the American law either by nationality, sex, sexual orientation, creed, religion, race, and/or even by one's social outlooks on life; are all being led up by the Spirit of Righteousness to do the righteous things unto God, by doing right toward all mankind. To them, this is a reasonable sacrifice and sensible service done by them unto God. They know that it is prudent to do right unto all who may use perverse words against them. This isn't a fight of blood against blood, but against principality and power. AMEN!

(1Cor.15:51-58) By faith their walks are not and will not be vain. As they take a stand for the sake of receiving righteous judgment, they also consider making righteous judgments of others. When righteousness come, also comes the zeal to yearn for heavenly knowledge; to learn and understand how people are sought out to be destroyed by the lawmakers, because of their distinguished subtil differences and social outlooks on life.

All who the earlier composers of law of the land sought to religiously prove are ill-favored, were sought out by a murderous traditional religion. Although some people are mistreated as an ill favored person or group by those who live under a murderous traditional religious law, the anointed teachings of the Holy Ghost teaches them that whosoever looks down upon them as to belittle or to destroy their faith on the Lord God in a despising or vengeful like manner are not worker of the Lord. The un-forbidden fruit which worldly law-abiding citizens of such murderous religions bear, religiously teach people during the 21st century to think its okay for them to despise one sort of sinner or another. Without consulting the Lord, these religious followers sow the seed of hatred which defines their religious love for another kind of doctrine.

The kind of Love, which is maliciously given isn't easily entreated nor does it come from a kind heart. (1John3:11-18, 4:8, Gal.5:22-23, Col.3:1, & 3:12-16) God is love, and love is longsuffering and kind. Love enables all sorts of mankind to put up with one another while keeping in mind that we are all imperfect and all have sin. Keeping these things in mind helps us all to be what the Lord is, and the Lord is considerate and forgiving. Those who are despised the most of all, are despised because of their subtil differences and social outlooks on life. As despised as they maybe, God still gives unto them the ability to love him and be loved by him. Through the Lord's mercy and grace those who are despised can identify with the Spirit of God working through them in spite of what a religious person may say or do against them.

After being ridiculed, persecuted, used, and abused by traditional religious people, a despised person who is converted into having a forgiving and an understanding heart may discern the spirit of a despiser whom are beguiled to misjudge and use perverse words against them. The most despised are granted an undeniable gift of discernment as a blessing from God to indentify with the way such acts condemned them, and with the power of forgivingness they desire to not treat others the same way they were mistreated by such traditional religious people who made a mockery of them. The righteous fruits of the Lord God, teach those who are truly converted the difference between the fruit of righteousness from the un-forbidden fruits of Satan so that they may learn how to make righteous judgments (St. Matt. 16/St. Luke 12). With the ability to identify the difference between the two, they may spiritually compare and understand the differences between the children of God from a child of Satan. The children of God are despised, but they yet can righteously identify the discriminations within every hateful traditional religion and sympathetically understand the emotional adherence and strong aversion of hatred which Satan planted for mankind to either be feed or too eat. Satan's children captivate the minds of men to be despisers of men. It is traditional for the beguiled to mislead men to think they are sorting out the signs of the light of Christ as they despise others. Like a fish taking the bait, many orthodox religions practice searching the world over for the signs of the times and misunderstands the true sign of Jonah. The sign of Jonah resides within the sympathetic understanding of the will and way of the Lord God. The illusion of Satan has coerced many to seek for revenge and restitution, while using the signs of darkness of the world to conclude their selves to have religious justification in discriminating. The will and the way of the Lord urges all to recognize the goodness of God's love, mercy, and grace as he distributes all of his goodness unto all sinners.

All believers on the Son of God are of Christ even though the followers of the Pharisees' Old Law of the world seek to discriminate against them. In fact they can expect to be persecuted. (St. Luke21:12-28) The religions of the world love to try to shape people up to be like Christ, but their worldly love is conditional and deceitful. Religious people of the world have an overly excessive desire to have God on their side to the point of them mentally predisposing peoples whom they traditionally despise, as they traditionally practice reviling and casting people out of the assembly of men like they did the blind man in St. John9.

The Lord's Divine order of righteousness separates false apostles from his chosen apostles by blinding the false ones and prevents them from receiving or being granted God's spiritual equitable. False apostles are given eyes for seeing but they can't see, and ears for hearing but they can't hear the voice of the Lord, because they choose to live under the law of the worldly definition of indivisible liberty and justice for all. The world's definition of granting equal equitable is defined by the lips of worldly people whose hearts are far from the Lord. If the law of the world stood for the Lord's Divine order of righteousness and truth, then all men who are created equally by God wouldn't have ever had to spiritually fight a physical war to gain their indivisible liberty and justice.

St. Luke21:17 "And ye shall be hated of all men for my name sake."

Some people who are noticeably marked with a subtle difference are still being discriminated against by the old-time traditional religious governing body of lawmakers, during the 21st century. Howbeit that America can stand as a divided Nation and yet set an example for other Nations of the world? God for bid! Therefore he requires of the United States of America to first remove the dictating mote in their own governing eyes, and then they'll understand how to also remove the beam of dictatorship out of the eyes of others. Americans are fully aware of how the earlier generations who fought evil with evil created more wars and rumors of wars, whether the wars were foreign or domestic.

All who have stood strong in the Word of God and fought meekly against the evil prince of the world as God instructs of them, meekly

425

humbles themselves while fighting evil with love and kindness, knowing that they have the protection of the Armor of God. In despite of the differences of walks of life, every individual who believes on God are in pursuit of the same things; Salvation, Equality, and Peace. (Rom.12:14-21/1Cor.4:4-7)

Many Americans today are living witnesses of an inevitable dream which was first dreamed up but not seen by the founding forefathers and the American ancestors. Some had dreams and others had nightmares of there someday being an African American President of the United States of America. The nightmares consisted of the black slaves killing all the white owners and masters. The nightmare was a mere image of their guilt which turned into their worst fears. The image of such fears kept the earlier composers of the American law striving for world domination.

The testimonies of the elder African American citizens of the United States are mighty and powerful as they speak openly about being taught by their parents and grandparents to believe that it was inevitable for the composers of the American law of the land to stop ruling despotically as dictators, while misusing the Word of God to create unlawful laws as a cloak of maliciousness against the entire African American population.

We the people of the United States are made-up of all sorts of races. Together we have learned to live in love on one accord, and we all individually desire to live in peace with one of another with equality and justice being our key desire concerning us sharing a fair form of democracy. Throughout the years we've learned to humble ourselves to be of one race; the human race. Together we've grown as a group of understandable, lovable, and forgivable people towards one another. (1Peter 2:16-18/Gal. 5:13-14)

THEORETICAL CONCLUSION

Is it a dream come true or is it a nightmare? A man who proclaims to be in associations with the Black Muslims & White Christians became the 44th President of the United States of America. His sure name is Barak Hussein Obama. He isn't God, but he is a symbolic symbol of peace, liberty, and justice for all Americans, whom appears to have the righteous nature of God sown in his heart. Those who are beguiled by Satan desires to use the signs of darkness of the world to ridicule and persecute the intent of his Presidency, as he works to bring balance into the American dream. He's not perfect, and doesn't brag or boast of himself as if he has no marks or mistakes. He speaks highly about making lawful changes which is also desired by the hearts of a great multitude of all races of American citizens. That change includes equality, justice, and peace. He was voted into office by those who have gained the spiritual power of God to subject their hearts towards restraining their inner spirits from yielding to the acts of discrimination, so that all races in America may have equal rights of liberty.

This don't mean that the time has come for the gays of America and the gays worldwide to gain their equal share of rights to be treated as an equal under Barak Obama's presidency leadership, but it does mean that more people around the world are acknowledging the struggles of one sort of people are the same struggles of all others whom have been oppressed. Despotism has the same affect on every sort of people everywhere it may lurk. Although God gives man the knowledge to fear the Lord, all are greatly aware that change doesn't come over night. Eventually, in due time the season of equality by faith will expand to all mankind alike concerning democracy, just as the Lord's key to Salvation is expanded unto all whom believes on him.

As a united front under the belief of the Christian faith the peace makers around the whole world within all nations can conclude the difference between God's works from the works of Satan, and self examine their own deeds their own selves; instead of examining the sin of others. The day will come when man will see themselves, for

427

themselves, and through godly sorrows they will repent of their irreligious ways of spreading ungodly fears and hatred which divides and separates them from God's love. This is an inevitable prophesy, of the Lord's chosen prophet, but certain things must first come to past as the Lord says it must; before this inevitable prophecy takes place. In the end, every knee shall bow and every mouth shall confess Jesus is Lord.

2Cor.7:6 "Nevertheless God, that comforteth those that are cast down, comforted us by the coming of Titus;"

2Cor.7:7 "And not by his coming only, but by the consolation wherewith he was comforted in you, when he told us your earnest desire, your mourning, your fervent mind toward me; so that I rejoice the more."

2Cor.7:8 "For though I made you sorry with a letter, I do not repent, though I did repent: for I perceive that the same epistle hath made you sorry, though it were but for a season."

Chapter 11 THE FRUIT OF THE SPIRIT OF RIGHTEOUSNESS SHALL NOT BE MOVED

There's an old time hymn called "I shall not be moved," which was song by many who believed that one day righteous judgment would prevail on earth and create an open gateway for all people to be treated righteously and equal, without partiality nor hypocrisy and deceit. Many oppressed lives during the earlier generations didn't believe in the inevitable measured gifts of God, which unites all people of a different origin, sex, sexual orientation, creed, nationality, and religion etc., because God didn't give it to them to receive an understanding thereof. They were blinded by the earthy things that befit them as seekers of earthy empowerment. When they were a child all things were pure unto them, but they were brought up under the dictatorship of worldly tutors.

> Romans11:29 "For the gifts and calling of God are without repentance."
>
> Romans11:30 "For as ye in times past have not believed God, yet have now obtain mercy through their unbelief."

MANY ARE CALLED

During the 21st Century are many who live without righteousness, being neither apart of their judgment nor apart of their faith. Righteousness to them is to be vengefully unrighteous towards those who they believe are unrighteous. This sort of faith is the opposite kind of faith which the Lord God requires of all men. The Lord's righteous faith leads men to follow the faith of the Lord God's Commandment, to stop the desiring hearts of them from lusting after envy. The reasoning which explains why people submit to the opposite perceptive of traditional religions' faith is because after being born again they no longer are blind and destitute of the truth.

Spiritual peoples don't have the same mindset as that of a traditional religious person. What the Lord promised to do for all is the same things which he promise to do for one, but traditional religious people don't preach this sort of gospel. Instead, they think everyone's mindset should be set exactly on the same things as their own as if their minds religiously were incline to be of the same belief. Traditional religious men do not know that if someone doesn't believe in something that someone else may believe in, it's because God gave all men a free spirit.

Therefore, they religiously misjudge the status of a spiritual person and incorrectly react to those of them who don't think, feel, or believe on the same said perceptive message of the Word of God as they. Under the terms of their self-righteous religions' agreed misconception of Christ's Doctrine, they negatively wind up telling whosoever disagrees with their religious judgments that they automatically are hell bound. Traditional religious tutors of men think that whosoever they can't mentally or spiritually control, automatically goes to Hell. While misusing the Word of God as a cloak of maliciousness, they use the Lord's name in vain. Through vain teachings, they blasphemously preach and teach against the Holy Ghost; by educating men to not believe they are saved by the Lord's mercy and grace.

GOD HAS MERCY FOR ALL, BUT SATAN TRICKS MAN INTO FORSAKENING THEIR OWN MERCY

The holy war which Satan has mankind fighting looks a little something like he has beguiled Self-righteous men into killing themselves." Satan has them taking this eye for an eye bit, a-bit too far out of context. Satan's followers are forsaking their own mercy by seeking to find truth in vengeance within certain parables of the Lord's. They take much away from themselves like grace, mercy, love, and hope of being saved, while misusing the Word of God. They live in false hope of providing physical written evidence within the Lord's written parables to support the beliefs of their own bellies, because they hope to continue coercing those whom they religiously despise into believing in a lie. Satan since the beginning was a liar and his lie has convinced his followers to believe that vengeance is theirs' for the picking. According to their actions which are lead by the desires of their own bellies, the judgment of God comes by the judgment of the despisers who loves to debate the Word of God to prove they are justified keep the old inner man alive instead of being spiritually renewed or born again. They seem to not fully understand that the old man within them doesn't agree with the new inner man, and their judgment by which they judge others by, has no support from God due to the intent of their dead deeds.

Satan's warriors may profess to know the Lord with their lips, but the Lord's nobleness is far from their hearts. Meanwhile they suggest for all others to believe that they by words are religiously fighting righteously for righteousness in a holy war. Therefore; many malnourished pupils under such tutorship are fooled by their false teachings, and for this cause them to suffer not knowing God for their selves.

Meanwhile, the true Ministers of God who can spiritually hear, see, and discern the Lord's Word through the singleness of the eye; acknowledges to all whom are lost that crosses their path in life of howbeit that they are blessed to recognize the followers of the wiles of Satan walking the wide and broad path of life. As they explain the Lord's Parable of the one who sows, they clearly discern the different things which many prophets and righteous men have desired to see, hear, and know of. (St.Matt.13/St. Mark4/St. Luke10:21-24/Heb.5:11)

The walk of Satan's warriors may resemble the walk of God's children in the eyes of the weak and simple babes. Therefore, it is their duty as the supporting strength of God to continue walking the straight and narrow path of the Lord, to help the weak and simple babes to learn that the wiles of Satan's walk is not done in love; so that the simple and weak may see and understand that without agape love, they too maybe in danger of walking the wide and broad path of life against God. In such

431

case point, a true Minister of God may point out the Lord's Truth unto the Lord's lost sheep's which indeed are working for nothing.

We all ought to Thank God for the Lord's New Testament, but the heart of the followers of destruction reads the eye for an eye or tooth for tooth scriptures with a misapprehension. The delusions of these men concerning the scriptures may cause other men who desire to know the Lord, to physically view life double-mindedly with a wrong spirit. Satan's stratagems are unchanging, and so are the Lord's. In other words, there's nothing new going on under the sun. What God required of mankind to do in the beginning after the first sin was committed, in regards of mankind receiving the gift of life also known as the First Fruit from the Tree of Life; mentioned in the Book of Genesis; still is required of mankind during today's generation.

Mercy is given to mankind by God, and all who believes that they may obtain the Lord's mercy indeed by following and commending the traditional religious men of the world; are worshipping the Lord in vain. As time draws nearer to the coming of the Lord for those whom believes on Jesus, the Anointed Spirit of the Holy Ghost ceases the liars' tongues. When the liars' tongue is silenced then the deaf and blind may hear and shall understand what they'd been too blind to see and too deaf to hear concerning the Word of God. Before their life in this world is over all whom confess Jesus is Lord will come to understand that mankind is created by and for God equally. Everyone that believes on the Lord will also confess that the Lord came to save all from sin, even the most despised.

THE CRUEL WORLD

As an illustration; the traditional (KKK) Ku-Klux-Klan organizers are alive and living well in America, during the 21st century. Their identities are secretively hidden, but they are recognized by the fruits that they. Everything that is done in the dark is brought out by the glorious light of Christ. Although they aren't going out into the world and lynching the people like they use to do to those whom they are trained to religiously hate, everyone knows that their murderous principles are of the same standard. During the year 2009, certain news broadcasting companies reported that the KKK had re-emerged in the Southern states of the United States and were seen at a hotel, trying to reorganize the troopers of their Kingdom. They reported the disturbance in the local area of the state of Tennessee. It was also reported that they even went to Florida and past out flyers on the windshields of peoples cars in the form of recruiting more members.

The blacks, Jews, and all other races didn't appear to be as frightful in response to the report as they were during the 1940's-1980, but they did take precautious measures, because they now recognize that they have legal protection under the governing law against such tyrants. Sure, there are active KKK members in the American governing body, trying to secretly retain the power of their ancestors, but in doing so they oppress their own race. It's a shame how a southern Caucasian is ridiculed by those of the citizens of northern states, because they stereotypically think all whites from the south are racists.

Apparently most white Americans aren't interested in being a member of an ungodly organization like the KKK clan. Everybody who knows God, whether they are religious, nonreligious, young, or old have the desire to receive the Kingdom of God. They know God has given unto all of them the faith to believe on his righteousness, which out weighs the desolate beliefs of the KKK clan. Not all peoples are interested in abusing the Power of God. In fact there are a lesser amount of supporters of the abusive behaviors of such organizations during today's generation than there were during the Civil Rights Movement.

All glory goes to God for converting the hearts of the people by which more of them now can recognize which of the despotic American laws are irrationally demanding for the spirit of them to feel obligated to yield to an ungodly spirit of hate, all for the sake of committing an unreasonable sacrifice unto God. After being converted, the Children of God no longer are willing to be easily misled by the Prince of the World. Therefore, they desire to let neither anything nor anyone to change their devoted hearts and minds which are set on receiving heavenly rewards from the Lord for being doers of the Word of God. That's why they boldly stand together in love and in peace with all mankind. They know that they by mercy and grace are fighting a good fight of faith against every manmade rule, policy, and law which supports the cruel world's legal but unlawful acts of despotism.

The renewed mindset of those who the children of Satan has targeted to recruit, are well aware of the evil doers of the past and present who may have placed a negative influence on the new reformed governing law of the land. The liberal minds of men may wonder amongst themselves why people still desire to spread hatred during the 21st century. For the sake of gaining an understanding heart to learn and know the undeniable logic behind a hater's thinking process, requires a righteous judgment of God. This is done by those who judge not man but man's circumstances which surround the point of view of a troublemaker's heart.

A reprobate person undoubtedly withstand against God, therefore they still desire to spread hatred. With a sympathetic heart a person who knows how to make a righteous judgment, can empathize with the resourceful holy source of reasoning to identify with such a person's situation; to understand that many are mislead to hate and despise one of another for the sake of maintaining a sense of majestic controlling powers. The embrace of such temporal powers awards those of them which work indeed to receive dominion over people. Therefore, their overly excessive desire causes them to misuse their worldly powers on earth. Their hidden agendas is to reign as lords of the land and as gods on earth, but their evil desirous hearts shall not prevail over the goodness of God's love, mercy, and grace.

IN YOUR HOUSE DO YOU & THE TARES THEREOF SERVE YOUR FATHER SATAN? (St. Matt.13:37-39, 52)

Some immoral people are pros at hiding themselves behind the unfair governing laws, which they politically maintain as an earthy duty of their own, because religiously they are like the scribe who profits from the unreasonable rules and regulations thereof; by bring forth out of their own hearts the treasure of things of the old and new. (St. Matt.7:11) The devil sows unto his tares to provide the world with an unrighteous, unfair, and iniquitous law which supports his evilly implied theoretical perceptions of the Lord's Truth. Under an unjust decree, Satan's children are commanded to take the leadership role over every society in the manner of belittling the least of all people of the field which God has made, while making themselves look more like their father the devil who teaches them. The devil whom they serve teaches them of how to fulfill the desires of their own bellies, which is guided by the adversary's evil excessive needful desire; to reign over the Lord's sheep's with dominion. (Prov.13:12) While lacking spiritual wisdom and sympathetic understandings of the holiness of the Lord, the tares of the field also lacks the ability to do the will of God and of his good pleasures. Loving God is impossible for the deferred hearts of the 21st century. Those who follow the cruel, vindictive, and malicious ways of Satan hope that every race of people would put them up on a pedestal like the tutors of the old time religion did unto themselves, because their hearts are sick. (Proverbs 13:12)

By the Lord's love, mercy, and grace; God's people are being spiritually deterred from the immoral ways of the adversary by the Power of God to do good and not evil. This means, the Holy Spirit is causing them to be discouraged by their own lying vanities, and encouraged into preventing themselves from repeating the same vain acts of the old-man which the Power of the Holy Sprit has renewed. The Power of God keeps the hearts of them unwilling or incapable of treating mankind unjustly with prejudice tendency! "United We Stand and Divided We Fall," is an Old American Motto, which reflects the Lord's order of righteous truth for all.

Throughout the years from one generation unto the next, the American legal system has been twinning together with the spiritual truth of God as it made gradual changes. Little by little the heart of America's society learned to charge and lay blame against the terrain acts of vanity instead of accusing one of another unto God. They have learned that judging one of another only misleads the heart to fall into the ditch of destruction and into a spiritual wall of death.

Not all Americans which claim to be Christians are converted. After all of the righteous fighting which has been won throughout history, the oppressors today still misuse the Word of God maliciously by twisting the denote meaning of the Word, because they religiously are encouraged to physically rule over the lives of others. No man alive can send another man to heaven nor send anyone to Hell. The way the Lord's Adversary teaches men to worship God is by teaching them how not to worship God at all. Satan is soul seeking to win souls, by coercing men to desire to use the Vail acts of hatred. He misleads people to destructively cause a war of some sort to come between people. The Vail acts of Satan's deeds today continue to come from those of them who are committed to receiving his earthy rewards above their heavenly rewards. As a person entrust in such acts of vainness and pass Satan's unfruitful deeds unto others, they fail to see that it is they whom the Apostle Paul speaks of in the Holy Scriptures whom causes misery and great despair unto the followers of Christ by persecuting them. Through their ignorance they can only see how happy it makes them feel as they love causing others a life time of pain and misery. They love to debate the Word of God with envy and strife in their hearts!

Satan's unfruitful deeds distort the hearts of people and trick them into having hate for and by their own cultural heritages as well as for the heritage and culture of other sorts of people. Not only does the Vail act of Satan's hateful desires corrupt the hearts of the people in America, but it also seduces the citizens of all countries on earth, whom are giving the wrong impression about God by the dictatorship of certain sorts of traditional religious martyrs. For instance, some people are tricked into desiring to believe that it's God the Father who wants them to either kill or break the Spirit of another man as to murder the blameless desire of those whom hope for deliverance and redemption.

The truth of the matter is, without hope of receiving salvation; man shall not be saved. Therefore the hearts of them who speaks to destroy the free willing spirit of mankind desires to keep certain people from desiring to have faith on being delivered by the Lord. The intent of their hearts are all vexed and filled with vanity. They blasphemously coax people into sinning without evaluating the blasphemous ways of their own religious self-righteous enticements. In other words the insensitive way in which they may wrong a person is the least of their concern, as they falsely minister the Word by lying against the Holy Ghost (St. Mark3:23-30). Satan's spirits work to condemn the Spirit of mankind not to save any; but to destroy all. The Stratagem of Satan coerces people to deceptively believe in false ministries which suggest that his unclean spirits aren't evil. Meanwhile, the goodness of God's Spirit works to revive and restore the faith back into the Spirit of mankind whom may have a condemned conscience, because God is more powerful than a condemned conscience.

Satan wants his unclean spirits to appear to be cleaner than the cleanest and purest of all, but spirit of his children carries a false simulate of an agape love which includes a hidden dissimulation, and there's no dissimulation in the Spirit of God's Love. For example, if a man who makes himself an apostle of God shows his love for Christ Church through the way he treats his wife by beating his wife and then living to lie about it, hides the truth of his impure love; by pretending that his love for Christ Church is honest and pure. Satan adds more misunderstandings to the earthy and fleshly fears of mankind. That's why one sort of people religiously loves to devour another. It is prudent for all to beware of the wiles of Satan.

The Lord's message to the people of the world is spoken quite clearly, but due to their deafened ears; they cannot hear nor understand the voice of the Lord instructing them. When the Comforter of the Lord comes and shares the good news of an inevitable spiritual desire being upon the Spirit of all believers of the Son of God, the despisers of men refuses to hear the Spirit of God teaching them to live happily on one accord and in peace with all mankind; including those who speaks perverse words against them. The Comforter has come along by the anointing teachings of the Holy Ghost to spread the heavenly desire of LOVE abroad, and love covers a multitude of sin.

Many people who are called by God ends up being misdirected by numerous attractions of the world, and they start taking their focus off of heavenly things and put their hearts upon receiving earthy rewards and simple pleasures. As they unfairly work against the living souls of others, they with prejudice in their hearts also work as if they think their own sanctimonious self-righteous misleading ideas of GOD'S WILL & GOODPLEASURES are either more considerable or significant than the idea of all others. The desires of their bellies are enmity against the LORD'S WILL and GOODPLEASURES. Therefore, they fail to understand the significance of the LORD'S WILL which contains self-control and peace. It is the Lord's Will and Good Pleasures that causes the Holy Spirit to make intersession for us. The Holy Spirit brings people a closeness with God to the point of them receiving an understanding of Christ's Spirit, which fills the hearts of mankind with the good pleasures of the Lord's godly spirit that exist in contentment. The Spirit of Christ is like a Tree of Life unto all who diligently seek for the Kingdom of Heaven. The Tree of Life has many godly forms and one form within it is more precious than gold and rubies. The Tree of Life is Heaven's Wisdom, and all who diligently seeks for the Kingdom of God shall find HER.

Many are afraid to publically confess of loving those whom they are traditionally trained to religiously and deeply despise, because of the profound prejudice of their hearts which was religiously established over the trial of time. In order for the nature of them to religiously declare others to be unworthy of being saved by the Blood of Jesus, they sent comfort unto themselves by glorifying and commending themselves. They believe in such heresies, because they've been spoiled for far too long by religion's orthodox principalities and vain philosophies of deceits. Such religions draws the minds of many people who traditionally regard and commend themselves in the manner of speaking well of their discriminating acts of hating and despising their neighbors and strangers alike.

In the eyes of the lost, the act of discrimination is viewed as a godly act of punishment, retaliation, and vengeance. Therefore, the hearts of them selectively loves to despise and hate their neighbors instead of loving their neighbors as they love themselves. They haven't the power to prevail against the predestined desire of the people of God who as one unit under the heavens, are living witnesses of an historical and spiritual change of heart. During every generation that comes to pass, the godly hearted are constantly reforming laws and are bringing comfort, peace, and joy unto every nation by the renewing of their hearts. Little by little the USA's custom-made traditional form of democracy are being made over for the people and by the people of every walk of life, and the root of their new reforms which works righteousness shall not be moved. (Prov.12:3)

Fearing what they can't understand by their own judgments and their yearnings for improvement or perfections, many who are not chosen by God, still love to draw up complaints about other people's dignities only to up hold their own dissatisfactions as they lack godly compassion. For example; a person who bullies another commonly engages in the very act thereof, because they themselves are suffering from a lack of self-esteem. This custom profoundly has worked its way into the political grounds and minds of all sorts of different religious denominations during today's society. The identity of all races whom are trained up under the traditional yokes of bondage also are trained up to have respectful regards to the earth's physical features, which represents what traditional religion have taught mankind from one generation unto the next.

Some people believe that "Prosperity" resides in having MONEY and having money is the Key to their contentment, because their hearts desire for their MONEY to bring unto them love, peace, joy, and happiness here on earth." This is a fine example of how worldly men seek to receive worldly rewards. This brings about an understanding to the factoring of those who say, "More money more; more problems."(St. Mark4:13-19) As the Rich becomes Richer, and the Poor becomes Poorer, more people are realizing that contentment is godliness and that godliness isn't found in money. Contentment is being happy and thankful.

Although the conservative laws of the land are constantly been reproached, reproved, and reformed many manmade congregational houses continuously are being built today by the hands and minds of those who were raised under the terrain ideas and orders of a supremacy power of ministers whose nationalities aren't of the white American race, but their religions are like that of the KKK's teachings, because they too are coerced to desire to have an excessive relationship with the Lord (Col.2:8/1Tim.1:3-11). Their excessive desire to have lordship is causing their members to wickedly target the weakness of others as if ones weakness symbolically proves the weaker parts of mankind are wicked and are hellhound.

As they preach to commend themselves, they sought out the weak to receive worldly glory and edification by manipulating the weak babes and elders of all ages into believing in the traditional misinterpreted and false mentioning's of the Holy Scriptures which originally was derived by false apostles. (1Tim1:12-16) These false teachers murder the character of the Lord's dignity unto their own kindred and hinder their offsprings from believing that Jesus is who he says he is and he will do what he says he'll do for all who believes on him.

Men pleasers use the Word of God to condemn or retain a person from spiritually believing that God loves them. Men pleasers also believe they have the power and the consent from God to use the Old and New Testament together to compare ones physical sin or their physical differences; to per-say who shall or shall not enter into either the Heaven above or the Hell below. After comparing physical with physical, these men only provide evidence that they maliciously judge a person's spirit by the physical eyes of the world and not by the spiritual sight of God.

A FEW ARE CHOSEN

Meanwhile, the comforter comes and consult the conscience of the simple, weak, and the weary all while instructing them all to submit to every ordinance of all kinds of people who has the worldly power to rule with authority like Caesar, the Roman Emperor and the sovereign of Judaea (St. John19:12, 15; Acts17:7) and other Kings and Governors etc., because the Lord set all men free from the same law of bondage and placed all who believes on him under the New Law of Christ. Under the Law of Christ all are concluded by God to be sinners and he also concluded all in unbelief so that he could save those who believe on him. Those who believe on the Lord are not neither obligated by God to carry out the whole Old Law, nor are they faulted for not doing the whole law, but traditional religions are known for subconsciously teaching men to fault and blame one of another as if one sort of people have an inalienable right to rule unfairly with dominion over others. The Lord blesses those who submit unto world's authorities. (Romans13:8-11/Gal.5:14) It is ordered for all who understands, to give to the world whatsoever the people of authority in the world says is owed them and owe them nothing where love is concerned; without obligating their complete devotion and loyalty unto serving or worshipping the worldly authority. This is one of many great successes of a Christian who are saved from worldly sorrows, misery, and from the grievous bondage of the Old Law.

The newness of the Lord's Spirit of Righteousness desires for no man to resist the Power of God. Since the fleshy desire of the world wants God's children to be apart of man's demandable sacrificial religion which profits men nothing, the Lord provides mankind with exactly what they really need in order for any to be delivered out of the temptations of the world. The Lord knows that certain men will speak evil against his servants who doesn't submit to every ordinance of mankind. Therefore, the Power of God gives all believers an escape route so that the simple, the weak, and the weary can be revived by the teachings of the Holy Ghost and strengthened to live up to the ordinance of God.

THE OLD LAW IS FULFILLED, LIKE A FULL GLASS OF WATER

Although the simple and the weak who believes on the Lord may feel as if their backs are pinned against a wall by the world who coerces them to think that they must complete the whole Old Law, the Lord leaves them not to be ignorant. The Holy Scriptures reveals to them by the anointed teachings of the Holy Ghost that God doesn't expect the faith of those of us who believes on the Lord to carry out the Old Law. The Old Law is a curse to all whom indeed are indistinguishable workers of a dead act indeed under the law. For example, the workers of the law don't free the spirit of any man; neither does the work of the law save anyone. Like two peas in a pod the works and the old law both interchangeably do the same ungodly things unto man. Under the Old Law it is impossible to differentiate the workers of the law from the workers of evil. Men aren't justified by the law in the sight of God, they are justified by faith, and the old law isn't of faith.

(Romans 10:1-7)Instead of misusing the Word God to per-say who shall ascend into heaven or who shall descend into the deep, we disclaim every traditional religious organization which teaches such things; as if they can either descend Christ down from above or ascending him up again from the dead. We have the Word of Faith written in our hearts to speak of and we preach as Evangelists who understands that the Lord Jesus was raised from the dead by God the Father. The Word of Faith is what we preach and the Lord holds us accountable to individually learn know and understand that whosoever shall call upon the name of the Lord shall be saved. (Romans 10:8-17/Gal.3)

No man with the exception of Jesus Christ can walk in the flesh as a perfect man without sin. The more a person try to do what they cannot, the hearts of them becomes condemned. There's no way possible that we in the flesh can obligate our full devotion into doing that which doesn't agree with the New Commandment of the Lord. The mercy of the Lord's kindness knows that if we live after the flesh, we surely will die. Therefore; if we through the Spirit do mortify the deeds of the body, we shall live as sons and daughters of God. (Romans 8)

442

We are the children of God and we are assured by the Comforter which builds our confidence, and strengthens our faith to be able to give or render to the violent lords of the land what they claim is due, so that we may in the end be unbound and liberated to not owe them anything. (Romans8, 13:1-10/1Peter2:11-13, 14 & 25/1Peter3:12-17)

The Comforter secures the conscience of the simple, the weak, and the weary into believing that the evils and perverse words of the evil Kings and governors; are a terror to the evil worker thereof, but is not a terror to those of us that are good workers of the Lord, because GOOD always will conquer EVIL.

Therefore, the babes should not be afraid of the evil terror of the worldly Kings and governors, because it is God's Will for their ignorant reign of evil terror to be put to silence. Those of us whom the tyrannous authority figures cause to suffer worldly sorrow and grief would rather suffer for well doing, rather than for evil doing. Unfortunately, many black Americans and other races have been drawn to the same desires of false dictating ministries. For this cause the leaders of such ministries to do unto their own members the same things, which the oppressors also known did unto their ancestors during times past. Everyone are highly urged to remember where we come from, because that source of information is necessary for us all too individually understand where we presently stand in life concerning our faith on the Lord. Knowing where we presently stand is necessary in the spiritual process of us growing in faith. Knowledge is power considering how we individually embrace the Lord's Holy Truth which guides and direct our steps. When we all get where the Lord wants us to be spiritually, we then can remember seeing the way the Lord saw us through the storms.

Some people appear to be more discerned with the expectations of seeking physical signs from heaven, and they don't regard the sign of the prophet Jonas nor can they understand the sufferings of Christ and the glory that should follow. (St.Matt.16:3-4/1Peter1:7-25) This trend of terror being past down from one generation onto the next eventually turned into blacks hating blacks, and whites hating whites etc.

443

As spiritual evidence of the things hoped for unfolds before the necked eyes of mankind, the increasing of black on black crime took the world by storm between the years of 1980's thru 1990's. These evil acts of events changed the ideological perceptive of unity and peace within the black community for all who fought for freedom and won the good fight of faith during prior years. The concept of love hasn't ever nor will it ever be changed. Love to the world is hate in reverse, but to the children of God; love is God. By the grace of God even the haters have received mercy, and have hope of being redeemed. (1Peter 1:9-25)

Like Jonah, jealous hearted haters who despise men, forsaken their own mercy within all of their complaining against other people. The Word of God, reprove the repining complaints made by the founding forefathers and their indentured servants the same way as his Words reproved Jonahs' repining or complaints against the people in the great city of Nineveh (Jonah2:8 & 4:9-11). It is by faith that the Lord also will reprove the repining and complaints made against the dignity other sinners who are greatly hated, like the gays. The Word of God convicts the haters' non-compassionate spirits and strengthens them all to stand boldly for righteousness. For goodness sakes they repent compassionately and use the Word of God to edify the despised ones while also edifying the Lord God. Not all white people were oppressors during or after slavery, and not all blacks were plotting to kill the whites while desiring to be treated equally and fair. No man can judge the true conscience of another man's heart, but if you ever doubt whether or not a person is of God's, believe their works are of God if you can see beyond their physical sin. Mark and remember that we all have faults and imperfections and stop judging.

A DILAPIDATED DOCTRINAIRE: [Latin word dilapidare to destroy", from dis+lapidare "to throw stone", from lapis "stone"]

For centuries the despotic principles and theories of man's laws have been throwing stones while being either unable or unwilling to grant equality and freedom to all mankind alike, especially on religious matters. As one generation pass onto the next, the manmade governing laws of the land remains to rule with unlimited tyrannous, abusive, and oppressive powers of authority over the minority class. In the beginning the least of mankind had no rights according to the written law of man, to vote on any policies which were made into law. Greed and ravenousness began to over throw even those who were of the same origin like the earlier composers of the American law. In other words the earlier American ancestors also oppressed and abused the lives of their own offspring.

During the year 2008-09 all American citizens received the fiery and rage which have set the world up in a great recession, and a global environmental crisis. The United States of America is only one nation out of many, which can relate to the fellowship of such tyrannous governing laws. The foundation or the root of these worldly laws has been revered too as an idol god for centuries. In the beginning creation of the American laws the white American men either worshiped them honorably or were forcefully coerced to adapt themselves to the prevailing standards, customs, and principles; which caused an inward corruption to be bestowed towards many whom compromised their spiritual consciences to not be engaged in a worldly revolutionized existence of a desolated environment. Therefore, the earlier American revolutionized doctrines left a legacy of a desolated genocide for those of us today to follow after, reprove, rebuke, or repent thereof.

THE HIDDEN MYSTERY

Until a new season of a new generation of God's people, the laws of the land will continue to deliberately and systematically up hold the dark spirit, which is known to be enmity against God. The wile of Satan's method also brings confusion unto the hearts of even the godly Christians, only to condemn and not to save them. The vexatious and greedy hearts of men intended to make the laws' unlawful principles and standards appear to be honest, but they ignorantly created an imitation or a simulation of God's Greatest Commandment; which is summed up in one word, (LOVE?).

445

(1Cor.13:13, St. Matt.22:36-40/Mark12:28-33/Rom.8:39/12:9-10). Love is to be without dissimulations, but vain hearted men composed laws together that put on a false appearance of love to hide their personal agenda behind. Meanwhile, others are required to live under the submission of a vain love and a traditional religious falsehood of love as a religious customary routine or a curse. (Romans12:9-18/13:10/St. John13:34-35/15:12/1John4:7-11 &20/Eph.3:16-19)

Eph.1:9 "Having made known unto us the mystery of his will, according to his good pleasure which he hath purposed in himself:"

Eph.3:3 "How that by revelation he made known unto me the mystery; "(as I wrote afore in few words,"

Eph.3:4 "Whereby, when ye read, ye may understand my knowledge in the mystery of Christ)"

Eph.3:5 "Which in other ages was not made known unto the sons of men as it is now revealed unto his holy apostles and prophets by the Spirit;"

Gal.3:28 "There is neither Jew nor Greek, there is neither bond nor free, there is neither male nor female: for ye are all one in Christ Jesus."

Gal.3:29 "And if ye be Christ's, then are ye Abraham's seed, and heirs according to the promise."

> Eph.3:6 "That the Gentiles should be fellowheirs, and of the same body, and partakers of his promise in Christ by the gospel:"
>
> Eph.3:7 "Wherefore I was made a minister, according to the gift of the grace of God given unto me by the effectual working of his power."

All things that go on in the dark are brought to the light. The truth of the greatest egotistical intent and agendas of the composers of the world's longest reigning dogmatic religious ordinances are being brought to the light. For centuries the spiritual truth has been concealed by the world's oldest traditional religions, which have hid the ungodly and boastful pride of the earlier composer's of the law. Therefore; due to the arrogance of the false pretenders thereafter they publically confess that they religiously stand for freedom, justice, equality, and peace for all mankind alike, but they are revealed as liars by the Holy Ghost. The Holy Ghost manifest the characterization of what freedom, justice, equality, and peace denote unto God, and gives righteous judgment to God's chosen ministers so that they may spiritually compare what Christ represents to the dictating representation provided by mankind which resides within the world's highly regarded and respected customary position of a high power of authority.

The American laws also were partially configured from the Holy Bible text which has depreciated the spiritual statues of the Word of God over a period of time. From one generation to the next the act of dissimulation which came from the hearts of the beginning composers of the laws of the land tremendously grew. During the 20th Century, the impression of most American's and non-Americans yet still honored the conventional unfair laws of the past with extravagant respect. The intuitions of unlawful dissimulations are seen today within the duty of the political idolaters who lacks clarity of their own ungodly actions and deeds. In most cases, these idolaters don't have the desire to reprove their own ways and are unwilling to repent, because they don't see anything wrong with their ancestors' traditional religious ways of life.

The religious technique of belittling one of another or having one to rule despotically over another living soul, transferred from the church houses which men built with their bare-hands and immediately entered into the White House of America after it was physically built brick by brick, by African American slaves. When the earlier American ideas were incorporated into laws, the minority were gruesomely mismanaged from one generation unto the next and the chauvinism, sexism, bigotry, and other prejudice behaviors of the earlier political generations gradually were dealt in a genuine manner of expression by each modified generation of the past onto this present day. The pattern of such dealing has always required for American citizens to make the selective vote for humility over the arrogant votes made by certain conceited American politicians.

The elected Commandeering Chiefs of the past and present are also known as the Presidents of the United States of America were hired by the electoral vote of the majority, who use their voting rights to help rule and govern this country. The people of the 21st century have set aside the old dogmatic way of thinking as a reformed group of Americans, and they elected the first African America president of the USA. This 44th president of the United States of America mentioned how he intended to make a fair change about the laws of the land. He talk about how he wanted to do things to better suit the inalienable rights of all Americans; including the ones on Main Street, which suffers the most from the abuse of governing powers that had been distributed by the rich lobbyists.

To universally explain the transitioning of the American peoples' change of heart requires one to look diligently into the conflict of interests between two parties; God and Satan. With an understanding heart, a seeker of truth may see the agape love of God residing in the deed of the awarders of righteous judgments. The awarders of righteous judgments consists of those whose deeds revealingly relates to bringing justice and peace in a meek manner unto the deprived. The hearts of them are different from the hearts of those whose uproars support the arrogant hatred of Satan.

The hatred of Satan resides in the deeds of the awarders of immoral dishonorable arrogance and boastful pride. Like Satan, those whose boastful pride desires to divide and conquer in the religious realm, casts people out of the public synagogues where they themselves as hypocrites pray. A diligent seeker of truth can see the evil workers of Satan vehemently casting down wrath and desolation against whosoever they desire to cast out from among them. The key to the evil substance of such religion is the poisoning religious hoax, which false teachers feed one of another in efforts of them keeps themselves separated from those whom they misjudge. This is one of the main sources of differences between the interests of the two parties. **If God is for all, then who can be against any?**

Those who coherently think they are right as they unjustly judge sinners, indeed make unrighteous judgments against sinners. This is where injustice is formed and why it is revered by the ignorance of traditional religious men. As one generation fades onto another, the ignorance of every beginning ordinance of the composed American laws from one decade unto the next may still remain the same during the 21st century, but due to the spiritual growth of the earlier minority class of people; the interests of the vote of the majority has evidently changed hands. For this cause, the old laws are to be preserved and sealed as the new reformation of the laws is being restructured.

Every godly change is attributed to the standard concept of the New Covenant of Jesus Christ within the Constitution of the United States of America which requires a certified change of heart from the majority of American voters. In order for any future spiritual changes to give attribution to the Lord, the sworn duty of the born again American citizens who are blessed with the power to vote responsibly should make sure that their vote correctly are accounted for. As a peculiar people, they must also learn to take heed to say and do what the intent of the Lord desires for them to do. For instance, not everyone who says they are seeking for peace has the lowliness of heart which God has instructed all to use, while submissively honoring the Lord and all of his glory.

Democracy is defined as the rule for the people and by the people whose deliberated votes on rules and policies are made into fair laws. Certain premeditated laws were considered and intended by the earlier composers who desired for all Americans to live humbly together in peace, but the intent of their hearts was clouded by the perverseness of many. Not all earlier Americans who voted for peace within their own community wanted to extend the humility of their freedom as an American citizen to the indifferent ones whom were born and raised on American soil, but were naturally born outside of the original white American race of people.

Putting on an unassuming nature of humility wasn't apart of their perverse intentions when they first thought of how life would be unto them if they humbled themselves as an equal to those who weren't pure-breed Americans. The very thought of showing meekness unto another race of people placed an awkwardness upon their hearts, because they were over zealous at seeking for mastery of the universe. As the foundation of certain worldly laws continue teaching people to follow after the despot ancestors' evil traditional religious customs and beliefs, the today's idolaters of such powers may imprudently fail to see how their hypocritical standing for the unjust laws places them in the same unwarrantable oppressive category as their ancestors.

The Holy Ghost still convert's people from being carnally minded, (just like Apostle Paul in the Book of Acts or Jonah in the Book of Jonah etc.) but many today have not yet received God to do the same. Unlike how alert an overly protective sleeping mother maybe to their babies' cry, some human beings today just aren't alert at all to hear the voice of the Lord. Although we today weren't born when the old American laws were being composed, we still must give an account for our own actions. As we know and learn the parable of the reaper and the sower, if we support the unchanged oppressive condemning ordinances of the old laws, we shall continue to reap destruction through the unfairness of our unjustifiable wrong doings.

Some world leaders may proclaim that it's not possible to change the law for the sake of righteousness, because they haven't received the Holy Ghost. Without the teachings of the Holy Ghost, no man can spiritually determine nor detect which laws are genuinely righteous. In such case, it is unknown unto them of which law neither to keep nor to void. Without the Holy Ghost many laws have been wrongfully instated by many worldly theoretical idealists, and these laws coerce the hearts of people into observing the worldly laws as if they were the Lord's laws of Righteousness. The blind and the lost sheep's are incapable of being a deviser of the Word of God, but this fact doesn't change the matter of how the false ministers attempt to justify their wrong. The worldly would rather continue worshiping a false image of God by yielding their hearts to the false image of love that is sown into the hearts of different prejudices for discrimination to be identified as the key elements of life which support the unlawful idea of having heaven on earth. Most leaders are constantly taunted by the true perceptive teachings of the Holy Ghost, and they'd rather be defaulted rather than to take fault for their wrong.

Meanwhile, the idea to change the laws of the land causes them to fear the inevitable. It is inevitable for every living despot to face the fact that the tyrannous desires of their ancestors religiously taught them wrongfully. If the anointed teachings of the BIBLE are right, then a whole lot of BODIES are bibliographically living wrong. It is profitable for thee that one of thy members should perish, and not that thy whole body should be cast into hell. (St. Matt.5:29-30)

Being godly or spiritually mortified simply means a person or a group of persons have received the Holy Ghost which changes their evil ways of thinking and their evil way of living. The worldly gods of love

451

encourages traditional religious people to engage in the acts of vileness, which consist of despising and hating an inferior group of people. The worldly god of love leads them into believing that their hate will make those who they despise and love to hate to susceptibly live preferably to what their orthodox but vain religion teaches unto them to be the Lord's Divine Order of Law. After the Holy Ghost has come and manifest the truth of their deeds are evil, only the scorners today continue desiring to live in that old time religion. The inferior group of peoples, whom the superiors of the world once considered last; are gaining recognition in the account of numbers, to the point of being considered first as the Holy Scriptures have mentioned.

The superiors of the world whom the prince has coerced for so many generations are taunted by the truth, and they are set in their own ways to the point of them not clearly seeing their faults. Therefore, they aren't influenced by the Word of God to be of a good quality of moral virtues, but are tempted by the cunning persuasive perverse words of Satan to do evil. Their no good thoughts are spiritually turned over by the spirit of condemnation and are evil and reprobate, and Satan is happy with their evil works and their evil deeds, because morally they haven't any godly morals aligned with the things they either do or say. They are uncompassionate towards the godly universal idea of treating others as they would like for others to treat them, because in being good to all others would cause them to be inwardly divided against the hateful desires of their own hearts. Satan can not rebuke Satan and any house divided against its self shall fall, because it cannot stand.

While the idolaters are busy making judgments against those whose subtle differences stands to be either not clearly expressed or not easily understood, the ordinance of their manmade laws' oppressively, abusively, and unfairly works to condemn those whom they don't understand. The ordinance of their laws legalizes the broad spread of hatred to be bestowed or used against all whom they religiously despise. Their ungodly religious ordinance turns lovers of GOD into haters of men. The idolaters of these forms of governed desolated laws; fearing what they don't understand, are easily misled by Satan's spirit of condemnation. Therefore, they make the outer appearance of themselves to be above those whom they constantly oppress.

Can you explain why so many traditional religious people think they are holier or closer to GOD than they really are?

In the mist of worshiping the traditional religious form of dissimulation, false teachers believe as haters of men that they are either doing the works of GOD or are working for GOD. In their own eyes, they see their evil deeds of entreating ill-will on other believers of the Son of God as an acceptable religious act. To help them to not live with a guilty conscience, Satan seduces their mindset to disbelief.

For instance, they are coerced by Satan to disbelieve a person (**a sinner**) is saved, even after one profess Jesus as their Lord and Saviour. They seek for a fault in such person's to accuse them unto God, because they are misled to believe that a person who confesses Jesus as their Lord and savoir shouldn't be seen lacking anything that they religiously think they are to possess. Some of the most traditional religious people of the world are beguiled and are professionally trained by Satan to be debaters, doubters, skeptics, and nonbelievers of the Power of God's ability to deliver an escape route for all sinners who are tempted. In other words, they are trained to believe that God gave them the power to judge the conscience of a sinner who cries out that they do believe on the Lord; only to falsely accuse those whom do cry out; of not believing on the Lord or of not being saved by, through, nor for him. They curse themselves while making such false judgments against those whom they religiously hate by thinking that they are making righteous judgment against whosoever they accuse unto God. They preferably base their false judgment and decision making skills on the unreasonable false judgments which religiously states or suggests for traditional religious people to count a person's slackness against them; in hopes of grafting themselves into the protection of the Lord, while cutting and carving those whom they hate out of his protection.

Those who make themselves an apostle of Christ, often times misuse the Holy Scriptures to build an outline for themselves which summarize how to work their way into heaven. Due to their misinterpretation of the scriptures, they believe that it's acceptable unto God for them to despise and hate sinners. This explains why people commonly use the discriminating features of the old traditional religions' vain philosophies and theories to suggest that God is a partial God whom shows them favoritism.

Theoretical religious suggestions such as this hypocritically bring a dissimulation of peace into false teachers' chaotic religious and worldly point of views. In fact, being threatening towards others is how they engage in religious recreations. The plan of their daily walk of life is to be prepared to satisfy their own religion's sinister characteristics. They think that their best ideal religious factor in life will ultimately prove unto others that they definitely know who God shall save and who shall perish (2Peter3:9). In vain they use the name of Jesus as they proclaim to believe in their traditional religious way of life, and they also believe they will be pardon from the wrath of God upon the Day of Judgment for preaching another doctrine other than that of Jesus Christ.

The heart of the false prophets' manmade doctrines or laws, are like a sham. They have a poor quality acting intentionally so as to give unto all mankind a false impression of love, peace, equality, unity, and joy. These worldly supporters subvert certain parts of the Holy Bible and other historical legal documents to sanction discrimination so that they may easily pass the mischievous impulse of iniquity to a deep unreasoning dislike within the motive of their fleshly desire to cause suffering for others by the evils which stresses the intensity and driven forces of malevolence. Filled with shameful injustice, their laws work abomination with froward words, which teach men to hate or to dislike one of another greatly and often with disgust. Such laws and teachings of such laws also are filled with lies against God. Although these teachings are an abomination, blind followers are yet still in pursuit of having dominion in the religious realm of life, and they find happiness by causing others pain, grief, and worldly sorrows. This too is evil and vexed.

The heart of all historical laws expresses the thoughts, feelings, and qualities of the composers' state of being. Today many of the things that were of their vexed hearts have been silenced and preserved by the teachings of the Holy Ghost; not by man. The true intentions of the Holy Ghost is to cause one alliance to form and rise up and glorify the will and good pleasures of God, by guiding the hearts of mankind into overcoming the abusive, oppressive, and tyrannous reign of terrors that are lurking amongst the fights between the Democrat vs. Republic Party and every similar fight that exist amongst the living Americans and non-Americans.

After the truth of their intentions are made manifest, an inner alliance often builds within the hearts of the members of the opposite party, because when the Holy Ghost comes God's spiritual and heavenly wisdom comes in peace of those who makes peace; in love and without deception. What the Lord put together nothing on earth can destroy, and for this cause, the afflictions of pain and suffering caused by the wisdom of the princes of the world comes to naught or nothing, and the last enemy which the Lord shall destroy is death. (St. John14:30/St. John12:30-36/1 Cor.1:28 &2:6) The crucifix of Jesus Christ has been written for all to mark as a reminder and for all to know and understand that the wisdom of the princes of this world would not have crucified Christ, if the people would have understood the hidden wisdom of God's love, mercy, and grace.

Towards that same aspect, the people of today's generation if they could understand the hidden wisdom of God, they would stop seeking to find happiness in another person's misery, because such acts symbolically represents the hearts of those who crucified Christ under the old law. The prince of this world and all whom are willing to die the second death in efforts to live on one accord with the wisdom of this world; fails to understand the hidden wisdom of God. As they continue condemning those of today's society, they no not of who it is they truly are serving. Therefore, they symbolically continue condemning and crucifying Jesus Christ over and over again, because Christ lives in us all in spite of our sin, and died to save us all from sin.

The wisdom from above is first pure, then peaceable, gentle, and easy to be entreated, full of mercy and good fruits, without partiality, and without hypocrisy (James 3:17). Heavenly wisdom enters the heart of all who believes on the Son of God. The power of the Holy Ghost reforms and makes intercessions for and by the Spirit which enables God's creation (MAN) to be spiritually empowered with the ability to distinguish the Lord's moral virtues and values from the unethical qualities of the adversary.

The adversary is establish as immoral, partially biased, and is not ethnically in sequence with the teachings of the Holy Ghost, when spiritually is compared by the saved saints; who compare spiritual things with spiritual (1Cor.2). His children are dissatisfied and are unhappy as they immorally judge the spirit of others. Satan cannot rebuke Satan and the children of the Lord's adversary are given to sin. They support the unforgivable sin which they are given unto each time they blaspheme against the teachings of the Holy Ghost and condemn those who confess or are caught committing a sinful act.

The idolater of the wisdom of this world worships the immoral, partially biased, and non-ethnical principles and values of the vain manmade laws, with extravagant respect. They use vehement words or deeds to condemn, harass, injure, annoy and afflict pain and suffering within their efforts to persecute and crucify another who differs from them either in origin, religion, nationality, creed, sex, sexual orientation, and social out looks etc. These forms of doctrines have existed for centuries and their partially biased words are sown into the hearts of many, during today's society. The biased hearts choose to commend, glorify, serve, praise, and revere discrimination, because it provides them with a false sense of godly empowerment on earth. This also causes their ideas and deeds to follow after their vexed and folly hearts. Their acts of foolish conduct are extremely unprofitable for the righteous to put themselves under the obligation to perform. Therefore, the conflict of interest on earth continues.

The worldly can't comprehend the Lord's predestined order of law. Therefore they from one generation to the next; passes down their own sown false judgments, false hopes, and false promises of liberty to their children and their children's children. In their many congregational houses they continue teaching their off springs to worship the Lord with their lips although their hearts are far from God. Nothing new lies under the sun, and this act was spoken of by the prophet Esaias (Isaiah6:8-13/St. John12:23-43).

> 1Cor.9:18 "What is my reward then? Verily that, when I preach the gospel, I may make the gospel of Christ without charge, that I abuse not my power in the gospel."

THE POOR ARE TRULY BLESSED

During today's society, children of many nations are living witnesses of how chiefs, kings, and other authority rulers use their money to give themselves control in powers. Many have been known to use their authority to rule despotically to gain self benefits or more worldly riches. Some use their authority to degrade the poor by judging their character. A rare few have ruled justly and fair. Some call the poor lazy and uneducated; they also accuse them of being beggars of government funding. One with a clear conscience can easily say, "Work is work, and the difference that man makes between one sorts of laborer from the other is their pay-rate. This concern were particularly seen on WALL STREET during 2008-2009 calendar years in the USA, where the income bracket of certain workers were put out in the open and was uncovered to be more than what the President of the United States of America makes through added bonuses.

In reality the American people whom were in need of government assistance were minimum wage recipients who worked hard at making a living, but their earnings barely covered the cost of an average householder's living expenses. America is turning into the type of country which the ancestors fled from when they sought to find freedom and equality in America so many generations ago.

Some whom were born and raised as poor Americans show off and blow their own horns about how they struck it rich, and they act as if they've forgotten what it was like to be a poor American. They return to their old neighborhoods and toot their own horns in an insulting manner to those whom weren't so lucky to be blessed with worldly riches. While comparing themselves among themselves they insinuate to the poor Americans that there isn't any excuse for them to not be able to make it out of poverty as if it is easy. Redundantly, they draw up most of their conclusions after seeing how other poverty societies outside of the United States are forced to live. Hypocritically, through pity; they are more willing to help the poor that resides outside of the United States more than they'd be willing to help those whom they know within the States that suffers.

The price for food in the United States has sky rocked and the big business lobbyists suggest that the increase of American products were due to the increase of oil prices. Of course they too are profiting from it all as well. That's why most of them are not very interested in producing a natural resource for the modern American society. A gallon of milk shot up from $2-$3 a gallon to $5 plus tax per gallon. In other words a minimum wage earner in America has to work for 2 hours before they are able to purchase a 12 oz. box of brand named cereal and a gallon of milk for their children. The other minimum 6 six hours which they are scheduled to work has to pay for 10 gallon of gas for their vehicle to get back and forth to work. Unfortunately, the rural areas of the United States where many well educated citizens' resides haven't public transportation like buses and trains. In other words, either the prices of the American consumer products are excessively too high or the wages earned by the American people are excessively too low. As rough as it is for the poor American families, some lobbyists publically stated that minimum wage earners were making too much money. They recommended decreasing the minimum wage pay rate to help boost the failing economy deficient during a recession. Fortunately, their proposal was rejected and so were they at the voting polls.

Meanwhile, the functioning of the American government came into clear sight by all American citizens and non American citizens, to be held hostage by rich lobbyists. Throughout the years the rich lobbyists made legal but unlawful rules and policies, which disqualified most low income and middle class workers from receiving government assistance. The survival figure of the American government's standardized low income bracket, which determines the amount of governing assistance was manipulated under the rules and policies of the rich lobbyists.

Therefore, many children and elders of all ages either were discontinued from the qualification bracket of the Americans' Government Assistance Programs and they were disallowed a reasonable increase in services during the time when the American low and middle classes dramatically needed an increase or an adjustment to their FDC or EBT cards. The Americans who lives on Main Street are in trouble as they struggle with the sudden and unexpected overly excessive increase of the cost of living. The price of everything is going up except a pay increases, they actually are going down. Normally every year the disabled SSI and minimum wage recipients receive a cost of living increase in their check, but during the recession this too came to an end.

Disturbingly, the Department of Human Services in America refuses to increase the unreasonably low amount of funds and services which the government provides to the low and middle income families. The USA government also refuses to decrease the income allowance rate, and this too makes the needy ineligible to receive government assistance. The rich lobbyists may have assumed that the average low income and middle class American workers should be happy and thankful with their living situations. Unfortunately, such joy is unreal to those who haven't enough food to last from one paycheck to the next. Some Americans are too ashamed to admit their struggles and are tricked into supporting the despot leaders which creates laws that places burdens around their necks, but even a blind man can see that they too are suffering. These poor employees are like a gambler, they invest their money in the failing economy's stocks and bonds and 401-K Retirement Plans to try to stay ahead, but like a get rich scandal; they always seems to loose money and profit nothing due to certain laws which allows a company owner to fire them, file bankrupt, and reestablish their businesses under a different name.

Rich American's either is born with a silver spoon in their mouths, struggled all their life time and received a rich blessing, or became a swindler by misusing the laws of the land to take an unfair advantage of others. Some people gain riches after being in the right place at the right time. For instance, sometimes a person may luck up and hit the Jack Pot or gain recognition to fame and fortunes by something they either accomplished or by a skill which they seemed to possess like acting, singing, writing, sports, etc. Whether it is by a great invention like the automobile, the airplane, a pooper scooper, a song, or a popular catch phrase of some sort, some people's pay-rates will always be better off than others.

As a receiver of earthy rewards, some who receives a college degree are automatically placed in a higher pay-rate bracket than those who are without a degree, but this isn't the outcome for all college degree holders. Hypocritically, during the years of oppression, depression, or recession; professional jobs aren't as easy to hold onto and are just as hard to find. Due to greed, an unstable economy has become the end result thereof. College graduates are forced to work two jobs outside of their educational fields just to survive.

Homeowners are rapidly foreclosing in the USA. These people have college degrees of some sort. Many are classified to be of the middle income pay-rate bracket. They too are in need of government assistance. They've lost their jobs and their homes due to the economic instability. They are victimized by the nature of greed and the disorder of liberal fairness which cause their current wages to either decline or become of no existence. Meanwhile, the cost of living constantly is rising. Although the cost of living is on the rise, minimum wages are not.

This is a government issue that hasn't been properly addressed nor properly handled by past governing officials for the past 8 to 12 years although these rulers have always had the controlling power to change the laws of the land. There's an old-time country saying about the rich, "They live high on a hog". They don't consider what goes on outside of their own box and they fail to view the life's issues of all others.

Where is Robin Hood when you need him? Is President Barack Obama the 21st Century Robin Hood? Can he fix this broken economy which was made before he entered the Presidential office in America? Or will his own supporters turn on him and put him down along with his oppressors by using perverse words and not give him a fair chance to complete his projects as a new leader of this country because of his race. His works are different from the past conservative idealists' works, which have failed to uphold the entire population for the past decade.

During every American generation of the past and present, the people of all sorts of physical and social differences generally unites together to form a godly alliance; which seeks for fairness by rising up against the unfair governing laws in hopes of gaining freedom in the common pursuit of happiness for all American citizens to be treated as an equal. This brave act started so many generations ago, but the authorized rulers of the laws of the land during the last past decade elaborated policies into law which were rebellious against the things which the united America societies felt were imperative rules of laws. The conservative formations of regulations were more so of a dictatorship rather than a compromiser.

After a decade of treasonable rulings that are domestically established by the improper use of Americans' government, came the peaceable 44th President of the United States of America who was accused of being non-patriotic during his presidential campaign because he is against those who love having the American economy set up in the seditious

461

way that it is. President Barak Obama's name in general was targeted by his accusers. His citizenship as an American and his religion was questioned by them as well, although he was legally recognized to had been birth in Hawaii and noted as a born again Christian who believes in God the Father, the Son, and the Holy Spirit. His main focus and promises to the American people were to reform the traditional laws of the land to befit the current needs for the present issues of the 21st century.

During the latter days ending the 1900's, the diversified American citizens publically challenged the detestable unlawful laws that were enforced by the American government, and they desired to bring about godly changes within the laws' ambiguous perspective outlooks towards clarifying equality, justice, and peace for all. These citizens recognized the acts of inequality tarring them down and their suggestive acts of reforming such laws expanded into a political and religious conflict of interest. Many elected officials failed to comply with the American citizens ideas of reforming such laws. By their own discretion, they lied to the people about being for making righteous reforms for the people, but after being elected they refused to do so. Those who refused the citizens suggested reforms, pledged their allegiance to up hold the prejudice original purposes for the misusage of the US laws. Such allegiances didn't deter the hearts of a majority of American citizens who had repented of the evil doings of the past, because the hearts of them desired for the prejudices to end as times had changed, and they wanted a democracy which represented the true meaning of peace and justice for all.

Today certain politicians whom either are holding a political position or are trying to get into a political office, protess with their mouths to believe in God, but judging by their actions their hearts are far from him. They accept the religious vows of the worldly, and the saints recognize their works being evilly implied. They today are seen following the ways of many despot politicians of the past whom falsely spoke openly of the Lord's predestined order of law, all the while they disloyally deliberate on policies that brings and creates tyranny against 90% of the American population and causes confusion and conflict of interest by severally contradicting and dishonoring the Lord's greatest of all Commandment. In the end, the fate of the Americans and the people of every other country are prophesized by biblical prophets just as it is said by the Lord himself; that in the end, all will acknowledge God's sovereignty (Is.45:23/Romans14:8-23/Eph.3:1-21).

Every knee shall bow and their tongues shall confess to God. The fate of the saints on earth is to live as it is in Heaven, and as they live and let live; they let every individual man be fully persuaded in his own mind to believe on the Lord. They do so without judging and despising anyone because they understand that whether a person stand or fall God is able to make them stand. (Roman14:1-10/James4:12-17) Those who don't know of this mystery seek to destroy those whom they religiously despise with the meats which they religiously eat concerning the Word of God, because they regard those whom they despise to be unclean. (Titus1:15/Romans14:14)

> Romans14:22" Hast thou faith. Have it to thyself before God. Happy is he that condemneth not himself in that thing which he alloweth."
>
> Romans14:23 "And he that doubteth is damned if he eat, because he eateth not of faith: for whatsoever is not of faith is sin."

ASK THE LORD FOR UNDERSTANDING AND YOU SHALL RECEIVE THE LORD'S ANSWER

Is it possible that the elected governing officials whom were found to be liars after getting voted into a political office were coerced to use their political position to manipulate the already unfair laws by influencing the pre-established governing system to do even more unfair biddings against the minority class of people who resides on Main Street? Or do they make things worse for the people on Main Street because they themselves are distracted by the din, noise, and clamor of the world? Could it be possible that the reason why the covenant breakers lie to get into office is because they really don't hear the voice of the Lord telling them of the errors of their own ways and instructing them to do right by all people? Or is because they really don't believe in God, they simply blaspheme against the Holy Ghost by sating that they do believe? Do they purposely lie and take the position as an overseer of the American government to make a mockery of God? Or do they really believe in God, but are afraid that they themselves would be put out of the assembly of men, if they suffer themselves for righteousness sake and do what is righteous and fair unto all citizens; especially onto the citizens on Main Street? Is it possible that the ideas of being put out of the assembly of men have an overbearing psychological effect which constantly places pressure and frustration on politicians?

Who are they who use their political positions to help the people on Main Street by working truthfully and openly for the Lord without partiality and deceit in fear of the Lord without fear of being put outside of the assembling of men? Are they the children of God? Yes, they are! It is possible for the children of God whom have political positions to be hindered by the traditional expectations and gruesome principles and standards, which reside within the hearts of their rivals, but the strong stands strong for the weak. Since the Lord's adversary is well known for purposely targeting all who spiritually seek to use everything God blesses them with to serve, honor, and obey the Lord's greatest Commandment, it is reasonable to conclude that they who uphold the traditional laws of tyranny and dictate their religious beliefs against the will of God are not of God. They use their political powers on earth to persecute and destroy the innocent bystanders just as the crowd persecuted and crucified Jesus Christ.

Is it possible that the Lord's enemy sways the hearts of the rich politicians who makes false judgments of themselves and think more of their selves than they ought? The living saints are witnessing those who the living God has placed in a political position speaking truthfully and openly on loving their neighbors and strangers alike. Without a doubt, this indeed is proven by the Fruit of the Spirit of God to accurately be in accordance with the Lord's Divine Law of Love. Unfortunately, not all voters are aware of the Lord's Divine ordinance of law. They only know of what the worlds' most powerful religious Sects have reverenced as they vote more and more despot leaders into political offices unwisely.

Is it possible that the political ones during the 21st century who loves the spiritual disorders of the old law are responsible for keeping division as an inner development of wars, conflicts, and confusions arises and keeps the domestic residents living as a segregated body within their own homelands? Who are they who presently support the historical prejudices and shameful foundations of the earlier debasing of the worldly religious defilements that productively subvert, threaten, and undermine the Great Commandment of the Lord, which is hidden within the passages of the Holy Bible text from the world?

It has been written that we all shall reap what is sown. Those who sow vanity shall also reap vanity. Nevertheless, the Lord has blessed the people of the United States of American to understand his plan for them as a leading nation worldwide; is not to use their powers maliciously to reign with dominion over one of another, but to live in love and in peace.

St. John12:42 "Nevertheless among the chief rulers also many believed on him; but because of the Pharisees they did not confess him, lest they should be put out of the synagogue:"

St. John12:43 "For they loved the praise of men more than the praise of God."

It will be a commonly fair expectation to find in the future that our children and our children's children onto the next generations will also be faced with false teachers who will still be standing by the traditional religious teachings that passes down false judgments, false hope and false promises of liberty. It is also a commonly fair expectation to find in the future that God will empower our children with the proper spiritual tools which will guide their hearts away from being coerced into applying the false teachers' fixations of worldly ideas, theories, religious beliefs, and non spiritual requests and demands into the future laws of the land. The false teachers of the future will be like those of every generation of past times. They will work indeed and strive for domination in hope that they themselves may be respectfully revered by the weak.

The workers of Satan are well known for holding God's children hostage against God. It shouldn't be a surprise to anyone in the future to find false prophets still building congregational houses for them-selves to gather together and worship God with their lips, even though their hearts are far from him; as it is written by the prophet Esaias. (Isaiah6:8-13/St. John12:23-43) Therefore to assure good works will come out of our off springs, those of us who believes on the power of the Son of God must teach them the difference between the wiles of Satan from the magnificence of God's works without hypocrisy and deceit; so that they'll know which way they ought to go. The living eyewitnesses of today's American society consist of many descendants of the earlier Saints whom now are living in peace with all sorts of people from different cultures and people of a variety of different religions, races, creeds, and nationalities etc.

Ephesians4:11 "And he gave some, apostles; and some, evangelists; and some, pastors and teachers;"

Ephesians4:12 "For the perfecting of the saints, for the work of the ministry, for the edifying of the body of CHRIST:"

Ephesians4:13 "Till we all come in the unity of the faith, and of the knowledge of the Son of GOD, unto a perfect man, unto the measure of the stature of the Fulness of CHRIST:"

Ephesians4:14 "That we henceforth be no more children, tossed to and fro, and carried about with every wind of doctrine, by the sleight of men, and cunning craftiness, whereby they lie in wait to deceive;"

The year 2008A.D. has been one of the most memorable years throughout the entire world, especially for the American citizens. The United States of America has been known for its many successful war stories of the past as well as that of the present. The USA is historically characterized to have always had the strongest military in the world and is one of the wealthiest countries. In spite of the financial burdens, the USA has been at its lowest of lows financially but at its highest of high spiritually, simultaneously.

The greatest and most powerful nation of the world dove into a recession. While in great debt with other countries, the American citizens fell to their knees under the heavens on one accord. Although the American people for centuries have been divided by either ones

467

nationality, sex, sexual orientation, creed, religion, race, or pay rate bracket, etc.; the things which symbolize the gaps that once put a wedge between us have been closed up by the spiritually moral virtues of reality. Patience is a virtue. Our moral values signify the One True Gospel of Jesus Christ which elaborates on the fact that Americans' believe treating each others the way they want to be treated which is equal and fair. All Americans acknowledge that the Holy Scriptures states that all men are created equal by God. Therefore, we the people of the United States are now riding in the same boat singing, "United We Stand & Divided We Fall." We are like a pot of vegetable soup being stirred around and about together as a unit of one society. When the laws of the land conflict with the prosperity of one, it conflicts with us all. While serving the same principles of God for the same purpose, we intend to provide flavor and satisfy the hunger of the hungered. Yes, we all ambitiously hungry for the same things; equality, justice, and peace.

No matter the district where we may live here in the United States, whether we live in the suburbs, the country, the city, the ghetto, a gully, an alley, the plains, the mountains, the ridges, the valleys, or within a village we all want a peace of mind from the same troubles of the world which our neighbors also suffer. Within our present trials and tribulations we've received a spiritual understanding of our ancestors, but the hour during their time period on earth wasn't set for them to have the honor of experiencing such great unity, except within their dreams.(Col 1:19-24)

Col.1:25 "Whereof I am made a minister, according to the dispensation of God which is given to me for you, to fulfil the word of God;"

Col.1:26 "Even the mystery which hath hid from ages and from

**generations, but now is made
manifest to his saints:"**

Today's Christians are being brought out of the darkness and into the glorious light of Truth. We the people of the United States can now see that we as a whole united nation are all equal to each other {Ecclesiastes 3:1-22/Exodus 2:1-25 THE SEASON OF MOSES}. Therefore we all should be grateful and thankful to God for sending us all through this financial storm, which is bring us all to unity not just in the American lands, but also worldwide.

**Psalms1:3 "And he shall be like a
tree planted by the rivers of water,
that bringeth forth his fruit in his
season; his leaf also shall not
wither; and whatsoever he doeth
shall prosper."**

We the people of the USA during today's generation are a society of **GOD's** children, whom are made up of a mixed variety of various and diverse nations. It is by the true works of God that we all have come together as one Nation under GOD. We are living witnesses of the spiritual change which is remarkably different from that of the first American colonists. We are often reminded of how the self-centered deeds of the first American colonists were like that of the unsure spirit which causes people to drift to and fro like a leaf in the wind. We the people today are partakers of Christian leadership and we recognize the Lord is the major leading controller of our governed political powers. We can perceive the differences and the similarities in President Barak Obama's ideas and principles from the earlier 43 elected presidents prior to him, by the Spirit of the Holy Ghost. With this knowledge, by the power of God we can use our voices which is counted on the 44th

United States Presidential election ballads to be 10 million more than the voices of the martyrs of American's traditional form of government, and defend for ourselves and others from the unrighteous and abusive political policies of the old American laws that represents injustice. We today are working together as One Body in Christ with Barak Obama for the sake of reproving and reforming the old tyrannous laws, to make wise changes of the tyrannous laws in hops of making them equally fair to all American citizens as we set an example for all other people of other nations worldwide.

The American politicians are authorized by the governing laws of the land of democracy to use the governing powers to gain and maintain a righteous order of security, peace and justice for all mankind alike. By choice, some Americans and non-Americans reluctantly prefer to misuse the political powers of the American laws as a reason to desire to either rule despotically; to have complete dominion over others' conscience minds while misusing the name of JESUS or to utilize the laws' political powers to disallow the decision makings of one's own conscience to be of PRO-CHOICE. They hope to maintain peace by dictating to the people of all nations, by the earthy desires of their own bellies as leading politicians.

During today's generation the idea to misuse democracy are being strongly reproached by saints like President Obama, because peace comes to those who make peace. The misuse of the old political stratagems in today's reformed generation will only continue to divide the people and create wars. GOD gives no man the power to retain, confine, or restrain another man's spirit, but some US governing officials have been coerced to believe that it is righteous for them to attempt to do so.

The present rulers of today's society are classified or categorize by their consumed titles such as Rev., Dr., Pastor, Bishop, Senators, Mayors, Governors, kings, lords, lords of lords, gods, goddess and Commandeering Chiefs/Presidents etc., but none of them are GOD. Some of them may profess with their mouth to be a believer in GOD, but their ungodly actions and leading roles as tyrannous and greedy leaders, does not represent nor agree with GOD's predestined order of Law. The Saints can identify good leadership from the bad by the fruit bared by the leaders thereof.

Of course the nation of GOD is biblically recognized to be the Nation of Israel by many who fail to study the Word of God to show them-selves approved unto God, but those who does study, understands that GOD's predestined order of law is for all people of every nation. God is the Father of the circumcised and uncircumcised, the just and unjust, and the dead and the living alike. Jesus Christ and his chosen apostles, whom Christ appointed to preach and teach the spiritual teachings of the Holy Ghost; went out unto every corner of the earth preaching the Gospel. Afterwards, the Holy Ghost is now made manifest by the appearing of the First Fruit; known as the Spirit of the Lord and Savior JESUS CHRIST. Therefore we all ought to know that before we individually were born into the sins of the world, under the New Testament JESUS CHRIST saved and called us all individually with a holy calling; not according to our works, but according to his own purpose and grace.(1Timothy1:4-16/2Timothy4:1-9/1Thessalonians 2:1-17/4:1-9)

> 1Tim.1:15 "For this is a faithful saying and worthy of all acceptation, that Christ Jesus came into the world to save sinners; of whom I am chief."
>
> 1Tim.1:16 "Howbeit for this cause I obtained mercy, that in me first Jesus Christ might shew forth all long sufferings, for a pattern to them which wives' should hereafter believe on him to life everlasting."

1Tim.4:7 "But refuse profane and old fables, and exercise thyself rather unto godliness."

1Tim.4:8 "For the bodily exercise profiteth little: but godliness is profitable unto all things, having promise of the life that now is, and of that which is come."

1Tim.4:9 "This is a faithful saying and worthy of all acceptation."

1Tim.4:10 "For therefore we both labour and suffer reproach, because we trust in the living God, who is the Saviour of all men, specially of those that believe."

1Tim.4:11 "These things command and teach."

THEORETICAL CONCLUSION

We as followers of Christ during the 21st century must make a pack to bring salvation back. Love is everywhere, and wheresoever's there is love; God is there providing an escape route known as deliverance. Just as fair as it is to say that Jesus died to save all from sin, it is also fair to propose after seeing the revealing of the Lord's Divine Love repeating itself by the Power of Man's forgiveness, that the kindly works of many believers of the Son of God who are selected and elected to inherit the earthy political dispositions in earth, charitably oversees the world's affairs by the grace of God.

Knowledge is power, but ignorance makes a man to be weak and unwise. We know that worldly people are evilly influenced and coerced to violently live under the high-ranked teachings of the beguiled. Therefore, in having such knowledge the saints can expect to find certain elected officials of the world whom are too afraid to speak openly of the evidence proven unto them by the Fruit of the Spirit of God, because they are overwhelmed with fear of being publicized by the religious assembly of men. Clearly the Fruit of the Spirit of God indicates unto all saints that the old tyrannous traditional religious manmade laws of the land which the entire world may revere, respect, and admire; is good for nothing, because it shows no love.

This truly explains how and why many traditional religions' that governs the oppressed nations of the world are made enmity against God's Divine order of law? The manmade laws of the land has no heart and haven't any compassion. Spitefully and unruly is how such laws subversively make a mockery of God throughout the land of the living. After misusing the Holy Scriptures and the Word of God maliciously against one of another for so long, many law abiding citizens in the earth are yet spoiled enough to view their selves to be spiritually equal to the sound doctrine of Jesus Christ.

After being exposed to the righteous comparisons of the inspiring law of God, maybe many more will willingly convert from the spiteful and ungodly manmade standardized laws with a clear conscience unto God and be made whole. The physical evidence of the earthy things that people are hoping to come into possession of consists of the worldly value of money and powers thereof. Such insights have been the top agenda of the despot leaders and followers of traditional religions for far too long. Therefore, it is fair to say that the root of all the evils of the world is the assessment of money and the estimated powers which many are tricked to believe money will bring to those who possess the most thereof. Money can be used to pay bills, buy merchandise, and provide other temporal things, but it can't be used for paying for a person's Salvation.

Stereotypically speaking, the possessors of worldly riches are believed by some of the most respected traditional religious teachers to have supreme controlling powers on earth. As a result thereof, many rich peoples think they can do whatsoever they want whenever they want; without repercussions. Those whose hearts are given unto this stereotypical image are followers of a false emulated image of God. Provokingly they strive to approach their appearance of equality unto God through the value of money. This is the reason why so many people think that the desire and the reward of having the riches of the world are equally compared to receiving a heavenly reward from God. The season has changed for the children of God, and they now know today of the majestic powers of God that were hidden from the earlier generations. All things are possible through Christ Jesus, and nothing can be done without him.

CHAPTER 12 THE TEACHINGS OF APOSTLE PAUL ARE ACQUAINTED WITH THE TEACHINGS OF GOD

The life of Apostle Paul spiritually elaborates clearly on what moral and ethical virtues denote signifies in the Book of Acts. If a diligent seeker can perceive the true concept of Paul's life story and God's purpose for his life, then one may also understand God's purpose of ones' own life. Like us all today, Paul was once a child who was born in bondage under the elements of the world. None of us are born a sinner, but like Paul we all are born under or into sin. During the early years of his life he was under tutors and governors after the straightest Sect of the Pharisee's religion, until the time appointed of God the Father; then he was converted. (Acts 26, Gal.4:1-5, Gal.4:11 & 12)

> Gal.3:22 "But the scripture hath concluded all under sin, that the promise by faith of Jesus Christ might be given to them that believe."
> Gal.3:23 "But before faith came. We were kept under the law, shut up unto the faith which should afterwards be revealed."

Paul, whose surname was Saul; before the Holy Ghost filled him with heavenly wisdom and understanding of the promise made of God unto his father's; (ANCESTORS), his preceptor (or teacher) Gamaliel; taught him according to the perfect manner of the law of the fathers, which is after the manner of Moses. Connately he lived after the Pharisees doctrine; he was zealous toward God as we are today. Yet, he was not converted until after Jesus death. Therefore, he spoke of himself saying he was born out of due time.

Bared a Jew in Tarsus; a city in Cilicia Paul was of the tribe of Benjamin and circumcised the eighth day of the stack of Israel. Although both his parents were Jews, his birth place was a free city of Rome. This gave him the honor and beneficial advantage of Roman citizenship. During his early years of life he was a blasphemer, a persecutor, and injurious (1Tim 1:13).

> Acts9:1 "And Saul, yet breathing out threatened and slaughter against the disciples of the Lord, went unto the high priest women,"
> Acts9:2 "And desired of him letters to Damascus to the Synagogues, that if he found any of this way, whether they were men or he might bring them bound unto Jerusalem."

As Saul journeyed near Damascus the Word of Truth convicted his spirit and personally manifested his deeds unto him to be enmity or an enemy against God (Acts9/Rom8). The Lord then spoke to a disciple at Damascus name Ananias in a vision.

> Acts9:11 "And the Lord said unto him, Arise, and go into the street which is called Straight, and inquire in the house of Judas for one called Saul, of Tarsus: for, behold, he prayeth,"
> Acts9:12 "And hath seen in a vision a man named Ananias coming in,

476

and putting his hand on him, that
he might receive his sight."

Acts9:15 "But the Lord said unto
him, Go thy way: for the is a chosen
vessel unto me, to bear my name
before the Gentiles, and Kings, and
the children of Israel:"

Acts9:16 "For I will shew him how
great things he must suffer for my
name sake."

After living as a carnally minded man, Paul reputation was broadly
known not only as a respectable Jew of the Pharisee religion, but also as
a terrorist of the Sect of Nazarenes. Yet, this was reversed through the
mercy and grace of God; who chose him to minister unto the people of
his own religious heritage as well as unto those whom he once desired
to persecute. (Acts9:5/22:5 &14/26:16-18/Titus3:3-7)

Acts22:6 "And it comes to pass,
that, as I made my journey, and was
come nigh unto Damascus about
noon, suddenly thee shone from
heaven a great light around about
me."

Acts22:7 "And I fell unto the ground
and heard a voice saying unto me,
"Saul, Saul, why persecutest thou
me."

Acts22:8 "And I answered, who art
thou, Lord? And he said unto me, "I
am Jesus of Nazareth, whom thou
persecutest."

477

Acts9:5 "And he said, who art thou? And the lord said, I am Jesus whom thou persecutest: it is hard for thee to kick against the pricks."

Acts26:16 "But rise, and stand upon thy feet: for I have appeared unto thee for this purpose, to make thee a minister and a witness both of these things which thou hast seen, and of those things in the which I will appear unto thee;"

Acts26:17 "Delivering thee from the people, and from the Gentiles, unto whom now I send thee,"

Acts26:18 "To open their eyes, and to turn them from darkness to light, and from the power of Satan unto God, that they may receive forgiveness of sins, and inheritance among them which are sanctified by faith that is in me."

A disciple, name Ananias; submitted to do what was instructed of him by the Lord, and he went to Saul who was said by the Lord that he might be given his sight. In so doing Saul received his sight, and was filled with the Holy Ghost. He then arose and was baptized, washed away his sins, and called on the name of the Lord. (Acts 22:13-17)

Being filled with the Holy Ghost, Paul was strengthened with heavenly wisdom to understand the will of God. Spiritually comparing spiritual things with spiritual, he recognized the religious teachings of his fathers had compelled their hearts to be ill will against their neighbor. By the help of the good Lord, Paul whose sure name is Saul; was converted and he committed his life's work of witnessing both to the small and great saying none other things than those which the prophets and Moses did say should come (Numbers 6). Those things which the prophets and Moses did say should come consisted of the teachings of Jesus Christ such as..."that Christ should suffer, and that he should be the first that should rise from the dead, and that he should show light unto the Gentiles and the people.(Acts 26:23)

He then walked and served the God of his fathers' in the newness of spirit and life, and not by the oldness of the letter (Romans 6:4 and 7:6). His new spirit of life was shown broadly first unto them of Damascus, and at Jerusalem, and throughout all the coasts of Judea and then to the gentiles; that they should repent and turn to God, and do work's meet for repentance. (Acts 26:20)

> Acts26:21 "For these causes the Jews caught me in the temple, and went about to kill me."

They accused him of being dangerous to society, and of one who persuades Jews throughout the world to be disobedient or disloyal to their traditional laws of religion. Also they accused him to be the ring leader of the Sect of the Nazarenes. (Numbers6/Acts18:18-20/21:28/24:5)

> Acts18:28 "For he mightly convinced the Jews, and that publicly, shewing by the scriptures that Jesus was Christ."(Acts9:22/Numbers6)

None who accused Paul could prove any of their accusations against him, but he succeeded in proving too many that he acquainted his teachings with the teachings of the God of his fathers and of the prophets. (Acts 25:7/24:12-13/26:23)

> **Acts 26:22 "Having therefore obtained help of God, I continue unto this day, witnessing both to small and great, saying none other things than those which the prophets and Moses did say should come:"**

Again, within all men including women and children, lives the Spirit of God. It's like a birth mark, but it isn't seen by the physical eye. (Gen 1:26-27)The Spirit of God lives in the heart of all human beings, but after we've been tutored by the perverse cunning words of Satan just as Satan did in the Garden of Eden; our hearts are subverted and carried about with divers and strange doctrines. Cunningly the Adversary's teachings universally seduce the hearts of both sexes to be re-established with meats, which have not profited them that have been occupied therein (Heb 13:9/Gen 3: 1-17/2 Cor.11:3). Therefore with every temptation which tempts us, God gives us all an escape route. He will not put more on us than we can bear. Though many people prefer to use this particular scripture when they are going through trials and tribulations, this passage provides comfort unto the world as it relates to God's spiritual escape route which delivers us out of the carnalities of our own minds.

THEORETICAL CONCLUSION

The Spirit of Righteousness and Truth is instilled in the heart of all men. God gives unto us all who believes in Jesus Christ, the authority to be consciously aware of the significance of the distinctive qualities and importance of moral virtues and their contrary vices. The Book of Proverbs chapter 11-24 lays a solid base and is filled with many spiritual illustrations of desirable and undesirable behaviors where one's moral virtues are concerned. Man's moral defaults or failings, cause us to have a false balance which destroys the godliness in man's heart. All throughout the Holy Bible Text, are spiritual patterns found for us all to use to self examine ourselves or reprove our selves with the Word of Truth. These patterns help us to distinguish whether or not we ourselves are in compliance and are on one accord morally with the Spirit of Righteousness. We then can self examine our deeds which can spiritually prove to our inner conscience or our inner selves whether or not we are truthfully living in an accurate manner with a righteous heart, as we worship the Lord during our daily walk of life; in spirit and truth or not.

Although the vote of a majority in today's society appears to possess more godly values than the majority of votes made in times past, the conjecturing idea that the vote of a majority justifies, clarifies, and determines what is morally right, remains to be faulty. Many unrighteous and despotic votes made today still bring desolation, dissimulation, and wars. Desolation causes division and wars, not unity or peace, and there's no dissimulation in love and God is love. Therefore, the true fact remains to be the same today as it did during times past. The vote of a majority doesn't justify, clarify, nor determine what is morally right or wrong, but man's conscience does; when it's lead by the Spirit of the Lord! When the Lord prepared the heavens and appointed the foundations of the earth, the Spirit of Wisdom was there by him as one brought up with him: and was daily his delight. She rejoices always before him. (Prov.8)

Gen.3:22 "And the Lord God said, Behold, the man is become as one of us, to know good and evil: and now, lest he put forth his hand, and take also of the tree of life, and eat, and live forever:"(Prov.3 & 8)

Prov.3:18 "She is a tree of life to them that lay holds upon her: and happy is everyone that retaineth her."

Prov.3:19 "The Lord by wisdom hath founded the earth; by understanding hath he established the heavens."

Prov.8:35 "For whoso findeth me findeth life, and shall obtain favour of the Lord."

Prov.11:30 "The fruit of the righteous is a tree of life; and he that winneth souls is wise."

Prov.13:12 "Hope deffered maketh the heart sick: but when the desire cometh, it is a tree of life."

> **Eph.6:5** "Servants, be obedient to them that are your masters according to the flesh, with fear and trembling, in singleness of your heart, as unto Christ;"

A clergyman in charge of a church may think they are always right, as long as they teach from the Holy Bible. In fact, they may biblically be correct within their teachings, but if they don't learn how to spiritually connect and talk to people concerning their salvation; they can mishandle the situation and this inaccuracy of their ministry is wrong.

The Holy Spirit intercedes between the fleshly desires of men, which are coerced cunningly and temptingly by the prince of this world. The Holy Spirit Comforts our hearts and directs our steps; to not be spiritually influenced or ignorant of the stratagems of Satan. This chapter will be dealing with self righteousness, morals, respect, and above all love. God made us in his image, but we all are different. Therefore, we should love and respect each other and not judge one another. **That's the Word!** (Romans 8:24-34/11:25/12:13-21/Heb.7:22-28)

After obtaining heavenly wisdom, man then are enabled to clearly detect the works of God from the wiles of the Devil. The wile's of Satan and the stratagems of the Adversary are the tools of vanity, which Satan uses to lure, beguile, and entice men by cunning means of trickery; to keep us from doing good works and the Will of God. The religious conflict, which I've seen or witnessed as a child of God; has helped me to understand how and why certain religious people inaccurately define their theoretical ideas with the Word of God concerning them accepting a difference concept of a sin and a sinner, than that in which the Anointed teaches. Religious peoples speak and live as hypocrites.

Although they say they believe they are sinners who are saved by the blood of Jesus, they speak evil of the dignity of others and live irreligiously, as if the Lord didn't give himself a ransom for all to be testified in due time. Maybe they are too religious to be spiritual minded.

> 2Peter3:9 "The Lord is not slack concerning his promise, as some men count slackness; but is longsuffering to us-ward, not willing that any should perish, but that all should come to repentance."

However, spiritual people have faith in the Word of God to believe he is who he says he is and works to have all men to come to the knowledge of Heavenly Wisdom to be saved.(1Tim.2:4-8). Those of us, who follow after Jesus Christ, acknowledge his sound doctrine as the Word of Truth. Being led by the Spirit, the Fruit of the Spirit of God authorizes us all to stand boldly against the wiles of the devil. As we boldly stand against the ungodly subverters, gainsayers, men pleasers, and people who despise truth etc., the Fruit of the Spirit of God being instilled in our hearts empowers us all regardless of our religion, nationality, origin, sex, creed or social outlooks; the power to cease from resenting one another as well as anyone who may offend us regardless of the offense. In other words we are able to obey the laws of the land as we use the power of forgiveness as the Son of Man has the power upon earth to forgive sins.(St. Luke5:20-24)

The power to forgive is a spiritual weapon for us all to use against the worldly soldiers of warfare. Not only do they physically kill as an addictive habit with bows and arrows, knives and guns, sticks and stones, swords and spears, explosives and bombs; but they also spiritually murder with perverse words which leads to destruction by using an untamed, unruly, evil and deadly poison tongue which is a fire.(James 3:5-8)

> St. Matt.15:18 "But those things which proceed out of the mouth come forth from the heart; and they defile the man."
> St. Matt.15:19 "For out of the heart proceed evil thoughts, murders, adulteries, fornications, thefts, false witness, blasphemies:"

Regardless of one's denominational religious name, religious views, religious practices, or religious beliefs; the Holy Ghost's teachings of Heavenly Wisdom and Truth are unchanging. The Holy Ghost's teachings shall cease the liar's tongues and bring them all to shame as the Just One and the Spirit of Righteousness and Truth are made manifest.

> Philippians 2:12 "Wherefore, my beloved, as ye have always obeyed, not as in my presence only, but now much more in my absence, work out your own salvation with fear and trembling."
> Philippians 2:13 "For it is God which worketh in you both to will and to do of his good pleasure."
> St. Luke 12:4 "And I say unto you my friends, Be not afraid of them that

kill the body, and after that have no
more that they can do."
St.Luke12:5 "But I will forewarn you
whom ye shall fear: Fear him, which
after he hath killed hath power to
cast into hell; yea, I say unto you,
Fear him."

TRUE REPENTANCE

Instead of letting Satan get an advantage of us, we ought to study to
show ourselves approved of unto God. We ought not to lie about the
truth. (James3:14-18, 5:16 & 19-20)If discriminators have jealousy,
envy, bitterness and strife in their hearts they ought not to lie about it.
Lies only conceal the wounds, but the truth heals the wounds.
Confessing the truth unto ourselves helps us to undergo a healing
process from all of the unwarrantable earthy sensations of the flesh
such as anger, hatred, prejudice, and jealousy etc. As we purge our
conscience from desiring to do dead works and serve the living God, we
should take heed of the Anointed teachings of the Holy Ghost and
reproach, reprove, and rebuke the evils which are sown into our hearts.
If we confess our faults with the intent to repent of our inward
vexatiousness, then our hearts shall be mortified with great sorrow.

2Cor.7:9 "Now I rejoice, not that ye
were made sorry, but that ye
sorrowed to repentance: for ye
were made sorry after a godly
manner, that ye might receive
damage by us in nothing."
2Cor.7:10 "For godly sorrow
worketh repentance to salvation
not to be repented of: but the

sorrow of the world worketh death."

There's no pretense in true repentance. Anyone, who is mortified with great sorrow will humble them-selves, in either their own eyes or in the eyes of others, as one subjects to humiliation or shame. Before true repentance is established within anyone's mind, the severity of God and his goodness of quality or state of being humble must first be established. It is through the godly feelings of humility within us, which grants us the desire and the motivation to change or repent.

James4:6 "But he giveth more grace. Wherefore he saith, God resisteth the proud, but giveth grace unto the humble."

James4:7 "Submit yourselves therefore to God. Resist the devil, and he will flee from you."

James4:8 "Draw nigh to God, and he will draw nigh to you. Cleanse your hands, ye sinners; and purify your hearts, ye double minded."

James4:10 "Humble yourselves in the sight of the Lord, and he shall lift you up."

Ps.51:17 "The sacrifices of God are a broken spirit: a broken and a contrite heart, O God, thou wilt not despise."

Romans12:1 "I beseech you therefore, brethren, by the mercies of God, that ye present your bodies a living sacrifice, holy, acceptable

487

unto God, which is your reasonable service."

THE LIFE OF HYPOCRITES

The Worldly are judges of God's law and not doers. They condemn themselves, while their sole criterion in life has been deluded by the ungodly predisposed governed or controlling systems which they believe justifies the discernment of their own vexed ideas, which spreads hatred and is enmity unto God. (James 4:1-11) From the vexed hearts of men and women, young and old come divisions, wars, and fighting. Imprudently they live by derived passages which are traced back to the original origin of the Sect of the Pharisees, Sadducees, and the Scribes traditional religious doctrine. Subversively they intermix and confuse their traditional religious doctrine with the new spiritual Doctrine of Jesus Christ.

Like one who mends an old garment with a new patch, worldly leaders and follows of all sorts of bound religions, subconsciously lessens the values of what the One True Gospel of Jesus Christ represent, and clearly signifies. They are like a man who drunk of old wine straightway and said the old is better than the new (St. Luke 5:39). Instead of preserving the old, they are strongly influenced to believe in the method of mending the old with the new; despite the fact that the new doesn't agree with the old.

> **St. Luke5:36 "And he spake also a parable unto them; No man putteth a piece of new garment upon an old; if otherwise, then both the new maketh a rent, and the piece that was taken out of the new agreeth not with the old."**

488

The hidden agenda of the idolaters who supports these hypocritical principles and standards is to pretend to be more virtuous or religious than they really are. Putting others down by speaking against the dignities of them, in false hopes of lifting themselves up are apart of their worldly every day walks of life. The worldly has built their own churches by their own hands, which represents their hypocritical beliefs and perceived concepts of the Bible text. Since they can't comprehend the Word of God, they derive facts mentioned in the Holy Bible Text to arrive at false propositions that are partially based on scanty evidence preferably to fit their own bellies. (St. John16:13-16)

Eccl.1:9 "The thing that hath been, it is that which shall be; and that which is done is what shall be done: and there is no new thing under the sun."

St. Luke9:44 "Let these sayings sink down into your ears: for the sun of man shall be delivered into the hands of men."

St. John16:1 "These things have I spoken unto you, that ye should not be offended."

St. John16:2 "They shall put you out of the synagogues: yea, the time cometh, that whosoever killeth you will think that he doeth God service."

St. John16:3 "And these things will they do unto you, because they have not known the Father, nor me."

St. John16:4 "But these things have I told you, that when the time shall come, ye may remember that I told you of them. And these things I said not unto you at the beginning, because I was with you."

St. John16:5 "But now I go my way to him that sent me; and none of you asketh me, Whither goest thou?"

St. John16:6 "But because I have said these things unto you, sorrow hath filled your heart."

St. John16:7 "Nevertheless I tell you the truth; It is expedient for you that I go away: for if I go not away, the Comforter will not come unto you; but if I depart, I will send him unto you."

St.John16:8 "And when he is come, he will reprove the world of sin, and of righteousness, and of judgment:"

St.John16:9 "Of sin, because they believe not on me;"

St.John16:10 "Of righteousness, because I go to my Father, and ye see me no more;"

St.John16:11 "Of judgment, because the prince of this world is judged."

St.John16:12 "I have yet many things to say unto you, but ye cannot bear them now."

Satan's method to seduce one's spiritual mind fold is the same today, yesterday, and days yet to come. He cunningly beguiles God's followers including the Lord's servants, friends, and children the same exact way as he did God's heavenly angles during the first war in heaven. His beguiling methods hypnotize and mesmerize the minds of many to convince their hearts to become jealous, spiteful, envious, hateful, etc. The beguiled living souls on earth are as innocent as the angels whom were coerced to follow Satan's captivating lead during the first war in Heaven, as they are caught up in Satan's cunning attempt to overthrow the Kingdom of God the Father, the Son, and the Holy Ghost. After being tricked by Satan, the living souls on earth are known for deriving certain passages from the Word of God and suggesting to God's angles on earth that the ideas of Satan's theoretical studies and interpretations of what thus saith the Lord thy God are sufficiently supported by God. Satan's implicit theories and implications draws men's spiritual mind set away from godliness, and into his own implicit false propositions which are befitting to his own occasions to divide with the intent to conquer. (Rev.12:7-17/St. Matt.25:41-46/St. Luke10:1-24)

The dark angle's theoretical, implicit, and stereotypical religious practices are implicated to that of his evil thoughts, beliefs, ideas, and desires. Since Satan's greatest desire is to be as God is, he tricks people to live without the goodness, which comes with the position of being as God is. He desires to subdue as many hearts as he possibly can and to delude as many minds as he can to also desire to be gods by bringing them under his control, subjection, and dominion. **If love** is partial and prejudice, then many traditional religions are in order. **But God is love** and isn't a partial God, which means the most respected traditional religions are **NOT** in order.

Satan being more subtle or more difficult to understand or distinguish than any other beast of the field which God made, brings forth unfruitful false doctrines, false promises, false teachings, and false hope to all mankind alike. All these things are the works of iniquity and also are vanity and vexed. Therefore God predestined such works as these to be hewn down, because they don't bring forth good fruit. (St. Matt.3:9-10/7:18-27/12:33/St. John15:2-8, 13-14) Satan makes it impossible for those who choose to follow after his kind, to enter into the Kingdom of Heaven. (Gen3:1-15/Gal.4:4-9)

James3:17 "But the wisdom that is from above is first pure, then peaceable, gentle, and easy to be entreated, full of mercy and good fruits, without partiality, and without hypocrisy."(1Cor.2:6-7)

James3:18 "And the fruit of righteousness is sown in peace of them that make peace."(St. Luke6:34-38)

BEING NURTURED INTO REBIRTH

Meanwhile, true men of God humble themselves as they minister God Words of Truth as the One True Gospel of Jesus Christ instructs. Not exalting themselves or any other man to be greater than the creator of the heavens and earth. They live as brethren and sisters who aren't influenced or desirous to be like the Prince of the Gentiles, whom excised dominion or lordship. Nor are they like those that are great, like the scribes and the Pharisees, whom exercised authority (St. Matt20:25-28/St. Matt21:21-32/St. Matt.23:1-13/St. Mark10:42-45). Instead of desiring to reign with dominion, men, women, and children of God free willingly humbles themselves to be exalted and they also humble themselves to become as those who are persecuted and are evil spoken of under the traditions of the scribe and Pharisees by false apostles of Christ whom yet still today idolize the idea of exercising lordship. They humble themselves by being strong enough to empathize with the weak as to be also persecuted with the weak that they might by all means according to the Word of God; save some.

Jesus Christ who has begotten all believers through the gospel, and instructs all to be followers of him as his chosen Apostles like Paul followed him (1Cor.4:1-16), and through the Power of the Gospel of Jesus Christ all believers will willingly humble themselves to be servants unto all mankind alike, that they may gain heavenly understanding to

492

minister to all who are under the law by also humbling themselves as if they too were under the law hypothetically speaking. (1Cor.9:11-27)

Being not without law to God, but under the law of Christ, they as servants to all mankind; humble themselves as without law to receive heavenly wisdom to understand the godly sorrows of those that are without law that they may also gain those who are without. This is likened of the physical sacrifice of ones' life to save the life of another, but in a spiritual sense. Christ died to save all, but a religious person lacks to understand how to follow the Lord as he instructs for all who believes on him to do, because they live under the law, which views Christ's birth, life, death, and resurrection in the physical sense. To die to save a stranger to them brings about an image of them physically taking a bullet for someone they don't know.

A spiritual person is more susceptible to understand what it clearly means to be like Christ and be willing to die to save the lives of strangers. Being willing to die means, they willingly becomes weak to those who may be weak in the spirit to also gain the weak as well. In other words, true men of God humbles themselves to be made of all things to all men, like Jesus did in the flesh that they might by all means have compassion and empathy for those whom they seek to save.

Spiritual men of God are normally drawn to nondenominational religions, because they are more willing to humble themselves unto all mankind alike; so that they may gain the godly ability to revive all mankind from the traditional religious influence of the spirit of condemnation, which traditional religious leaders and followers historically uses to persecute people by and kill a person's faith and hope of being saved by the Blood of Jesus.

Spiritual people aren't easily influenced by any traditional religious law which symbolizes death through the condemned law which supports the spirit of condemnation. They may have their dignities evil spoken of by traditional religious dictators, tutors, and persecutors of the Word of God whom despises them for humbling themselves to be made equal unto the least of mankind. Such persecutions of this kind is what a spiritual person understands to be a reasonable sacrifice made by them unto God, because they by faith are freed from the yoke of bondage of the traditional religious dictators, tutors, and persecutors of the Word of God. In other words, they take up their cross and follow Christ as instructed by Christ. (1Cor.4:1-16)

Although they are despised and are evilly spoken of by non-believers and haters of men whom live under the law and don't understand why a spiritual person would choose to walk meekly with those whom traditional religious tutors and persecutors for centuries have spoken evilly of; a spiritual person continues to humble themselves to be made equal unto the least of mankind because they seek not for their own profit, but for the profit of many; that many of the least of mankind may be saved. The Lord didn't leave a spiritual person to be ignorant. They spiritually realize that they too are being evilly spoken of by traditional religion, but that doesn't stop them from humbling themselves. In fact, it increases their humility even more too also treat the traditional religious leaders and followers who speaks evil of their dignity with kindness so that their conscience may remain clear unto God. (Lev.11:44-45)

1Peter1:15 "But as he which hath called you is holy, so be ye holy in all manner of conversation;"

St. Luke10:19(JESUS spake) "Behold, I give unto you power to tread on serpents and scorpions, and over all the power of the enemy: and nothing shall by any means hurt you."

Eph.2:18 "For through him we both have access by one Spirit unto the Father."

> Eph.3:12 "In whom we have
> boldness and access with
> confidence by the faith of him."

WHO SUFFERS FROM HOMO-PHOBIC
(St John15:1-27/Romans2:11/Romans11:18-22)

Oil and water don't mix! Today's discriminations are differentiated by the quality or state of being apart of either the heterogeneous population or of the homogenous population. Some people are deluded into thinking that God didn't give man the power of authority to love all mankind, therefore they go through life bidding themselves by the false tutors misinterpretations of the Holy Scriptures to choose to love one sinner and hate another. Like the false tutors of past time, traditional religious teachers during today's generation organize themselves together, and speak as if they have the power to open the gates of Hell and close the gates of Heaven for or against whomever they religiously despise. They go through life having neither the knowledge nor the compassion of Christ to desire to love all mankind, by presenting themselves as a lowly spirit of God which gives a gentle reproof to save those whom they despise. The spirit of those who lacks the Compassion of Christ is incapable of humbling themselves to be poor in Spirit, because their murderous spirit isn't of God, but is of the adversary. It is impossible to serve the Lord with hatred ruling their hearts. Therefore, they harass, injure, taunt, and persecute people with the desire to expel, revile, or force whosoever they despise out from the protection of God's love, mercy, and grace. Of course they are not pardoned by God in doing so, but they are coerced to think that they are right for treating people wrong. Therefore, they go out into the political world with others whom also are convinced that they are obligated by God to react evilly, in hopes of banishing those whom they are trained to religiously keep from being protected by their home land's governing laws.

They use the original distorted governing laws of the land, which were full of preconceived notions that were intended to be bias against most of their own heritages. During the 21st century, the traditional religious desire of these people simulates the old laws which misled the people who hunted, captured, and persecuted Jesus Christ. As they desire to do well unto God, evil is present within them and deters their hearts to do evil biddings that are enmity against God and against whosoever they religiously despise. Due to the oldness of its age, the method of such religious evil thinking is being persuasively influenced by Satan to be good works; by his children on earth.

Everyone has heard many stories concerning the world's history on slavery, but not everyone has asked the Lord for the wisdom to understand from whereby does wars come from. After asking the Lord, this is a sample of the author's spiritual perception. "Long before slavery was abolished, discrimination was on the rise. The sinful white American martyrs domestically treated the sinners, who were born outside of their race; poorly. The sinners who were born outside of the white sinful martyrs' race were pursued by them, because they as sinners themselves were traditionally trained to believe in the idea of using the law of the land to govern those of them who they loved to hate. Therefore they created murderous laws to support their theory."

Long after slavery was abolished in America, discrimination in America did not cease. The belligerent traditional religious warring attitudes between the divided spirits of the earlier American governed Republic party members fought aggressively among themselves, because not all white republic Americans agreed with creating despotic laws of tyranny. The tyrants vehemently desired to protect their worldly rights to reign with dominion over all other races and different classes of people which too were born in America. Meanwhile, the peaceable Americans simply wanted to serve the Lord God and treat people of all races in the way in which they themselves wanted to be treated; which was an equal, fair, and acceptable sacrifice made by the inner conscience of them unto God.

The influence of the earlier American tyrants' traditional religious ideas continues during the 21st century, and these causes many Americans and their off springs; to yearn for the ungodly desire to uphold the God forbidden need to keep the prejudicial and bias traditions of the old injurious American laws intact. These old laws originally gave authoritative consent and freedom to the tyrants who desired to use religion as a dependable offensive resource of defense, for those who presently represent the ideology of the original clans of America. By the desires of their own bellies, they are legally equipped by the preexisting tyrannous American laws; to take it upon themselves to use religion to justify the illogic and irrational reason for them to continue creating a desolated environment amongst themselves.

The most common logical reasoning for them to accept the practice of one religion over another is based upon how closely drawn they are towards being on the controlling end of the inspiring flows of despotism, racism, and repression. Since they desire to have complete domination, they respect the oldness or the age of certain bias traditional governing laws of the land. It is highly believed that these unlawful but legal laws of the land were full of preconceived notions which falsely gave unto the domineering masters on earth, a sign of a guaranteed promise made-up by the Prince of the World. The Prince of the world assured them that they would obtain complete satisfaction with the outcome of their life; for as long as they live, if they vehemently fought to keep themselves and their off springs from being oppressed by the same sort of dictatorship which they distributed as haters of men, unto other citizens of their own society.

The guaranteed promise of the oppressor is similar to the Lord's promise of everlasting life, but the Prince of the World is a partial god who promises to only give a good life full of worldly riches unto the masters on earth who willingly oppress all others. Therefore, each generation of every society consists of those who historically lived as masters, gods, and lords without considering that they themselves have a Master in Heaven who urges, warns, pleas, and commands them to treat their noble slaves the way that they themselves wanted to be treated. Unfortunately, those who don't know God; fails to desire to treat all others respectfully by a lowly spirit of God, because inwardly they lack the desire to obtain a humbled spirit. Inwardly they themselves are ravening wolves.

THE LIFE OF THE BULLIED LESBIANS, GAYS, AND BI-SEXUAL (LGB) TEENAGERS & ADULTS

Without encouraging or discouraging anyone to support the acts of a gay person's trend of life, the author of Discerning Perceptive believes that it is vital to express to her readers how they must beware of the evils that resides in the hearts of all who loves to gay bash them. She realizes that if she attempts to discourage you from supporting the acts, there will always be those of you who will continue doing so. Therefore, she dedicates this section of her book towards the spiritually analyzed contradictions of gay history without naming anyone in particular.

Theoretically speaking, during the Civil Rights Movement the oppressed ones who meekly fought for equality, peace, and justice were privately accompanied by gay people who too were discriminated against by the orthodox religious laws of the land. Those laws were creatively designed by the followers of the oppressor to show favoritism due to their race, nationality, and religion etc. The gays understood that their fight for equality was much bigger than themselves. As a separate group from amongst all others, the non-gay Gay Rights Activists believed that the odds of them obtaining justice, peace, and equality for the gay Americans were slim to none during the Civil Rights Movement. Therefore, they proceeded to humble themselves to work together with all other heterosexual Americans who rejected the theoretical concept of gays being created by God under the orthodox religious law of the land. They inwardly knew that they weren't fighting only for the sake of their selves being treated fair, but they had high hopes of obtaining civil and human rights for every race of Americans.

Among the Civil Right members were a few gay rights activists, who weren't gay but were against gay bashing, and they humbled the identity of them and laid down their own life as a friend; to save a friend. They knew that they would be humiliated as they fought for equality for all mankind. As they recognized, believed, and acknowledged the Lord's calling on their life, they also accepted the Holy Spirit which gave them the reliance of a Christian who knew that the battle for justice, peace, and equality for all Americans required of them to hold onto their faith in God and patiently wait for God to work it out for them.

As a Christian, they realized that a divided house would not stand, so they patiently waited until after the Civil Rights battle was over before involving themselves in pursuing the Human Rights issue of the gay community. They back then thought they were fighting the good fight of faith, not only to gain their own rights to be granted equality as an American citizen, but also to gain their rights to be granted equality as human-beings and as children of God.

By mercy and grace with empathy, the God fearing heterosexual Gay Rights Activists humbled themselves through their faith on the Anointed teachings of God; to gain a godly understanding of the homosexuals' point of view as an oppressed society. They yearn more so than ever during the 21st century, to boldly stand on the Word of God and meekly fight for all mankind; and not just for their own-kind. They also spiritually believe that the time has come for all humanity to acknowledge and praise the Lord God for sending the Comforter to convert the mindset of the oppressors and for setting all who believes on him free from the dictator's traditional religious laws of bondage. It is highly believed by many Christians that the righteous deeds of the Christian heterosexual Gay Right Activists' are spiritually settling their different opinion of the Word of God. They independently are working on working out their own Salvations in fear and trembling of the Lord, to fulfill the Lord's Law of Love. Instead of destroying the Lord's Law, as many traditional religious dictators who judge the Word of God predicted such workers would, many believe that the works of the Gay Right Activists which doesn't include giving the gays the right to be married; are reviving the Spirit of Forgiveness unto all of Mankind alike. The Gay Rights Activists who are Christians neither agree to the acts of homosexuality or to the evil acts which creates hate crimes against the gay community. According to their concept of the Word of God, the preaching of the oppressors of today's generation who oppose them, desires to sit in Moses' seat and are subconsciously preventing the fulfillment of the Lord's Law of Love from taking place as they work to keep the partial laws of the land bias, uncompassionate, and unforgiving towards such sinners.

Whether truth or fable; many believe that the earlier heterosexual Gay Rights Activists in America ceased from speaking out for what they truly believed in when their fight for equality in the USA had first began, because if they shared their spiritual beliefs which were semi for/against the beliefs of the majority, they more than likely would have strengthened the heterosexual supporters of despotism. Those who supported despotism were seducing the minds of others to believe that a person could be a Christian if they only supported part of the despots' religious beliefs and not fully support their beliefs. The majority of authoritative persons in America, who were historically recognized as followers of Christ before most Americans received their Civil Rights, encouraged the evil acts of partiality and hatred to be issued as an earthy but religious punishment against all Americans who openly confessed that they either had homosexual desires or openly owned up to being gay. Since the time had not yet come for certain peculiar Christians, who were semi for and semi against such deluded religious prevision and principles; to fully explain the merit of their faith on the Power of God, they were misjudged as servants of the Devil.

Whether truth of fable: before, during, and immediately after the Civil War was won, the American hearts which supported despotism made it legally possible for the authoritative persons in America to evilly react vengefully as discriminators against new born babies who were born outside of their race. Disgustingly, most of them desired to kill any child that was born outside of the race or origin of the original American despot leaders and followers. In those days a massive majority of voting Americans who claimed they were Christians, also disgustingly desired to murder gay people without a cause. The despots who created such laws were protected by the laws, and they coerced others to believe that they could save themselves from damnation and hellfire by supporting the laws of their vanity.

The murderous laws existed because the hearts of majority of American voters back then; inwardly desired to uphold the dogmatic traditional religious expectations, which falsely obligated them to believe that God had called and sent them out into the world to rule evilly with brutal dominance. During the 21st century, since murdering is frowned upon in America and the old laws which support vanity still exist in the hearts of the followers of certain long-established despotic traditional religions; it is common to learn that certain religious individuals are demanding for the gay children and young adults to kill themselves. Even the peers of the gay children are instructed by the adult religious despots of their household, to place them in a hostile and bully like environment. After being stressfully pushed over the edge by such persons, some gay children reportedly have taken their own lives as a result thereof.

A MOVEMENT FOR PEACE IS ON THE RISE AGAINST GAY BASHING BULLIES

The heterosexuals of the 21st century have formed a movement of peace, which meekly fights against all sorts of bullying. Two of the worst types of bullying are cyber bullying on social networks over the internet and random unprotected job/school bullying. The America Civil Rights members are well aware and are acknowledging openly, that the gays had joined together with them during the Civil Rights Movement to independently gain their civil rights to be treated as an equal. These people recognize and acknowledge that gay people are apart of every human-race known unto man. When America was at war within itself; fighting for equality, freedom, justice, and peace the votes of the gay community were totally warranted and were properly added to the Civil disputing which consented to the Civil Rights Movement.

The Civil Rights Act of 1964 is a powerful United States law that was proposed by President John F. Kennedy in 1963. This law has become one of the nation's toughest Civil Rights Laws. Whether truth or fable, certain elected Republican State Governors in A.D. 2011 distinctively are working subconsciously on ridding this Civil Rights Law all together; by first attacking and ridding the powers of the Union which gave a great foundation in the creation of the Civil Rights Act of 1964. Without the Union, the fair labor laws that support all working class Americans will be destroyed.

Due to greed, certain political conservatives want to remove the power of fairness from the hands of the citizens, who demands protection and equality. As a result thereof, the conservatives are threatening to restore all discriminating powers back into the rich hands of big business lobbyists. In other words, under their leadership, the American workers are threatened to return to slavery in the 21st century, but that's a different subject all together.

Let's get back to the subject at hand, concerning the 21st century movement of peace against such bullies. Although Americans fought together as a diverse arrangement of all sorts of different races and classes of religious people to gain their civil and human rights, many today refuse to acknowledge the complaints made by the earlier Gay Rights Activists. They have refused to accept the existence of the gay community being apart of the Civil and the Human Rights Movement. In fact, they act like the Gay Rights organization is something new.

Civil rights are also mentioned in the body of the United States Constitution and later it was added to other amendments. Every individual state of the United States has a bill or a declaration of rights, but the system of the Supreme Court have almost for certainty done foremost the most essential part towards defining civil rights. Historically, the judges of the Supreme Courts often define the boundaries of civil rights by trying to balance the limited civil rights of a particular individual or group; who stands against the traditional societal rights of the original heritage of America's society.

As an illustration, when ever the original Americans raise questions about the limitations of civil rights, which violates the civil rights of others; they request and expect for the Supreme Court's decisions to provide them with the answer. The typical American conflict of the 21st century involves the Christian heterosexual American population fighting amongst themselves about the moral value of right and wrong.

The never ending political battle of the ages, in America; consists of prejudice wars of intolerance as the rich vs. the poor and the straights vs. the gays. These battles have progressed over the years into a crucial struggle for the oppressed citizens of the United States of America, as religious men of the world who are lip worshippers of God; concern themselves with unanswered or unsettled questions regarding worldly affairs. These worldly battles pertain to the counted slackness or the gains of one's worldly possessions, and the genealogy of a person's sexuality.

Therefore, it is reasonable to understand why so many denominational religious members in America publically profess that they don't have a problem with transitioning their mindset, to peacefully admit with their faith consecrated on the Lord; that they support the moral political values that previously were written in their hearts by the Lord concerning his love for all mankind. They vitally point out each moral value of the Lord's non-bias law of love that had been rewritten within the American Constitution as well as within other American amendments. The objective of their case and point reveals how certain particular American laws were ordained by the authority of the Word of God; to protect, guard, and secure all American citizens from violence; without partiality and deceit.

More Christians worldwide during this generation are righteously judging the circumstances of each individual situation where they are deprived by their own government; concerning the sown fruit of discrimination, and they are convinced into believing that social equality hasn't ever been given a fair examination by their home land regime. This theory to them is a natural fact, due to the historical unfairness which they've personally experienced as living witnesses thereof. Maybe that's one of the main reasons why so many American citizens are protesting against discrimination during the 21st century, as they proclaim that they believe that some Americans have never had fair representation within the legislative governing body of the United States of America serving their class or origin.

Due to their unique and undefiled faith on the Power of God's ability to save their lowly and poor spirits; the heterosexual Gay Rights Activists who are a peculiar people; refuse to give in to the same said doubtful disputations of another man's religious faith, which believes that the most despised American may not ever have fair representation within the legislative governing body on earth as they do in heaven.

These peculiar protestors believe that they have spiritually come to the knowledge of God to comprehend that although the deity of their Christian faith gives them the spiritual integrity of the Lord, to desire to get rid of the old enticing violent laws of the land; not all American Christians shares that same desire. Due to the unwavering faith of these peculiar people, they are willing to allow themselves to be degraded by the religious faith of other Americans and non-Americans, whose religious ethnic code of morality consist of them disbelieving that God predestined them to peacefully stand up as lowly spirits; against every sort of bigotry and worldly law of despotism.

Protecting the civil rights of a homosexual has been placed on the back burner of the traditional American political views every since America was first established based on democracy and social equality, because homosexuality has been biblically perceived for centuries as a wicked and evil act; committed by a wicked and evil individual or group of people within every generation. In other words, never in recorded history has any government on earth ever given civil rights to the homosexual community. The American oxymoron within the traditional limitations of providing civil rights to the gay community has always been denied, because these human beings have always been classified in the same category as illegal aliens and devil worshippers by all dictators who proclaim to run their country based on a democratic system of equality.

After gaining the ability to personally perceive the anointed classified meaning of what wicked and evil signifies, the 20th and 21st century homosexual community in America are historically noted for challenging the biblical perceptions of every religious organizational member who have sought to persecute, revile, and discriminate against them. After being exploited by the worldly perception of what wickedness is or what religious men think the word means, even the heterosexual American Christian community have started to rise up and demand for their government or regime to disband and terminate any and every idea that grants authority unto those who sought to make miserable of the lives of the gay community.

Of course those who reproach such laws of the land believe that these laws are indeed enmity against God and are the leading cause of the agony and worldly sorrows which others go through. They believe that whosoever suggests that the troubles of the world are due to the Lord's Commandments, are coerced by the hypocrites and false preachers who also have seduced many into believing that the Lord's Law is what causes the gays and other sinners in the world to suffer worldly sorrows.

The American laws are found guilty by the singleness of the eyes of every Christian who perceives how the laws of the land is giving the religious tyrants of every race the legal authority to freely live under the root mandate of a governing policy which provides security, equality, and justice unto the prejudice hearts of all who religiously believe God gave them the unalienable Rights to demand for the government or regime to give them the legal authority to stalk and impair the lives of whosoever they religiously despise.

The idea of disbanding such laws has always been argued by those who judge the Word of God. The judgers religiously believe that disbanding such governing laws would serve as a conflict to their religious interests of being a vengeful soldier or fighter for the Lord. They preach with envy in their hearts about how the Holy Bible describes the wickedness of the gay community as an abomination. As they seek the Holy Scriptures to find the sin of others, they find themselves as sinners. For example, the description of an abomination within the Holy Bible also describes everything that gives an offense unto God; like idolatry (Deut.7:25, 27:15, 32:16), self righteousness (St. Luke16:15), lying lips (Prov.12:22), and a perverse heart (Prov.11:20) etc. I say again, "A half truth is still a lie!" There's no sin too big for Jesus!

Every since America was founded on the idea of peace, liberty, and justice for all; the Gay Right's issue was treated like dirt on a floor and was swept under the rug, but the American Christians of the 20th and 21st century generation made this an essential topic. The subject of their spiritual concerns includes the present existence of discrimination.

Therefore, the heterosexual American Gay Right Activists are peacefully protesting against the unfair American laws that are aimed at inciting riots, because the main intent of such unlawful laws are designed to give Americans the consent to be unforgiving, as they thrash and bash all gays. The Christian Gay Right Activists have united together with religious people of all sorts of denominations for the better of good over evil. Together they humbly are requesting for the US government and the American court system to grant gays the right to work and live without being harassed or discriminated against due to their sexuality. They don't want to stop any person from religiously believing of God's disapproval of homosexuality, but they do want to eliminate the evil acts of hate crimes that are legally committed by a Nation of people who supports the idea of equality, justice, and peace should be granted to all mankind.

Many have lost their lives from working for the Lord in hopes of providing freedom, peace, and justice for all. As they risked their life and humbled themselves to the humiliations of the world, they stood firm on the Word of God in every act of devoting their love unto God by loving their neighbors and strangers alike; whether domestic or foreign. The works of them weren't done in vain, because the Lord's Law represents freedom and justice for all without partiality or deceit. After they've lost their lives, the American laws of the land slowly but surely are starting to include equal protection unto the gays and straights alike.

The Lord's Law is made perfect; not to be partial, but his ordinance makes the fulfillment of the entire human race complete and whole.

Being treated fairly by the heterosexual community is indispensable, and there are people on both walks of life that are in agreement with the fact that the seriousness of this matter needs not to be swept under the rug any longer, and needs to be sensibly dealt with. In harmony, both parts agree that the gays should have the rights to receive an education and have job security without being violated by a setup law that authorizes employees, employers, teachers, students, and faculty staff the sanction to show favoritism for or against them and to stop all harassments which injures them or causes a hostile and unstable environment.

This includes the ending of the "Don't Ask Don't Tell" policy for the gay militants who are putting their lives on the line to serve and protect their country in the military. The 21 century Gay Right Activists also are focusing on meeting the requirements of the domestic safety issues and concerns of their conservative opponents including all American non-militants and citizens, concerning the transitioning safety hazards of their everyday livelihood. The safety concerns of the heterosexual non-militants were put to silence after several polls were taken in the military which detected that most heterosexual militants didn't feel that ending the Don't Ask Don't Tell policy would jeopardize their safety.

To conclude the author's thoughts and concerns of the present supporters of peace, justice, and equality she believes it is fair to say that during today's generation the hope for civility is in progress for and by all individuals, but having complete justice for all Americans is a mere illusion, because equality isn't a clear cut for all Americans to have the same equal rights and freedoms. A person who takes pride in sociability isn't wicked nor does it make the weak, but it is good and is a test of their faith on the Lord God. When used properly, their compassion strengthens the faith of the weak, but if used inappropriately sociability can weaken one's faith on the Lord. Faith is not impossible to obtain. Some are lead to believe that the acts of a peace making socialist is really evil, but others believe that if Christ did it, then so should all who follows him. President Barak Obama has been called a socialist, because he appears to be interested in make the laws fair for the survival of all Americans. This message is written for a self examination and shouldn't be used to stir up an argument, so those of you who likes to point fingers need to recognize that you have three pointing right back at you.

THE UNTOLD HISTORICAL TRUTH, OPINION, AND THEORY OF ANOTHER EXHIBITION OF HOMOPHOBIC

Up until the 20th century, the American form of democracy was like the ancient Athens' Direct Democracy. It discriminated and worked to silence the working class Americans who did most of the work which helped to build and support the economy. Just like the ancient Athens who prevented their women and slaves from helping with deliberating any policy into law, the history of the American governing body prevented the gays from retaining certain equitable rights all throughout history. Like the ancient Athenian women and slaves, the gays in America were disallowed to speak and protest against the unfairness within the legislative and executive branches of government which were used against them. The governments which forcefully silenced the lambs of God explains the reason why historians noted the Athens for not having division between their legislative and executive branches of government and also why American Christians were historically noted for not having religious division between their Church and State laws concerning the gay rights issue.

The historical American appointees who generated laws which supported the US governing affairs, made the true topic of equality for all mankind the least of importance to discuss; when the discussion pertained to granting gays the right to be treated as an equal amongst their neighbors, strangers, co-workers, colleagues etc. Some suggest that the past appointees hid themselves from the subject as if the issues of injustice would simply go away in the mist of ignoring the matter.

Tyranny has been displayed by the despots of every religious heterosexual community as a debt of persecution that should be led against the entire gay community. This theoretically implies that the tyrannous works of the most respected traditional religious denominations against the gays are good works. Hypothetically speaking, the spiritual appearance of the detestable subject is manifesting, and many are able to identify the works of these despot leaders and followers are evil. Apparently, the Christians are realizing that they have mistaken the gay's tolerance and lenience to the despots insulting method of rebuking Satan out of them is also insulting unto God. This concludes the source of the religious ideas and point of views of the most respected religious denominations', which involves why their members have been swayed to believe; that if the majority of them unreasonably deliberate within their ministry to cause anguish, misery, and despair against the gays, their outspoken religious creation of desolation will break the spirit of the gays and cause them to disbelieve that the blood of Jesus was shed to save them from sin.

DOES GAY CHRISTIANS EXIST?

(Acts5:14)My dear brethren and sisters have you not heard or do you not believe that the name Christian is given to all who believes on God. Who knows the mind of God's children to know whether or not if they will turn and repent? Who knows the mind of God to know whether or not if God will turn away from his fierce anger that the gays perish not? Why do so many religious people believe God sent the Word into the world in vain? The Fruit of the Spirit of God, which is greater than any witness on earth, proves what is acceptable unto God. After spiritually analyzing the surrounding acts of events that troubles a great multitude; the Lord's heavenly evidence reveals to all believers that desolation creates wars and not peace. All doers of the Word of God have heard and believe that the gates of Hell will not prevail against the church which the Lord built upon the Rock. Therefore, man cannot make nor break the Spirit of another man's conscience unto God. God didn't give any man the power to restrain the Spirit of another man's conscience, and this maybe why such shameful historical attempts that were made by the majority of traditional religious tutors, have timelessly failed to break the Spirit of the minority. Gays are pressured into being physically oppressed and demoralized by all religious groups on earth, but some of them still believe they have hope of being redeemed by the Lord. The humanity of their leniency towards their oppressors has been their strength which helps them to cope with such worldly things that causes the hearts of most of them despair.

The Spirit of Christ wasn't given unto man by the ordinance and commandments of men. Therefore, the acts of cruelty that comes from the teachings of a majority of traditional religions can't prevail against the ordinance of the Spirit of God. Many Christians of the 21st century think its extraordinary how meekly the gays have kept their composure within every murderous generation worldwide. Even though they've been maliciously treated by the most respected religious organizations in the world, those who have confessed and repented have also waited patiently in an orderly fashion for the Lord of Host to intercede the spirit of their haters, without seeking vengeance against their oppressors.

The Christian community acknowledges that the lips of the dictators which are irreligiously worshiping the Lord during today's generation, are offending themselves. They and the author of Discerning Perceptive charge these dictators for professing that they believe that God authorized them to advantage themselves by downing the dignities of others believers. It is for certain that some religious dictators blasphemously use the Holy Scriptures maliciously, with the intent to encourage others among them to think more of themselves than they ought. When they heard that God gave Christians the authority to rebuke Satan, they taught they were given the power to rebuke the gay out of a person; by completely reviling and hating on the entire gay community. All who charge the religious dictators for such preaching's, believes that they blaspheme against the Holy Ghost, because the power of the Holy Spirit makes corrective intercessions to the Spirit of all whom believes on the Son of God, even those who are beguiled by such profanity, so that they may see their own faults as revilers of men; to repent thereof. If God is for redemption, than who is for damnation under God?

THE SEAL OF SILENCE IS BROKEN

After centuries of waiting, the gays have finally broken their silence and are demanding equality to be granted unto them by the unfair lawmakers of the land and they are much bolder now than ever. Some people who supports the American traditional laws, refuses to view the gay's complaints as a fight for justice. Instead they see their fight as an invasion against the religious beliefs of some of the most respected denominational leaders and followers thereof. Most religious dictators personally don't classify the gays' fight for justice to be equivalent to the defensive measures made by other groups whose reasons for fighting for their rights were due to them being demoralized and discriminated because of their nationality, creed, sex, or religion.

Hypothetically speaking, every group born in America which have sin; believe they should also have the legal right to live in a democracy which preserves their human rights equally with all others, without the tyranny of any domestic despotic governing body mentally and physically forcing them to devote their complete loyalty to live with an empty heart, which has no hope of being saved by the blood of Jesus Christ. (Prov.13:12) Only, the hypocrites think other wise, because they are beguiled to have an overly excessive desire to have a closer relationship with the Lord than any other.

One true reason why the original American Civil Rights members today are boldly standing up and demanding for the gays to have equal rights under the American law is because many heterosexuals believe all American citizens should be treated equally fair under the law of democracy. Back in the old days the Civil Rights members were limited to resources, and they were restrained by the boundaries and circumstances which mostly surrounded the warring ideas of the traditional religious martyrs of the world. After those traditional boundaries and borders were torn down, nothing has stopped them from speaking out on what they independently believe concerning the Gospel and the Compassion of Christ.

Some heterosexuals haven't forgotten what the Lord brought them out of, and others needs to be reminded thereof; so that they can put on the whole armor of God and do unto others as they would have others to do unto them. Their lost memory makes it easier for them to pretend to have no sin; as they condemn others. Meanwhile, the 21st century martyrs are constantly encouraging people to be more like the original religious despots, who despise people as a religious veneration or ritual. They have not learned that hating a person or a group of people isn't godly or righteous.

Simultaneously, many Christians and Ministers of God believe they all are directed by God; to sympathetically understand the will of God and of his good pleasure. They hate the sin of homosexuality, but they love the sinner. They desire to live by to the "Golden Rule of Life" and do righteous unto the Lord by treating all others the way they want to be treated, but the traditional religious despots accuses them of doing wrong and blame them unto God. Those who desire to live by the "Golden Rule of Life" are very tempted by their accusers, to be Gain-Sayers and men-pleasers under a religious doctrine other than the Doctrine of Jesus Christ. The tyrannical religious rulers of worldly matters swear they are not dictators when they are reproached by the Word of God concerning the Golden Rule of Life. They commonly attempt to justify their purpose for blaming the doers of the Word of God unto God; by accusing them of wrong doing. The despot rulers of the world desire to restrain the Lord's servants from desiring to seek for equality for all mankind. They are also recognized as religious instigators, who use seductive fair words and well put together speeches to convince the Lord's servants to trust and believe that the oldness of every religious motivation which spreads hatred abroad; holds the rationale proof which indicates their religious doctrines are more comparably the same as the Doctrine of Jesus Christ. Imprudently they don't understand that the compatibility of such doctrines doesn't have the heart or the Spirit of Christ to co-exist together in harmony with the Doctrine of Jesus Christ. In such case, there's no way for anyone who supports such doctrines to also support the greatest Commandment of the Lord.

Haters and despisers of men during today's generation are like the unawares mentioned in the Holy Bible text. As they scorn organizations that are made up of a diverse group of people, like the Civil Rights Organization they privately creep in and portray themselves to be on one accord with their ministry. Inwardly their ravening's for control and powers prevents them from believing in the fullness of human rights. Neither do they believe that the propitiation of Jesus Christ's Church is made up of many members and is made for everybody who confesses Jesus as their Lord and Savor. Therefore, they prefer to continue following the same preexisting course of actions and differentiations of all sorts of despotic religions, which promise false hope and liberty. The haters are susceptible to worship in the accordance to whatsoever the heart of their despotic religious leaders blasphemously specifies.

(Ps.10/Ps.50:16-23/Prov.1:10-19/Roman3:8-17) It's common for foolish thinkers to be swift to insult or shed the innocent blood of whosoever they think they are better than, because they hypocritically think that causing destruction and misery will earn them the ability to gain or regain the Lord's favor. They religiously think such actions appease the Lord God, because they view the Lord as a monstrous and angry god. According to their perception of the prophetic Word of God, they believe that their vengeful way is the righteous way to conciliate with the Lord. In other words, they believe that they can propitiate the angry god with such sacrifices.

While religiously making hatred perfect by their own understanding and by judging the Word of God, the despots are known for thinking that they can save others. As the foolishness of their own understandings cause their lips to imprudently speak froward and perverse things against other men who believe on the Son of God, the Holy Spirit perfectly works to please the Father by reconciling all things created by him and for him. Even those of you that were sometimes alienated and enemies in your mind by wicked works, yet are now reconciled. (Colo.1/Eph.2:1-2, 6:12-18/St. John5:24, 6:40)

These perverse speaking people hate being reproved by the Word of God. They despise the wisdom, knowledge, and the instructions of God. Their way of attempting to show and prove their love and devotion for God is by enticing people to follow their hateful religious ways of lurking privately to destroy the faith of the innocent; without a cause. They have no reason or no cause to seek to destroy anyone's faith on the Lord God, because all fall short to sin; including them.

It is fair to judge the circumstances of a person's reasons for hating another for the sake of discerning why one sinner love to hate another sinner. To hate a person because they are a sinner defines the ignorance of those of them which hates without a cause. The wiles of Satan deludes their minds into thinking his way brings peace unto them and brings them closer to God (Romans3:8-17), but within all of their doing they misrepresent what godly love clearly signifies.

> Titus2:1 "But speak thou the things which become sound doctrine:"
> Titus2:8 "Sound speech, that cannot be condemned; that he that is of the contrary part may be ashamed, having no evil thing to say of you."
> Titus2:9 "Exhort servants to be obedient unto their own masters, and to please them well in all things; not answering again;"
> (Titus2:10-15)

AN ORDINANCE OF LEGAL PROTECTION IS PROPOSED IN THE STATE OF TENNESSEE

The local news media of the North MS region stated that a transgendered male was arrested in TN and accused by the arresting officers for prostitution. They showed a video clip which clearly revealed the cross gendered male sitting in a chair in the booking department of the police station, and the arresting officer pulled out his handcuffs and used them like brass knuckles upside the male cross dresser's head over and over again. Simultaneously, another officer on the captured video stood behind the chair and held the defenseless suspect in the chair all the while the armed officer commenced to beat him in the face with the handcuffs.

After being released from jail, the battered suspect made a public statement during an interview with the same said local TV news media. He stated that he was falsely arrested and was verbally and brutally abused and beaten by the arresting officers because of his sexual orientation. He also stated he had hired an attorney to file a suit against the police dept. and that he had planned to leave the State of TN to live with his mother in the Northern States. Unfortunately, the suspect was found dead a day before he was scheduled to move with his mother and according to the news media, the TN police ironically filed the death of this homosexual as a homicide. There wasn't any evidence to prove his death was associated to neither his arrest nor to his law suit against the police force or to his sexual orientation. After a thorough investigation was done, the evidence within this case according to the news media; revealed that there were no protective services surrendered to the transgendered male by the police force upon them discharging or freeing him from the jail.

Now of course there's the matter of police brutality being in question during this incident, which caused the citizens of TN as well as others who may visit the State of TN to be shocked, disgusted, and dismayed by this story. The eyes of the frightened and apprehensive domestic gay citizens of TN who are well aware of this case also worry about their personal safety. Not only do they fear their neighbors and strangers but they also fear the law enforcement which is sworn in under oath to protect them.

As an illustration of the aftermath of the type of hate crimes that are reproduced by the traditional religious discriminations of men, in A.D.

515

2009 a public official of Shelby County, TN; created an ordinance of protection. It was proposed to the public as a solution for its gay citizens who are victimized, hated, and discriminated against because of their sexual orientation. This ordinance didn't propose to give gays the legal rights to marriage or to be married. It only proposed that those who were employed by the state should be treated equally fair to their heterosexual colleagues as instructed by the authority of the employer who in such case is the proposal made on the behalf of the State of TN in the form of a reformed government.

In order to discern between good and bad concerning what the proposal offers unto the people, requires a spiritual analysis of God to separate the proposal and break it down into parts. After spiritually comparing the good spirit of God with the bad spirit of the adversary, the saints are enabled to identify the inner part of the proposal which is not open to bribery as it debase the traditional despotic standard of the previous legal laws that at the time were unlawfully depriving and robbing the goodness from the heart of people of TN who religiously are tempted by anger to humiliate and injure others.

The proposal worked in the sense of honoring Lord, but it went against the false religious organizers who have always believed that God has always given them an inalienable right to mistreat whosoever they've been trained to religiously despise; even if their anger incite a riot. Since so many traditional religious people loved to inspire the sadistic acts of hatred, the outer part of the proposal is seen challenging the superiors of their corruptible authority to be weak-willed of the characteristic of what Jesus Christ signifies. God is love, and the proposal was designed to change the ordinance of the present heartless laws of TN; to defile the legalization of hate crimes. The corrupt structure of the old religious laws which the Jews used to Crucify Jesus Christ supports the acts of hate crimes, and hate crimes has always supported the outer appearance of the traditional religious members' rights; concerning fair justice under the manmade law of the land.

This proposal didn't in anyway form nor fashion, suggest authorizing the lawmakers or the citizens of Shelby Co. to give any TN gay resident the legal right to marry, but there was a religious dispute against the originality of the ordinance. The proposal suggested making a law which would grant legal authorization to the gays so that they may have the right to be treated fairly by their fellow employees and supervisors, only if they were employed by the government. This proposal didn't offer the same fairness to the average gay-workers of TN, who are employed at a non-government job.

During the religious uproar, local TV News interviewed a Rev. who proclaimed publically that he was a minister at a church in Tennessee. He publically singled out the name of this congregation as he announced that he opposed the ordinance which suggestively gives legal protection to the gay state employees of TN. There were a variety of other religious leaders in the area protesting with and against this Rev.'s concept of reason for disagreeing with the proposal.

This proposal of legal protection suggestively disallowed the reoccurrences of discrimination against gays in all government work places, in the State of TN. In other words, it proposed all to cease misusing religion as a reason to go against the ordinance of the Lord's golden rule of life, which commands all to love their neighbors as they love their selves and to treat others the way they would want to be treated. The local news media broadcasting service displayed this Rev.'s interview which revealed him speaking out publically about why he disagreed with the ordinance, which again was ONLY designed to protect the safety and the wellbeing of the gay employees of government jobs.

The absurd notion to persecute and cause misery to come upon a sinner were established by several recognized high caliber traditional religious men who publically announced that they believe all traditional religious people having an unalienable right to discriminate, persecute, and torment gay people; to show their religious disapprovals of the gays. The argument of such belief appears to win the majority voters who support the tyrannical Sect of the Pharisees' doctrine and traditional religious ways of thinking of stoning a sinner who is found with fault.

> 2Timothy2:23 "But foolish and unlearned questions avoid, knowing that they do gender strifes."
> 1Timothy1:3 "As I besought thee to abide still at Ĕph-ĕ-sŭs, when I went into Măc-ē-dō-nĭ-ă, that they teach no other doctrine," (Acts 20:1-3)
> 1Timothy1:4 "Neither give heed to fables and endless genealogies, which minister questions, rather than godly edifying which is in faith: so do."

Therefore, those who support such thinking within the 21st century's despotic American traditional religious laws also subconsciously think their support of the Pharisees' old religious laws; proves their theological vain philosophies are righteous. For centuries people have made the same attempt over and over again to justify their evil acts, by asking and answering the same old questions about genealogy which are of the records of lineage. They use the same old interpretations of the other doctrines which evolved during the earlier generations from Abraham to David; from David until the carrying away into Babylon, and from the carrying away into Babylon unto Christ. We today are living in the New Testament of Jesus Christ who didn't come into the world to destroy the law, but to fulfill it. The Law of Christ is fulfilled in one word, LOVE!

Therefore, when inhumane suggestions such as these are twined together against the Civil and Human Rights concept of the human nature of mankind, many today use an impure terminology to conclude that the Civil Rights Activists are in violation with the ordinance of the Lord and that this intolerance disallows their operational set to mandate a reasonable sacrificial expansion of the law of the land through the use of Civil and Human Rights laws; to defend the gay community.

The Civil Rights Activists aren't claiming the gays will make it to Heaven, because only the Lord can determine who will and will not make it to the Kingdom of Heaven. The Civil Rights Activists are only defending the Word of God concerning the Saints loving all mankind regardless of one's distinguished subtil differences, by standing boldly on the Word of God which teaches them treat everybody as they themselves would want to be treated.

During the interview made by the local News Broadcast, the same said Rev. of TN proclaimed he religious is in dispute against the new ordinance of Shelby Co. because he doesn't believe the ordinance of the proposal represented a Civil Rights issue. He stated that homosexuality is a moral issue, and his religious argument suggested that an ordinance which protects gays from discrimination violates the religious rights of him and every other person who the original law of the land has for centuries protected the religious rights thereof. He suggested that the proposal was unconstitutional because he believed that he should be treated equal and fair by the law to be able to express his religious disapproval of gay people through the acts of being ill-will towards them.

That which defiles such thinkers, is the ways of their speech which are filled with ungodliness and relates to the speeches made by those who biblically believe in the physical circumcision of life. The ways of their words closes the mindset of many whom also are lead to believe that the best way to convert a sinner regardless of their sin; is by being unruly and by speaking evilly unto them as if vain talking's would make them feel ashamed unto repentance. Have such traditional religious thinkers not yet heard that evil cannot rebuke evil?

Unfortunately most people all around the world religiously think the only way to make a sinner or a gay person choose to repent or make straight of that which is crooked; is by making them suffer worldly sorrows and have an ungodly fear of God. Their traditional religious way of making people feel dishonored is by spreading hatred and discriminating against them. Very willingly those who follow such ministries desire to be ill-will towards others, and they misguidedly think they are serving God. The hidden truth of all ill-willed ministries is that they love to despise their neighbors. As luck would have it, what goes around comes around. We all must reap what we've sown.

Fortunately for sinners, God isn't a hypocrite. Ironically, the ordinance of TN didn't propose to make it legal for gays to marry, it only proposed to give the gays which had government jobs their Civil and Human rights to work and be independently employed without being unfairly discharged or terminated during the worst time of an economic recession by their supervisors whose hearts desires to discriminate against ones' sexuality, sexual preference, or ones' different opinion concerning their personal and social outlooks on life.

Well, this particular Rev. and the members of his congregation still have the legal right to practice what they preach as they discriminate and spread hatred abroad; because the ordinance will keep them in the same predicament which they religiously believe will happen to them upon Judgment Day. For instance, they and every individual gay person they meet and despise will stand alone before God as they answer for what they do and say; whether their words and actions are good or evil. The actual ordinance which was proposed by a Public Official of Shelby Co. in TN was created into a law, and was very peculiar in its words as it gave this Rev. and his congregation the right to continue their religious ways of discriminating against gays who aren't employed by the government but are employed by private companies or organizations. This proposal was setup to only protect the inevitable rights of the gays who worked for the government.

Under the New Testament the Lord comes to unite all people as one Body in Christ in peace and in love, and to divide mankind in parts of soul and spirit (Heb.4). In other words, as certain ministers are coerced to live under the old law and labor in disbelief, they think that if they entreat one sort of mankind; like the entire gay population with evil that good would come unto them.(Rom.3:8)

Meanwhile, God's chosen ministers are standing boldly with confidence against such traditional ways of worship, because discriminating isn't relevant to their spiritual purpose of life. Certain religious members of the Body of Christ would rather attempt to provoke the Lord God by mending the renewed reborn way of spiritually thinking with the old Law of Moses, as if the New Written Commandment of the Lord takes away from the old.

The Lord God has prepared his chosen ministers, bishops, evangelists, servants, apostles, and prophets etc. with Heavenly Wisdom to understand how to put on a new way of thinking with a new way of living; to preserve both the new and old for the sake of living in love and having peace within one's own conscience towards the Lord God, like how one preserves new wine in new bottles. (St.Matt.9:16-17/St.Mark2:21-22/St.Luke5:36-39)

Many are called to do the works of the Lord all over the world. In the meantime, individually all are given a choice in the process of either supporting a bill which outlaws and prohibits discrimination or support a bill that creates and supports discrimination. Meanwhile, God's chosen few are humbling themselves as an equal to those whom are oppressed and free willingly they receive the same persecutions which Christ himself endured. For the moment, the oppressors are religiously suggesting that the supporters of any proposal which prohibits discrimination against sinners and against the gay community is a trick made up by the Devil, and these religious bullies are urging all of their congregational members to be not deceived by the supporters of such a proposal.

During the summer months of 2010, it was reported by the local News that a prominent woman in government who profess she believes on God the Father, the Son, and the Holy Ghost; received death threats by phone and had dead cats thrown on her lawn as a suggestive warning against her safety for supporting a bill which banned discrimination against gays in Memphis TN. The warning wasn't issued unto her by God as many religious dictators would like to promote was the actual culprit in this hate crime against her, but the premonition was issued as a warning sign against her by a evil person or a group who is guilty of spreading hatred. In despite of what the haters and despisers said and did against her, the council woman still stood strong with her mind made-up and she did not sway from the issue at hand. For a person of her stature to experience this extreme radical type of drastic intimidation through the demonstration of hatred and disorder, let's take a moment and halfway try to image what regular citizens who supports the idea of outlawing the acts of discrimination are going through.

> Gal.4:1 "Now I say, That the heir, as long he is a child, differeth nothing from a servant, though he be lord of all;"
>
> Gal.4:2 "But is under tutors and governors until the time appointed of the Father."
>
> Gal.4:3 "Even so we, when we were children, were in bondage under the elements of the world:"
>
> Gal.4:4 "But when the fulness of the time was come, God sent forth his Son, made of a woman, made under the law,"
>
> Gal.4:5 "But redeem them that were under the law, that we might receive the adoption of sons."

As it is written; "Love covers a multitude of sin." Jesus left an example for all mankind to follow, (St. John1:12-13) and he gave resourceful resources of powers over to mankind not by the works of the law but by grace and faith, for the followers of Christ to use during their everyday walk of life. God sent his only begotten son Jesus Christ in the flesh to save all from sin, because mankind didn't believe on the Lord. (St. John9:24-41, 15:5-6, 15:22-24, St.John16:9/St. Matt.3:7-11)

> St. John14:26 "But the Comforter, which is the Holy Ghost, whom the Father will send in my name, he

> shall teach you all things, and bring
> all things to your remembrance,
> whatsoever I have said unto you."
> St. John14:29 "And now I have told
> you before it come to pass, that,
> when it is come to pass, ye might
> believe."

The path which Christ led for us all to follow first started upon his birth. He was born of the Holy Ghost, which is left by him for all believers to reprove the world of sin, and of righteousness, and of judgment so all who lives after him could be guided into all truth in the way in which they ought to go (St. John3:3-7). By God's loving merciful grace, Jesus humbled himself to come into the world in the form of the flesh. He could've come in the spiritual form without being of a fleshly body, but he didn't. Symbolically, he was lowered to be as a man, and he became a partaker of the things, which mankind condemns without accusing any for accusing him. (St. John5:39-47)

After returning to the heavens, he sent the Spirit of the Holy Ghost, which teaches all believers how to humble their fleshly selves so that they too, like him can be reborn of the Spirit.

> St. John3:6 "That which is born of
> the flesh is flesh; and that which is
> born of the Spirit is spirit."
> St. John3:7 "Marvel not that I said
> unto thee, Ye must be born again."

By the flesh, Jesus felt the sorrows of the world which today still condemns men whom lives under the law which crucified him. By the Spirit, he felt a godly sorrow, which led him to teach repentance, reconciliation, redemption, and the resurrection of the dead unto salvation; for the living to be revived from the bondage of the world. In order for us to follow him we must study the Word of God to show ourselves approved unto God by humbling ourselves to feel what our neighbors feel in so doing that we may receive a spiritual understanding of what they are going through. If we lack the ability to humble ourselves to understand the sorrows of our neighbors, then we also will fail to receive the goodness of God's grace to know and to do the will of God and of his good pleasures as Good Samaritans and servants with the singleness of the heart. Without empathy can no man alive survive, because they can not gain a lowly heart to receive humility for their past shameful injustices!

St. John5:44 "How can you believe,
which receive honor one of another,
and seek not the honor that cometh
from God only?"

What is moral and ethical? Well, in this world they both require National apprehension in conforming to the world's ideas which agrees with the worldliest double minded specified standards and principles of right and wrong. What is morally and ethically right and wrong to the worldly is determined by the vote of a majority as they derive scriptures from the Bible Text to define what they've concluded or have understood to be a special requirement or request of the Lord Jesus Christ.

Along the wooden and concrete walls of many man made congregational houses are engraved two passages that are derived from the Holy Bible Text. "But seek ye first the Kingdom of God and his Righteousness; and all these things shall be added unto you." The second passage is, "The Kingdom of Heaven is at hand." These two scriptures are true, but what good are they if one can't grasp the one true concept of what's being requested, nor can understand the graphics of what either denotes signifies.

(Prov.8:32) A diligent seeker shall find wisdom and get understanding of the Word of God. With the heart of zeal, a diligent seeker becomes a deviser; to obtain in the mind the truth of what's requested. The Lord knows the heart of man and directs his steps to do his will which is the will of his Father. With heavenly wisdom and understanding by mercy and truth, the heart and mind of a spiritual deviser becomes free of impurities through a cleansing process (Prov.16:6).

> Prov.16:9 "A man's heart deviseth his way: but the Lord directeth his steps."

Receiving the Spirit of Righteousness, which is of God, give us heavenly wisdom that we might know the things that are freely given to us of God. Therefore, the anointing teaches us without lies and deceits, the hidden wisdom which God established or ordained as an order of law before the world. (1Cor.2/John 2:27)

CORRUPTIBLE OR INCORRUPTIBLE

None of the princes of this world acknowledges the order of law which God predestined. They've always been unable to make a solemn and formal declaration or an assertion in the placement or same rankings of God's order of law within their everyday walk of life, because they are blinded by the wisdom of this world. Instead, they affirm or agree to an implied declaration or assertion of the laws of the Pharisees and the Sadducees to satisfy their own curiosities and eager desires of learning the things of the old and new world orders. Being persuasively convinced in their own beliefs and understandings of the Word of God, they corrupt the conduct of many, by using the same stratagem as the doctrine of the Pharisees and Sadducees to govern the people by establishing laws, policies, and rules which suggests the exercise of arbitrary or despotic power of authority.

Being born under or into these particular defensive and offensive tactics, causes many to believe that it is righteous to create desolation in order to make peace. Symbolically, people believe in the illusion that by declaring war in the end will create peace. This corruptible seed has caused division and wars within the House of God as well as the House of many nations. The authoritativeness of the world is the exercise of power and authority over others in efforts to direct and control an unjust law for the common good and interests of the worldly to gain earthy treasures and rewards. According to the anointing teachings of the Holy Ghost, heavenly wisdom and knowledge spiritually strengthens a diligent seeker of the Kingdom of God with the power to clearly understand and obtain the Spirit of God. (Eph.3:16-21/1Peter2:1-3/Rom.12:2-8)

> **1Peter2:4** "To whom coming, as unto a living stone, disallowed indeed of men, but chosen of God, and precious,"
> **1Peter2:5** "Ye also, as lively stones, are built up a spiritual house, an holy priesthood, to offer up spiritual sacrifices, acceptable to God by Jesus Christ."
> **Prov.21:3** "To do justice and judgment is more acceptable to the Lord than sacrifice."
> **Hosea6:6** "For I desired mercy, and not sacrifice; and the knowledge of God more than burnt offerings."

RIGHTEOUS JUDGEMENTS

The Spirit of Knowledge is power, and with great power come great responsibility. Every purified heart undergoes a cleansing process as described by the predestined Divine orders of God ordained law. Receivers of the Spirit of God are subject to use God's issued spiritual gifts as a spiritual tool, in hopes of being spiritually freed from the bondage of this world. After understanding God's righteous judgments, we then as reborn Christians gains confidence in the Spirit of Righteousness to compare spiritual things with spiritual; for the proper usage to reprove, rebuke, and repent of our own fleshly deeds and dead works (Ps.118:8-9/Heb.4/Heb.10/Eph.2:18-22, 3:12/1John 4:17). It's all apart of the Lord's purification process, by which all born again Christians can gain the ability to spiritually change for the better. The righteous judgment is the proper name of this type of action, but the worldly perverse the meaning of God's righteous judgments, to place stumbling blocks in the way of their fellow brethren and sisters in Christ. The judgments made by the worldly in reality consist of whatsoever the worldly think about themselves, and their thoughts linger to judge others in the same manner (Prov.23:6-7). In so doing they tend to use the Word of God to justify their wrong without understanding that there's no justification in wrong doing. (St. Luke6:47) The Holy Spirit has revealed that it's godly to try the spirit and to identify which spirit it is (James4:1-2), but it's ungodly to judge or to confine the spirit whichever one it is. (St. Matt.7)

Carnally minded men use the wisdom of this world to delude the minds of other men by perversions the Word of God. They imprudently suggest God only gives to them special privileges or the rights to use the Word of God to Judge and to confine the spiritual minds of all men, who confess their sin. In doing so, their vexed hearts place stumbling blocks in the way of them that are weak, which are befitting to the occasion or to the purpose of the Adversary and not to God. (Rom.5:15/Rom.14:7-9, 13, 14/2Cor.5:14-15/1John1:8-9/Ps.51/1John2:3-4/Rom.10:10-11)

> James5:16 "Confess your faults one to another, and pray one for another, that ye may be healed. The effectual fervent prayer of a righteous man availeth much."

They oppress and confine the weak by falsely teaching those who desire God's love, mercy, and grace, to present unreasonable, unwarrantable, and non-profitable sacrifices unto God in hopes of receiving their Salvation. God knows that all the things which they falsely suggest for others to do, they themselves do not do. They pretend to be what they are not or believes in what they do not... "Hypocrites". They pretend to be children of God, but they seduce others faith into believing God doesn't love them and that they have no hope of being saved because of their sin, as if they themselves have no sin. (Rom.3:9 & 23/11:32/Gal.3:22-25/1Cor.4:15)

Jesus Christ is the only living soul who walked in the flesh as a perfect man. Therefore, we ought not to claim to be perfect as liars do. For our soul's sake the heavenly wisdom allows and strengthens our spirit to perceive the difference between good and evil, truth and lies, right and wrong, and the light from darkness. Not after our own understanding or after the understandings of another man, but after the Spirit of God. It's then left up to us as an individual to choose between the righteous and unrighteous path in our everyday walk of life (1John1). When we know to do right and do it not, then it is sin.

> Eph.5:9 "(For the fruit of the Spirit is in all goodness, and righteous and truth;)"
> Eph.5:10 "Proving what is acceptable unto the Lord."

THE LIFE OF SCORNERS DENIES THE WORKS OF THE FRUIT OF THE SPIRIT OF GOD

The Fruit of the Spirit of God is without evil, lies, and/or wrongful deceits. It implies to all men a kindly intention to express or signify God's disapproval of the works of the flesh. Without harshness nor force, the Spirit of Righteousness manifest to everyone that does evil deeds that they've yielded to iniquity and that their deeds are free from righteousness. The Lord said I stand at the door and knock, but he didn't say he will enter by way of force. If any man hears the voice of the Lord, and opens the door of their hearts unto him, he said he will come in and sup with him. This is his way of being gentle and persistent while requesting an invitation into each of our lives. (Rev. 3:20)

> **Romans6:18 "Being then mad free from sin, ye became the servants of righteousness."**
> **Romans6:20 "For when you were the servants of sin, ye were free from righteousness."**

The teachings of the Holy Ghost, reveals to us the wrought of our flesh as well as the wrought of the Spirit of Righteousness in God (St. John3:21/1John1:6-7/2Cor.1:21-22/5:5). After we receive heavenly wisdom which is not of this world, we then can spiritually understand and accept the heavenly truth.

The heavenly truth reveals that God is love and so is his Spirit which dwells in all whom believeth, loveth, and confesses that Jesus is the Son of God (1John4/Gal.5:22). In love and by faith, we then as spiritual devisers of the Word of God can reproach, rebuke, reprove, and repent of our fleshly deeds which consist of evil works. When our fleshly deeds are made obvious by the Spirit of God to be the acts of shameful injustice or wickedness our inner godly spirit convicts our conscience and repentance follows. Again, this is apart of the Lord's purification process, and not man's own will nor way of being cleansed and freed from sin. Mans' will and way of cleansing causes burden on the inner spirit and even kills the inner spirit of man's faith in God the Father, the Son, and Holy Ghost.

> **St. John3:21 "But he that doeth truth cometh to the light, that his**

deeds may be made manifest, that
they are wrought in God."

The Lord's words in all goodness, righteousness, and truth implies a stern and sharp reproving as it rebukes (St. John8:1-12), and brings forth great sorrow to the heart of the righteous. By sorrow of the heart, our spirit is broken (Prov.15). When the Spirit of Truth comes and manifest to us that our fleshly deeds are the work of iniquity, which has been sown into our heart, the Lord's words convicts our conscience and free willingly we then can repent or change our evil ways.

2Cor.7:10 "For godly sorrow worketh repentance to salvation not to be repented of: but the sorrow of the world worketh death."
James4:17 "Therefore to him that knoweth to do good, and doeth it not, to him it is sin."
Psalms34:18 "The Lord is nigh unto them that are of a broken heart; and saveth such as be of a contrite spirit."

THE NEED OF TRUE REPENTANCE & RECONCILIATION

The Contrite Spirit sets off a vehement feeling of godly sorrow upon ones own heart for a wrong that one has done whether self inflicted or onto another. It's the after effect of the heart which express one's deeply repentant. This is an illustration of how we as fellow servants of the Lord by the grace and mercy of God present our bodies a living sacrifice, holy, and acceptable unto God which is of a reasonable service. (Rom.12:1-2/2Cor.2:1-10)

> 1Cor.6:19 "What? know ye not that your body is the temple of the Holy Ghost which is in you, which ye have of God, and ye are not your own?"
> 1Cor.6:20 "For ye are bought with a price: therefore glorify God in your body, and in your spirit, which are God's."

The Lord Words of Truth may convict our spirit, but it doesn't condemn us like the words of the worldly does. Like a father does to his child the Lord express to us in a gentle or mild scolding of his displeasure or disappointment in our faulty deeds, and this he does for all man-kind alike. As a despiser of iniquity, the Lord views and treat the works of iniquity with contempt to convict and to declare unto them that their hearts are filled with iniquities and their deeds are wrong. It is by the Spirit of Righteousness that convicts the Spirit of iniquity, as the Spirit is made manifest unto us by the Lord. If we then refuse to repent or change due to our own contemptuous desires like a scorner, we then condemn our selves.

Although God clearly makes it known to all man-kind alike that he doesn't want our filthy bodies (Ashes to Ashes Dust to Dust), many religious people still focus more so on ones' physical sin made in the physical body, as if the physical body stands a chance at being presented unto God by man as a living sacrifice. For this causes them to submit themselves to be alive indeed unto sin (Romans6:10-16, 2Colo.2:18-22), by willingly sinning themselves while judging another man servant; whom God has received and has the ability to make him stand. They also sin indeed by yielding their members as instruments of unrighteousness. In doing so, they defraud themselves to have dominion over their members' life unto death. (Romans 14:1-4) After focusing on the physical sin for so many generations, like the psychopaths who misleads others into following the doctrine of the Pharisees and Sadducees under the New Testament; many people today may have a clear perception of reality, but they lack the divine sense of social and moral requirements of the Prophetic Word of God. Therefore, their idea of receiving the Kingdom of Heaven as a personal gain is sought by the criminal act of overseeing worldly dominance without the marked feeling of guilt. They deny the spiritual aspect of what's being requested of them by God the Father, the Son and the Holy Ghost, which is clearly revealed unto them by the Comforter which also manifests the Holy Truth unto us all; to teach us what is Holy and acceptable unto God.

Proverbs 15:12 "A scorner loveth not one that reproveth him: neither will he go unto the wise."

THEORETICAL CONCLUSION

After obtaining heavenly understandings of the Word of God, spiritual men of God can clearly detect the works of God from the wiles of Satan. The wiles of Satan are known as the stratagem of the Adversary. They are the tools Satan uses to lure beguile, and entice people of God by cunning means of trickery to keep us from doing good works or God's will.

Let's stop for a moment and meditate together. Self examine yourself, while I explain indirectly to you how I self-examine myself. Beware; no two are exactly alike. We all have faults and failings, and not every life experience or life learned lesson which evolves in our individual lives; is dealt unto no two pair in the form of the same measure of portion. Therefore, we all will not react to every situation in the exact same manner all the time. Some things we may be able to agree on, but others we may not. God is the One True Judge and we should not stop judging righteously in the form of our own similarities, but we need to stop feeling obligated to disband others from the Holy Root of the Fruit of Jesus Christ. Therefore, we ought not to compare ourselves to one of another. That's vanity! We are of the same body of Christ and we must learn to agree to disagree without allowing the things that are vanity to cause us despair. Some of us who are stronger than others in certain areas use God's love to strengthen the weak the same we God's love strengthens us when we too grow weak and weary. That's the way true love goes. If you understood the love of the Lord, you would be susceptible to also understand what God requires of your love as a servant of Christ. The strong should be strong for the weak, in the name of Christ Jesus. The one who brings you into the righteous knowledge of Christ without causing worry and doubt to come upon your already weary, weak, and simple heart; are doing so meekly and as gentle as a dove. True servants of God shall prevail at not breaking the Lord's Greatest Comment, because nothing of this world wins over the will of God. Only a person who knows God can prevail at obeying this great task, and we all aren't able to indentify the love of God flowing through a person's words, phrases, and their actions simultaneously, because not all of us are serving the right One and despising the other. Every time their despising hearts attempt to make righteous judgments, the evilness of their mammon hearts; speaks words and phrases which serve the works of Satan. Unfortunately the world shall not ever obtain the mystery of the Word of God and will not ever able themselves to be in sequence with the Holy Spirit of God. Their eyes are blind and their ears are deaf.

Some say and do not, and are called hypocrites by biblical annalists, and those of the world call such persons realists. The Lord didn't leave us to be ignorant my friends. We all know and understand that a scorner misconstrues the loving and peaceful Word of the Son of God to be inferior or unworthy, and they reject being reproved with bitter, angry, and hatred of knowledge residing in the debt of their hearts and minds. Their hearts reap the unrighteous judgments of their own sown feelings of contempt, and they're very unwilling and reluctant to reconsider or re-evaluate the evil deeds, which comes as a result of what's in their hearts. By the sown contempt of the heart; a scorner suffers to be defrauded, rather than to take spiritual right over worldly wrong, even after being reproved by the Spirit of Righteousness and Truth (2Peter2:10/ Jude4-10). What is truth? The truth is... "The people of the world have an evil custom by which they willingly will become unruly if such customs aren't legally met, but everyone that is of the Holy truth; hears and understands the instructions of the Lord."(St. John18:35-40)

1Peter3:17 "For it is better, if the will of God be so, that ye suffer for well doing, than for evil doing."

536

CHAPTER 15 OUT GOES THE OLD & IN COMES THE NEW

St. Matt.15:9 "But in vain they do worship me, teaching for doctrines the commandments of men."

Jesus Christ without committing sin rose up against and above the abusive and tyrannous laws of the doctrines of the Pharisees and Sadducees' religious sects and all others simulated after their kind. During the life of Christ, both of these organizations were members of an unbelieving group of citizens from the Jewish party. Like those unbelieving parties which claim they are apart of the body of Christ, their arbitrary rigid despotic rules and usage of power suggested restrictions to ones' faith on the Son of God and established limitations, which forcefully coerce people to feel obligated by their governed laws to follow after their commended orthodox beliefs and religious practices.

The Pharisees were widely and favorably known during ancient times to be one of the most noted denominations throughout the religious realm. They studied the Law and were truly exact or correct in the outward appearance of it, but inwardly they were either unable or unwilling to show through their deeds that they possessed godly compassion. They were firm and strong minded in their belief as servants of unfair practices of a martyr.

For instance, they fastened every second and fifth day of the week, and physically gave a false appearance of themselves being more holy than others. Due to the carnalities of their minds, they inwardly were prevented by the power of the Holy Ghost from grasping the true concept of what godly love clearly signifies (1Cor.2). Spiritually comparing the deeds of their hearts by the fruit of the Spirit of God, the manifested evidence has proven them to not be the holy ones as they had professed and commended and highly praised themselves to be.

537

Instead they were the Sinners whom the Lord Jesus Christ was sent to save.

One of the greatest crimes any man can commit against God is blaspheming against the Holy Ghost (St. Matt.12:31-33/St. Mark3:28-29/St. Luke12:10). Many may not clearly understand how Satan uses man's love for God against God, by persuading people to commit that unforgivable sin (HATE) while using one's own ignorance against them. (Romans 2:16-29/10:3-13 &14-21/Eph.2:1-4) Followers of Satan uses the word love to make it work for Satan's own use and service, and he also uses it at his own disposal. Having such an extreme affect over the inferior class and as for being the number one leaders of the set foundation for the worldly governing laws of the land, the majority of the people of the Nation over turned the inferior class and they coerced them to feel obligated to accept the Doctrine of the Pharisees and the Sadducees. Meanwhile, these laws define love by the things which are bounded by boundaries as if love comes by the works of the law. The boundaries which they established subverted the souls of many who heard the troubling words of the Pharisees sect.

As an illustration, there were two men of the sect of the Pharisees which taught and believed that it was needful to circumcise the brethren after the manner of Moses in order to be saved. Apostle Paul testifies in Gal chapter 5, that every man who's circumcised is a debtor to do the whole law. This is a curse for all who attempts to do the works of that law (Gal3:10-15). Although the Pharisees were reported by the Apostle of Jesus Christ to be liars and slanders, God still showed them love. (Acts15:18-24/Gal.1:6-8/2Cor.11:4/Jude/Titus1:10-16/2Peter2:1)

> **Acts15:8 "And God, which knoweth the hearts, bare them witness giving them the Holy Ghost, even as he did us;"**

Acts15:9 "And put no difference between us and them, purifying their hearts by faith."

Acts15:10 "Now therefore why tempt ye God, to put a yoke upon the neck of the disciples, which neither our Fathers nor we were able to bear?"

Acts15:11 "But we believe that through the grace of the Lord Jesus Christ we shall be saved, even as they."

Due to the long term influences of one of the most noted, (Well Known) and ancient denominational religious doctrine of the Pharisees, many religious rituals and vows have been capitalized from its same false teaching. During today's generation in the year 2008 A.D., their legacies persist to go on resolutely without being directly contested with boldness. Certain religious people think they are standing righteously as they stand for being the thorn in your side, in spite of God's oppositions, warnings, and earnest request or plea. Therefore, by the powers of God the strong are being called to stand boldly for sake of the Holy Truth.

It's traditional of the Pharisees to continue professing or proclaiming to be holier than any other religion. That's only one of many convenient ways of recruiting or coercing people into joining or following their teachings. They also use the same tactics of the Pharisees to teach along the same field of their beliefs about physical circumcision. They are unable to understand that the order of ordinances of the New Testament uses the physical things of the Old Testament as a symbolic symbol. They today believe that they can literally physically work their way into heaven.

(Gal.5:1-6)According to the doctrine of the Pharisees men are saved by the works of the law, but the descended spiritual wisdom from heaven teaches that the physical circumcision of ones appearance or physical sins don't purify the heart, but that it does cause division between people and desolation between the Lord's Word of Truth as man uses their physical eye to judge one another by the letter. (St. Matt 12:22-37/St. Mark 3:22-35)   Regardless of the name of the today's denominational congregations, if they during today's generation are yet still confining and basing their religion around the same beliefs of the Pharisees; they give God no glory. The Lord and his apostles warn for all to beware of such doctrines and to flee from man's traditional religion. (St. Matt.16:5-13/Col.2:20-23/St. Mark7:1-13)

> **St. Mark7:13 "Making the word of God to none effect through your tradition, which ye have delivered: and many such like things do ye."**

The other sect among the Jews was the Sadducee. They acknowledged the law, but were accused of rejecting all the scriptures of the other Books except for the five books of Moses.   The Sadducees are recognized in the religious realm to be the religious party which denies the existence of angles as well as spirits. Like scorners they without faith in the Lord Jesus totally reject the ideas of immortality of the soul and of the resurrection of the body of Jesus. (Matt. 22:23/Mark12/Luke 20:27)

> **Romans2:28 "For he is not a Jew, which is one outwardly; neither is that circumcision, which is outward in the flesh:"**
> **Romans2:29 "But he is a Jew, which is one inwardly; and circumcision is that of the heart, in the spirit, and**

> not in the letter; whose praise is not
> of men, but of God."

GOD IS HEALING/SATAN IS KILLING (2Cor.3:3-11)

Thanks to God, the Holy Ghost has predisposed of the inherited traditional religious beliefs and customs, which kills the godly spirit in the hearts of men. According to the anointing teachings of the Holy Ghost, purification is the spiritual circumcision of the heart, and the circumcision of heart is so done through the grace of the Lord Jesus Christ. It is by the Lord's mercy and grace that we are saved. Purification is like all other magnificent gifts from GOD, it too comes by faith and not by man. (Roman 12:1-3)

Many people have made themselves Apostles of Christ under false doctrines' of men, and they use their liberty or freedom as a cloak of maliciousness; to perversely delude the minds of men into becoming judges or masters of the acts of mental enslavement. Unwisely they condemn themselves as judges of the law. Not only do they blaspheme against men; which is a forgivable sin, but they also blaspheme against the Holy Ghost; which is an unforgivable sin.

They fail to obtain the true understandings of how God compassionately shows mercy for all sinners that reprove the works of their fleshly deeds. Even after his only begotten son was born, lived, died and was resurrected on the third day to forgive and save all sinners who believe in the Son of God, unbelievers being blinded by the destituteness of the Lord's godly truth; falsely accuse the Lord God of being bias and partial in efforts to justify their own wrong. God loves all sinners alike, and he gives equally to all sinners the same message concerning them all having the power of authority and favor in God to faithfully believe on the Son of God. (Romans 12:3/14:11-13/Philippians2:9/James 3:14-18)

Although no man has the power to open the gates of Heaven or Hell, false doctrinaires cause men to deliberate judgments against the truth;

to cause one to deviate their intellect of heavenly wisdom for worldly knowledge. No man has powers over the Spirit of God to hold it back or to keep the Spirit in possession from another living soul. Neither does anyone have the power to withhold another person from receiving the Lord's gift of life, which is giving within the Spirit and by all spiritual things concerning the Lord's promise of life everlasting. (Romans 5:15-21/8:1-16) The vexation of men's hearts causes them to commend themselves as they worship under the fellowship of men and they revere to the earthy desire to entreat the acts of ill will upon those whom they unjustifiably judge. Since Satan cannot rebuke Satan, neither can the in-treatment of ill will and wickedness; deliver anyone who religiously practices at doing it.

> Ecclesiastes 8:8 "There is no man that hath power over the spirit to retain the spirit; neither hath he powers in the day of death: and there is no discharge (burden) in that war: neither shall wickedness deliver those that are given to it."

REFORMED/TRANSFORMED

Biblically, during the dawning of the New Testament also came a new commandment. Of course it didn't bring a new written commandment, but that Old Commandment which we've all heard from the beginning. "We should love one another," is the same dissembling we've heard from the beginning. The newness of it has been written in all our hearts, which things are true in him and in us. It's new because the darkness of it has past, and the true teachings now shine. (1 John 2:7-12/3:11/St. John 8)

The newness of the Old Commandment is to love; being written in the hearts of all men; delivers unto us all a new spiritual life. The newness of the spirit converts our old desires from the unwarrantable or unjustifiable dissembling of perverse teachings, which traditional religious supporters use to veil or cover the evils which are embedded in their own hearts. With their hearts darkened, ears deafened, and eyes blinded to the truth of the New Commandment false brethren persist to abide in the Old Law of Moses which indicates sinners are to be stoned to death. (Romans 6 & 7)

> **St. Matt.9:16 "No man putteth a piece of new cloth unto an old garment, for that which is put in to fill it up taketh from the garment, and the rent is made worse."**
> **St. Matt.9:17 "Neither do men put new wine into old bottles: else the bottles break, and the wine runneth out, and the bottles perish: but they put new wine into new bottles, and both are preserved."**

TRADITIONAL RELIGIOUS MARTYRS

The leader of the beguiled has replaced the physical stones of the earth for the spiritual stone know today as the Lord's Word of Truth. Satan was a liar in the beginning; he's a liar today, and shall be a liar even for generations to come. Jesus spoke saying, "Upon this Rock I build my Church, and the Gates of Hell shall not prevail against it." The Lord's Words don't lie, but when men per verses it, it's then turned into words of corruptness. (St. John 8:4-12/St. Matt.16:18) The good words and fair speeches of the beguiled perverse the Word of God by twisting the origin of it's meaning. It also twists the hearers' sense of understanding.

It causes them to justify the liar's wrongful acts of condemning one another, while publicly proclaiming them-selves to be the protectors of the Lord's ordained law. In a vengeful manner they lure others into supporting their traditional religious interests and beliefs. Vengefully, they thrive to work the works of their own bellies to satisfy their own earthy desires. Through the physical eye; they see the physical sins of their neighbors, and they rush in quickly toward the vehement feelings and words of condemnation to vigorously persecute and despise the sinners physically and mentally. As they and their followers justify this wrongful act, they believe they are soul winning for Jesus. Meanwhile, the souls of the sinners which they physically and mentally torture finds no peace within the comfortless state which the perverse disputing of men attempts to turn all sinners' hearts towards believing in.

The Comforter says that he loves all sinners and forgives all sins except for that one unforgivable sin. Then the liar and all his followers creeps in and per say that because of the physical sins of man; that the all merciful Lord God will not have any mercy, compassion, nor love for the sinners who commits sin (2Thessalonians 2:7-17). Not only do they judge man, but they also judge the Word of God. They also blaspheme against the Holy Ghost, but they are blinded to not see that their acts or deeds blaspheme against the Holy Ghost as they ignorantly judge the Word of God.

As a martyr of men's traditional religion, the followers of the liar believe that if anyone is condemned by their teachings that they are not doing the condemning, but it is the Father, the Son, And, the Holy Spirit whose words condemn the conscience of them. Therefore, the liar convinces his followers to believe that as they blaspheme against the Spirit of God, their works are approved of by God. As the Holy Spirit manifest the Heavenly Truth, which implies that the Word of God convicts man's conscience to save their souls, puts or places all followers of the liar to shame, because the manifested truth reveals that the Lord Words don't remove hope and condemn, but it does restore hope and save all believers in the Son of God. (St. John 8:1-9/St. Matt 7:1) The Lord didn't exclude any churches in the New Testament from receiving the Holy

Ghost, but he did forewarn, plea, and advised them to correct the errors of their ways. As an illustration Apostle Paul wrote the Book of Romans which discusses the Lord God's spiritual terms and accommodations. This article includes the specified limits and everything in between both the universality of sin and the specified limits and everything in between God's saving methods, to set them both apart for the purpose of saving all believers in the Son of God from their sin. This systematic article insists that everyone should recognize the spiritual rights of one's faith.

> **St. John3:19 "And this is the condemnation, that the light is come into the world, and men loved the darkness rather than light, because their deeds were evil."**

It is the Comforter who spiritually brings comfort to the spirit of all of us who believes in the Son of God in spite of the religious stoning of false teachers and the oppressors. The Spirit of Condemnation deprives us from receiving the righteously implied truth of The One True Gospel of Jesus Christ, and it causes us to live in doubt of our own love for the Lord as well as the Lord's love for us. It is the Spirit of Righteousness which spiritually identifies the Fruit of the Spirit of God for us to bear witness within ourselves. (Gal.5:22/Col.3:12). It also reveals to us the elect of God being apart of our godly deeds. In so doing, we as sinners ought to be able to look at our deeds and determine if the hands of the Lord God are apart of our actions. When we see that it is not, then by the power of God we are given the power to reprove our own deeds. In the mist of doing so, comes a spiritual sorrow and repentance follows.

> **2Cor.13:5 "Examine yourselves, whether ye be in the faith; prove**

your own selves. Know ye not your own selves, how that Jesus Christ is in you, except ye be reprobates?"

Galatians5:22 "But the fruit if the Spirit is love, joy, peace, longsuffering, gentleness, goodness, faith,"

Galatians5:23 "Meekness, temperance: against such there is no law."

Colossians3:12 "Put on therefore, as the elect of God, holy and beloved, bowels of mercies, kindness, humbleness, of mind, meekness, longsuffering;"

Colossians3:13 "Forbearing one another, and forgiving one another, if any man have a quarrel against any: even as Christ forgave you, so also do ye."

Colossians3:14 "And above all these things put on charity, which is the bond of perfectness."

Colossians3:15 "And let the peace of God rule in your hearts, to the which also ye are called in one body; and be ye thankful."

Like their Father, the children of Satan when they become loose in the world they will deceive many (Rev. 20). Satan's children use his knowledge of what thus saith the Lord thy God against us as if they have no sin (1John1:8-10). It's another ritual of his followers who establishes a religious practice in using the power of coercing to retain the spirit of man. This is their known way of putting forth the effort to dominate in the religious realm. They entrust or commend themselves amongst themselves for having or exhibiting themselves to having moral excellent virtues, while spiritually killing other sinners' faith in believing they are saved. The destructive works of the children of wrath takes away the spiritual hope (faith) from the oppressed sinners and their unsympathetic hearts thrives to have dominion over them. The hope in which they yearn to kill is that which is freely given to all men by grace through Jesus Christ (Ephesians 2:1-10). Using fair speeches and good words, Satan coerces these people to either be disobedient or an unbeliever unto death. He's happy with those who follow and uses his bullying stratagems in obeying his coerce ways to be as gods, because they help him to cause babes and elders of all ages to live in doubt.

> **St. John 3:18 "He that believe on him is not condemned: but he that believeth not is condemned already, because he hath not believed in the name of the only begotten Son of God."**

THEORETICAL CONCLUSION

The Fruit of the Spirit proves what is acceptable unto God for the people today, yesterday, and days yet to come. Therefore, men are required to work in the Spirit of Christ, which is the light of Righteousness and Truth, without concerning themselves with another man's matter or the matter of the world. The vexation of a person's heart causes them to condemn themselves in their faulty deeds of misjudging the consciences of one another by the sights of ones' physical appearance or sin. Jesus Christ walked a strait and narrow pathway which leads unto life everlasting, and all are required to follow him and keep his commandments. (1Cor.11:28-33) Nowhere, within the Holy Scriptures concerning the New Testament does it say that Jesus used the Word of God as a cloak of maliciousness or accused any man unto God. Therefore, self examine self first and compare your Spirit to the Fruit of the Spirit of Christ to verify unto yourself who you are really serving in Spirit and in Truth. (1John3:1-8/St.Matt.7:1-12) Some of you are so twisted up in the religious things which concern the world, to the point of not recognizing that the Spirit which has you judging and condemning others; is the same evil spirit which Christ made void to have no affect on those whom believes on him. As a symbolic comparison start considering this, "Each time you judge and condemn others you too are guilty of persecuting and re-hanging Christ up on the Cross."

Heb.5:14 "But strong meat belongeth to them that are of full age, even those who by reason of use have their senses exercised to discern both good and evil."(1Cor.2:14-16)
Eph.6:17 "And take the helmet of salvation, and the sword of the Spirit, which is the word of God:"

> Hebrews3:4 "For every house is built by some man; but he that built all things is God."
>
> 1Tim.6:2 "And they that have believing masters, let them not despise them, because they are brethren; but rather do them service, because they are faithful and beloved, partakers of the benefit. These things teach and exhort."(Col.4:1-7, Eph.6:21)
>
> 1Tim.6:3 "If any man teach otherwise, and consent not to the wholesome words, even the words of our Lord Jesus Christ, and to the doctrine which is according to godliness;"
>
> 1Tim.6:4 "He is proud knowing nothing, but doting about questions and strifes of words, whereof cometh envy, strife, railings, evil surmisings,"(1Tim.6:5-6/Titus 1:10-11/Phil 4:11)

Regardless of our religious make up or back ground, there's only One God for the whole world to serve (1Cor. 8:5-7). If the Lord's unchanging hands aren't seen in the deeds of one's heart, it's because the heart of that person have not yet received him. (1Peter2:16/Gal.5:13-14) Being ill willed and using the Lord's gift of liberty or freedom for or as a cloak of maliciousness isn't the work nor the will of God, but vengefully and despitefully certain men religiously uses the Word of God during their fair speeches in an inappropriate manner against one another as to defend their doubtful disputations of the truth. (1John1:5) Jesus Christ is the light of the world, and there's no darkness in the light of Christ. Satan, being more subtle or more harder to distinguish and understand than any other beast in the field which God has made, causes us much hindrance.(Gen.3:1)

2Corinthians11:13 "For such are false apostles, deceitful workers, transforming themselves into the apostles of Christ."

2Corinthians11:14 "And no marvel: for Satan himself is transformed into an angle of light."

2Corinthians11:15 "Therefore it is no great thing if his ministers also be transformed as the ministers of righteousness; whose end shall be according to their works."

Romans16:17 "Now I beseech you, brethren, mark them which cause divisions and offences contrary to the doctrine which ye have learned and avoid them."

Romans16:18 "For they that are such serve not our Lord Jesus Christ, but their own belly; and by good words and fair speeches deceive the hearts of the simple."

THE YOKE OF BONDAGE

As we continue following the true light, the Holy Spirit reveals or manifests the simplicities of Satan's teachings, which beguiles to deceive and to control the minds of many men by cunning means. Many are beguiled by vague promises made by the teachings of Satan. These false promises are used by Satan only to draw men's attention to become interested in his wiles and charm. Some of us whom maybe weak, lack confidence in the Word of Truth either because we are coerced by the beguiled or are mentally enslaved and physically discriminated against by the good words and fair speeches, which are befitting to the charming occasion of the adversary by false prophets.

(St. Matt.16:1-12/1Cor.5:5-13)False prophets use Satan's stratagem against the simple and weak to impose unprofitable meats and unbearable restrictions or limitations that are destitute of the truth within their own way of defining godliness. Their vain traditional religious philosophies and deceitful words place stumbling blocks of offences in the way of the simple and weak. These stumbling blocks symbolically represents the spots & blemishes, which are associated with the old leaven of malice and wickedness of the Pharisees and Sadducees' traditional religion(Exodus 13:1-10/Eph.5:1-5,Eph.6/Col3:1-5/2Peter2:12-13).

The opposition of false teaching against the Doctrine of Jesus Christ is to work towards confining, condemning, and retaining men's minds to always be in doubtful disputations of their own faith as well as the faith of others. Meanwhile, the God of Hope works to fill us all with all joy and peace, as we individually fight for our own salvation by fighting for our rights to obey God by believing that we may abound in hope, through the power of the Holy Ghost (Romans 15:13). Being under the teachings of the false apostles and false prophets is what kill the godly spirit within men, because their false teachings persuasively keep peoples under the old law as unbelievers of the powers of God. (Gal5:18/Rom14:13-19)

> Galatians5:8   "This   persuasion
> cometh not of him that calleth
> you."
> Galatians5:13 "For brethren, ye
> have been called unto liberty; only
> use not liberty for an occasion to
> the flesh, but by love serve one
> another."

THE SPIRIT OF CONDEMNATION

Beware of the Leaven, which modifies the Doctrine of the Pharisees and the Sadducees.   These Leavens conflicts and alters the New Commandment of the New Testament.   The liar's stumbling-blocks places insecurities upon the hearts of the simple/weak, and like a child molester, the adversary uses God's love and fear against God. This act is similar to how a child molester uses a child's love and fear of their parents against their parents. A parent's worst fear is that their child would be physically or mentally harmed by someone who their child reveres and trust who easily scares them into not telling. In most cases the physical abuse or sexual abuse is repeatedly done to a child who keeps it a secret.

> St. Matt.16:6 "Then Jesus said unto
> them, Take heed and beware of the
> leaven of the Pharisees and of the
> Sadducees."

For instance, the mental state of being empowered by a child's worst fears influences molesters to create an image of the child's worst fears in the form of a personal threat unto the child. In other words, they know a child could be coerced to do the opposite of what the parent wants them to do, which is the simple act of telling them if someone hurts them. Instead of telling their parents of the person or persons who are abusing them or causes them harm; they tend to remain silent, because they believe that their silence is what protects them from worse experiences. They frightfully believe that if they did break their silence, that their worst fears would come to pass. One of the worst fears of a child is to be held responsible for their parents' or another loved one's injury or death. During many child molesting cases, a child molester is commonly known to threaten their victims by saying they will harm or kill someone that they love, if ever they should tell. In some cases, the abused child is afraid of telling, because the victimizer convinces them to think that being abused is their entire fault and they are coerced to think that they'll get into more trouble with their parents.

These examples also emotionally and spiritually describe how false prophets of every sort of ministry misuse the gift of God's love as a cloak of maliciousness against those who are weak in the spirit. This mental strategy of false ministering is a method of Satan's, and it kills two birds with one stone. It causes people to become unbelievers and blasphemers at the same time. For instance, the ministers who are subconsciously teaching people to hate and despise the weak are in danger for blaspheming against the Holy Ghost. They imprudently use the Word of God to spread the news of their own bellies, which confuses the simple and weak to be wicked people, who aren't worthy to be spared by God. For centuries Satan has been raping God's children of their life source (known as HOPE/FAITH) by causing them to have an ungodly fear of God. What makes one's fear of God ungodly is when Satan's lies trick an individual or a group of persons into believing that they are unloved by God.

The purpose of Satan's methods is to remove hope and faith from the hearts and minds of as many as he can, because he knows that a nonbeliever of the Word of God will not receive the Kingdom of Heaven. He's the author of confusion and his stratagem is to kill God's children with their love for God. Therefore, after being convinced of Satan's lies, some of those who are weakened in spirit, thinks it's normal to confusedly continue to linger in the congregational houses that are built by men's traditional religious philosophies and vain deceits under the dictatorship of the false prophets and false apostles whom receive worldly glory in their weak flesh. When making, an attempt to fit in, the weak and the simple finds themselves feeling split into two halves under false teachings, because that which they are being taught doesn't co-aside with the anointing teachings of the Spirit of God, which lives within their hearts.

The false prophets and false apostles commend themselves to be more virtuously closer to God than those who are weakened in spirit. In many instances they use condemning words and vain religious philosophies to lift themselves up, by putting down the simple and weak. The simple and weak babes who are in Christ need to be aware of the existence of these man-made churches, which supports and preach vehement words of condemnation, which indirectly or directly works with the intent to cast the devil out of their congregation by casting out certain sinners from their congregation. They do so because they think that the Lord has instructed them to do so.

Meanwhile, some who are weak but not wicked decides to leave these congregational houses, because they are coerced to believe that their presents and their worship are in vain. After being marked with doubtful disputations, they ask themselves why they should serve a God whose purpose of creating them is only to send them to Hell. A fool for Christ can easily recognize that God's purpose of creating every living soul aren't to send them to hell, but many who'd rather be fools for men are fooled by man and are coerced to believe in Satan's lies. (Heb.3:8-19) Many of them hardened their hearts as a result.

Some babes hearts are hardened to the point of them straying away from believing on God and they also stray away from the affiliations of all religions, because they assume that all denominations supports the preaching and teaching of the same traditional beliefs in areas where the spirit of condemnation is concerned. The weak often ask the Lord in prayer; "Why did you create me to send me to hell?", because they've been taught to believe that Hell is what God has in stores for them upon the day of their physical death or upon Judgment Day. They inwardly lack hope/faith of being saved, as the spirits of condemnation teach them that they are hell-bound and that the Lord hates them.

The conscience of the weak inwardly loves God and desires to receive love from God, but they are tricked into not believing that they have hope of that ever happening. Satan knows they still have hope and he knows that they love God; because God first loved them. Therefore, the wile of Satan's method continues to coerce people to believe in his lying spirits of condemnation. For as many as he can mentally and spiritually condemn, happy is he.(Gal.5:5/6:13) Satan knows that an unbeliever shall not enter the Kingdom of Heaven, and he uses this knowledge to drive his followers to use perverse words to drive many into unbelief.

PERVERSE DISPUTING

> 1Cor.9:22 "To the weak I became I as weak, that I might gain the weak: I am made all things to all men, that I might by all means save some."
> 1Cor.9:23 "And this I do for the gospel's sake, that I might be partaker thereof with you."
> Hebrews12:1 "Wherefore seeing we also are compassed about with so great a cloud of witnesses, let us lay aside every weight, and the sin which doth so easily beset us, and let us run with patience the race that is set before us,"
> 1Cor.9:24 "Know ye not that they which run in a race run all, but one

receiveth the prize? So run, that ye may obtain."

Philippians3:14 "I press towards the mark for the prize of the high calling of God in Christ Jesus."

1Cor.9:25 "And every man that striveth for the mastery is temperate in all things. Now they do it to obtain a corruptible crown; but we an incorruptible."

1Cor.9:26 "I therefore so run, not as uncertainly; so fight I, not as one that beateth the air:"

1Cor.9:27 "But I keep under my body, and bring it into subjection: lest that by any means, when I have preached to others, I myself should be a castaway."

1Cor.12:18 "But now hath God set the members every one of them in the body, as it hath pleased him."

1Cor.12:20 "But now are they many members, yet but one body."

1Cor.12:23 "And those members of the body, which we think to be less honourable, upon these we bestow more abundant honour; and our uncomely parts have more abundant comeliness."

1Cor.12:24 "For our comely parts have no need: but God hath tempered the body together, having given more abundant honour to that part which lacked:"

1Cor.12:25 "That there should be no schism (split) in the body; but that

the members should have the same
care one for another."

False teachers are desirers of vain glory. They are debtors to do the whole law and entangle themselves with the yoke of bondage, which is a curse. They idolize religious doctrines and commandments of men, and they cunningly persuade the weak to do things which they themselves CANNOT do. False teachers are afraid that they themselves should suffer persecution, harassment, or annoyance by their continual traditional religious teachings. Therefore, when they speak of the Word of GOD, they are seduced to place that same fear onto the hearts of the simple and the weak. Their vain efforts during their desperate attempt; works to constrain, confine, imprison, and condemn people by using the Lord's name in vain, because the intent of their spirit is to weaken the faith of the simple and weak babes of Christ by trying to keep them from believing that they too are saved by the Blood of Jesus. The works of their fleshly efforts of constraining the simple is driven by Satan's stratagem, which he used on Adam and Eve to lure them to be overly desirous to be like God, knowing good and evil.(1Cor.15:21-22)

1Cor.15:33 "Be not deceived: evil communications corrupt good manners." (Morals)

1Cor.15:34 "Awake to righteousness, and sin not; for some have not the knowledge of God: I speak this to your shame." (1Cor.15:35-58)

Satan is also using the false teachers' selfish zeal against them, to lead their hearts to be overly zealous in their pursuit to have a relationship with the Lord. Selfishly, they desire to have others kicked out of God's assembly and merciful grace, just like the carnal and worldly vexed hearted and partially biased manmade laws of the land unfairly kicks people out of its protection. The simple hearted may become weakened in faith by these false teachers, but the anointing power of The Holy Ghost teaches the simple and the weak to not harden their hearts and to remain alive and in love with the Lord Jesus Christ. (Gal.5 & 6) Therefore, by mercy and grace through faith, they still are comforted with the Spirit of Hope, in hopes of them receiving the Lord's promise of everlasting life.

> **Romans15:1 "We then that are strong ought to bear the infirmities of the weak, and not to please ourselves."**

The responsibility of the strong which are spiritual minded, is to restore the faith of the weak in the spirit of meekness. This is ought be done without being desirous of vain glory, provoking one another, or envying one another as one considers fulfilling the Law of Christ.(Gal.5:6) The Law of Christ is fulfilled in one word ...LOVE.

Unlike a scorner; the simple babes desires heavenly wisdom, and are willing to go unto the wise to receive it. Unfortunately, some are constrained or entangled like a bug in a spider's web that is set by false prophets. (1John 4:1) Seducers, Gain Sayers, idolaters, men pleasers, false accusers, false witnesses, deceivers, despisers, persecutors, judges, and ungodly subverters etc. are all like leeches. They feed on the simple by draining faith or the substance of hope from their hearts.

James1:5 "If any of you lack wisdom, let him ask of God, that giveth to all men liberally, and upbraideth not; and it shall be given him."

1John2:26 "These things have I written unto you concerning them that seduce you."

1John2:27 "But the anointing which ye have received of him abideth in you, and ye need not that any man teach you: but as the same anointing teacheth you all things, and is truth, and is no lie, and even as it hath taught you, ye shall abide in him."

FROWARD SPEECHES OF THE WICKED ARE LIES AGAINST THE TRUTH

The hearts of the false prophets and false apostles are all on one accord with the way in which they choose to use perverse words of vehement condemnation. The sequence of their teachings mostly surrounds the perverse disputing of men's traditional religious ideas, which are supported by the carnally minded beliefs in practicing the vain power of coercing. Some are more discreet than others, but the coercions of their teachings are clearly individually distinctive from the teachings of the Holy Ghost. (Act 20:30)

1John4:5 "They are of the world: therefore speak they of the world, and the world hearth them."

1John4:6 "We are of God: he that knoweth God heareth us; he that is not of God heareth not us. Hereby know we the spirit of truth, and the spirit of error."

1John5:5 "Who is he that over cometh the world, but he that believeth that Jesus is the Son of God?"

1John5:10 "He that believeth on the Son of God hath the witness in himself: he that believeth not God hath made him a liar; because he believeth not the record that God gave of his Son."{St. John5:11-12, 8:17-18}

St. John3:17 "For God sent not his Son into the world to condemn the world; but that the world through him might be saved."

Every man shall bear his own burden, and every one of us shall give an account of our individual selves to God upon Judgment Day (Romans14:12-14/Gal.6:5-7). The imprudent acts of placing stumbling blocks in the way of another to insinuate in a subtle and devious manner that someone is holier than someone else is absurd, and it does not advantage the one over another. The persons who place this type of stumbling block in the way of another imply falsely that one has superiority in the eyes of the Lord in hopes of producing a favorable impression or effect on a particular traditional religious outlook or a particular traditional religious belief. Therefore, we all should comfort and edify one of another as the Lord requires, knowing that we all have faults, because this deed represents a descriptive act of godly love. As we all shall one day stand before the judgment seat of Christ, we individually will receive the things done in the body, according to that we have done during our life time, whether it be good or bad

(2Cor.5:10). Therefore, we all ought to keep this in mind as we teach and preach onto the weak, because it's also written that we also shall give in account of the things we say. Whether we speak the Word of Truth, which convicts and restore hope to the faith of our brethren's spirit as the Holy Ghost teaches us to do, or speak words of falseness, which condemns our brethren, and cause confusions which brings doubt to our brethren's faith on the Lord's ability to save them.

St. Matt.12:36 "But I say unto you, That every idle word that men shall speak, they shall give account thereof in the day of judgment."

St. Matt.12:37 "For by thy words thou shalt be justified, and by thy words thy shalt be condemned."

St. Matt.7:15 "Beware of false prophets, which come to you in sheeps clothing, but inwardly they are ravening wolves."

St. Matt.7:16 "Ye shall know them by their fruits. Do men gather grapes of thorns, or figs of thistles?"

St. Matt.7:18 "A good tree cannot bring forth evil fruit, neither can a corrupt tree bring forth good fruit."(St. Matthew.7: 19-22/St. John15:1-11)

St. Matt.7:23 "And then will I profess unto them, I never knew you: depart from me, ye that work iniquity."

THEORETICAL CONCLUSION

Denominational religions and Non-Denominational religions don't make the people, but the people make the religion. Since there's only One God for all to serve, the people of all sorts of denominations and non-denominations are being urged by the Anointed One through the scriptures of the Holy Bible to take heed. Be strong for the weak and be aware of the will of God, as a minister of God, and teach all people to have and to hold onto the faith in the Deliverer.

> **Romans13:11 "And that, knowing the time, that Now it is high time to awake out of sleep: for now is our salvation nearer than when we believed."**

Let us cast off the works of darkness, and put on the armor of light. All things that are reproved first are made manifest or made obvious by the light to be dead works of the flesh. Therefore, be renewed in the spirit of the mind, and make no further provision or preparation for the flesh to fulfill the lusts there of {Rom.13/St John3:19-21/Eph.5:11-17}. The lust of the flesh goes beyond fornication and adultery. In fact, any thing which we may idolize whether it's money, control of power, envy, strife, and hatred are also the dead works of the flesh. If our deeds lead us to either devour ourselves or someone else in the process of working on working out our own Salvation, then we must sort out our priorities in the manner of reproving our own deeds so that we won't be of a curse of ourselves.

CHAPTER 17 A BIBLICAL ANAYLIZED THEORETICAL CONCLUSION OF DISCERNING PERCEPTIVE

These are for Self-Examinations:

> Romans 3:27 "Where is boasting then? It is excluded. By what law? of works? Nay: but by the law of faith."
>
> Acts 13:35 "Wherefore he saith also in another psalm, Thou shalt not suffer thine Holy One to see corruption."
>
> Acts 13:36 "For David, after he had served his own generation by the will of God, fell on sleep, and was laid unto his fathers, and saw corruption:"
>
> Acts 13:37 "But he whom God raised again, saw no corruption."
>
> Acts 13:38 "Be it known unto you therefore, men and brethren, that through this man is preached unto you the forgiveness of sins:"
>
> Acts 13:39 "And by him all that believe are justified from all things, from which ye could not be justified by the law of Moses."
>
> Romans 3:28 "Therefore we conclude that a man is justified by faith without the deeds of the law."
>
> Acts 16:5 "And so were the churches established in the faith, and increased in number daily."(Acts 16:1-3)
>
> Romans 3:29 "Is he the God of the Jews only? is he not also of the Gentiles? Yes, of the Gentiles also:"
>
> Romans 3:30 "Seeing it is one God, which shall justify the circumcision by faith, and uncircumcision through faith."
>
> 1 Corinthians 7:18 "Is any man called being circumcised? Let him not become uncircumcised. Is any called in uncircumcision? Let him not be circumcised."
>
> 1 Corinthians 7:19 "Circumcision is nothing, and uncircumcision is nothing, but the keeping of the commandments of God."
>
> 1 Corinthians 7:20 "Let every man abide in the same calling wherein he was called."

Romans 3:31 "Do we then make void the law through faith? God forbid: yea, we establish the law."

Romans 8:3 "For what the law could not do, in that it was weak through the flesh, God sending his own Son in the likeness of sinful flesh, and for sin, condemned sin in the flesh:"

Romans 8:4 "That the righteousness of the law might be fulfilled in us, who walk not after the flesh, but after the Spirit."

Gal.5:13 "For brethren, ye have been called unto (_freedom_) liberty; only use not (_freedom_) liberty for an occasion to the flesh, but by love serve one another."

Gal.5:14 "For all the law is fulfilled in one word, even as this; Thou shalt love thy neighbour as thyself."

Gal.5:15 "But if ye bite and devour one another, take heed that ye be not consumed one of another."

Gal.5:16 "This I say then, Walk in the Spirit, and ye shall not fulfil the lust of the flesh."

Gal.5:17 "For the flesh lusteth against the Spirit, and the Spirit against the flesh: and these things are contrary the one to the other: so that ye cannot do the things that ye would."(Rom 7)

Gal.5:18 "But if ye be led of the Spirit, ye are not under the law."(Rom.6:14)

Gal.5:7 "Ye did run well; who did hinder you that ye should not obey the truth?"

Gal.5:8 "This persuasion cometh not of him that calleth you."(Gal. 1:6)

Gal.6:7 "Be not deceived; God is not mocked: for whatsoever a man soweth, that shall he also reap."

Gal. 6:8 "For he that soweth to his flesh shall of the flesh reap corruption; but he that soweth to the Spirit shall of the Spirit reap life everlasting."(Hos.8:7)

May God Bless the Hears and Doers of his Word! AMEN!

CHAPTER 18 GOD GIVES A GLORIOUS REDEMPTION UNTO SISTER GLORY SANDERS THOMPSON

ONE LIFE

Sister Glory has a message for those who may believe that it is impossible for a wretch like her to be saved by the Blood of Jesus. After being redeemed, Sister Glory says, "You all may need to know that it was never impossible, but it was always inevitable; concerning the prevailing will and good pleasures of Jesus Christ the redeemer."

The major turn around of her spiritual journey started in December 2004, when the Lord sent Sister Glory Sanders Thompson into the world of Milwaukee WI where she encountered a personal contact with the Berean Family Worship Center (BFWC). Her first personal contact with the BFWC was with a certified daycare provider whose sure name was Vanessa. Within the godly foundation of their inevitable meeting resided a spiritual connection between the two.

Before moving from Abbeville, MS to Milwaukee, WI, she was under the care of a physician out of Memphis, TN. This physician verbally informed her after he performed a last resort type of surgery unto her lower back L-5 lumber that she wouldn't be physically able to do certain simple things, like run, jump, or lay flat on her back again. Like a butcher, her physician at the clinic; cut up her ruptured L-5, this presumably was the largest disc that held all of her bodyweight and made it the smallest. For the rest of her life she is expected to live in pain. Of course henceforth comes the pain, comes also pain medication. Unfortunately, after a long term of taking pain medication; other health issues and side affects later became another major factor of her life (KIDNEY DEFICIENCY in 2008).

Approximately in May of 2005 she received healing against the pain from her back surgery at the Berean Family Worship Center. This was the beginning era of a new life and the dawn of a new day for Sister Glory. She had spent the length of many years of her life traveling on an ordained spiritual journey in search of the Holy Truth, and the Holy Ghost led her to praise the Lord at the BFWC. She described her first visit at the Berean Family Worship Center as an amazing spiritual adventure. Prior to her first encounter with the BFWC, she prayed and asked the Lord to help her to find a Church Home where the true Gospel of Jesus Christ was taught in Milwaukee, WI. Not too long afterwards, the BFWC became the home which she had longed for. Approximately around the month of March in A.D. 2005, she was enlisted as a new member of the (BFWC) Berean Family Worship Center under the leadership of Pastor Dr. Walter Henderson III.

The story unfolds

One day she was invited to a prescheduled women's retreat at the BFWC. She expected the retreat to consist of a group of educated women who would use their knowledge to assist single parent mothers, with food, shelter, and cloths, but she wasn't expecting to witness herself personally experiencing a healing by the Holy Ghost power. Within this retreat the young female leaders and the elder ladies went to praising the Lord. After reciting a few scriptures out of the King James Version of the Holy Bible Text, they went into a zone of praying and laying hands. It all started when one of the ladies asked those who wanted prayer to stand and verbally report what exactly it was that they individually desired for them to pray for. When it was Sister Glory's turn to answer, she was a little shy and simply stated that she believed the Lord knew all about her troubles and he knew her heart. She explained to them that she entrusted herself totally in the Lord to give them utterance of what to pray for. The first Lady Evangelist Joycelyn Pernell Henderson called Sister Glory to the front of the room, and a young lady within the ministry held her hands and began to pray unto God. The lady started off her prayer to say unto God, that he was an all powerful and all knowing God whom knew all about her troubles. She continued on to pray that the Lord would provide her with what she was in need of, and suddenly Sister Glory past-out of consciousness. When she woke up, she was laying flat on her back; her right leg was pinned underneath her buttock.

With the Holy Ghost over my body, said Sister Glory; my eye ducts were filling with tears and flowed like a river of water without me crying. As she reminisce of what she could recollect about this holy moment, she characterized her experience to have felt like death was upon her.

"I remember not being able to breathe freely. As I mentally regained consciousness of my surrounding position, I earnestly thought of the back pain which oddly enough didn't exist at the time. Simultaneously, my leg without the help of anyone was pulled from underneath my body. Flat on my back phenomenally I laid there pain free. Although it wasn't time-consuming, to me the praying and lying of hands felt like it took forever. Immediately after gaining consciousness I simply wanted to get up, but I couldn't. As the prayers of the Christian women persisted, with every ounce of strength of my very being; I tried to yell three words, "I-CAN'T-BREATHE!", but out came a great whisper instead of a loud shout. I wanted them to stop praying and call 911, because I couldn't freely breathe. It was like I was having an anxiety attack. The more I tried to get up, the more impaired my breathing got. I just rested their on the floor uncompromisingly. In the back of my mind, I thought to myself, that I had reached the end of the rope. I wanted them to see that I was suffering from some sort of medical emergency, but without the energy or strength to move; I just laid there. I felt like I was suffocating. I couldn't get enough air into my lungs."

"This was the first time in my whole life that I had personally experienced the Power of the Holy Ghost like this. Up to this point, I was taught to believe that the jumping and shouting which I witnessed others doing was apart of a hoax. During my life time I had witnessed some of the biggest unconverted hypocrites doing it in church. They would jump scream and shout on Sunday morning in church and later that same day would be out acting a fool and raising hell. During my early maturity stage in the One True Gospel of Jesus Christ, I was led by the Spirit of God to learn that the Holy Ghost Power is built upon Heavenly knowledge; consecrated with faith on the Power of God and is set apart from the world. In other words I knew that it sanctifies a person in part, while cleansing their hearts and minds, which is a holy gift of knowledge. With all that which I knew, it wasn't completely clear to me to understand exactly what the full meaning of such knowledge consisted of. It wasn't until that moment that I realized that everything in which I wasn't a believer of, concerning the Word of God; I like many other hypocrites I had became a hypocrite and a judge of the Word of God. ***God is not done with me yet!***

At the time it was hard for me to think that I was going through a spiritual experience when I past out of consciousness at the BFWC, because every religion which I've abandoned, seductively beguiled me to disbelieve that the Holy Ghost power would cause a person to jump up and down, speak in tongue, or pass out of consciousness. The reason why I've renounced such blasphemous religious beliefs at that point of time is because I have become a living witness to the Power of the Holy Ghost concerning these very factors.

Speaking in tongue didn't come until 2years later in 2007 in the privacy of my own home during a private prayer, and even then it wasn't something that I could make my tongue control. Thus so far, I have not ever spoken in tongue in the public. When I did speak in tongue it wasn't an enforced deliberate act as many are disloyal to the Lord's truth to portray, but it was a spiritual reaction that caught me by surprise. To the same token, the act of passing out of consciousness while praising the Lord was something I had not ever experienced until this day at the BFWC women's retreat.

While in distress due to a desperate need of air, I felt like I had used my last breath to say "I can't breathe." I was falling in and out of consciousness, and the sound of the ladies praying got louder and the laying of hands continued. The sense of death felt nearer and nearer, and subconsciously I thought to myself that I was experiencing a medical emergency.

I wanted them to stop what I had misjudged to be the senseless acts of a ceremonial agenda, but I had neither the breath nor the strength to say another word. Predictably I thought about my life and death simultaneously. As I saw my life flash before my very eyes, I went into a silent prayer unto God and asked the Lord to give me the strength to speak loudly and give the women the ability to hear my voice saying, "Stop I can't breathe." Once again with all of my might I whispered, "I-CAN'T-BREATHE." The praying didn't stop, in fact it got louder and the laying of the hands on my head and body felt heavier.

Then I heard a soft gentle voice coming through the ladies' loud thunderous uncoordinated praying. The voice said, "Your not sick baby! Let go and Let God! Let go and say yes to Jesus!" With water running like a river from my eyes, I tried to open them wide to see if I could find a face to fit the voice, but I couldn't see anything through my tears except the glare of light, which were coming from the light fixtures from the loft top of the ceiling. Through the stream of tears rolling from my eyes, the light appeared to resemble the inside of a glassy diamond. The appearances of the images which I saw through the tears were sparkling and blurry.

Although I had desired my whole life to understand the power of the Holy Ghost, within all that was going on all around and about me; I was hindered by the ungodly spirit of doubt and I disbelieved that the Holy Ghost was upon me at that very moment. I believed I was sick and under the extreme circumstances, that was the only thing that made sense to me. After evaluating my situation, I prayed again unto the Lord. My last prayer was more like a negotiation. I said unto him, "Lord, if I say yes as the voice instructed; maybe these women will get up off of me and recognize that we are engaged in a medical emergency situation, and maybe they then will go call 911". At the end of my thoughts an inner voice entered my spiritual conscience and said unto me, "That's the wrong reason to say, (Yes)." Meanwhile, the soft voice consistently and repetitiously said, "YOU'RE NOT SICK BABY. LET GO AND LET GOD, JUST SAY YES TO JESUS. Let GO AND SAY YES TO JESUS."

The more I inwardly fought against the possibility of this being a real supernatural experience; I had the worst of a time trying to breathe. When my inward consciousness finally accepted a different truth of my reality, I received a different theoretical conclusion of my situation and said yes to Jesus for righteous reasons, but I didn't have enough strength to breathe more air into my lungs to actually physically say the words out loud. Therefore, within my inner Spirit; I repeatedly said YES! YES! YES! At that very moment, like a drowning swimmer coming up for air out of water, God had refilled my lungs and out loud I yelled the words "YES!" repeatedly.

Soon afterwards, the Lord blessed me with a security job at Potawatomi Bingo Casino in Milwaukee WI, which is where I resided until the Anoint One commanded for me to return to my birth home in Mississippi. I had already received verification from the Lord that he wanted me to return home and spiritually help my hometown peoples to spiritually understand the wonderful Power of God, but at the time I didn't want to completely let go of the worldly lifestyle and the worldly people which I had grown to know and love. As a security officer at Potawatomi Bingo Casino I didn't fully understand the holy things which were transpiring in my new life. Some may say I was running from the Lord, but in reality I was caught by the Lord.

In other words; I was going through a spiritual phase and the Lord had to humble me to spiritually change, because that was something that I as one of his own asked him to do for me. Seeing that I couldn't humble myself without his help, the Lord gave unto me a painful escape route out of my worldly life style. (St.Matt.6:13/2Peter2:9)In so doing, the Lord used the love which tempted me in the world, to deliver me out. Within my deliverance came also a mixture of great pain and joy simultaneously, which lacked worldly sorrows or shame. These various emotions were balanced out by the gifts of God's love, mercy, and grace. They provided relevance in my continuous reliance on him; by keeping me deeply rooted in his Word. My faith on the Lord comes in the form of me believing on the substance of the unseen things that are close to my heart, with Jesus Christ being the head thereof. The unseen things which I hope for are the Lord's heavenly gifts of knowledge which helps me to receive heavenly gifts like peace, joy, love, **Salvation** and **Redemption**. These gifts were not given to me to keep concealed all to myself, but it was given unto me to share with all others as well.

After sharing the Lord's gifts with one of her security supervisors at Potawatomi Bingo Casino and many other co-workers and strangers alike, more people became drawn to her. Some accepted the fullness of the Lord's Power working in her that which was good and loved her. The reactions of others appeared too had became jealous as if they were over taken by the evil spirit of hatred against her. She assumed that they were contrary against her, because she thought they feared what they couldn't understand about her. Through the jealousy of a few of her co-workers, came also the wrath of detestation against her. It was understandable to her of why certain associates of hers slowly started to fade away when most of her conversations with them had stopped being full of meaningless words and were solely on the Lord.

Before she gained the spiritual insight of what exactly God wanted her to do and say unto a great multitude of people concerning his love, she started to put her full focus on writing Discerning Perceptive. The start of the book was written things in which the Lord started to reveal unto her. At first she started writing down unanswered questions that she personally asked the Lord to help her to understand. These questions concerned the intent of the heart and mind of God's chosen apostles that wrote the epistles of Jesus Christ, and later were made available as an answer unto her life's purpose; by the anointed teachings of the Holy Ghost.

After being told so many times that she was an angle of God by people who thought that she was heavenly sent unto them; she became more desirous to find and to know the Holy Truth concerning the Lord's purpose for her life. It was extremely hard for any of them to convince her to believe that she was a child of God, because many traditional religious leaders and false teachers whom she trusted for many years of her life; convinced her to believe the total opposite. They convinced her to view God as a monstrous God, whom would have no mercy on her life.

For many years she thought that the God which created the Heavens and the earth had an insensitive sense of view of her, because her mind was deluded by false teachers to think that he created her with the intent to send her to Hell. She was setup by the religious designers of the world to fail at serving her true purpose as a servant of God. Her mind was abusively placed in a damned state of being. The measure of her faith was placed in an unreasonable position to think that she was damned if she did right and she was damned if she did wrong. Win, loose, or draw; the religious dictators of her life had deceived her so well that she automatically believed that they were always classified by the vote of a majority to be right and being of the least by number she figured she would always be wrong. The seed of condemnation was planted early into her spirit and gave her an ungodly feeling of shame, but for some reason unknown she kept showing up at the doorstep of those worship houses anyway. It was almost like she enjoyed being targeted, but in reality she desired to love the Lord and wanted to receive love from the Lord.

After the Anointed had taught her what man could not concerning the passion of Christ, the moment of truth came when her eyes were opened to know good and evil. She gained the sight to see herself being what strangers whom followed the path of Christ were saying that they saw in her. No longer was she ashamed to stand bold on the Word of God and all of his Righteousness and Truth. Due to worldly doubts and her sinful lusts for the world, she like many others whom came across that same path in life; feared what she didn't understand. "Why did you choose me Lord", became her makeup. She feared what others would say about her and against her, but she feared the Lord more.

As she started believing on the Lord's calling on her life; she feared loosing her friendship with the world and her sanity was jeopardized, but she never lost her mind to the things of the world. "I'd rather be a fool for the Lord than to be a fool for man," became her motivational motto. Although she didn't fully understand what was going on with herself at that present time nor did she understand what was to become of her in the near future, she completely surrendered herself unto the Son of God.

MAY GOD BLESS THE HEARERS AND DOERS OF HIS WORDS, AMEN!

For more information of the Berean Family Worship Center in Milwaukee, WI; go to www.bereanfwc.org **(© 1985-2010 for further and more in depth details.**

> Proverbs11:30 "The fruit of righteousness is a tree of life; and he that winneth souls is wise."
> Proverbs14:25 "A true witness delivereth souls: but a deceitful witness speaketh lies."
> Proverbs14:26 "In the fear of the LORD is strong confidence: and his children shall have a place of refuge."
> Proverbs14:27 "The fear of the LORD is a foundation of life, to depart from the snares of death."

In September 2007 while working as a security surveillance officer at Potawatomi Bingo Casino in Milwaukee, WI; Sister Glory was inevitably called to commune and empathize with many patrons and a few co-workers including two of her male security supervisors. One of them invited her to a Church Revival at The Greater New Birth Church located near downtown Milwaukee, WI. Upon her arrival on the first night, the subject of the Pastorate's sermon included a variety of testimonial declarative statements which she believes was intended to satisfy the curiosity of all visitors and members who may question the way a person praise God. That night she heard a lady motivational guest speaker whom came in from the South to share her strong inspiring testimony with The Greater New Birth congregation. The guest speaker lifted up her beautiful unique heavenly voice of song and praise. Through her own personal testimony, she was enabled to spiritually sing a touching song which edified Christ. There was nothing neither duplicated nor copied concerning the heavenly unique voice of this lady. The testimonial message within her compassionate song of praise did belong to Christ. The story that lies behind her praise was partially given within her song of praise. The words of her song edifies all whom has an ear to hear how the good Lord blesses all whom believes on him, especially those whom at some point or another can identify with how a person may feel after an experience of being demoralized, persecuted, and discouraged.

While listening to the guest speaker, the Lord ordained Sister Glory immediately to discern that the Spirit of the Lord ordained for her to tell the guest speaker, **"To tell the story that lies behind her praise."** Without knowing or understanding exactly what the message personally meant; Sister Glory knew that the Lord was testing her faith. She immediately thought the message was self-explanatory, but she previously had learned to stop assuming to know anything. In fear of being called crazy by her friends and co-workers, who also sat in the pews; she was greatly discouraged on many accounts to step out on faith and tell the guest speaker to tell the story that lies behind her praise.

Sister Glory was brought up in a domineering religious environment, which exposed her to several different religious outlooks of life. She detected how some people subverts and undermines certain messages from different scriptures of the King James Version of the Holy Bible. Since she once was coerced to waver like a leaf in the wind concerning her own destiny, it was very difficult for her to earnestly believe that she was chosen by God to exhort and encourage people to believe on the Power of God. The disfigured mental state of her religious outlooks on life almost totally spoiled her spiritually and consumed her in sin, because she had lived for so long under the dictatorship of vain religious philosophies and words of deceits. Although she had truly witnessed herself being prophesied too by strangers who oftentimes went out from among her and told others that she had also prophesied unto them, she yet lived in the shadows of doubt; fearing what she didn't understand.

The test of her faith was a matter of her questioning herself to either believe or disbelieve that the purpose of her life consisted of her trying to awaken religious enthusiasm as an Evangelist. She would be in awe after each time she stepped out on faith and say things to people which the Lord placed in her heart and mind to say. She made sense out of the unknown by thinking that it was simply coincidental that some of her conversations and speeches which were grounded on the Word of God actually brought Revelation to the lives of others as some point or another. Sometimes she would be hindered to take the initiative to step out on faith and deliver a message which comes unto her as a light bulb of an idea, because the inspiring insight sometimes is farfetched beyond her limited imagination.

On this Holy Revival night, she faced similar hindrances and wondered should she simply ignore what the Lord placed into her heart to say to the motivational guest speaker at the Greater New Birth Church or continue on as a nonbeliever. While deciding which way she ought to go, the Lord brought to her conscious mind of the many different righteous outcomes which he allowed her to witness the occurrences thereof prior to this glorious night; concerning her sharing her sympathetic insights of the inspiring Word of God. She immediately was able to build up her faith on the power of the Lord. After remembering how many times she mysteriously actually was spiritually blessed by God to use the Word to speak revelation unto the lives of others and awaken their religious enthusiasm, she once again offering her spiritual conscience unto the Lord as a spiritual sacrifice and allow the Lord to use her to do of his will and deliver the Word as a servant.

SHE REMEMBERED MYSTERIOUSLY SPEAKING REVELATION

One Sunday morning at the BFWC in Milwaukee, WI before church service began; an unknown elderly lady approached sitting in the pew and stated to her that she was told by a male member of the congregation that she had prophesied to him at a corner store near 35th and Wells Street. Sister Glory at the time was very fragile in faith, but was still yet properly being molded by God. She had a weak side which incapacitated her faith and caused her to waver in unbelief, because of certain irreligious traditional teachings, which had deluded her understandings of the Word of God. Therefore, she was incapable at the time to accept the Power of God working in her and denied prophesying to any man on 35th and Wells.

The lady went and found another lady who also witnessed the man saying the same thing. Again Sister Glory denied doing so. She honestly thought that the ladies had mistaken her identity with someone else whom may have prophesied to the man whom they spoke of. They both stuck with their story and repeatedly said, "HE SAID IT WAS YOU!" Sister Glory kindly explained to the ladies that she loved to talk about the Lord and she put great emphasis on how she talks about the Lord everywhere she goes, but she implied to them both that she couldn't recollect prophesying to anyone at the corner store on 35th and Wells.

The corner store on 35th and Wells Street was a common store that she visited in a rough part of the Downtown area of Milwaukee, but she wasn't aware at the time; of how the powerful Word of God was affecting the people whom she spoke with. She went on to explain to both ladies why she thought the man may had contemplated that she prophesied to him. Within her explanation she explained with much emphasis, that she likes sharing personal testimonial things and how she loves to talk about things which she has heard of concerning the Gospel of Jesus Christ with anyone who also loves the Lord enough to talk about how Good God is!. The logic of her explanation conclusively was in reference with the Word of God and neither of them reproached her thereafter. About a month later; the man whom they had mentioned unto her, excitedly approached her at that same said corner store. He went in debt to farther enlighten Sister Glory of how what she had said to him had a spiritual affect on him. Sister Glory very politely told him the same thing which she told the two ladies concerning her not being a prophet and departed from him.

The Lord brought back to her remembrance of many situations like this one, which repetitiously was happening long before she was invited to the Greater New Birth Church. Upon her arriving to the Greater New Birth Church she mentally contemplated on all kinds of spiritual things, which she had already encountered or experienced and her very thoughts encouraged her to believe that the Lord had a Divine calling on her life.

Although her conviction was powerful, she strongly feared what she didn't understand. With all of her flaws, she couldn't understand why God chose her. The fears of regretting to do the works of the Lord, straight-way arrived and almost took complete control over her heart. In order for her to stand bold for the Lord, she knew she had to emerge up out of the doubtful disputations which most religions consist of, and she knew that she had to let go of the world and the peoples of the world thereof; whom she had grown to know and love. This is what she feared more than fear itself.

During the first revival night she refused to comply with the first opportunity presented unto her to privately deliver the Lord's message at The Greater New Birth Church unto the guest speaker. She grievously left the church house that night, and all throughout the next following day she endured much regret for not doing what the Lord put on her heart to do and say what she believed the Spirit of the Lord intended for her to say. She regretted it so deeply to the point of her immediately asking the Lord for forgiveness and she repented. The spirit confirmed unto her that she would suffer a deeper regret if she continued to refuse to deliver the message. This was still the beginning era of Sister Glory answering as a true believer on the calling, which the Lord preordained of her life. In fact, the pressure of regret had set into her spirit so deeply that she repentantly decided to not let another day go by without answering the Lord's calling on her life. That moment she decided that if the Lord presented her with another opportunity, she would do the Lord's will and good works.

Therefore, on the next sunset she returned with that same said supervisor whom she also was convinced to believe, had coincidently received a spiritual message from God through her; concerning him writing and displaying a spiritual play like that resembling the style of Tyler Perry's. On their way to the second revival, she made him aware of her desiring to deliver what she believed was the Lord's message unto the guest motivational speaker. Upon reentering the church, she instantly recognized more of her co-workers either arriving or were already seated in the pews. Her and her supervisor almost sat in the same seats which they had on the first revival night. They sat in the pew that was located on the first floor close to the front row in close proximity to the pull-pit, but slightly over to the left side of the congregation.

The spirit of the Lord was highly intoxicating to Sister Glory and the Lord's stimulating duty of her calling at the Greater New Birth Church once again came unto her through the inspiring preaching of the pastorate that night. To her, the subject of the sermon was a heavenly confirmation which implicated the same spiritual message that the Lord personally had predestined unto her to tell the guest speaker. The sermon was like a boost of courage being engaged upon her heart as the preacher repeatedly stated to the congregation that nobody knew the story that lies behind his praise.

After the sermon was preached then came the lady guest speaker to close out on the revival session with her personalized testimonial song of praise. Within her testimony she shared a story of how the adversary coerced her when she was a little girl to stop singing. She explained how she was dramatize and demoralized as a child by a Christian leader whom she once looked up too. She said that she stopped singing after over hearing that Christian leader talking down on her singing. He murmured "I thought you said she could sing" to the person whom bragged on her and encouraged her to publically sing in the presents of the one whom belittled her.

Throughout her testimony she mentioned other discouraging obstacles that were in her way like the death of her loved ones. She gave details of everyone in her family whom she loved and loved her in return, had died. Surely, everyone whom knows how this lonely cruel world can depress the strongest soul alive can empathize. Within her testimony she informed the Greater New Birth congregation and visitors of how she had suffered a death in her family right before taking the trip to Milwaukee, WI for that revival. She stated that she started to cancel the trip, but the Lord stepped in and she felt as if she would miss out on a blessing that he had waiting for her if she didn't come.

When she was done with her testimonial song of praise, she exited the chapel doors and entered the main corridor. At that very moment, Sister Glory stepped out on faith and boldly approached her sitting at a table in the main corridor of The Greater New Birth Church and boldly stated to her that she believed that the Lord had ordained her to deliver her this message. She said, "I believe that the Lord ordained me to tell you that <u>he wants you to tell the story that lies behind your praise</u>." While telling her this, Sister Glory envisioned the future of the lady working along side a very popular minister of God known as T.D. Jakes on TV, but she refrained from telling her of that vision. She prayed to God to forgive her if he meant for her to tell her what she visualized.

With a personal interest to learn more about the message, which she didn't understand Sister Glory became engaged in a one on one conversation with the guest motivational speaker, and she kindly explained to the lady that she personally didn't understand the message herself, but she figured that it personally meant something to her. Then Sister Glory departed from her presence. While walking away she felt a load lifting up off of her shoulders. Inwardly she knew that the Lord wasn't done with her yet.

She didn't know how things would end, but she rose up to the occasion of using her liberty to edify God at the Greater New Birth Church anyway. She began taking evangelistic classes there, but she didn't complete her evangelistic orientation due to an immediate last minute decision to relocate to Mississippi. In October of 2007 the Lord called her to return to her birthplace in the outskirts of Oxford, MS in a small town of Abbeville, MS. She currently uses her liberty to edify God at the Springfield M.B. Church as a humbled servant of God. She's still being molded by God as she attend this church, but some are blind and can not see the Lord working something magnificent through her, because they no not God. Others do see and are in awe as her life unfolds before their very eyes. None claim her to be perfect, but all can see an agape love flowing through her personality and humbled characteristics.

Commonly northerners would conclude that all Baptist churches in the South have certain issues that aren't relevant to the teachings of the Doctrine of Jesus Christ, but except they humble themselves to visit Springfield they all will be misled. They are use to scrutinizing all Baptist congregations to be one of the same and they base this theory upon scanty evidence and not on the Holy truth. The truth is…The Lord makes every man a lie and the Word of God is the Truth. "If the Holy Spirit is right, then a whole lot of people are living bibliographically wrong." The old stereotypical hype which many false judges either practice or teach is being put to silence by the Lord. In spite of the bad reputations which stereotypically have been placed on all Baptist churches, there are those selective few true ministries like Springfield M.B. Church, which understands the love of God and they invite all sinners to also get to know, understand, and love God. The motto at Springfield M.B. Church evolves around the New Law of Christ and his greatest of all commandments which all has heard since the beginning.

SPRINGFIELD M.B. CHURCH MOTTO: "I love you and there's nothing you can do about it, except to love me back."

Proverbs3:13 "Happy is the man that findeth wisdom, and the man that getteth understanding."
Proverbs3:18" She is a tree of life to them that lay hold upon her: and happy is everyone that retaineth her."
May God bless the hearers and doers of his Word, Amen!

ONE YEAR LATER! (PROVERBS3:24-28)

In 2008 a year later, Sister Glory was diagnosed with a kidney deficiency and stayed in Tupelo, MS; at the Baptist Memorial Hospital in critical condition for approximately 3 weeks. Her entire body had massively swollen. She went from weighing 123lbs. to 175lbs. in four days. Fluids had quickly built-up and surrounded her vital organs such as her heart and lungs and made her health condition critical. Her breathing became impaired by the built-up fluids and the physicians couldn't get the fluids off of her with the administering of an extremely high dosage of Lasix orally as well as into her veins through an I-V bag.

In the mist of this terrible storm, she never accepted defeat as if it was the end of the world. She held onto her faith on the Lord who she believe ordained her to write and publish Discerning Perceptive. Nor does she accredit herself in writing the book. She fully believes that the making of Discerning Perceptive, which started off in 2001 as written questions that were later answered by the Anointed teaching of the Holy Ghost; were the work of the Lord and not of her own. Without God no man can do anything, but with God man can do everything that is of the Lord's will. She has always believed that the Lord had appointed her to publish the book upon its completion. It was never revealed unto her of her life timeline expectancy of being neither lengthened nor shortened, but by faith she believed that through mercy and grace; nothing on earth would prevail against the will of God making Discerning Perceptive available for peoples of all nations.

Once again all odds in the physical sense of men were against her concerning publishing "Discerning Perceptive". She knew nothing at all about writing a book or publishing one. On top of that she didn't have any extra money to spend on paying the expenses which a reliable book publishing company would charge an unpublished new author for their many services. She prayed to the Lord that if it be of his will to extend his gift of knowledge to others through her writing, then let his will be done. After putting her faith on the Lord, her zeal to do the will of God increased and she was led by Christ after choosing to serve him; onto the path of Righteousness and Truth.

Since the book was incomplete and non-published, at the time of her taking ill, by her faith she was encouraged to believe that there was another untold chapter to the story that lies behind her praise. Therefore, she refused to give into the doubtful disputations of the physical things of the world, which covered the mindset of her siblings concerning her illness. They were calling out-of-town relatives and friends of the family with bereaving news, because they without faith believed her life was coming to an immediate end. Her kidneys were failing.

While lying on her sick bed, she faced one of the greatest challenges of her life in concern of her faith on the Lord. The state of her very being had given her divided attention to the Lord of Host, and she once again cried out to him. In return she heard the voice of the Lord inwardly fighting against the spirit of condemnation in her inner-most consciousness. Subconsciously she started to remember every religious person during her lifetime that she at some point idolized and looked up too, whom had said that the Lord didn't love her. Simultaneously, she thought of all the wrong choices she made in life as a result thereof. Subliminally, she single-mindedly remembered every individual whom told her that the Lord doesn't hear her prayers. At the same time, the Holy Spirit made it obvious for her to understand that those busy bodies were the spots and blemishes of her life, which gloried in her flesh. They were of the world and did not know God, and without knowing him they could not lift one finger to help her out of the bonds of her infirmities because they were blinded by their own self-centered infirmities. The Holy Spirit revealed unto her that such persons of the world were under the false impression that they could maliciously misuse the Word of God to build a case against her, and they were inclined to believe they were obligated to religiously judge her. According to their-own understandings, when she prays; she prays in vain.

The voice of the Lord brought her spiritual comfort and righteous glory, as the Holy Ghost fought and won against every evil aspect of repressive memory that was presented unto her by the evil spirit of condemnation, as she helplessly was lying in the hospital bed. The Holy Spirit of God reminded her, as the Father reprimands his children; of all the prior times when the Lord answered her prayers and did things for her that no man dead or alive could do. The reprimanding of the Lord reminded her of how he provided for her during troubled times, and how he delivered her up out of the temptations of the world. As her life flashed before her very eyes, the loving voice of the Lord made manifest unto her of every un-forgiven false teacher whom told a lie to her against the Holy Ghost. The spiritual conviction of the Lord made it visible for her to clearly see that every false tutor of her past and present were hypocrites and liars. In the mist of despair, Sister Glory with a clear sight of the Holy Truth, felt woe unto the hypocrites and liars who privately waits to deceive others; in the same aspect of speaking, teaching, and preaching. (Prov.1:11-18)

On the night when she was going through these spiritual phases, a couple of nephrology specialists visited her bedside and updated her of their diagnosis. Actually, they really confirmed what she already knew. Their prognosis of her condition concluded that her body was rejecting every medication which they medically recommended for her condition. They felt that there was nothing left to do except start seeking chemotherapy and dialysis. Soon after they left the room, the Lord brought a great sense of spiritual peace upon her and she fell fast asleep.

In the middle of the night she was blessed to be awakened by the Lord; to hear a very familiar heavenly voice covering the air waves of the television set in her hospital room. When she opened and adjusted her eyes to the TV screen, the Lord blessed her to see that same said guest motivational speaker from The Greater New Birth Church in Milwaukee, WI. She was lifting up her voice of praise and telling the story that lies behind her Praise. The lady amazingly was standing on stage with a few well-known religious tutors and among them was a famous Bishop. To

Sister Glory whom recognized the working of the Lord's ministry, it was like a dream come true.

At that very moment Sister Glory's faith shot through the roof, because she then realized what the Spirit of the Lord clearly meant a year a beforehand in 2007 concerning her not having to regret stepping out on faith at The Greater New Birth Church. She once thought that it meant that the Lord was going to punish her severally, but the all merciful God proved to her that he isn't the monster which many traditional religious men portray him to be.

As a newly established missionary for the Lord, with all joy and no regrets; Sister Glory's eyes became weighed down with tears. She began to praise and give thanks unto the Lord God as the mind of her spirit was **feed the Lord's wisdom**, which reminds and reprimands her daily of how merciful and strong the powerful Spirit of the Lord really is. All glory is to God, for enlightening her to know for certainty that it was the Power of God who pricked her heart to stand bold and speak by Divine inspiration to people concerning what the Lord gave her sight to spiritually see. It is evident that sometimes the Lord blesses her to have a second encounter with the same people who she inspires, and sometimes he doesn't. Like a ship, she sees herself as a vessel that is just passing through. It was amazing to Sister Glory to witness a whole year later, the lady praising the Lord on the television set while carrying the title of her Hymn of Praise to be equivalent to the message which she articulated unto her at the Greater New Birth Church in September of 2007, by the mercy and grace of God.

As she rejoiced without feeling repentant or regretful for being obedient to do what the Lord had simplified into her heart to do and say, the works of God indeed increased her stature of faith; without her exploiting herself to go beyond what the Lord's measured amount of faith had issued for her to do. The Spirit of the Lord manifest to Sister Glory of his Divine order of mercy and grace, for she boldly stood obedient to correspond in faith with others as instructed by the Spirit of the Holy Ghost.

While watching the TV scene, she became conscious of the fulfillment of the Holy Spirit which encouraged her to believe that she would be made whole upon following through and completing her spiritual laboring for the Lord. She immediately realized that her works for the Lord were not in vain. She finally realized that working for the Lord was never about trying to prove herself to others; it was always about her showing herself approved unto the Lord. As she rejoiced, the Lord revealed unto her that if she would have chosen not to go and tell that sister that he wanted her to tell they story that is behind her praise, the sister would've still been blessed by him to do of his will and his good pleasures. With that form of knowledge; Sister Glory realized just how bad she would've grievously regretted it, if she wouldn't have stepped out on faith when God gave her the ability to do so. She figured that if she hadn't step out on faith and spoke up for the Lord at the Greater New Birth Church, that she herself would have spiritually suffered a major void of emptiness while lying on her sick bed watching the works of God unfold before her very eyes.

She knew that God gave her the ability to reap what she had sown, as she simultaneously reaped the works of another man's labor. All glory is to God for helping her to see how important it is for her to continue doing what she can, while she still can; concern her laboring for the Lord. Tomorrow isn't promised to any man. She thought to herself while she was praising the Lord in tears on her sick bed, that if she wouldn't have done what the Lord had appointed her to do a year prior; she would have regretfully been lying on her sick bed feeling like she was facing all of these things alone. With lesser faith she may would've wanted to repent, but wouldn't have had the ability to do so. God is a good God for allowing the Lord to fulfill yet another empty void in her life by helping her to understand the meaning of having a deeper regret than she has ever known of, without causing her to feel neither regretful or to experience the self inflicted spirit of grief of being physically born.

The all knowing Lord God knew she would be lying in the hospital in great need of hope. The Spirit of the Comforter evaluated the situation and concluded to her that the fulfillment of the Holy Spirit couldn't have come unto her at a better time. The intersession of the Holy Spirit concluded unto her that she had met the Lord's requirements. Therefore, she has no regrets in understanding that it was by faith that she did what he intended for her to do. Seeing the lady on TV was an amazing experience. The Holy Spirit revived the righteousness of her Spirit and got her to truly believe without wavering in doubt that life for her wasn't over, because in faith a newness of life for her was being set in motion.

She modestly wondered why the Lord didn't advise her to pay attention to the lady's name upon delivering the message or why he didn't instruct for her to get too personal. It was done in such a righteous way that all glory and praise in the end would be given to him and not man. Sister Glory couldn't help for thinking to herself while inwardly rejoicing on her sickbed, that if her faith would've been just a little bit stronger at The Greater New Birth Church in Milwaukee, WI a year earlier; she would've told the motivational guest speaker that she had envisioned or foreseen her sharing her inspiring gift in the form of a testimony with a larger multitude of people, while standing along side of Bishop T.D. Jake on the television. Simultaneously, the Spirit of the Lord comforted the inner-conscience of her and reprimanded her thoughts; that she shouldn't have **ANY** regrets after doing no more or less than that which he instructed. The Comforter clarified unto her that her envision was intended for her to see, but it wasn't meant for the motivational speaker to receive yet from her. The blessing of knowing of the personal impact of having such foresight came unto her as a gift from God. This was astoundingly the breaking point for Sister Glory to wisely grow and understood her new outlook of her new life of hope, faith, and redemption.

In 2008 God blessed Sister Glory to once again hear the voice of the lady which was predestined "to tell the story that lies behind her praise." This time, she heard that same said lady's voice over the air waves of a spiritual radio broadcasting stations, in North Mississippi; The Anointed F.M.102.1. The lady explained how and why she decided to entitle her spiritual hymn of praise in associations to the personal story that lies behind her praise, and she even mentioned her visit to the Ministry of The Greater New Birth Church in Milwaukee WI in September 2007.

While listening to the live radio broadcast, Sister Glory gave all honor and praise to the Lord God as she related personally to the lady's spiritual story. She heard the motivational speaker perfectly explain how the Spirit of the Lord motivated her to name the title of her spiritual hymn in relations to the subject of the Pastorate's sermon at The Greater New Birth Church's revival in 2007. Sister Glory immediately recognized on a personal note, that the same subject of the Pastorate's sermon at the Greater New Birth Church also related to her to have faith and deliver unto the guest speaker the spiritual message. Sister Glory believes that the Lord's words which had already pierced her heart were speaking through the pastorate to confirm unto her that the Lord wanted her to deliver that sister the message.

NOBODY UNDERSTANDS THE STORY THAT LIES BEHIND MY PRAISE

Every living soul on earth has a testimony, and there's a story that lies behind each one. Without knowing what lies behind a converted person's praise makes it impossible for anyone to know why they praise the Lord the way they do. It is up to each of us to independently use our testimonies to edify and uplift one of another, while edifying Jesus Christ. For instance, prior to the Lord blessing Sister Glory with a good medical report from her nephrologists concerning her cured chronic kidney deficiency, she was also blessed by God with the ability to use the Word of God to discern the difference between good and evil with a Holy aptitude to uplift others whom are exploited, demoralized, and oppressed.

Sister Glory hopes that Discerning Perceptive will uplift the spirits of those whom are either exiled or are beguiled by false teachers to believe that they have no hope of being saved by the blood of Jesus. In fact, within certain parts of her testimony her personal uniqueness; sympathetically empathize with the unconstitutional fate of those who have been belittled for a mighty longtime by the nature of false teachers.

For example, she now perseveres on the idea that God chose her to make the most of her spiritual experiences in life without doubting the Power of God's ability to save her; especially after he delivered her out of the worldly mental oppressed state of being. She now realizes that the Lord allowed her to go through many experiences, which in the end gave her self-assurance when her confidence on him was made shallow. Her old self-belief of being loved by God was shallow, because she didn't completely understand the spiritual changes that were manifesting within her. For a certain period of her life time, she struggled with understanding the Lord's truth, even though the Lord had made certain spiritual things obvious unto her. Her old self-belief concerning her faith on the Power of God was once deluded and she was misled to believe on irreligious things that consist of the unreasonable sacrifices that are in agreement to what false teachers had religiously seduced her to believe. She speaks much on how she has been religiously persecuted and beguiled to believe that God hated her. She explains how the false tutors whom she had trusted for a long period of time, gloried in her flesh as they caused her to disbelieve that God would grant his mystical Divine power to come unto her. She implicates that this was the reason why she wavered in faith, and for such cause her explanation also clarify why she thought she wasn't good enough for God to use; in the way in which he actually does. Her mind today concerning her faith is devoted to help revive the spirit of the readers and hearers of false tutors of the Word of God through her book.

In despite of all the clouded religious ideologies and false dogmatic ideas and beliefs which others want her to observe, worship, and revere; deep down inside of her very being she now knows that her purpose in life is to serve God and not the profound irreligious theories of men whom used the Word of God maliciously against the weak and simple babes of Christ. It wasn't until after God redirected her heart to spiritually believe on him and step out on faith did her confidence increase to a brand new high. She today continues to use her testimony as a living witness whom the Lord uses to clearly put in plain words of how God can use the least of all mankind to do his bidding.

Although those who disbelieve may attempt to use the Word as a cloak of maliciousness against her, Sister Glory refuses to deny the power of the Lord because she fears he would in return deny her unto his Father. After allowing the Lord to use her for the occasion of edifying Christ by speaking to others of his ministry, some of her Christian brothers and sisters describe her as being converted, but her worldly friends considers her to be a sellout. Meanwhile, she humbly considers herself to be a servant and a living witness of the Power of God.

A GLORIOUS EPIPHANY: A LIFE CHANGING EXPERIENCE

Those that are of the world who may have been acquainted with Sister Glory may never be on familiar terms with how uplifted she actually became upon hearing the live radio broadcast of the motivational guest speaker telling the story of how she was blessed with the ideal title to her inspiring voice of hymns and praise, unless they comprehend how the Lord used the testimony of that same woman to confirm unto Sister Glory in an indirect way of how Powerful the Almighty God truly is. During the moment in time when her faith was taking the greatest test ever known unto her, as she laid on her sick bed; the Lord revealed himself as the light of her life. The light is the truth and Christ is that light.

Therefore, to better explain it to you readers of the story that lies behind her praise, she had what some may call an epiphany on her sickbed. Her seeing the Lord reveal the woman on TV made her realize how good and powerful God really is. Some says it's a coincidence, but she doesn't believe in coincidence. She believes everything happens for a reason.

While lying in the hospital bed like a wasting vegetable, she inwardly rejoiced and celebrated in high hopes of receiving a full recovery from the Lord. Such hope gave her a fair balance of peace and joy. With her faith on the Lord she had a stronger desire and a more zealous will to live for the Lord than ever before. This epiphany also provided her closure in the sense of her truly acknowledging and accepting her calling.

Due to her lacking medical insurance, she was discharge from the hospital after three weeks had past. Before being discharged, the doctors confirmed unto her that her body was rejecting the medications which they prescribed. Immediately after being discharged she avowed to her entire family and friends that the Lord had revealed to her that she was healed. In the eyes of all whom were made aware of her medical condition the odds of her being healed were against her, but it didn't stop her from believing that she was healed. Within her new life, she walks by faith and not by sight.

Of course nobody honestly believed she was healed, because they were use to seeing life through the physical eye, and according to many of them; she was living in denial of her illness. Many false religious tutors and pupils even went beyond themselves to say that God placed that illness on her to punish her, but by her faith she believe that the Lord allowed her to become ill to show unto her and unto all whom knew him; that he is the Lord of lords. She also believes that the Lord revealed his true power of repentance and forgiveness in the form of a test of her faith which strengthened her confidence to believe the Lord, has the ability to convert even a retch like her.

Like Apostle Paul, Sister Glory stated "I speak as a man." Then she added; "If man believes I'm a sinner and don't believe that the Lord hears a sinner's prayer, then to them this marvelous miracle means that I am not a sinner." Since the Word of God is true and every man is a liar, says Sister Glory, then this miracle simply means that all falls short to sin, and the Lord is the redeemer of all whom believes on him. All who truly knows of Sister Glory's condition are also called to be a living witness of the true Power of God. Be not misled, her physical healing isn't a sign of her not having any faults or failings, but it is evidence of the merciful God's power of forgiveness. Her many spiritual accomplishments are evident that if she were not of God, she could do nothing. (St.John9)

She even suggest for all who are the disciples of Moses and don't believe the Lord hears a sinners prayer to privately study the scriptures from whence false teachers have turned aside unto vain jangling; desiring to be teachers of the law; understanding neither what they say, nor whereof they affirm. (1Tim.1:7-8) Pray for understanding and privately study for yourself the story of the blind man whom spoke to the Jews whom accused Jesus of casting out devils and healing the sick by the powers of Bē-ĕĺ-zĕ-bŭb. In the Book of St. John 9 the blind man explained to those of them that accused Jesus of being a sinner that he didn't know whether Jesus was a sinner or not, but he did know that he himself was born blind and now he can see; by the works of Jesus whom work the works of his Father; God.

This is the section where false ministers love to go when trying to either mislead a person to believe that a parent can pass down their sin to their unborn or new born child and that God doesn't hear the prayers of a sinner.   They take the scriptures out of context; because they are made blind by the Lord (St.John9:39).   The blind man from St. John whom the Jews had hated, despised, and reviled was simply reminding those who were in doubt of Jesus being of God, of the Moses law which they revered which also concludes Jesus to be of God by the description of his works. (St. John9:30-31)

> **St. John9:32 "Since the world began was it not heard that any man opened the eyes of one that was born blind."**
>
> **St. John9:33 "If this man were not of God, he could do nothing."**

Upon being discharged from the hospital the medical physicians didn't believe she was healed. She was assigned to a specialist, whom scheduled for her to return to a nephrology clinic in Tupelo, MS at a later date; to undergo more tests to prep her for farther medical treatments that included chemotherapy and dialysis. Her scheduled appointment date was the day when she was listening to the Anointed 102.1 spiritual radiobroadcast and heard the motivational guest speaker from the Greater New Birth Church testifying of how she was encourage by God to entitle a spiritual hymn which expressed the story that lies behind her praise. Surprisingly, after listening to many uplifting spiritual songs; the D.J interrupted the normal broadcast and did an interview with the same lady whose testimony provided her closure in the sense of acknowledging the destiny of her true calling.

When she arrived at the nephrologists' office, she with boldness; asked the nurse whom was taking a sample of her blood for tests if she had ever known of a person to be cured of the kidney disease which she had. The nurse stated with a sad look upon her face, "No I have not." Sister Glory looked up at her with a big smile and sad, "Well, I'll be your first." Not too long after sitting and waiting, her nephrology doctor came in and said, "How are you doing?" and Sister Glory replied with a smile, "I'm doing fine doc., but I want you to tell me how I'm doing." The doctor's eye's appeared to be in a state of skepticism. He said, "I got to send your lab work off for confirmation, because my lab work says you're clear; and I don't believe it." Sister Glory never stopped smiling and she asked the doctor if he believed in God. She carried on saying that she believes on the Lord God and that by faith she had told her supervisor at work, her family and friends, and his nurse that she was healed.

She believes the Lord's first confirmation was given unto her on the same day that she heard and saw the lady guest speaker on the TV screen while lying on her sick bed in the hospital. She heard the lady's voice once again on the radio during her trip from Oxford, MS to Tupelo, MS to receive her second confirmation from that same said doctor. The third confirmation came from a different lab, and the forth confirmation came into existence after her regular family physician in Oxford, MS personally retested her and verified the accuracy of the medical report provided by the nephrologists' lab from Tupelo, MS.

Some people whom personally knows of Sister Glory's past life style, either aren't able to forgive her or aren't able to believe that God could convert her. In fact, when they heard the good news; they reacted disapprovingly in a very negative and disturbing way towards her. Contemptuously they acted as if they had become angry at God for not doing what they thought that he should have done. They thought like Jonah in the Book of Jonah 3-4:1 concerning their anger at God for repenting and turning away from his fierce anger as a gracious and merciful God that Sister Glory perished not after he saw her good works and within her heart that she had turned from the evil life of a disbeliever and repented thereof. They thought of course; that God should have had her to suffer unto death. Though she saw all of this, she was not discouraged. She knew that when bad things happen to people which such persons despise, happy are the despisers. She remarkably forgave all who desired for their monstrous god to make an example out of her and make her suffer to death. No man knows how they life shall end. Some suffer unto death and others suffer not, but one thing is for sure; all shall be judged by God upon Judgment Day.

Like all other imperfect humans, Sister Glory sought to find and found refuge in Jesus Christ. By the flesh she shall one day physically die, but after being born again; it is by the spirit that she lives. The mercy of the Lord is upon her and no man will ever know the complete state of her inner spirit. Nor will they know of the hour when the Lord may call her home and neither does she. That's why it's so important to Sister Glory to teach as many as she can, while she still can; concerning all the things that the Lord instructs unto her which she with the voice of thanksgiving have vowed. She didn't vow to never commit another sin, but she did vow to explain to every Nation that Salvation is of the Lord.

Not too many days subsequently following after the time of her being pronounced cured, did the Lord direct her to telephone The Anointed

F.M.102.1 radio station's business phone line, and she was connected on a three way phone call with that same said lady motivational guess speaker. Without desiring vain glory, Sister Glory thanked her for being a strong faithful servant of God and informed her of what a great deal it was to her too witness how everything had worked out for the best concerning her taking heed to the Lord's message. This is a fine example to the significance of the scriptures that states "Faith without works is dead."

The lady stated that she did remember Sister Glory from the Greater New Birth Church in Milwaukee, WI telling her that she believed that she was ordained by God to tell her that the Lord wanted her to tell the story that lies behind her praise. After a few other brief discussions about Sister Glory being called out of the world, she advised Sister Glory to hold on to her FAITH on the LORD. Without the greedy desire of being praised by man and without, jealousy, or any other fleshly sensation overthrowing the innermost conscience of her heart and mind, Sister Glory continues today edifying the Lord by acknowledging that she received healing from the Lord. She honestly believes her healing was designed by the Power of God for her to give as a testimonial test of her faith on him to others who are in doubt, and she accepts the Word of God as the truth which gives heavenly reward unto her in the account of her being redeemed.

During her weakest hour she recognized the Lords' Heavenly Wisdom, comforting her daily while enabling her to identify and understand that he gave unto her a sacred holy gift which comes in the measured balance of strengthening her faith. As she accredit the Lord for this blessing, she realizes that she has no reason at all to feel apologetic or regretful for stepping out on faith neither in Milwaukee, WI nor within the good old southern state of Mississippi. The power of her faith resides not in what man thinks of her or what they do against her, but her faith is within the powerful Word of God which healed her broken-spirit and her sickened body simultaneously. By her faith and through the mercy and grace of the Lord; she is healed.

She prudently understands that her body is of the flesh and to the flesh she is made weak, but her Spirit is the Lord's and for that she is made strong. Sickness may come and go, but the Spirit of the Lord is forever. Therefore, she cleaves to her faith on the Power of God and rejoices in sickness and in good health; knowing that tribulations don't last always. Things may not ever be as good as a person may think it should be, but for those who are in Christ; they rejoice knowing that things never gets to be as bad as it could be. The loving Power of God's mercy and grace sent his only begotten son Jesus in the form of the flesh, to save all whom believes on him. It is now the end of the old year of 2010 and the beginning year of 2011, and Sister Glory has not ever needed a kidney transplant, chemotherapy, or dialysis. All glory and praise be to God! AMEN!

CHAPTER 20 SISTER GLORY SANDERS THOMPSON'S PERSONAL OVERVIEW OF SPRINGFIELD M.B. CHURCH©

> *St. Luke10:24 "For I tell you, that many prophets and kings have desired to see those things which ye see, and have not seen them; and to hear those things which ye hear, and have not heard them."(St.Matt.13:10-17/St.Luke10:1-23)*

The best expression which the author of Discerning Perceptive has concerning the teachings of the Gospel which she has personally received within the walls of this congregation, resides solely on her comparing the spiritual sense of her earlier childhood experiences and her many life learned lessons; to the spiritual sense which she has passionately grown up in the Word to acquire. She edifies the Lord daily while carefully explaining how the Lord has opened her heart and mind to know and understand the Holy Truth.

Meanwhile, she personally amplifies all the things which the Lord has blessed her to spiritually distinguish with clarity through the complete published writing of Discerning Perceptive. She has been blessed with the ability to add clear details for the hears of the Word of God while explaining what she sees and hears; by putting in plain words of how the powerful Fruit of the Spirit of the Lord is inevitably intervening, overriding, and superseding the provoking methods of Satan in her life. She clearly sees the inevitable and unavoidable chain reactions within the spiritual hearts of many which once loved to glory in her flesh, transforming into brand new creatures of GOD. The new creatures aren't surely new, but they are the same. What differs about them is their inward devotion, which has transferred from being haters© of men into lovers of God. Therefore, the transformation which Sister Glory sees occurring isn't by her own doing, but it is the work of the Lord, whom directs her steps and encourages her to do and say certain things concerning the Lord and the Lord's enemy.

597

The Lord has revealed unto her of his precious Heavenly Wisdom. She doesn't claim to know anything, but she does speak truthfully of the things which she has either experienced or experimented with. As she encouragingly goes out seeking to get more understandings of the Lord's truth, she discovers the evil intentions which lies behind the motives of the one's who love to provoke the pureness of her heart to be troubled with grief and anger. Since she was taught by the Anointed to know how to recognize the children of the provoker and the haters of men by their fruits, she daily walk through the valley of the shadow of death without fearing their greatest of all evil. Their **HATRED** is often provoked by **GREED!**"

The evil ones potentially are known for corruptibly comparing themselves by themselves and amongst themselves. The old traditional religious method of men worshiping one of another is of the religion of the adversary. His old method is the same today, yesterday and will remain forever to go on unchanged as he continues to cause confusion within the hearts of many. Satan keeps causing confusion by provoking the members of all sorts of congregations to remain envious and jealous of one of another.

The Anointed teaches all true Christians of how to recognize Satan's followers who carry on with a false impression of what Christianity signifies. Satan coerces the hearts and minds of his followers to work against the will of God. Some people are not chosen by God, but yet they make themselves an apostle of Christ. Instead of them properly using the Word of God to convince the people of God that the whole duty of them ought to be to enlighten and encourage one of another as a new creature of God, Satan coerces the hearts of many to feel condemned as he indeed works to kill the godly Spirit of hope and faith from the hearts of the people.

The Lord has rebuked the desires of such vain thoughts from entering the heart of Sister Glory as well as most members of Springfield M.B. Church, and the Spirit of God is continuing to make intercessions to the godly Spirit within them all; to allow all of them to worship together without frustrating or oppressing the Spirit of GOD.

The Spirit of GOD makes a righteous plea for all to self examine themselves and compare them-selves with the spiritual perfected inspiring Word of God. In so doing, all evil works are put to death, such as jealousy, hatred, backbiting, envy, etc. On the behalf of doing the will of God, Sister Glory asked the Lord to stop her from following the wrong unrighteous path of the old spoiled religious method of Satan, which has been known for provoking people to hate and despise one of another. Not only did the Lord answer her prayer, but the Saviour also revealed to her of his plan to make peace and not war. Not all whom says, "Lord, Lord" shall enter into the Kingdom of Heaven. In other words, not all shall truly believe on him or carryout his ministry.

In the Word, it is written that what God said he'd do for one, he'd do for all. In order for anyone to righteously be converted, they must see themselves for themselves through the eyes of Christ. Therefore, the uncovering of the war which Sister Glory sees consists of God revealing unto each individual individually, of the evil and wrong which they individually do and say. This too became a popular prayer of hers, because she herself couldn't change until she saw her evil self for herself through the Word of God. In so doing, became the desired need to change. True repentance to Sister Glory is likened of the sign of Jonah, which without a shout of a doubt is a reasonable sign from the Heavens above, but the world understands it not.

She was instructed to stop running from her destiny which includes her being persecuted by religious leaders who are willing to charge her unto God and falsely accuse her to be of Satan. The voice of the Lord living within her heart reminds her daily that if she rebuke Satan daily and stand firmly on the Word of God, like the tree planted by the rivers of the water, she shall not be moved. It has always been strongly believed by her even when she was a little child that in order for her to stop running from the old methods' of Satan in the small Lafayette, Co. community of Oxford, MS; the Wisdom of the Heavens would have to provide a spiritual tutor of the Anointed whom is enabled by God the Father, the Son, and the Holy Ghost; to righteously divide the difference between good and evil as a discerner of the Spirit; to intercept and interrupt the evil traditional religious dictatorship all around the world including within her hometown community.

On May 7, 2006 the ordained Pastor Jerry L. Malone answered the Lord's calling on his life and became the Springfield M. B. Church's head Pastor. Sister Glory and many others believe he was predestined by God upon the day of his birth to add more blessings unto Springfield M.B. Church. As an added leader whom the Lord gives wonderful works unto, Pastor Malone has allowed the people of Springfield M.B. Church to see and understand the trueness of their way of conduct and habits, without condemning or defiling the Spirit of any man and without judging and falsely accusing any man unto God. In the Spirit, he minister as if he has grown to understand that evil cannot rebuke evil and God gave no man the power to judge the Spirit of another man's conscience.

Those who come and join with him as to congregate together, tends to learn and recognize the inaccurate fault and failings of their own idol ways. They grow to see their evil ways are equivalent to Satan's approach and not God's, as the Anointed ordains him to sincerely warn, urge, and teach all to repent. After gaining their sight on the righteous order of the Lord, the ministry of Springfield consists of evangelizing disciples and missionaries and encouraging them to grown tremendously in the form of agape love for God; as One Body of Christ.

On October 19, 2007 the author of Discerning Perceptive answered the Lord's calling on her life, and returned to the land where she was born. On October 21, 2007 Sister Glory Sanders Thompson returned to Springfield M.B. Church, which is where she presently attends; under the leadership of the same said Anointed Pastor Jerry L. Malone.

PASTOR JERRY L. MALONE MISSION STATEMENT®

QUOTE: "I will commit to doing the works of the one who has sent me. My main objective is to do the will of God. It is God's will for me to use most of my energy in organizing and equipping the saints to carry out their ministries."

ALL GLORY AND THANKS BE TO GOD

I would like to take this time to thank God for showering me with his love on earth through the ways of his love, mercy, and grace. His unconditional love just keeps on blessing me. Even though I'm undeserving, he blessed me of all people with the ability to write and publish the things which he has allowed me to see and understand; concerning the teachings of his anointed and prophetic inspiring Word of Hope. After gaining a sympathetic understanding of the Lord's purpose for forgiving me and giving me a new walk in life, I've sincerely chosen to stand bold on my faith as a believer on the Power of God. In the name of Jesus, I am crying out to all peoples in hopes of saving some from the bondage of misery, worldly sorrows, grief, and pain. For the psychotic religious leaders and followers of the world who are misled to twist the concept of my message, I pray to God for you. I dare not to commend any religious dictator who supports discrimination of any kind, because the Lord didn't leave me to be ignorant. Nor do I claim to know anything except what the Lord has presented unto me. He left my with the Word of God to encourage love not hate. I fight evil with kindness as instructed by the Word and I advise all others to do the same.

As I say and do whatsoever the Lord directs my heart to say and do, I pray that the lost sheep's may find love, peace, joy, and hope of being redeemed. Within all the things that the lost may go out and get; I pray that they get heavenly understanding of the truth of God's Divine order and nature, so that they may become spiritually wise. God is; who he says he is. God is Love and there's no dissimulation in love. Love doesn't hate anybody nor does love seek to hurt the givers or the receivers thereof. The Kingdom of God is at Hand for all whom seeks for it.

May God Bless the Hearers and the Doers of His Word!

Amen! Amen! Amen!

The love which my grandparents had for the Lord during their life time was built upon a rock of faith in the accordance of the Word of God, and was passed down to me in a genuine way. As the old time saying goes, "It takes a whole village to raise a child".

I'm thankful to God for sending me to be born to my mom; the late Ella Mae Sanders Gators, and my dad; Clarence W. Sanders. When I was a child, they both shared their knowledge of what the Lord's unconditional love and the world's conditional style of love consist of simultaneously. The Lord used them to help prepare me when I was a child for the different changes which I later experienced through force and through self inflictions of my own doings. They illustrated the Lord's love for me not by words alone, but by actually loving me unconditionally. Even though I strayed away and didn't always stick to the Lord's standard principles of life, which they both by the grace of God exhibited unto me when I was a child; they indisputably loved me in spite of.

Thanks pop, for sharing your knowledge of God's unfailing and unfaultable love for me. If I wouldn't have been taught the right way in which God wanted me to go as a child, after I had grown up and strayed away from the goodness of the Lord's teachings; I wouldn't have had the confidence nor the strength to stand bold on the Word of God's love, mercy, and grace and spiritually returned in my right mindset as a discerner of the Holy Truth. Being a discerner of the Spirit doesn't mean I'm a perfect person who has no sin or doesn't fall short thereof, but it does mean I'm blessed by the Lord for working by the perfection of the Word of God. The Lord isn't done with me yet. I'm presently being spiritually molded by the Potter Maker. Therefore, I dare myself to claim to know everything as some may inaccurately misjudge me and say that I think I do. In this race called life, no person knows when their days in this old world will be over. Therefore, it is prudent for us all to stop waddle in the earlier starting gleam of our past faults, failings, and misfortunes and start focusing more so on how we all finish the race of time. Pop, thanks for being my hero! **May God continue to keep on blessing you!**

SON-DEION 1stFIRST PHOTO/ DAUGHTER-JUSTINE 2nd PHOTO

I personally would like to thank my children Deion and Justine. God has truly blessed me by sending me two extremely strong spiritual souls whom the Lord molded to be my strength where I'm weak. I thank God for my children. The Lord promised me, that he would not put any more on me than I could bare, and I believe that he knew that I could not bare the troubles of this world as a single parent, if I would have given birth to a weaker side of myself. Therefore, he sent unto to me two of his strongest angles to comfort me. He also built me up and blessed me with the ability to also love and comfort them during the worst times of duress when threats are made up against us by the followers of that old Adversary, who works enmity against us and God.

My message to you is this,

"Faith isn't what you say you believe, but it's how you live. Keep your faith on the Lord, and put the Lord first in everything you do." **May God Continue to Protect and Bless You Both!**

The authenticity of my passion for writing this book was inspired by God and the articulation thereof is driven by my fascination as a poet. When I was a young teen, I wrote unpublished poems and raps. During my later teenage years I became an MC in the local community of my birthplace. Being a poetic writer has always helped me to express myself to others whom also can relate to how I feel.

The group on this CD cover is "THE NAWTY 1'z" and neither their lyrics nor the spelling of their name is to be duplicated. I believe these four young men are the newest undiscovered HOT-BOYS' Hip-Hop/Rap prodigy of the 21st century. Through their genius lyrics they too express to all who has an ear to hear of all of the similar struggles that persist in their daily walk of life and in the lives of the people of their Hood. Like most Hip-Hop artists, they have two versions to most of their lyrics. Beware; some of their lyrics may contain unequivocal language, which may not be suitable for children. I myself love listening to the rated PG versions of their songs. As they express their love for their family and for God, they also express their anger, frustrations, and pain.

The articulation of their music expresses how they hustle in the South to survive during this struggling recession. Through their music, they provide their fans with in-depth details of their great efforts to survive their underground label as undiscovered rappers in the music industry. They nobly are known for using their talent to improvise and compensate for what they lack as providers for their families.

They now are hopeful towards broadening their horizons. They are striving to receive more exposure as they now independently seek to carry their rap legacy throughout the world on different social network sites over the internet. Within the foundation of their individual hearts resides a true form of poetic justice. They connect to their audiences and fans by keeping it 100nurd% real, instead of faking it to make it. They even have a song titled "Keepin' It 100Nurd%" which their fan-based audience can relate too. Again the unique spelling and the tile of their song isn't to be duplicated. They don't believe in dividing the articulations of rappers between the East Coast and West Coast nor do they believe in isolating the unique virtuous style of the North and South, because they believe all rappers are in the same game. I thank God for you all and I'm proud to have had the pleasure in working with you. You all have grown into a mature group of young men. My message to you is this, "With God all things are possible." **May God Continue Blessing You!**

I would like to thank my oldest brother Vernon and his wife Gloria for their infallible love and support. Although you're my big brother, you've always been more like a second dad to me. Thanks for helping me to stay encouraged during the darkest hours of my life. I love you Bro! **May God Bless You!**

I would like to thank Evangelist Sister Freddie Brown in Milwaukee, WI for reprimanding and reminding me that the Lord called me out of the world to do his business. **May God Bless You!**

I would like to thank all of my friends and church family whom attends Springfield M.B. Church and Clear Creek M.B. Church in Abbeville, MS; and Philadelphia M.B. Church in Oxford, MS for reminding me that I am not what the liars, false prophets, and worldly men says I am. I am who the Lord says I am, and I am "REDEEMED!" **May God Continue Blessing You All!**

I would like to thank Sister Jennifer Buford; the loving daughter of Sister Bessie (*Smith*) Buford of Oxford, MS and the deceased Rev. William Buford of Abbeville, MS for caring about soul winning and for carrying on the Divine legacy of Christ's Ministry just as your dad ministered unto me when I was a mere child. In fact, the entire Buford family has been a great key to my spiritual growth from the earlier part of my youth until this present day. **"May God Bless You All!"**

Also I would like to thank Minister Alfred Harris and his wonderful wife Sister Wilma Harris of Oxford, MS whom personally has helped to see me through a great upbringing in the House of God. Minister Harris conducted many holy messages to me at the Philadelphia M. B. Church when I was a child under the Pastorate of Pastor William M. Kelly Jr. The end result of your dedication as a servant of God has sown many prudent seeds of an agape love. **May God Continue Blessing You All!**

I would like to thank my half-sister Earnestine whom made it mandatory for me to attend a Church of Christ in Milwaukee, WI in 1993 during the 3 months which I lived under her roof. I believe that you sincerely wanted to save me, and in a certain way you did. At that church house,

I became aware of the dangers of involving myself unworthily with false teachers. The beginning psychological advancement of my spiritual growth started increasing while attending that congregation. I must admit, that I did learn more about Christ establishing his church in one day of attendance at that building than I had ever learned in my lifetime at any other religious organization. After attending that particular religious institution, my desire to learn, know, and understand more about God escalated. Over all, I've learned that I belong to the Lord; I am the Church, and Salvation is the Lord's. With my faith on the Lord, I believe I'm saved by the Blood of Jesus through his mercy and grace. **May God Continue Blessing You!**

I would like to thank my half-sister Faristeen for helping me to recognize that I am more than a conqueror. God isn't going to put no more on me than I can bear. No matter how much another person may wish for worse things to happen to me, he's my protector and my Rock. **May God Bless You!**

I would like to thank my big sister Deborah for always being there for me through good times and bad. We have never allowed the evils of this world to cause conflict to come between us and for that I feel truly blessed. True love is unconditional and unconditional love is hard to find, but it's great to recognize that I've always had a friend in you. Thanks Sis for being true. **May God Continue to Walk With You and Bless You and Your Family!**

I would like to thank my brother Robert for encouraging me to stay strong and stand bold for the Lord against those whom pretend to be without sin. I'm not perfect nor do I pretend to be, but I'm working towards perfection by properly using the perfected prophetic Word of God during my daily walk of life. The truth is the light, and the Light is Christ. Thanks for helping me to shake my fears of what others may say against me or think of me. I understand that every ear which hears my mouth confessing that Jesus is my Lord and Savior, also have faults and failings. **May God Continue to Bless You!**

LAFAYETTE HIGH SCHOOL IN OXFORD, MS

This book is dedicated to all teachers, coaches, and staff of the Lafayette County School District in Oxford, MS whom are linked to the Graduated Class of 1992. Thanks for helping me to believe in myself, when the odds of me succeeding were against me. You all were more than school teachers to me. I believe you all were heavenly sent, because you guided me throughout my childhood to be a better person. **May God Bless You All!**

SPECIAL DEDICATION

THE BEREAN FAMILY WORSHIP CENTER IN MILWAUKEE, WI

This book is dedicated to the Berean Family. The Fruit of your Spirit beyond a shout of a doubt is apart of the Holy Root of the First Fruit of Jesus Christ. You have truly blessed me in the presence of the Lord God. When I was lost, I prayed to the Lord for a church home in Milwaukee, WI. God led me straightway to you. I sought for a God fearing and a knowledgeable family of God, and I found you. **May God Continue Blessing You All!**

PASTOR DR. WALTER HENDERSON III & (The First Lady) Evangelist Joycelyn Pernell Henderson

They are the founders of BFWC which was established in their home on Dec. 6, 1985. (© By BFWC 1985-2010)

God gave Pastor Henderson the name **BEREAN** which was taken from the City of **Berea** in Acts 17:10-12. On August 30, 1992 with approximately 25 members BFWC were able to purchase their first facility. In 2004 God showed favor for BFWC once again and they relocated to a larger facility. (© BY BFWC 1985-2010)

> Acts17:10-11 "And the brethren immediately sent away Paul and Silas by night unto Berea; who coming thither went into the synagogue of the Jews. These were more noble than those in Thessalonica, in that they received the word with readiness of mind, and searched the scriptures daily, whether those things were so."

THE BEREAN FAMILY WORSHIP CENTER IS A NON-DENOMINATIONAL MINISTRY. IT SEEKS TO UPHOLD THE FOLLOWING: ©

BFWC Vision "To disciple Sons and Daughters that will enlarge the Kingdom of God"

BFWC Mission "Evangelize the Lost; Disciple Those Won; Send Those Disciples"

BFWC Moto "Making perfect that which is lacking in your faith."

SPECIAL DEDICATION

SPRINGFIELD M.B. CHURCH IN ABBEVILLE, MS

PASTOR JERRY L. MALONE & (First Lady) Sister Darlene Malone

This book is dedicated to the Springfield M.B. Church family, which is where I currently reside. Upon my return home to Mississippi, the Lord placed you heavenly on my mind and in my heart. He sent me to you and you welcomed me back with open arms. We've been through many heartaches and pain together, and through it all we've learned to have an agape love and forgiveness for one of another. **May God Continue to Bless Each of You!**

THE SPRINGFIELD M.B. CHURCH'S IMPLICATION OF THE WORD...
"CHURCH" ®

—At its root, the word church means "a called-out group." It is used of the National Israel (Acts 7:38), which was a group of people who were called out of the rest of the people of the world to have a special national relationship to God.

THE PURPOSE OF SPRINGFIELD M.B. CHURCH ®

—See Ephesians 3:21...The ultimate purpose of the church is to bring honor and glory to its head, Jesus Christ. It does this as it fulfils its two purposes related to God's program for the world.

—The one purpose of the church, as it relates to the world, is evangelism. See also the [Great Commission] in Matthew 28:19, 20, where you'll find that the program wasn't ever rescinded, neither cancelled, nor repealed, or made void. The program or the agenda of Springfield M.B. Church is to **"Make Disciples of all the Nations"**

—Another purpose of the Church, as it relates to the world, is edification (building one up). See also Ephesians 4:12

614

The year in which this organization came into exists is unknown, but what is known is the one-room church building was originally located in the Hurricane Creek area of Abbeville, MS in the 1800's. ®

In the 1940's, Springfield Church moved to its present location on Springfield Road in Abbeville, MS. It is 75-100 yards from the family old homestead of the author of Discerning Perceptive; Sister Glory Sanders Thompson. The church building was a one room building that was built out of wood plank materials, and was torn down and rebuilt in the form of a brick building during the years of 1954-1955. The one room building didn't include bathrooms, baptizing pools, or a foyer. These things were added a few years later.

According to the Springfield's historical overview in 1994, by the grace of God; the church was remolded and upgraded again under the new leadership of the deceased (*DECEASED YEAR 2010*) Pastor Willie James Lumpkin. According to the Springfield M.B. Church history, Pastor Lumpkin was notably recorded as the head minister from 1989-January 22, 2006. During the time of his leadership the growth of the church included an additional makeover in 1994. The additions included bathrooms in the foyer, a pastor's study and suite, a fellowship hall, a kitchen, plus renovations of the sanctuary, as well as other amenities.

In 2008 under the leadership of Pastor Jerry L. Malone, the church started building a Christian Life Center. According to the church's construction logbook, this center was completed in 2009. It includes a conference room, several classrooms, a fellowship hall, gymnasium, and fitness center and resource areas.

The Springfield community of Abbeville, MS is truly blessed by God to have such a good strong stable foundation. As the members of Springfield M.B. Church follow the Lord whom directs their steps, they are stepping out on faith into the streets of reality; to unify people of all nations and nationalities. The people of the same said community are continuously being led up together as One Body of Christians for the edification of Christ Jesus. Some members are stronger than others in different areas of life, but by the mercy and grace of God; all whom believes on the Lord understands that they all are apart of the same Holy Root of the First Fruit of Jesus Christ. In the area where one maybe weak they indeed are spiritually helped by those whom are strong in that same area. AMEN!

This book is also dedicated to the following close family members of the author: (Sanders, Wilson, Keys, Gators, Gilliom, Liggins, and Hilliard)

May God bless all of you!

Contact Info for Seminars and Discussion Groups:
Contact Sister Glory Sanders Thompson a spiritual motivational speaker gloriouswonenterprisellc@yahoo.com. Include name of organization, phone number, and a brief detailed message concerning future seminars.